ORACLE   *Oracle Press*

Oracle DBA Handbook

Kevin Loney

Osborne **McGraw-Hill**

Berkeley New York St. Louis San Francisco
Auckland Bogotá Hamburg London Madrid
Mexico City Milan Montreal New Delhi Panama City
Paris São Paulo Singapore Sydney Tokyo Toronto

Osborne **McGraw-Hill**
2600 Tenth Street
Berkeley, California 94710
U.S.A.

For information on software, translations, or book distributors outside of the U.S.A., please write to Osborne **McGraw-Hill** at the above address.

Oracle DBA Handbook

234567890 DOC 9987654

ISBN 0-07-881182-1

Publisher
 Lawrence Levitsky

Acquisitions Editor
 Jeff Pepper

Project Editor
 Claire Splan

Copy Editors
 Gary Morris
 Jan Jue

Proofreader
 Pat Mannion

Computer Designer
 Jani Beckwith

Illustrator
 Rhys Elliott

Series Design
 Jani Beckwith

Quality Control Specialist
 Joe Scuderi

This effort is dedicated to those
who have borne its weight most heavily:

to my family
for their steadfastness and love,
their endurance and understanding,
their patience and support.

About the Author

Kevin Loney, a veteran Oracle developer and DBA, has written "User Help" columns for *ORACLE Magazine* since 1990. He frequently makes presentations at international conferences.

Contents At A Glance

Contents

PART 2
Database Management

PART 3
Supporting Packages

PART 5
Appendixes

Acknowledgments

In addition to my family, a number of other folks were key contributors to this effort:

Thanks to the amazing I/T staff at Astra/Merck—particularly the Information Integration Team (presently Mary, Mary, Pat, John, Edmund, Joseph, Steve, and Eric), my users, and Cheryl Bittner and Rob Cohen. They have allowed and encouraged me to write this book during an intense development period. Without their contributions, this book could not have been written.

Thanks to John Hunt and Jay Warshell of Astra/Merck and Michele Becci of Wyeth-Ayerst Research for their technical input.

Julie Gibbs, the editor of *ORACLE Magazine*, played a role in my involvement in this project and has helped with those areas that related to articles I have previously published in *ORACLE Magazine*. Jeff Pepper led the charge as editor-in-chief of Osborne/McGraw-Hill, and the support of him, Ann Wilson, Claire Splan, Gary Morris, Jan Jue, Jani Beckwith, and the rest of the OMH crew has been invaluable. Thanks to David McClanahan and Brian Quigley for their technical review and input. The quality of the final product is directly attributable to their talent and efforts.

Thanks to Decky & Bill, Jan, Marie, Rob, and all those who helped me make this possible. To Skipper, Charlie, Angelo, Chris, Doreen, and Ming-Hwa for hiring me. And a nod to the past and present support staffs for the JCTS and FMIS.

In terms of supporting documentation, most of the Oracle7 Server documentation set was used as a reference in the creation of this book. This includes the *Server Administrator's Guide, Server Concepts Manual, Application Developer's Guide, Server Migration Guide, Utilities Users Guide,* and the *SQL Language Reference Guide.* The *Installation and Users Guides* for VAX/VMS and UNIX and the *Technical Reference Guide for UNIX* were also used, as were the *Performance Tuning Guides* for both of those operating systems. For SQL*Net issues, the *SQL*Net 2.0 Administrator's Guide, MultiProtocol Interchange Administrator's Guide, Oracle*Names Administrator's Guide, TCP/IP Adapter for Windows,* and *Setting up SQL*Net TCP/IP for DOS* guides were used. For Oracle Version 6 issues, the *Database Administrator's Guide, Utilities Users Guide,* and the *Performance Tuning Guide* were constant companions. A number of Oracle technical bulletins, available via the Oracle support bulletin board, were also used as reference material, as was the *SQL*Plus Reference Guide.* "An Optimal Flexible Architecture for Oracle RDBMS Version 6.0," by Cary Millsap of Oracle, provided the foundation for Chapter 3.

Several non-Oracle publications were also important. George Koch's *Oracle7: The Complete Reference* provided advice on application design, and Julie Gibbs of *ORACLE Magazine* supported the use of a number of my previous articles in that magazine in this effort. For this handbook, the most important of those were "System-Level Roles in Oracle7" (July 1994), "On-Line Free Space Defragmentation" (September 1993), "Integrating Oracle Backup Strategies" (July 1993), and "Export by Tablespace: The Missing Utility" (April 1992).

The structure for Chapter 5, "Managing the Development Process" is inspired by the work of Donald Marquardt, leader of the US delegation to the committee that wrote the ISO 9000 standard for Quality Systems. His emphasis on the "success triad," along with the work of Joseph Juran and W. Edwards Deming, provides the philosophical basis for that chapter. Deming's version of the Shewhart cycle is used as the foundation for the database design methods described here.

Introduction

Whether you're an experienced DBA, a new DBA, or an application developer, you need to know how the internal structures of the Oracle database work and interact. Properly managing the database's internals will allow your database to meet two goals: it will work, and it will work *well*.

In this book, you'll find the information you need to achieve both of these goals. The emphasis throughout is on managing the database's capabilities in an effective, efficient manner to deliver a quality product. The end result will be a database that is dependable, robust, secure, extensible, and designed to meet the objectives of the applications it supports.

Several components are integral to these goals, and you'll see all of them are covered here in depth. A well-designed logical and physical database architecture will improve performance and ease administration by properly distributing database objects. Determining the correct number and size of rollback segments will allow your database to support all of its transactions. You'll also see appropriate monitoring, security, and tuning strategies for standalone and networked databases. Optimal backup and recovery procedures are also provided to help ensure the database's recoverability. The focus in all of these sections is on the proper planning and management techniques for each area.

You'll also find information on how to manage the support of specific packages, such as Oracle*CASE, Oracle Financials, the Oracle utilities, and third-party utilities.

Networking issues and the management of *distributed* and *client-server* databases are thoroughly covered. SQL*Net, networking configurations, snapshots, location transparency, and everything else you need to successfully implement a distributed or client-server database is described in detail here. You'll also find real-world examples for every major configuration.

By following the techniques in this book, you'll no longer have to worry about disasters striking your databases. And they'll be designed and implemented so well that tuning efforts will be minimal. So administering the database will become easier as the users get a better product, while the database works—and works well.

PART 1

Database Architecture

CHAPTER 1

The Oracle Architecture

Putting together a jigsaw puzzle can be a difficult task—even more so when the pieces are all turned upside down. And although putting together an upside-down puzzle is a distressingly easy task for some four-year-olds I know, most people muddle through the process slowly. Each piece is considered in relation to its neighbors, rather than as part of a bigger picture.

This chapter provides the big picture of the Oracle architecture. It also provides details on its pieces and the basic implementation concepts that guide their usage. It describes the physical, memory, and process structures that provide data to users. Administering an Oracle database requires knowing how these different structures interact, where they fit in the big picture, and how to best customize the system to meet your needs. In many ways, this chapter is a road map to the detailed discussions of database administration in the rest of the book.

An Overview of Databases and Instances

Two basic concepts have to be understood in order to make any sense out of the Oracle architecture: databases and instances. In the following two major sections you will see descriptions of both of these concepts and their implementation in Oracle.

Databases

An Oracle *database* is a set of data. Oracle provides the ability to store and access this data in a manner consistent with a defined model known as the Relational Model. Because of this, Oracle is referred to as a relational database management system (RDBMS). Most references to a "database" refer not only to the physical data but also to the combination of physical, memory, and process objects described in this chapter.

Data in a database is stored in tables. Relational tables are defined by their *columns*, and are given a name. Data is then stored as *rows* in the table. Tables can be related to each other, and the database can be used to enforce these relationships. A sample table structure is shown in Figure 1-1.

An Oracle database stores its data in files. Internally, there are database structures that provide a logical mapping of data to files, allowing different types of data to be stored separately. These logical divisions are called tablespaces. The next two subsections describe tablespaces and files.

Tablespaces

A *tablespace* is a logical division of a database. Each database has at least one tablespace (called the *SYSTEM* tablespace). Other tablespaces may be used to group users or applications together for ease of maintenance and for performance benefits. Examples of such tablespaces would be USERS for general use and RBS for rollback segments (which will be described later in this section). A tablespace can belong to only one database.

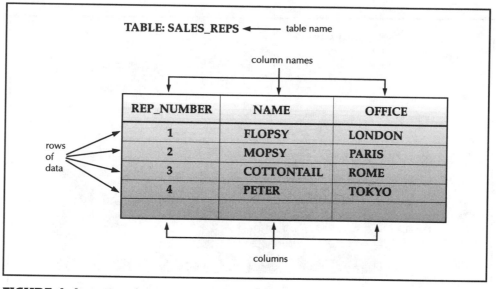

FIGURE 1-1. *Sample Table Structure*

Files

Each tablespace is comprised of one or more files, called *datafiles,* on a disk. A datafile can belong to one and only one tablespace. Datafiles are fixed in size at the time of their creation; when more space is needed, new files must be added. Creating new tablespaces requires creating new datafiles.

Dividing database objects among multiple tablespaces thus allows for those objects to be physically stored in separate datafiles, which may be placed on separate disks. This is an important tool in planning and tuning the way in which the database handles the I/O requests made against it. The relationship between tablespaces and datafiles is illustrated in Figure 1-2.

Instances

In order to access the data in the database, Oracle uses a set of background processes that are shared by all users. In addition, there are memory structures that are used to store the most recently queried data from the database. These memory areas

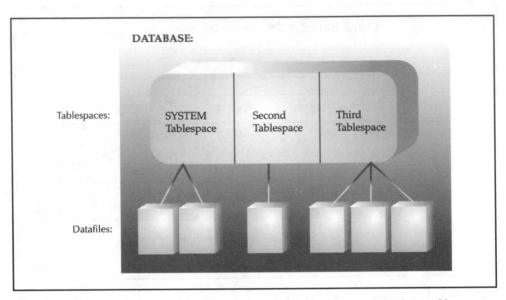

FIGURE 1-2. *Relationship Between Databases, Tablespaces, and Datafiles*

help to improve database performance by decreasing the amount of I/O performed against the datafiles.

A database *instance* (also known as a *server*) is a set of memory structures and background processes that access a set of database files. It is possible for a single database to be accessed by multiple instances (this is the Parallel Server option). The relationship between instances and databases is illustrated in Figure 1-3.

The parameters that determine the size and composition of an instance are stored in a file called INIT.ORA. This file is read during instance startup and may be modified by the DBA. Any modifications made to this file will not take effect until the next startup that uses this file.

Internal Database Structures

Given this overview of databases and instances, Oracle's database structures can be divided into three categories:

■ Those that are internal to the database (such as tables)

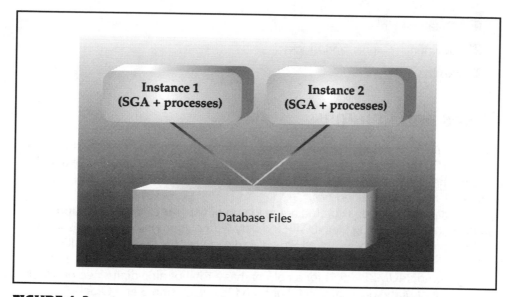

FIGURE 1-3.   *Instances and Databases in Oracle*

- Those that are internal to memory areas (including shared memory areas and processes)
- Those that are external to the database

In the following sections, you will find descriptions of each of the elements within each category. The categories will be presented in the order listed above.

First, those elements that are internal to the database will be described. These include:

- Tables, Columns, Datatypes, and Constraints
- Users and Schemas
- Indexes, Clusters, and Hash Clusters
- Views
- Sequences
- Procedures, Functions, Packages, and Triggers
- Synonyms
- Privileges and Roles

■   Database Links

■   Segments, Extents, and Blocks

■   Rollback Segments

Tables and Columns

Tables are the storage mechanism for data within an Oracle database. As shown in Figure 1-1, they are comprised of a fixed set of columns. The columns of a table describe the attributes of the entity being tracked by the table. Each column has a name and specific characteristics.

The characteristics of a column are made up of two parts: its *datatype* and its *length*. For columns using the NUMBER datatype, the additional characteristics of precision and scale can be specified. *Precision* determines the number of significant digits in a numeric value. *Scale* determines the placement of the decimal point. A specification of NUMBER (9,2) for a column has a total of nine digits, two of which are to the right of the decimal point. For both Oracle Version 6 and Oracle7, the default precision is 38 digits, which is also the maximum precision.

The available datatypes for Oracle Version 6 are listed in Table 1-1.

DATATYPE	DESCRIPTION
CHAR	A variable-length field, up to 255 characters in length.
DATE	A fixed-length, seven-byte field used to store all dates. The time is stored as part of the date. When queried, the date will be in the format DD-MON-YY, as in 13-APR-94 for April 13, 1994.
NUMBER	A variable-length number column. Allowed values are zero, and positive and negative numbers with magnitude 1.OE-129 to 9.99..E124.
LONG	A variable-length field, up to 65,535 characters in length.
RAW	A variable-length field used for binary data, up to 255 characters in length.
LONG RAW	A variable-length field used for binary data, up to 65,535 characters in length.

TABLE 1-1.   *Oracle Version 6 Datatypes*

The available datatypes for Oracle7 are listed in Table 1-2.

The tables owned by the user SYS are called the *data dictionary* tables. They provide a system catalog that the database uses to manage itself.

Tables are related to each other via the columns they have in common. The database can be used to enforce these relationships via *referential integrity*. In Oracle7, referential integrity is enforced at the database level via table constraints.

Table Constraints

A table can have *constraints* placed upon it; when this is done, every row in the table must satisfy the conditions specified in the constraint clauses. Consider the following CREATE TABLE command, which creates a table called EMPLOYEE.

DATATYPE	DESCRIPTION
CHAR	A *fixed-length* field, up to 255 characters in length.
VARCHAR	Presently synonymous with VARCHAR2, but its functionality may change in future releases. Therefore, use the VARCHAR2 datatype to store variable-length character strings.
VARCHAR2	A variable-length field, up to 2,000 characters in length.
DATE	A fixed-length, seven-byte field used to store all dates. The time is stored as part of the date. When queried, the date will be in the format DD-MON-YY, as in 13-APR-94 for April 13, 1994.
NUMBER	A variable-length number column. Allowed values are zero, and positive and negative numbers with magnitude 1.OE-130 to 9.99..E125.
LONG	A variable-length field, up to 2Gb in length.
RAW	A variable-length field used for binary data, up to 2,000 characters in length.
LONG RAW	A variable-length field used for binary data, up to 2Gb in length.
MLSLABEL	For Trusted Oracle only. This datatype uses between two and five bytes per row.

TABLE 1-2.   *Oracle7 Datatypes*

```
CREATE TABLE employee
(empno              NUMBER(10)      PRIMARY KEY,
 name               CHAR(40)        NOT NULL,
 deptno             NUMBER(2)       DEFAULT 10,
 salary             NUMBER(7,2)     CHECK salary<1000000,
 birth_date         DATE,
 soc_sec_num        CHAR(9)         UNIQUE,
 FOREIGN KEY (deptno) REFERENCES dept.deptno)
TABLESPACE users;
```

First, note that the table is given a name (EMPLOYEE). Each of its columns is named ("EMPNO", "NAME", etc.). Each column has a specified datatype and length. The "EMPNO" column is specified as a NUMBER datatype, with no scale—this is the equivalent of an integer. The "NAME" column is specified as a CHAR(40); in Oracle Version 6, this would be a variable-length column up to 40 characters in length. In Oracle7, it is a fixed-length column; any values less than 40 characters in length would be padded with spaces to reach a 40-character length.

The *primary key* of the table is the column or set of columns that makes every row in that table unique. A primary key column will be defined within the database as being *NOT NULL*—this means that every row that is stored in that table must have a value for that column; it cannot be left NULL. The NOT NULL constraint can be applied to the columns in the table, as used for the NAME column in the above example.

A column in an Oracle7 database can have a *DEFAULT* constraint. This will be used to generate a value for a column when a row is inserted in a table, but no value is specified for a column. The *CHECK* constraint is also unique to Oracle7; it is used to ensure that values in a specified column meet a certain criterion (in this case, that the SALARY column's value is less than 1,000,000).

Another Oracle7 constraint, *UNIQUE*, is used to specify uniqueness for columns that should be unique but are not part of the primary key. In this example, the "SOC_SEC_NUM" column has a UNIQUE constraint. This means that every record in this table must have a unique value for this column.

A *foreign key* constraint is used to specify the nature of the relationship between tables. A foreign key from one table references a primary key that has been previously defined elsewhere in the database.

For example, if another table, called DEPT, had a primary key of DEPTNO, then the records in that table would list all of the valid DEPTNO values. The DEPTNO column in the EMPLOYEE table shown above *references* that DEPT.DEPTNO column. By specifying EMPLOYEE.DEPTNO as a foreign key to DEPT.DEPTNO, you guarantee that no DEPTNO values can be entered into the EMPLOYEE table unless those values already exist in the DEPT table.

Both foreign and primary keys can be defined in Oracle7 and in Oracle Version 6. However, the enforcement of these constraints changed between the two versions. In Oracle7, the constraint is enforced for each row, so that all relationships are maintained at the data level. In Oracle Version 6, there is no enforcement at the data level; the only enforcement is that a table that has a primary key constraint cannot be dropped if that primary key is referenced by foreign keys elsewhere in the database.

In Oracle 7, the constraints in the database help to ensure the *referential integrity* of the data. This provides assurance that all of the references within the database are valid, and all constraints have been met.

Users

A *user* account is not a physical structure in the database, but it does have important relationships to the objects in the database: users own the database's objects. The user SYS owns the *data dictionary tables*; these store information about the rest of the structures in the database. The user SYSTEM owns views that access these data dictionary tables, for use by the rest of the users in the database.

When objects are created in the database in support of applications, they are created under user accounts. Each such account can be customized to use a specific tablespace as its default tablespace.

Database accounts can be connected to an operating system account; this allows users to access the database from the operating system without having to enter passwords for both the operating system and the database. They can then access the objects they own or to which they have been granted access.

Schemas

The set of objects owned by a user account is called the user's *schema*. In Oracle7, it is possible to create users who do not have the ability to log into the database. Such user accounts provide a schema that can be used to hold a set of database objects separate from other users' schemas.

Indexes

In a relational database, the physical location of a row is irrelevant—unless, of course, the database needs to find it. In order to make it possible to find data, each row in each table is labeled with a *ROWID*. This ROWID tells the database exactly where the row is located (by file, block within that file, and row within that block).

An index is a database structure used by the server to quickly find a row in a table. There are two types of indexes: cluster indexes and table indexes.

Indexes contain a list of entries; each entry consists of a key value and a ROWID. The key value is the value of a column in a row or the combination of values of columns in a row. Entries in table and cluster indexes in an Oracle database are stored using a B*-tree mechanism guaranteeing a short access path to the key value. The I/O required to find a key value is minimal, and once found, the ROWID is used to directly access a row.

Indexes are used in both Oracle Version 6 and Oracle7 for performance and to ensure uniqueness of a column.

In Oracle Version 6, if the UNIQUE constraint clause is specified for a column in a CREATE TABLE command, the constraint is not enforced unless a table index is created for the column.

In Oracle7, an index is automatically created when a UNIQUE or PRIMARY KEY constraint clause is specified in a CREATE TABLE command.

Indexes can be created on one or multiple columns of a table. In the example of the EMPLOYEE table given earlier, an Oracle7 database will automatically create unique indexes on the EMPNO and SOC_SEC_NUM columns since they have been specified as PRIMARY KEY and UNIQUE, respectively. In an Oracle Version 6 database, the indexes would have to be created via separate commands. Dropping an index will not affect the data within the previously indexed table.

Clusters

Tables that are frequently accessed together may be physically stored together. To store them together, a *cluster* is created to hold the tables. The data in the tables is then stored together to minimize the number of I/Os that must be performed and thus improve performance.

The related columns of the tables are called the *cluster key*. The cluster key is indexed using a cluster index, and its value is only stored once for the multiple tables in the cluster.

Hash Clusters

In Oracle7, a second type of cluster is supported. *Hash clusters* use *hashing functions* on the row's cluster key to determine the physical location where the row should be stored. This will yield the greatest performance benefit for queries of the form shown in the following listing.

```
SELECT name
FROM employee
WHERE empno = 123;
```

In this example, the EMPLOYEE table is queried for an exact match of the EMPNO column. If that table was part of a hash cluster, and EMPNO was part of the cluster key, then the database could use the hashing function to quickly determine where the data was physically located. The same performance gains would not be expected if the WHERE clause had specified a range of values, as in the following listing.

```
SELECT name
FROM employee
WHERE empno > 123;
```

Views

A *view* appears to be a table containing columns and is queried in the same manner that a table is queried. Conceptually, a view can be thought of as a mask overlaying one or more tables, such that the columns in the view are found in one or more underlying tables. Thus, views do not use physical storage to store data. The definition of a view (which includes the query it is based on, its column layout, and privileges granted) is stored in the data dictionary.

When a view is queried, it then queries the tables that it is based on, and returns the values in the format and order specified by the view definition. Since there is no physical data directly associated with them, views cannot be indexed.

Sequences

Sequence definitions are also stored in the data dictionary. Sequences are used to simplify programming efforts by providing a sequential list of unique numbers.

The first time a sequence is called by a query, it returns a predetermined value. Each subsequent query against the sequence will yield a value that is increased by its specified increment. Sequences can cycle, or may continue increasing until a specified maximum value is reached.

Procedures

A *procedure* is a block of PL/SQL statements that is stored in the data dictionary and is called by applications. Procedures allow you to store frequently used application logic within the database. When the procedure is executed, its statements are executed as a unit. Procedures do not return any value to the calling program. They are not available in Oracle Version 6.

Stored procedures can help enforce data security. To accomplish this, do not grant users access directly to the tables within an application. Instead, grant them the ability to execute a procedure that accesses the tables. When the procedure is executed, it will execute with the privileges of the procedure's owner. The users will be unable to access the tables except via the procedure.

Functions

Functions, like procedures, are blocks of code that are stored in the database. Unlike procedures, though, functions are capable of returning values to the calling program. They are not available in Oracle Version 6.

Packages

Packages are used to arrange procedures and functions into logical groupings; their definitions are stored in the Oracle7 data dictionary. Packages are very useful in the administrative tasks required for the management of procedures and functions. Their usefulness stems from the ability to organize related procedures.

Different elements within the package can be defined as being "public" or "private." Public elements are accessible to the user of the package, while private elements are hidden from the user. Private elements may include procedures that are called by other procedures within the package.

Triggers

Triggers are procedures that are executed when a specified database event takes place against a specified table in an Oracle7 database. You may use them to augment referential integrity, enforce additional security, or enhance the available auditing options.

There are two types of triggers:

Statement triggers	Fire once for each triggering statement
Row triggers	Fire once for each row in a table affected by the statements

For each of these types, a BEFORE trigger and AFTER trigger can be created for each type of triggering event. Triggering events include INSERTs, UPDATEs, and DELETEs.

Statement triggers are useful if the code in the trigger action does not rely on the data affected. For example, you may create a BEFORE INSERT statement trigger on a table to prevent INSERTs into a table except during specific time periods.

Row triggers are useful if the trigger action relies on the data being affected by the transaction. For example, you may create an AFTER INSERT row trigger to insert new rows into an audit table as well as the trigger's base table.

Synonyms

To completely identify a database object (such as a table or view) in an Oracle distributed database, you must specify the host machine name, the server name, the object's owner, and the object's name. Depending on the location of the object, between one and four of these parameters will be needed. To screen this process from the user, developers can create synonyms that point to the proper object; thus, the user only needs to know the synonym name. Public synonyms are shared by all users of a given database. Private synonyms are owned by individual database account owners.

For example, the EMPLOYEE table that was previously described must be owned by an account—let's say that the owner is HR. From a different user account in the same database, that table could be referenced as HR.EMPLOYEE. However, this requires that the second account knows that the HR account is the owner of the EMPLOYEE table. To avoid this, a public synonym called EMPLOYEE can be created to point to HR.EMPLOYEE. Any time this synonym is referenced, it will point to the proper table. The following SQL statement creates such a synonym.

```
CREATE PUBLIC SYNONYM employee FOR hr.employee;
```

Synonyms can be used to provide pointers for tables, views, procedures, functions, packages, and sequences. They can point to objects within the local database or in remote databases. Pointing to remote databases is accomplished via the use of database links, as described later in this section.

Privileges and Roles

In order to access an object owned by another account, the *privilege* to access that object must first have been granted. Typically, non-owners are granted the privilege to INSERT, SELECT, UPDATE, or DELETE rows from a table or view. Privileges to SELECT values from sequences and EXECUTE procedures and functions may also be granted. No privileges are granted on indexes or triggers, since they are accessed by the database during table activity. Privileges may be granted to individual users or to PUBLIC, which gives the privilege to all users in the database.

In Oracle Version 6, the management of user privileges for a large application can very quickly escalate into a time-consuming ordeal. Each privilege must be granted to each user account as needed by the application. In Oracle7, *roles,* which are groups of privileges, can be used to simplify this process. Privileges can be granted to a role, and the role in turn can be granted to multiple users. Adding new users to applications then becomes a much easier process to manage, since it is simply a matter of granting or revoking roles for the user.

The relationship between privileges and roles is shown in Figure 1-4. In Figure 1-4 (a), the privileges required to grant SELECT access on two tables to four users are shown as lines. In Figure 1-4(b), the Oracle7 role capability is used to simplify the privileges administration. The privileges are granted to a single role, and that role is granted to the four users.

Oracle7 role groups can also be used to grant system-level privileges, such as CREATE TABLE. This will be discussed in detail in Chapter 5, "Managing the Development Process," and in Chapter 9, "Database Security and Auditing."

Database Links

Oracle databases that are using SQL*Net have the ability to reference data that is stored outside of the local database. When referencing such data, the fully qualified name of the remote object must be specified. In the synonym example

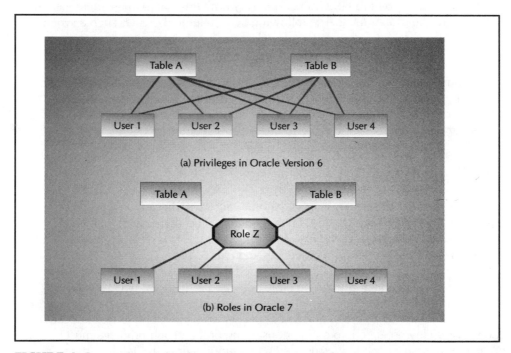

FIGURE 1-4. *Relationship between Privileges and Roles*

given earlier, only two parts of the fully qualified name—the owner and the table name—were specified. What if the table is in a remote database?

To specify an access path to an object in a remote database, you will need to create a *database link*. Database links can either be public (available to all accounts in that database) or private (created by a user for only that account's use). The options available when creating a database link vary depending on which version of SQL*Net is in use; see Chapter 15, "SQL*Net V1 and V2," for more details. The following syntax will work for either version.

```
CREATE PUBLIC DATABASE link my_link
CONNECT TO hr IDENTIFIED BY puffinstuff
USING 't:host1:db1';
```

In this example, the link specifies that when it is used, it will open up a session in the database "db1" on the server named "host1" (the "t:" specifies the TCP/IP driver; the proper driver is system-specific). When it opens the session in the db1 instance, it will log in as the user account HR, with the password "puffinstuff."

To use this link for a table, it must be specified in the FROM clause, as in the following example.

```
SELECT * FROM employee@my_link;
```

This will access the table described earlier. It is possible to create a synonym for this table, as shown in the following SQL command.

```
CREATE SYNONYM employee FOR employee@mylink;
```

Note that the fully qualified designation for the database object has been defined—its host (host1), its database (db1), its owner (HR), and its name (EMPLOYEE).

The location of the EMPLOYEE table is thus completely transparent to the end user. SQL*Net V2 developers may also take advantage of *service names* to make the data location even more transparent. You may also leave out the "connect to" line if the same account and password will be used in the remote database as is used in the local database. These options are fully explained in Chapter 15, "SQL*Net V1 and V2."

Segments, Extents, and Blocks

Segments are the physical counterpart to logical database objects that store data. Index segments, for example, store the data associated with indexes. The effective management of segments requires that the DBA know the objects that an application will use, how data will be entered into those objects, and the ways in which it will be retrieved.

Because a segment is a physical entity, it must be assigned to a tablespace in the database (and will thus be placed in one of the datafiles of that tablespace). A segment is made up of sections called *extents*—contiguous sets of Oracle blocks. Once the existing extents in a segment can no longer hold new data, the segment will obtain another extent. This extension process will continue until no more free space is available in the tablespace's datafiles, or until an internal maximum number of extents per segment is reached. If a segment is comprised of multiple extents, there is no guarantee that those extents will be contiguous.

Information about the management of specific types of segments is provided in Chapter 4, "Physical Database Layouts," and in Chapter 7, "Managing Rollback Segments."

Rollback Segments

In order to maintain read consistency among multiple users in the database and to be able to roll back transactions, Oracle must have a mechanism for reconstructing a "before image" of data for uncommitted transactions. Oracle uses *rollback segments* within the database to accomplish this.

Rollback segments will grow to be as large as the transactions they support. The effective management of rollback segments is described in Chapter 7, "Managing Rollback Segments."

Internal Memory Structures

There are two different types of memory structures used by the Oracle database: global areas and process areas. Process areas will be described in the next section. This section will focus on the global memory areas used by all Oracle database users.

Depending on the database server option used, the implementation of the memory options available may vary widely. The most common implementations will be described here and in Chapter 2, "Hardware Configurations and Considerations."

The elements described in this section include

■ System Global Area (SGA)

■ Data Block Buffers

■ Dictionary Cache

■ Redo Log Buffer

- Shared SQL Pool
- Context Areas
- Program Global Area (PGA)

System Global Area (SGA)

If you were to read a chapter of this book (say, Chapter 4 on planning physical database layouts), what would be the quickest way of passing that information on to someone else? You could have the other person read that chapter as well, but it would be quickest if you could hold all of the information in memory, and then pass that information from your memory to the second person.

The *System Global Area (SGA)* in an Oracle database serves the same purpose—it facilitates the transfer of information between users. It also holds the most commonly requested structural information about the database.

The SGA is divided into three main sections in Oracle Version 6. These sections are also found in Oracle7, along with additional shared areas that were process-specific in Oracle Version 6.

The composition of the SGA is shown in Figure 1-5. Figure 1-5(a) shows the SGA structure for Oracle Version 6, Figure 1-5(b), the same structure for Oracle7. The shared areas in the figures are described in the following sections.

Data Block Buffers

The *data block buffers* are a cache in the SGA used to hold the data blocks that are read from the data segments in the database, such as tables, indexes, and clusters. The size of the data block buffer cache is determined by the DB_BLOCK_BUFFERS parameter in the INIT.ORA file for that database server. Managing the size of the data block buffer cache plays an important part in managing and tuning the database.

Since the data block buffer cache is fixed in size, and is usually smaller than the space used by database segments, it cannot hold all of the database's segments in memory at once. Oracle will manage the space available by using a *Least Recently Used (LRU)* algorithm. When free space is needed in the cache, the least recently used blocks will be written out to disk. New data blocks will take their place in memory. In this manner, the most frequently used data is kept in memory.

However, if the SGA is not large enough, then different objects will contend for space within the data block buffer cache. This is particularly likely when multiple applications share the same SGA. In that case, the most recently used segments from each application constantly contend for space in the SGA with the most recently used segments from other applications. As a result, requests for data from the data block buffer cache will result In a lower ratio of "hits" to "misses." For information

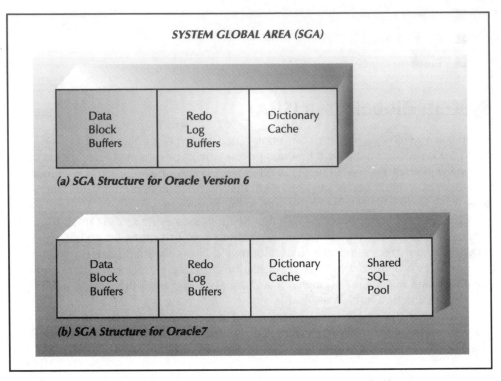

FIGURE 1-5. *SGA Structures in Oracle Version 6 and Oracle7*

on monitoring the usage of the data block buffer cache, see the "Interpreting the Statistics Reports" section of Chapter 6, "Monitoring Multiple Databases."

Dictionary Cache

Information about database objects is stored in the data dictionary tables. This information includes user account data, datafile names, segment names, extent locations, table descriptions, and privileges. When this information is needed by the database (for example, to check a user's authorization to query a table), the data dictionary tables are read and the data that is returned is stored in the SGA in the *dictionary cache.*

This cache is also managed via an LRU algorithm. In Oracle7, the size of the dictionary cache is managed internally by the database; it is part of the shared SQL pool whose size is set via the SHARED_POOL_SIZE parameter in the database's INIT.ORA parameter. In Oracle Version 6, the size of each cache within the dictionary cache is set manually via separate entries in the database's INIT.ORA file (such as DC_TABLES for the number of entries in the table definition cache).

If the dictionary cache is too small, then the database will have to repeatedly query the data dictionary tables for information needed by the database. These queries are called *recursive hits,* and are slower to resolve than are queries that can be handled solely by the dictionary cache in memory. For information on monitoring the usage of the dictionary cache, see the "Interpreting the Statistics Reports" section of Chapter 6, "Monitoring Multiple Databases."

Redo Log Buffer

Redo log files are described in the section, "Redo Logs," later in this chapter. Redo entries describe the changes that are made to the database. They are written to the online redo log files so that they can be used in roll-forward operations during database recoveries. Before being written to the online redo log files, however, they are first cached in the SGA in an area called the *redo log buffer.* The database then periodically writes batches of redo entries to the online redo log files, thus optimizing this operation.

The size (in bytes) of the redo log buffers is set via the LOG_BUFFER parameter in the INIT.ORA file.

Shared SQL Pool

In Oracle7 databases, the dictionary cache is stored in an area called the *shared SQL pool.* This memory area also includes information about statements that are run against the database. Thus, while the data block buffer and dictionary cache enable sharing of structural and data information between users in the database, the shared SQL pool allows the sharing of commonly used SQL statements.

The shared SQL pool contains the execution plan and parse tree for SQL statements run against the database. The second time that an identical SQL statement is run (by any user), it is able to take advantage of the parse information available in the shared SQL pool to expedite its execution. For information on monitoring the usage of the shared SQL pool, see the "Interpreting the Statistics Reports" section of Chapter 6, "Monitoring Multiple Databases."

Context Areas

Within the Oracle7 shared SQL area, there are both public and private areas. Every SQL statement issued by a user requires a private SQL area, which continues to exist until the cursor corresponding to that statement is closed. The analogous structure in Oracle Version 6 is called a *context area*; however, since there are no shared SQL pools in Oracle Version 6 (and thus no public SQL areas), the context areas must manage all of the information tracked by the Oracle7 shared SQL pool.

Program Global Area (PGA)

The *Program Global Area* (*PGA*) is an area in memory that is used by a single Oracle user process. In Oracle Version 6 it contains the user's context areas, as well as process control information. The memory in the PGA is not shareable.

If you are using Oracle7, then part of the PGA may be stored in the SGA. This occurs when the Oracle7 *multithreaded server* is used. The multithreaded server architecture allows multiple user processes to use the same server process, thus reducing the database's memory requirements. If this option is used, then the user session information is stored in the SGA rather than in the PGA.

Process Structures

The relationships between the database's physical and memory structures are maintained and enforced by *process structures.* These are the database's own background processes, which may vary in number depending on your database's configuration. These processes are managed by the database and require little administrative work.

The following sections describe each background process and the role it plays in managing the database. The relationships between the physical structures and the memory structures in the database, along with the major processes, are shown in Figure 1-6.

System Monitor: SMON

The *SMON* background process serves the same basic system monitoring functions in both Oracle7 and Oracle Version 6. When the database is started, SMON performs instance recovery as needed (using the online redo log files). It also cleans up the database, eliminating transactional objects that are no longer needed by the system.

In Oracle7, SMON serves an additional purpose: it coalesces contiguous free extents into larger free extents. The free space fragmentation process is conceptually described in Chapter 4, "Physical Database Layouts." Oracle Version 6 DBAs must manually perform the free space coalescence; a utility for performing this task is given in Chapter 8, "Database Tuning."

Process Monitor: PMON

The *PMON* background process cleans up behind failed user processes in both Oracle Version 6 and Oracle7. PMON frees up the resources that the user was using. Its effects can be seen when a process holding a lock is killed; PMON is responsible for releasing the lock and making it available to other users. Like SMON, PMON wakes up periodically to check if it is needed.

Database Writer: DBWR

The *DBWR* background process is responsible for managing the contents of the data block buffer cache and the dictionary cache. It reads the blocks from the datafiles and stores them in the SGA. It performs batch writes of changed blocks back to the datafiles. Tuning the activities of the DBWR process (efficiency of reads from datafiles, efficiency of reads from memory) comprises much of the tuning effort that DBAs perform.

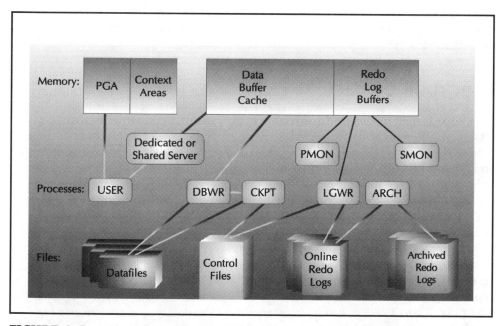

FIGURE 1-6.   *Physical, Memory, and Process Structures in Oracle*

Although there is only one SMON and one PMON process running per database instance, it is possible to have multiple DBWR processes running at the same time, depending on the platform and operating system. Using multiple DBWR processes helps to minimize contention within DBWR during large queries that span datafiles. The number of DBWR processes running is set via the DB_WRITERS parameter in the database's INIT.ORA file.

Log Writer: LGWR

The *LGWR* background process manages the writing of the contents of the redo log buffer to the online redo log files. It writes log entries to the online redo log files in batches. The redo log buffer entries always contain the most up-to-date status of the database, since the DBWR process may wait before writing changed blocks from the data block buffers to the datafiles.

Note that LGWR is the only process that writes to the online redo log files and the only one that directly reads the redo log buffers during normal database operation. The online redo log files are written to in sequential fashion, as opposed to the fairly random accesses that DBWR performs against the datafiles. If the online redo log files are mirrored (as they can be in Oracle7), LGWR writes to the mirrored sets of logs simultaneously. See Chapter 2, "Hardware Configurations and Considerations," for details on this mirroring capability.

Checkpoint (Oracle7): CKPT

Checkpoints help to reduce the amount of time needed to perform instance recovery. Checkpoints cause DBWR to write all of the blocks that have been modified since the last checkpoint to the datafiles and update the datafile headers and control files to record the checkpoint. They occur automatically when an online redo log file fills; the LOG_CHECKPOINT_INTERVAL parameter in the database instance's INIT.ORA file may be used to set a more frequent checkpoint. In Oracle Version 6, setting LOG_CHECKPOINT_INTERVAL is the only method available to change checkpoint frequency.

In Oracle7 only, an additional background process, *CKPT*, may be created to separate the two functions of LGWR (signaling checkpoints and copying redo entries) between two background processes. The CKPT background process is enabled by setting the CHECKPOINT_PROCESS parameter in the database instance's INIT.ORA file to TRUE. It is not necessary unless the database experiences a high transaction volume, which in turn causes delays at log switches.

Archiver: ARCH

The LGWR background process writes to the online redo log files in a cyclical fashion; after filling the first log file, it begins writing the second, until that one fills, and then begins writing to the third. Once the last online redo log file is filled, LGWR begins to overwrite the contents of the first redo log file.

When Oracle is run in ARCHIVELOG mode, the database makes a copy of each redo log file before overwriting it. These archived redo log files are usually written to a disk device. They may also be written directly to a tape device, but this tends to be very operator-intensive.

The archiving function is performed by the *ARCH* background process. Databases using this option will encounter contention problems on their redo log disk during heavy data transaction times, since LGWR will be trying to write to one redo log file while ARCH is trying to read another. They may also encounter database lockups if the archive log destination disk fills. At that point, ARCH freezes, which prevents LGWR from writing, which in turn prevents any further transactions from occurring in the database until space is cleared for the archived redo log files.

Recoverer (Oracle7, Distributed Option): RECO

The *RECO* background process is used to resolve failures in Oracle7 distributed databases. This process attempts to access databases involved in in-doubt transactions and resolve the transactions. This process is only created if the Oracle7 Distributed Option is supported on the platform and the DISTRIBUTED_TRANSACTIONS parameter in the INIT.ORA file is set to a value greater than zero.

Lock (Parallel Server): LCKn

Multiple *LCK* processes, named LCK0 through LCK9, are used for inter-instance locking when the Oracle7 Parallel Server and Oracle 6.2 Parallel Server options are used. In Oracle Version 6.2, the number of LCK processes is set via the MI_BG_PROCS parameter in the database's INIT.ORA file; in Oracle7, it is set via the GC_LCK_PROCS parameter.

Dispatcher (Oracle7, SQL*Net V2): Dnnn

Dispatcher processes are part of the SQL*Net V2 multithreaded server (MTS) architecture; they help to minimize resource needs by handling multiple connections. At least one dispatcher process must be created for each protocol that is being supported on the database server. These processes are described in Chapter 15, "SQL*Net V1 and V2." Dispatcher processes are created at database startup, based on the SQL*Net configuration, and can be created or removed while the database is open.

Server: Snnn

Server processes are created to manage connections to the database that require a dedicated server. These are typical of pre-SQL*Net V2 connections.

External Structures

The database's datafiles, as described earlier in the "Files" portion of the overview section of this chapter, provide the physical storage for the database's data. Thus, they are both "internal" structures, since they are tied directly to tablespaces, and "external," since they are physical files. The planning process for their distribution across devices is described in Chapter 4, "Physical Database Layouts."

The following types of files, although related to the database, are separate from the datafiles. These files include

- Redo Logs
- Control Files

Redo Logs

Oracle maintains logs of all transactions against the database. These transactions are recorded in a file called an *online redo log file*. These logs are used to recover the database's transactions in their proper order in the event of a database crash. The redo log information is stored external to the database's datafiles.

Redo log files also let Oracle streamline the manner in which it writes data to disk. When a transaction occurs in the database, it is entered in the redo log buffers, while the data blocks affected by the transaction are not immediately written to disk. This allows the database to perform batch writes to disk, thus optimizing the performance of this function.

Each Oracle database will have two or more online redo log files. Oracle writes to online redo log files in a cyclical fashion: after the first log file is filled, it writes to the second log file, until that one is filled. When all of the online redo log files have been filled, it returns to the first log file and begins overwriting its contents with new transaction data. If the database is running in Archivelog mode, then the database will make a copy of the online redo log files before overwriting them. These archived redo log files can then be used to recover any part of the database to any point in time (see Chapter 10, "Optimal Backup and Recovery Procedures").

In Oracle7, redo log files may be mirrored (replicated) within the database. This allows the DBA to mirror the redo log files without relying on the operating system or hardware capabilities of the operating environment. See Chapter 2, "Hardware Configurations and Considerations," for details on this mirroring capability.

Control Files

A database's overall physical architecture is maintained by its control files. These record control information about all of the files within the database. They are used to maintain internal consistency and guide recovery operations.

Since the control files are critical to the database, multiple copies are stored online. These files are typically stored on separate disks to minimize the potential damage due to disk failures. The database will create and maintain the control files specified at database creation. An example of this is shown in the database creation scripts in Appendix A, "Database Creation Procedures."

Basic Database Implementation

In its simplest form, an Oracle database consists of

- One or more datafiles
- One or more control files
- Two or more online redo logs

Internally, that database contains

- Multiple users/schemas
- One or more rollback segments
- One or more tablespaces
- Data dictionary tables
- 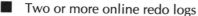 User objects (tables, indexes, views, etc.)

The server that accesses that database consists of (at a minimum)

- An SGA (includes the data block buffer cache, dictionary cache, redo log buffer cache, and in Oracle7 the shared SQL pool)
- The SMON background process
- The PMON background process
- The DBWR background process
- The LGWR background process
- User processes with associated PGAs

This is the base configuration; everything else is optional or dependent on the Oracle version and options you are using.

The remainder of this section will provide an overview of the recovery and security capabilities of the database, as well as sample logical and physical layouts for Oracle databases.

Backup/Recovery Capabilities

The Oracle database features a number of backup and recovery options. Each of these will be described in detail in Chapter 10, "Optimal Backup and Recovery Procedures." The available options are described in the following sections.

Export/Import

The *Export* utility queries the database and stores its output in a binary file. The portions of the database that it reads may be customized. You may direct it to read the entire database, a user's or a set of users' schema(s), or a specific set of tables. It also has options that allow it to only export the tables that have changed since the last export (called an *incremental* export) or since the last full system export (called a *cumulative* export).

Full system exports read the full data dictionary tables as well. A full export can thus be used to completely re-create a database, since the data dictionary tracks users, datafiles, and database objects. It is commonly used to eliminate fragmentation in the database (see Chapter 8, "Database Tuning").

Export performs a logical read of the database. To read information out of the binary dump file created by the export, the *Import* utility must be used. Import can selectively choose objects or users from the dump file to import. It will then attempt to insert that data into the database (rather than overwriting existing records).

Offline Backups

In addition to logical (export) backups of the database, physical backups of its files can also be made. To make a physical backup of the database, there are two options available: *online backups* and *offline backups*. Offline backups are performed by first shutting down the database; the files that comprise the database can then be backed up to a storage device (disk-to-disk copies or tape writes). Once the backup is complete, the database can be reopened. It is not possible to perform incremental physical backups of the Oracle database.

Even if it is not the main backup and recovery option being implemented, it is still a good idea to make a offline backup of the database periodically (such as when the host it resides on undergoes routine maintenance).

Online Backups

Online backups are available for those databases that are being run in ARCHIVELOG mode (described in the "Archiver: ARCH" process section). They allow the DBA to make physical database backups while the database is open. This is accomplished by placing tablespaces temporarily into a backup state, then restoring them to their normal state when their files have been backed up. This capability was introduced with Oracle Version 6.

Security Capabilities

The full security-related capabilities within Oracle will be described in detail in Chapter 9, "Database Security and Auditing." This section will provide an overview of these capabilities within Oracle.

Account Security

Database accounts may be password-protected. This protection is separate from the operating-system password protection. Accounts may also be created using an autologin capability; this allows users who have accessed a host account to access a related database account without entering a database password. Having an account or privileges in one database does not give a user an account or privileges in any other database.

Database Privileges

In Oracle Version 6, there are only three levels of system privileges within the database: CONNECT, RESOURCE, and DBA. All users need CONNECT, and those who will be creating segments need to have RESOURCE privilege.

In Oracle7, system-level roles can be created from the full set of system-level privileges (such as CREATE TABLE, CREATE INDEX, SELECT ANY TABLE) to extend the basic set of system-level roles. CONNECT, RESOURCE, and DBA are still available in Oracle7, but they are now roles instead of privileges.

Object Security
Users who have created objects may grant privileges on those objects to other users via the GRANT command. They may also grant to other users the ability to make further grants on their objects. In Oracle7, the GRANT ANY TABLE privilege gives accounts the ability to grant privileges on any object to any user.

Auditing
User activities that involve database objects may be audited via the AUDIT command. These may include table accesses, login attempts, and DBA-privileged activities. The results of these audits are stored in an audit table within the database. Oracle7 offers the full set of Oracle Version 6 auditing capabilities, plus additional options such as the use of database triggers to supplement regular audits.

Sample Logical Database Layout

The logical layout of an Oracle database has a great impact on the administrative options the DBA has. The tablespace layout shown in Table 1-3 is based on the design considerations given in Chapter 3, "Logical Database Layouts." The

TABLESPACE	USE
SYSTEM	Data dictionary
DATA	Standard-operation tables for an application
DATA_2	Static tables used during standard application operation
INDEXES	Indexes for the standard-operation application tables
INDEXES_2	Indexes for the static application tables
RBS	Standard-operation rollback segments
RBS_2	Specialty rollback segments used for data loads
TEMP	Standard-operation temporary segments
TEMP_*USER*	Temporary segments created by a particular user
TOOLS	RDBMS tools tables
TOOLS_I	Indexes for RDBMS tools tables
USERS	User objects, in development databases

TABLE 1-3. *Sample Logical Database Layout*

objective of this layout is to isolate database segments based on their usage and characteristics.

Sample Physical Database Layout

The proper physical layout for the database files is database-specific; however, certain general rules can be applied to correctly separate database files whose I/O requests will conflict with each other. A detailed discussion of this topic is given in Chapter 4, "Database Physical Layouts." The configuration shown in Figure 1-7 is given as a sample configuration for a 12-disk Production system. The procedures given in Chapter 4 should be followed to determine the proper distribution of files that will meet your needs.

Understanding Logical Modeling Conventions

In the previous section on table constraints, several data-modeling terms were defined. This section will show how the relationships implied by those terms are graphically depicted. The information in this section will assist DBAs in interpreting application data models (some of which are used in this book).

```
Disk        Contents
1           Oracle software
2           SYSTEM tablespace, Control file 1
3           RBS tablespace, RBS_2 tablespace, Control file 2
4           DATA tablespace, Control file 3
5           INDEX tablespace
6           TEMP tablespace, TEMP_USER tablespace
7           TOOLS tablespace, INDEX_2 tablespace
8           Online Redo logs 1, 2, and 3
9           Application software
10          DATA_2
11          Archived redo log destination disk
12          Export dump file destination disk
```

FIGURE 1-7. *Sample 12-Disk Configuration for Physical Database Files*

A *primary key (PK)* is the column or set of columns that makes each record in a table unique. A *foreign key (FK)* is a set of columns that refers back to an existing primary key.

Tables can be related to each other via three types of relationships: *one-to-one*, *one-to-many*, and *many-to-many*. In a one-to-one (*1:1*) relationship, the tables share a common primary key. In a one-to-many (*1:M*) relationship, a single record in one table is related to many records in another table. In a many-to-many (*M:M*) relationship, many records in one table are related to many records in another table. The following sections provide examples of each type of relationship.

These graphical standards for depicting various types of relationships will be used throughout this book.

One-to-One Relationships

It is rare to have two tables that share the exact same primary key. This is usually done for performance or security reasons. For example, Oracle recommends that when a LONG datatype is used in a table, it should be stored in a separate table, with the two tables related to each other in a 1:1 fashion.

Consider the SALES_REPS table from Figure 1-1. What if an additional column, RESUME, with a datatype of LONG, were to be added to the data being stored? Since there is one resume for each sales rep, the RESUME column should be stored in the SALES_REP table. However, this will force the database to read through the LONG value every time the table is queried, even if only the NAME field is being sought.

To improve performance, create a second table, called SALES_REPS_RESUME. This table will have the same primary key (REP_NUMBER), and one additional column (RESUME). The two tables thus have a 1:1 relationship. This is shown graphically in Figure 1-8.

The solid line between the two entities indicates that the relationship is mandatory. Had the relationship been optional, the line would have been partially dashed.

One-to-Many Relationships

One-to-one relationships are rare. It is far more common for a relationship to be of the one-to-many (1:M) variety. In this type of relationship, one record in one table is related to many records in another table.

Consider the SALES_REPS table again. For the records given in Figure 1-1, there is only one sales rep per office. However, it is possible that the data analysis may reveal that multiple sales reps can report to the same office. In this case, a new entity, OFFICE, would be created. The OFFICE column of the SALES_REPS table would then be a foreign key to this new table.

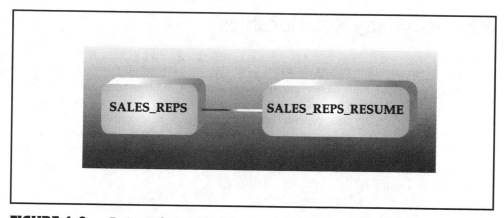

FIGURE 1-8.   *Entity Relationship Diagram for a 1:1 Relationship*

Since many sales reps (records in the SALES_REPS table) can report to a single office (record in the OFFICE table), there is a 1:M relationship between these tables. This is shown graphically in Figure 1-9. Note two differences in the connecting line: the addition of a crow's-foot on the "many" side of the relationship, and the use of a dashed line on the "one" side. The dashed line is used to signify that the relation is not mandatory on that side—in other words, that it is possible to have an office with no sales reps assigned to it.

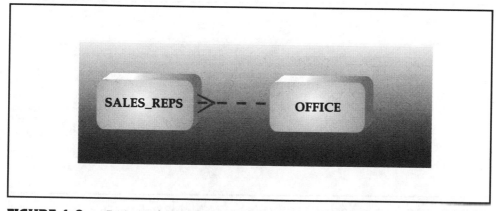

FIGURE 1-9.   *Entity Relationship Diagram for a 1:M Relationship*

Many-to-Many Relationships

It may also be possible that many rows of a table are related to many rows of another table. Consider the SALES_REPS table (Figure 1-1) again. For this example, assume that the data analysis reveals that sales reps contact multiple companies. Furthermore, a single company can be called upon by multiple sales reps. Thus, there is a many-to-many relationship between the SALES_REPS entity and the COMPANIES entity. To understand this relationship, note that a single sales rep (record in the SALES_REPS table) can correspond to multiple companies (records in the COMPANIES table), and that the reverse is also true. This relationship is shown graphically in Figure 1-10.

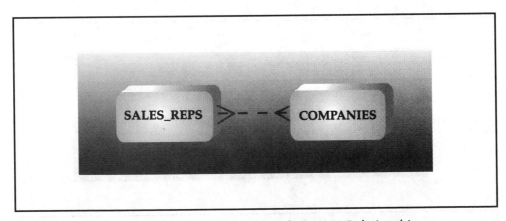

FIGURE 1-10. *Entity Relationship Diagram for a M:M Relationship*

CHAPTER 2

Hardware Configurations and Considerations

Although each Oracle database will be built from the same basic pieces, the options available to you depend on your hardware platform and operating system. For most platforms, you will have a number of options to choose from. This chapter describes the standard architectures available—the ways that the pieces are usually put together. Since Oracle supports over 70 hardware platforms, it will not be possible to cover all of the options in this chapter. Rather, the focus will be on the most common implementations.

Architecture Overview

An Oracle database is comprised of physical files, memory areas, and processes. The distribution of these components varies depending on the database architecture chosen.

The data in the database is stored in physical files (called *datafiles*) on a disk. As it is used, that data is stored in memory. Oracle uses memory areas to improve performance and to manage the sharing of data between users. The main memory area in a database is called the *System Global Area (SGA)*. To read and write data between the SGA and the datafiles, Oracle uses a set of background processes that are shared by all users.

A database *server* (also known as an *instance*) is a set of memory structures and background processes that accesses a set of database files. The relationship between servers and databases is illustrated in Figure 2-1.

The characteristics of the database server—such as the size of the SGA and the number of background processes—are specified during startup. These parameters are stored in a file called INIT.ORA. This file is only read during startup; modifications to it will not take effect until the next startup that uses this file.

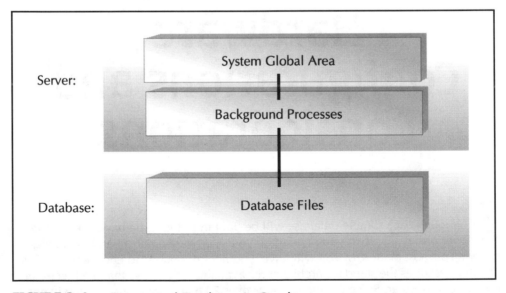

FIGURE 2-1. *Servers and Databases in Oracle*

Stand-Alone Hosts

The simplest conceptual configuration for a database is a single server accessing a single database on a stand-alone, single-disk host. In this configuration, shown in Figure 2-2, all of the files are stored on the server's sole device, and there is only one SGA and one set of Oracle background processes on the server.

The architecture shown in Figure 2-2 represents the minimum configuration. All of the other database configurations are modifications to this base structure.

The files stored on the disk include the database datafiles and the host's INIT.ORA file. As shown in Figure 2-2, there are two main interface points in the database:

- Between the database files and the background processes

- Between the background processes and the SGA

Tuning efforts are mostly comprised of improving the performance of these interface points. If the memory area dedicated to the database is large enough, then fewer repetitive reads will be performed against the database files. If the file

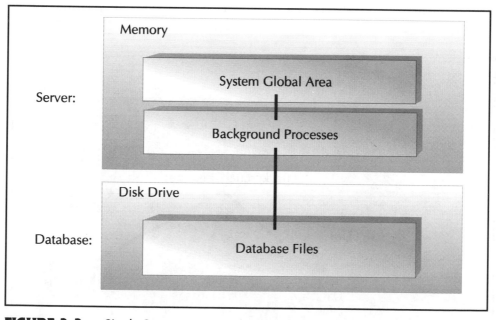

FIGURE 2-2.   *Single Server on a Stand-Alone Host*

distribution is properly planned, then the reads and writes performed against those files by the background processes will be optimized. These topics are covered in detail in Chapter 4, "Physical Database Layouts, " and in Chapter 8, "Database Tuning."

Stand-Alone Hosts with Disk Arrays

If multiple disks are available, then the database files can be separated onto separate devices. This is done to improve database performance by reducing the amount of contention between the database files. During database operation, it is common for information from multiple files to be needed to handle a transaction or query. If the files are not distributed across multiple disks, then the system will need to read from multiple files on the same disk concurrently. The separation of files across multiple disks is shown in Figure 2-3.

The database uses several types of files. These file types, and guidelines for their optimal distribution across multiple disks, are described in Chapter 4, "Physical Database Layouts."

Control File Mirroring

The INIT.ORA file for the server that accesses the database is stored in the Oracle software directories, usually in ORACLE_HOME/dbs. It does not list the names of

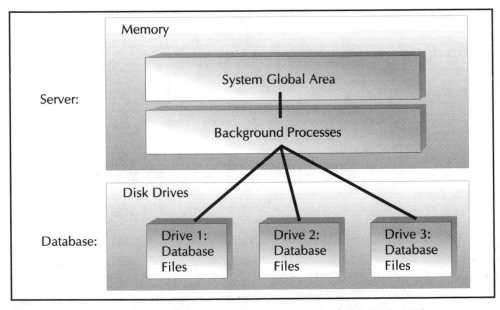

FIGURE 2-3. *Single Server on a Stand-Alone Host with Multiple Disks*

the datafiles or online redo log files for the database; these are stored within the data dictionary. However, it does list the names of the control files for the database. On a multiple disk host, the control files should be stored on separate disks. The database will keep them in sync. By storing them on multiple disks, you greatly reduce the risk from media failures.

In Oracle7, a second server configuration file, CONFIG.ORA, is called by INIT.ORA. This file is used to set values for those parameters that typically do not change within the database. The control files' names are among those parameters. The following listing shows the entry for the CONTROL_FILES parameter in an Oracle Version 6 INIT.ORA file and an Oracle7 CONFIG.ORA file.

```
control_files              = (/db01/oracle/ORA1/ctrl1ora1.ctl,
                              /db02/oracle/ORA1/ctrl2ora1.ctl,
                              /db03/oracle/ORA1/ctrl3ora1.ctl)
```

This entry names the three control files. If it is used during the database creation, then the database will automatically create the three control files listed here. If you want to add additional control files to an existing database, follow this procedure:

1. Shut down the database.

2. Copy one of the current control files to the new location.

3. Edit the INIT.ORA (Oracle Version 6) or CONFIG.ORA (Oracle7) file, adding the new control file's name to the CONTROL_FILES entry.

4. Restart the database.

The new control file will then be activated.

Redo Log File Mirroring

As noted in the previous section, the database will automatically mirror control files. In Oracle7, the database can also mirror online redo log files. This is accomplished via the use of *redo log groups*. If redo log groups are used, then the operating system does not need to perform the mirroring of the online redo log files; it is done automatically by the database.

When using this functionality, the LGWR (Log Writer) background process simultaneously writes to all of the members of the current online redo log group. Thus, rather than cycling through the redo log files, it instead cycles through *groups* of redo log files. Since the members of a group are usually placed on separate disk drives, there is no disk contention between the files, and LGWR thus experiences little change in performance. See Chapter 4, "Physical Database Layouts," for further information on the placement of redo log files.

Redo log groups can be created via the CREATE DATABASE command. They can also be added to the database after it has been created, via the ALTER DATABASE command. The following listing shows an example of the addition of a redo log group to an existing database. The group is referred to in this example as "GROUP 4." Using group numbers eases their administration; number them sequentially, starting with 1. The ALTER DATABASE command in this example is executed from within SQLDBA.

```
sqldba lmode=y
SQLDBA> connect internal
SQLDBA> ALTER DATABASE
    2> ADD LOGFILE GROUP 4
    3> ('/db01/oracle/CC1/log_1c.dbf',
    4> '/db02/oracle/CC1/log_2c.dbf') size 5M;
```

To add a new redo log file to an existing group, use the ALTER DATABASE command shown in the following listing. As in the previous example, this command is executed from within SQLDBA. It adds a third member to the "GROUP 4" redo log group.

```
sqldba lmode=y
SQLDBA> connect internal
SQLDBA> ALTER DATABASE
    2> ADD LOGFILE MEMBER '/db03/oracle/CC1/log_3c.dbf'
    3> TO GROUP 4;
```

When the ADD LOGFILE MEMBER option of the ALTER DATABASE command is used, no file sizing information is specified. This is because all members of the group must have the same size. Since the group already exists, the database already knows how large to make the new file.

Stand-Alone Hosts with Disk Shadowing

Many operating systems give you the ability to maintain duplicate, synchronized copies of files via a process known as *disk shadowing* or *volume shadowing*. (This practice is also known as *mirroring*.)

There are two benefits to shadowing your disks. First, the shadow set of disks serves as a backup in the event of a disk failure. In most operating systems, a disk failure will cause the corresponding disk from the shadow set to automatically step into the place of the failed disk. The second benefit is that of improved performance. Most operating systems that support volume shadowing can direct file I/O requests to use the shadow set of files instead of the main set of files. This reduces the I/O load on the main set of disks and results in better performance for file I/Os. The use of disk shadowing is shown in Figure 2-4.

The type of shadowing shown in Figure 2-4 is called RAID-1 shadowing. In this type of shadowing, each disk in the main set of disks is paired up, one-to-one, with a disk in the shadow set. Depending on your operating system, other shadowing options may be available. In RAID-3 and RAID-5 shadowing, for example, a set of disks is treated as a single logical unit, and each file is automatically striped across each disk. A parity check system is then used to provide a means of recovering a damaged or failed member of the set of disks.

The method of shadowing that is used will affect how the files are distributed across devices. For example, datafiles that store tables are usually stored on a different disk than the datafiles that store those tables' indexes. However, if RAID-3 or RAID-5 is used, then the distinction between disks is blurred. Accessing a datafile when using those options will almost always require that all of the disks in the set be accessed. Therefore, contention between the disks is more likely.

Despite this, the contention should not be severe. In RAID-5, for example, the first block of data is stored on the first disk of a set, and the second block is stored on the next disk. Thus, the database only has to read a single block off a disk before moving on to the next disk. In this example, any contention that results from multiple accesses of the same disk should therefore last only as long as it takes to perform a single block read.

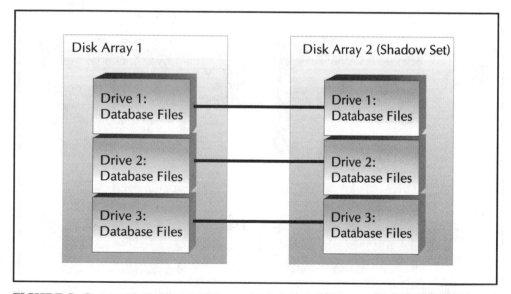

FIGURE 2-4. *Disk Shadowing*

Stand-Alone Hosts with Multiple Databases

You may create multiple databases on a single host. Each database will have a separate set of files and will be accessed by a different server. Guidelines for appropriate directory structures are provided in Chapter 4, "Physical Database Layouts."

Figure 2-5 shows a single host that is supporting two databases. Since each server requires an SGA and background processes, the host must be able to support the memory and process requirements that this configuration will place upon it.

As noted earlier, these configurations are modifications to the base database architecture. In this case, you simply create a second database that mimics the structure of the first. Note that although the two databases are on the same host, they do not (in this case) communicate with each other. The server from the first database cannot access the database file from the second database.

Multiple databases on the same server typically share the same Oracle source code directories. If the INIT.ORA files for the two databases in Figure 2-5 are both stored in the same directory (ORACLE_HOME/dbs), then their INIT.ORA files should contain the server names. This will make the file names unique. For example, if the two server names were ORA1 and ORA2, then the associated INIT.ORA files would be named initora1.ora and initora2.ora, respectively. Their server

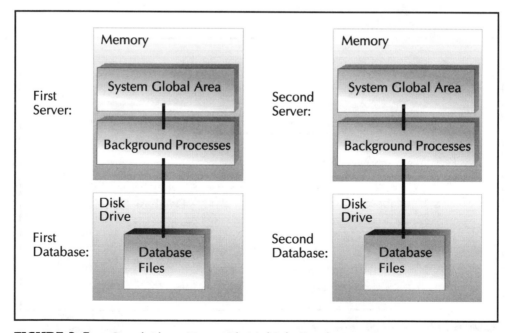

FIGURE 2-5.   *Stand-Alone Host with Multiple Databases*

parameters, like their datafiles, are completely independent of each other. If they are Oracle7 databases, then their CONFIG.ORA files will also include the server name in the filename (for example, configora1.ora and configora2.ora).

Although they will share the same source code directories, their datafiles should be stored in separate directories—and, if available, separate disks. Directory structures for datafiles are provided in Chapter 4, "Physical Database Layouts." If multiple databases have datafiles stored on the same device, then neither database's I/O statistics will accurately reflect the I/O load on that device. Instead, you will need to sum the I/O attributed to each disk by each database.

Networked Hosts

When hosts supporting Oracle databases are connected via a network, those databases can communicate via SQL*Net. Depending on the version of SQL*Net you are using, the integration of SQL*Net with the communications software differs.

As shown in Figure 2-6, the SQL*Net drivers rely on the local networking protocol to achieve connectivity between two servers. The SQL*Net portion then supports communications between the application layers on the two servers. In SQL*Net V2, the SQL*Net driver is split into two sections: a protocol adapter and the Transparent Network Substrate (TNS). These are described in Chapter 15, "SQL*Net V1 and V2."

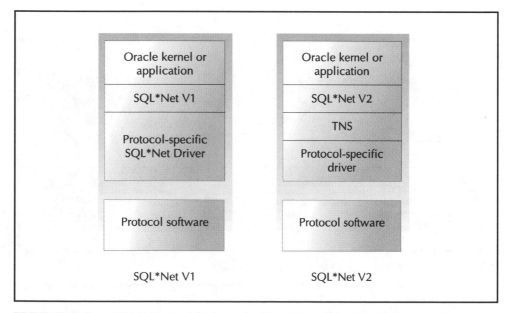

FIGURE 2-6. *SQL*Net Architecture for Host-Host Communications*

The database configuration options available in a networked environment depend on the network's configurations and options. The following sections describe the main architectures:

- Networks of databases (including non-Oracle databases), used for remote queries

- Distributed databases, used for remote transactions

- Parallel server databases, on which multiple server access the same database

- Client-server databases

Networks of Databases

SQL*Net allows Oracle databases to communicate with other databases that are accessible via a network. Each of the servers involved must be running SQL*Net. This configuration is illustrated in Figure 2-7.

In Figure 2-7, two hosts are shown. Each host can operate a database in stand-alone fashion, as was previously shown in Figure 2-2 and Figure 2-3. Each

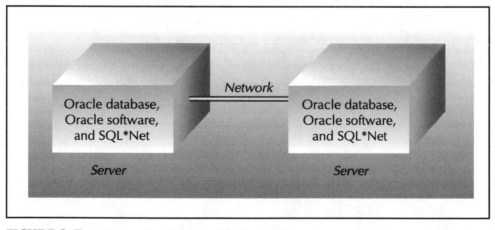

FIGURE 2-7. *Networked Hosts with Databases*

host in this example maintains a copy of the Oracle software and one or more Oracle databases.

For the databases to be able to communicate, their respective servers must be able to communicate with each other. As shown in Figure 2-6, the database layers of communication rely on the networking software and hardware to establish the communications link between the servers. Once that communications link is created, the database software can use it to transport data packets between remote databases.

The Oracle software used to transfer data between databases is called SQL*Net. In its simplest configuration, it is comprised of a host process that waits for connections via a specific connection path. When those connections are detected, it follows the instructions passed via the connection, and returns the requested data. A full description of SQL*Net V1 and V2 is found in Chapter 15, "SQL*Net V1 and V2." Implementation examples are provided in Chapter 16, "Networking in UNIX," and in Appendix D, "Configuration Guidelines for Client-Server Environments."

In SQL*Net V1, the host process is named *orasrv*. This is the process that must be running on each host that will be involved in the database communications. Each server must be configured to assign this process to a specific communications port (see Chapter 16, "Networking in UNIX," for an example of this). In SQL*Net V2, the host process is referred to as the *Listener*.

Examples of the use of database connections are shown in the following sections. They include queries against remote databases, queries against non-Oracle databases, and transactions against remote databases.

Remote Queries

Queries against remote Oracle databases use *database links* to identify the path that the query should take to find the data. The options available for managing database links changed between SQL*Net V1 and V2, although their functionality and syntax remained largely unchanged. See Chapter 17, "Managing Distributed Databases," for detailed information on their management.

A database link specifies, either directly or indirectly, the host, database, and account that should be used to access a specified object. It does this by referring to the SQL*Net connect string (SQL*Net V1) or service name (SQL*Net V2) that is to be used. When a database link is referenced by an SQL statement, it opens a session in the specified database and executes the SQL statement there. The data is then returned, and the remote session stays open in case it is needed again. Database links can be created as public links (by DBAs, making the link available to all users in the local database) or as private links.

The following SQL*Net V2 example creates a public database link called HR_LINK.

```
CREATE PUBLIC DATABASE LINK hr_link
CONNECT TO hr IDENTIFIED BY puffinstuff
USING 'hq';
```

The CREATE DATABASE LINK command, as shown in this example, has several parameters:

- The optional keyword PUBLIC, which allows DBAs to create links for all users in a database.

- The name of the link (hr_link, in this example).

- The account to connect to (if none is specified, then the local username and password will be used in the remote database).

- The service name ("hq"). For SQL*Net V1, the connect string is used instead. See Chapter 15, "SQL*Net V1 and V2," for information on this.

To use this link, simply add it as a suffix to table names in commands. The following example queries a remote table by using the HR_LINK database link.

```
SELECT * FROM employee@hr_link
WHERE office='ANNAPOLIS';
```

Database links cannot be used to return values from fields with LONG datatypes.

Database links allow for queries to access remote databases. They also allow for the information regarding the physical location of the data—its host, database, and schema—to be made transparent to the user. For example, if a user in the local database created a view based on a database link, then any access of the local view would automatically query the remote database. The user performing the query would not have to know where the data resides.

The following listing illustrates this. In this example, a view is created using the HR_LINK database link defined earlier in this section. Access to this view can then be granted to users in the local database, as shown here.

```
CREATE VIEW local_emp
AS SELECT * FROM employee@hr_link
WHERE office='ANNAPOLIS';

GRANT SELECT ON local_emp TO public;
```

When using a database link to access a remote database that is from an earlier version of Oracle, you are limited to using those commands that are available in the remote database. If the local database is Oracle7 and the remote database is

Oracle Version 6, then you can only perform Oracle7-type functions on the data after it has been retrieved from the remote database.

Connections to Non-Oracle Databases

Oracle allows connections to non-Oracle databases via its *SQL*Connect* product. The non-Oracle database being accessed must be supported by SQL*Connect for this to be an available option. The syntax and usage of SQL*Connect depend on the database resident on the remote server.

When performing queries against remote non-Oracle databases, you are limited to the capabilities of the remote database. Extensions to SQL, such as Oracle's CONNECT BY option, may be performed at the local database rather than at the remote database. This typically involves sending a much larger set of data across the network than would be needed during Oracle-to-Oracle communications. Refer to the SQL*Connect documentation that is specific to your database and gateway for information on the specific SQL capabilities available to you.

Remote Updates: The Distributed Option

In addition to querying data from remote databases, Oracle7 databases using the Distributed Option can update databases that are located on remote hosts. The updates against these remote databases can be combined with updates against the local database into a single logical unit of work: either they all get committed or they all get rolled back.

A sample set of transactions is shown in Figure 2-8. One of the transactions goes against a database on a remote host, and one against the local host. In this example, a local table named EMPLOYEE is updated; a remote table named EMPLOYEE, in a database defined by the HR_LINK database link, is also updated as part of the same transaction. If either update fails, then both of the transactions will be rolled back. This is accomplished via Oracle7's implementation of Two-Phase Commit, which is described in greater detail in Chapter 17, "Managing Distributed Databases."

The databases involved in this remote update are functionally separate. They each have their own sets of datafiles and memory areas. They each must be running the Oracle7 Distributed Option. The hosts involved must be running SQL*Net, and must be configured to allow host-host communications.

After SQL*Net is set up for each host, any files associated with it must be properly configured. This requirement is specific to SQL*Net V2, which adds a layer of location transparency to database links by maintaining several configuration files on the host. These configuration files allow the database to interpret the service names shown in the CREATE DATABASE LINK command earlier in this chapter.

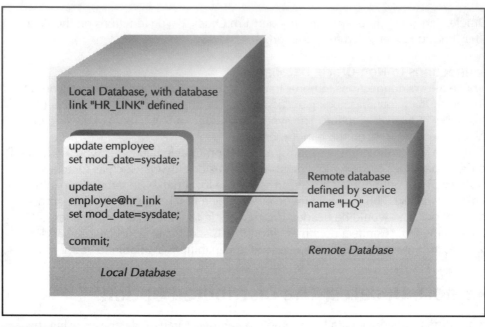

FIGURE 2-8. *Sample Distributed Transaction*

Each host that runs SQL*Net V2 must maintain a file called TNSNAMES.ORA. This file defines the connect descriptors for the service names that are accessible from that host. For example, the following listing shows the TNSNAMES.ORA file entry for the "HQ" service name used in the HR_LINK example.

```
HQ =(DESCRIPTION=
       (ADDRESS=
            (COMMUNITY=TCP.HQ.COMPANY)
            (PROTOCOL=TCP)
            (HOST=HQ)
            (PORT=1521))
       (CONNECT DATA=
            (SID=loc)))
```

This example shows a number of different aspects of the connection process (its parameters are specific to TCP/IP, but the underlying connection needs are the same for all platforms). First, there is the hardware addressing information—the SQL*Net community, the protocol, the host name, and the communications port to use. The second section defines the instance name—in this case, "loc." Since the TNSNAMES.ORA file tells the database all it needs to know to connect to remote databases, it is important to keep the contents of this file consistent across hosts. See Chapter 17, "Managing Distributed Databases," for information on this and other aspects affecting the management of location transparency.

The listing for the "HQ" service name shows an entry for its "community." This is needed when different communications protocols are used for the hosts in the network. When that is the case, a *MultiProtocol Interchange* is used to perform the protocol translation. This is a feature of SQL*Net V2, and is described in Chapter 15, "SQL*Net V1 and V2." When you are using SQL*Net V1, the same communications protocol must be run on all of the servers involved in distributed queries.

The logical unit of work for distributed transactions is processed via Oracle7's implementation of Two-Phase Commit (2PC). If there is a network or server failure that prevents the unit of work from successfully completing, then it is possible that the data in the databases affected by the transactions will be out of sync. The Oracle7 RECO (Recoverer) process automatically checks for incomplete transactions and resolves them as soon as all of the resources it needs become available.

The maximum number of concurrent distributed transactions for a database is set via the DISTRIBUTED_TRANSACTIONS parameter of its INIT.ORA file. If it is set to 0, then no distributed transactions will be allowed, and the RECO process will not be started when the instance starts.

Clustered Servers: The Parallel Server Option

Up to this point, all of the configurations discussed have featured databases that are accessed by a single server. However, depending on your hardware configurations, it may be possible to use multiple servers to access a single database. This configuration, called the *Parallel Server* Option, is illustrated in Figure 2-9.

As shown in Figure 2-9, two separate servers share the same set of datafiles. Usually, these servers are located on separate hosts of a hardware cluster (such as a VAX cluster). Using this configuration provides the following benefits:

- More memory resources are available, since two machines are being used.

- If one of the hosts goes down, the other can still access the datafiles, thus providing a means of recovering from disasters.

- Users can be separated by the type of processing they perform, and high-CPU users will be kept on a separate host from regular online processing transactions.

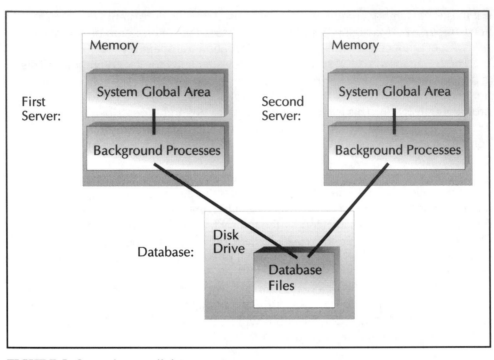

FIGURE 2-9.   *The Parallel Server Option*

Despite these advantages, there is a significant potential problem with this configuration— what if both servers try to update the same records? Following a transaction, Oracle does not immediately write modified blocks from the SGA back to the datafiles. While those blocks are in the SGA, another instance may request them. To support that request, Oracle will write the blocks out to disk, and *then* read them into the second SGA. The result is a database request that becomes very I/O-intensive.

The best way around this potential problem is to plan the distribution of users *not* by their CPU usage, but rather by their data usage. That is, users who update the same table should use the same instance to access the database.

When setting up a set of servers to use the Parallel Server Option, a number of database structures and parameters must be specified.

First, the central database must be configured to handle separate servers. Its primary requirement is a set of rollback segments that each server can use. To best manage these, create a separate rollback segment tablespace for each server, using the server name as part of the tablespace name. For example, if the server names were ORA1 and ORA2, then the rollback segment tablespace names should be RBS_ORA1 and RBS_ORA2.

To specify which rollback segments to use, each server must name them in its INIT.ORA file. This method for activating rollback segments is described in Chapter 7, "Managing Rollback Segments." There are several other database initialization parameters that must be set for the parallel servers. Since many of these must be the same for each server, the INIT.ORA "IFILE" parameter should be used. This specifies an "*include file*," which lists values for additional parameters. If both instances refer to the same IFILE, then you will not need to worry about the common values.

Table 2-1 lists the INIT.ORA parameters that must be unique for each server in a Parallel Server environment.

The INIT.ORA parameters that must be identical for all servers in a Parallel Server environment are listed in Table 2-2. The file that contains these parameters should be referenced by the IFILE parameter from the server-specific INIT.ORA files.

Further details on all of these parameters are found in the *Oracle7 Parallel Server Administrator's Guide.* Note that a number of them are tied to the number of servers used. Because of that relationship, the common INIT.ORA parameters must be reevaluated every time a new server is added to the set of servers for a database.

Client-Server Database Applications

In a host-host configuration, as described earlier in this chapter, an Oracle database exists on each host, and the databases communicate via SQL*Net. However, it is possible for a host without a database to access a remote database. This is typically

PARAMETER	DESCRIPTION
instance_number	Identifies the instance to the database.
rollback_segments	The private rollback segments to be used by the instance. See Chapter 7, "Managing Rollback Segments," for more information.
thread	Identifies the instance's redo log thread. Each instance has its own set of redo log groups, which maintain the instance's *thread*, or redo history.

TABLE 2-1. *Host-Specific Parameters for INIT.ORA for the Parallel Server Option*

PARAMETER	DESCRIPTION
control_files	The names of the control files in the database, separated by commas. See example earlier in this chapter.
db_block_size	The block size for the database.
db_files	The maximum number of open datafiles in the database. This value is superseded by the value of MAXDATAFILES set during database creation.
db_name	The name of the database.
gc_db_locks	The total number of instance locks.
gc_files_to_locks	Controls the database file locks.
gc_lck_procs	The total number of Oracle7 distributed locks for the SGAs.
gc_rollback_locks	The number of rollback locks; use the default for two instances, or ten per instance for more than two instances.
gc_rollback_segments	The total number of rollback segments used by all of the instances.
gc_save_rollback_locks	The number of rollback save locks; use the default for two instances, or ten per instance for more than two instances.
gc_segments	The maximum number of segments which may have space management activities performed simultaneously by different instances. Use the default for two instances, or ten per instance for more than two instances.
log_files	The maximum log group number; see examples earlier in this chapter.
row_locking	Defaults to "ALWAYS," which signifies that only row locks are obtained when a table is updated.
serializable	Defaults to "FALSE," which allows updates of a table to occur while a query is performed against the table.
single_process	Must be set to "FALSE" for the Parallel Server Option.

TABLE 2-2. *Common Parameters for INIT.ORA for the Parallel Server Option*

done by having application programs on one host access a database on a second host. In that configuration, the host running the application is called a *client* and the other is called the *server*. This configuration is illustrated in Figure 2-10.

As shown in Figure 2-10, the client must have the ability to communicate across the network to the server. The application programs are run on the client side; therefore, the database is used mainly for I/O. The CPU costs for running the application programs are thus charged to the client PC rather than to the server.

For this configuration to work, the client must be running SQL*Net. When the client's application program prompts the user for database connection information, the SQL*Net connect string (for SQL*Net V1) or service name (for SQL*Net V2) should be specified. The application will then open a session in the remote database.

Using a client-server configuration thus helps to reduce the amount of work that is being done by the server. However, shifting an application to a client-server configuration will not automatically improve the system's performance, for two main reasons:

■ CPU resources may not have been a problem before. Usually, CPU resources are used often during the day and infrequently during off-hours. Effective scheduling of batch programs can help resolve this situation.

■ The application may not have been redesigned. Designing for a client-server environment requires you to take into account the data

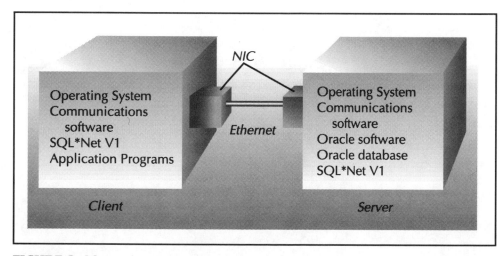

FIGURE 2-10. *Client-Server Configuration*

volumes that are sent across the network for every database access. In server-based applications, this is not a problem. In client-server applications, the network traffic must be considered during planning and tuning.

There are many different ways to implement the client-server configuration, depending on the hardware that is available. The implementation shown in Figure 2-10 is fairly common; it would be used by an ad hoc query tool running on a PC to access an Oracle database running on a server.

If you have file servers available in your environment, or if your clients are workstations instead of PCs, then you have a great deal of flexibility with your system architecture. See Appendix D, "Configuration Guidelines for Client-Server Environments," for examples. These include using the file server to prevent users from directly accessing the database server, and using the file server to store the Oracle software.

The examples in that appendix also use as examples the most common types of client machines, including IBM-compatible PCs running Microsoft Windows. Installation guidelines specific to that environment are provided in Appendix D. In that environment, the PC will also have configuration files that specify how SQL*Net should perform connections. The available parameters depend on the client environment and the version of SQL*Net in use.

CHAPTER 3

Logical Database
Layouts

The logical configuration of a database has a dramatic effect on its performance and its ease of administration. This chapter provides a guideline for choosing the proper tablespace layout for any Oracle database.

A sample database creation script suite, showing the steps involved in creating a database with multiple tablespaces, appears in Appendix A, "Database Creation Procedures." These scripts are provided for both Oracle Version 6 and Oracle7.

The effective distribution of the database's logical objects was first formalized by Cary Millsap of Oracle, who named the resulting architecture the *Optimal Flexible Architecture* (OFA). The logical database design described here will define and extend OFA. Planning the layout using this architecture will greatly ease database administration while allowing the DBA greater options when planning and tuning the physical layout.

The End Product

The objective of the database design described here is to configure the database so that its objects are separated by object type and activity type. This configuration will greatly reduce the amount of administrative work that must be done on the database, while decreasing the monitoring needs as well. Problems in one area thus will not affect the rest of the database.

Distributing the database objects in the manner described here will also allow the DBA greater flexibility when planning the database's physical layout. That exercise, described in Chapter 4, "Physical Database Layouts," is easiest to do when the logical design is as distributive as possible.

In order to distribute the objects, a system of classification must first be established. The logical objects within the database must be classified based on how they are to be used and how their physical structures impact the database. This includes separating tables from their indexes and high-activity tables from low-activity tables. Although the volume of activity against objects can only be determined during post-production, a core set of highly used tables can usually be isolated.

The Optimal Flexible Architecture (OFA)

In the following sections you will see the object categories as defined by OFA. Thereafter, you will be introduced to suggested OFA extensions.

The Starting Point: The SYSTEM Tablespace

It is possible, though not advisable, to store all of the database's objects in a single tablespace; this is analogous to storing all your files in your root directory. The SYSTEM tablespace, which is the Oracle equivalent of a root directory, is where the data dictionary tables (owned by SYS) are stored. It is also the location of the SYSTEM rollback segment, and during database creation the SYSTEM tablespace is temporarily used to store a second rollback segment (which is then deactivated or dropped).

There is no reason for anything other than the data dictionary tables and the SYSTEM rollback segment to be stored in the SYSTEM tablespace. Storing other segment types in SYSTEM increases the likelihood of space management problems there, which may require the tablespace to be rebuilt. Since the only way to rebuild the SYSTEM tablespace is to re-create the database, anything that can be moved out of SYSTEM should be moved.

The *data dictionary* segments that always reside in the SYSTEM tablespace and are fairly static tables that store all of the information about all of the objects in the database. They are created during the database creation process and are fairly small; in a moderately sized Oracle Version 6 database, they take less than 10M of space. Oracle7 data dictionary tables and indexes will have greater resource requirements if procedural objects such as triggers and procedures are stored in the database. These objects store PL/SQL code in the database, and their definitions are stored in the data dictionary tables. This requires additional space in those tables.

To move objects out of the SYSTEM tablespace, other tablespaces must first be created. The database creation scripts shown in Appendix A, "Database Creation Procedures," create databases that contain tablespaces for non-data dictionary database objects.

To prevent users from creating objects in the SYSTEM tablespace, their RESOURCE privilege on SYSTEM (which gives them the ability to create objects there) must be revoked:

```
revoke RESOURCE from user;
revoke RESOURCE ON SYSTEM from user;
```

Users in Oracle Version 6 databases are created with SYSTEM as their default tablespace. In Oracle7, the CREATE USER command can be used to specify an alternate default tablespace.

```
CREATE USER username identified by password
DEFAULT TABLESPACE tablespace name;
```

In both Oracle7 and Oracle Version 6, the

```
ALTER USER username DEFAULT TABLESPACE tablespace name;
```

command can be used to reassign the default tablespace. Specifying a default tablespace for users and developers will direct objects created without a tablespace specifier to be stored outside of the SYSTEM tablespace.

The following sections describe each type of database object, its usage, and why it should be stored apart from the rest of the database. The end result will be a standard database configuration with up to 12 standard tablespace types, depending on the manner in which the database is to be used.

Separating Application Data Segments: DATA

Data segments are the physical areas in which the data associated with tables and clusters are stored. These segments tend to be very actively accessed by the database, experiencing a high number of data manipulation transactions. Managing the access requests against the data segments is the main goal of a production database.

A typical DATA tablespace contains all of the tables associated with an application. The high traffic volumes against these tables make them ideal candidates for isolation in their own tablespace, since this allows them to be isolated into their own datafile, which can then be placed on a separate disk drive.

Segments in a DATA tablespace are likely to be fragmented. This means that the segments were not properly sized when created; the database then acquires more space by allocating additional space in the tablespace. This problem, which is described in greater detail in Chapter 4, "Physical Database Layout" and is resolved in Chapter 8, "Database Tuning," also drives the need to separate DATA from SYSTEM. Doing so makes it much easier to resolve fragmentation problems.

Separating Application Index Segments: INDEXES

The indexes associated with tables are subject to the same I/O and growth/fragmentation considerations that encouraged the movement of data segments out of the SYSTEM tablespace. Index segments should not be stored in the same tablespace as their associated tables, since they have a great deal of concurrent I/O during both data manipulation and queries.

Index segments are also subject to fragmentation due to improper sizing or unpredicted table growth. Isolating the application indexes to a separate tablespace greatly reduces the administrative efforts involved in defragmenting either the DATA or the INDEXES tablespace.

Separating existing indexes from their tables may be accomplished by using the INDEXFILE option of export/import. Export the user, then perform an import using the command

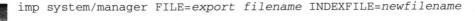

```
imp system/manager FILE=export filename INDEXFILE=newfilename
```

Nothing will be imported, but a file will be created which will show the DDL for all of the tables (commented out) and indexes. The tablespace specification clauses for the indexes can then be easily modified to point to INDEXES. Drop the original indexes and run the indexfile script to re-create them in the chosen tablespace.

Separating Tools Segments: TOOLS

Despite the previous sections' admonitions about not storing data segments in the SYSTEM tablespace, many tools do exactly that. They do this not because they specifically call for their objects to be stored in the SYSTEM tablespace, but rather because they store them under the SYSTEM database account, which normally has the SYSTEM tablespace as its default area for storing objects. To avoid this, change the SYSTEM account's default tablespace to the TOOLS tablespace and revoke its RESOURCE privilege on the SYSTEM tablespace. The steps to accomplish this are shown in the scripts in Appendix A, "Database Creation Procedures."

SQL*Forms, SQL*Menu, SQL*ReportWriter, and a number of third-party tools (such as PowerBuilder) all create tables owned by SYSTEM. If they have already been installed in the database, their objects can be moved by exporting the database, dropping the old tools tables, revoking RESOURCE privilege from the System account, granting it access only to the TOOLS tablespace, and importing the tables.

The following listing shows this process. In the first step, RESOURCE privilege is revoked from the SYSTEM user. In the second step, SYSTEM's RESOURCE privilege on the SYSTEM tablespace is revoked. The final step grants RESOURCE privilege on the TOOLS tablespace to the SYSTEM user.

```
revoke RESOURCE from SYSTEM;
revoke RESOURCE on SYSTEM from SYSTEM;
grant resource on TOOLS to SYSTEM;
```

Separating Rollback Segments: RBS

Rollback segments maintain the data concurrency within the database. In order to create non-SYSTEM tablespaces, you must first create a second rollback segment within the SYSTEM tablespace. To isolate rollback segments (which incur I/O for every transaction in the database) from the data dictionary, create a rollback segment tablespace that contains nothing but rollback segments. Splitting them out in this fashion also greatly simplifies their management (see Chapter 7, "Managing Rollback Segments").

Once the RBS tablespace has been created, and a rollback segment has been activated within it, the second rollback segment in the SYSTEM tablespace can be dropped. You may find it useful to keep this rollback segment in

SYSTEM inactive but still available in the event of a problem with the RBS tablespace.

Rollback segments dynamically expand to the size of the largest transaction (and, in Oracle7, shrink to a specified optimal size). I/O against rollback segments is usually concurrent with I/O against the DATA and INDEXES tablespaces. Separating them thus helps avoid I/O contention while making them easier to administer.

Separating Temporary Segments: TEMP

SYSTEM
DATA
INDEXES
TOOLS
RBS
TEMP

Temporary segments are dynamically created objects within the database that store data during large sorting operations (such as SELECT DISTINCT, UNION, and CREATE INDEX). Due to their dynamic nature, they should not be stored with any other types of segments. The proper structure of temporary segments is described in Chapter 4, "Physical Database Layouts." When a TEMP tablespace is "at rest," there are no segments stored within it. Separating temporary segments from SYSTEM thus removes a problem child from the data dictionary area and creates a tablespace that is simple to administer.

Users in Oracle Version 6 databases are created with SYSTEM as their temporary tablespace. In Oracle7, the CREATE USER command can be used to specify an alternate temporary tablespace, as follows.

```
CREATE USER username IDENTIFIED BY password
DEFAULT TABLESPACE some tablespace
TEMPORARY TABLESPACE TEMP;
```

In both Oracle7 and Oracle Version 6, the

```
ALTER USER username TEMPORARY TABLESPACE TEMP;
```

command can be used to reassign the temporary tablespace. This will cause all future temporary segments created for that user's account to be created in TEMP.

Separating Users: USERS

Try as we might, we can't forget users. Although they typically do not have object creation privileges in production databases, they may have such privileges in development databases. User objects are usually transient in nature and unplanned by default. Their sizing efforts are usually nonexistent. As a result, these objects should be separated from the rest of the database. This will help to minimize the impact of user experimentation on the functioning of the database.

To do this, revoke users' RESOURCE privilege on other tablespaces and change their default tablespace settings to the USERS tablespace. Users in Oracle Version 6 databases are created with SYSTEM as their default tablespace. In Oracle7, the CREATE USER command can be used to specify an alternate default tablespace, as shown here.

```
CREATE USER username IDENTIFIED BY password
DEFAULT TABLESPACE USERS
TEMPORARY TABLESPACE TEMP;
```

In both Oracle7 and Oracle Version 6, the

```
ALTER USER username DEFAULT TABLESPACE USERS;
```

command can be used to reassign the default tablespace. Doing so will direct objects created without a tablespace specifier to be stored in USERS.

Beyond OFA

The previous section was the last major section called for by traditional OFA. However, there are several extensions that may be appropriate for your database. These extensions, described in the following sections, help to further isolate objects with differing usage requirements while handling exceptions without impacting the production setup.

Separating Low-Usage Data Segments: DATA_2

SYSTEM
DATA
INDEXES
TOOLS
RBS
TEMP
USERS

DATA_2

When reviewing your list of data tables, it is likely that they can very easily be combined into two or more groups based on their characteristics: some will contain very dynamic, others very static data; the latter type of table may contain a list of states, for example. The static data tables tend to experience less I/O than the active data tables; when queried (as in a SQL*Forms application), the access against a static data table is usually concurrent with an access against a dynamic data table.

This concurrent I/O can be split among multiple files (and thus among multiple disks, to improve performance) by placing static data tables in their own data tablespace. Administrative functions performed against the DATA tablespace, such as defragmentation, now only occur against those tables most likely to require assistance. Meanwhile, the tablespace for static data tables, DATA_2, should remain static and simple to maintain.

Separating Low-Usage Index Segments: INDEXES_2

SYSTEM
DATA
INDEXES
TOOLS
RBS
TEMP
USERS

DATA_2

INDEXES_2

The indexes for low-usage, static data tables also tend to be low usage and static. To simplify the administrative actions for the INDEXES tablespace, move the static tables' indexes to a separate INDEXES_2 tablespace. This also helps to improve performance tuning options, since concurrent I/O among indexes can now be split across disk drives.

If the low usage indexes have already been created in the INDEXES tablespace, then they must be dropped and re-created in INDEXES_2. This is usually done concurrent with the moving of low usage tables to DATA_2. If the index was created via an Oracle7 PRIMARY KEY or UNIQUE constraint definition, then that constraint will need to be modified.

The following listing shows a sample tablespace specification for an automatically created index. This example creates a unique constraint on the "DESCRIPTION" column in a static table called EMPLOYEE_TYPE. The unique index that the database will create for this constraint is directed to be stored in the

INDEXES_2 tablespaces.

```
ALTER TABLE employee_type
     add constraint uniq_descr
     UNIQUE(description)
     USING INDEX TABLESPACE INDEXES_2;
```

Separating Tools Indexes: TOOLS_I

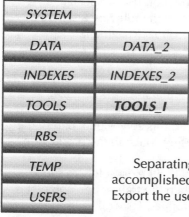

If your database shows a lot of activity against the TOOLS tablespace (as would be expected for a development environment that featured SQL*Forms 3.0, for example), then the indexes for those tools tables may be moved to a separate tablespace. This is most applicable to those environments in which the TOOLS tablespace is treated as a DATA tablespace; that is, its tables are the subject of much of the I/O in the database.

Separating existing indexes from their tables may be accomplished by using the INDEXFILE option of export/import. Export the user, then perform an import using the command

```
imp system/manager FILE=export filename INDEXFILE=newfilename
```

Nothing will be imported, but a file will be created which will show the DDL for all of the tables (commented out) and all of the indexes. The tablespace specification clauses for the indexes can then be easily modified to point to TOOLS_I. Drop the original indexes and run the indexfile script to re-create them in the chosen tablespace.

Separating Specialty Rollback Segments: RBS_2

SYSTEM	
DATA	DATA_2
INDEXES	INDEXES_2
TOOLS	TOOLS_I
RBS	RBS_2
TEMP	
USERS	

The rollback segments in the RBS tablespace should be of the proper size and number to support production usage of the application (see Chapter 7, "Managing Rollback Segments"). There will almost always be a transaction whose size is unsupported by the production rollback segment configuration. When it is executed, it will take over one of the production rollback segments and extend it heavily, using up as much free space as it can before the transaction succeeds or fails.

It doesn't have to be that way. The production rollback segments should be used by production users. Special transactional requirements should be handled by a separate rollback segment. To specify this rollback segment, the user must use the

```
SET TRANSACTION USE ROLLBACK SEGMENT segment name
```

command prior to executing the transaction. However, this solves only part of the problem, since the chosen rollback segment is still using space in the production rollback segment tablespace.

Create a separate rollback segment tablespace that will exist solely to support this type of transaction (such as large data loads). When the transaction completes, the rollback segment may be either deactivated or dropped (as well as its tablespace, thus saving disk space). Once again, separating logical objects based on their functional requirements serves to greatly simplify their administration.

Separating User-Specific Temporary Segments: TEMP_USER

SYSTEM	
DATA	DATA_2
INDEXES	INDEXES_2
TOOLS	TOOLS_I
RBS	RBS_2
TEMP	**TEMP_USER**
USERS	

The final major tablespace is, like RBS_2, a specialty tablespace designed to address specific needs of the application users. Certain users, such as GL in an Oracle Financials application, may require much larger temporary segments than the rest of the application's users. In such a case, it makes sense to separate those temporary segments from the standard TEMP tablespace. This eases administration, since you can now design for the common usage of the system, while handling the exceptions via TEMP_*USER*. In practice, name this tablespace after the name of the user, as in TEMP_GL or TEMP_SCOTT.

Users in Oracle Version 6 databases are created with SYSTEM as their temporary tablespace. In Oracle7, the CREATE USER command can be used to specify an alternate temporary tablespace.

```
CREATE USER username IDENTIFIED BY password
DEFAULT TABLESPACE tablespace name
TEMPORARY TABLESPACE TEMP_user;
```

In both Oracle7 and Oracle Version 6, the

```
ALTER USER username TEMPORARY TABLESPACE TEMP_user;
```

command can be used to reassign the temporary tablespace. This will cause all future temporary segments created for that user's account to be created in the user's custom TEMP_*USER* tablespace.

Common-Sense Logical Layouts

The resulting logical design of the database should meet the following criteria:

- Segment types that are used in the same way should be stored together.
- The system should be designed for standard usage.
- Separate areas should exist for exceptions.
- Contention among tablespaces should be minimized.
- The data dictionary should be isolated.

Note that meeting these criteria requires the DBA to know the application being implemented: which tools it will use, which tables will be most active, when data loads will occur, which users will have exceptional resource requirements, and how standard transactions behave. Gaining this knowledge requires a very high level of involvement of the DBA in the application development process (see Chapter 5, "Managing the Development Process").

It results in a system whose varied segment types do not interfere with each other's needs. This makes it much simpler to manage the database, and to isolate and resolve performance problems. When fragmentation of segments or free space does occur (see Chapter 4, "Physical Database Layouts," and Chapter 8, "Database Tuning"), it is much simpler to resolve when the database is laid out in this manner.

The only potential tablespace in which multiple types of segments may exist is the USERS tablespace. If the development environment is also used as a testing environment, then it would be a good idea to separate users' indexes into a USERS_I tablespace.

The combination of a sensible logical database layout with a well-designed physical database layout (see Chapter 4, "Physical Database Layouts") results in systems that require very little tuning after the first post-production check. The up-front planning efforts pay off immediately in both the flexibility and the performance of the database. The cost of implementing this design from the start is minimal; it can be built into all of your database creation scripts automatically, as shown in the database creation scripts in Appendix A, "Database Creation Procedures." The final overall design of the system should be an appropriate combination of the logical divisions shown in Table 3-1.

TABLESPACE	USE
SYSTEM	Data dictionary
DATA	Standard-operation tables
DATA_2	Static tables used during standard operation
INDEXES	Indexes for the standard-operation tables
INDEXES_2	Indexes for the static tables
RBS	Standard-operation rollback segments
RBS_2	Specialty rollback segments used for data loads
TEMP	Standard-operation temporary segments
TEMP_*USER*	Temporary segments created by a particular user
TOOLS	RDBMS tools tables
TOOLS_I	Indexes for RDBMS tools tables
USERS	User objects, in development databases

TABLE 3-1.   *Logical Distribution of Segments in an Optimal Database*

CHAPTER 4

Physical Database Layouts

Picture a crowded lecture hall, in which every seat is taken. Now, eliminate half of the seats by combining groups of attendees onto seats. For the combinations to work, characteristics of the people must be estimated: their relative weights, their space needs, etc. Now eliminate half of the remaining seats. The cycle of planning the appropriate distribution of attendees must be repeated.

This same repetitive reallocation of resources happens to DBAs every day. In the DBA's case, it occurs when the number of database-related files exceeds the number of disks available. The characteristics of those files must then be considered in order to arrive at the optimal combinations.

If you're looking for the definitive word on the placement of database files, you might encounter the following advice:

"Data files should not *be stored on the same disk drive that stores the database's redo log files."*
—Oracle7 Server Administrator's Guide [my emphasis]

However, further down the same page, you'll see this:

"... you can *store data files on the same drive as some redo log file."*
—Oracle7 Server Administrator's Guide [my emphasis]

The sad thing is both statements are true.

The documentation describing the proper distribution of Oracle database files across devices is sparse and contradictory (even when on the same page, as shown in this example). Most of the contradictions are due to a failure to define the circumstances under which each design is advisable.

In this chapter, you will see the manner in which Oracle manages physical data storage, along with the optimal physical database layouts for any number of disks. These layouts will be the result of understanding the ways in which various database files operate and interact.

Too often, the physical layout of the database is not planned; it is only considered when the database is experiencing performance problems. Just as the logical layout of the database should be planned (see Chapter 3, "Logical Database Layouts"), the physical layout of the database's files must be designed and implemented to meet the database's goals. Failure to plan the layouts before creating the database will result in a recurring cycle of layout-related problems and performance tuning efforts.

In this chapter, you will see where to place database-related files relative to each other to ensure optimal recoverability and performance. A method for verifying the planned layout will be provided. The directory structure for the system's disks will also be covered, and an overview on database space usage will be presented. These four sections, taken together, provide an understanding of the impact of system-level file layout decisions on each level of an Oracle database.

Database File Layout

By establishing the clear goals of the file distribution design, and by understanding the nature of the database (e.g., transaction-oriented versus read-intensive), the proper design can be determined for distributing the files across any number of devices. This chapter will provide designs for the most common configurations, as well as guidelines for applying them to any situations not directly covered.

This process will be accomplished via the following steps:

- ■ Identifying I/O contention among datafiles
- ■ Identifying I/O bottlenecks among all database files
- ■ Identifying concurrent I/O among background processes
- ■ Defining the security and performance goals for the database
- ■ Defining the system hardware and mirroring architecture
- ■ Identifying disks that can be dedicated to the database

In most cases, only the datafile contention, hardware mirroring, and disk acquisition tasks are performed before creating databases, thus designing contention into the system. By accomplishing all of the steps listed here, the end product will be a physical database layout that has your needs designed into it.

I/O Contention among Datafiles

When designing a database that will hold an application, follow the design procedures given in Chapter 3, "Logical Database Layouts." Doing so should result in a database that contains some combination of the tablespaces shown in Table 4-1.

TABLESPACE	USE
SYSTEM	Data dictionary
DATA	Standard-operation tables
DATA_2	Static tables used during standard operation
INDEXES	Indexes for the standard-operation tables
INDEXES_2	Indexes for the static tables
RBS	Standard-operation rollback segments
RBS_2	Specialty rollback segments used for data loads
TEMP	Standard-operation temporary segments
TEMP_*USER*	Temporary segments created by a particular user
TOOLS	RDBMS tools tables
TOOLS_I	Indexes for RDBMS tools tables
USERS	User objects, in development databases

TABLE 4-1. *Logical Distribution of Segments in an Optimal Database*

Each of these tablespaces requires a separate datafile. Oracle allows you to monitor database I/O among datafiles *after* the database has been created; this capability is only useful during the planning stages if an analogous database is available for reference. If no such database is available, then the DBA must estimate the I/O load for each datafile.

Start the physical layout planning process by estimating the relative I/O of the datafiles. Assign the most active tablespace an I/O "weight" of 100. Then estimate the I/O against the other data tablespaces relative to that tablespace. Assign the SYSTEM tablespace files a weight of 35, and the index tablespaces a value equal to one-third of the weighting for their associated data tablespaces.

What about the TOOLS, RBS, and TEMP tablespaces? The I/O against these tablespaces varies widely, depending on the nature of the database. TOOLS will experience very little I/O in a production environment. If the database will be very transaction-oriented, RBS's weight may go as high as 75 (in most cases, it should be between 10 and 40). TEMP, in production, will only be used by large sorts; its weight will therefore vary widely during usage, ranging from 0 to 75. Choose a value that is reflective of the database you are implementing.

The message in this weighting procedure is twofold: first, the file I/O weight has to be estimated before the files are created; and second, this procedure has to be done for each database. Table 4-2 shows the I/O weights for a sample transaction-oriented production database.

In this example, the DATA tablespace has been given a weight of 100. Its associated index tablespace, INDEXES, has a weight of one-third of that, 33. The SYSTEM tablespace has been given a weight of 35, and RBS (the rollback segments tablespace) has been given an estimated I/O weight of 40. TEMP and TOOLS have been estimated to have weights of 5 and 1, respectively. The DATA_2 and

TABLESPACE	WEIGHT	PERCENT OF TOTAL
DATA	100	45
RBS	40	18
SYSTEM	35	16
INDEXES	33	15
TEMP	5	2
DATA_2	4	2
INDEXES_2	2	1
TOOLS	1	1
Total:	220	

TABLE 4-2. *Estimated I/O Weights for Sample Tablespaces*

INDEXES_2 tablespaces have been estimated to be very lightly used, with weights of 4 and 2, respectively.

Note that 94 percent of the I/O is concentrated in the top four tablespaces. In order to properly distribute the datafile I/O, you would therefore need at least five disks: one for each of the top four tablespaces (by I/O weight) and one for the lower I/O tablespaces. The DBA of this database should also avoid putting additional database files on the disks holding the top four tablespaces.

These weightings serve to reinforce several cardinal rules about database file placement on disks: the DATA tablespaces should be stored separate from their INDEXES tablespaces, the RBS tablespaces separate from the DATA tablespaces, and the SYSTEM tablespace separate from the other tablespaces in the database. The weightings and characteristics of the lower I/O tablespaces will be used to determine which of them should be stored on the same devices when that becomes necessary.

Scripts that will monitor the database (and thus verify the I/O weighting estimates) are given in the "Verification of I/O Weighting Estimates" section of this chapter.

I/O Bottlenecks Among All Database Files

Once the I/O weightings of the datafiles have been estimated, the location of the datafiles relative to each other can be designed. However, this is only part of the picture. Other database file types must be considered as well.

Redo Logs

The most confusing aspect of database file placement concerns online *redo logs.* These are the files that store the records of each transaction in the database. Each database must have at least two redo log files available to it. The database will write to one log file in a sequential fashion until it is filled, then it will start writing to the second redo log file. When the last redo log file is filled, the database will begin overwriting the contents of the first redo log file with new transactions.

In Oracle Version 6, online redo log files are the database's Achilles' heel. Since they maintain information about the current transactions in the database, they cannot be recovered from a backup. They are the only type of file in the database that cannot be recovered via the database backup utilities.

Because of this, DBAs need to make sure that the online redo log files are mirrored by some means. In Oracle7, *redo log "groups"* can be set up to allow the database to dynamically maintain multiple sets of the online redo log files. This uses the database to mirror the online redo log files, thus minimizing the recovery problems caused by a single disk failure.

In Oracle Version 6, redo log "groups" are not available. The DBA must rely on the operating system to mirror the redo log files. One of the quotes given at the start of this chapter stated that "you can store data files on the same drive as some redo log file." Given this mirroring information, the reasoning behind this advice can be seen: the advice is given with the assumption that the redo log files will be physically mirrored via the operating system. Since critical files should be mirrored, you may take advantage of the mirroring of the redo log files and place other files on these disks, which will therefore also be mirrored. Your ability to recover from media failures is thus improved.

However, that advice considers only the recoverability of the database. It ignores the performance impact of placing datafiles on the same disk as online redo log files. Understanding this impact requires knowing how the two types of files (datafiles and online redo log files) are used.

Every transaction is recorded in the redo log files. Transaction entries are written to the redo log files by the *LGWR (Log Writer)* background process. The data in the transactions is concurrently written to several tablespaces (such as the RBS rollback segments tablespace and the DATA tablespace). The writes to the tablespaces are done via the *DBWR (Database Writer)* background process. Thus, even though the datafile I/O may be properly distributed, contention between the DBWR and LGWR background processes will occur if a datafile is stored on the same disk as a redo log file. This is reflected in the first of the two quotes at the beginning of this chapter.

Redo log files are written sequentially. Thus, if there is no concurrent activity on the disk, then the disk hardware will already be properly positioned for the next log write. By contrast, datafiles are read and written to in a comparatively random fashion. Since the log files are written sequentially, they will process I/O the fastest if they do not have to contend with other activity on the same disk.

If you must store a datafile on the same disk as a redo log files, then it should not belong to the SYSTEM tablespace, the RBS tablespace, or a very active DATA or INDEX tablespace. All of these will have direct conflicts with the redo log files and will increase the likelihood of the log writes being affected by the database reads.

Control Files

Control files can be internally mirrored in both Oracle Version 6 and Oracle7. The number and name of the control files should be specified via the CONTROL_FILES parameter in the database's INIT.ORA file. If the control file names are specified via this parameter during database creation, then they will be automatically created during the database creation process. The database will thereafter maintain the control files as identical copies of each other. The database creation scripts shown in Appendix A, "Database Creation Procedures," make use of this capability.

Each database should have a minimum of three copies of its control files, located across three drives. Very little I/O occurs in these files relative to that of the other database files.

Archive Logs

The LGWR background process writes to the online redo log files in a cyclical fashion; after filling the first log file, it begins writing the second, until that one fills, and then begins writing to the third. Once the last online redo log file is filled, LGWR begins to overwrite the contents of the first redo log file.

When Oracle is run in ARCHIVELOG mode, the database makes a copy of each redo log file before overwriting it. These archived redo log files are usually written to a disk device. They may also be written directly to a tape device, but this tends to be operator-intensive.

The archiving function is performed by the ARCH background process. Databases using this option will encounter contention problems on their redo log disk during heavy data transaction times, since LGWR will be trying to write to one redo log file while ARCH is trying to read another. The only way to avoid this is to distribute the redo log files across multiple disks. Therefore, if you are running in ARCHIVELOG mode on a very transaction-oriented database, avoid LGWR-ARCH contention by splitting up your online redo log files across devices.

You should also be careful with the placement of the archived redo log on disk. Remember that this device, by its nature, will have the same amount of I/O as the online redo logs device. Therefore, the rules regarding placement of online redo log files apply also to the archived redo log files. They should not be stored on the same device as the SYSTEM, RBS, DATA, or INDEXES tablespace, and they should not be stored on the same device as any of the online redo log files. Since running out of space on the archived redo log device will freeze the database, archived redo log files should only be stored with small, static files.

Oracle Software

The specific Oracle software files that are accessed during normal database operation vary according to the packages that are licensed for the host on which the server resides. The I/O against these files is not recorded within the database. Since the location of the files is also variable (particularly in a distributed or client-server architecture), a system or network monitor should be used to determine the I/O against these files. The actual I/O against these files can then be compared with the actual I/O measurements for the database files to determine if the files need to be redistributed.

To minimize contention between the database files and the database code, avoid placing database files on the same disk device as the code files. If datafiles must be placed on that disk device, then the least frequently used datafiles should be placed there.

Concurrent I/O among Background Processes

When evaluating contention among various processes, it is important to identify the type of I/O being performed and its timing. Files contend with each other if I/O from one file interferes with I/O for the second file, so two random-accessed files that are never accessed at the same time can be placed on the same device.

Based on the discussion in the previous section, two types of I/O contention can be defined: *concurrent I/O* and *interference*. Concurrent I/O contention occurs when multiple accesses are performed against the same device at the same instant. This is the kind of contention that is eliminated by isolating tables from their associated indexes. Interference contention occurs when writes to a sequentially written file are interrupted by reads or writes to other files on the same disk, even if those reads or writes occur at a different time than the sequential reads and writes.

There are three database background processes that actively access the database files on disk: the Database Writer (DBWR), the Log Writer (LGWR), and the Archiver (ARCH). DBWR reads and writes to files in a fairly random manner, LGWR writes sequentially, and ARCH reads and writes sequentially. Eliminating the contention possibilities between these three background processes will effectively eliminate all contention at the database level.

Note that LGWR and ARCH are always writing to one file at a time. DBWR, on the other hand, may be attempting to read or write to multiple files at once. There is thus the potential for DBWR to cause contention with itself! To combat this problem, certain operating systems (including UNIX) can create multiple DBWR processes for each instance. The number of DBWRs is set via the initiation parameter DB_WRITERS; Oracle recommends setting DB_WRITERS to a value between n and $2n$, where n is the number of disks. If this option is not available on your system, then you may be able to use asynchronous I/O to reduce internal DBWR contention. With asynchronous I/O, only one DBWR process is needed, since the I/O processing is performed in parallel.

The nature of the contention that will occur between the background processes is thus a function of the backup scheme used (ARCH), the transaction load on the system (LGWR), and the host operating system (DBWR). Designing a scheme that will eliminate contention between files and processes requires a clear understanding of the ways in which those files and processes will interact in the production system.

Defining the Recoverability and Performance Goals for the System

Before designing the database's disk layout, the goals for the layout must be clearly defined. Otherwise, you'll end up with the contradictory advice given in the quotes that started this chapter.

The database goals that relate directly to disks are (1) *recoverability* and (2) *performance.* The recoverability goals must take into account all processes that impact disks. These should include, at a minimum, the storage area for archived redo logs (if used) and the storage area for export dump files.

The performance tuning goals must take into account the projected database file I/O distribution and the relative access speeds of the disks available (since heterogeneous systems may feature some disks that are faster than others).

Recoverability considerations were the basis for the second quote at the beginning of this chapter (which stated that datafiles can be stored with online redo log files). In order to avoid conflicting advice on disk layouts, the goal of the layout must be clearly defined: Are you trying to optimize performance or recoverability? If recoverability is the primary goal of the layout, then all critical database files should be placed on mirrored drives, and the database should be run in ARCHIVELOG mode. In such a scenario, performance is a secondary consideration.

Recoverability of a database should always be a primary concern. But once the database has been secured, the performance goals of the system should be taken into consideration. For example, the server on which the database resides may have fully mirrored disks, in which case performance is the only real issue.

To ensure database recoverability, you must mirror your online redo log files. This can be done via the operating system or via mirrored redo log groups (in Oracle7), but it must be done. The architecture put in place for recoverability should complement the performance tuning architecture; the two goals will yield two different file layouts. If the performance tuning design conflicts with the recoverability design, then the recoverability design must prevail. Recoverability issues should only involve a few disks; once the database recovery options have been chosen (see Chapter 10, "Optimal Backup and Recovery Procedures"), the performance issues can be addressed.

Defining the System Hardware and Mirroring Architecture

Since the Systems Management group allocates and manages the server's disk farm, DBAs must work with that team to manage the system's hardware and mirroring architecture. This involves specifying

- the number of disks required
- the models of disks required (for performance or size)
- the appropriate mirroring strategy

The number of disks required will be driven by the size of the database and the database I/O weights. Wherever possible, those disks should be dedicated to Oracle files to avoid concurrent I/O and interference contention with non-Oracle files. If the disk farm is heterogeneous, then the size and speed of the drives available should be taken into consideration when determining which are to be dedicated to Oracle files.

Disk mirroring is used to provide fault tolerance with regard to media failures. Mirroring is performed either by maintaining an exact duplicate of each disk online (known as *RAID-1* or *volume shadowing*) or by using a *parity-check* system among a group of disks (usually *RAID-3* or *RAID-5*). The parity-check systems implicitly perform file striping across disks. In RAID-5, for example, each file is striped on a block-by-block basis across the disks in the mirroring group. A parity check is then written on another disk in the set so that if one disk is removed, its contents can be regenerated based on knowing the parity check and the contents of the rest of the mirrored set.

The system mirroring architecture thus impacts the distribution of database files across those disks. Disks that are mirrored on a 1-to-1 basis (RAID-1) can be treated as stand-alone disks. Disks that are part of a parity-check system (such as RAID-3 or RAID-5) must be considered as a set, and can take advantage of the implicit striping.

Identifying Disks That Can Be Dedicated to the Database

Whatever mirroring architecture is used, it is important that the disks chosen be dedicated to the database. Otherwise, the non-database load on those disks will impact the database, and that impact is usually impossible to forecast correctly. User directory areas, for example, may experience sudden increases in size—and wipe out the space that was intended for the archived redo log files, bringing the database to a halt. Other files may have severe I/O requirements that were not factored into the database I/O weights estimated earlier.

Choosing the Right Layout

The basis for deciding the appropriate disk layout can now be deduced:

- The database must be recoverable.

- The online redo log files must be mirrored via the system or the database.

- The database file I/O weights must be estimated.

- Contention between DBWR, LGWR, and ARCH must be minimized.

- Contention between disks for DBWR must be minimized.

- The performance goals of the system must be defined.
- The disk hardware options must be known.
- The disk mirroring architecture must be known.
- Disks must be dedicated to the database.

The Dream Database Physical Layout: The 22-Disk Solution

The layouts presented in this section assume that the disks involved are dedicated to the database, and that the online redo log files are being mirrored via the operating system. It is also assumed that the disks have identical size and performance characteristics.

The configuration shown in Figure 4-1 is not likely to be available, but it's important to start with goals that aim high. This configuration eliminates contention

```
Disk       Contents
1          Oracle software
2          SYSTEM tablespace
3          RBS tablespace
4          DATA tablespace
5          INDEXES tablespace
6          TEMP tablespace
7          TOOLS tablespace
8          Online Redo log 1
9          Online Redo log 2
10         Online Redo log 3
11         Control file 1
12         Control file 2
13         Control file 3
14         Application software
15         RBS_2
16         DATA_2
17         INDEXES_2
18         TEMP_USER
19         TOOLS_I
20         USERS
21         Archived redo log destination disk
22         Export dump file destination disk
```

FIGURE 4-1. *The 22-Disk Solution*

between datafiles completely by giving each a separate disk to occupy. It also eliminates LGWR-ARCH contention by giving each redo log a separate disk. It also assigns a disk (number 14) to the software for the application that will access the database.

This configuration is unlikely because of the capital resources that are required; on the control file disks, an entire disk (usually up to 2Gb) is used to maintain a single, low-access file that seldom exceeds 200K. To reach a more realistic configuration, the disk layout should be iteratively revised until the available number of disks is reached.

The First Iteration: The 17-Disk Solution

Each successive iteration of the disk layout will involve placing the contents of multiple disks on a single disk. The first iteration (in Figure 4-2) moves the three control files onto the three redo log disks. Control files will cause interference contention with the online redo logs, but only at log switch points and during database recovery. During normal operation of the database, very little interference will occur.

Assuming that this will be a production database, the TOOLS_I tablespace's contents will be merged with the TOOLS tablespace (they are usually only separated in intense development environments). For production environments,

```
Disk        Contents
1           Oracle software
2           SYSTEM tablespace
3           RBS tablespace
4           DATA tablespace
5           INDEXES tablespace
6           TEMP tablespace
7           TOOLS tablespace
8           Online Redo log 1, Control file 1
9           Online Redo log 2, Control file 2
10          Online Redo log 3, Control file 3
11          Application software
12          RBS_2
13          DATA_2
14          INDEXES_2
15          TEMP_USER
16          Archived redo log destination disk
17          Export dump file destination disk
```

FIGURE 4-2. *The 17-Disk Solution*

```
Disk        Contents
1           Oracle software
2           SYSTEM tablespace
3           RBS tablespace, RBS_2 tablespace
4           DATA tablespace
5           INDEXES tablespace
6           TEMP tablespace, TEMP_USER tablespace
7           TOOLS tablespace
8           Online Redo log 1, Control file 1
9           Online Redo log 2, Control file 2
10          Online Redo log 3, Control file 3
11          Application software
12          DATA_2
13          INDEXES_2
14          Archived redo log destination disk
15          Export dump file destination disk
```

FIGURE 4-3.   *The 15-Disk Solution*

users will not have resource privileges, so the USERS tablespace will not be considered in these configurations.

The Second Iteration: The 15-Disk Solution
The second iteration of file combinations (in Figure 4-3) begins the process of placing multiple tablespaces on the same disk. In this case, the RBS and RBS_2 tablespaces are placed together because they are seldom used concurrently; as previously defined, RBS_2 contains specialty rollback segments that are used during large data loads. Since data loads should not be occurring during production usage (which RBS is used for), there should be no contention between RBS and RBS_2, so they can be placed together.

The TEMP and TEMP_*USER* tablespaces can also be placed on the same disk. The TEMP_*USER* tablespace is dedicated to a specific user (such as GL in Oracle Financials) who has temporary segment needs that are far greater than the rest of the system's users. The TEMP tablespace's weighting, as previously noted, can vary widely; however, it should be possible to store it on the same device as TEMP_*USER* without overly impacting its I/O.

The Third Iteration: The 12-Disk Solution
Before putting any more combinations of tablespaces on multiple disks, the online redo logs should be placed together on the same disk (see Figure 4-4). In databases

```
Disk      Contents
1         Oracle software
2         SYSTEM tablespace, Control file 1
3         RBS tablespace, RBS_2 tablespace, Control file 2
4         DATA tablespace, Control file 3
5         INDEXES tablespace
6         TEMP tablespace, TEMP_USER tablespace
7         TOOLS tablespace, INDEXES_2 tablespace
8         Online Redo logs 1, 2, and 3
9         Application software
10        DATA_2
11        Archived redo log destination disk
12        Export dump file destination disk
```

FIGURE 4-4. *The 12-Disk Solution*

that use ARCHIVELOG backups, this will cause concurrent I/O and interference contention between LGWR and ARCH on that disk. Thus, this combination is not appropriate for very high-transaction systems running in ARCHIVELOG mode.

Because the online redo log file disks have been combined into one, the control files must be moved. I have moved them to coexist with the three most critical tablespaces (SYSTEM, RBS, and DATA). As previously stated, the control files are not I/O intensive and should cause little contention. The only other change for this configuration is the combination of the TOOLS tablespace with the INDEX_2 tablespace.

The Fourth Iteration: The 9-Disk Solution

As you may have noted, most of the changes have consisted of moving items from the highest-numbered disks onto the lower-numbered disks. This is because the first disks were assigned to those files that were judged to be most critical to the database. The later disks were assigned to files that would be helpful to have on separate devices, but whose isolation was not a necessity.

This iteration (shown in Figure 4-5) combines the three highest-numbered disks (disks 10, 11, and 12) with good matches for their characteristics. First, the DATA_2 tablespace (weighted as 2 percent of the total datafile I/O) is combined with the TEMP tablespaces, creating a disk that now handles 4 percent of the datafile I/O. This should be a good match because the static tables are less likely to have large group operations performed on them than are the tables in the DATA

```
Disk          Contents
1             Oracle software
2             SYSTEM tablespace, Control file 1
3             RBS tablespace, RBS_2 tablespace, Control file 2
4             DATA tablespace, Control file 3
5             INDEXES tablespace
6             TEMP tablespace, TEMP_USER tablespace, DATA_2
                 tablespace
7             TOOLS tablespace, INDEXES_2 tablespace
8             Online Redo logs 1, 2, and 3, Export dump file
                 destination disk
9             Application software, Archived redo log destination
                 disk
```

FIGURE 4-5.   *The 9-Disk Solution*

tablespace. Second, the export dump files have been moved to the online redo log file disk. This may seem an odd combination at first, but they are well suited to each other, since the online redo log files never increase in size (and usually take less than 15M), while the process of exporting a database causes very little transaction activity (and therefore little contention between the redo log file and the export dump file). The third combination in this iteration is that of the application software (such as SQL*Forms and SQL*Menu applications) with the archived redo log destination area. The application software is assumed to be both static and small, using less than 10 percent of the available disk space. This leaves the Archiver ample space to write log files to while avoiding conflicts with DBWR.

The Fifth Iteration: The 7-Disk Compromise
From this point onward, the tablespace combinations should be driven by the weights assigned during the I/O estimation process. For the weightings given earlier in this chapter, the distribution of I/O among the disks after the fourth iteration is shown in Table 4-3.

The weighting for disk 1 is not shown because it is installation-specific, since applications may be of widely varying size and different Oracle software is licensed for different sites. Also, sites running Oracle CASE will find that the I/O against the CASE software files counts against the Oracle software disk, not against the Application software disk.

DISK	WEIGHT	CONTENTS
1		Oracle software
2	35	SYSTEM tablespace, Control file 1
3	40	RBS tablespace, RBS_2 tablespace, Control file 2
4	100	DATA tablespace, Control file 3
5	33	INDEXES tablespace
6	9	TEMP tablespace, TEMP_*USER* tablespace, DATA_2 tablespace
7	3	TOOLS tablespace, INDEXES_2 tablespace
8	40+	Online Redo logs 1, 2, and 3, Export dump file destination disk
9	40+	Application software, Archived redo log destination disk

TABLE 4-3. *Estimated I/O Weightings of the 9-Disk Solution*

The weightings for disks 8 and 9 are based on the weighting for the rollback segments tablespaces, since transactions written to RBS will also be written to the online redo log files. If the database is running in ARCHIVELOG mode, then disk 9's archived redo log files will have the same I/O as disk 8's online redo log files. Because other files are on these disks (the export dump files and the application software), their weight is indicated as being some value greater than the RBS disk's I/O weight.

From the weightings shown above, there are no good solutions going forward. In order to compress the disk farm further, you must either store data on the same disk as its associated index (by combining disks 6 and 7, which feature DATA_2 and INDEXES_2, respectively), or you must store extra tablespaces on one of the top four weighted disks (disks 2, 3, 4, and 5). The last two disks, which are being used to support the online redo log files, exports, application software, and archived redo log files, which are key to the database's recoverability, should not be further burdened.

The I/O weighting for the fifth iteration results in the compromise distribution of files shown in Figure 4-6.

For this iteration, the TOOLS and INDEXES_2 tablespaces are moved from old disk 7 to the disk that contains the SYSTEM tablespace. The TEMP, TEMP_*USER*, and DATA_2 tablespaces are moved from old disk 6 to the disk that features the INDEXES tablespace (since temporary segments dynamically extend, they should be kept separate from the SYSTEM tablespace).

The database's tablespace files are shown in bold in Figure 4-6. They are now spread over just four disks (disks 2, 3, 4, and 5). Each of these four disks features

```
Disk    Weight    Contents
1                 Oracle software
2       38        SYSTEM, TOOLS, INDEXES_2 tablespaces, Control
                     file 1
3       40        RBS, RBS_2 tablespaces, Control file 2
4       100       DATA tablespace, Control file 3
5       42        INDEXES, TEMP, TEMP_USER, DATA_2 tablespaces
6       40+       Online Redo logs 1, 2, and 3, Export dump
                     file destination disk
7       40+       Application software, Archived redo log
                     destination disk
```

FIGURE 4-6.   *The 7-Disk Compromise*

one of the top four I/O weighted files for the database; their relative weightings will be the same for most databases. If systems have a very high transaction volume, then this design will not change, since the rollback segment tablespaces (RBS and RBS_2) are already isolated.

Going beyond this level of file combinations forces the DBA to compromise even further. Since the database's recoverability should not be compromised, disks 6 and 7 should remain as they are. Additional combinations of tablespace files will compromise performance. Therefore, any further combinations of datafiles must be based on actual measurements of database I/O against these datafiles.

Verification of I/O Weighting Estimates

"I often say that when you can measure what you are talking about and express it in numbers, you know something about it; but when you cannot measure it, when you cannot express it in numbers, your knowledge is of a meagre and unsatisfactory kind."

—Lord Kelvin

The statistics tables within the data dictionary record the amount of I/O for each datafile. A query against the statistics tables, modeled after the BSTAT/UTLBSTAT file I/O queries (see Chapter 6, "Monitoring Multiple Databases"), can be used to verify the weightings assigned in the estimation process. The following listings provide the Oracle Version 6 and Oracle7 queries for generating the actual I/O weights.

Note that this script is not run for a specific time interval, but instead records all I/O against the database since it started up; the I/O against the SYSTEM tablespace will therefore be slightly higher than its value during everyday usage. Also note that the weightings are relative to the largest single file's I/O, not to the total I/O in the database. These scripts must be run from the SYS account.

The SQL*Plus scripts first create a view called MAX_TOTAL_VIEW that will be used to determine the datafile with the maximum I/O. This file will be assigned an I/O weight of 100. The second part of the script queries the kernel tables accessed by the file I/O portions of the database's statistics scripts. It adds together the values for the physical reads and writes to determine the total I/O against the file. This value is then compared with the maximum total I/O to determine the file's actual I/O weighting. The output from the query is written to a file called "io_weights.lis" via the "spool" command.

```
rem Oracle7 Version
rem
rem file: io_weights.sql
rem This is an ad hoc report against current statistics, based
rem on the queries used for UTLBSTAT/UTLESTAT.
rem
rem This report generates the file I/O weights based on actual
rem I/Os against the database, for use in verifying file layout
rem design.
rem
rem NOTE: This assumes that the drive designation is the first 5
rem       letters of the file name (e.g. /db01). If your drive
rem       designation is a different length, change the script
rem       where noted***
rem
rem
rem View creation.
rem This step creates the view MAX_TOTAL_VIEW that will retrieve
rem the maximum total I/O for a datafile in the database.
rem The view query is based on the UTLBSTAT/UTLESTAT queries.
rem
DROP VIEW max_total_view;
CREATE VIEW max_total_view
AS SELECT
   max(x.phyrds+x.phywrts) max_total
FROM v$filestat x, ts$ ts, v$datafile i,file$ f
WHERE i.file#=f.file#
and ts.ts#=f.ts#
```

```
and x.file#=f.file#;
rem
rem Column formatting for the query. If the drive name is not
rem  5 characters long, then adjust the format for the drive
rem  column.
rem
column drive format A5
column filename format a32
column total_io format 999999999
column weight format 999.99
rem
rem Establish a break after each drive.
rem
break on drive skip 1
rem
rem Sum the I/O weights for each drive.
rem
compute sum of weight on drive
rem
rem Page formatting
rem
set linesize 80 pagesize 60 newpage 0 feedback off
ttitle skip center "Database File IO Weights" skip center—
"Ordered by Drive" skip 2
rem
rem The Query. This is based on the UTLBSTAT/UTLESTAT file I/O
rem queries. If the drive name is not 5 characters long then
rem adjust the substr command.
rem
SELECT
    substr(i.name,1,5) "DRIVE",    /*assumes a 5-letter drive name*/
    i.name filename,
    x.phyrds +
    x.phywrts "total_io",
    round(100*(x.phyrds+x.phywrts)/m.max_total,2) weight
FROM v$filestat x, ts$ ts, v$datafile i,file$ f, max_total_view m
WHERE i.file#=f.file#
and ts.ts#=f.ts#
and x.file#=f.file#
ORDER BY 1,2

spool io_weights.lis
```

```
/
spool off


rem Oracle Version 6 Version
rem
rem file: io_weights.sql
rem This is an ad hoc report against current statistics, based
rem on the queries used for BSTAT/ESTAT.
rem
rem This report generates the file I/O weights based on actual
rem I/Os against the database, for use in verifying file layout
rem design.
rem
rem NOTE: This assumes that the drive designation is the first 5
rem       letters of the file name (ex: /db01). If your drive
rem       designation is a different length, change the script
rem       where noted***
rem
rem
rem View creation.
rem This step creates the view MAX_TOTAL_VIEW that will retrieve
rem the maximum total I/O for a datafile in the database.
rem The view query is based on the BSTAT/ESTAT queries.
rem
DROP VIEW max_total_view;
CREATE VIEW max_total_view
AS SELECT
   max(p.kcfiopyr+p.kcfiopyw) max_total
FROM x$kcffi n, x$kcfio p
WHERE n.kcffiidn=p.kcfiofno and
n.kcffinam is not null;
rem
rem Column formatting for the query. If the drive name is not
rem  5 characters long, then adjust the format for the drive
rem  column.
rem
column drive format A5
column filename format a32
column total_io format 999999999
column weight format 999.99
rem
```

```
rem Establish a break after each drive.
rem
break on drive skip 1
rem
rem Sum the I/O weights for each drive.
rem
compute sum of weight on drive
rem
rem Page formatting
rem
set linesize 80 pagesize 60 newpage 0 feedback off
ttitle skip center "Database File IO Weights" skip center—
"Ordered by Drive" skip 2
rem
rem The Query. This is based on the BSTAT/ESTAT file I/O
rem queries. If the drive name is not 5 characters long then
rem adjust the substr command.
rem
SELECT
    substr(n.kcffinam,1,5) drive, /*assumes a 5-letter drive name*/
    n.kcffinam filename,
    p.kcfiopyr+
    p.kcfiopyw total_io,
    round(100*(p.kcfiopyr+p.kcfiopyw)/m.max_total,2) weight
FROM x$kcffi n, x$kcfio p, max_total_view m
WHERE n.kcffiidn=p.kcfiofno and
n.kcffinam is not null
ORDER BY 1,2

spool io_weights.lis
/
spool off
```

The following listing shows sample output from this query.

```
                    Database File I/O Weights
                        Ordered by Drive

DRIVE    FILENAME                          total_io    WEIGHT
-----    --------------------------        --------    -------
/db01    /db01/oracle/DEMO/sys01.dbf          31279     40.65
         /db01/oracle/DEMO/tools.dbf           2112      2.74
*****                                                   -------
sum                                                      43.39


/db02    /db02/oracle/DEMO/rbs01.dbf           3799      5.94
         /db02/oracle/DEMO/rbs02.dbf           2465      3.20
         /db02/oracle/DEMO/rbs03.dbf           1960      2.55
         /db02/oracle/DEMO/rbs04.dbf           1675      2.18
*****                                                   -------
sum                                                      13.87


/db03    /db03/oracle/DEMO/ddata.dbf          76950    100.00
*****                                                   -------
sum                                                     100.00


/db04    /db04/oracle/DEMO/demondx.dbf        36310     47.19
         /db04/oracle/DEMO/temp.dbf            4012      5.21
*****                                                   -------
sum                                                      53.40
```

In this example, the main data tablespace (DDATA, using the *ddata.dbf* datafile on /db03) is rated at a weight of 100. The index tablespace associated with that data (DEMONDX, using the *demondx.dbf* datafile on /db04) is rated at 47.19, and the SYSTEM tablespace (using the *sys01.dbf* datafile on /db01) has a weight of 40.65. The biggest difference between these actual values and the estimates made earlier are in the rollback segments' RBS tablespace, which has a weight of only 13.87, rather than its estimated weight of 40. This information should be used to reorganize the database file layout to take advantage of the lighter-than-forecast transaction load in the database.

The Sixth Iteration: Back to the Planning Stage

Given these actual I/O weights for this database, the disk layout should be reevaluated. The disk layout for this example, with the estimated and actual I/O weights, is shown in Figure 4-7. Note that this example, for a small demo database, did not use the RBS_2, DATA_2, INDEXES_2, USER, or TEMP_USER tablespaces.

Disk	Est Weight	Actual Weight	Contents
1			Oracle software
2	38	43.39	SYSTEM, TOOLS tablespaces, Control file 1
3	40	13.87	RBS tablespace, Control file 2
4	100	100	DATA tablespace, Control file 3
5	42	53.40	INDEXES, TEMP tablespaces
6	40+	13.87+	Online Redo logs 1, 2, and 3, Export dump files
7	40+	13.87+	Application software, Archived redo logs

FIGURE 4-7. *Estimated and Actual I/O Weights for the 7-Disk Compromise*

Clearly, the INDEXES tablespace is being much more actively used than had been forecast (by about 25 percent). Also, the rollback segment usage is much lower than the estimates (13.87 instead of 40). As a result, two moves can be made for this system to better distribute the I/O weight; first, move TEMP from the INDEXES disk to the RBS disk, then move TOOLS from the SYSTEM to the RBS disk as well. This will result in a more leveled distribution of the I/O weight, as shown in Figure 4-8.

Disk	Actual Weight	Contents
1		Oracle software
2	40.65	SYSTEM tablespace, Control file 1
3	21.82	RBS, TEMP, and TOOLS tablespaces, Control file 2
4	100	DATA tablespace, Control file 3
5	47.19	INDEX tablespace
6	13.87+	Online Redo logs 1, 2, and 3, Export dump files
7	13.87+	Application software, Archived redo logs

FIGURE 4-8. *The 7-Disk Compromise, Revised for the Example's Actual Weights*

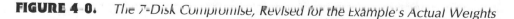

It is worth noting that the final example configuration process consisted of five iterations during the planning stage, and only one iteration during the tuning stage. The single tuning iteration's cost, in terms of database downtime, CPU usage, and time for completion, was greater than that of all of the planning stage's costs combined. Planning must not be an afterthought.

File Location

In order to simplify database management, the files associated with a database should be stored in directories created specifically for that database. Database files from different databases should not be stored together.

Furthermore, the database's datafiles should be separated from the software used to access the database (despite the fact that this is the default for some of the installation programs). The disk layouts shown in the previous sections all featured "Oracle software" as their Disk #1. This disk (Figure 4-9) includes all active versions of all Oracle software, and should not be allowed to cause contention with the datafiles.

Storing the datafiles at the same level in a directory hierarchy will simplify the management procedures. It also allows you to avoid putting the instance identifier in the file name, using it instead as part of the directory path, as in the following sample directory structure listing. A sample disk hierarchy for data disks in Oracle7 is shown in Figure 4-10.

```
        Disk 1        (/orasw)
/orasw
   /v636
        /rdbms
        /dbs
                initcase.ora
                initcc1.ora
                initdemo.ora
   /v715
        /rdbms
        /dbs
   /dba
```

FIGURE 4-9. *Disk Layout for Oracle Software*

```
        Disk 2        (/db01)
/db01
   /oracle
        /CASE
               control1.dbf
               sys01.dbf
               tools.dbf
        /CC1
               control1.dbf
               sys01.dbf
               tools.dbf
        /DEMO
```

FIGURE 4-10.   *Disk Hierarchy for a Sample Data Disk*

Note that this layout allows the same file names to be used across instances. In this configuration, the files are logically separated from each other in a consistent fashion. This allows wildcards or search lists to be used when referencing them (if the disks are named in a consistent fashion). For example, in UNIX environments, all of the files belonging to a specific instance could be copied to a tape device with a single command:

```
> tar /dev/rmt/1hc /db0[1-8]/oracle/CASE
```

In this example, the system will write out to the tape device (/dev/rmt/1hc) the contents of the /oracle/CASE subdirectory on the devices named /db01 through /db08.

Database Space Usage Overview

In order to understand how space should be allocated within the database, you first have to know how the space is used within the database. This section will provide an overview of the Oracle database space usage functions.

When a database is created, it is divided into multiple logical sections called tablespaces. The SYSTEM tablespace is the first tablespace created. Additional tablespaces are then created to hold different types of data, as described in Chapter 3, "Logical Database Layouts."

When a tablespace is created, datafiles are created to hold its data. These files immediately allocate the space specified during their creation, and never expand in size. (Resizing of datafiles will be accomplished in a future Oracle release.) There is thus a one-to-many relationship between databases and tablespaces, and a one-to-many relationship between tablespaces and datafiles.

A database can have multiple users, each of whom has a *schema*. Each user's schema is a collection of logical database objects such as tables and indexes. These objects refer to physical data structures that are stored in tablespaces. Objects from a user's schema may be stored in multiple tablespaces, and a single tablespace can contain objects from multiple schemas.

When a database object (such as a table or index) is created, it is assigned to a tablespace via user defaults or specific instructions. A *segment* is created in that tablespace to hold the data associated with that object. The space that is allocated to the segment is never released until the segment is dropped, shrunk (Oracle7 rollback segments only), or truncated (Oracle7 tables only, when TRUNCATE is used with the DROP STORAGE option).

A segment is made up of sections called *extents*. The extents themselves are contiguous sets of Oracle blocks. Once the existing extents can no longer hold new data, the segment will obtain another extent. This extension process will continue until no more free space is available in the tablespace's datafiles, or until an internal maximum number of extents per segment is reached. If a segment is comprised of multiple extents, there is no guarantee that those extents will be contiguous.

The logical interrelationships between these database objects are shown in Figure 4-11.

As shown in Figure 4-11, a tablespace may contain multiple segments. The segment types available in Oracle are

TABLE
INDEX
ROLLBACK
TEMPORARY

Managing the space used by each is one of the basic functions of the DBA. Chapter 6, "Monitoring Multiple Databases," Chapter 7, "Managing Rollback Segments," and Chapter 8, "Database Tuning," contain detailed information on the monitoring and tuning of these segments. The intent of this overview is to aid in the planning of their physical storage.

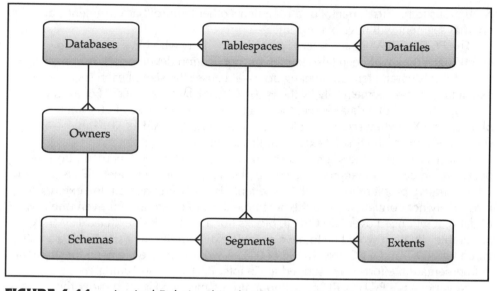

FIGURE 4-11.   *Logical Relationships between Database Structures*

Implications of the STORAGE Clause

The amount of space used by a segment is determined by its storage parameters. These parameters are determined by the database at segment creation time; if no specific storage parameters are given in the CREATE [TABLE¦INDEX¦CLUSTER¦ ROLLBACK SEGMENT] command, then it will use the default storage parameters for the tablespace in which it is to be stored. The storage parameters specify the INITIAL extent size, the NEXT extent size, the PCTINCREASE (a factor by which each successive extent will geometrically grow), the MAXEXTENTS (maximum number of extents), and MINEXTENTS (minimum number of extents). After the segment has been created, the INITIAL and MINEXTENTS values cannot be altered. The default values for the storage parameters for each tablespace are contained in the DBA_TABLESPACES and USER_TABLESPACES views.

When a segment is created, it will acquire at least one extent (other values can be set via MINEXTENTS). This extent will be used to store data until it no longer has any free space available (the PCTFREE clause can be used to reserve, within each block in each extent, a percentage of space that will remain available for updates of existing rows). When additional data is added to the segment, the segment will extend by obtaining a second extent of the size specified by the NEXT parameter. There is no guarantee that the second extent will be physically contiguous to the first extent. For all segments other than rollback segments, an optimal segment will have one extent.

The PCTINCREASE parameter is provided for users who have no clue how much space they will need (also known as "application developers"). A non-zero value for this parameter can be dangerous—it causes the size of each successive extent to increase geometrically by the PCTINCREASE factor specified. For example, consider the case of a data segment with an INITIAL extent size of 20 Oracle blocks, a NEXT extent size of 20 blocks, and a PCTINCREASE of 50. Table 4-4 shows the sizes of the first 10 extents in this segment.

In just 10 extents, the segment's size has increased by 7,655 percent. Besides being an indicator of inappropriate space planning by the developer, this is also an administrative problem for the DBA. The table is badly fragmented, the extents are most likely not contiguous, and the next time this table extends (for even one row of data), it will need over 750 Oracle blocks (for a 2K block size, that's 1.5M). A preferable situation would be to have a single extent of the right size, with a small value for NEXT and a PCTINCREASE of 0. This would obviate the need for segment defragmentation efforts (as described in Chapter 8, "Database Tuning").

Never change PCTINCREASE without also changing NEXT. Consider the example given above. Note that the size of each successive extent is calculated by going back to the storage parameters for the table; the size of the last extent added is not considered. If, for example, you were to now change the PCTINCREASE value to 0 for that segment, then extent number 11 would have a size of 20 Oracle blocks (NEXT*1.0*1.0 etc.), *not* 518 blocks.

EXTENT NUMBER	SIZE (IN ORACLE BLOCKS)	TOTAL	COMMENTS ON EXTENT SIZE
1	20	20	INITIAL
2	20	40	NEXT
3	30	70	NEXT*1.5
4	45	115	NEXT*1.5*1.5
5	68	183	NEXT*1.5*1.5*1.5
6	102	285	etc.
7	153	438	
8	230	668	
9	345	1013	
10	518	1531	

TABLE 4-4. *The Effect of Using a Non-Zero PCTINCREASE*

Table Segments

Table segments, also called *data segments*, store the rows of data associated with tables or clusters. Each data segment contains a header block that serves as a space directory for the segment.

A properly sized table will have one extent. The more extents a data segment has, the more work is involved in retrieving data from it. In some cases, it is not possible to have single-extent data segments; since extents cannot span datafiles, a segment that is larger than the largest datafile available will have to be comprised of multiple extents. Multiple extents can also be used to stripe a segment across disks; this operation, though, is better handled outside of the database (for example, by using RAID-3 or RAID-5 disk mirroring, as described earlier in this chapter).

Once a data segment acquires an extent, it keeps that extent until the segment is either dropped or truncated (in Oracle7, when the DROP STORAGE clause is specified). Deleting rows from a table has no impact on the amount of space that has been allocated to that table. The number of extents will increase until either (1) the MAXEXTENTS value is reached, (2) the maximum number of extents allowable for the operating system is reached, or (3) the tablespace runs out of space.

To minimize the amount of wasted space in a data segment, tune the PCTFREE parameter. This parameter specifies the amount of space that will be kept free within each data block. This free space can then be used when null-valued columns are updated to have values, or when updates to other values in the row force the row to lengthen. The proper setting of PCTFREE is database-specific, since it is dependent on the nature of the updates that are being performed. For information on setting this and other storage parameters for tables and indexes, see Chapter 5, "Managing the Development Process."

Index Segments

Like table segments, *index segments* hold the space that has been allocated to them until they are dropped; however, they can also be indirectly dropped if the table or cluster they index is dropped. To minimize contention, indexes should be stored in a tablespace that is separated from their associated tables.

Indexes are subject to the same space problems that tables experience. Their segments have storage clauses that specify their INITIAL, NEXT, MINEXTENTS, MAXEXTENTS, and PCTINCREASE values, and they are as likely to be fragmented as their tables are. They must be sized properly before they are created; otherwise, their fragmentation will drag down the database performance—exactly the opposite of their purpose.

Rollback Segments

Rollback segment functionality will be discussed in detail in Chapter 7, "Managing Rollback Segments." The same principles of sound design apply to rollback segments as did to tables. However, while optimal tables have one extent that is suited to their size requirements, optimal rollback segments will have multiple evenly sized extents that add up to their optimal total size (they will have a minimum of two extents when created). Each extent should be large enough to handle all of the data from a single transaction. If it is not, or if too many users request the same rollback segment, then the rollback segment may extend.

In Oracle Version 6, rollback segments are like any data segment: they cannot shrink back and release previously acquired extents—the only recourse is to drop and re-create the rollback segment. For this reason, it is advisable to have a second rollback segment tablespace if your users will be periodically performing very large transactions (such as large data loads) and you do not wish to assign that space to the rollback segment tablespace on a permanent basis. The specialty rollback segments tablespace can be added and removed as needed; the rollback segments can be specified via the following command.

```
SET TRANSACTION USE ROLLBACK SEGMENT segment name
```

The OPTIMAL clause in Oracle7, which allows rollback segments to shrink to an OPTIMAL size after extending, is like the PCTINCREASE clause; it helps to provide interim support to systems that have not been properly implemented for the way they are being used. Frequent shrinks (see the "Interpreting the Statistics Reports" section of Chapter 6, "Monitoring Multiple Databases," and Chapter 7, "Managing Rollback Segments") indicate the need for the rollback segments to be redesigned. Since Oracle7 gives DBAs much greater flexibility in the management of rollback segments, they can be maintained much more easily.

This does not address the most commonly asked question: How many rollback segments should you have? The answer to that is database-dependent; it's like asking how large your DATA tablespace should be. For guidance in choosing the right number and size of rollback segments, see the "Choosing the Number and Size" section of Chapter 7, "Managing Rollback Segments."

Temporary Segments

Temporary segments are used to store temporary data during sorting operations (such as large queries, index creations, and unions). Each user has a temporary tablespace specified when the account is created via CREATE USER (Oracle7) or ALTER USER (Oracle Version 6 and Oracle7). This should be pointed to someplace other than SYSTEM (the default).

When a temporary segment is created, it uses the default storage parameters for that tablespace. While it is in existence, its storage parameters cannot be altered by changing the default storage parameters for the tablespace. It extends itself as necessary, and drops itself when the operation completes or encounters an error. Since the temporary segment itself can lead to errors (by exceeding the maximum number of extents or running out of space in the tablespace), the size of large sorting queries and operations should be taken into consideration when sizing the temporary tablespace.

The temporary tablespace, usually named TEMP, is fragmented by its nature (in Oracle Version 6, this is especially true). Temporary segments are constantly created, extended, and then dropped. It is therefore necessary to maximize the reusability of dropped extents. To accomplish this, choose an INITIAL and NEXT extent size of 1/20th to 1/50th of the size of the tablespace. INITIAL and NEXT should be equal for this tablespace. Choose a PCTINCREASE of 0; the result will be segments made up of identically sized extents. When these segments are dropped, the next temporary segment to be formed will be able to reuse the dropped extents.

Oracle7 automatically recombines contiguous free extents, so the reusability of extents is not as big an issue as it is in Oracle Version 6 (although proper sizing is still important). This free space defragmentation also removes an important diagnostic tool, since the number of fragments in an Oracle Version 6 TEMP tablespace serves as an indicator of the number of extents that were acquired during the most active temporary segment usage. In Oracle7, this information can only be detected while the transactions are taking place, by querying the DBA_SEGMENTS view where the segment_type = 'TEMPORARY'.

Free Space

A *free extent* in a tablespace is a collection of contiguous free blocks in the tablespace. When a segment is dropped, its extents are deallocated and are marked as free. However, these free extents are not recombined with neighboring free extents in Oracle Version 6 databases; the barriers between these free extents are maintained (see Figure 4-12b)). In Oracle7 databases, SMON periodically coalesces neighboring free extents (see Figure 4-12(c)).

The Oracle Version 6 methodology affects the allocation of space within the tablespace during the next space request (such as by the creation or expansion of a table). In its quest for a large enough free extent, the database will not merge contiguous free extents unless there is no other alternative; thus the large free extent at the rear of the tablespace tends to be used, while the smaller free extents toward the front of the tablespace are relatively unused, becoming "speed bumps" in the tablespace because they are not, by themselves, of adequate size to be of use. As this usage pattern progresses, the database thus drifts further and further from its ideal space allocation.

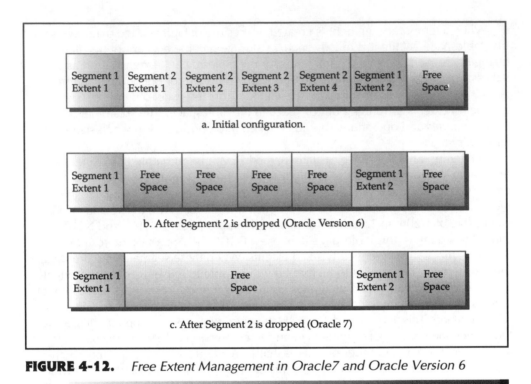

| Segment 1 Extent 1 | Segment 2 Extent 1 | Segment 2 Extent 2 | Segment 2 Extent 3 | Segment 2 Extent 4 | Segment 1 Extent 2 | Free Space |

a. Initial configuration.

| Segment 1 Extent 1 | Free Space | Free Space | Free Space | Free Space | Segment 1 Extent 2 | Free Space |

b. After Segment 2 is dropped (Oracle Version 6)

| Segment 1 Extent 1 | Free Space | Segment 1 Extent 2 | Free Space |

c. After Segment 2 is dropped (Oracle 7)

FIGURE 4-12. *Free Extent Management in Oracle7 and Oracle Version 6*

However, you can force the Oracle Version 6 database to recombine the contiguous free extents, thus emulating the Oracle7 SMON functionality. This will increase the likelihood of the free extents near the front of the file being reused, thus preserving the free space near the rear of the tablespace file. As a result, new requests for extents are more likely to meet with success. Scripts for accomplishing this are provided in Chapter 8, "Database Tuning."

In an ideal database, all objects are created at their appropriate size (in one extent), and all free space is always stored together, a resource pool waiting to be used. In reality, the image shown in the bottom half of Figure 4-12 is often encountered: fragmented tables, fragmented free space (in Oracle Version 6), and free space that is separated from other free space by data extents. Resolutions to these fragmentation issues are described in Chapter 8, "Database Tuning." Monitoring scripts to determine the severity of these conditions are given in Chapter 6, "Monitoring Multiple Databases."

Physically Fit

In both Oracle Version 6 and Oracle7 databases, the file allocation must be planned (using I/O weightings) and the weightings must be verified once the system goes into production. The file layout can then be modified to better balance the I/O requirements of the files. The result will be a database that achieves its performance goals without sacrificing recoverability, and its recoverability goals without sacrificing performance.

Each main facet of the database—tables, indexes, rollback segments, and temporary segments—must be sized correctly as well. Correct sizing requires knowing the way in which the data is to be entered, how it is to be stored, and the processes that will be performed on it once it gets there. The costs of planning the storage parameters are minimal when compared to the costs of manipulating the system once it has been released to production. Post-production tuning should be a final, minor step in the database physical design planning process.

PART 2

Database Management

CHAPTER 5

Managing the Development Process

Controlling application developers is like herding cats. Since developers can't be controlled, the best way to manage the development process is for DBAs to become an integral part of it. This chapter will discuss the activities involved in migrating applications into databases, and will provide the technical details needed for implementation. These will include system role specifications and sizing formulas for database objects.

This chapter focuses on controlling the activities that create objects in the database at various stages. These activities should follow the database planning activities that were described in Chapter 3, "Logical Database Layouts," and Chapter 4, "Physical Database Layouts." Chapter 6, "Monitoring Multiple

Databases," and Chapter 8, "Database Tuning," address the monitoring and tuning activities that follow the database creation.

Implementing an application in a database by merely running a series of CREATE TABLE commands fails to integrate the creation process with the other major areas (planning, monitoring, and tuning). The DBA must be involved in the application development process in order to correctly structure the database that will support the end product. The methods described in this chapter will also provide important information for structuring the database monitoring and tuning efforts.

The Three Critical Elements of Success

The life cycle of a database is defined by the four actions referred to previously: planning, creating, monitoring, and tuning. The elements of a successful implementation of this cycle can be identified as belonging to three key categories: *cultural processes*, *management processes*, and *technology*.

Managing the implementation efforts of database developers requires action on all three points:

1. Cultural: The corporate culture and the development team must support the DBA's involvement in this level of activity.

2. Management: The developers' adherence to a life cycle methodology must be enforceable.

3. Technology: The developers and DBAs must define mechanisms for making sure the appropriate level of involvement and attention to detail is taking place.

Attempting to implement a development life cycle methodology without corporate buy-in or without technology that allows for the tracking of deliverables will yield no long-term benefit.

Cultural Processes

In order to break down the traditional barrier between DBAs and developers, the relationship between them must be formalized. The revised nature of the relationship must be accepted by all of the parties involved. This can only be accomplished if the groups being brought together feel that the new team's structure adds value to the development process. There must be a corporate commitment to the team structure to overcome the initial turf wars that may otherwise disrupt the process from the start.

A joint DBA/developer team adds value by

- Building applications that are easier to maintain

- Building applications that are properly sized and organized, and thus require no downtime for reorganizations

- Creating appropriate indexes to maximize performance

- Building into each application an understanding of the interface needs of outside applications

- Identifying technical problems earlier in the development process

- Allowing the DBA, who will eventually provide much of the application's support, to accept partial ownership of the application during its development

Difficult to maintain, fragmented, slow, and isolated database applications cost the organization in terms of downtime, tuning time, and user frustration. These costs can be avoided by entering into true team relationships between developers and DBAs. The methodology must clearly define the roles and responsibilities within these relationships. It must be accepted by all levels within the personnel groups responsible for applications development. This will greatly ease the need for third-party enforcement of the methodology.

Management Processes

In order to properly manage development efforts, the methodology must not only spell out the relationships between the different functional areas, but must also clearly define the deliverables required in phase of application development. For example, when does an application move out of "Development" and into "Test," or from "Test" to "Production"? Who decides?

The answer is, the methodology decides. If the deliverables for the "Development" section are complete, reviewed, and approved, then the application can be moved into the "Test" environment, under whose constraints the developers must now work.

Defining the Environment

Most application environments are divided into two to four areas. They are *Development, System Test, Acceptance Test*, and *Production*. For the purposes of this discussion, the two Test areas will be combined. The exact number of areas maintained is methodology-specific.

Consider each of the areas. The methodology needs to specify what the finished product will be from each area, and what completing that section will provide to subsequent areas. Once this has been defined, the database needs for the different areas can be deduced.

In Development, for instance, users may have free reign to make table changes, test new ideas, and create new objects. An integrated CASE dictionary such as Oracle*CASE should be used to maintain a constantly synchronized logical model. The CASE database should be used to generate the first set of database objects in each environment; the developers should be responsible for maintaining the CASE dictionary thereafter.

Once the system enters the Test phase, its final configuration should be within sight. At this point, the table volumes, user accounts, and performance needs should be identified. These will allow the DBA to create a proper database for the application on the first try, and to monitor for performance problems that are outside of the defined acceptable bounds.

In Production, developers are locked out. From the database's perspective, they are just another set of users. All changes to database objects in the Production database should have first passed through the Test environment. Any modifications to the system's needs should have been clearly defined in Test.

In order to maintain the proper level of user system-level privileges, developer accounts must be configured differently for each area. The next section will describe the proper system role definitions for developers in Oracle Version 6 and Oracle7 databases, given the Development-Test-Production areas previously described.

Role Definitions

In Oracle Version 6, there is little flexibility in the assignment of system-level roles; only *Connect*, *Resource*, and *DBA* are available. Since developers should not have DBA privileges (despite their protests to the contrary), this greatly reduces the number of options that must be considered. In Production, users should only have Connect (unless the application for some reason requires the users to be able to create segments in the database, in which case they will need Resource as well). In Development, developers will need both Connect and Resource.

The only real question for Oracle Version 6 databases, then, is what privileges the developers will be granted in a Test environment. The answer depends on the nature of the testing being done. If the applications are relatively small in size and the testing area is used to perform system acceptance tests, then developers do not need the Resource privilege. However, if it is being used as test area for small portions of large applications, then developers may need the ability to modify the sections of the application that interface with other sections. In this case, they would need Resource. The final decision on this privilege issue is determined by the usage of the Test area, and should be clearly defined in the methodology.

In Oracle7, the DBA can create *system-level roles* to define system privileges beyond Connect, Resource, and DBA. These can be customized for the different areas (Development, Test, and Production), depending on what privileges are determined to be necessary.

Oracle7 Development Roles

In the Development database, users need the privileges required to create and test database application objects such as tables and views. All users in that database should be treated as developers. Granting them the APPLICATION_DEVELOPER role described in the next section will ease administration and create a consistent set of privileges for each developer.

Application Developers   For developers in an Oracle7 Development area, create a role called *APPLICATION_DEVELOPER.* This role should allow a developer to create objects in his or her own account, and should be analogous to the Oracle Version 6 Resource privilege. The APPLICATION_DEVELOPER role should not be explicitly granted UNLIMITED TABLESPACE; developers in Development database should only be granted resource access to tablespaces specific to their applications.

The APPLICATION_DEVELOPER role's privileges are:

- CREATE, ALTER SESSION
- CREATE, ALTER, or DROP CLUSTER
- CREATE, ALTER, or DROP DATABASE LINK
- CREATE, ALTER, or DROP PROCEDURE
- CREATE, ALTER, or DROP ROLE
- CREATE, ALTER, or DROP SEQUENCE
- CREATE, ALTER, or DROP SNAPSHOT
- CREATE, ALTER, or DROP SYNONYM
- CREATE, ALTER, or DROP TABLE
- CREATE, ALTER, or DROP TRIGGER
- CREATE, ALTER, or DROP VIEW
- CREATE, ALTER, or DROP TABLE

The APPLICATION_DEVELOPER role, once created, can be granted to users The following commands can be used to create the role and grant it to users.

Note that not all of the privileges are listed, allowing for the role to be customized to your needs.

```
create role APPLICATION_DEVELOPER;
grant CREATE SESSION, ALTER SESSION, other privileges to
APPLICATION_DEVELOPER;
grant APPLICATION_DEVELOPER to username;
```

Oracle7 Production Roles

In the Production database, users are divided into several classes: Application Creators, Application Owners, and Application Users. Each class of users requires a separate role. Using the APPLICATION_CREATOR, APPLICATION_OWNER, and APPLICATION_USER roles described in the following sections will ensure consistency and ease of administration.

Application Creators   In Oracle Version 6, users could only create objects in their own *schemas* (accounts). In Oracle7, users can be granted privileges to create objects in remote schemas. This allows a privileged user to create tables in the schema of an application owner. Taking advantage of this capability allows the application ownership and the application administration to be divided among multiple users. This, in turn, allows the application owner to be an account that lacks CREATE SESSION privilege, thus avoiding the security issues inherent in having an application owner account which users can directly log in to.

An APPLICATION_CREATOR role is therefore used to remotely manipulate the objects owned by the application owner account.

The APPLICATION_CREATOR role's privileges are:

- ANALYZE ANY
- CREATE, ALTER, or DROP ANY CLUSTER
- CREATE or DROP [PUBLIC] DATABASE LINK
- CREATE, ALTER, or DROP ANY INDEX
- GRANT ANY PRIVILEGE
- CREATE, ALTER, DROP, or EXECUTE ANY PROCEDURE
- CREATE or DROP PUBLIC SYNONYM
- CREATE or ALTER SESSION
- CREATE, ALTER, DROP, or SELECT ANY SEQUENCE

- CREATE, ALTER, or DROP SNAPSHOT

- CREATE or DROP ANY SYNONYM

- CREATE, ALTER, DROP, LOCK, COMMENT, SELECT, INSERT, UPDATE, or DELETE ANY TABLE

- CREATE, ALTER, or DROP ANY TRIGGER

- CREATE or DROP ANY VIEW

Create the role and grant it to users via the following commands. Note that not all of the privileges are listed, allowing for the role to be customized to your needs.

```
create role APPLICATION_CREATOR;
grant CREATE SESSION, ALTER SESSION, other privileges to
APPLICATION_CREATOR;
grant APPLICATION_CREATOR to username;
```

Application Owners   The APPLICATION_OWNER role that accompanies the APPLICATION_CREATOR role will serve only to identify a schema that is being used as the holding area for an application's objects. It will not even have CREATE SESSION privilege, so no one can log in to it directly. Its objects can only be manipulated by remote users (Application Creators) who have the proper authority. In order to create objects in an account that has been granted this role, the DBA must first give the Application Owner account resource quotas for the tablespaces in which the database objects will be stored.

The APPLICATION_OWNER role's privileges are:

- No privileges.

Create the role and grant it to users via the following commands.

```
create role APPLICATION_OWNER;
grant APPLICATION_OWNER to username;
```

Application Users   The Oracle Version 6 CONNECT role is supported in Oracle7. In addition to CREATE SESSION, it includes CREATE VIEW, CREATE SYNONYM, and the other Oracle Version 6-style privileges. But are they necessary? In a controlled Production environment, users should not be creating their own views, synonyms, or database links. If you need to create such objects in users' schemas, you can do so by virtue of the privileges granted via the APPLICATION_CREATOR role. This very restricted APPLICATION_USER role permits only the log in capability of the standard CONNECT privileges.

The APPLICATION_USER role's privilege is:

■ CREATE SESSION

Create this role and grant it to users via the following commands.

```
create role APPLICATION_USER;
grant CREATE SESSION to APPLICATION_USER;
grant APPLICATION_USER to username;
```

Oracle7 Test Roles

The appropriate role designations for the Test environment depend on how that environment is to be used. If it is to be used as a true Acceptance Test region, mirroring the eventual production database, then its roles should be assigned to mirror the Production roles. If, however, developers will be allowed to make modifications to the Test database, then they will require the APPLICATION_DEVELOPER role described in the previous section.

Deliverables

How do you know if the methodology is being followed? Doing so requires establishing a list of items called *deliverables* that must be completed during the application development. The methodology must clearly define, both in format and in level of detail, the required deliverables for each stage of the life cycle. These should include specifications for each of the following items:

- Entity Relationship diagram
- Physical Database diagram
- Space requirements
- Tuning goals
- Data requirements
- Execution plans
- Acceptance test procedures

Each of these items is described in the following sections.

Entity Relationship Diagram

The *Entity Relationship (E-R) diagram* illustrates the relationships that have been identified among the entities that make up the application. E-R diagrams are critical for providing an understanding of the goals of the system. They also help to identify interface points with other applications, and to ensure consistency in definitions across the enterprise. Modelling conventions for E-R diagrams are described in Chapter 1, "The Oracle Architecture."

Physical Database Diagram

A *Physical Database diagram* shows the physical tables generated from the entities, and the columns generated from the defined attributes in the logical model. A physical database diagramming tool is usually capable of generating the DDL necessary to create the application's objects. Modelling conventions for physical database diagrams are described in Chapter 1, "The Oracle Architecture."

Space Requirements

The space requirements deliverable should show the initial space requirements for each database table and index. The calculations necessary to determine the proper size for tables, clusters, and indexes are shown in the "Sizing Database Objects" section later in this chapter.

Tuning Goals

It is important to identify the performance goals of a system *before* it goes into production. The role of expectation in perception cannot be overemphasized. If the users have an expectation that the system will be at least as fast as an existing system, then anything less will be unacceptable. The estimated response time for each of the most-used components of the application must be defined and approved.

It is important during this process to establish two sets of goals: reasonable goals and "stretch" goals. *Stretch goals* represent the results of concentrated efforts to go beyond the hardware and software constraints that limit the system's performance. Maintaining two sets of performance goals helps to focus efforts on those goals that are truly mission-critical versus those that are beyond the scope of the core system deliverables.

Security Requirements

The development team must specify the account structure that the application will use. This should include the ownership of all objects in the application and the manner in which privileges will be granted. If it is an Oracle7 database, then roles and privileges must be clearly defined. The deliverables from this section will be used to generate the account and privilege structure of the production application.

Depending on the application, it may be necessary to specify the account usage for batch accounts separately from that of online accounts. This may occur in situations in which the batch accounts will use the database's autologin features, while the online users have to manually sign in.

Like the space requirements deliverable, this is an area in which the DBA's involvement is critical. The DBA should be able to design an implementation that meets the application's needs while fitting in with the enterprise database security plan.

Data Requirements

The methods for data entry and retrieval must be clearly defined. They will need to be tested and verified while the application is in the Test environment. Any special data archiving requirements of the application must also be documented, since they will be application-specific.

You must also describe the backup and recovery requirements for the application. These requirements can then be compared to the site database backup plans (see Chapter 10, "Optimal Backup and Recovery Procedures," for guidelines). Any database recovery requirements that go beyond the site's standard will require modifying the site's backup standard or adding a module to accommodate the application's needs.

Execution Plans

Execution plans are the steps that the database will go through while executing queries. They are generated via the EXPLAIN PLAN statement, which is described in Chapter 8, "Database Tuning." Recording the execution plans for the most important queries against the database will aid in planning the index usage and tuning goals for the application. Generating them prior to production implementation will simplify tuning efforts and identify potential performance problems before the application is released. This will also facilitate the process of performing code reviews of the application.

Acceptance Test Procedures

The developers and users should very clearly define what functionality and performance goals must be achieved before the application can be migrated to production. These goals will form the foundation of the test procedures that will be executed against the application while it is in the Test environment.

The procedures should also describe how to deal with unmet goals. They should very clearly list the functional goals that must be met before the system can move forward. A second list of noncritical functional goals should also be provided. This separation of functional capabilities will aid in both resolving scheduling conflicts and structuring appropriate tests.

Sizing Database Objects

Choosing the proper space allocation for database objects is critical. Developers should begin estimating space requirements before the first database objects are created. Afterwards, the space requirements can be refined based on the actual usage statistics. The following sections give the space requirement calculations for tables, indexes, and clusters. The proper setting of PCTFREE is also discussed.

Sizing Non-Clustered Tables

In addition to showing the initial space requirements for a table, the space requirements deliverable should show the estimated yearly percentage increase in number of records for each table. If applicable, a maximum number of records should also be defined.

Once the table's column definitions and data volumes are known, its storage requirements can be determined. This is a process of educated guessing, since the true data volumes and row lengths will not be known until after the table is created. It is important that sample data be available at this point in order to make the results of these calculations as accurate as possible.

First, calculate the *average row length*. This is the total of the average length of each value in a row. If no data is available, then estimate the actual length of the values in a column. Do not use the full length of a column as its actual length unless the data will always completely fill the column. This is the case with the Oracle7 fixed-length CHAR column.

For example, consider a table comprised of three columns, all of which are VARCHAR2(10). The average row length cannot exceed 30; its actual length depends on the data that will be stored there.

If the sample data is available, then the VSIZE function can be used to determine the actual space used by the data. Again, assume a table has three columns. To determine its average row length, perform the following query.

```
select
    avg(nvl(vsize(column1),0))+
    avg(nvl(vsize(column2),0))+
    avg(nvl(vsize(column3),0))    avg_row_length
from tablename;
```

In this example, the average length of each column is determined, and the averages are totalled to determine the average row length.

Each row has *row header* information stored with it. This also takes up space. The header space requirements can be calculated via the following formula, in which two types of columns are considered: the "short" column (less than 250 characters long) and the "long" column (more than 250 characters long). This distinction is necessary because of the number of length bytes that the database must store for the values.

```
Header space per row=3+
                number of short columns+
                (3*number of long columns)
```

Adding the average row length and the header space per row yields the total space required by each row.

```
Bytes per row=        Header space per row+
                average row length
```

Now that the space requirements of each row are known, the data volumes can be used to estimate the total space requirements of the table's rows.

```
Total bytes required=Bytes per row*number of rows
```

This is the space that is required to store all of the data in the table. However, the database will have additional overhead. There will be overhead to store *block header* information, and there will be overhead to handle rows that expand (*PCTFREE*). Calculating the proper PCTFREE value will be explained in the following section (called "Determining the Proper PCTFREE"). The space allocation within a block is shown in Figure 5-1.

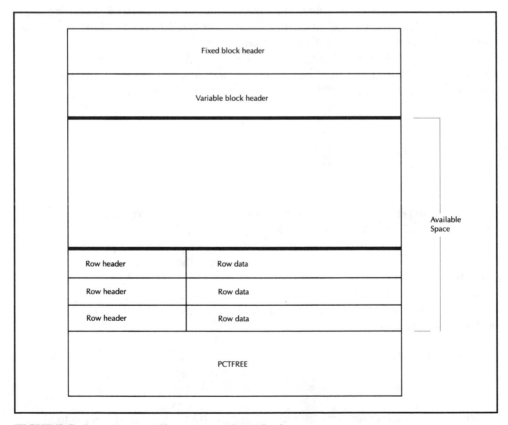

FIGURE 5-1. *Space Allocation within Blocks*

Determining the block header size requires knowing how the data will be used. The block header consists of a fixed section and a variable section. The fixed section is at least 80 bytes in length, and the variable header is at least 6 bytes in length. Both of these are dependent on the way in which the data is stored, as shown in the following formulas.

```
Fixed block header size (in bytes)=57+23*INITRANS
Variable block header size (in bytes)=4+2*number of rows per block
```

In the fixed block header calculation, the *INITRANS* parameter for the table is important. This parameter is used to preallocate space in the block header for transactions that will access the block's rows. Its default value is 1 for tables. If multiple transactions will simultaneously access the same data block, then the INITRANS parameter should be set to the number of transactions that will concurrently access a single data block. If the value is not set high enough to support these transactions, then the database will dynamically use the available free space in the data block to support the block header's space needs.

The variable portion of the block header stores the table directory (4 bytes) and the row directory (2 bytes per row).

The block header size and the data requirements are thus interrelated. The more rows there are in a block, the larger the block header must be, leaving less space for the data. This relationship makes the calculation of space requirements more complicated than it would otherwise be.

First, calculate the available space per block as a function of the number of rows per block. Estimate a value for PCTFREE, using the guidelines in the next section.

```
Available space per block=       total block size-
                          fixed block header size-
                          variable block header size
                    =     (block size-fixed block header size
                               -variable block header size)
                          -(block size-fixed block header size)
                               *(PCTFREE/100)
                          -4-2R
                    =     (block size-(57+23*INITRANS))
                          -(block size-(57+23*INITRANS))
                               *(PCTFREE/100)
                          -4-2R
where R is the number of rows per block.
```

Since the number of rows per block is the available space in the block divided by the average row size, R can be calculated now. For this example, an INITRANS of 1 will be used; this is valid if only one transaction will access the same data block at any time.

```
Number of rows per block (R)=available space per block /
                    bytes per row
             =((block size-(57+23*INITRANS))-
                  (block size-(57+23*INITRANS))
                       *(PCTFREE/100)-4-2R) /
             (Header space per row + average row length)
```

For our sample three-column table, the average row length will be estimated at 25 bytes. The row header for the data will be 6 bytes (3 bytes plus 1 byte for each column). The total row length is therefore 31 bytes (25 for the data + 6 bytes for the header).

For the block size, use the block size that your database was created with. If you do not know what this is, either check the database's INIT.ORA DB_BLOCK_SIZE parameter or go into SQLDBA and enter the command

```
SQLDBA> SHOW PARAMETERS db_block_size
```

This value will be used in the equation above. For this example, use a block size of 2048 (2K). For this example, a PCTFREE value of 20 will be used; this value will force 20 percent of each block to be set aside to handle expansions of rows already stored in the block. Like the INITRANS value of 1 chosen earlier, its correct value may be different for each table. These calculations also assume a block size of 2048 bytes.

```
Number of rows per block (R)=((block size-(57+23*INITRANS))-
               (block size-(57+23*INITRANS))
                    *(PCTFREE/100)-4-2R) /
               (Header space per row+average row length)
Number of rows per block (R)=
   ((2048-80)-(2048-80)*(20/100)-4-2R)/31
31*R=(1968)-(1968*.2)-4-2R
31*R=1968-393-4-2R
31R+2R=1968-393-4
33R=1968-393-4
33R=1571
R=47 rows per block
```

The total number of blocks required to store this table is thus equal to the number of rows, divided by 47 rows per block. Note that if you had ignored the database's overhead and PCTFREE space, you would have estimated 81 (2048/25) rows per block.

Note that this calculation was dependent on several variables, including the block size, average row length, PCTFREE, and INITRANS. If any of these variables changes, then the space requirements for the table will have to be recalculated.

Determining the Proper PCTFREE

The proper *PCTFREE* value must be determined for each table. This value represents the percentage of *each data block* that is reserved as free space. This space is used when a row that has already been stored in that data block grows in length, either by updates of previously NULL fields or by updates of existing values to longer values.

There is no single value for PCTFREE that will be adequate for all tables in all databases. But since PCTFREE is tied to the way in which updates occur in an application, determining the adequacy of its setting is a straightforward process. The following description will work in both Oracle Version 6 and Oracle7; a shortcut for Oracle7 users will also be described.

PCTFREE controls the number of records that are stored in a block in a table. To check to see if it has been set correctly, first determine the number of records per block. This is done by first querying the number of records in the table:

```
select count(*) from tablename;
```

The second query looks solely at the ROWID of the records in the table. The ROWID identifies the physical location of a row in a database. It is comprised of three parts: the Block ID (positions 1-8), the sequence within that block (positions 10-13), and the File ID (positions 15-4). For example, a ROWID of 00008791.0001.0003 would refer to row 0001 in block 00008791 of file 0003.

The importance of this is that the block ID and file ID are stored with each row—and since each row can be queried, the blocks in which that data is stored can be determined. The following query determines how many distinct blocks are used to store data. In order to make sure the location is unique, the block ID is concatenated with the file ID.

```
select
    count(distinct(                    /*How many distinct */
         substr(rowid,1,8)||           /*combinations of block ID */
         substr(rowid,15,4)))          /*and file ID are there? */
from tablename;
```

As a result of these two queries, you now know how many rows of data there are, and how many blocks they are stored in. Dividing the number of rows by the number of blocks gives you the number of rows per block. This is the number that will be checked against later to determine if PCTFREE has been set correctly.

In Oracle7, you can use the ANALYZE command to speed up this process.

```
ANALYZE TABLE tablename COMPUTE STATISTICS;
```

Once the table has been analyzed, query its record in the USER_TABLES view and record its NUM_ROWS and BLOCKS values. Dividing NUM_ROWS by BLOCKS yields the number of rows stored per block, as shown in the following query.

```
select
    num_rows,                       /*number of rows*/
    blocks,                         /*number of blocks used*/
    num_rows/blocks                 /*number of rows per block*/
from user_tables
where table_name='TABLENAME';
```

Once the number of rows per block is known, update records in the table in a manner that mimics its production usage. Once the updates are done, check the number of rows per block by rerunning these queries. If PCTFREE was not set high enough, then some of the rows may have been moved to new data blocks to accommodate their new lengths. If the value has not changed, then the PCTFREE value is adequate.

This PCTFREE value, though, may be too high, resulting in wasted space. The Oracle7 ANALYZE command shown earlier also generates values for the AVG_SPACE column of the USER_TABLES view. This column shows the average number of bytes that are free in each data block. If this value is high after the update test, then the PCTFREE value can be decreased.

Sizing Indexes

The process of sizing indexes is very similar to the table sizing process described previously. There are several differences due to the way in which they are structured. These will be explained in this discussion.

Once an index's column definitions and data volumes are known, its space requirements can be determined. This is a process of educated guessing, since the true data volumes and row lengths will not be known until after the table is created. It is important that sample data be available at this point in order to make the results of these calculations as accurate as possible.

First, calculate the *average index entry length*. This is the total of the average length of each value in the index, plus overhead. If no data is available, then estimate the actual length of the values in the columns. Do not use the full length of a column as its actual length unless the data will always completely fill the column. This is the case with the Oracle7 fixed-length CHAR column.

For example, consider a table comprised of three columns, all of which are VARCHAR2(10). Assume that a unique index will be created on its first two columns. Estimate the actual length of the entries in both of those columns.

If the sample data is available, then the VSIZE function can be used to determine the actual space used by the data. For the two-column index in this example,

```
select
   avg(nvl(vsize(column1),0))+
   avg(nvl(vsize(column2),0)) avg_index_entry_length
from tablename;
```

In this example, the average length of each column in the index is determined, and the averages are totalled to determine the average index length.

Each index entry has *entry header* information stored with it. This also takes up space. The header space requirements can be calculated via the following formula, in which two types of indexed columns are considered: the "short" column (less than 128 characters long), and the "long" column (more than 128 characters long). This distinction is necessary because of the number of length bytes that the database must store for the values.

```
Header space per entry=3+
                number of short columns+
                (3*number of long columns)
```

Adding the average index entry length and the header space per entry yields the total space required by each row.

```
Bytes per entry=Header space per entry+
                average index entry length
```

For this example, the two columns being indexed will have an average total column length of 20 bytes. The entry headers will have 5 bytes (3 bytes + 1 byte for each of the columns), so the average index entry size will be 25 bytes.

Now that the space requirements of each entry are known, the data volumes can be used to estimate the total space requirements of the index.

```
Total bytes required=Bytes per entry*number of entries
```

This is the space that is required to store all of the data in the table. However, the database will have additional overhead. There will be overhead to both store *block header* information and handle rows that expand (PCTFREE). PCTFREE for indexes is typically set to a small value (around 5 percent) unless the columns being indexed are frequently updated.

Determining the block header size requires knowing how the data will be used. The block header consists of a fixed section and a variable section. The fixed section is at least 113 bytes in length, and the variable header is at least 46 bytes in length. Both of these are dependent on the way in which the data is stored, as shown in the following formulas.

```
Fixed block header size (in bytes)=113
Variable block header size (in bytes)=23*INITRANS
```

In the fixed block header calculation, the INITRANS parameter for the index is important. This parameter is used to preallocate space in the block header for transactions that will access the block's entries. Its default value is 2 for indexes. If multiple transactions will simultaneously access the same data block, then the INITRANS parameter should be set to the number of transactions that will concurrently access a single data block. If the value is not set high enough to support these transactions, then the database will dynamically use the available free space in the data block to support the block header's space needs.

Indexes will also require overhead to account for their internal management of index blocks. This overhead is usually estimated to be 5 percent.

The available space per block is a function of the total block size, the block header size, and the PCTFREE setting.

```
Available space per block=block size-block header-
                (block size-block header)*(PCTFREE/100)
            =(2048)-(113+23*2)
            -(2048-(113+23*2))*(5/100)
            =2048-159-(2048-159)(.05)
            =1889-94
            =1795 bytes available per block
```

The number of blocks required to store an index can be calculated from the following formula, based on the numbers already calculated.

```
Number of blocks=(overhead*number of rows in index*
                average entry size)/
        ( Floor(available space per block/average entry size)
            *average entry size))
        =1.05*((number of rows*25 bytes) /
            (floor(1795/25)*25))
        =26.25*number of rows/(71*25)
        =0.0148*number of rows
```

In other words, a single row in the table requires 0.0148 blocks in the associated index. Taking the inverse of this, a single block in the index stores the index entries of 67 (1/0.0148) rows in the table.

Note that this calculation was dependent on several variables, including the block size, average row length, PCTFREE, and INITRANS. If any of these variables changes, then the space requirements for the table will have to be recalculated.

Sizing Clustered Tables

Clusters are used to store data from different tables in the same physical data blocks. They are appropriate to use if the records from those tables are frequently queried together. By storing them in the same data blocks, the number of database block reads needed to fulfill such queries decreases, thereby improving performance. They may have a negative performance impact on data manipulation transactions and on queries which only reference one of the tables in the cluster.

Because of their unique structure, clustered tables have different storage requirements than non-clustered tables. Each cluster stores the tables' data, as well as maintaining a *cluster index* that it uses to sort the data.

The columns within the cluster index are called the *cluster key*. This is a set of columns that the tables in the cluster have in common. Since these columns determine the physical placement of rows within the cluster, they should not be subject to frequent updates. The cluster key is usually the foreign key of one table that references the primary key of another table in the cluster.

After the cluster has been created, the cluster index is created on the cluster key columns. After the cluster key index has been created, data can then be entered into the tables stored in the cluster. As rows are inserted, the database will store a cluster key and its associated rows in each of the cluster's blocks.

Sizing a cluster thus involves elements of table sizing and index sizing. For this example, consider the table used in the previous sections: a three-column table, each column of which has a datatype and length of VARCHAR2(10). If this table is very frequently joined to another table, then it may be appropriate to cluster the two tables together. For the purposes of this example, assume that the second table has two columns: a VARCHAR2(10) column and a VARCHAR2(5) column, the former of which is used to join the tables together.

Since the two tables are joined using the VARCHAR2(10) column which they have in common, that column will be the cluster key.

As with tables and indexes, the amount of header space needed for each block must be calculated. It is comprised of a fixed section and a variable section. For clusters, a table and row directory area must also be accommodated in the block header.

```
Block header size=fixed block header size+variable block header size
             +table directory+row directory
```

The fixed block header size is 57 bytes (as it was for tables). The variable block header size is 23*INITRANS bytes.

```
Block header size=57+23*INITRANS
             +table directory+row directory
```

Since clusters use cluster indexes, the default INITRANS value for a cluster is the same as that of an index: 2. The cluster's table directory will require 4N+1 bytes per block, where "N" is the number of tables in the cluster. Its row directory will require 2 bytes for every row in the block. The following equation assumes the default INITRANS value.

```
Block header size=57+23*INITRANS+(4N+1)+2R
               =58+23*INITRANS+4N+2R
               =58+46+4N+2R
               =104+4N+2R
where R is the number of rows per block.
```

For this example, there are two tables in the cluster, so the block header size becomes

```
Block header size=104+4N+2R
               =104+8+2R
               =112+2R
```

The available space in each block will be the difference between the block size and the block header size. Since the block header size is dependent on the number of rows per block (R), the available space per block will also be dependent on this factor. This example assumes a 2K (2048 byte) block size.

```
Available space per block=block size-block header size
               =2048-(112+2R)
               =1936-2R
```

Next, calculate the space required for a single row in each of the tables, excluding the length due to the column(s) in the cluster key.

If the sample data is available, then the VSIZE function can be used to determine the actual space used by the data. Again, assume a table has three columns. To determine its average row length, perform the following query.

```
select
   avg(nvl(vsize(column1),0))+
   avg(nvl(vsize(column2),0))    avg_row_length_1
from table1;
select
   avg(nvl(vsize(column1),0))    avg_row_length_2
from table2;
```

In this example, the average length of each column that is not in the cluster key is determined, and the averages are totalled to determine the average row length. This example assumes that the cluster key is "Column3" in "Table1," and "Column2" in "Table2."

Each row in the cluster has *row header* information stored with it. This also takes up space. The header space requirements can be calculated via the following formula, in which two types of columns are considered: the "short" column (less than 250 characters long) and the "long" column (more than 250 characters long). This distinction is necessary because of the number of length bytes that the database must store for the values.

```
Row length=header space per row+
            number of "short" columns+
             (3*number of "long" columns)+
             total of average row lengths
```

Remember that the average row lengths used here do not include the space used by the cluster key columns.

The header space per row for a clustered table is 4 bytes. Therefore,

```
Row length=4+number of "short" columns+
            (3*number of "long" columns)+
            total of average row lengths
```

The row lengths for each table must be calculated separately. For Table1 in this example, both columns are "short" (<250 byte) columns (so there are no "long" columns). Assuming the average row length for Table1 is 20 bytes,

```
Row length for Table1    =4+2+20=26 bytes
```

For Table2 in this example, the only non-cluster key column is a VARCHAR2(5) column. Assuming that the average length of this column is 3 bytes,

```
Row length for Table2    =4+1+3=8 bytes
```

However, 8 bytes is not a valid row size. The absolute minimum row length for a clustered row is 10 bytes. Therefore, 10 bytes should be used as the row length for Table2.

```
Row length=Greatest(10, calculated row length)
Row length for Table2    =10 bytes
```

The next step in the cluster sizing process is to determine the value of the SIZE parameter, which is unique to clusters. SIZE is the estimated number of bytes required by a cluster key and its associated rows.

SIZE is dependent on the distribution of the data. That is, how many rows are there in a table for each distinct value in the cluster key? To determine these values, query the clustered tables and divide the number of records in the table by the number of distinct cluster key values.

```
select
    count(distinct(column name))/    /* Num of records in table*/
    count(*)  rows_per_key           /* Num of cluster key values*/
from tablename;
```

For this example, assume that in Table1, there are 30 rows per cluster key value. In Table2, there is one row per cluster key value for this example.

SIZE also needs to know the average length of the cluster key value. Query the clustered tables using the VSIZE query shown previously. Since it should be the same in both tables (via referential integrity), only one table has to be queried.

```
select
    avg(nvl(vsize(cluster key column),0)) avg_key_length
from table1;
```

For this example, assume that the average key column value is 5 bytes. The value for SIZE can now be calculated.

```
SIZE=
  (Rows per cluster key in Table1*Average row size for Table1)+
  (Rows per cluster key in Table2*Average row size for Table2)+
  (if more tables are in the cluster, add their rows*row size here)+
  cluster key header+
  column length of the cluster key+
  average length of cluster key+
  2*(Rows per cluster key in Table1+Rows per cluster key in Table2+
       Rows per cluster key for any other tables in the cluster)
```

The "cluster key header" is 19 bytes in length. Thus, for the example data,

```
SIZE     = (30 rows per key in Table1*26 bytes per row)+
     (1 row per key in Table2*10 bytes per row)+
     19  bytes for the cluster key header+
     10  bytes for the column length of the cluster key+
     5   bytes for the average length of the cluster key+
     2*(30 rows+1 row)
   = (30*26)+(1*10)+34+(2*31)
   = 780+10+34+62
   = 886 bytes
```

Thus, each cluster key will require 886 bytes, rounded up to 900 bytes. This will be placed in the available space in the block. Earlier in this section, that was calculated to be

```
Available space per block=block size-block header size
                    =2048-(112+2R)
                    =1936-2R
```

(assuming block size = 2048, INITRANS = 2, and there are two tables in the cluster).
The number of cluster keys per block is

```
Number of cluster keys per block=
            FLOOR((available data space+2R)/(SIZE+2*rows per key))
        =FLOOR((1936-2R+2R)/(900+2*31))
        =FLOOR(1936/962)
        =FLOOR(2.01)
        =2
```

So in every block in the cluster, there will be entries for two cluster keys. To determine the total number of blocks required, simply divide the number of cluster keys by this value. The number of cluster keys is the number of distinct values for the column(s) that comprises it.

```
select
    count(distinct(column name))  /* Number of distinct values*/
from table2;                       /* from the primary key table */
```

For this example, divide the resulting number of keys by 2 (cluster keys per block) to get the number of blocks the cluster will need.

Iterative Development

Iterative development methodologies typically consist of a series of rapidly developed prototypes. These prototypes are used to define the system requirements as the system is being developed. These methodologies are attractive because of their ability to show the customers something tangible as development is taking place. However, there are a few common pitfalls that occur during iterative development that undermine its effectiveness.

First, effective *versioning* is not always used. Creating multiple versions of an application allows certain features to be "frozen" while others are changed. It also allows different sections of the application to be in Development while others are in Test. Too often, one version of the application is used for every iteration of every feature, resulting in an end product that is not adequately flexible to handle changing needs (which was the alleged purpose of the iterative development!).

Second, the prototypes are not thrown away. Prototypes are developed to give the customer an idea of what the final product will look like; they should not be intended as the foundation of a finished product. Using them as a foundation will not yield the most stable and flexible system possible. When performing iterative development, treat the prototypes as temporary legacy systems. You wouldn't want to base a brand new system on a legacy system; think of the prototypes in the same light.

Third, the Development-Test-Production divisions are clouded. The methodology for iterative development must very clearly define the conditions that have to be met before an application version can be moved to the next stage. It may be best to keep the prototype development completely separate from the development of the full application.

Lastly, unrealistic timelines are often set. The same deliverables that applied to the structured methodology apply to the iterative methodology. The fact that the application is being developed at an accelerated pace does not necessarily mean that the deliverables will be any quicker to generate.

Technology

Following the methodology is not enough if it is done in isolation. The in-process deliverables must be made available while development is underway. Since most development teams include multiple developers (and now, at least one DBA), a means of communication must be established. The communications channels will help maintain consistency in planning and execution.

Four technological solutions are needed in order to make the methodology work. At present, this will require four separate technologies, since no integrated product development package is available. They are CASE tools, shared directories, project management databases, and discussion databases. The use and impact of each of these will be discussed.

CASE Tools

A *CASE* (Computer-Aided Software Engineering) tool can be used to generate the Entity Relationship diagram and the Physical Database diagram. Oracle*CASE version 5 is a multiuser CASE tool that can create the Entity Relationship diagram and has an integrated data dictionary. It allows for entities to be shared across applications, and can store information about table volumes and row sizes. This functionality will help to resolve several of the deliverables that have been defined here. Its multiuser capability helps to ensure consistency between developers. It also allows for different versions of a data model to be maintained or frozen. Oracle*CASE 5.1 also supports the database objects that are unique to Oracle7 (such as stored PL/SQL procedures).

The SQL commands that create the database objects for the application should be generated directly from the CASE tool. The CASE tool may also be used to create generic versions of applications based on the defined database objects.

Shared Directories

Several of the deliverables, such as the backup requirements, have no specific tool in which they must be created. These deliverables should be created in whatever tools are most appropriate and available at your site. The resulting files should be stored in shared project directories so that all involved team members can access them. The formats and naming conventions for these files must be specified early in the development process.

Project Management Databases

In order to communicate the status of the application and its deliverables to people outside the development team, a project management database should be maintained. It should provide an outsider with a view of the project and its current milestones. This will allow those people who are not directly involved in the project (such as systems management personnel) to anticipate future requirements. It also allows for the impact of scheduling changes or delays on the critical-path milestones to be analyzed. This analysis may result in modifications to the resource levels assigned to the tasks in the project.

Discussion Databases

Most of the information in these three shared areas—the CASE tool, the shared deliverables directories, and the project management databases—represents a consensus of opinion. For example, several team members may have opinions about the backup strategy, and the system management and DBA staffs must have input as well. To facilitate this communication, a set of discussion databases (usually using a groupware product on a local area network) can be created. Drafts can be posted to these areas before the final resolution is placed in the shared deliverables directory.

Managing Package Development

Imagine a development environment with the following characteristics: none of your standards are enforced; objects are created under the SYS or SYSTEM accounts; proper distribution and sizing of tables and indexes is only lightly considered; and every application is designed as if it were the only application you intend to run in your database.

Welcome to the management of packages.

Properly managing the implementation of packages involves many of the same issues that were described for the application development processes in the previous sections. This section will provide an overview of how packages should be treated so they will best fit with your development environment.

Generating Diagrams

Most CASE tools have the ability to *reverse-engineer* packages into a Physical Database diagram. This consists of analyzing the table structures and generating a Physical Database diagram that is consistent with those structures. This is usually accomplished by analyzing column names and indexes to identify key columns. However, normally there is no one-to-one correlation between the Physical Database Diagram and the Entity Relationship diagram. Entity Relationship diagrams for packages can usually be obtained from the package vendor. They are helpful in planning interfaces to the package database.

Space Requirements

Most packages provide fairly accurate estimates of their database resource usage during production usage. However, they usually fail to take into account their usage requirements during data loads and software upgrades. For this reason, it is wise to create a special rollback segment tablespace (RBS_2) to be used to handle large data loads. A spare data tablespace may be needed as well if the package creates copies of all of its tables during upgrade operations.

Tuning Goals

Just as custom applications have tuning goals, packages must be held to tuning goals as well. Establishing and tracking these control values will help to identify areas of the package in need of tuning (see Chapter 8, "Database Tuning").

Security Requirements

Unfortunately, most packages that use Oracle databases fall into one of two categories: either they were migrated to Oracle from another database system, or they assume they will have full DBA authority for their object owner accounts.

If the packages were first created on a different database system, then their Oracle port very likely does not take full advantage of Oracle's functional capabilities. These include row-level locking, the use of sequence objects, and

Oracle7 features such as roles and database triggers. Tuning such a package to meet your needs may require modifying the source code.

If the package assumes that it has full DBA authority, then it must not be stored in the same database as any other critical database application. This is particularly true in Oracle Version 6, since the DBA-privileged accounts have full access to all data in all tables in the database.

Most packages that require DBA authority do so in order to add new users to the database. Oracle7 DBAs should determine exactly which system-level privileges the package administrator account actually requires (usually just CREATE SESSION and CREATE USER). A specialized system-level role can then be created to provide this limited set of system privileges to the package administrator.

Packages that were first developed on non-Oracle databases may require the use of the same account as another Oracle-ported package. For example, ownership of a database account called SYSADM may be required by multiple applications. The only way to resolve this conflict with any confidence is to create the two packages in separate databases.

Data Requirements

Any processing requirements that the packages have, particularly on the data entry side, must be clearly defined. These are usually well documented in package documentation.

Execution Plans

Generating execution plans requires accessing the SQL statements that are run against the database. In Oracle Version 6, the only way to access this is via the source code; if that is not available, then the execution plans are not available. In Oracle7, the shared SQL area in the SGA (see Chapter 1, "The Oracle Architecture," and Chapter 6, "Monitoring Multiple Databases") maintains the SQL statements that are executed against the database. Matching the SQL statements against specific parts of the application is a time-consuming process. It is best to identify specific areas whose functionality and performance are critical to the application's success, and work with the package's support team to resolve performance issues.

Acceptance Test Procedures

The acceptance test procedures for a package are typically created after the application has been installed. However, packages should be held to the same functional requirements that custom applications must meet. The acceptance test procedures should therefore be developed before the package has been selected; they can be generated from the package selection criteria. By testing in this manner, you will be testing for the functionality that you need, rather than what the package developers thought you wanted.

Be sure to specify what your options are in the event the package fails its acceptance test for functional or performance reasons. Critical success factors for the application should not be overlooked just because it is a purchased application.

The Managed Environment

The result of implementing the three critical elements—cultural processes, management processes, and technology—will be a development environment that has quality control built into it. This will allow for improvements to be made in the development process. The production applications will benefit from this in the form of improved performance, better integration with other enterprise applications, and simpler maintenance.

CHAPTER 6

Monitoring Multiple Databases

t the risk of tipping off future interview candidates, here are two questions that I always ask when interviewing to fill DBA positions:

1. "What are the critical success factors for your database?"

2. "How do you monitor them?"

These seem like fairly straightforward questions, but many candidates suddenly realize that they don't know their database's critical success factors—"Something with space, right?" And without knowing those factors, their monitoring systems are either insufficient or overkill. The database must be monitored in a fashion that takes its specific structure and usage into account. Monitoring should focus on revealing problems with the system implementation, rather than tracking the problems' symptoms.

Putting out a fire in a hotel results in an extinguished fire, but it does not make the hotel any less likely to catch fire in the future. This analogy illustrates the point that most systems problems are caused by design flaws. Reacting to problems requires understanding the underlying system faults that led to them; otherwise, only the symptom is being treated while the cause remains.

To avoid falling into permanent DBA fire-fighting mode, four things are necessary:

1. A well-defined understanding of how the database will be used by its applications

2. A well-structured database

3. A set of metrics that gauge the database's health

4. A systematic method for making those measurements and determining trends

The first two points, on database design, have been covered in Chapter 3, "Logical Database Layouts," Chapter 4, "Physical Database Design," and Chapter 5, "Managing the Development Process." This chapter addresses the third and fourth points, providing measurement guides and a method for monitoring them. The first part of this chapter will concentrate on measuring physical elements of the database via a "Command Center" database; the second section will focus on monitoring memory objects via the Oracle statistics scripts.

Common Problem Areas

There are several potential problem areas in all Oracle databases. These include

■ Running out of free space in a tablespace

■ Insufficient space for temporary segments

■ Rollback segments that have reached their maximum extension

■ Fragmentation of data segments

■ Improperly sized SGA areas

An effective database monitoring system, such as the one whose details are provided in this chapter, should be able to detect unacceptable values for each of these areas.

In the following sections you will see a brief synopsis of the problem areas to be tracked, followed by details for creating a system tailored for their monitoring.

Running Out of Free Space in a Tablespace

Each tablespace in the database has datafiles assigned to it. The total space in all of the datafiles in a tablespace serves as the upper limit of the space that can be allocated in the tablespace.

When a segment is created in a tablespace, space is allocated for the initial extent of the segment from the available free space in the tablespace. When the initial extent fills with data, the segment acquires another extent. This process of extension continues either until the segment reaches a maximum number of extents or until the free space in the tablespace is less than the space needed by the next extent.

The free space in a tablespace therefore provides a cushion of unallocated space that can be used either by new segments or by the extensions of existing segments. If the available free space falls to a value that does not allow new segments or extents to be created, then additional space will have to be added to the tablespace (in the form of additional datafiles).

Therefore, you should monitor not only the current available free space in tablespaces, but also the trend in the available free space—is there more or less available today than there was a week ago? You must be able to determine the effectiveness of the current space allocation, and predict what it will look like in the near future.

Insufficient Space for Temporary Segments

Temporary segments are used to store temporary data during sorting operations (such as large queries, index creations, and unions). Each user has a temporary tablespace specified when the account is created via the CREATE USER (Oracle7) or ALTER USER (Oracle Version 6 and Oracle7) command. This should be pointed to someplace other than the SYSTEM tablespace (the default).

When a temporary segment is created, it uses the default storage parameters for that tablespace. While it is in existence, its storage parameters cannot be altered by changing the default storage parameters for the tablespace. It extends itself as necessary, and drops itself when the operation completes or encounters an error. Since the temporary segment itself can lead to errors (by exceeding the maximum number of extents or running out of space in the tablespace), the size of large sorting queries and operations should be taken into consideration when sizing the temporary tablespace.

If the temporary tablespace runs out of free space during the execution of a sorting operation, then the operation will fail. Since it is difficult to accurately size such segments, it is important to monitor whether the temporary tablespace created to hold them is large enough. As we did with data tablespaces, both the current value and the trend will be monitored via the utility provided in this chapter.

In Oracle Version 6, the total amount of space used at any one time by temporary segments can be easily measured after the fact. In Oracle7, only the currently used temporary segments can be measured.

Rollback Segments That Have Reached Their Maximum Extension

Rollback segments are involved in every transaction that occurs within the database. They allow the database to maintain read consistency between multiple transactions. The number and size of rollback segments available is specified by the DBA during database creation.

Since rollback segments are created within the database, they must be created within a tablespace. The first rollback segment, called *SYSTEM*, is stored in the SYSTEM tablespace. Further rollback segments are usually created in at least one other separate tablespace. Because they are created in tablespaces, their maximum size is limited to the amount of space in the tablespaces' datafiles.

Since they allocate space in the same manner as data segments, they are subject to two potential problems: running out of available free space in the tablespace and reaching the maximum allowable number of extents. When either situation is encountered, the transaction that is forcing the rollback segment to extend will fail. A single transaction cannot span multiple rollback segments.

Thus, in addition to tracking the free space (current and trends) for tablespaces that contain rollback segments, the number of extents in each segment must also be monitored.

In Oracle7, there is a new storage parameter, OPTIMAL, that is available for rollback segments. This parameter is used to set the optimal length of a rollback segment; when it extends beyond this length, it dynamically eliminates its unused extents to shrink itself. This capability makes it difficult to determine whether the rollback segments are extending just by looking at the segment's space usage. Instead, the dynamic performance tables, which track the number of times each rollback segment extends and shrinks, must be used. The monitoring system provided here monitors both rollback segment space usage and the number of times they extend and shrink.

Fragmentation of Data Segments

As noted earlier in this chapter, Oracle manages space in segments by allowing a segment to acquire multiple extents. While this allows for flexibility when sizing tables, it can also cause performance degradation. Ideally, a segment's data will be stored in a single extent. That way, all of the data is stored near the rest of the data in the segment, and there are fewer pointers needed to find the data.

If a segment is comprised of multiple extents, there is no guarantee that those extents are stored near each other. A query against a single table in the database may thus require data that is stored in several different physical locations. This will have a negative impact on performance.

Each segment in the database has a maximum allowable number of extents. There is also a maximum number of extents allowable for each Oracle block size—for a 2048-byte block size, no segment can exceed 121 extents.

Any transaction that causes a segment to attempt to exceed its maximum number of extents will fail. Any segment that continually extends has been improperly sized and contributes to poor performance. Compressing segments into single extents is described in Chapter 8, "Database Tuning." The monitoring utility provided in this chapter will track the current extension and extension trends for segments in the database.

Fragmented Free Space

Just as data segments can become fragmented, the available free space in a tablespace can become fragmented. This problem is much more prevalent in Oracle Version 6 than it is in Oracle7.

When a segment is dropped, its extents are deallocated and are marked as being "free." However, these free extents are not recombined with neighboring free extents in Oracle Version 6 databases; the barriers between these free extents are maintained. The free space available to a new data extent can be affected by this.

Oracle7 automatically combines neighboring free extents into single, large extents. However, it is possible that free extents may be physically separated from each other by data extents, blocking their combination with other free extents.

To detect these potential problems, the utility provided in this chapter tracks the number and size of the available free extents in each tablespace.

Improperly Sized SGA Areas

The size of the System Global Area (SGA) used to store shared memory objects for a database is usually set once, and rarely monitored or tuned after that. However, the proper sizing of the SGA is critical to the performance of the database. Thus, the scripts in the second half of this chapter focus on ways in which the usage of the SGA can be tracked.

Target Selection

Based on the "Common Problem Areas" described, the following statistics are important:

- Free space in all tablespaces

- Rate of changes in free space for all tablespaces

- Total space usage by temporary segments at any one time

- Sizes and number of extents for rollback segments

- Number of extents for all segments

This list is a minimum acceptable starting point that should be customized for each database in a system. It should be expanded to include those statistics that, combined, determine the success or failure of the system. For each statistic, upper and lower control limits must be defined. Once the acceptable ranges have been defined, the monitoring system can be designed. Note that the ranges may be related to either the physical measurements (such as free space in a tablespace) or to the rate at which they change.

The End Product

Before describing the configuration and implementation of the monitoring system, decide what the output should provide. Here are sample listings from the system that will be described in this chapter. If further detail or different information is needed, the system can be easily modified.

The first report, shown in Figure 6-1, is a trend report of free space by tablespace, for all databases. This report shows the current percentage of unallocated ("free") space in each tablespace (the "TS" column) of each database (the "DB_NM" column). This value is shown in the "Today" column of the sample report. The other columns show the free space percentage for each tablespace for the last four weeks. The

```
                    Percent Free Trends for Tablespaces

                         4Wks  3Wks  2Wks  1Wk
DB_NM            TS       Ago   Ago   Ago   Ago   Today  Change
----------       ----------   ----  ----  ----  ----  -----  ------
CASE             CASE      56    56    55    40    40     -16
                 USERS     86    64    75    77    76     -10
                 SYSTEM    22    22    22    21    21     -1
                 TOOLS     25    25    25    25    25
                 RBS       32    32    32    32    32
                 TEMP     100   100   100   100   100


CC1              CC        94    94    93    92    92     -2
                 TESTS     71    70    70    70    70     -1
                 SYSTEM    24    24    24    24    24
                 RBS       32    32    32    32    32
                 CCINDX    51    51    51    51    51
                 TEMP     100   100   100   100   100
```

FIGURE 6-1. *Percent Free Trends for Tablespaces Sample Report*

change between today's free space percentage and its value as of four weeks ago is shown in the "Change" column. The tablespaces experiencing the greatest negative changes in free space percentage are listed first.

The report shown in Figure 6-1 shows the current values, the previous values, and the trend for the percentage of free space in each tablespace. This report is part of the output from the monitoring application provided in this chapter.

The SQL scripts used to generate this report include a variable that can be set to restrict the output to only those tablespaces whose free space percentages have changed more than a given threshold value. It may also be restricted to only show specific databases or tablespaces. Note that these threshold limits, which are used to define whether the system is "in control" or "out of control," can also be hard-coded into the reports. That allows this report to function as an exception report for the databases.

Extent allocation among segments may be seen in the report shown in Figure 6-2. This report, also generated from the monitoring application provided here, shows the trends in extent allocation for all segments that presently have more than 10 extents. It shows all rollback segments regardless of their extent procurement.

```
              Extent Trends for Segments with 10 or more Extents

                                         4Wks 3Wks 2Wks 1Wk
DB_NM TS    Owner    Name     Type    Blocks Ago  Ago  Ago  Ago  Today Change
----- ----- -------- -------- -------- ------ ---- ---- ---- ---- ----- -------
CASE  CASE  CASEMGR  TEMP_TBL TABLE    100                        20   20    20
                     TEMP_IDX INDEX     80                        16   16    16

      RBS   SYSTEM   ROLL1    ROLLBACK 3800   19   19   19   19   19
                     ROLL2    ROLLBACK 3800   19   19   19   19   19

      USERS AL1      TEST1    TABLE    120         12   12   12   12   12
                     TEST2    TABLE    140         14   14   14   14   14

CC1   RBS   SYSTEM   ROLL1    ROLLBACK 3800   19   19   19   19   19
                     ROLL2    ROLLBACK 3800   19   19   19   19   19
```

FIGURE 6-2. *Extent Trends for Segments Sample Report*

This report shows the current number of extents (the "Today" column) for each of the segments listed. The segment's database ("DB_NM"), tablespace ("TS"), owner ("Owner"), name ("Name"), and type ("Type") are listed to fully identify it. Its current size in Oracle blocks (the "Blocks" column) is also shown. The current and previous number of extents are shown, as well as the change in the number of extents during the past four weeks (the "Change" column).

The report shown in Figure 6-2 shows the current values, the previous values, and the trend for the number of extents for badly fragmented segments. It also shows these statistics for all rollback segments. This report is part of the output from the monitoring application provided in this chapter.

This report can also be customized to show only those values which have changed. However, it is more informative when all of the alert (>9 extents) records are shown. It can then be compared with the free space trends report to reach conclusions about the database. Given these two example reports, one could conclude that

■ All rollback segments appear to be appropriately sized. None of them have increased in size despite the creation of new tables in the databases. (Note: This assumes that this is either an Oracle Version 6 database, or an Oracle7 database in which the OPTIMAL size of the rollback segments has not yet been reached.)

■ The AL1 user in the CASE database has created several tables in the USERS tablespace. Although they have contributed to the decline in the free space in that tablespace, they cannot by themselves account for the dip down to 64% three weeks ago. That dip appears to have been caused by transient tables (since the space has since been reclaimed).

■ The CASE_MGR account has impacted a production tablespace by creating a temporary table and index in the CASE tablespace. These segments should be moved unless they are part of the production application.

These two reports, which are generated from the application described in the rest of this chapter, are sufficient to measure all of the variables listed as targets earlier in this section—free space, rollback segments status, extent allocation, and trends for these. More importantly, they provide information about the appropriateness of the database design, given the application's behavior. The sample reports show that the rollback segments were sized correctly, but that the CASE_MGR account has created developmental tables in a production database. This reveals a lack of control in the production system that may eventually cause a production failure.

Since it may be helpful to see a summary of each database, the final sample report summarizes the CC1 database. It lists all files and tablespaces and the space details for each. The CC1 database is the Command Center database, which will be defined in the next section of this chapter.

The sample output shown in Figure 6-3 is divided into two sections. In the first section, each of the datafiles in the databases is listed (the "File nm" column), along with the tablespace it is assigned to (the "Tablespace") column. The number of Oracle blocks ("Orablocks") and disk blocks ("DiskBlocks") in each datafile is also displayed in this section.

In the second half of the report, the free space statistics for the tablespaces are displayed. For each tablespace, the number of free extents is displayed ("NumFrExts"). This column shows how many fragments the available free space in a tablespace is broken into. The largest single free extent, in Oracle blocks, is shown in the "MaxFrExt" column, as well as the sum of all free space in the tablespace ("SumFrBl"). The percentage of the tablespace that is unallocated is shown in the "PERCENTFR" column.

The "MaxFrPct" column displays the ratio of the largest single free extent to the total free space available. A high value for this column indicates that most of the free space available is located in a single extent. The last two columns display the free space available, in disk blocks ("DiskFrBl") out of the total available disk blocks ("DiskBlocks") for each tablespace.

```
                      Oracle Tablespaces in CC1
                      Check Date = 07-AUG-94


  Tablespace    File nm                         Orablocks      DiskBlocks
  -----------   --------------------------      ------------   ------------
  CC            /db03/oracle/CC1/cc.dbf         30,720         122,880
  CCINDX        /db04/oracle/CC1/ccindx.dbf     20,480         81,920
  RBS           /db02/oracle/CC1/rbs01.dbf      5,120          20,480
                /db02/oracle/CC1/rbs02.dbf      5,120          20,480
                /db02/oracle/CC1/rbs03.dbf      5,120          20,480
  SYSTEM        /db01/oracle/CC1/sys01.dbf      10,240         40,960
  TEMP          /db01/oracle/CC1/temp01.dbf     15,360         61,440
  TESTS         /db04/oracle/CC1/tests01.dbf    15,360         61,440


                    Oracle Free Space Statistics for CC1
                      (Extent Sizes in Oracle blocks)
                        Check Date = 07-AUG-94


  Tablespace    NumFrExts MaxFrExt  SumFrBl  PERCENTFR MaxFrPct DiskFrBl DiskBlocks
  -----------   --------- --------  -------  --------- -------- -------- ----------
  CC            1         21504     21504    70.00     100      86016    122880
  CCINDX        1         15360     15360    75.00     100      61440    81920
  RBS           3         2019      2057     13.39     98       8228     61440
  SYSTEM        1         6758      6758     66.00     100      27032    40960
  TEMP          6         12800     15360    100.00    83       15360    15360
  TESTS         1         21504     21504    70.00     100      86016    122880
```

FIGURE 6-3.   *Sample Space Summary Report*

This listing is for a database that uses a 2K database block size, with a 512-byte operating system block size (as found in most VMS and UNIX environments).

The report shown in Figure 6-3 provides an overview of the space usage in the database. The first section shows where the free space is coming from—the datafiles assigned to the tablespaces—and the second section shows how that free space is currently being used. This report is part of the output of the monitoring application provided in this chapter.

The combination of the reports shown in Figures 6-1, 6-2, and 6-3 is sufficient to measure all of the targets listed above. They were all generated based on queries against a single "command center" database. The database design is given in the next section, followed by instructions for data acquisition and a set of standard queries to provide a baseline for your reporting needs.

Creating the Command Center Database

Establishing a separate database that is used solely for monitoring other systems resolves three problems with traditional Oracle database monitoring capabilities:

- Monitoring activities can be coordinated across multiple databases.

- The monitoring activities will not affect the space usage in the system they are monitoring.

- Trends can be detected for the parameters being monitored.

This section will describe the creation, structure, and implementation of a stand-alone monitoring database.

The system described here is a *reactive monitor*. It is not designed to perform proactive, real-time monitoring of systems, since our well-designed, well-implemented, and well-monitored systems are fundamentally sound. It should ideally be called from a system or network monitor, since focusing solely on the database will fail to address the factors that affect the performance of client-server or distributed databases (and this entire function can then be given to the Systems Management team).

The monitoring database in this example is given the instance name "CC1" to designate it as the first command center database in the system. Based on your system architecture, you may wish to have multiple databases to perform this function. The database architecture is

SYSTEM tablespace:	20M
RBS tablespace:	30M
	two 10M rollback segments, 10M free
CC tablespace	30M
CCINDX tablespace	20M
TESTS tablespace	30M
TEMP tablespace	15M
Redo Logs	three 2M redo logs

The CC1 database is used as the example in Appendix A, "Database Creation Procedures." Follow those instructions to create it in your environment.

The design of the application that will store the monitoring results is fairly simple. For each instance, we will store descriptive information about its location and usage. Information about each file in each database will also be stored (this is very useful information to have during recoveries when the database being recovered is not open). Each tablespace's free space statistics will also be stored, and every segment will be checked for excessive extents. Figure 6-4 shows the physical database diagram for the monitoring tables.

A view of the FILES table, called FILES_TS_VIEW, is created by grouping the FILES table by instance ID, tablespace (ts), and check date. This view is needed when comparing data in the FILES table (allocated space) with data in the SPACES table (used and free space). The DDL for creating these objects is given in the following listings. The objects are described in Table 6-1.

If this is being used in an Oracle Version 6 database, use the CHAR datatype instead of the VARCHAR2's shown. If the primary key constraints are declared at

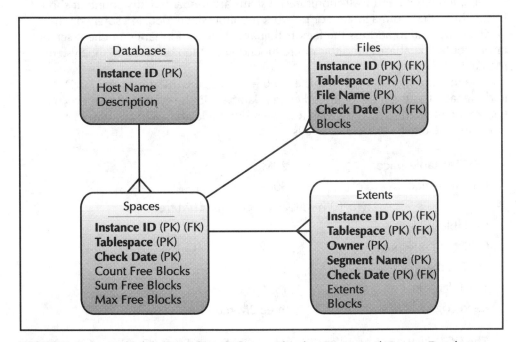

FIGURE 6-4. *Physical Database Diagram for the Command Center Database*

OBJECT	DESCRIPTION
DBS	Table for storing descriptive information about instances
FILES	Table for storing information about files
FILES_TS_VIEW	View of the FILES table, grouped by tablespace
SPACES	Table for storing information about free space
EXTENTS	Table for storing information about used extents

TABLE 6-1. *Tables Used in the Command Center Database*

table creation time, then the unique indexes will be automatically created by the database (when using Oracle7).

```
drop table dbs;

rem * This table will store descriptive information about instances*/

create table DBS
(db_nm          varchar2(8),      /*instance name*/
 host_nm        varchar2(8),      /*host (server) name*/
 description    varchar2(80))     /*instance description*/
tablespace CC;

drop table FILES;

rem /*This table will store information about datafiles*/

create table FILES
(db_nm          varchar2(8),      /*instance name*/
ts              varchar2(30),     /*tablespace name*/
check_date      date,             /*date entry was made into table*/
file_nm         varchar2(80),     /*file name*/
blocks          number,           /*size of the file, in blocks*/
primary key(db_nm, ts,
```

```
     check_date,file_nm))
tablespace CC;

drop view FILES_TS_VIEW;

rem /*This view groups the file sizes by tablespace*/

create view FILES_TS_VIEW as
select
     db_nm,                        /*instance name*/
     ts,                           /*tablespace name*/
     check_date,                   /*date entry was made into table*/
     sum(blocks) sum_file_blocks   /*blocks allocated for the ts*/
from files
group by
     db_nm,
     ts,
     check_date;

drop table SPACES;

rem /*This table will store information about free space*/

create table SPACES
(db_nm           varchar2(8),    /*instance name*/
ts               varchar2(30),   /*tablespace name*/
check_date       date,           /*date entry was made into table*/
count_free_blocks number,        /*number of free extents*/
sum_free_blocks   number,        /*free space, in Oracle blocks*/
max_free_blocks   number,        /*largest free extent, in Oracle blocks*/
primary key (db_nm, ts, check_date))
tablespace CC;

drop table EXTENTS;

rem /*This table will store information about extent concerns*/

create table EXTENTS
(db_nm    varchar2(8),          /*instance name*/
ts        varchar2(30),         /*tablespace name*/
seg_owner    varchar2(30),      /*segment owner*/
seg_name varchar2(32),          /*segment name*/
```

```
seg_type varchar2(17),        /*segment type*/
extents   number,            /*number of extents allocated*/
blocks number,               /*number of blocks allocated*/
check_date      date,        /*date entry was made into table*/
primary key (db_nm, ts, owner, segment_name))
tablespace CC;

rem
rem ** Indexes for Oracle Version 6 databases.  In Oracle7, they
rem      will be created automatically via the "primary key"
rem      specifications in the "CREATE TABLE" commands.
rem

create unique index IU_FILES$DB_TS_CD_FILE on
    files(db_nm, ts, check_date, file_nm)
tablespace CCINDX;

create unique index IU_SPACES$DB_TS_CD on
    spaces(db_nm, ts, check_date)
tablespace CCINDX;

create unique index IU_EXTENTS$DB_TS_OWN_SEG on
    extents(db_nm, ts, owner, segment_name)
tablespace CCINDX;
```

These database structures will allow the DBA to track all of the "targets" listed previously, across all databases. Note that there is no table for rollback segments. These segments will be tracked via the EXTENTS table.

Getting the Data

The first object listed in Table 6-1, DBS, is provided as a reference for sites where there are multiple DBAs. It allows the entry of descriptive information about instances, and is the only component of this application that requires manual entry of the data. All other data will be automatically loaded into the tables. All of the standard data reports will also be automated, with ad hoc capabilities available as well.

The data that is needed to populate these tables is accessible via the SYSTEM account of each database. (A secondary DBA account may also be used for this purpose; this account requires access to DBA-privileged tables, so a specialized system role may be created in Oracle7 for this purpose.)

Within the CC1 database, you can create an account that will own the monitoring application. This account does not require DBA privileges (Oracle

Version 6) or the DBA role (Oracle7). Within that account, create private database links to a DBA-privileged account in each remote database. The database link's name should be the same as the name of the instance that it links to. For example:

```
create database link CASE
connect to system identified by manager
using 't:server1:case';
```

This link uses the TCP/IP driver (t:) to access the CASE database on a host called "server1." When used, it will log into that database as the user "system," with a password of "manager."

If you are able to use SQL*Net V2 (against Oracle7 databases), then two changes can be made to this link. First, the connect string can be replaced by a "service name," whose translation is specified in an external file called TNSNAMES.ORA. This simplifies the management of database links. Second, the "connect to" line is not necessary if the username and password will be the same on the remote system as they are on the local system.

The outline of the data acquisition process is shown in Figure 6-5.

A batch scheduler will be used to call a command script that will start the process. The job should be scheduled to run daily, at off-peak hours.

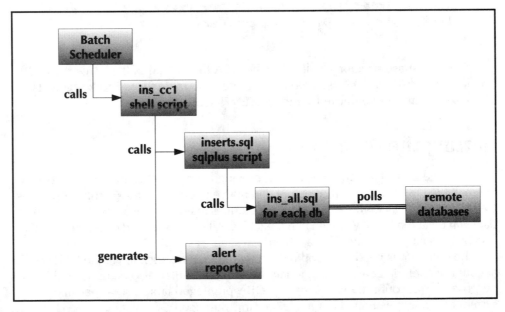

FIGURE 6-5.   *Process Flow for Database Monitoring*

As shown in Figure 6-5, the monitoring application will perform the following steps:

1. The command script (called ins_cc1) calls a SQL*Plus script (named inserts.sql) that lists all of the databases to monitor.

2. Each of those databases is checked via a SQL*Plus script (named ins_all.sql).

3. The results of those queries are stored in tables in the Command Center database by ins_all.sql.

4. The command script then generates alert reports based on the latest values in the Command Center database.

To start the system, construct a command file that is run using the operating system's batch scheduler. A sample shell file for UNIX (to be called via cron) is shown below. This file first sets up its environment variables to point to the CC1 database. It then goes into SQLDBA and opens the CC1 database. Once the database is open, a sqlplus command is executed to start the inserts.sql script. After it completes, the CC1 database is again shut down.

```
# file:   ins_cc1
#
# This script is run once daily to insert records into the CC1
# database recording the space usage of the databases listed in
# inserts.sql file called by this file.  New databases need to
# have new links created in CC1 and have to have entries in the
# inserts.sql script.
#
ORACLE_HOME=/orasw/v7;export ORACLE_HOME
ORACLE_SID=cc1; export ORACLE_SID
PATH=$PATH:$ORACLE_HOME/bin; export PATH
cd /orasw/dba/CC1
sqldba lmode=y <<EOF
connect internal
startup mount cc1 exclusive;
alter database open;
!sqlplus / @inserts
shutdown
EOF
```

Note that this file assumes that the database is closed when this monitoring is not taking place. This allows the memory normally used by CC1's SGA and background processes to be freed during regular working hours. Monitoring is assumed to be taking place once a day, at a fixed time when the system is lightly loaded.

If CC1 was an Oracle Version 6 database, then the "connect internal" command line would *follow* the startup command line, rather than preceding it. Also, a "disconnect" command line would be necessary prior to the "shutdown" command line, and the "lmode=y" clause would not be necessary.

The shell script shown in the previous listing calls a file named inserts.sql, located in the /orasw/dba/CC1 directory. A sample inserts.sql file is shown below. This script calls the ins_all.sql script for each database that is to be monitored. Once that is complete, two alert reports, named space_watcher.sql and extent_watcher.sql, are executed.

```
rem
rem   file:  inserts.sql
rem   location:  /orasw/dba/CC1
rem   Called from ins_cc1 shell script.
rem   New entries must be made here every time a new database
rem   is added to the system.
rem
set verify off
@ins_all CASE
@ins_all CC1
@space_watcher
@extent_watcher
```

This file lists all of the databases for which monitoring statistics will be gathered. When new databases are added to the system, an additional line should be added for each. This file thus provides a layer of process management that allows easy changes without altering the submitted batch program or the SQL statements that access the remote databases.

The last two lines in this script call a pair of SQL scripts named space_watcher.sql and extent_watcher.sql. These script will generate versions of the "Percent Free by Tablespace" and "Segments with over 10 Extents" reports shown earlier in Figures 6-1 and 6-2, respectively. Since they will be used for alerting purposes, only rows with changes exceeding defined limits will be shown.

So far, we've seen the first two layers of the data acquisition system. Continuing down the process path depicted in Figure 6-5, the next step is to run a script (ins_all. sql) that inserts records into all applicable monitoring tables, based on queries against remote databases. These queries use the database links created earlier to search each instance in turn and record the statistics returned. A sample ins_all.sql SQL*Plus script, for inserts into the FILES, SPACES, and EXTENTS tables, is shown below.

The first part of the ins_all.sql script inserts records into the FILES table. It queries each database for information about all of its datafiles, the tablespaces to which they are assigned, and their sizes.

The second part of the script queries the free space statistics of each database. It stores the output in the SPACES table, recording the number of free extents in each tablespace, the total free space available, and the size of the largest single free extent.

The third part of the script checks the space usage by segments and stores its results in the EXTENTS table. It records the information needed to identify the segment (such as its owner and name), as well as its current size and number of extents. To limit the number of records returned by this query, only rollback segments and segments with greater than 9 extents are selected.

```
rem
rem    file:  ins_all.sql
rem    location:  /orasw/dba/CC1
rem    Used to perform all inserts into CC1 monitoring tables.
rem    This script is called from inserts.sql for each instance.
rem    For best results, name the database links after the
rem    instances they access.
rem
insert into files
    (db_nm,
    ts,
    check_date,
    file_nm,
    blocks)
select
    upper('&&1'),        /*insert database link name as instance name*/
    tablespace_name,    /*tablespace name*/
    trunc(sysdate),     /*date query is being performed*/
    file_name,          /*full name of database file*/
    blocks              /*number of database blocks in file*/
from sys.dba_data_files@&&1
/
commit;
rem
insert into spaces
    (db_nm,
    check_date,
    ts,
    count free blocks,
```

```
    sum_free_blocks,
    max_free_blocks)
select
    upper('&&1'),        /*insert database link name as instance name*/
    trunc(sysdate),      /*date query is being performed*/
    tablespace_name,     /*tablespace name*/
    count(blocks),       /*num. of free space entries in the tablespace*/
    sum(blocks),         /*total free space in the tablespace*/
    max(blocks)          /*largest free extent in the tablespace*/
from sys.dba_free_space@&&1
group by tablespace_name
/
commit;
rem
insert into extents
    (db_nm,
    ts,
    seg_owner,
    seg_name,
    seg_type,
    extents,
    blocks,
    check_date)
select
    upper('&&1'),        /*insert database link name as instance name*/
    tablespace_name,     /*tablespace name*/
    owner,               /*owner of the segment*/
    segment_name,        /*name of the segment*/
    segment_type,        /*type of segment (ex. TABLE, INDEX)*/
    extents,             /*number of extents in the segment*/
    blocks,              /*number of database blocks in the segment*/
    trunc(sysdate)       /*date the query is being performed*/
from sys.dba_segments@&&1
where extents>9                  /*only record badly extended segments*/
or segment_type = 'ROLLBACK'     /*or rollback segments*/
/
commit;
rem
undefine 1
```

Note that the inserts into the EXTENTS table only take place for rollback
segments and those segments that have exceeded nine extents. This is therefore an

incomplete listing of the segments in the database. Since these two WHERE clauses establish the threshold for the extent alert report, change the extent limit to best suit your needs.

This series of scripts will perform all of the data acquisition functions necessary to generate the reports shown earlier. It is assumed throughout that they will be run on a daily basis. If more frequent monitoring is needed, then the primary keys of the tables will need to be modified to include both CHECK_DATE and CHECK_HOUR (for hourly reporting).

Now that the data has been inserted into the CC1 monitoring tables, Oracle can automatically generate alert reports. This will be accomplished via the space_watcher.sql and extent_watcher.sql files that are called from the inserts.sql file shown earlier.

Generating Alert Reports

The composition of the alert scripts, described in the previous section, depends entirely on the nature of the databases being monitored. They are simply modifications to the generic free space and extent trends reports shown in Figures 6-1 and 6-2. They feature WHERE and GROUP BY clauses to eliminate those entries that have not exceeded some threshold value. The setting of these values should be customized for each site—they are based on the control limits defined during the target variable selection process.

Since these reports are called automatically following the insertion of records into the Command Center database, the DBA may wish to have them automatically mailed or printed so they are seen each morning before the production users begin to access the databases.

```
rem
rem   file:  space_watcher.sql
rem   location:  /orasw/dba/CC1
rem   Called from inserts.sql
rem
rem   ...like some watcher of the skies
rem   when a new planet swims into his ken (Keats)
rem
column db_nm format A8
column ts format A20
```

```
column week4 format 999 heading "4Wks¦Ago"
column week3 format 999 heading "3Wks¦Ago"
column week2 format 999 heading "2Wks¦Ago"
column week1 format 999 heading "1Wk¦Ago"
column today format 999
column change format 999

set pagesize 60
break on db_nm skip 2
ttitle center 'Tablespaces whose PercentFree values have -
decreased 5 pct this month' skip 2

select
   spaces.db_nm,
   spaces.ts,
   max(decode(spaces.check_date, trunc(sysdate-28),
        round(100*sum_free_blocks/sum_file_blocks),0)) week1,
   max(decode(spaces.check_date, trunc(sysdate-21),
        round(100*sum_free_blocks/sum_file_blocks),0)) week2,
   max(decode(spaces.check_date, trunc(sysdate-14),
        round(100*sum_free_blocks/sum_file_blocks),0)) week3,
   max(decode(spaces.check_date, trunc(sysdate-7),
        round(100*sum_free_blocks/sum_file_blocks),0)) week4,
   max(decode(spaces.check_date, trunc(sysdate),
        round(100*sum_free_blocks/sum_file_blocks),0)) today,
   max(decode(spaces.check_date, trunc(sysdate),
        round(100*sum_free_blocks/sum_file_blocks),0)) -
   max(decode(spaces.check_date, trunc(sysdate-28),
        round(100*sum_free_blocks/sum_file_blocks),0)) change
from spaces, files_ts_view ftv
where spaces.db_nm = ftv.db_nm          /*same database name*/
and spaces.ts = ftv.ts                  /*same tablespace name*/
and spaces.check_date = ftv.check_date  /*same check date*/
and exists                              /*does ts still exist?*/
   (select 'x' from spaces x
   where x.db_nm = spaces.db_nm
   and x.ts = spaces.ts
   and x.check_date = trunc(sysdate))
group by
   spaces.db_nm,
   spaces.ts
having                  /*has percentfree dropped 5 pct in 4 weeks?*/
```

```
(   max(decode(spaces.check_date, trunc(sysdate),
            round(100*sum_free_blocks/sum_file_blocks),0)) -
    max(decode(spaces.check_date, trunc(sysdate-28),
            round(100*sum_free_blocks/sum_file_blocks),0))
    >5      )
or                       /*is percentfree less than 10?*/
(  max(decode(spaces.check_date, trunc(sysdate),
                round(100*sum_free_blocks/sum_file_blocks),0)) <10)
order by spaces.db_nm, decode(
    max(decode(spaces.check_date,trunc(sysdate),
            round(100*sum_free_blocks/sum_file_blocks),0)) -
    max(decode(spaces.check_date, trunc(sysdate-28),
            round(100*sum_free_blocks/sum_file_blocks),0)),0,9999,
    max(decode(spaces.check_date,trunc(sysdate),
            round(100*sum_free_blocks/sum_file_blocks),0)) -
    max(decode(spaces.check_date, trunc(sysdate-28),
            round(100*sum_free_blocks/sum_file_blocks),0))),
    max(decode(spaces.check_date,trunc(sysdate),
            round(100*sum_free_blocks/sum_file_blocks),0))

spool space_watcher.lst
/
spool off
```

If the "exists" section is left out of the above query, then all tablespaces will be shown, even after they have been dropped from the database. The two HAVING clauses define the threshold for the alert report. In this example, only those tablespaces whose percentfree values have decreased by more than 5 percent in the past 28 days will pass the first HAVING clause. The second HAVING clause identifies those tablespaces whose current percentfree value is less than 10 percent, regardless of its trends.

If incremental changes in specific databases are critical to their success, then you may wish to add a HAVING clause to this report that lists those specific databases regardless of their trends.

Sample output (based on the percent free trend report in Figure 6-1) is shown in Figure 6-6.

Note that this alert report does not show fluctuations that have since been resolved (for example, a 4-week trend of 70-70-20-70-70 would not be shown). It is expected that this alert will be run and viewed on a daily basis; thus, if a tablespace's space problems have been resolved, then it is no longer shown on the alert reports.

```
         Tablespaces whose Percent Free values have
                 decreased 5 pct this month

                        4Wks   3Wks   2Wks   1Wk
DB_NM         TS        Ago    Ago    Ago    Ago    Today   Change
----------    ----------  ----   ----   ----   ----   ----    -----
CASE          CASE        56     56     55     40     40      -16
              USERS       86     64     75     77     76      -10
```

FIGURE 6-6.   *Sample Alert Report for Tablespace Percent Free Trends*

The second report is the extent watcher (extent_watcher.sql). Like the space watcher report, this SQL*Plus query uses the Oracle GROUP BY clause to transpose multiple rows into multiple columns for a single row. It will provide a subset of the data listed in the generic extent trends report that was shown in Figure 6-2.

```
rem
rem   file:  ext_watcher.sql
rem   location:  /orasw/dba/CC1
rem   Called from inserts.sql
rem
rem   ...like some watcher of the skies
rem   when a new planet swims into his ken (Keats)
rem
column db_nm format A8
column ts format A18
column seg_owner format a14
column seg_name format a32
column seg_type format a8
column blocks format 99999999
column week4 format 999 heading "4Wks|Ago"
column week3 format 999 heading "3Wks|Ago"
column week2 format 999 heading "2Wks|Ago"
column week1 format 999 heading "1Wk|Ago"
column today format 999
column change format 999

set pagesize 60 linesize 132
```

```
break on db_nm skip 2 on ts skip 1 on seg_owner
ttitle center 'Segments whose extent count is over 10' skip 2

select
    extents.db_nm,
    extents.ts,
    extents.seg_owner,
    extents.seg_name,
    extents.seg_type,
    max(decode(extents.check_date, trunc(sysdate),
            blocks,0)) blocks,
    max(decode(extents.check_date, trunc(sysdate-28),
            extents,0)) week1,
    max(decode(extents.check_date, trunc(sysdate-21),
            extents,0)) week2,
    max(decode(extents.check_date, trunc(sysdate-14),
            extents,0)) week3,
    max(decode(extents.check_date, trunc(sysdate-7),
            extents,0)) week4,
    max(decode(extents.check_date, trunc(sysdate),
            extents,0)) today,
    max(decode(extents.check_date, trunc(sysdate),
            extents,0)) -
    max(decode(extents.check_date, trunc(sysdate-28),
            extents,0)) change
from extents
where exists  /*did this segment show up today during the inserts?*/
    (select 'x' from extents x
    where x.db_nm = extents.db_nm
    and x.ts = extents.ts
    and x.seg_owner = extents.seg_owner
    and x.seg_name = extents.seg_name
    and x.seg_type = extents.seg_type
    and x.check_date = trunc(sysdate))
group by
    extents.db_nm,
    extents.ts,
    extents.seg_owner,
    extents.seg_name,
    extents.seg_type
order by extents.db_nm, extents.ts, decode(
    max(decode(extents.check_date,trunc(sysdate),
```

```
        extents,0)) -
max(decode(extents.check_date, trunc(sysdate-28),
      extents,0)),0,-9999,
max(decode(extents.check_date,trunc(sysdate),
      extents,0)) -
max(decode(extents.check_date, trunc(sysdate-28),
      extents,0))) desc,
max(decode(extents.check_date,trunc(sysdate),
      extents,0)) desc

spool extent_watcher.lst
/
spool off
```

Note that the only portion of this query that limits the records to be shown is the exist clause that queries to see if the segment was returned from the current day's query. It is assumed that the threshold values for the "number of extents" variable was enforced during the insert into the EXTENTS table (see ins_all.sql, shown in the "Getting the Data" section of this chapter). The EXTENTS table is the only one that has the threshold enforced during inserts rather than during querying, since there may be thousands of segments in a database.

If incremental changes in specific segments are critical to their success, then you may wish to add a WHERE clause to the portion of the ins_all.sql script that inserts the rows for those segments into the EXTENTS table. The report will then list those specific segments regardless of their trends.

Sample output from the extent_watcher.sql report is shown in Figure 6-7, which is identical to Figure 6-2. This is because the queries used for the inserts into the EXTENTS table only selected those segments that were already fragmented. No additional restrictions were needed to produce an alert report.

The Space Summary Report

Since every day's statistics are being stored in the CC1 Command Center database, a summary report can be generated for any database, for any specified date. This report should be generated on a weekly basis via the batch scheduler. It does not have to be printed out at that time. It should, however, be available online to the DBA. This will shorten the time delay in getting the report, since the CC1 database is usually kept closed after its daily batch run is completed (as specified in the ins_cc1 shell script).

This SQL*Plus report should be run once for each database. It generates an output file whose name includes the name of the database link that was used in the query. It takes three parameters. They are, in order:

```
          Extent Trends for Segments with 10 or more Extents


                                          4Wks 3Wks 2Wks 1Wk
DB_NM  TS     Owner   Name     Type     Blocks Ago  Ago  Ago  Ago  Today Change
-----  -----  ------- -------  -------  ------- ---- ---- ---- ---- ----- ------
CASE   CASE   CASEMGR TEMP_TBL TABLE    100                    20   20    20
                      TEMP_IDX INDEX    80                     16   16    16

       RBS    SYSTEM  ROLL1    ROLLBACK 3800    19   19   19   19   19
                      ROLL2    ROLLBACK 3800    19   19   19   19   19

       USERS  AL1     TEST1    TABLE    120          12   12   12   12    12
                      TEST2    TABLE    140          14   14   14   14    14

CC1    RBS    SYSTEM  ROLL1    ROLLBACK 3800    19   19   19   19   19
                      ROLL2    ROLLBACK 3800    19   19   19   19   19
```

FIGURE 6-7. *Sample Alert Report for Extent Usage Trends*

1. The database link name (since this will be stored in the output file name, it should have the same name as the instance it accesses).

2. The check date (since this report can be run for any date).

3. The ratio of the Oracle block size (such as 2K) to the host operating block size (such as 512 bytes). For these block sizes, the ratio is 2048/512 = 4.

The report is divided into two sections. The first part queries the FILES table to determine the current file names and sizes for the database. The second part of the query compares the values in the SPACES table (free space sizes) to those in the FILES table (via the FILES_TS_VIEW view). Since these tables contain information about the space allocated to a tablespace, and the amount of it that has yet to be allocated, the percentage of free space remaining in each tablespace can be measured.

```
rem
rem space_summary.sql
rem  parameter 1:  database link name
rem  parameter 2:  check date
rem  parameter 3:  ratio of Oracle block size to operating sytem block size
rem
```

```
rem  to call this report from within sqlplus:
rem  @space_summary link_name check_date block_ratio
rem
rem  Example:
rem  @space_summary CASE 07-AUG-94 4
rem
rem  Should be called weekly for each database.
rem
set pagesize 60 linesize 132 verify off feedback off newpage 0
column ts heading 'Tablespace' format A18
column file_nm heading 'File nm' format A40
column blocks heading 'Orablocks'
column percentfree format 999.99
column diskblocks format 99999999
column cfb format 9999999 heading 'NumFrExts'
column mfb format 9999999 heading 'MaxFrExt'
column sfb format 9999999 heading 'SumFrBl'
column dfrb format 9999999 heading 'DiskFrBl'
column sum_file_blocks heading 'DiskBlocks'
column maxfrpct heading 'MaxFrPct' format 9999999

break on ts
ttitle center 'Oracle Tablespaces in ' &&1 skip center -
'Check Date = ' &&2 skip 2 center
spool &&1._space_summary.lst

select
   ts,                    /*tablespace name*/
   file_nm,               /*file name*/
   blocks,                /*Oracle blocks in the file*/
   blocks*&&3 diskblocks  /*operating system blocks in the file*/
from files
where check_date = '&&2'
and db_nm = upper('&&1')
order by ts, file_nm
/

ttitle center 'Oracle Free Space Statistics for ' &&1 skip center -
 '(Extent Sizes in Oracle blocks)' skip center -
  'Check Date = ' &&2 skip 2

select
```

```
    spaces.ts,                           /*tablespace name*/
    spaces.count_free_blocks cfb,  /*number of free extents*/
    spaces.max_free_blocks mfb,     /*lgst free extent, in Orablocks*/
    spaces.sum_free_blocks sfb,     /*sum of free space*/
    round(100*sum_free_blocks/sum_file_blocks,2)
        percentfree,                 /*percent free in ts*/
    round(100*max_free_blocks/sum_free_blocks,2)
        maxfrpct,                    /*ratio of largest extent to sum*/
    spaces.sum_free_blocks*&&3 dfrb, /*disk blocks free*/
    sum_file_blocks*&&3 sum_file_blocks /*disk blocks allocated*/
from spaces, files_ts_view ftv
where spaces.db_nm = ftv.db_nm
and spaces.ts = ftv.ts
and spaces.check_date = ftv.check_date
and spaces.db_nm = upper('&&1')
and spaces.check_date = '&&2'
/
spool off
undefine 1
undefine 2
undefine 3
```

A sample output report is shown in Figure 6-8. Based on the spool command listed in the query, the output file will be called CC1_space_summary.lst. This is based on using the period (.) as the concatenation character in SQL*Plus.

Figure 6-8 is identical to Figure 6-3 earlier in this chapter. The sample output shown in Figure 6-8 is divided into two sections. In the first section, each of the datafiles in the databases is listed (the "File nm" column), along with the tablespace it is assigned to (the "Tablespace" column). The number of Oracle blocks ("Orablocks") and disk blocks ("DiskBlocks") in each datafile is also displayed in this section.

In the second half of the report, the free space statistics for the tablespaces are displayed. For each tablespace, the number of free extents is displayed ("NumFrExts"). This column shows how many fragments the available free space in a tablespace is broken into. The largest single free extent, in Oracle blocks, is shown in the "MaxFrExt" column, as well as the sum of all free space in the tablespace ("SumFrBl"). The percentage of the tablespace that is unallocated is shown in the "PERCENTFR" column.

The "MaxFrPct" column displays the ratio of the largest single free extent to the total free space available. A high value for this column indicates that most of the free space available is located in a single extent. The last two columns display the free space available, in disk blocks ("DiskFrBl") out of the total available disk blocks ("DiskBlocks") for each tablespace.

```
                         Oracle Tablespaces in CC1
                          Check Date = 07-AUG-94


  Tablespace     File nm                         Orablocks      DiskBlocks
  ------------   ---------------------------     ------------   ------------

  CC             /db03/oracle/CC1/cc.dbf         30,720         122,880
  CCINDX         /db04/oracle/CC1/ccindx.dbf     20,480         81,920
  RBS            /db02/oracle/CC1/rbs01.dbf      5,120          20,480
                 /db02/oracle/CC1/rbs02.dbf      5,120          20,480
                 /db02/oracle/CC1/rbs03.dbf      5,120          20,480
  SYSTEM         /db01/oracle/CC1/sys01.dbf      10,240         40,960
  TEMP           /db01/oracle/CC1/temp01.dbf     15,360         61,440
  TESTS          /db04/oracle/CC1/tests01.dbf    15,360         61,440


                   Oracle Free Space Statistics for CC1
                     (Extent Sizes in Oracle blocks)
                          Check Date = 07-AUG-94


  Tablespace   NumFrExts MaxFrExt SumFrBl PERCENTFR MaxFrPct DiskFrBl DiskBlocks
  ------------ --------- -------- ------- --------- -------- -------- ----------

  CC           1         21504    21504   70.00     100      86016    122880
  CCINDX       1         15360    15360   75.00     100      61440    81920
  RBS          3         2019     2057    13.39     98       8228     61440
  SYSTEM       1         6758     6758    66.00     100      27032    40960
  TEMP         6         12800    15360   100.00    83       15360    15360
  TESTS        1         21504    21504   70.00     100      86016    122880
```

FIGURE 6-8.   *Sample Space Summary Report*

This listing is for a database that uses a 2K database block size, with a 512-byte operating system block size (as found in most VMS and UNIX environments).

Monitoring Memory Objects

Oracle's memory objects, such as the System Global Area (SGA) and the background processes, can also be monitored. Since most of the monitoring of the background processes is done at the operating system level (and is operating system specific), this section will focus on tuning the SGA.

Oracle continuously updates a set of internal statistics. These statistics should only be stored in tracking tables (such as the tables used in the space monitoring section of this chapter) when you can be sure that the database will not be shut down between monitoring checks. This is necessary because these internal statistics are reset each time the database is shut down and restarted.

In order to facilitate monitoring of these statistics, Oracle provides two scripts which should be modified: in Version 6, they are called BSTAT.SQL and ESTAT.SQL; in Oracle7, they are called UTLBSTAT.SQL and UTLESTAT.SQL. They are located in the /admin subdirectory of the ORACLE_HOME/rdbms directory. The first file, BSTAT/UTLBSTAT (Begin Statistics) creates a set of tables and populates them with the statistics in the database at that time. The second file, ESTAT/UTLESTAT, run at a later time, creates a set of tables based on the statistics in the database at that time and then generates a report (called REPORT.TXT) that lists the changes in the statistics during the interval between the run times for the beginning and ending scripts.

Necessary Modifications to BSTAT/UTLBSTAT and ESTAT/UTLESTAT

Before running the statistics scripts provided by Oracle, change them. First, modify the scripts to include database links as part of the FROM clause—this will allow them to be run from a Command Center database. Second, add a TABLESPACE clause to allow the segments to be stored in a data or scratch area tablespace.

Why make these modifications? Failing to do so causes two problems: First, since these scripts insert records into tables, storing the tables in a database that is being monitored automatically skews the file I/O statistics for the database (since the monitoring activity is being factored into the I/O activity). Second, the scripts are written to be run from within SQLDBA, connected INTERNAL. If no alternate tablespace is named, then the SYSTEM tablespace will be fragmented by the create-and-drop table operations of these scripts.

The Oracle7 version differs slightly from the Oracle Version 6 monitoring scripts. In Oracle7, both the beginning and ending statistics tables are created by UTLBSTAT.SQL. UTLESTAT.SQL then creates a series of tables to store the differences between the beginning and ending statistics before generating REPORT.TXT. The script must still be run under a DBA account in Oracle7 due to a reference to the SYS.FILE$ table (in Version 6 there are several file-related tables that require SYS access). All other tables referenced by these scripts are accessible to users who have been granted access to the monitoring tables.

To reference a remote database from within the statistics scripts, add a database link that points to the target database. In order to access all of the tables needed by these scripts, you will need to either create a link to the target SYS account or grant the remote SYSTEM account privileges on the SYS tables used by the scripts. To minimize your risk, create a link to SYS specifying a temporary password:

```
create database link CASE_STAT
connect to sys identified by only_for_a_minute
using 't:server1:case';
```

> **NOTE**
> This link uses the SQL*Net TCP/IP driver (t:) to access the CASE instance on a host called "server1."

Once the link is established, log in to the CASE database, change the SYS password to "only_for_a_minute" (or whatever you choose), go back to CC1, and run the statistics script. When it completes, reset the SYS password.

To tell the query to use this link, append the database link name to the table name being queried. The following listing shows the table creation portion of UTLBSTAT.SQL, after it has been modified to use this link. If you are managing multiple databases, then use a variable in place of the database link name.

For this example, the tables will be stored in the "CC" data tablespace of the CC1 Command Center database. Each "CREATE TABLE" command will have the "TABLESPACE CC" clause appended to it, and each query of a remote table will have the "@CASE_STAT" clause added to it so the database link named CASE_STAT will be used.

After this script has been run, all of the statistics from the remote database's dynamic performance tables will be stored in the CC tablespace of the local database.

```
rem
rem  Modified version of $ORACLE_HOME/rdbms/admin/utlbstat.sql
rem  Note the addition of TABLESPACE clauses and database links
rem
rem  ***********************************************************
rem              First create all the tables
rem  ***********************************************************

drop table stats$begin_stats;
create table stats$begin_stats
TABLESPACE CC
as select * from v$sysstat@CASE_STAT where 0 = 1;
```

```
drop table stats$end_stats;
create table stats$end_stats
TABLESPACE CC
as select * from stats$begin_stats;

drop table stats$begin_latch;
create table stats$begin_latch
TABLESPACE CC
as select * from v$latch@CASE_STAT where 0 = 1;

drop table stats$end_latch;
create table stats$end_latch
TABLESPACE CC
as select * from stats$begin_latch;

drop table stats$begin_roll;
create table stats$begin_roll
TABLESPACE CC
as select * from v$rollstat@CASE_STAT where 0 = 1;

drop table stats$end_roll;
create table stats$end_roll
TABLESPACE CC
as select * from stats$begin_roll;

drop table stats$begin_lib;
create table stats$begin_lib
TABLESPACE CC
as select * from v$librarycache@CASE_STAT where 0 = 1;

drop table stats$end_lib;
create table stats$end_lib
TABLESPACE CC
as select * from stats$begin_lib;

drop table stats$begin_dc;
create table stats$begin_dc
TABLESPACE CC
as select * from v$rowcache@CASE_STAT where 0 = 1;

drop table stats$end_dc;
create table stats$end_dc
```

```
TABLESPACE CC
as select * from stats$begin_dc;

drop table stats$begin_event;
create table stats$begin_event
TABLESPACE CC
as select * from v$system_event@CASE_STAT where 0 = 1;

drop table stats$end_event;
create table stats$end_event
TABLESPACE CC
as select * from stats$begin_event;

drop table stats$dates;
create table stats$dates (stats_gather_times varchar2(100))
TABLESPACE CC;

drop view stats$file_view;
create view stats$file_view
as                  /*NOTE:  Have to change the FROM clause here*/
   select ts.name    ts,
          i.name     name,
          x.phyrds pyr,
          x.phywrts pyw,
          x.readtim prt,
          x.writetim pwt,
          x.phyblkrd pbr,
          x.phyblkwrt pbw
   from   v$filestat@CASE_STAT x,
          ts$@CASE_STAT ts,
          v$datafile@CASE_STAT i,
          file$@CASE_STAT f
 where i.file#=f.file#
   and ts.ts#=f.ts#
   and x.file#=f.file#;

drop table stats$begin_file;
create table stats$begin_file   /*No link needed here*/
TABLESPACE CC
as select * from stats$file_view where 0 = 1;

drop table stats$end_file;
```

```
create table stats$end_file
TABLESPACE CC
as select * from stats$begin_file;
```

The UTLESTAT.SQL script also needs to be changed, since it creates tables too. Since all of the tables it uses are local, no additional database links are necessary. The following is the table creation portion of UTLESTAT.SQL, assuming that the original tables have been created in the CC tablespace of the CC1 Command Center database.

For this example, the tables will once again be stored in the "CC" data tablespace of the CC1 Command Center database. Each "CREATE TABLE" command will have the "TABLESPACE CC" clause appended to it, and each query of a remote table will have the "@CASE_STAT" clause added to it so the database link named CASE_STAT will be used.

```
create table stats$stats
TABLESPACE CC
as select  e.value-b.value change , n.name
   from v$statname n ,  stats$begin_stats b , stats$end_stats e
   where n.statistic# = b.statistic# and n.statistic# = e.statistic#;

create table stats$latches
TABLESPACE CC
as select e.gets-b.gets gets,
   e.misses-b.misses misses,
   e.sleeps-b.sleeps sleeps,
   e.immediate_gets-b.immediate_gets immed_gets,
   e.immediate_misses-b.immediate_misses immed_miss,
   n.name
   from v$latchname n ,  stats$begin_latch b , stats$end_latch e
   where n.latch# = b.latch# and n.latch# = e.latch#;

create table stats$event
TABLESPACE CC
as select  e.total_waits-b.total_waits event_count,
         e.time_waited-b.time_waited time_waited,
         e.event
   from  stats$begin_event b , stats$end_event e
   where b.event = e.event
 union
 select  e.total_waits event_count,
         e.time_waited time_waited,
```

```
          e.event
   from   stats$end_event e
   where e.event not in (select b.event from stats$begin_event b);


create table stats$roll
TABLESPACE CC
as select   e.usn undo_segment,
        e.gets-b.gets trans_tbl_gets,
    e.waits-b.waits trans_tbl_waits,
    e.writes-b.writes undo_bytes_written,
    e.rssize segment_size_bytes,
        e.xacts-b.xacts xacts,
    e.shrinks-b.shrinks shrinks,
        e.wraps-b.wraps wraps
    from stats$begin_roll b, stats$end_roll e
        where e.usn = b.usn;


create table stats$files
TABLESPACE CC
as select b.ts table_space,
        b.name file_name,
        e.pyr-b.pyr phys_reads,
        e.pbr-b.pbr phys_blks_rd,
        e.prt-b.prt phys_rd_time,
        e.pyw-b.pyw phys_writes,
        e.pbw-b.pbw phys_blks_wr,
        e.pwt-b.pwt phys_wrt_tim
   from stats$begin_file b, stats$end_file e
        where b.name=e.name;


create table stats$dc
TABLESPACE CC
as select b.parameter name,
        e.gets-b.gets get_reqs,
        e.getmisses-b.getmisses get_miss,
        e.scans-b.scans scan_reqs,
        e.scanmisses-b.scanmisses scan_miss,
        e.modifications-b.modifications mod_reqs,
        e.count count,
        e.usage cur_usage
   from stats$begin_dc b, stats$end_dc e
        where b.cache#=e.cache#
```

```
        and  nvl(b.subordinate#,-1) = nvl(e.subordinate#,-1);

create table stats$lib
TABLESPACE CC
as select e.namespace,
       e.gets-b.gets gets,
       e.gethits-b.gethits gethits,
       e.pins-b.pins pins,
       e.pinhits-b.pinhits pinhits,
       e.reloads - b.reloads reloads,
       e.invalidations - b.invalidations invalidations
  from stats$begin_lib b, stats$end_lib e
       where b.namespace = e.namespace;
```

The before and after "snapshots" of these statistics tables will provide information about all of the relevant memory objects that can be monitored in Oracle. These include the dictionary cache, the Hit Ratio ((db block gets + consistent gets)/physical reads) and the I/O statistics on a file-by-file basis. Information about rollback segment usage and latch usage is also reported.

Interpreting the Statistics Reports

The UTLBSTAT/UTLESTAT scripts, like their Oracle Version 6 predecessors, create a report called REPORT.TXT which lists information about all sections of the database. The Oracle7 REPORT.TXT contains all six of the sections found in the Oracle Version 6 version, plus five new sections. The report structures are shown in Table 6-2.

Since the Oracle7 REPORT.TXT file contains all of the sections of the Oracle Version 6 report, the following discussion will focus on the Oracle7 report. The descriptions of the report sections that they have in common will be applicable to both versions.

Library Cache Statistics

The Library Cache (LC) contains shared SQL and PL/SQL areas in Oracle7 databases. The statistics in this section of the report help determine if shared SQL statements are being reparsed due to insufficient memory being allocated to the LC. The listing shown in Figure 6-9 shows sample data that will be used for this discussion.

The "Pins" column shows the number of times that an item was executed, while "Reloads" shows the number of misses. The ratio of reloads to pins indicates the percentage of executions that resulted in reparsing. For this sample data, that ratio is 6/378, or 1.6 percent. That means that 1.6 percent of the time, a statement had to be reparsed prior to execution. An ideal value for this ratio is 0; Oracle recommends

ORACLE VERSION 6	ORACLE7
	Library Cache statistics
Overall statistics	Overall statistics
	Systemwide wait events
	Average length of dirty buffer write queue
File I/O	File I/O
	File I/O, summed by tablespace
Latch statistics	Latch statistics
	No-wait gets of latches
Rollback segments	Rollback segments
Dictionary cache	INIT.ORA values
INIT.ORA values	Dictionary cache

TABLE 6-2. *REPORT.TXT Structures for Version 6 and Oracle7*

adding memory to the shared SQL pool if the value is greater than 1 percent (as in this example). Memory is added to this pool via the INIT.ORA SHARED_POOL_SIZE parameter.

Overall Statistics

The "overall statistics" section of the report shows the total changes for many system statistics, as well as giving "per transaction" and "per logon" values (but since running ESTAT or UTLESTAT requires logging in to the database, the "per logon"

```
LIBRARY          GETS    GETHITRATI  PINS    PINHITRATI    RELOADS  INVALIDATI
-------------    -----   ----------  ------  ------------  -------  ----------
BODY             0       1           0       1             0        0
SQL AREA         89      .843        282     .879          5        0
TABLE/PROCED     106     .83         96      .802          1        0
TRIGGER          0       1           0       1             0        0

Note: Sum of Pins column = 378. Sum of Reloads column = 6.
```

FIGURE 6-9. *Sample Library Cache Statistics*

numbers will always reflect one more logon than actually took place). In the Oracle7 version, only nonzero changes are shown. This section of the report is useful for determining the overall Hit Ratio and for detecting indications of possible problems in the database setup.

To determine the Hit Ratio, use the formula (Logical Reads-Physical Reads)/Logical Reads. "Logical Reads" is the sum of the "consistent gets" and "db block gets" statistics; "Physical Reads" is shown on the report as "physical reads." For the statistics shown in Figure 6-10, the Hit Ratio is 93.4 percent ((1358+214)-103)/(1358+214).

When analyzing the other statistics, note that many of them should be zero or very low for best results. These include "recursive calls" (which should also show up in the "Dictionary cache" section of the report), "Table scans (long tables)" and "enqueue timeouts." High values for these statistics indicate that the database and the applications that use it should be altered in order to improve performance.

Systemwide Wait Events

This part of the report lists the count, total time, and average time for a number of system events. There is no documentation in the report to establish ranges for the values shown, and there is no description of the base performance table it accesses (V$SYSTEM_EVENT) in the Oracle7 Server Administrator's Guide. Since the query for this part of REPORT.TXT calculates the time spent per event, the initiation parameter, TIMED_STATISTICS, should be set to TRUE to get nonzero values.

Average Length of Dirty Buffer Write Queue

The query for this portion of the report revisits the statistics tables used by the "Overall statistics" section. It compares two of the entries there, calculating the ratio of the change in the "summed dirty queue length" record to the change in the "write requests" record. If the average length (the value returned by the query) is greater than the value of the db_block_write_batch INIT.ORA parameter (see "INIT.ORA values" section), then either (1) the database I/O is unevenly distributed among the datafiles, or (2) the db_block_write_batch parameter is set low. In either case, the database writer operations are performing poorly.

Statistic	Total	Per Transact	Per Logon
consistent gets	1358	1358	226.33
db block gets	214	214	35.67
physical reads	103	103	17.17

FIGURE 6-10. *Sample Hit Ratio Statistics*

File I/O

This section records the physical and logical I/O against the datafiles in the database. A description of the most relevant columns is provided in the "Extensions to the Statistics Reports" section of this chapter.

File I/O, Summed by Tablespace

This section of the report provides the same information as the "File I/O" section, except that it is summed at the tablespace level instead of the file level. For a description of the most relevant columns in this report, see the "Extensions to the Statistics Reports" section of this chapter.

Latch Statistics

This section of the report varies slightly in Version 6 and Oracle7, because of changes in the internal latch mechanisms. However, both reports will allow you to determine the proper number of redo log allocation latches and redo log copy latches that are appropriate for your database.

Redo log copy latches are used on multiple-CPU servers to distribute the processing that is normally done via the redo log allocation latch. In such a setup, the copy latches are used to copy a process' redo information into the redo log buffer area in the SGA. If copy latches are not used, then the allocation latch must both manage the latch allocation and perform the copy, thus slowing down the transaction logging process.

If the "Timeouts" value for redo allocation is greater than 10 percent of the sum of the "Timeouts" and "Immediate" columns, and if you have multiple processors on your server, then consider adding redo log copy latches. To do this, decrease the INIT.ORA parameter LOG_SMALL_ENTRY_SIZE and increase the LOG_SIMULTANEOUS_COPIES and LOG_ENTRY_PREBUILD_THRESHOLD values. These will determine the number of latches and the maximum size of a redo entry that should be copied using the allocation latch (all others will be passed on to the copy latches). After changing these values, regenerate the statistics reports to see if further latch changes are necessary. Figure 6-11 shows sample values for the latch statistics.

In Figure 6-11 (which uses the Oracle Version 6 column names), the "Timeouts" are only .005 percent of the total waits, so additional copy latches are not necessary.

NAME	WAITS	IMMEDIATE	TIMEOUTS	NOWAITS	SUCCESSES
redo allocation	82658	82654	4	0	0

FIGURE 6-11. *Sample Latch Statistics*

No-wait Gets of Latches

This section is specific to Oracle7. In the Oracle Version 6 latch report, "No-wait" requests for latches, which immediately time out without waiting for the latch to become free, are shown in the full latch report. In Oracle7, the "No-wait" entries are shown via a separate query. The Oracle7 report adds a "No-wait Hit Ratio" column to calculate the percentage of no-wait latch requests that were satisfied immediately. For the sample data shown in Figure 6-12, all of the No-wait Hit Ratios are calculated to be 100 percent.

Rollback Segments

The Oracle7 version of this part of the report includes all of the Version 6 report's columns, plus four new columns:

- ■ UNDO_SEGMENT, which identifies (by number) the rollback segment the line refers to

- ■ XACTS, the number of active transactions

- ■ SHRINKS, the number of times the rollback segment shrank

- ■ WRAPS, the number of times the rollback segment wrapped from one extent to another

The actions that these columns track are described in Chapter 7, "Managing Rollback Segments."

The UNDO_SEGMENT column's value can be used to determine the rollback segment name by querying the V$ROLLNAME table:

```
select name from v$rollname
where usn = &UNDO_SEGMENT;
```

LATCH_NAME	NOWAIT_GETS	NOWAIT_MISSES	NOWAIT_HIT_RATIO
cache buffers chai	60643	0	1
cache buffers lru	1021	0	1
library cache	96	0	1
library cache pin	14	0	1
row cache objects	11	0	1

FIGURE 6-12. *Sample No-wait Latch Gets Statistics*

Waits for the rollback segment, as indicated in the "TRANS_TBL_WAITS" column of the report, indicate that more rollback segments may be needed in the database. Nonzero values for "SHRINKS" and "WRAPS" indicate that the rollback segments are dynamically expanding and shrinking (back to their "OPTIMAL" settings in Oracle7). This activity shows that the rollback segments need to be redesigned in order to reflect the kinds of transactions being performed against the database.

INIT.ORA Values
This section is slightly different between Version 6 and Oracle7. In Version 6, all of the INIT.ORA parameters were shown. In Oracle7, only the nondefault parameters are shown. You may wish to remove the WHERE clause in the Oracle7 version of this query so that all of the parameters and their values will be listed.

Dictionary Cache
The Dictionary Cache (DC) portion of REPORT.TXT contains one new column for Oracle7. This column, COUNT, reflects the setting of the parameter in the database (while USAGE shows the number of current entries in that cache). The Oracle7 report only shows those parameters that have nonzero values for the time interval being reported. In both Oracle Version 6 and Oracle7, the ratio of "misses" to "gets" should be low (generally less than 10 percent). Figure 6-13 shows the DC portion of REPORT.TXT for an Oracle7 database.

NAME	GET_REQS	GET_MISS	SCAN_REQ	SCAN_MIS	MOD_REQS	COUNT	CUR_USAG
dc_free_extents	246	0	0	0	0	97	82
dc_segments	2	1	0	0	0	128	126
dc_rollback_seg	36	0	0	0	0	17	7
dc_users	46	0	0	0	0	14	13
dc_user_grants	32	0	0	0	0	43	10
dc_objects	60	10	0	0	0	221	218
dc_tables	116	5	0	0	0	195	190
dc_columns	446	27	53	5	0	1880	1871
dc_table_grants	54	24	0	0	0	1626	764
dc_indexes	17	1	37	2	0	261	140
dc_constraint_d	1	0	9	0	0	396	13
dc_synonyms	3	0	0	0	0	18	17
dc_usernames	15	0	0	0	0	20	15
dc_sequences	5	0	0	0	0	7	1

FIGURE 6-13. *Sample Dictionary Cache Statistics*

If you are using Oracle Version 6, these parameters are set via individual lines in the INIT.ORA file. In Oracle7, they are set internally by the database, based on the INIT.ORA SHARED_POOL_SIZE parameter. High Misses/Gets ratios call for additional memory to be added to the appropriate caches (V6) or the shared pool (V7).

Extensions to the Statistics Reports

By using the queries that generated the REPORT.TXT file, you can generate very useful reports that can be run in an ad hoc manner. These queries will be run against the current values of the statistics in the database, rather than against the tables created by the BSTAT/UTLBSTAT and ESTAT/UTLESTAT scripts. The statistics generated from these queries will thus reflect all of the activities in the database since it was last started.

File I/O

The following SQL*Plus script generates a listing of all database files, by disk, and totals the I/O activities against each disk. This helps to illustrate how well the file I/O is currently being distributed across the available devices.

Because these scripts reference kernel tables that changed between Oracle Version 6 and Oracle7, there are two distinct scripts provided here. Also, these scripts assume that the drive designation comprises the first five letters of the file name (as in "/db01"). If this is not the case for your databases, then modify the lines indicated.

The first script is the Oracle Version 6 version. It queries several of the cryptically named kernel tables owned by the SYS user. Each script queries the same tables twice—first to determine the file I/O by drive, then a second time to show the I/O attributed to each file. The queries themselves come from the BSTAT/ESTAT scripts, and should not be modified.

```
rem   ORACLE Version 6 Version
rem
rem   file:  file_io.sql
rem   This is an ad hoc report against current statistics, based
rem   on the queries used for BSTAT/ESTAT.
rem
rem   There are two queries:  the first sums the IOs at a drive level,
rem   the second at a file level.
rem
rem   NOTE:  This assumes that the drive designation is the first 5
rem       letters of the file name (ex:  /db01).  If your drive
rem       designation is a different length, change the script
```

```
rem     where noted***
rem
column drive format A5
column filename format a30
column physrds format 99999999
column physwrt format 99999999
column blk_rds format 99999999
column blk_wrt format 99999999
column total   format 99999999
set linesize 80 pagesize 60 newpage 0 feedback off
ttitle skip center "Database File Information" skip center -
"Ordered by IO per Drive" skip 2

break on report
compute sum of physrds on report
compute sum of physwrt on report
compute sum of blk_rds on report
compute sum of blk_wrt on report
compute sum of total on report

select
   substr(n.kcffinam,1,5) "DRIVE",   /*assumes a 5-letter drive name*/
   sum(p.kcfiopyr)+
   sum(p.kcfiopyw) "total",        /*total IO*/
   sum(p.kcfiopyr) "PHYSRDS",      /*Physical reads*/
   sum(p.kcfiopyw) "PHYSWRT",      /*Physical Writes*/
   sum(p.kcfiopbr) "BLK_RDS",      /*Block Reads*/
   sum(p.kcfiopbw) "BLK_WRT"       /*Block Writes*/
from x$kcffi n, x$kcfio p
where n.kcffiidn=p.kcfiofno and
n.kcffinam is not null
group by
   substr(n.kcffinam,1,5)          /*assumes a 5-letter drive name*/
order by 2 desc

spool file_io_by_drive.lis
/
spool off

set linesize 132 pagesize 60
ttitle skip center "Database File IO Information" skip 2
clear breaks
```

```
break on drive skip 1 on report
compute sum of total on drive
compute sum of physrds on drive
compute sum of physwrt on drive
compute sum of blk_rds on drive
compute sum of blk_wrt on drive

select
    substr(n.kcffinam ,1,5) drive,     /*assumes a 5-letter drive name*/
    n.kcffinam filename,
    p.kcfiopyr+
    p.kcfiopyw total,                   /*Total IO*/
    p.kcfiopyr physrds,                 /*Physical Reads*/
    p.kcfiopyw physwrt,                 /*Physical Writes*/
    p.kcfiopbr blk_rds,                 /*Block Reads*/
    p.kcfiopbw blk_wrt                  /*Block Writes*/
from x$kcffi n, x$kcfio p
where n.kcffiidn=p.kcfiofno and
  n.kcffinam is not null
  order by 1,2


spool file_io_by_file.lis
/
spool off
```

The Oracle7 version of this report is based on the queries in the UTLBSTAT/UTLESTAT scripts. It queries the same tables twice: first to generate a report of I/O by drive, then a second time to report on the I/O for each file. It should be run by the SYS user, who owns the cryptically named tables this report accesses.

```
rem   Oracle7  VERSION
rem
rem   file:  file_io.sql
rem   This is an ad hoc report against current statistics, based
rem   on the queries used for UTLBSTAT/UTLESTAT.
rem
rem   There are two queries:  the first sums the IOs at a drive level,
rem   the second at a file level.
rem
rem   NOTE:  This assumes that the drive designation is the first 5
rem        letters of the file name (ex:  /db01).  If your drive
rem        designation is a different length, change the script
```

```
rem         where noted***
rem
column drive format A5
column filename format a30
column physrds format 99999999
column physwrt format 99999999
column blk_rds format 99999999
column blk_wrt format 99999999
column total    format 99999999
set linesize 80 pagesize 60 newpage 0 feedback off
ttitle skip center "Database File Information" skip center -
"Ordered by IO per Drive" skip 2

break on report
compute sum of physrds on report
compute sum of physwrt on report
compute sum of blk_rds on report
compute sum of blk_wrt on report
compute sum of total on report

select
    substr(i.name,1,5)"DRIVE",   /*assumes a 5-letter drive name*/
    sum(x.phyrds) +
    sum(x.phywrts) "total",          /*Total IO*/
    sum(x.phyrds) "PHYSRDS",         /*Physical Reads*/
    sum(x.phywrts) "PHYSWRT",        /*Physical Writes*/
    sum(x.phyblkrd) "BLK_RDS",       /*Block Reads*/
    sum(x.phyblkwrt) "BLK_WRT"       /*Block Writes*/
from v$filestat x, ts$ ts, v$datafile i,file$ f
where i.file#=f.file#
and ts.ts#=f.ts#
and x.file#=f.file#
group by
    substr(i.name,1,5)              /*assumes a 5-letter drive name*/
order by 2 desc

spool file_io_by_drive.lis
/
spool off

set linesize 132 pagesize 60
ttitle skip center "Database File IO Information" skip 2
```

```
clear breaks
break on drive skip 1 on report
compute sum of total on drive
compute sum of physrds on drive
compute sum of physwrt on drive
compute sum of blk_rds on drive
compute sum of blk_wrt on drive

select
    substr(i.name,1,5) "DRIVE",    /*assumes a 5-letter drive name*/
    i.name filename,
    x.phyrds +
    x.phywrts "total",                 /*Total IO*/
    x.phyrds "PHYSRDS",                /*Physical Reads*/
    x.phywrts "PHYSWRT",              /*Physical Writes*/
    x.phyblkrd "BLK_RDS",             /*Block Reads*/
    x.phyblkwrt "BLK_WRT"            /*Block Writes*/
from v$filestat x, ts$ ts, v$datafile i,file$ f
where i.file#=f.file#
and ts.ts#=f.ts#
and x.file#=f.file#
order by 1,2

spool file_io_by_file.lis
/
spool off
```

Figure 6-14 shows a sample output from these queries. The first part of the report shows a drive-by-drive comparison of the database I/O against datafiles. It shows that the device called "/db03" is the most heavily used device during database usage. The second half of the report shows that the I/O on device "/db03" is due to one file, since no other database files exist on that drive for the CC1 database. It also shows that accesses against the file on "/db03" are read-intensive by an overwhelming margin. The ratio of physical reads to block reads is roughly analogous to a file hit ratio—in this case, the system had to read 84,710 blocks to find the 56,820 blocks requested by the database.

The second most active device is "/db01," which has two database files on it. Most of the activity on that disk is against the SYSTEM tablespace file, with the TEMP tablespace demanding much less I/O. The SYSTEM tablespace's readings will be high during these queries because you are not looking at I/O for a specific interval, but for the entire time that the database has been opened. Since this is the case, all of the I/O involved in database startup and initial SGA population show up here.

```
                        Database File Information
                         Ordered by IO per Drive

    DRIVE   TOTAL      PHYSRDS    PHYSWRT    BLK_RDS    BLK_WRT
    ----    -------    -------    ---------  -------    ---------
    /db03   57217      56820      397        84710      397
    /db01   39940      27712      6228       171657     6228
    /db04   15759      14728      1031       14728      1031
    /db02   1898       10         1888       10         1888
    *****   ---------  -------    -------    -------    ---------
    sum     108814     99270      9544       271105     9544


                      Database File IO Information

    DRIVE   FILENAME                   TOTAL   PHYSRDS  PHYSWRT  BLK_RDS  BLK_WRT
    ----    -------------------------  ------  -------  -------  -------  ---------
    /db01   /db01/oracle/CC1/sys.dbf   29551   27708    1843     171653   1843
            /db01/oracle/CC1/temp.dbf  4389    4        4385     4        4385
    *****                              ------  -------  -------  -------  ---------
    sum                                33940   27712    6228     171657   6228

    /db02   /db02/oracle/CC1/rbs01.dbf 1134    3        1131     3        1131
            /db02/oracle/CC1/rbs02.dbf 349              349               349
            /db02/oracle/CC1/rbs03.dbf 415     7        408      7        408
    *****                              ------  -------  -------  -------  ---------
    sum                                1898    10       1888     10       1888

    /db03   /db03/oracle/CC1/cc.dbf    57217   56820    397      84710    397
    *****                              ------  -------  -------  -------  ---------
    sum                                57217   56820    397      84710    397


    /db04   /db04/oracle/CC1/ccindx.dbf 15759  14728    1031     14728    1031
    /db04   /db04/oracle/CC1/tests01.dbf
    *****                              ------  -------  -------  -------  ---------
    sum                                15759   14728    1031     14728    1031

    *****                              ------  -------  -------  -------  ---------
    sum                                108814  99270    9544     271105   9544
```

FIGURE 6-14. *Sample File I/O Statistics Report*

This report is excellent for detecting possible conflicts among file I/O loads. Given this report and the I/O capacity of your devices, you can correctly distribute your database files to minimize I/O contention and maximize throughput. See Chapter 4, "Physical Database Layouts," for further information on minimizing I/O contention.

Dictionary Cache

The following SQL*Plus query shows the current status of the dictionary cache in the SGA. This report is written to be run from the CC1 Command Center database, using a previously defined database link. It stores the name of the database link in the output file name.

This report has two checks in its WHERE clause. The first part of the WHERE clause retrieves those rows whose "Usage" value (how much is currently in use) is over 90 percent of its "Count" value (what the setting is for that cache). The second part of the WHERE clause retrieves those rows that have a miss rate (getmisses/gets) of greater than 10 per cent.

In Oracle Version 6, the "Count" parameter for each cache is set by the DBA via the INIT.ORA file. In Oracle7, the system manages these caches automatically; the size of the shared SQL area determines their settings.

This report generates these values by querying the V$ROWCACHE dynamic performance table, which tracks the performance of the dictionary cache.

```
rem
rem   file:  rowcache_check.sql
rem   This script queries the dictionary cache to verify adequacy
rem   of settings.
rem
rem   parameter:  database link name
rem
ttitle 'RowCache Report for '&&1 center skip 2
column parameter format A25
set pagesize 60 linesize 132 newpage 0 verify off

select
    parameter,                      /*cache name*/
    count,                          /*current setting*/
    usage,                          /*current usage*/
    gets,                           /*accesses against cache*/
    getmisses,                      /*misses*/
```

```
    round(decode(gets,0,0,100*getmisses/gets),2) pctmiss
from v$rowcache@&&1
where decode(count,0,0,usage/count) > .9
or decode(gets,0,0,getmisses/gets) > .1

spool &&1._rowcache_report.lst
/
spool off
undefine 1
```

The output file for the report will contain the database link name in its title. This is based on using the period (.) as the concatenation character in SQL*Plus.

Segments at Maximum Extension

The alert reports in this chapter use control limit criteria that are established at the system level (for example, 10 extents per segment). However, it is useful to compare the current extent usage of segments against the limits defined specifically for that segment, via the MAXEXTENTS storage parameter.

The following SQL*Plus report queries remote databases to detect any segment that is within a specified factor of its maximum extension. It is written to access those databases via a database link, and the link name is stored in the output file name. The multiplier value should always be greater than 1—it is the value by which the actual extent count will be multiplied when it is compared with the maximum extent count. To determine which segments are within 20 percent of their maximum extension, set the multiplier value to 1.2.

This query checks four different types of segments: clusters, tables, indexes, and rollback segments. For each one, it determines whether the current number of extents is approaching the maximum number of extents that segment can have (as set via the MAXEXTENTS storage parameter). The "multiplier" variable is used to determine how close to its maximum extension a segment must be before it is returned via this query. If the segment is approaching its maximum extension, then its owner, name, and current space usage information will be returned.

```
rem
rem   file:  over_extended.sql
rem   parameters:  database link name (instance name), multiplier
rem
rem   The "multiplier" value should always be greater than 1.
rem   Example:  To see segments that are within 20 per cent of their
rem        maximum extension, set the multiplier to 1.2.
rem
```

```
rem   Example call:
rem   @over_extended CASE 1.2
rem

select
    owner,                      /*owner of segment*/
    segment_name,               /*name of segment*/
    segment_type,               /*type of segment*/
    extents,                    /*number of extents already acquired*/
    blocks                      /*number of blocks already acquired*/
from dba_segments@&&1 s
where                           /*for cluster segments*/
(s.segment_type = 'CLUSTER' and exists
(select 'x' from dba_clusters@&&1 c
where c.owner = s.owner
and c.cluster_name = s.segment_name
and c.max_extents <= s.extents*&&2))
or                              /*for table segments*/
(s.segment_type = 'TABLE' and exists
(select 'x' from dba_tables@&&1 t
where t.owner = s.owner
and t.table_name = s.segment_name
and t.max_extents <= s.extents*&&2))
or                              /*for index segments*/
(s.segment_type = 'INDEX' and exists
(select 'x' from dba_indexes@&&1 i
where i.owner = s.owner
and i.index_name = s.segment_name
and i.max_extents <= s.extents*&&2))
or                              /*for rollback segments*/
(s.segment_type = 'ROLLBACK' and exists
(select 'x' from dba_rollback_segs@&&1 r
where r.owner = s.owner
and r.segment_name = s.segment_name
and r.max_extents <= s.extents*&&2))
order by 1,2

spool &&1._over_extended.lst
/
spool off
undefine 1
undefine 2
```

The output file for this report will contain the database link name in its title. This is based on using the period (.) as the concatenation character in SQL*Plus.

The Well-Managed Database

The effective management of any system requires strategic planning, quality control, and action to resolve out-of-control parts of the system. The database management systems described in this chapter provide a broad foundation for the monitoring of all of your databases. Individual databases may require additional monitoring to be performed, or may have specific thresholds. These can be easily added to the samples shown here.

Establishing a Command Center database allows the other databases in the system to be monitored without impacting the measures being checked. It also allows for easy addition of new databases to the monitoring system and trend analysis of all statistics. It should be tied in to your existing operating system monitoring programs in order to coordinate the distribution and resolution of alert messages.

Like any system, the Command Center database must be planned. The examples in this chapter were designed to handle the most commonly monitored objects in the database, and threshold values were established for each. Do not create the CC1 database until you have fully defined what you are going to monitor and what the threshold values are. Once that has been done, create the database—and in a great example of recursion, use the monitoring database to monitor itself.

CHAPTER 7

Managing Rollback Segments

Rollback segments are Oracle's version of time machines. They capture the "before image" of data as it existed prior to the start of a transaction. Queries by other users against the data that is being changed will return the data as it existed *before* the change began.

Rollback segments are the problem children of an Oracle database. No matter how well-behaved the rest of the database is, they will almost always require special attention. And since they control the database's ability to handle transactions, they play a key role in the database's success.

This chapter will cover the key managerial tasks that DBAs need to perform for rollback segments. You will see:

- The basic functional aspects of rollback segments

- The unique way in which they use available space

- How to monitor their usage

- How to select the correct number and size of rollback segments for your database

Rollback Segments Overview

The SQL command *ROLLBACK* allows users to undo transactions that have been made against a database. This functionality is available for any UPDATE, INSERT, or DELETE transaction; it is not available for changes to database objects (such as ALTER TABLE commands). To support the need to undo transactions, Oracle introduced rollback segments in Oracle Version 6. Their base functionality stayed the same in Oracle7, although their administration became easier.

How the Database Uses Rollback Segments

Rollback segments are involved in every transaction that occurs within the database. They allow the database to maintain read consistency between multiple transactions. The number and size of rollback segments available are specified by the DBA during database creation. See Appendix A, "Database Creation Procedures," for an example of this.

Since rollback segments are created within the database, they must be created within a tablespace. The first rollback segment, called *SYSTEM*, is stored in the SYSTEM tablespace. Further rollback segments are usually created in at least one other separate tablespace. Because they are created in tablespaces, their maximum size is limited to the amount of space in the tablespaces' datafiles. Appropriate sizing of rollback segments is therefore a critical task. Figure 7-1 depicts the storage of rollback segments in tablespaces.

A *rollback segment entry* is the set of before-image data blocks that contain rows that are modified by a transaction. Each rollback segment entry must be completely contained within one rollback segment. A single rollback segment can support multiple rollback segment entries. This makes the number of rollback segments available a critical factor for the database's performance. Figure 7-2 illustrates the relationship between rollback segments and rollback segment entries.

The database assigns transactions to rollback segments in a round-robin fashion. This results in a fairly even distribution of the number of transactions in each rollback segment. Although it is possible to specify which rollback segment a transaction should use (see "Specifying a Rollback Segment for a Transaction," later

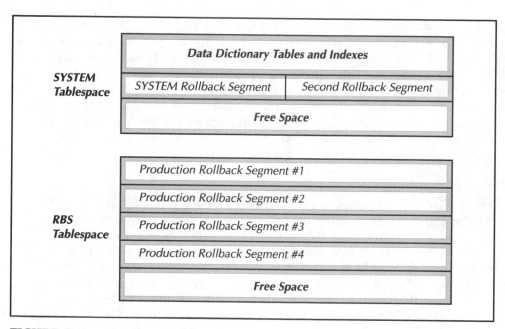

FIGURE 7-1.   *Storage of Rollback Segments in Tablespaces*

in this chapter), this is usually not done. It is therefore not advantageous to have rollback segments of varied sizes.

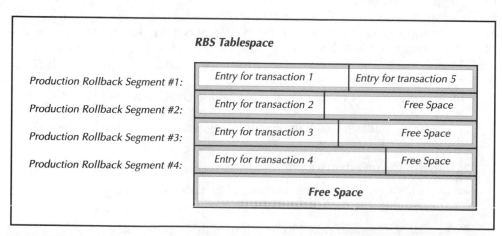

FIGURE 7-2.   *Storage of Rollback Segment Entries in Rollback Segments*

It is possible to create rollback segments that are designated as *private* or *public*. These designations refer to whether the rollback segment is available to a single instance or to multiple instances that access that database. Private rollback segments are explicitly acquired when an instance opens a database (as shown in the "Activating Rollback Segments" section of this chapter). If a second instance accesses the same database, then it may not use the same private rollback segment that the first instance has already acquired. Instead, it can either use its own private rollback segments or it can draw from a pool of public rollback segments. The administrative discussions in this chapter will focus on private rollback segments.

The SYSTEM Rollback Segment

The SYSTEM rollback segment is created automatically during database creation. Its name and storage parameters are not specified in the CREATE DATABASE command. Rather, it is implicitly created in the SYSTEM tablespace.

The usage of the SYSTEM rollback segment varies depending on your configuration. If your database has multiple tablespaces, then you will have to create a second rollback segment to support them. When other rollback segments are available, the database will attempt to use them to manage all of the transactions. The SYSTEM rollback segment is then used only to manage the database-level transactions. Such transactions include the modifications to the data dictionary tables that record information about free space usage and user privileges.

The Second Rollback Segment

If your database will have multiple tablespaces, then you will have to create a second rollback segment. During database creation, this must be created in the SYSTEM tablespace. However, it should not be made available for production transactions; doing so would put the SYSTEM tablespace's free space in jeopardy during large transactions.

Therefore, the second rollback segment should be used only during database creation. As soon as a tablespace for rollback segments has been created, create rollback segments in it and deactivate or drop the second rollback segment in the SYSTEM tablespace. This process is illustrated in the database creation code shown in Appendix A, "Database Creation Procedures."

With regard to rollback segments, those database creation procedures

1. Create a database, which implicitly creates a SYSTEM rollback segment in the SYSTEM tablespace.

2. Create a second rollback segment, named r0, in the SYSTEM tablespace.

3. Make the new rollback segment available. Other tablespaces can then be created.

4. Create a tablespace called RBS for further rollback segments.

5. Create additional rollback segments in the RBS tablespace.

6. Deactivate the second rollback segment (r0) in the SYSTEM tablespace and activate the new rollback segments in RBS.

Although it is no longer needed after database creation, you may wish to keep the second rollback segment available but inactive. To do this, deactivate the rollback segment (see "Activating Rollback Segments" later in this chapter) but do not drop it. This rollback segment can then be quickly reactivated during emergency situations that affect the RBS tablespace.

The Production Rollback Segments

Non-SYSTEM *production rollback segments* support the rollback segment entries generated by production usage of the database. They support the use of the ROLLBACK command to restore the previous image of the modified records. They also roll back transactions that are aborted prior to completion, either because of a problem with the rollback segment or because of the user cancellation of the transaction. During queries, rollback segments are used to construct a consistent "before image" of the data that was changed—but not committed—prior to the execution of the query.

The database assigns rollback segment entries to the production rollback segments in a round-robin fashion. This is designed to distribute the transaction load being carried by the rollback segments (as seen in Figure 7-2). Since a single rollback segment can support multiple transactions, it is possible to create a single, large rollback segment to handle all transactions in a database. Such a design would result in performance problems due to contention for the rollback segment.

Conversely, the DBA may choose to create many small rollback segments, so that each transaction will be guaranteed its own rollback segment. This implementation will run into performance problems if the rollback segments are created so small that they must dynamically extend in order to service their transactions. Planning a database's rollback segment design involves finding the proper balance between the two extremes. The "Choosing the Number and Size" section of this chapter addresses this critical design issue.

Activating Rollback Segments

Activating a rollback segment makes it available to the database users. A rollback segment may be deactivated without being dropped. It will maintain the space already allocated to it, and can be reactivated at a later date. The commands for activating a rollback segment changed between Oracle Version 6 and Oracle7. The following sections provide the full set of rollback segment activation commands for both versions.

Oracle7 Commands

In Oracle7, an active rollback segment can be deactivated via the command

```
ALTER ROLLBACK SEGMENT segment_name OFFLINE;
```

Dropping the rollback segment requires a separate command:

```
DROP ROLLBACK SEGMENT segment_name;
```

Creating a rollback segment requires the following command:

```
CREATE PUBLIC ROLLBACK SEGMENT segment_name
TABLESPACE RBS;
```

Note that this command creates a public rollback segment (via the PUBLIC keyword) and that it creates it in a non-SYSTEM tablespace called RBS. Since no storage parameters are specified, it will use the default storage parameters for that tablespace.

Although the rollback segment has been created, it is not yet in use by the database. To activate it, bring it online using the following command:

```
ALTER ROLLBACK SEGMENT segment_name ONLINE;
```

Oracle Version 6 Commands

In Oracle Version 6, activating a rollback segment requires that the rollback segment's name be listed in the database's initialization (INIT.ORA) file. This file is only read during database startups. Thus, taking a rollback segment offline requires changing the INIT.ORA file, followed by shutting down and restarting the database.

Consider an INIT.ORA file that contains the following line:

```
rollback_segments     = (r0,r1,r2)
```

NOTE
The SYSTEM rollback segment should never be listed here. The SYSTEM rollback segment can never be dropped; it is always acquired along with any other rollback segments the instance may acquire.

For this database, the rollback segments named r0, r1, and r2 are online. To take the r0 rollback segment offline, modify the line by removing r0 from the list of active rollback segments. The modified line will now read:

```
rollback_segments     = (r1,r2)
```

This change will not take effect until the database is shut down and restarted using this INIT.ORA file. After this occurs, the rollback segment r0 will be OFFLINE, and can be dropped. The following command is used to drop rollback segments.

```
DROP ROLLBACK SEGMENT segment_name;
```

Creating a rollback segment requires the following command:

```
CREATE PUBLIC ROLLBACK SEGMENT segment_name
TABLESPACE RBS;
```

Note that this command creates a public rollback segment (via the PUBLIC keyword) and that it creates it in a non-SYSTEM tablespace called RBS. Since no storage parameters are specified, it will use the default storage parameters for that tablespace.

Although the rollback segment has been created, it is not yet in use by the database. To activate it, modify the database's INIT.ORA file to list its name. For example, if a rollback segment named r3 had been created, the "rollback_segments" line of the INIT.ORA file will now read:

```
rollback_segments    = (r1,r2,r3)
```

In order to have this change take effect, the database would have to be shut down and restarted using this INIT.ORA file.

Specifying a Rollback Segment for a Transaction

As of Oracle Version 6.0.33, a new SET TRANSACTION command was made available that allows users to specify which rollback segment their transaction should use. This should be used before large transactions to ensure that they use rollback segments that are created specifically for them.

The settings that are specified via this command will be used only for the current transaction. The following example shows a series of transactions. The first transaction is directed to use the DATA_LOAD_1 rollback segment. The second transaction (following the second "COMMIT;") will be randomly assigned to a production rollback segment.

```
COMMIT;

SET TRANSACTION USE ROLLBACK SEGMENT DATA_LOAD_1
```

```
INSERT INTO table_name SELECT * FROM data_load_table;

COMMIT;

REM*  The commit command clears the rollback segment assignment.
REM*  Implicit commits, like those caused by DDL commands, will
REM*  also clear the rollback segment designation.

INSERT INTO table_name SELECT * FROM some_other_table;
```

Space Usage within Rollback Segments

When a transaction begins, Oracle starts writing a rollback segment entry in a rollback segment. The entry cannot expand into any other rollback segments, nor can it dynamically switch to use a different rollback segment. The entry begins writing sequentially to an extent within the rollback segment. Each block within that extent must contain information for only one transaction. Blocks from different transactions can be stored in the same extent. This is shown in Figure 7-3.

In Figure 7-3, the first five blocks of an extent of a rollback segment are shown. Two separate transactions are storing active rollback information in that rollback extent.

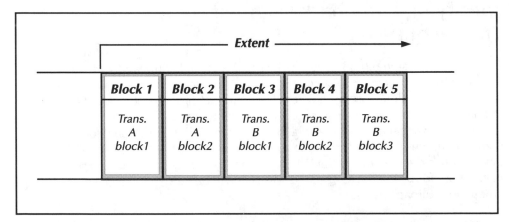

FIGURE 7-3.   *Two Transactions in a Single Rollback Segment Extent*

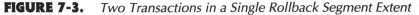

In an ideal database, each transaction will fit within a single extent. However, this is rarely the case. When a transaction can no longer acquire space within an extent, the rollback segment looks for another extent to which it can continue writing the rollback segment entry.

The database will first try to extend the entry into the next extent within the rollback segment. If the current extent is the last extent within the rollback segment, then the database will attempt to extend the entry into the first extent.

However, that extent may already be in use. If it is, then the rollback segment will be forced to acquire a new extent. The entry will then be continued in this new extent. This process of selective extension is illustrated in Figure 7-4.

As shown in Figure 7-4(a), a transaction (referred to here as "Transaction A") presently has its entry data stored in four extents of rollback segment r1. Since it started in Extent #3 of this rollback segment, the first two extents must have been unavailable when the transaction started. At this point, it has acquired four extents and is in search of a fifth.

Since it already occupies the last extent (Extent #6) of the rollback segment, the database checks to see if the first extent of that rollback segment contains any active transaction data. If it does not, then that extent is used as the fifth extent of Transaction A's entry (see Figure 7-4(b)). If, however, that extent is actively being used by a transaction, then the rollback segment will dynamically extend itself. Extent #7 will then be used as the fifth extent of Transaction A (see Figure 7-4(c)).

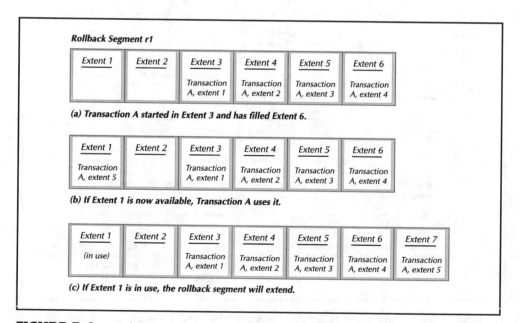

FIGURE 7-4. *Selective Extension of Rollback Segments*

Note that once a transaction is complete, its data is not deleted from the rollback segment. It remains there to service the queries and transactions that began executing before it was committed. This may cause a problem with long queries; namely, they may get the error message

ORA-1555: snapshot too old (rollback segment too small)

This problem arises from the definition of "active" data. Consider the large transaction referred to as "Transaction A" in Figure 7-4. If a long-running query accesses the same table as Transaction A, then it will need to use the data blocks stored by Transaction A's rollback segment entry. However, once Transaction A has completed, those blocks are marked as being "*inactive.*" Those blocks may then be overwritten by other transactions, even though the separate long-running query against those blocks has not completed. The query, upon attempting to read the blocks that have been overwritten, will fail. This situation is depicted in Figure 7-5.

There are two problems that are the true cause of the query's failure. First, a long-running query is being executed at the same time as data manipulation transactions. In other words, batch processing and online transaction processing are being performed simultaneously in the database. From the earlier discussions of rollback segment functionality, the problems with this strategy should be clear: the

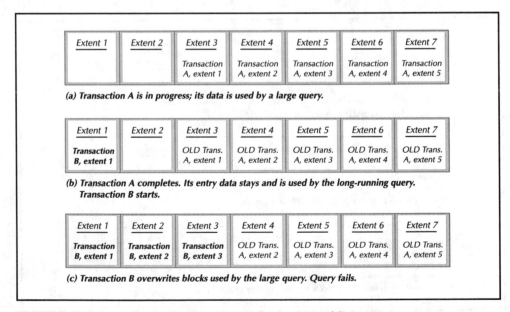

FIGURE 7-5. *Query Failure Due to "snapshot too old" Error*

long-running query must not only access all of the tables and indexes it needs to complete, but must also access data stored in the rollback segments to return a consistent version of the data.

Since it must continue to access the rollback segments until it completes, the long-running query requires that the rollback segment entries it is using not be overwritten. But once those entries have completed, there is no guarantee that this will be the case. The advice given in the error message ("rollback segment too small") solves the problem by resolving the second, related problem: to avoid overwriting existing entries in the rollback segment, add more space to it so it will take longer to wrap around back to the first extent.

This is not a true solution. It is only a delaying tactic, since the rollback segment may eventually overwrite all of its data blocks. The proper solution is to schedule long-running queries at times when online transaction processing is at a minimum.

The Oracle7 OPTIMAL Storage Clause

As shown previously in Figure 7-4, rollback segments dynamically extend to handle large transaction entry loads. Once the transaction that forced the extension completes, the rollback segment *keeps* the space that it acquired during the extension. This is a major cause of rollback segment space management problems in Oracle Version 6. A single large transaction may wipe out all of the available free space in the rollback segment tablespace. This prevents the other rollback segments in that tablespace from being able to extend.

In Oracle7, this problem is solved via two changes in the STORAGE clause used for rollback segments. First, the *PCTINCREASE* parameter is no longer available. This is important because it forces rollback segments to grow at an even pace, rather than at a geometrically increasing rate (see Chapter 4, "Physical Database Layouts," the "Implications of the STORAGE Clause" section for an illustration of this problem). In Oracle Version 6, PCTINCREASE must be set to 0 during rollback segment creation.

The second change in the STORAGE clause for rollback segments is the addition of a parameter called *OPTIMAL*. This allows DBAs to specify an optimal length of the rollback segment (in bytes). When the rollback segment extends beyond this length, it dynamically *shrinks* itself by eliminating its oldest extent.

At first glance, this seems like a terrific option. It prevents a single rollback segment from using all of the free space in a tablespace. However, note that the database is

1. Dynamically extending the rollback segment, causing a performance hit
2. Dynamically choosing and eliminating old extents, causing a performance hit

3. Eliminating inactive data earlier that it would have under the old method

The last point causes databases with OPTIMAL sizes set too low to experience a greater incidence of the "snapshot too old" scenario depicted in Figure 7-5. This is because old transaction data may now be eliminated in two ways: by being overwritten, and by being discarded during shrinks.

The process of extending and shrinking a rollback segment via the OPTIMAL parameter is shown in Figure 7-6. Note that this parameter is very useful for handling situations in which the transaction size is completely unknown, and the available free space in the rollback segment tablespace is limited. However, it is not a substitute for the correct sizing of the rollback segments. This topic will be covered in the "Choosing the Number and Size" section later in this chapter.

As shown in Figure 7-6, when an Oracle7 rollback segment must extend itself, it checks its OPTIMAL size value. If it is already beyond its OPTIMAL size, it will eliminate the oldest inactive extent (Extent #1 in Figure 7-6(a)), and acquire a new extent (Extent #7 in Figure 7-6(b)). This keeps the rollback segment to a prespecified size while servicing queries. It has the side effect of reducing the amount of inactive rollback data available to current transactions.

What would have happened if there had been no inactive extents in the rollback segment when it exceeded its OPTIMAL size? The rollback segment would have continued to extend to support the transaction. Each time the transaction

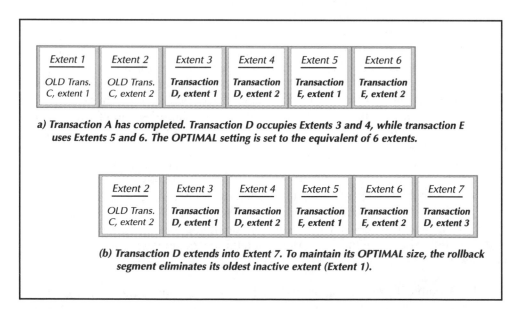

a) Transaction A has completed. Transaction D occupies Extents 3 and 4, while transaction E uses Extents 5 and 6. The OPTIMAL setting is set to the equivalent of 6 extents.

(b) Transaction D extends into Extent 7. To maintain its OPTIMAL size, the rollback segment eliminates its oldest inactive extent (Extent 1).

FIGURE 7-6. *Dynamic Shrinking of Rollback Segments to an OPTIMAL Size*

forced the rollback segment to extend again, it would check to see if it could reclaim any inactive extents. If the rollback segment is forced (for instance, by a single, large transaction) to extend beyond its OPTIMAL size, then the space it acquired would remain part of that rollback segment temporarily. The next transaction that wrapped into a second extent would force the database to reclaim any space that forced it to exceed its OPTIMAL setting.

Monitoring Rollback Segment Usage

The monitoring requirements for rollback segments are similar to those for data segments. Monitoring the space and memory usage of segments was described in Chapter 6, "Monitoring Multiple Databases." Since rollback segments are dynamic objects that are accessed during transactions, they have additional features that should be monitored.

Monitoring Current Space Allocation

The current space allocation for a database's rollback segments can be determined by querying the DBA_SEGMENTS dictionary view, where the SEGMENT_TYPE column equals 'ROLLBACK':

```
SELECT * FROM dba_segments
WHERE segment_type = 'ROLLBACK';
```

Table 7-1 lists the columns of interest that will be returned from this query.
There's one column missing. The value for the OPTIMAL parameter is not stored in DBA_SEGMENTS. Rather, it is stored in the OPTSIZE column of the dynamic performance table named V$ROLLSTAT. To retrieve this value, query V$ROLLSTAT, joining it to V$ROLLNAME to get the rollback segment's name.

```
SELECT
     n.name,              /* rollback segment name */
     s.optsize            /* rollback segment OPTIMAL size */
FROM v$rollname n, v$rollstat s
WHERE n.usn=s.usn;
```

If no OPTIMAL size was specified for the rollback segment, then the OPTIMAL value returned by this query will be null.
Since rollback segments are physical segments in the database, they are included in the space monitoring scripts given in Chapter 6, "Monitoring Multiple Databases." The tablespace space monitoring programs will report any change in

COLUMN NAME	DESCRIPTION
SEGMENT_NAME	Name of the rollback segment.
TABLESPACE_NAME	Tablespace in which the rollback segment is stored.
HEADER_FILE	File in which the first extent of the rollback segment is stored.
BYTES	Actual allocated size of the rollback segment, in bytes.
BLOCKS	Actual allocated size of the rollback segment, in Oracle blocks.
EXTENTS	Number of extents in the rollback segment.
INITIAL_EXTENT	Size, in Oracle blocks, of the initial extent.
NEXT_EXTENT	Size, in Oracle blocks, of the 'NEXT' parameter.
MIN_EXTENTS	Minimum number of extents for the rollback segment.
MAX_EXTENTS	Maximum number of extents for the rollback segment.
PCT_INCREASE	PCTINCREASE parameter for the rollback segment. In Oracle7, this parameter is not allowed during rollback segment creation and is always 0. In Oracle Version 6, it must be manually set to 0.

TABLE 7-1. *Rollback Segment-Related Columns in DBA_SEGMENTS*

the free space available in the RBS or SYSTEM tablespace. The extent monitoring scripts store records for all of the rollback segments regardless of their number of extents. By doing this, all changes in the rollback segment space allocations can be detected immediately.

The queries for the Command Center space monitoring scripts in Chapter 6, "Monitoring Multiple Databases," query the DBA_SEGMENTS view, the main columns of which are listed in Table 7-1.

Monitoring Current Status

Information about the rollback segments' status is accessible via the DBA_ROLLBACK_SEGS view. This view contains the storage parameters (TABLESPACE_NAME, INITIAL_EXTENT, NEXT_EXTENT, MIN_EXTENTS,

COLUMN NAME	DESCRIPTION
STATUS	Status of the rollback segment.
INSTANCE_NUM	Instance the rollback segment belongs to. For a single-instance system, this value is null.

TABLE 7-2. *Additional Columns in DBA_ROLLBACK_SEGS*

MAX_EXTENTS, PCT_INCREASE) provided in DBA_SEGMENTS. It includes two additional columns, which are listed in Table 7-2.

The status of a rollback segment will be one of the values listed in Table 7-3.

Monitoring Dynamic Extensions

Rollback segments can extend and shrink. In addition, rollback segment entries "*wrap*" from one extent to another within a rollback segment each time they grow beyond their present extent. All three of these actions require the database to perform additional work to handle transactions. This extra work affects performance.

STATUS	DESCRIPTION
IN USE	The rollback segment is online.
AVAILABLE	The rollback segment has been created, but has not been brought online.
OFFLINE	The rollback segment is offline.
INVALID	The rollback segment has been dropped. Dropped rollback segments remain listed in the data dictionary with this status.
NEEDS RECOVERY	The rollback segment contains data that cannot be rolled back, or is corrupted.
PARTLY AVAILABLE	The rollback segment contains data from an unresolved transaction involving a distributed database.

TABLE 7-3. *Rollback Segment Status Values in DBA_ROLLBACK_SEGS*

Consider the case of a large transaction that extends beyond its OPTIMAL value when an entry wraps and causes the rollback segment to expand into another extent. The sequence of events to handle this looks like:

1. The transaction begins.

2. An entry is made in the rollback segment header for the new transaction entry.

3. The transaction entry acquires blocks in an extent of the rollback segment.

4. The entry attempts to wrap into a second extent. None is available, so the rollback segment must extend.

5. The rollback segment checks to see if it is past its OPTIMAL value. It is.

6. The rollback segment chooses its oldest inactive extent.

7. The oldest inactive extent is eliminated.

8. The rollback segment extends.

9. The data dictionary tables for space management are updated.

10. The transaction completes.

If the rollback segment had been sized so that the entry fits in one extent, the sequence of events would instead look like:

1. The transaction begins.

2. An entry is made in the rollback segment header for the new transaction entry.

3. The transaction entry acquires blocks in an extent of the rollback segment.

4. The transaction completes.

The savings in the amount of overhead needed for space management are clear.

The incidence of shrinks, wraps, and extensions can be monitored via the *V$ROLLSTAT* dynamic performance table. The records from this view may be retrieved for a specified time interval or via ad hoc queries, as described in the next two sections.

Dynamic Extensions During a Time Interval
To determine the changes in the values of the V$ROLLSTAT columns during a specific time interval, the system statistics scripts can be used. These are called *BSTAT.SQL* and *ESTAT.SQL* in Oracle Version 6, and *UTLBSTAT.SQL* and *UTLESTAT.SQL* in Oracle7. Running these scripts is described in Chapter 6, "Monitoring Multiple Databases."

The BSTAT/UTLBSTAT script creates a table that stores the current values in the V$ROLLSTAT table. When ESTAT/UTLESTAT is run at a later date, V$ROLLSTAT's values at that time will be compared to those that were stored. The difference will be reported. It is important that the database not be shut down between the running of the BSTAT/UTLBSTAT script and the ESTAT/UTLESTAT script. This is because the database resets the statistics in the V$ROLLSTAT table during system startup; therefore, the baseline values generated by BSTAT/UTLBSTAT would be of no use following a database restart.

In the UTLBSTAT script, the following commands are used to create the tables at the beginning of the time interval. The first two CREATE TABLE commands create tables called STATS$BEGIN_ROLL and STATS$END_ROLL, both with no records in them. The INSERT command then stores the current values from the V$ROLLSTAT table into STATS$BEGIN_ROLL.

```
DROP TABLE stats$begin_roll;
CREATE TABLE stats$begin_roll
AS SELECT * FROM v$rollstat WHERE 0 = 1;

DROP TABLE stats$end_roll;
CREATE TABLE stats$end_roll
AS SELECT * FROM stats$begin_roll;

INSERT INTO stats$begin_roll SELECT * FROM v$rollstat;
```

When UTLESTAT is run, it populates the STATS$END_ROLL table by querying the V$ROLLSTAT table for the then-current values. A table called *STATS$ROLL* is then created. Its sole purpose is to hold the results of a query that determines the difference between the records in STATS$BEGIN_ROLL and STATS$END_ROLL. This is the table that is queried to generate the output report from UTLESTAT.

```
INSERT INTO stats$end_roll SELECT * FROM v$rollstat;

CREATE TABLE stats$roll
AS SELECT   e.usn undo_segment,
        e.gets-b.gets trans_tbl_gets,
    e.waits-b.waits trans_tbl_waits,
    e.writes-b.writes undo_bytes_written,
    e.rssize segment_size_bytes,
        e.xacts-b.xacts xacts,
    e.shrinks-b.shrinks shrinks,
        e.wraps-b.wraps wraps
    FROM stats$begin_roll b, stats$end_roll e
        WHERE e.usn = b.usn;
```

COLUMN NAME	DESCRIPTION
TRANS_TBL_GETS	The number of rollback segment header requests.
TRANS_TBL_WAITS	The number of rollback segment header requests that resulted in waits.
UNDO_BYTES_WRITTEN	The number of bytes written to the rollback segment.
SEGMENT_SIZE_BYTES	The size of the rollback segment, in bytes. Note that this column only considers the ending value.
XACTS	The number of active transactions.
SHRINKS	The number of shrinks that the rollback segment had to perform in order to stay at the OPTIMAL size.
WRAPS	The number of times a rollback segment entry wrapped from one extent into another.

TABLE 7-4.   *Columns Available in STATS$ROLL for Oracle7*

The data in the STATS$ROLL table lists each rollback segment, and the statistics that accumulated during the time between the running of UTLBSTAT and UTLESTAT.

Querying the STATS$ROLL table will return the columns listed in Table 7-4 for the interval.

You may wish to make two modifications to UTLESTAT.SQL. First, the XACTS reference in the UTLESTAT query should be changed. This column reflects the *current* number of active transactions, not the *cumulative* number of transactions. As such, the difference between the beginning and ending values for XACTS has no significance. Change that line from

```
e.xacts-b.xacts xacts,
```

to

```
e.xacts        xacts,
```

if you care about this value. Otherwise, remove it entirely.

Second, you may wish to include the EXTENDS column (which *is* cumulative) in the report. This column shows the number of times the rollback segment was extended to include a new segment. It is most appropriate for those rollback segments whose OPTIMAL size has not yet been reached.

COLUMN NAME	DESCRIPTION
TRANS_TBL_GETS	The number of rollback segment header requests.
TRANS_TBL_WAITS	The number of rollback segment header requests that resulted in waits.
UNDO_BYTES_WRITTEN	The number of bytes written to the rollback segment.
SEGMENT_SIZE_BYTES	The size of the rollback segment, in bytes. Note that this column only considers the ending value.

TABLE 7-5. *Columns Available in STATS$ROLL for Oracle Version 6*

The BSTAT/ESTAT reports of Oracle Version 6 function in a similar manner to the UTLBSTAT/UTLESTAT reports shown above. The rollback segment output contains the columns listed in Table 7-5 for the interval.

The XACTS, SHRINKS, and WRAPS columns are not shown in the Oracle Version 6 report—and of the three, only the XACTS column exists in Oracle Version 6's V$ROLLSTAT table.

The monitoring of dynamic extension, wrapping, and shrinking of the rollback segments is thus fairly simple in Oracle7. The rollback segment portions of the UTLBSTAT/UTLESTAT reports can be used to determine the nature of all dynamic extension within the rollback segments.

In Oracle Version 6, this is not possible. After all, Oracle Version 6 rollback segments can't shrink, so there are no shrinks to monitor. Extensions have to be monitored as changes in a segment's extent allocation (see "Monitoring Current Space Allocation" previously in this chapter). Wraps cannot be directly monitored.

A final note of caution: these scripts insert records into tables. In other words, they perform transactions, which in turn generate rollback segment entries, skewing the results. I have found that the number of bytes generated via these queries is less than 100. This skew can be avoided by performing the queries from a remote database (see Chapter 6, "Monitoring Multiple Databases," for information on this topic).

Ad Hoc Querying

The V$ROLLSTAT table can be queried in an ad hoc fashion by anyone who has been granted access to it. This access is usually granted via the MONITOR.SQL (Oracle Version 6) or UTLMONTR (Oracle7) script found in the $ORACLE_HOME/rdbms/admin directory.

The columns available in V$ROLLSTAT are shown in Table 7-6. The columns with an asterisk are found only in the Oracle7 version of this table.

When querying V$ROLLSTAT, you will also want to query V$ROLLNAME. This table maps the rollback segment number to its name (for example, 'SYSTEM','R0').

Unfortunately, the method of joining the two tables changed between Oracle Version 6 and Oracle7.

Good news first. In Oracle7, there is a one-to-one relationship between the two tables. They both have a primary key called USN ("Undo Segment Number"). When querying the tables in an ad hoc fashion, join them on this key as shown in the following example.

```
SELECT
    n.name,                          /* rollback segment name */
    s.rssize                         /* rollback segment size */
FROM v$rollname n, v$rollstat s
WHERE n.usn=s.usn;
```

COLUMN NAME	DESCRIPTION
*USN	Rollback segment number.
EXTENTS	Number of extents in the rollback segment.
RSSIZE	The size of the rollback segment, in bytes.
WRITES	The number of bytes of entries written to the rollback segment.
XACTS	The number of active transactions.
GETS	The number of rollback segment header requests.
WAITS	The number of rollback segment header requests that resulted in waits.
*OPTSIZE	The value of the OPTIMAL parameter for the rollback segment.
*HWMSIZE	The highest value (High Water Mark), in bytes, of RSSIZE reached during usage.
*SHRINKS	The number of shrinks that the rollback segment has had to perform in order to stay at the OPTIMAL size.
*WRAPS	The number of times a rollback segment entry has wrapped from one extent into another.
*EXTENDS	The number of times that the rollback segment had to acquire a new extent.
*AVESHRINK	The average number of bytes freed during a shrink.
*AVEACTIVE	The average size of active extents.
*STATUS	Status of the rollback segment; similar to the status values listed earlier. Values are ONLINE (same as 'IN USE') and PENDING OFFLINE (same as 'PARTLY AVAILABLE').

TABLE 7-6. *Columns Available in V$ROLLSTAT*

Okay, now the difficult one. Oracle Version 6 also has a one-to-one relationship between these tables. However, there is no common key. This is because the V$ROLLSTAT table lacks the USN number. It simply has the attribute columns (RSSIZE, WRITES, etc.). So there is no way to directly join the tables during a query.

Several options are available. The first involves creating a view (under the SYS owner) that queries the V$ROLLSTAT table and adds the pseudocolumn ROWNUM. The value ROWNUM-1 is equal to the USN for that row. This view can be joined to the V$ROLLNAME table.

```
CREATE VIEW modified_v$rollstat
AS
SELECT
    *,
    rownum-1  usn
FROM v$rollstat;

SELECT
    n.name,                    /* rollback segment name */
    s.rssize                   /* rollback segment size */
FROM v$rollname n, modified_v$rollstat s
WHERE n.usn=s.usn;
```

Although this is an option, I prefer not to create views in the SYS schema. The second option available for Oracle Version 6 DBAs is to simply query V$ROLLSTAT exclusively. When a rollback segment has been identified as needing further study, query V$ROLLNAME. The first row in V$ROLLNAME will map to the first row in V$ROLLSTAT, and so on.

Transactions Per Rollback Segment

Determining the users who own active entries in each rollback segment effectively answers two questions: how are the rollback segments currently distributed, and who is where.

Understanding this query requires knowing that transactions acquire locks within the rollback segment header. The V$LOCK table can thus be joined to V$ROLLNAME. Since locks are owned by processes, the V$LOCK table can be joined to V$PROCESS. The result is a mapping of user processes in V$PROCESS to rollback segment names in V$ROLLNAME.

The following query is for Oracle Version 6:

```
REM*
REM*   Username to Rollback Segment mapping for Oracle Version 6.
REM*
SELECT
    r.name rollback_seg,
    l.pid   oracle_pid,
    p.spid  system_pid,
    nvl(p.username,'NO TRANSACTION') transaction,
    p.terminal
FROM v$lock l, v$process p, v$rollname r
    WHERE l.pid = p.pid (+)
    and trunc(l.id1(+)/65536)=r.usn
    and l.type(+) = 'TX'
    and l.lmode(+) = 6
    ORDER BY r.name;
```

Sample output is shown in the following listing.

```
ROLLBACK_SEG            ORACLE_PID SYSTEM_PI TRANSACTION     TERMINAL
--------------------    ---------- --------- --------------  ---------
R1                                           NO TRANSACTION
R2                                           NO TRANSACTION
R3                                           NO TRANSACTION
R4                          14 23C09442      SMITHJ          VTA3905:
R5                          15 23C0A8D3      IDL1            VTA3992:
R6                          22 23C07727      SCOTT           VTA3869:
SYSTEM                                       NO TRANSACTION
```

This shows that only three users are actively writing to the rollback segments
(SMITHJ, IDL1, and SCOTT). Each is writing to a rollback segment that no one else
is using. Rollback segments R1, R2, R3, and SYSTEM are presently inactive. If there
were more than one user using a rollback segment, there would be multiple
records for that rollback segment. You may wish to add a break on the
ROLLBACK_SEG column to make this stand out.

For Oracle7, two minor changes must be made to account for a change in the
Oracle7 V$LOCK table. That table no longer has a 'PID' (Process ID) column, so
the ADDR (address) column is used in its place for the join to V$PROCESS. The
PID selected is now retrieved from V$PROCESS.

```
REM*
REM*   Username to Rollback Segment mapping for Oracle7.
REM*
SELECT
```

```
      r.name rollback_seg,
      p.pid   oracle_pid,
      p.spid  system_pid,
      nvl(p.username,'NO TRANSACTION') transaction,
      p.terminal
FROM v$lock l, v$process p, v$rollname r
      WHERE l.addr = p.addr (+)
      and trunc(l.id1(+)/65536)=r.usn
      and l.type(+) = 'TX'
      and l.lmode(+) = 6
      ORDER BY r.name;
```

DBAs using the UNIX operating system may not be able to see the actual usernames via these queries. That is because of the way in which database processes are managed under UNIX. In those systems, a second process will be started to access the database during database connections, and its username may be null. In that case, the NVL performed for the 'TRANSACTION' field will return the value 'NO TRANSACTION', even though the PID (Process ID) will be shown.

Data Volumes in Rollback Segments

The number of bytes written to a rollback segment can be determined via the dynamic performance table V$ROLLSTAT. This table contains a column called WRITES, which records the number of bytes that have been written to each rollback segment since the database was last started.

To determine the amount of activity in a rollback segment for a specific time interval, select the WRITES value at the start of the test period. When the testing completes, query that value for the then-current value. The difference will be the number of bytes written to the rollback segment during that time interval. Since shutting down the database resets the statistics in the V$ROLLSTAT table, it is important that the database remain open during the testing interval.

Select the WRITES value from the V$ROLLSTAT table using the following query. For Oracle Version 6, the USN (Undo Segment Number) column has been replaced by a column that uses the ROWNUM pseudo-column. This is necessary because Oracle Version 6 does not have a USN column in its V$ROLLSTAT table.

```
REM*
REM*      Oracle7 version
REM*
SELECT
   n.name,                       /* rollback segment name */
   s.writes                      /* bytes written to date */
```

```
FROM v$rollname n, v$rollstat s
WHERE n.usn=s.usn;

REM*
REM* Oracle Version 6 version
REM*
SELECT
    rownum-1 usn,                /* rollback segment number */
    writes                       /* bytes written to date */
FROM v$rollstat;
```

Detecting the size of the rollback segment entry created by a single transaction requires combining these queries with a command given earlier in this chapter. First, isolate the transaction by performing it in a database in which it is the only process. Direct the transaction to a specific rollback segment via the

```
SET TRANSACTION USE ROLLBACK SEGMENT segment_name
```

command. Then query the WRITES column of the V$ROLLSTAT table for that rollback segment. When the transaction completes, requery V$ROLLSTAT. The exact size of the transaction's rollback segment entry will be the difference between the two WRITES values.

Choosing the Number and Size

The descriptions of rollback segment entries given in this chapter can be used to properly design the appropriate rollback segment layout for your database. Note that the final design will be different for each database—unless your databases are functionally identical with respect to their transactions.

The design process involves determining the transaction volume and estimating the number and type of transactions. In the following sections you will see this process illustrated for a sample application.

From this transaction data, the proper number, size, and structure of the rollback segments can be derived.

Transaction Entry Volume

The first step in the design process is to determine the total amount of rollback segment entry data that will be active or in use at any instant. Note that there are two distinct types of entries being considered here:

■ *Active* entries, which have not yet been committed or rolled back

■ *Inactive, In-Use* (IIU) entries, which have been committed or rolled back, but whose data is in use by separate processes (such as long-running queries)

Rollback segment entries that are inactive, and are not in use by separate processes, are unimportant in these calculations.

The key to managing rollback segments effectively is to minimize the amount of "Inactive, In-Use" (IIU) entry data. As a DBA, you have no way of detecting the amount of rollback segment space being used by inactive, in-use entries. Their existence only becomes evident when users begin reporting the ORA-1555 "snapshot too old" error described previously in this chapter (see Figure 7-5).

Minimizing the amount of IIU data in rollback segments involves knowing when long-running queries are being executed. If they are occurring concurrently with multiple transactions, there will be a steady accumulation of IIU rollback segment entries. No matter how large the rollback segments are, this poor transaction distribution will ultimately cause queries to fail.

To solve this problem, isolate all large queries so that they run at times when very little transaction activity is occurring. This minimizes the amount of IIU rollback segment entry data while also helping to prevent potential concurrent I/O contention between the queries and the transactions.

To determine the amount of rollback segment entry data being written to the rollback segments, use the queries given in the "Data Volumes in Rollback Segments" section shown previously. Each large transaction should be sized via the methods described there (in a Test environment). Sizing of transaction should be a standard part of the database sizing process during application development.

Care should also be taken to minimize the amount of inactive, in use rollback data that is shared between transactions. This would result from concurrent transactions in which one transaction referenced a table that the other was manipulating. If this is minimized, the result will be a system whose rollback segment data needs are distributed and measurable.

There is overhead associated with each transaction. However, this header information is counted in the statistics queries given earlier. Thus, those queries give a very accurate report of the amount of rollback segment space that is needed.

Number of Transactions

Once the total amount of rollback segment entry data is known, the number of transactions must be considered. Segregate the transactions into types by their relative volume. For each group, determine the maximum and average transaction

TRANSACTION TYPE	NUMBER	TOTAL ENTRY SIZE	AVERAGE ENTRY SIZE	LARGEST ENTRY
FEEDING_LOG	3	210K	70K	70K
NEW_BIRTH	1	500K	500K	500K
VISITOR_LOG	20	800K	40K	40K
VISITOR_EATEN	1	700K	700K	700K
TIME_SHEETS	<u>10</u>	500K	50K	50K
Total	35	2710K		

TABLE 7-7. *Sample Transaction Distribution*

size. For this part of the rollback segment sizing process, only consider the transactions that occur during normal production usage of the system, excluding all data loads.

Create a spreadsheet of the structure shown in Table 7-7. Sample data is shown for reference. The "Transaction Types" for this table are for a data entry application at a zoo safari exhibit. The "Number" column refers to the number of *concurrent* transactions of each type. The "Total Entry Size" column refers to the total entry size, in bytes, of all the *concurrent* entries of this type.

Note that the "Number" column refers to the number of separate transactions. If multiple records are being updated in a single transaction, then that still counts as only one transaction.

The transactions listed in Table 7-7 reflect that for this application, users commit after every 10 to 100 records. For example, the average "Visitor Log" transaction is 40K in size—which may be 10 4K records or 100 400-byte records, depending on the record length and the frequency of commits.

According to the data in Table 7-7, there are, on average, 35 concurrent transactions in the database. They take, on average, 2710K bytes of data at any one time.

The largest single transaction in the database is 700K bytes long. Use this as the starting point for the rollback segment sizing. That transaction must fit in a single rollback segment. That rollback segment will contain rollback segment header space as well, and may also contain inactive data. To calculate the minimum possible size for a rollback segment that can support this single transaction, use the following formula. This formula makes the following assumptions:

■ 20 percent of the rollback segment will remain as free space.

■ 15 percent of the rollback segment will be used for inactive, in use data.

■ 5 percent of the rollback segment will be used by the rollback segment header area.

```
Minimum Possible Size (MPS) = Largest Transaction Size *100 /
                                 (Free Pct + In Use Pct + Header Pct)
                            = Largest Transaction Size *100 /
                               (20+15+5)
                            = Largest Transaction Size *100/40
                            = Largest Transaction Size * 2.5
                            = 700K bytes * 2.5
                            = 1750K bytes
```

Since the database chooses a rollback segment to use in a round-robin fashion, each rollback segment that may have to handle this transaction must be at least this size.

The total rollback segment space needed at any one time can also be calculated. The same space assumptions will be used.

```
Minimum Total Size (MTS)    = Sum(Total Entry Size) *100 /
                                 (Free Pct + In Use Pct + Header Pct)
                            = Sum(Total Entry Size) *100 /
                               (20 + 15 + 5)
                            = Sum(Total Entry Size) * 100/40
                            = Sum(Total Entry Size) * 2.5
                            = 2710K bytes * 2.5
                            = 6775K bytes
```

So the minimum total rollback space available at any one time must be at least 6775K bytes for this example.

How many rollback segments should this space be divided between? Since the rollback segments should all be of the same size, the minimum value is easy to estimate. You have already seen that the minimum size of each rollback segment is 1750K bytes. The total minimum size of all rollback segments is 6775K bytes. The following equation compares these two values to determine the minimum number of rollback segments needed.

```
Minimum Num of Rollback Segs (MNRS) = Minimum Total Size /
                                        Minimum Possible Size
                                    = 6775K bytes / 1750K bytes
                                    = 3.8 (round up to 4)
```

This will be our starting point for the number of rollback segments needed. Note that it only considers the space requirements at this point.

To refine this calculation, consider the number of concurrent transactions. The fewer transactions there are in a rollback segment, the less work the database will have to do to manage its space needs. The maximum number of rollback segments is the number of concurrent transactions (assuming one transaction per rollback segment). For the example data shown in Table 7-7, this number is 35.

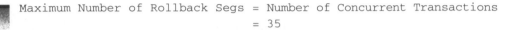

```
Maximum Number of Rollback Segs = Number of Concurrent Transactions
                                = 35
```

So the production database requires somewhere between 4 and 35 rollback segments. To restrict this range further, you must determine the number of transactions per rollback segment. Each transaction will now be fit into its own extent, rather than into its own rollback segment. To do this, you must evaluate the distribution of transaction sizes.

As shown in Table 7-8, there are two distinct groupings of the safari transactions. These groups are shown in Table 7-8. The first group features entries whose average entry sizes are between 40K and 70K bytes. The second grouping contains entries whose average sizes are between 500K and 700K bytes. Since there is an order of magnitude of difference between average entry size for these two groups, it will not be possible to resolve their space needs without wasting space or forcing wraps to occur.

The transactions in the large-entry size group are very few in number. Of the 35 concurrent transactions, they comprise just 2. So you can design to handle the small-entry group, while leaving space to handle the exceptions in the large-entry

TRANSACTION TYPE	NUMBER	TOTAL ENTRY SIZE	AVERAGE ENTRY SIZE	LARGEST ENTRY
VISITOR_LOG	20	800K	40K	40K
TIME_SHEETS	10	500K	50K	50K
FEEDING_LOG	3	210K	70K	70K
Subtotal:	33	1510K		
NEW_BIRTH	1	500K	500K	500K
VISITOR_EATEN	1	700K	700K	700K
Subtotal:	2	1200K		
Total:	35	2710K		

TABLE 7-8. *Sample Transaction Distribution, Grouped by Average Entry Size*

group. The sizing for the small-entry group will thus form the lower bound for the design requirements.

For the small-entry size group, the sum of the total entry sizes is 1510K bytes. So the minimum total size of the rollback segments needed just for that group is

```
MTS = 1510K * 2.5  = 3775K bytes
```

The minimum extent size for that group is the size of the largest transaction in that group.

```
Minimum Extent Size (MES) = 70K bytes
```

A 70K byte extent size will handle each of the small-entry transactions. For the large-entry transactions, it will require a minimum of seven wraps (eight 70K byte extents for the 500K-byte entry). To minimize the number of wraps for the large-entry transactions, consider a larger extent size. An extent size of 125K would require fewer wraps, at the cost of increased storage space. An extent size of 250K bytes would require even fewer wraps for all transactions. However, it would require a great deal of additional physical space, as shown in Table 7-9.

In Table 7-9, three different extent sizes are compared. The first, 70K bytes, was based on the calculated minimum average extent size. The second, 125K bytes, was proposed to reduce the number of wraps needed to support the larger transactions. The third, 250K bytes, was proposed to reduce even further the number of wraps needed to support the larger transactions.

The "Space Req" column in Table 7-9 shows that with a 70K extent, and one transaction per extent, 3570K bytes of rollback segment space would be needed while incurring 16 wraps. Increasing the extent size to 125K bytes increases the space requirements by a third, to 5350K, while decreasing the number of wraps to 7. Doubling that extent size, to 250K, increases the space requirement to 9500K while only reducing the number of wraps to 3. The space calculations all assume one transaction per extent. That assumption may result in overestimating the space requirements, but it is usually accurate.

Based on Table 7-9, it is possible to cut this example's number of wraps in half by increasing the extent size by only two-thirds. Extending it much beyond that will not reduce the number of wraps appreciably. Note that these calculations still assume one transaction per extent, even for the larger extent sizes.

You have to be able to estimate your transaction volume in order to reach this point. Since this calculation assumes that only 15 percent of the rollback segment is being used to support IIU entries, such entries must be minimized via scheduling. You have to be able to estimate the type, quantity, and nature of the system's transactions in order to be able to reach this decision point.

Given the trade-off between the two options in Table 7-9, a small extent size will almost always be the proper choice, since it is usually the most common type

EXTENT SIZE	TRANSACTION ENTRY TYPE	NUMBER	SPACE REQ	NUMBER OF WRAPS
70K bytes	small (<70K)	33	2310K	0
	large (500K)	1	560K	7
	large (700K)	1	<u>700K</u>	9
	Total:		3570K	16
125K bytes	small (<70K)	33	4125K	0
	large (500K)	1	500K	3
	large (700K)	1	<u>750K</u>	5
	Total:		5350K	8
250K bytes	small (<70K)	33	8250K	0
	large (500K)	1	500K	1
	large (700K)	1	<u>750K</u>	2
	Total:		9500K	3

TABLE 7-9. *Extent Sizing Tradeoffs*

of transaction. The deciding factor will be the distribution of the number of transactions. Since 33 of 35 concurrent transactions are small in this example, the largest extent size can be discarded. The choice is then between the two smaller extent sizes (70K and 125K). Since the number of wraps falls so rapidly with the small increase in extent size, choose the 125K size. Note that the choice of an extent size, falling between the minimum extent size (MES) and the minimum extent size necessary to eliminate all wraps, should always be the best compromise. This compromise assumes that (1) the additional disk space needed is available and (2) the performance penalties due to the wraps are acceptable.

The Minimum Total Size of all rollback segments for the database was previously calculated as 6775K bytes. The Minimum Possible Size for a rollback segment was calculated as 1750K bytes, yielding a minimum of four rollback segments.

In that configuration, each of the four rollback segments would support 9 transactions at a time (35 transactions divided by 4 rollback segments, rounded). Oracle recommends a number closer to 4 transactions per rollback segments. For this implementation, split the difference and start with 6 transactions per rollback segment, yielding 6 rollback segments (35/6, rounded). The actual space requirements for them can now be determined.

Each of the six rollback segments will contain an extent that is used for the rollback segment header. Its extent distribution is listed in Table 7-10.

The resulting rollback segment consists of a total of 2250K bytes, in 18 evenly sized extents. It can handle the high transaction load of the small-entry transactions. It can support the large transactions. And it contains free space in the event that the transaction volume or the transaction load is greater than has been predicted.

For details on monitoring the adequacy of this design, see Chapter 6, "Monitoring Multiple Databases." The next section describes the calculations used to reach this final layout.

Determining the OPTIMAL Size

The optimal size of a rollback segment must accommodate the transaction volume and the overhead needed to manage the transactions. The design should allow most of the transactions to be handled within a single extent.

EXTENT NUMBER	DESCRIPTION
1	Rollback segment header
2	Transaction #1
3	Transaction #2
4	Transaction #3
5	Transaction #4
6	Transaction #5
7	Transaction #6
8	Inactive, in use data
9	Inactive, in use data
10	Expansion space for large transactions
11	Expansion space for large transactions
12	Expansion space for large transactions
13	Expansion space for large transactions
14	Expansion space for large transactions
15	Expansion space for large transactions
16	Free space
17	Free space
18	Free space

TABLE 7-10. *Extent Distribution within the Sample Rollback Segments*

The amount of transaction data in a rollback segment should therefore be measured in extents. The number of extents required for each rollback segment is

```
Min Num of Extents/Segment = Number of Single-Extent Transactions
                  +((Number of Wraps in Long Transactions +1)*
                  Average Number of Long Transactions)
```

Applying this to our sample data,

```
Min Num of Extents/Segment     = (33 small-entry transactions
                                 /6 rollback segments) +
                                 (5 wraps +1 )*1
                               = 5.6 + 6
                               = 11.6, rounded up to 12
```

The longest transaction is 700K, which will require six 125K extents. This requires five wraps. Since only one such transaction is active at a time, a rollback segment needs to have an extent for each transaction, plus an additional extent for each wrap.

Using this many extents will allow the rollback segment to handle its share of the small-entry transaction load while also having room to support an average large-transaction load. This distribution of extents was shown graphically in Table 7-10. In that table, Extents 2 through 7 support the first extents of six different transactions. Extents 10 through 15 handle the expansion needs of the large transactions.

The transaction data thus requires 12 extents. The overhead needs of the rollback segment must now be estimated. They consist of three parts:

```
Rollback Segment Overhead = Rollback segment header space +
                            Inactive, In-Use space +
                            Free Space
```

The rollback segment header should always be estimated to take an extent (shown as Extent #1 in Table 7-10).

The IIU space is determined by the transaction scheduling for the application. If long-running queries are executing concurrently with online transactions that use the same data, then this value will have to be set high. It is possible that the amount of IIU data may exceed the currently used transaction volume.

If the transactions have been distributed correctly, then no long-running queries will be run concurrently with data manipulation transactions. Even so, there may be some overlap between the transactions. This overlap results in IIU space, and usually comprises at least 10 percent of the rollback segment's transaction volume.

For the safari example, I have estimated a 15 percent overlap between the transactions.

```
IIU Space          = (Per cent Inactive, In-Use) *
                       Number of Data Extents
                   = .15*12
                   = 1.80, rounded up to 2 extents.
```

These two extents are shown as Extents 8 and 9 in Table 7-10.

The final overhead factor is the Free Space. The Free Space must accommodate the worst case scenario of transaction allocations. In this case, that would be for both of the large-entry transactions to be assigned to the same rollback segment.

The space needed for a single large transaction has already been factored into the Minimum Number of Extents per Segment calculation. Therefore, you only need to add the number of wraps that would occur for a second large transaction. Since that is listed as 500K bytes (Table 7-8), and the extent size is 125K bytes (Table 7-9), such a transaction would require four extents (three wraps).

```
Free Space Extents  = Maximum Number of Additional Extents Needed
                    = 3
```

These extents are shown as Extents 16, 17, and 18 of Table 7-10.

The optimal size of the rollback segment, and the value for the OPTIMAL storage parameter, is thus

```
OPTIMAL   = (Minimum Number of Data Extents per Segment
                 + Rollback Segment Header extents
                 + Inactive, In Use extents
                 + Free Space extents)
             * Extent Size

          = (12+1+2+3)* 125K bytes/extent
          = 18 * 125K bytes /extent
          = 2250K bytes
```

To minimize the dynamic extension of the rollback segment in reaching this size, set MINEXTENTS to 18. The optimal size of the rollback segment will then be preallocated.

Creating the Rollback Segments

The rollback segments can now be created. They should all be created with the same storage parameters. The storage parameters for the safari application are listed in Table 7-11.

All of the production rollback segments will be created in the RBS tablespace. Therefore, the default storage settings for that tablespace can be used to enforce the desired storage values for the rollback segments. Use the following command to set these parameters (Oracle7 version shown).

```
ALTER TABLESPACE RBS
DEFAULT STORAGE
(INITIAL 125K NEXT 125K MINEXTENTS 18 MAXEXTENTS 999)
```

When creating rollback segments in that tablespace, you now only have to specify the tablespace and the OPTIMAL value, as shown in the following set of commands (Oracle7 version shown).

```
CREATE ROLLBACK SEGMENT r4 TABLESPACE RBS;
    STORAGE (OPTIMAL 2250K);
ALTER ROLLBACK SEGMENT r4 ONLINE;
```

The RBS tablespace will have to contain at least enough space to hold six 2250K-byte rollback segments (13500K bytes). When planning its space requirements, it is helpful to think of it graphically. Figure 7-7, which should call to mind Figures 7-1 and 7-2, shows a potential layout for the RBS tablespace.

PARAMETER	VALUE
INITIAL	125K bytes
NEXT	125K bytes
*PCTINCREASE	0
MINEXTENTS	18
MAXEXTENTS	999
**OPTIMAL	2250K bytes

* not applicable for Oracle7
** not applicable for Oracle Version 6

TABLE 7-11. *Storage Parameters for the Sample Rollback Segments*

In the layout shown in Figure 7-7, six equally sized rollback segments are shown. An additional area of free space of the same size is added at the bottom. That space will be available for adding a seventh segment (if rollback segment header contention is a problem) or for temporary extensions of the six rollback segments.

Figure 7-7 also shows that these rollback segments may be separated into their own files. In such files, a small amount of space will be reserved for overhead. For this example, I have created seven 2300K-byte files. Using multiple files will improve your options during database tuning efforts, since these files could be placed on different disks to distribute the transaction I/O load.

Production Versus Data Load Rollback Segments

All of the calculations performed here assumed that the application had no way of assigning transactions to specific rollback segments. The rollback segments thus had to support both large and small entry sizes. This is acceptable for most production usage, but it is not acceptable for handling data load transactions.

Data load transactions are used to manipulate large volumes of data in an application. These may include initial data loads, or the creation of large summary

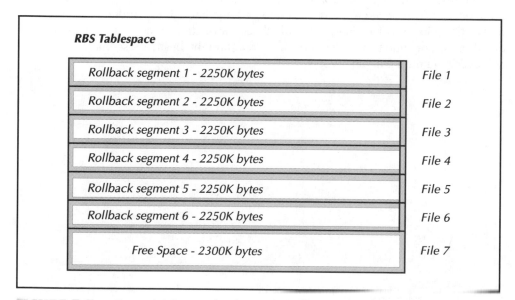

FIGURE 7-7. *Potential Layout for the Sample RBS Tablespace*

tables from detail tables. Either way, they involve transaction volumes that are orders of magnitude greater than those designed for here.

Data loads not only deal with large volumes of data, but the transactions within those loads are larger. For example, when using the Oracle *Import* utility, its default functionality is to perform one commit for each table's data. To support that, a rollback segment the size of the table would be needed. See Chapter 10, "Optimal Backup and Recovery Procedures," for alternatives to Import's default transaction size.

Data load transactions must be assigned to specific rollback segments. This can be done via the

```
SET TRANSACTION USE ROLLBACK SEGMENT segment_name
```

command, or it may be done by deactivating all but one production rollback segment (during off-peak hours). The size of the data load transactions should be measured using the V$ROLLSTAT queries shown previously in this chapter.

Once the data load transactions have been isolated to specific rollback segments, those rollback segments should be isolated in the RBS_2 tablespace. This tablespace, as described in Chapter 3, "Logical Database Layouts," is used solely for rollback segments that have extraordinary space requirements. Placing them in RBS_2 allows their extensions into the RBS_2 free space to be performed without impacting the free space available to the production rollback segments (in the RBS tablespace).

The result will be production rollback segments that are properly sized and preallocated. Their extents are designed to be large enough to handle an entire transaction. Space is allocated to handle those transactions that are not properly distributed. The worst case scenario is covered, and the best case scenario is achieved: the time machine works.

CHAPTER 8

Database Tuning

Like the cavalry riding up to save the day, tuning steps in to rescue systems suffering poor performance. As noted in previous chapters, most performance problems are not isolated symptoms, but rather are the result of the system design. Tuning efforts should therefore focus on identifying and fixing the underlying flaws that yield the unacceptable performance.

Tuning is the final step in a four-step process: Planning (Chapters 3 and 4), Doing (Chapter 5), and Monitoring (Chapter 6) must precede it. If you tune only for the sake of tuning, then you are failing to address the full cycle of activity, and will likely never resolve the underlying flaws that were planned into the system.

Most of the database objects that can be tuned are discussed elsewhere in this book—for example, rollback segments are covered very thoroughly in Chapter 7, "Managing Rollback Segments." This chapter will only discuss the tuning-related activities for such objects, while their own chapters cover planning and monitoring activities.

Tuning activities will be described for the following areas:

- Application design
- SQL
- Memory usage
- Data storage
- Data manipulation
- Physical storage
- Logical storage
- Network traffic

Tuning Application Design

Why should a DBA tuning guide include a section on application design? And why should this section come first? Because *nothing* you can do as a DBA will have as great an impact on the system performance as the design of the application. The requirements for making the DBA's involvement in application development a reality are described in Chapter 5, "Managing the Development Process." In designing an application, several steps can be taken to make effective and proper use of the available technology, as described in the following sections.

Effective Table Design

> *"No major application will run in Third Normal Form."*
> George Koch—*Oracle7, The Complete Reference*

No matter how well designed your database is, poor table design will lead to poor performance. Not only that, but overly rigid adherence to relational table designs will lead to poor performance. That is due to the fact that while fully relational table designs (said to be in the *Third Normal Form*) are logically desirable, they are physically undesirable.

The problem with such designs is that although they accurately reflect the ways in which an application's data is related to other data, they do not reflect the normal access paths that users will employ to access that data. Once the user's access requirements are evaluated, the fully relational table design will become unworkable for many large queries. Typically, the first problems will occur with queries that return a large number of columns. These columns are usually scattered among several tables, forcing the tables to be joined together during the query. If one of the joined tables is large, then the performance of the whole query may suffer.

In designing the tables for an application, developers should therefore consider denormalizing data—for example, creating small summary tables from large, static tables. Can that data be dynamically derived from the large, static tables on demand? Of course. But if the users frequently request it, and the data is largely unchanging, then it makes sense to periodically store that data *in the format in which the users will ask for it.*

User-centered table design, rather than theory-centered table design, will yield a system that better meets the users' requirements. Design options include separating a single table into multiple tables, and the reverse—combining multiple tables into one. The emphasis should be on providing the users the most direct path possible to the data they want in the format they want.

Distribution of CPU Requirements

When effectively designed, and given adequate hardware, an Oracle database application will be *CPU-bound.* That is, the limiting factor to its performance will be the availability of CPU resources. Short of purchasing additional CPU power for the available servers, there are several options that should be used.

First, the CPU load should be scheduled. This topic was mentioned in Chapter 7, "Managing Rollback Segments," with regard to reducing rollback segment overhead. However, it applies in general as well: schedule long-running batch query or update programs to run at off-peak hours. Rather than run them at lower operating-system priority while online users are performing transactions, run them at normal operating-system priority *at an appropriate time.* This will minimize potential locking, rollback, and CPU conflicts.

Second, as distributed computing becomes more widespread, take advantage of the opportunity to physically shift CPU requirements from one server to another. Wherever possible, isolate the database server from the application's CPU requirements. This can be done via the data distribution techniques described in Chapter 15, "SQL*Net V1 and V2," and Chapter 17, "Managing Distributed Databases." This will result in data being stored in its most appropriate place, and the CPU requirements of the application may be separated from the I/O requirements against the database.

Effective Application Design

In addition to the application design topics described later in this chapter, there are several general guidelines for Oracle applications.

First, they should minimize the number of times they request data from the database. Options for doing this include the use of sequences and using PL/SQL blocks. The denormalization of tables discussed earlier in this chapter also applies here. Distributed database objects such as snapshots may also be used to help reduce the number of times a database is queried.

Second, different users of the same application should query the database in a very similar fashion. This will increase the likelihood that their requests may be resolved by information that is already available in the SGA. This sharing of data includes not only the tables and rows retrieved, but also the actual queries that are used. If the queries are identical, then the parsed version of a query may already exist in the Shared SQL Pool (Oracle7 only), reducing the amount of time needed to process the query.

Stored procedures are available with the Oracle7 Procedural Option. When they are used, it is very likely that the same code will be executed multiple times, thus taking advantage of the Shared SQL Pool. You can also manually compile procedures, functions, and packages to avoid runtime compilation. For example, to create a procedure, use a CREATE PROCEDURE command, as shown in the following listing.

```
CREATE PROCEDURE my_raise (my_emp_no IN NUMBER, raise IN NUMBER)
AS BEGIN
     UPDATE employee
     SET salary = salary+raise
     WHERE empno = my_emp_no;
END;
/
```

When you create a procedure, Oracle automatically compiles it. If the procedure later becomes invalid, the database must recompile it before executing it. To avoid incurring this compilation cost at runtime, use the ALTER PROCEDURE command shown in the following listing.

```
ALTER PROCEDURE my_raise COMPILE;
```

The SQL text for all procedures in a database can be viewed via the "TEXT" column in the DBA_SOURCE view. The USER_SOURCE view will display the procedures owned by the user performing the query. Text for packages, functions, and package bodies is also accessible via these views. These views reference a table named SYS.SOURCE$. Since this table is part of the data dictionary, the procedural code is stored in the SYSTEM tablespace. Therefore, if you use these objects, you must be sure to allocate more space to the SYSTEM tablespace—usually doubling its size.

The two design guidelines discussed—limiting the number of user accesses and coordinating their requests—require that the application developer know as much as possible about how the data is to be used, and the access paths involved. For this reason, it is critical that users be as involved in the application design as they are in the table design. If the users spend long hours drawing pictures of tables with the data modelers, and little time with the application developers discussing the access paths, then the application will most likely not meet the users' needs.

Tuning SQL

As with application design, the tuning of SQL statements seems far removed from a DBA's duties. However, DBAs should be involved in reviewing the SQL that is written as part of the application. A well-designed application may still experience performance problems if the SQL it uses is poorly constructed. Application design and SQL problems cause most of the performance problems in properly designed databases.

In a relational database, the physical location of data is not as important as its logical place within the application design. However, the database has to find the data in order to return it to a user performing a query. The key to tuning SQL is to minimize the search path that the database uses to find the data.

Each row of data in a database has a ROWID in the following format.

```
00000027.0000.0003
```

Columns 1-8	The block ID.
Columns 10-13	The sequence number of the row within that block (row 0000 is the first).
Columns 15-18	The file ID.

Taking these three parts of the ROWID together, the database will be able to locate the row by going to the appropriate file, finding the right block, and then finding the right row within that block. The ROWID thus points to a specific physical location within a datafile.

Which datafile? The File ID portion of the ROWID can be compared to the FILE_ID column of the DBA_DATA_FILES view to determine which file is being used, as shown in the following listing.

```
SELECT
      file_name,          /*Name of the datafile*/
      tablespace_name,    /*Name of the datafile tablespace*/
      bytes,              /*Size of the datafile,in bytes*/
      blocks              /*Size of the datafile,in Oracle blocks*/
FROM dba_data_files
WHERE file_id = file id;
```

When a query with no WHERE clause is performed, the database will usually perform a *full table scan*. This involves reading every block from the table. To do this, the database locates the first extent of the table and then reads sequentially through all other extents in the table. For large tables, this can be a very time-consuming process.

When specific rows are queried, the database may use an index to help speed the retrieval of the desired rows. An index maps logical values in a table to their ROWIDs—which in turn map them to a specific physical location. Indexes may either be unique—in which case there is no more than one occurrence for each value—or non-unique. They only store ROWIDs for NOT NULL values in the indexed columns.

You may index several columns together. This is called a *concatenated* index, and it will be used if its leading column is used in the query's WHERE clause. Simply throwing an index at a query will not necessarily make it run faster—the index must be tailored to the access path needed.

Consider the case of a three-column, concatenated index. As shown in the following listing, it is created on the CITY, STATE, and ZIP columns of the EMPLOYEE table.

```
CREATE INDEX city_st_zip_ndx
ON employee(city, state, zip)
TABLESPACE INDEXES;
```

If a query of the form

```
SELECT * FROM employee
WHERE state='NJ';
```

is executed, then the index will *not* be used, because its *leading* column (CITY) is not used in the WHERE clause. If users will frequently run this type of query, then the index's columns should be reordered with STATE first in order to reflect the actual usage pattern.

It is also important that the table's data be as ordered as possible. Again, this is unimportant in relational theory, but plays a critical role in retrieving data for queries. If users are frequently executing *range* queries—selecting those values that are within a specified range—then having the data ordered may require fewer data blocks to be read while resolving the query, thus improving performance. The ordered entries in the index will point to a set of neighboring blocks in the table, rather than blocks that are scattered throughout the datafile(s).

For example, a range query of the type shown in this listing

```
SELECT * FROM employee
WHERE empno BETWEEN 1 and 100;
```

will require fewer data blocks to be read if the physical records in the EMPLOYEE table are ordered by the EMPNO column. This should improve the performance of the query. To guarantee that the rows are properly ordered in the table, extract the records to a flat file, sort the records in the file, and then delete the old records and reload them from the sorted file.

If two tables are frequently queried together, then *clusters* may be effective in improving performance. Clusters store rows from multiple tables in the same physical data blocks, based on their logical values (the cluster key). See Chapter 5, "Managing the Development Process," for more information on clusters.

Queries in which a column's value is compared to an exact value are called *equivalence* queries. In Oracle7, a new type of cluster, called a *hash cluster,* is made available. This type of cluster stores a row in a specific location based on its value in the cluster key column. Every time a row is inserted, its cluster key value is used to determine which block it should be stored in; this same logic can be used during queries to quickly find data blocks that are needed for retrieval. These are designed to improve the performance of equivalence queries; they will not be as helpful in improving the performance of the range queries discussed earlier.

How can you determine which access path the database will use to perform a query? This information can be viewed via the EXPLAIN PLAN command. This command will evaluate the execution path for a query and will place its output into a table (named PLAN_TABLE) in the database. A sample EXPLAIN PLAN command is shown in the following listing.

```
EXPLAIN PLAN
SET statement_id = 'TEST'
FOR
SELECT * FROM employee
WHERE city > 'Y%';
```

The first line of this command tells the database that it is to explain its execution plan for the query without actually executing the query. The second line labels this query's records in the PLAN_TABLE with a STATEMENT_ID equal to "TEST". Following the keyword "FOR", the query to be analyzed is listed.

The account that is running this command must have a PLAN_TABLE in its schema. Oracle provides the CREATE TABLE commands needed for this table. In Oracle Version 6, the file is called XPLAINPL.SQL and is located in $ORACLE_HOME/rdbms/admin. In Oracle7, the file is located in the same directory, but is named UTLXPLAN.SQL. Users may run this script to create the table in their schemas.

Query the plan table using the query in the following listing. Records in that table are related to each other, so the CONNECT BY clause of the SELECT statement can be used to evaluate the hierarchy.

```
SELECT
  LPAD(' ',2*LEVEL)||operation||' '||options||' '||object_name
  q_plan
FROM plan_table
WHERE statement_id = 'TEST'
CONNECT BY PRIOR id = parent_id and statement_id = 'TEST'
START WITH id=1;
```

This query will report on the types of operations the database must perform to resolve the query. Sample output is shown in the following listing.

```
Q_PLAN
-------------------------------------------------------
TABLE ACCESS BY ROWID EMPLOYEE
  INDEX RANGE SCAN CITY_ST_ZIP_NDX
```

This plan shows that the data that is returned to the user comes via a "Table Access by ROWID." The ROWIDs are supplied by an index range scan, using the CITY_ST_ZIP_NDX index described earlier in this section.

Please see the *Oracle7 Server Application Developer's Guide* and the *Oracle7 Server Concepts Manual* for further details on tuning SQL.

Tuning Memory Usage

Monitoring the usage of Oracle's memory areas is discussed in Chapter 6, "Monitoring Multiple Databases." Specifically, that chapter describes the proper use of the Oracle statistics scripts, and the interpretation of their output. These scripts, called BSTAT/ESTAT in Oracle Version 6 and UTLBSTAT/UTLESTAT in Oracle7, summarize the changes in system statistics for a given period. They help point out areas to which not enough resources have been given.

In Oracle Version 6, there are several areas to worry about: the dictionary cache and the data buffer cache are the two most significant memory areas to tune.

In Oracle7, the dictionary cache is not directly sized or tuned, but is part of the Shared SQL Pool in the SGA. The Shared SQL Pool also contains the parsed versions of the statements run against the database.

All of these memory areas are managed via a *least recently used (LRU)* algorithm. A preset area is set aside to hold values; when it fills, the least recently used data is eliminated from memory and written back to disk. An adequately sized memory area keeps the most frequently accessed data in memory; accessing less frequently used data requires physical reads.

Sizing of both the dictionary cache and the Shared SQL Pool is described in Chapter 6, "Monitoring Multiple Databases." The Hit Ratio calculation in that chapter also helps to alert you to an improperly sized data buffer cache. But how do you know if the data buffer cache is set too high? If it is, then memory is being wasted, and may possibly lead to performance problems.

The Hit Ratio is a measure of how well the data buffer cache is handling requests for data. It is calculated as

```
Hit Ratio = (Logical Reads - Physical Reads)/Logical Reads
```

Thus, a perfect Hit Ratio would have a value of 1.00. In that instance, all requests for database blocks (logical reads) would be fulfilled without requesting any data from datafiles (physical reads); all requests would be handled by the data that is already in memory.

In general, the online transaction portion of applications should have Hit Ratios in excess of 0.90. The overall Hit Ratio for an application will be lowered by its batch activity. The method for measuring the Hit Ratio is described in Chapter 6, "Monitoring Multiple Databases."

Even if your Hit Ratio is within the allowable range you set, it should still be checked. It is possible that you can reduce the size of the data buffer cache and still maintain the same Hit Ratio. To check this, you must first add the following line to your database's INIT.ORA file:

```
DB_BLOCK_LRU_STATISTICS = TRUE
```

Then shut down and restart the database. This will cause the database to maintain memory statistics in a table called SYS.X$KCBCBH. This table is described in Table 8-1.

COLUMN	DESCRIPTION
INDX	The potential number of buffers in the data buffer cache, minus 1.
COUNT	The number of cache hits attributable to INDX+1 buffers.

TABLE 8-1. *Columns in the SYS.X$KCBCBH Table*

There will be one row in this table for each buffer in your buffer cache. Thus, for each buffer in the data buffer cache, you will be able to see how many *cache hits* (that is, logical reads that require no physical reads) it contributed.

This information will tell you how many of your data buffers are being actively used. Since these buffers contribute cache hits, you may use this table to determine how many additional *cache misses* would result if the number of buffers was decreased.

To do this, query the table to determine how many cache hits (the COUNT column) would be lost if you were to eliminate buffers (the INDX column). The number of lost hits can be shown via the following query.

```
SELECT
   sum(count) lost_hits
FROM sys.x$kcbcbh
WHERE indx >= new_number_of_buffers;
```

Since these "lost hits" will require additional physical reads, the Hit Ratio for this new number of data buffers can be calculated as

```
Hit Ratio = (Logical Reads - Physical Reads - Lost Hits)
                     /Logical Reads
```

Running the database in this statistics-gathering mode will make it run slower (since the database is constantly monitoring its memory areas). Once your testing is complete, be sure to remove the DB_BLOCK_LRU_STATISTICS parameter from your INIT.ORA file and restart the database.

Another option for memory management will become available with Oracle7.1. This option, called CACHE, will automatically load an entire table into the SGA the first time that table is accessed. That table's data will still be subject to the LRU algorithms that manage the SGA caches. It is most useful for frequently accessed tables that change infrequently. You can then run queries that will reload the most-used tables into the SGA caches each time the database is restarted.

With all of the areas of the SGA—the data block buffers, the dictionary cache, and, in Oracle7, the Shared SQL Pool—the emphasis should be on sharing data among users. Each of these areas should be large enough to hold the most commonly requested data from the database. In the case of the Shared SQL Pool, it should be large enough to hold the parsed versions of the most commonly used queries. When they are adequately sized, the memory areas in the SGA can dramatically improve the performance of individual queries and of the database as a whole. Instructions for proper sizing of tables, indexes, and clusters are provided in Chapter 5, "Managing the Development Process."

Tuning Data Storage

How the database actually *stores* data also has an effect on the performance of queries. If the data is fragmented into multiple extents, then resolving a query may cause the database to look in several physical locations for related rows.

Fragmentation may also slow performance when storing new records. If the free space in a tablespace is fragmented, then the database may have to dynamically combine neighboring free extents to create a single extent that is large enough to handle the new space requirements. Tuning data storage thus involves tuning both used space and free space, as described in the next sections.

Defragmentation of Segments

Space: The INITIAL Frontier.

As described in Chapter 4, "Physical Database Layouts," when a database object (such as a table or index) is created, it is assigned to a tablespace via user defaults or specific instructions. A *segment* is created in that tablespace to hold the data associated with that object. The space that is allocated to the segment is never released until the segment is dropped, shrunk (Oracle7 rollback segments only), or truncated (Oracle7 tables only, when TRUNCATE is used with the DROP STORAGE option).

A segment is made up of sections called *extents*. The extents themselves are contiguous sets of Oracle blocks. Once the existing extents can no longer hold new data, the segment will obtain another extent. This extension process will continue until no more free space is available in the tablespace's datafiles, or until an internal maximum number of extents per segment is reached. If a segment is comprised of multiple extents, there is no guarantee that those extents will be contiguous.

Thus, a fragmented data segment not only causes performance problems, but it may also lead to space management problems within the tablespace. It is therefore beneficial to have each data segment comprised of only one extent; its INITIAL storage parameter, which specifies the size of its initial extent, should be set large enough to handle all of the segment's data. The monitoring system provided in Chapter 6, "Monitoring Multiple Databases," checks for fragmented data segments via its EXTENTS table.

That monitoring system checks the DBA_SEGMENTS data dictionary view to determine which segments are comprised of ten or more extents. A general query of the DBA_SEGMENTS view is shown in the following listing. This query will retrieve the tablespace name, owner, segment name, and segment type for each segment in the database. The number of extents and blocks used by the segment will be displayed.

```
SELECT
        tablespace_name,    /*Tablespace name*/
        owner,              /*Owner of the segment*/
        segment_name,       /*Name of the segment*/
        segment_type,       /*Type of segment (ex. TABLE, INDEX)*/
        extents,            /*Number of extents in the segment*/
        blocks,             /*Number of db blocks in the segment*/
        bytes               /*Number of bytes in the segment*/
FROM sys.dba_segments
/
```

Segment types include TABLE, INDEX, CLUSTER, ROLLBACK, TEMPORARY, DEFERRED ROLLBACK, and (Oracle7 only) CACHE. The DBA_SEGMENTS view does not list the size of the individual extents in a segment. To see that, query the DBA_EXTENTS view, as shown in the following listing.

```
SELECT
        tablespace_name,    /*Tablespace name*/
        owner,              /*Owner of the segment*/
        segment_name,       /*Name of the segment*/
        segment_type,       /*Type of segment (ex. TABLE, INDEX)*/
        extent_id,          /*Extent number in the segment*/
        file_id,            /*File_ID for the extent*/
        block_id,           /*Starting block number for the extent*/
        bytes,              /*Size of the extent, in bytes*/
        blocks              /*Size of the extent, in Oracle blocks*/
FROM sys.dba_extents
WHERE segment_name = 'segment_name'
ORDER by extent_id;
```

This query selects the extent information for a single segment (identified via the WHERE clause). It returns the storage information associated with the segment's extents, including the size and location of each data extent. A similar query is used when mapping the distribution of free extents and used extents in a tablespace. This query, which is covered in the "Measuring Fragmentation" section of the coming "Defragmentation of Free Extents" section, results in the output shown later in this chapter in Figure 8-2.

If a segment is fragmented, the easiest way to compress its data into a single extent is to rebuild it with the proper storage parameters. Since the INITIAL storage parameter cannot be changed after a table has been created, a new table must be created with the correct storage parameters. The old data can then be inserted into the new table, and the old table can be dropped.

This process can be automated via the Export/Import utilities. As noted in Chapter 10, "Optimal Backup and Recovery Procedures," the Export command has a COMPRESS flag. This flag will cause Export, when reading a table, to determine the total amount of space allocated to that table. It will then write to the export dump file a new INITIAL storage parameter—equivalent to the total of the allocated space—for the table. If the table is then dropped, and Import is used to re-create it, then its data should all fit in the new, larger initial extent.

Note that it is the *allocated,* not the *used,* space that is compressed. An empty table with 300M allocated to it in three 100M extents will be compressed into a single, empty 300M extent. No space will be reclaimed. Also, the database will not check to see if the new INITIAL extent size is greater than the size of the largest datafile for the tablespace. Since extents cannot span datafiles, this would result in an error during Import.

The data segment compression procedure is shown in the following example. First, export the tables.

```
exp system/manager file=exp.dmp compress=Y grants=Y indexes=Y
    tables=(HR.T1,HR.T2)
```

Next, if the Export succeeded, then go into SQL*Plus and drop the exported tables. Then import the tables from the export dump file.

```
imp system/manager file=exp.dmp commit=Y buffer=64000 full=Y
```

In this example, the DBA exported two tables, named T1 and T2, owned by the user HR. The tables were exported with the COMPRESS=Y flag, which modified their storage parameters during the Export. The tables were then dropped. When they were then imported, the Import utility created the tables with the new, compressed storage parameters.

This method may also be used on the entire database. Export the database with the COMPRESS=Y flag, re-create the database, and then perform a full Import. With some restrictions, it may also be applied to the defragmentation of tablespaces. See Chapter 10, "Optimal Backup and Recovery Procedures," for further details on tablespace rebuilds.

Defragmentation of Free Extents

As noted in Chapter 4, "Physical Database Layouts," a *free extent* in a tablespace is a collection of contiguous free blocks in the tablespace. When a segment is dropped, its extents are deallocated and are marked as free. However, these free extents are not recombined with neighboring free extents in Oracle Version 6 databases; the barriers between these free extents are maintained. In Oracle7 databases, the SMON background process periodically coalesces neighboring free extents.

The Oracle Version 6 methodology affects the allocation of space within the tablespace during the next space request (such as by the creation or expansion of a table). In its quest for a large enough free extent, the database will not merge contiguous free extents unless there is no other alternative; thus the large free extent at the rear of the tablespace tends to be used, while the smaller free extents toward the front of the tablespace are relatively unused, becoming "speed bumps" in the tablespace because they are not, by themselves, of adequate size to be of use. As this usage pattern progresses, the database thus drifts further and further from its ideal space allocation. Free space fragmentation is particularly prevalent in environments in which database tables and indexes are frequently dropped and re-created, especially if their storage parameters are changed in the process.

However, you can force the Oracle Version 6 database to recombine the contiguous free extents, thus emulating the Oracle7 SMON functionality. This will increase the likelihood of the free extents near the front of the file being reused, thus preserving the free space near the rear of the tablespace file. As a result, new requests for extents are more likely to meet with success.

In the ideal Oracle V6 tablespace, each database object is stored in a single extent, and all of the available free space is in one large contiguous extent. This will minimize recursive calls during retrievals while maximizing the likelihood of acquiring a large enough free extent when an object needs additional storage space. The utility presented here will provide a means of accomplishing the second goal, that of automated free space defragmentation, as well as mapping database space allocations and providing a means of evaluating the severity of the free space fragmentation problems you may experience.

Measuring Fragmentation

To judge whether a tablespace could benefit from a free space rebuild, it is necessary to establish a baseline on an arbitrary scoring system. Since free space fragmentation is made up of several components (number of extents, size of largest extent), I created a scoring index that considers both. It is important to note that the weightings I set up are arbitrary, and were chosen to reflect the potential for the database to acquire a large extent. Thus, the number of extents is given little importance. The critical factor is the size of the largest extent as a percentage of the total free space (that is, how close is the tablespace to the ideal?). I refer to this as the *Free Space Fragmentation Index* (FSFI). You may wish to tailor your index to give greater importance to other criteria. Note that it does not consider how much free space is available, only its structure.

$$\text{FSFI} = 100 * \text{sqrt}\left(\frac{\text{largest extent}}{\text{sum all extents}}\right) * \frac{1}{(\text{number of extents})^{1/4}}$$

The largest possible FSFI (for an ideal single-file tablespace) is 100. As the number of extents increases, the FSFI rating drops slowly. As the size of the largest extent drops, however, the FSFI rating drops rapidly. The following script calculates the FSFI values for all tablespaces in a database:

```
rem
rem   file: fsfi.sql
rem   location: /orasw/dba/contig
rem
rem   This script measures the fragmentation of free space
rem   in all of the tablespaces in a database and scores them
rem   according to an arbitrary index for comparison.
rem
set newpage 0 pagesize 60
column fsfi format 999.99

SELECT
      tablespace_name,
      sqrt(max(blocks)/sum(blocks))*
      (100/sqrt(sqrt(count(blocks)))) fsfi
FROM dba_free_space
GROUP BY
      tablespace_name
ORDER BY 1

spool fsfi.lis
/
spool off
```

Output from this query, showing the FSFI values for a sample database, is shown in Figure 8-1.

Given your database's FSFI ratings, you must then establish a baseline. You should rarely encounter free space availability problems in tablespaces which had adequate free space available and FSFI ratings over 30. If a tablespace appears to be approaching that borderline, you may wish to generate a mapping of space usage in the tablespace. The following script will show all space marked as free or used by database objects. This is useful (1) to show the distribution and size of the free extents, and (2) to determine which database objects are barriers between free extents.

```
rem
rem    file: mapper.sql
rem    location: /orasw/dba/contig
rem    Parameters: the tablespace name being mapped
rem
rem    Sample invocation:
rem    @mapper DEMODATA
rem
rem    This script generates a mapping of the space usage
rem    (free space vs used) in a tablespace. It graphically
rem    shows segment and free space fragmentation.
rem
set pagesize 60 linesize 132 verify off
column file_id heading "File¦Id"

SELECT
       'free space' owner,     /*"owner" of free space*/
       '   ' object,           /*blank object name*/
       file_id,                /*file ID for the extent header*/
       block_id,               /*block ID for the extent header*/
       blocks                  /*length of the extent, in blocks*/
FROM dba_free_space
WHERE tablespace_name = upper('&&1')
UNION
SELECT
       substr(owner,1,20),        /*owner name (first 20 chars)*/
       substr(segment_name,1,32), /*segment name*/
       file_id,                   /*file ID for extent header*/
       block_id,                  /*block ID for block header*/
       blocks                     /*length of the extent in blocks*/
FROM dba_extents
WHERE tablespace_name = upper('&&1')
ORDER BY 3,4

spool &&1._map.lst
/
spool off
undefine 1
```

Sample output from this mapping query is shown in Figure 8-2. It displays the owner and segment name for each extent in the tablespace. If their extent is a free extent, then the owner is listed as "free space," and the segment name (the "OBJECT" column) is left blank.

```
Tablespace_Name      FSFI
----------------     -------
DEMODATA             87.91
DEMONDX              30.39
RBS                  68.24
SYSTEM               73.78
TEMP                 100.00
TOOLS                100.00
```

FIGURE 8-1. *Sample Free Space Fragmentation Ratings*

The output in Figure 8-2 shows 12 rows. Five of them are of free space extents, and seven are from data segments. Note that the first three free space extents are contiguous; in an Oracle7 database they would be automatically coalesced into a single extent with 15 blocks. In Oracle Version 6, they are left separate, and largely unusable. Following two more data extents, there is another free space extent. Because it is separated from the other free extents in the tablespace, it cannot be combined with any of them unless the tablespace is defragmented.

Owner	OBJECT	File Id	BLOCK_ID	Blocks
OPS$CC1	FILES	6	2	20
OPS$CC1	SPACES	6	22	20
OPS$CC1	EXTENTS	6	42	20
OPS$CC1	FILES	6	62	20
free space		6	82	5
free space		6	87	5
free space		6	92	5
OPS$CC1	SPACES	6	97	20
OPS$CC1	EXTENTS	6	117	20
free space		6	137	10
OPS$CC1	FILES	6	147	20
free space		6	167	14,833

FIGURE 8-2. *Sample Extent Map*

Evaluating Contiguous Space

Depending on the manner in which the free space is distributed in the tablespace, it may be impossible to combine any of the free extents without performing an Import/Export (tablespace defragmentation). This next pair of scripts will determine if any benefit is to be gained. The first script, CONTIG_TABLE.SQL, uses PL/SQL to check every entry in the DBA_FREE_SPACE data dictionary view. It builds a table (called CONTIG_TABLE) that lists every extent, the extent's starting position, and the starting position that it would have if all contiguous free extents were combined. Note that the numbers will be inaccurate for the tablespace in which this table is being stored; you may wish to create a transient tablespace to hold this data during the evaluation and defragmentation process.

In the script, the "Block_ID" column of every entry in DBA_FREE_SPACE is added to the value in its "Blocks" column. If this is equal to the next entry's Block_ID (and if they are in the same file), then the two extents can be compressed into one.

```
rem
rem     file: contig_table.sql
rem     location: /orasw/dba/contig
rem
rem     This script creates and populates a table called CONTIG_SPACE.
rem     It evaluates the starting position and length of each free extent
rem     and compares that to the starting position of the next extent
rem     to determine if the two extents are contiguous.
rem
DROP TABLE contig_space;
CREATE TABLE contig_space
(tablespace_name   char(30),
 file_id                  number,
 block_id                 number,
 starting_file_id         number,
 starting_block_id        number,
 blocks                   number,
 bytes                    number)
TABLESPACE TEMPDATA
/

declare
  cursor query is SELECT *
      FROM dba_free_space
      ORDER BY tablespace_name, file_id, block_id;
  this_row          query%rowtype;
  previous_row          query%rowtype;
```

```
        old_file_id            integer;
        old_block_id           integer;

begin
  open query;
  fetch query into this_row;
  previous_row := this_row;
  old_file_id := previous_row.file_id;
  old_block_id := previous_row.block_id;
  while query%found loop
    if this_row.file_id = previous_row.file_id and
       this_row.block_id = previous_row.block_id +
                 previous_row.blocks
      then insert into CONTIG_SPACE
             (tablespace_name,
              file_id,
              block_id,
              starting_file_id,
              starting_block_id,
              blocks,
              bytes)
      values
             (previous_row.tablespace_name,
              previous_row.file_id,
              this_row.block_id,
              old_file_id,
              old_block_id,
              this_row.blocks,
              this_row.bytes);
      else insert into CONTIG_SPACE
             (tablespace_name,
              file_id,
              block_id,
              starting_file_id,
              starting_block_id,
              blocks,
              bytes)
      values
             (this_row.tablespace_name,
              this_row.file_id,
              this_row.block_id,
              this_row.file_id,
```

```
                this_row.block_id,
                this_row.blocks,
                this_row.bytes);
        old_file_id := this_row.file_id;
        old_block_id := this_row.block_id;
      end if;
      previous_row := this_row;
      fetch query into this_row;
    end loop;
end;
.
/
commit;
```

The data in the CONTIG_SPACE table can be used to determine whether combining all of the free extents would have a significant impact on the FSFI rating of the tablespaces. To automate this process, create a view called NEW_LOOK, defined by the following script.

```
rem
rem     file: new_look.sql
rem     location: /orasw/dba/contig
rem
rem     This file creates a view of the CONTIG_SPACE table
rem     that shows what the free space would look like
rem     if all contiguous free space was combined.
rem     This view will be used to evaluate whether the operation
rem     will yield any benefit.
rem
DROP VIEW new_look;
CREATE VIEW new_look
as SELECT
        tablespace_name,
        starting_file_id,
        starting_block_id,
        sum(blocks) sum_blocks,
        count(blocks) count_blocks,
        max(blocks) max_blocks,
        sum(bytes) sum_bytes
FROM contig_space
GROUP BY
        tablespace_name,
```

```
        starting_file_id,
        starting_block_id
/
```

The BEFORE_AFTER.SQL script, shown next, displays the FSFI values before and after free space defragmentation for a given tablespace to allow the DBA to evaluate whether such fragmentation would be worthwhile. It uses the current values in the DBA_FREE_SPACE view to measure the current FSFI and uses the NEW_LOOK view to measure the projected FSFI. The details of the free extents location and size are retrieved from the CONTIG_SPACE table.

```
rem
rem     file: before_after.sql
rem     location: /orasw/dba/contig
rem
rem     This SQL*Plus script evaluates a target tablespace to determine
rem     the potential benefit of coalescing the neighboring free space
rem     extents. If the "New FSFI" value is beneath your threshold,
rem     then the tablespace must be defragmented.
rem
set verify off pagesize 60
ttitle center 'Before-After Changes Report for '&&1 skip 2
break on starting_file_id skip 1
column new_length format 99999999
column num_fragments format 99999999
column current_top format 99999999

SELECT
        starting_file_id,              /*starting file ID for extent*/
        starting_block_id,             /*starting block ID for extent*/
        sum(blocks) new_length,        /*comb. length for extents*/
        count(blocks) num_fragments,   /*number of frags combined*/
        max(blocks) current_top        /*largest extent of the set*/
FROM contig_space
WHERE tablespace_name = upper('&&1')
GROUP BY
        starting_file_id,
        starting_block_id
HAVING count(*)>1
ORDER BY 1,2
spool before_after.lis
/
```

```
ttitle center 'Old FSFI rating for '&&1 skip 1
column fsfi format 999.999

SELECT
     sqrt(max(blocks)/sum(blocks))*
     (100/sqrt(sqrt(count(blocks)))) fsfi
FROM dba_free_space
WHERE tablespace_name = upper('&&1')
/

ttitle center 'New FSFI rating for '&&1 skip 1
column new_fsfi format 999.999
SELECT
     sqrt((max(sum_blocks))/sum(sum_blocks))*
     (100/sqrt(sqrt(count(sum_blocks)))) new_fsfi
FROM new_look
WHERE tablespace_name = upper('&&1')
/
spool off
```

Figure 8-3 shows sample output from this set of queries. The first section shows the free space as it would exist if all neighboring free extents were combined. This section of the report also shows how many extents would be combined for each new free extent, and how large the current largest extent is within each such group. The second section of the report shows the current FSFI rating for the tablespace. The third section of the report shows what the FSFI rating would be if all neighboring free extents were coalesced.

If the tablespace's new FSFI rating is still below your threshold score, a tablespace rebuild should be considered (see Chapter 10, "Optimal Backup and Recovery Procedures"). The output in Figure 8-3 is for the DEMONDX tablespace listed earlier. Before defragmentation, it had 27 free extents, the largest of which was 120K (out of 250K). After defragmentation, it will have 5 free extents, the largest of which is 210K, improving its FSFI rating from 30.39 to 56.17.

Prior to this combination, a request for an extent of 10 blocks in size would have taken space in the large free space chunk at the end of the tablespace, since none of the uncombined extents had a length of 10 blocks (see the "Current_Top" column in the report). As a result of combining the free extents, such a request could be satisfied by the first free extent in the tablespace. Potential speed bumps in the free space have been turned into usable areas.

Combining the Free Extents
If a tablespace would benefit from having its free extents compressed (as shown in its Before/After FSFI numbers), then the following scripts should be run. They will

```
            Before-After Changes Report for DEMONDX

Starting_File_ID   Starting_Block_ID   New_Length   Num_Frag   Current_Top
----------------   -----------------   ----------   --------   -----------
       7                    74             10           3            6
                           204             10           3            4
                           334              8           2            6
                           385             12           3            4
                           420            210          16          120


            Old FSFI Rating for DEMONDX
    FSFI
    -------
    30.39


            New FSFI Rating for DEMONDX
    FSFI
    -------
    56.17
```

FIGURE 8-3.   *Sample Output from the Before-After Query*

automatically create and execute "create table" scripts. Since they will temporarily use all free space in a tablespace, they should not be run during periods when new extent requests are likely. These tables will be sized to use every free extent in the tablespace, forcing all contiguous free extents to be combined. When the tables are then dropped, the extents will now be coalesced rather than separate, improving the tablespace's FSFI rating and moving it closer to the ideal space usage model. After compressing the free extents, rerun the CONTIG_TABLE.SQL script to update the free space extent mappings.

The spool files created by this script contain the tablespace names in their filenames. This is done by using the period (.) as the SQL*Plus variable concatenation character.

```
rem
rem     file: gen_creates.sql
rem     location: /orasw/dba/contig
rem     Parameters: the tablespace name
rem
rem     Sample usage:
rem     @gen_creates DEMONDX
```

```
rem
rem   This script automatically generates and runs the create table
rem   and drop table scripts that will force the database to combine
rem   the available free space in a designated tablespace.
rem
set verify off echo off termout off feedback off
set pagesize 0 linesize 80 newpage 0
column X format A80 word_wrapped

SELECT 'create table '||'&&1'||rownum||'(dummy char(1))'||
' storage(initial '||sum_bytes||' next '||sum_bytes||
' minextents 1 maxextents 1)'||' tablespace '||'&&1'||';' X
FROM new_look
WHERE tablespace_name = upper('&&1')
ORDER BY sum_bytes desc /*Important!*/

spool &&1._creates.sql
/
spool off

SELECT 'drop table '||'&&1'||rownum||';'
FROM new_look
WHERE tablespace_name = upper('&&1')

spool &&1._drops.sql
/
spool off

start &&1._creates.sql
start &&1._drops.sql
```

Identifying Chained Rows

When a data segment is created, a PCTFREE value is specified. This parameter tells the database how much space should be kept free *in each data block*. This space is then used when rows that are already stored in the data block extend in length via UPDATEs.

If an update to a row causes that row to no longer completely fit in a single data block, then that row may be moved to another data block, or the row may be *chained* to another block. If you are storing rows whose length is greater than the Oracle block size, then you will automatically have chaining.

Chaining affects performance because of the need to look in multiple physical locations for data from the same logical row. By eliminating unnecessary chaining, you reduce the number of physical reads needed to return data from a datafile.

Chaining can be avoided by setting the proper value for PCTFREE during creation of data segments. For instructions for setting this value, see the "Determining the Proper PCTFREE" section of Chapter 5, "Managing the Development Process."

In Oracle Version 6, the only way to detect chaining is to search for rows that are longer than the available space in an Oracle block. In Oracle7, a new command is available that automates this process.

The Oracle7 ANALYZE command is used to collect statistics about database objects. These statistics may then be used by the cost-based optimizer to determine the best execution path to use. This command has an option that detects and records chained rows in tables. Its syntax is

```
ANALYZE TABLE table_name LIST CHAINED ROWS INTO chained_rows;
```

This command will put the output from this operation into a table called CHAINED_ROWS in your local schema. The SQL to create this table is in a file named UTLCHAIN.SQL, in the $ORACLE_HOME/rdbms/admin directory. The following query will select the most significant columns from the CHAINED_ROWS table.

```
SELECT
        owner_name,      /*Owner of the data segment*/
        table_name,      /*Name of the table with the chained rows*/
        cluster_name,    /*Name of the cluster, if it is clustered*/
        head_rowid       /*Rowid of the first part of the row*/
FROM chained_rows;
```

The output will show the ROWIDs for all chained rows. This will allow you to quickly see how much of a problem chaining is in each table. If it is prevalent in a table, then that table should be rebuilt with a higher value for PCTFREE.

Increasing the Oracle Block Size

The effect of increasing the database block size is stunning. In most environments, at least two block sizes are supported—for example, 2K and 4K. Most of the installation routines are set to use the lower of the two. However, using the next higher value for the block size may improve the performance of query-intensive operations by up to 50 percent.

This gain comes relatively free of charge. To increase the database block size, the entire database must be rebuilt, and all of the old database files have to be deleted.

The new files will be created in the same location as the old files, with the same size, but will be managed more efficiently by the database. The performance savings comes from the way that Oracle manages the block header information. Doubling the size of the Oracle blocks has little effect on the block header; thus, a smaller percentage of space is used to store block header information. This will not be true if the table is transaction-intensive, since the variable block header will then require more space; see Chapter 5, "Managing the Development Process," for more information on this topic.

To change the block size, modify the INIT.ORA parameter called DB_BLOCK_SIZE. Note that in Oracle7 databases, this parameter has been moved to the CONFIG.ORA file that the database's INIT.ORA file calls.

Be careful when doing this, since several of the database's INIT.ORA parameters are set in terms of the number of Oracle blocks. For example, the DB_BLOCK_BUFFERS parameter, which sets the size of the data buffer cache, is set in this manner. If you double the block size, you should cut the DB_BLOCK_BUFFERS parameter in half. Failing to do this will double the size of the data buffer cache, possibly causing problems with the memory management on your server.

Tuning Data Manipulation

There are several data manipulation tasks that may involve the DBA. These tend to involve manipulation of large quantities of data. You have several options when loading and deleting large volumes of data, as described in the following sections.

With Oracle Version 6 data manipulation commands, you should try to maximize the number of database blocks that are written to the database in a single batch. This is controlled by the DB_BLOCK_WRITE_BATCH parameter in the database's INIT.ORA file. Check its default setting; its optimal setting is operating-system dependent.

In Oracle7, you can improve the performance of database reads and writes by creating multiple DBWR (Database Writer) processes. This will prevent access requests against multiple disks from causing performance bottlenecks. Oracle recommends creating at least as many DBWR processes as you have disks. The number of database writers that should be created for an instance is set via the DB_WRITERS parameter in the database's INIT.ORA file.

Bulk Inserts: Using the SQL*Loader Direct Path Option

When used in the Conventional Path mode, SQL*Loader reads a set of records from a file, generates INSERT commands, and passes them to the Oracle kernel. Oracle then finds places for those records in free blocks in the table and updates any associated indexes.

With Oracle7, a new option, called Direct Path, is available. In this mode, SQL*Loader creates formatted data blocks and writes directly to the datafiles. This requires occasional checks with the database to get new locations for data blocks, but no other I/O with the database kernel is required. The result is a data load process that is dramatically faster than Conventional Path.

If the table is indexed, then the indexes will be placed in "DIRECT PATH" state during the load. After the load is complete, the new keys (index column values) will be sorted and merged with the existing keys in the index. To maintain this temporary set of keys, the load will create a temporary index segment that is at least as large as the largest index on the table. The space requirements for this can be minimized by presorting the index and using the SORTED INDEXES clause in the SQL*Loader control file.

To use the Direct Path option, a series of views must be created in the database. These views are created during database creation via the script CATLDR.SQL, located in $ORACLE_HOME/rdbms/admin.

To get the best performance from the load, the data segment that you are loading into should already be created, with all of the space it will need already allocated. This will minimize the amount of dynamic space allocation necessary. You should also presort the data on the columns of the largest index in the table. Sorting the data and leaving the indexes on the table during a Direct Path load will yield better performance than if you were to drop the indexes before the load and then re-create them after it completed.

To take advantage of this option, the table cannot be clustered, and there can be no other active transactions against it. During the load, only NOT NULL, UNIQUE, and PRIMARY KEY constraints will be enforced; after the load has completed, the CHECK and FOREIGN KEY constraints can be automatically reenabled. To force this to occur, use the

```
REENABLE DISABLED_CONSTRAINTS
```

clause in the SQL*Loader control file.

The only exception to this reenabling process is that table Insert triggers, when reenabled, are not executed for each of the new rows in the table. A separate process must manually perform whatever commands were to have been performed by this type of trigger.

Bulk Deletes: The TRUNCATE Command

Occasionally, users attempt to delete all of the records from a table at once. When they encounter errors during this process, they complain that the rollback segments are too small, when in fact their transaction is too large.

A second problem occurs once the records have all been deleted. Even though the segment no longer has any records in it, it still maintains all of the space that was allocated to it. Thus, deleting all those records saved you not a single byte of space.

The new Oracle7 TRUNCATE command resolves both of these problems. It is a DDL command, not a DML command, *so it cannot be rolled back*. Once you have used the TRUNCATE command on a table, its records are gone, and none of its Delete triggers are executed in the process. However, the table retains all of its dependent objects—such as grants, indexes, and constraints.

The TRUNCATE command is the fastest way to delete large volumes of data. Since it will delete all of the records in a table, this may force you to alter your application design so that no protected records are stored in the same table as the records to be deleted.

A sample TRUNCATE command for a table is shown in the following listing.

```
TRUNCATE TABLE employee DROP STORAGE;
```

This example, in which the EMPLOYEE table's records are deleted, shows a powerful feature of this command. The DROP STORAGE clause is used to deallocate the non-INITIAL space from the table (this is the default option). Thus, it is now possible to delete all of a table's rows, and to reclaim all but its initial extent's allocated space, without dropping the table.

This command also works for clusters. In this example, the REUSE STORAGE option is used to leave all allocated space empty, within the segment that acquired it.

```
TRUNCATE CLUSTER emp_dept REUSE STORAGE;
```

When this command is executed, all of the records in the EMP_DEPT cluster will be instantly deleted.

Tuning Physical Storage

Although the database should be CPU-bound, this can only happen if its physical I/O is evenly distributed and handled correctly. Chapter 4, "Physical Database Layouts," describes a process for planning file distribution across disks. This process involves understanding the interactions of the DBWR, LGWR, and ARCH background processes. A means of verifying the adequacy of the final layouts is also provided there.

In addition to that level of physical storage tuning, several other factors should be considered. The following sections address factors that are external to the database, but may have a profound impact on its ability to access data quickly.

Tuning File Fragmentation

Back in Oracle Version 5, there was a command called CCF—Create Contiguous File. This command created datafiles that were contiguous on the physical disk. In Oracle Version 6 and Oracle7, there is no way to guarantee that any of the database's files are created in contiguous areas on their disks.

Why is this significant? Consider the case of a perfectly sized and compressed table. All of its data is in a single extent. However, that extent is located in a datafile—and that datafile may not be contiguous on the disk. Thus, the disk hardware has to keep moving to find the data, even though the database considers the table to be contiguous.

The method for determining whether a file is contiguous or not is operating-system dependent. In most cases, you will have to dump the header of the file, and analyze the output to determine how many fragments the file is physically broken into. This process should be done in coordination with the Systems Management personnel.

Their participation is important because they hold the key to resolving the situation. To have the best chance at creating a contiguous file, create a new file on an unused disk, and then check its fragmentation. To minimize file fragmentation, keep non-database files off of database disks, and avoid dropping and re-creating files. This highlights the need for disks that are dedicated to your database files.

Using Raw Devices

Raw devices are available with some UNIX operating systems. When they are used, the DBWR process bypasses the UNIX buffer cache and eliminates the file system overhead. For I/O-intensive applications, they may result in a performance improvement of around 20 percent.

Raw devices cannot be managed with the same commands as file systems. For example, the *tar* command cannot be used to back up individual files; instead, the *dd* command must be used. This is a much less flexible command to use and limits your recovery capabilities.

Tuning Logical Storage

From a logical standpoint, like objects should be stored together. As discussed in Chapter 3, "Logical Database Layouts," objects should be grouped based on their space usage and user interaction characteristics. Based on these groupings, tablespaces should be created that cater to specific types of objects.

A suggested tablespace layout is presented in Table 8-2, along with details about the characteristics of the types of objects stored in each tablespace.

For further information on this distribution of segment types and my extensions to the Optimal Flexible Architecture (OFA), see Chapter 3, "Logical Database Layouts." For information on detecting and managing contention for rollback segments, see Chapter 7, "Managing Rollback Segments."

Reducing Network Traffic

As databases and the applications that use them become more distributed, the network that supports the servers may become a bottleneck in the process of delivering data to the user. Since DBAs typically have little control over the network management, it is important to use the database's capabilities to reduce the number of network packets that are required for the data to be delivered. Doing so will reduce your reliance on the network, and thus eliminate a potential cause of performance problems.

Replication of Data

As described in Chapter 15, "SQL*Net V1 and V2," and Chapter 17, "Managing Distributed Databases," it is possible to query data from remote databases. However, it is not desirable to have large volumes of data constantly sent from one database to another. To reduce the amount of data being sent across the network, different data replication options should be considered.

In a purely distributed environment, each data element exists in one place, as shown in Figure 8-4. When data is required, it is accessed from remote databases via SQL*Net queries.

TABLESPACE	USE
SYSTEM	Data dictionary tables and indexes. Created during the database creation. No other objects should be stored here.
DATA	Standard-operation tables for an application. They tend to be actively used and to be the most likely to grow.
DATA_2	Static tables used during standard operation of an application. They tend to be fixed in size and infrequently accessed other than as reference tables.
INDEXES	Indexes for the standard-operation tables. They tend to be actively used and to be likely to grow.
INDEXES_2	Indexes for the static tables. They tend to be fixed in size.
RBS	Standard-operation rollback segments.
RBS_2	Specialty rollback segments used for data loads. When no data loads are taking place, they may be taken offline.
TEMP	Standard-operation temporary segments for all regular users of an application.
TEMP_*USER*	Temporary segments created by a particular user. This is intended to isolate exceptional space requirements from the main application.
TOOLS	RDBMS tools tables for tools such as SQL*Forms, SQL*Menu, etc.
TOOLS_I	Indexes for RDBMS tools tables.
USERS	User objects, in development databases. In Production databases, this tablespace typically does not exist.

TABLE 8-2. *Logical Distribution of Segments in an Optimal Database*

This purist approach is similar to implementing an application in Third Normal Form—and as was stated earlier in this chapter, that approach will not support any major production application. Modifying the application's tables to improve data retrieval performance involved denormalizing data. This process deliberately stores redundant data in order to shorten users' access paths to the data.

In a distributed environment, replicating data accomplishes this goal. Rather than force queries to cross the network to resolve user requests, selected data from remote servers is replicated to the local server. This can be accomplished via a number of means, as described in the following sections.

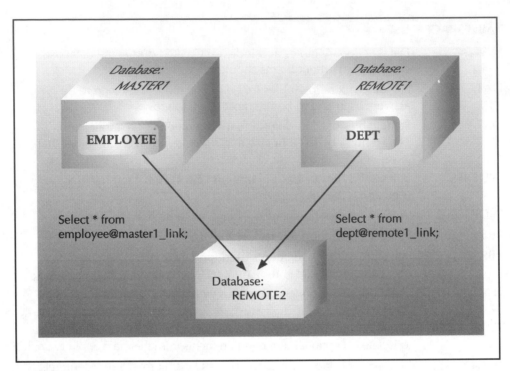

FIGURE 8-4. *Sample Distributed Environment*

Using the COPY Command to Replicate Data

In the first option the data can be periodically copied to the local server. This is best accomplished via the SQL*Plus COPY command, as described in Chapter 15, "SQL*Net V1 and V2." This command allows selected columns and rows to be replicated to each server. This option is illustrated in Figure 8-5.

For example, the remote server may have a table called EMPLOYEE. The local server would be able to replicate the data that it needs by using the COPY command to select records from the remote EMPLOYEE table. The COPY command can be used to store those selected records in a table in the local database. This command includes a query clause; thus, it is possible to return only those rows that meet the specified criteria.

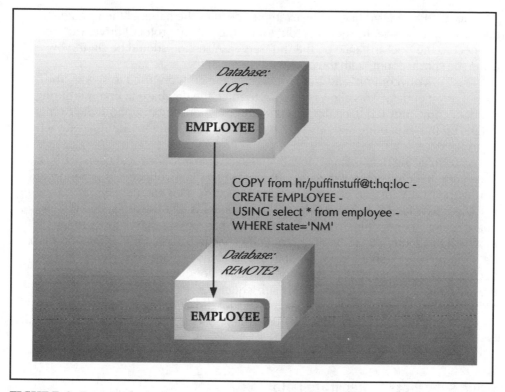

FIGURE 8-5. *Data Replication Using the COPY Command*

In this example, a portion of the EMPLOYEE table is copied down from the headquarters database to a local database. A WHERE clause is used to restrict which records are selected.

```
set copycommit 1
set arraysize 1000
COPY FROM hr/puffinstuff@t:hq:loc -
CREATE employee -
USING -
SELECT * FROM employee -
WHERE state = 'NM'
```

The "COPY FROM" line in this example specifies the name of the remote database. In this case, the query is told to use the TCP/IP protocol driver ("t:") to connect to the "loc" instance on the "hq" server. A session should be started by using the "hr" account, with the password "puffinstuff".

The "set copycommit" and "set arraysize" commands are used to specify the size of array of data. This allows the DBA to force the database to commit during the data copy, thus reducing the size of the transactions to be supported. For more details on this capability and other COPY options, see Chapter 15, "SQL*Net V1 and V2."

As soon as the data is stored locally, it is accessible to the local users. They can thus query the data without traversing the network; a network access is performed during the COPY instead of separate network accesses for each query.

The downside to replicating data in this manner is that the replicated data is out of date as soon as it is created. This option is thus most useful for those situations in which the source data is very infrequently changed. The COPY command must be performed frequently enough so that the local tables contain useful, sufficiently accurate data. The REPLACE option of the COPY command can be used to replace the contents of the local tables during subsequent COPYs. See Chapter 15, "SQL*Net V1 and V2," for further usage notes for the COPY command.

Although the local table may be updatable, none of the changes made to it will be reflected in the source table. Thus, this scenario is only effective for improving the performance of query operations.

Using Snapshots to Replicate Data

The Oracle7 Distributed Option offers a means of managing the data replication within a database. This option uses *snapshots* to replicate data from a master source to multiple targets. It also takes care of refreshing the data, updating the targets at specified time intervals. This option is illustrated in Figure 8-6.

Snapshots are read-only; updatable snapshots are expected to be available in production release six months after the release of Oracle7.1. This section will focus on their performance tuning aspects. Managing snapshots is covered in Chapter 17, "Managing Distributed Databases."

Before creating a snapshot, a database link to the source database should first be created. The following SQL*Net V1 example creates a private database link called HR_LINK.

```
CREATE DATABASE LINK hr_link
CONNECT TO hr IDENTIFIED BY puffinstuff
USING 'T:hq:loc';
```

The CREATE DATABASE LINK command, as shown in this example, has several parameters:

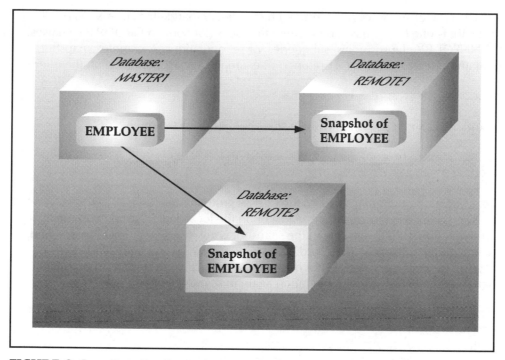

FIGURE 8-6. *Data Replication Using Snapshots*

- The name of the link ("hr_link," in this example).

- The account to connect to (if none is specified, then the local username and password will be used in the remote database).

- The connect string. In this case, it tells the database to use the TCP/IP protocol driver ("T:") to connect to the instance named "loc" on the server named "hq".

For more information on this command, see Chapter 15, "SQL*Net V1 and V2." There are two styles of snapshots available: simple snapshots and complex snapshots. The proper type to use for your environment depends on the amount of replicated data and the manner in which it is queried. The type of snapshot used affects which data refresh options are available.

The type of snapshot is determined by the query that defines it. A *simple* snapshot is one that is based on a query that does not contain GROUP BY clauses, CONNECT BY clauses, joins, subqueries, or set operations. A *complex* snapshot contains at least one of these options. For example, a snapshot based on the query

```
SELECT * FROM employee@hr_link;
```

would be a simple snapshot, while a snapshot based on the query

```
SELECT dept, max(salary) FROM employee@hr_link
GROUP BY dept;
```

would be a complex snapshot because it uses grouping functions.

The syntax used to create the snapshot on the local server is shown in the following listing. In this example, the snapshot is given a name ("local_emp"), and its storage parameters are specified. Its base query is given, as well as its refresh interval. In this case, the snapshot is told to immediately retrieve the master data, then to perform the snapshot operation again in seven days ("sysdate+7").

```
CREATE SNAPSHOT local_emp
PCTFREE 5
TABLESPACE DATA_2
STORAGE (INITIAL 100K NEXT 100K PCTINCREASE 0)
REFRESH FAST
      START WITH sysdate
      NEXT sysdate+7
AS SELECT * FROM employee@hr_link;
```

The REFRESH FAST clause tells the database to use a *snapshot log* to refresh the local snapshot. This capability is only available with simple snapshots. When a snapshot log is used, only the changes to the master table are sent to the targets. If a complex snapshot is used, then the REFRESH COMPLETE clause must be used instead; in that scenario, the refresh completely replaces the existing data in the snapshot table.

Snapshot logs must be created in the master database, via the CREATE SNAPSHOT LOG command. An example of this command is shown in the following listing.

```
CREATE SNAPSHOT LOG ON employee
TABLESPACE data
STORAGE (INITIAL 10K NEXT 10K PCTINCREASE 0);
```

The snapshot log is always created in the same schema as the master table.

Using simple snapshots with snapshot logs allows you to reduce the amount of network traffic involved in maintaining the replicated data. Since only the changes to the data will be sent via a snapshot log, the maintenance of simple snapshots should use fewer network resources than complex snapshots require. This is particularly true if the master tables for the snapshots are large, fairly static tables. If this is not the case, then the volume of transactions sent via the snapshot log may not be any less than would be sent to perform a complete refresh.

This plays a part in your application design as well. If your data access paths require joining information from multiple remote tables, then you have two choices, as shown in Figure 8-7. The first option (see Figure 8-7(a)) is to create multiple simple snapshots, and then perform the join query on the local server. The second option

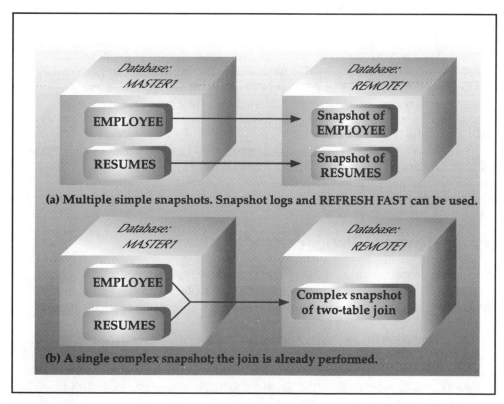

FIGURE 8-7. *Data Replication Options for Joins*

(see Figure 8-7(b)) is to create a single complex snapshot on the local server, based on multiple remote tables.

Which option will retrieve data the fastest? The answer to that depends on several factors:

- The size of the master tables. How long does a complete refresh take?

- The volume of transactions against the master tables. How large are the snapshot logs?

- The frequency of the refreshes. How often will the data be replicated?

If the data is rarely refreshed, and there are few transactions against the master tables, then it should be quicker to use a complex snapshot (Figure 8-7(b)). If the data is frequently updated and refreshed, then the time savings from using fast refreshes should outweigh the cost of performing the join when the query is executed (rather than ahead of time, via the snapshot). In that case, using a set of simple snapshots would result in a faster response time.

There is a potential data inconsistency problem with using multiple simple snapshots. If the tables are related to each other (via a foreign key to primary key relationship), and they have different refresh times, then it is possible that their snapshots will not reflect their referential integrity. Their snapshots may have foreign key references that do not have matching primary keys. This consistency problem will be resolved in Oracle7.1.

The goal is to minimize the time it takes to satisfy the user's data request. The decision on the proper type of snapshot configuration to use can only be made if you know most common joins ahead of time. For further information on the management of snapshots, see Chapter 17, "Managing Distributed Databases."

Using Remote Procedure Calls

When using procedures in a distributed database environment, there are two options: to create a local procedure that references remote tables, or to create a remote procedure that is called by a local application. These two options are illustrated in Figure 8-8.

The proper location for the procedure depends on the distribution of the data, and the way it is to be used. The emphasis should be on minimizing the amount of data that must be sent through the network in order to resolve the data request. The procedure should reside within the database that contains most of the data that is used during the procedure's operations.

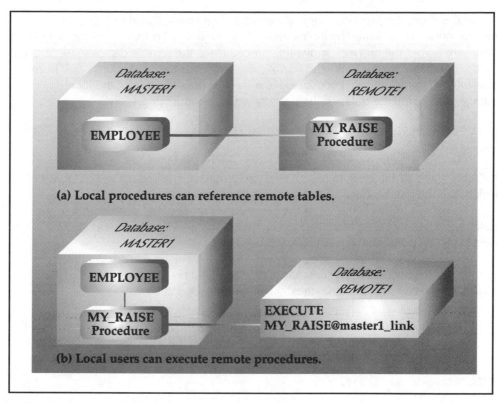

(a) Local procedures can reference remote tables.

(b) Local users can execute remote procedures.

FIGURE 8-8. *Options for Procedure Location*

For example, consider this procedure:

```
CREATE PROCEDURE my_raise (my_emp_no IN NUMBER, raise IN NUMBER)
AS BEGIN
      UPDATE employee@hr_link
      SET salary = salary+raise
      WHERE empno = my_emp_no;
END;
/
```

In this case, the procedure only accesses a single table (EMPLOYEE) on a remote node (as indicated by the database link "hr_link"). To reduce the amount of data sent across the network, move this procedure to the remote database identified by the database link "hr_link" and remove the reference to that database link from the "FROM" clause in the procedure. Then call the procedure from the local database by using the database link, as shown in the following listing.

```
EXECUTE my_raise@hr_link(1234,2000);
```

In this case, two parameters are passed to the procedure—MY_EMP_NO is set to '1234', and RAISE is set to '2000'. The procedure is invoked using a database link to tell the database where to find the procedure.

The benefit of this is that all of the procedure's processing is performed in the database where the data resides. This minimizes the amount of network traffic necessary to complete the procedure's processing.

To maintain location transparency, you may create a local synonym that points to the remote procedure. The database link name will be specified in the synonym, so that user requests will automatically use the remote database.

```
CREATE SYNONYM my_raise FOR my_raise@hr_link;
```

A user could then enter the command

```
EXECUTE my_raise(1234,2000);
```

and it would execute the remote procedure defined by the synonym MY_RAISE.

CHAPTER 9

Database Security and Auditing

Dead bolt locks, secret passwords, iron bars, gated driveways, access cards, security patrols—the elements of physical security in the real world are found in the database world as well.

Creating and enforcing security procedures helps to protect what is rapidly becoming the most important corporate asset: data. And while storing that data in a database makes it more useful and available companywide, it also makes it susceptible to unauthorized access. Such access attempts must be prevented and detected.

The Oracle database has several layers of security, and the ability to audit each level. Each layer will be described in this chapter, as will the auditing process. The implications of distributed database environments will also be covered, along with methods for setting impossible passwords in both Oracle Version 6 and Oracle7.

Security Capabilities

Oracle makes several levels of security available to the DBA:

- Account security for validation of users
- Access security for database objects
- System-level security for managing global privileges

Each of these capabilities is described in the following sections; the "Implementing Security" sections of this chapter provide details for effectively using the available options.

Account Security

In order to access data in an Oracle database, you must have access to an account in that database. This access can be direct—via user connections into a database—or indirect. Indirect connections include access via preset authorizations within database links. Each account must have a password associated with it. A database account can also be tied to an operating system account.

Passwords are set for a user when the user's account is created. They may then be altered by either the DBA or the user. The database stores an encrypted version of the password in a data dictionary table. If the account is directly related to an operating system account, then it is possible to bypass the password check.

Object Security

Access to objects within a database is accomplished via *privileges*. These allow specific database commands to be used against specific database objects via the GRANT command. For example, if the user THUMPER owned a table called EMPLOYEE, and executed the command

```
GRANT SELECT ON employee TO public;
```

then all users (PUBLIC) would be able to select records from THUMPER's EMPLOYEE table. In Oracle7, *roles*—named groups of privileges—can be used to simplify the administration of privileges. For applications with large numbers of users, this greatly reduces the number of GRANT commands needed. Since roles can be password-protected and can be dynamically enabled or disabled, they also add an additional layer of security to the database.

System-Level Roles

Roles can also be used to manage the system-level commands available to users in Oracle7. These include commands such as CREATE TABLE and SELECT ANY TABLE. In Oracle Version 6, the only system-level privileges available are CONNECT, RESOURCE, and DBA. All users who will access the database need CONNECT privilege; those who will be creating segments need RESOURCE. A user with the DBA privilege has authority to view and manage all data in the database.

In Oracle7, CONNECT, RESOURCE, and DBA are roles, comprised of sets of system-level privileges. Actions against each type of database object are authorized via separate privileges. That is, whereas the Oracle Version 6 RESOURCE privilege granted a user the capability to both alter and create tables, an Oracle7 user might be granted the CREATE TABLE privilege, but not the ALTER TABLE privilege. RESOURCE is included as a role in Oracle7 for upward compatibility with Oracle Version 6 users, but Oracle7 DBAs should take advantage of the granularity of privileges now available. You can create customized system-level roles that grant users the exact privileges they need without granting them excessive authority within the database.

Implementing Security in Oracle Version 6

How should these capabilities be used? In the following sections you will see the usage of all of these features in Oracle Version 6. The proper combination of account, object, and system-level security can then be implemented.

The Starting Point: Operating System Security

You cannot access a database unless you can first access, either directly or indirectly, the server on which the database is running. The first step in securing your database is to secure the platform on which it resides. Once that has been accomplished, the operating system security must be considered.

Oracle uses a number of files that its users do not require direct access to. For example, the datafiles and the online redo log files are written and read only via Oracle's background processes. Thus, only DBAs who will be creating and dropping these files require direct access to them at the operating system level. Export dump files and other backup files must also be secured.

Creating Users

In Oracle Version 6, user account creation is a two-step process. First, the account is granted CONNECT privilege and a password is set. Next, the account is altered via the ALTER USER command to set the available parameters.

There are three system-level security options in Oracle Version 6. They are named CONNECT, RESOURCE, and DBA. The capabilities that they grant to users are listed in Table 9-1.

The following listing shows a sample user creation. In the first line of the listing, the CONNECT privilege is granted to THUMPER, and a password is assigned (in this example, "rabbit"). The second command in the listing uses the ALTER USER command to set the default and temporary tablespaces for the account. The third command uses the GRANT RESOURCE command to establish a space quota in the USERS tablespace for the user.

```
GRANT CONNECT TO thumper IDENTIFIED BY rabbit;

ALTER USER thumper
DEFAULT TABLESPACE users
TEMPORARY TABLESPACE temp;

GRANT RESOURCE (100M) ON users TO thumper;
```

The parameters that may be set via the ALTER USER command in Oracle Version 6 are listed in Table 9-2.

PRIVILEGE	CAPABILITIES GRANTED
CONNECT	Can connect to the database; perform data manipulation commands; create views, synonyms, and database links; and perform User and Table exports.
RESOURCE	Can create tables, indexes, clusters, and sequences; and grant privileges on these objects.
DBA	Can access any user's data; grant and revoke privileges; administer database-wide objects (such as rollback segments); create public objects (such as public synonyms); create and alter users; audit all database activities; and perform all types of exports.

TABLE 9-1. *System-Level Privileges for Oracle Version 6.*

PARAMETER	USAGE
Password	Password for the account; may also be tied directly to the operating system host account name.
Default tablespace	The default tablespace in which objects created in this schema will be stored. This setting does not give the user rights to create objects.
Temporary tablespace	The tablespace in which temporary segments used during sorting transactions will be stored.

TABLE 9-2. *Parameters for the ALTER USER Command in Oracle Version 6.*

Setting a resource quota via the GRANT RESOURCE command implicitly grants the user the ability to create objects in the database. By specifying a tablespace in this command, the user is authorized to create objects only in that tablespace. If no quota or tablespace is specified, then the user can create objects of any size anywhere in the database.

Revoking Users

In Oracle Version 6, all users, whether active or inactive, remain in the data dictionary. That is, the information about their account never gets deleted by the database. This may cause problems when account names are reused (see the "Listing Invalid Grants" section of this chapter).

The REVOKE CONNECT command is used to deactivate an account. The account will continue to own any objects it had created, and any grants that had been made to it. A sample REVOKE CONNECT command is shown in the following listing.

```
REVOKE CONNECT FROM thumper;
```

This command does not drop the THUMPER user; it only revokes its ability to access the database. This is significant because any grants made to the THUMPER user stay in the data dictionary. If, in the future, another account is created in the same database with the same name, then that new account will inherit all of the old account's objects and privileges that were not cleaned out. That is, if a

```
GRANT CONNECT TO thumper IDENTIFIED BY nowpassword;
```

command is executed for a new user, the database will not create a new account. Rather, it will reactivate the *old* THUMPER account and use that; the new user will inherit all of the objects and privileges that the old user had, unless they have been manually dropped.

The REVOKE RESOURCE and REVOKE DBA commands are used to revoke the RESOURCE and DBA system-level privileges, respectively.

System-Level Roles

In Oracle Version 6, performing backup and recovery operations requires the DBA privilege. Since there is no ability to separate system-level privileges (such as SELECT ANY TABLE) from the DBA Privilege in Oracle Version 6, anyone who has the ability to back up the database also has the ability to query every table in it. Thus, the Systems Management team is often indirectly granted full access to the data in the database. This problem is not resolved in Oracle Version 6; in Oracle7, customized system-level roles can be used to grant users only those privileges they need to perform their job functions.

Tying Database Accounts to Host Accounts

Users are allowed to access a database once they have entered a valid username and password for that database. However, it is possible to take advantage of the operating system to provide an additional level of user authentication.

A database account may be paired with an operating system account on the same server. The two account names will differ only in the prefix of the database account name. In Oracle Version 6, the prefix is "OPS$".

For example, consider an operating system account named FARMER. The matching database account name for this user is OPS$FARMER. When the FARMER user is logged into his operating system account, he can access his OPS$FARMER account without specifying a password, as shown in the following listing.

```
> sqlplus /
```

The "/" takes the place of the username/password combination that would normally be required for access.

In Oracle Version 6, all accounts must be created with passwords. Considering the OPS$FARMER account again, its creation command would be in the following format.

```
GRANT CONNECT TO ops$farmer IDENTIFIED BY some_password;
```

Even though the password will not be needed by the user, it still must be specified. Because of this, it is possible to access the OPS$FARMER database account from a different operating system account if you know the password for the database account. The following listing shows a sample connection to the OPS$FARMER account from a different operating system account.

```
> sqlplus ops$farmer/some_password
```

The only way to get around this problem in Oracle Version 6 is to create the account with an impossible password. This method, described in the "Setting Impossible Passwords" section of this chapter, prevents the user from logging into the database account other than through the operating system account associated with it.

Password Protection

User accounts can be protected via passwords. Passwords are set when accounts are created, and may be modified via ALTER USER commands.

In Oracle Version 6, the initial password for an account is set via the GRANT CONNECT command, as shown in the following example. In this example, the THUMPER account is created with an initial password of RABBIT.

```
GRANT CONNECT TO thumper IDENTIFIED BY rabbit;
```

The passwords for accounts should be changed via the ALTER USER command. It is possible to use the GRANT CONNECT command for this purpose, but this is not advisable, since a typing error would result in a new account being created. A sample ALTER USER command is shown in the following listing.

```
ALTER USER thumper IDENTIFIED BY newpassword;
```

Managing Privileges

Privileges give users access to data that they do not own. Privileges are created via the GRANT command, and are recorded in the data dictionary. Access to tables, views, sequences—as well as synonyms for these—may be granted in both Oracle Version 6 and Oracle7. The privileges that may be granted on objects are listed in Table 9-3.

The WITH GRANT OPTION clause is used to pass along to the grantee the ability to make further grants on the base table. The following listing from SQL*Plus shows an example of this. In this example, the user named THUMPER grants the user named MCGREGOR both SELECT and partial UPDATE access on a table

PRIVILEGE	CAPABILITIES GRANTED
SELECT	Can query the object.
INSERT	Can insert records into the table or view.
UPDATE	Can update records in the table or view. This privilege may be granted for specific columns in the table or view.
DELETE	Can delete records from the table or view.
ALTER	Can alter the table or sequence.
INDEX	Can create indexes on the table.
REFERENCES	Can create foreign keys that reference the table.

TABLE 9-3. *Available Privileges in Oracle Version 6*

called EMPLOYEE, WITH GRANT OPTION. This user then grants one of these privileges to another user (named JFISHER).

```
GRANT SELECT, UPDATE (employee_name, address)
ON employee TO mcgregor
WITH GRANT OPTION;

CONNECT mcgregor/farmer
GRANT SELECT ON thumper.employee TO jfisher;
```

Granting the privileges to PUBLIC would have made them available to all users in the database.

To grant another user all of the available privileges on an object, use the GRANT ALL command, as shown in the following listing.

```
GRANT ALL ON employee TO jfisher;
```

This command is equivalent to individually granting each available privilege to the user.

Listing Invalid Grants

Information about privileges that have been granted is stored in the data dictionary. This data is accessible via the data dictionary views.

The views listed in Table 9-4 are used in Oracle Version 6 to determine which privileges exist in the database.

DATA DICTIONARY VIEW	CONTENTS
DBA_USERS	Users who have been granted CONNECT, RESOURCE, or DBA
DBA_TAB_GRANTS	Users who have been granted privileges on objects
DBA_COL_GRANTS	Users who have been granted privileges on columns of tables

TABLE 9-4.   *DBA Views of Privileges in Oracle Version 6*

These views can be used to determine which grants are no longer valid. Invalid grants are those that have been granted to users who no longer have the ability to connect to the database. This is particularly troublesome in Oracle Version 6, since there is no DROP USER command available for that version. A user account whose CONNECT privilege has been revoked in Oracle Version 6 will maintain all its object grants unless the grantor of those privileges revokes them.

To view privileges that still exist in the data dictionary for Oracle Version 6 users who no longer have CONNECT privilege, query the DBA_TAB_GRANTS view for those users (grantees) whose accounts have been deactivated. A deactivated account will have a CONNECT_PRIV value of '0' in the DBA_USERS view.

```
rem
rem    This query retrieves information about invalid grants
rem    in Oracle Version 6 databases.
rem
break on grantor skip 1 on owner on table_name
SELECT
   grantor,       /*Grantor of the privilege.*/
   owner,         /*Owner of the object.*/
   table_name,    /*Name of the object.*/
   grantee        /*Account to which the privilege was granted.*/
FROM dba_tab_grants
WHERE exists
(SELECT 'x' from dba_users
WHERE dba_users.username=dba_tab_grants.grantee
and connect_priv = '0');
```

The rows retrieved by this query will show the grantor of the privilege, the owner of the object on which the privilege is granted, the object name, and the user to whom the privilege is granted. These privileges may then be revoked by the grantors.

Revoking privileges is done via the REVOKE command. You may revoke either some (by explicitly listing them) or all of the user's privileges (via the ALL keyword). In the following example, a specific privilege is revoked for the EMPLOYEE table from one user, while another user's privileges are completely revoked.

```
REVOKE DELETE ON employee FROM peter;
REVOKE ALL ON employee FROM mcgregor;
```

The REVOKE ALL command is often used when cleaning up revoked accounts in Oracle Version 6.

Implementing Security in Oracle7

The security capabilities in Oracle7 build on the Oracle Version 6 security foundation. The means of creating and revoking users has changed, and *roles*—named groups of privileges—have been added to the security options available. In the following sections you will see the usage of all of these features, including several undocumented capabilities.

The Starting Point: Operating System Security

You cannot access a database unless you can first access, either directly or indirectly, the server on which the database is running, The first step in securing your database is to secure the platform on which it resides. Once that has been accomplished, the operating system security must be considered.

Oracle uses a number of files that its users do not require direct access to. For example, the datafiles and the online redo log files are written and read only via Oracle's background processes. Thus, only DBAs who will be creating and dropping these files require direct access to them at the operating system level. Export dump files and other backup files must also be secured.

Creating Users

The commands used for creating users changed between Oracle Version 6 and Oracle7. In both versions, the goal of the account creation process is the same: to establish a secure, useful account that has adequate privileges and proper default settings.

In Oracle7, the CREATE USER command is used to create a new database account. When the account is created, it will not have any capabilities—and will not even be able to log in until that privilege is granted.

All of the necessary settings for a user account can be specified within a single CREATE USER command. These settings include values for all of the parameters listed in Table 9-5.

The following listing shows a sample CREATE USER command. In this example, the user THUMPER is created, with a password of RABBIT, a default tablespace of USERS, a temporary tablespace of TEMP, no quotas, and no profile.

```
CREATE USER thumper
IDENTIFIED BY rabbit
DEFAULT TABLESPACE users
TEMPORARY TABLESPACE temp;
```

Since no profile was specified, the default profile for the database will be used. This is an actual profile named DEFAULT; its initial settings are for all resource consumption limits to be set to UNLIMITED. See the "User Profiles" section of this chapter for further details on this topic.

Since no quotas were specified, the user cannot create objects in the database.

PARAMETER	USAGE
Username	Name of the schema.
Password	Password for the account; may also be tied directly to the operating system host account name.
Default tablespace	The default tablespace in which objects created in this schema will be stored. This setting does not give the user rights to create objects.
Temporary tablespace	The tablespace in which temporary segments used during sorting transactions will be stored.
Quota [on tablespace]	Allows the user to store objects in the specified tablespace, up to the total size specified as the quota.
Profile	Assigns a profile to the user. Profiles are used to restrict the usage of system resources such as CPU time; they are described in the "User Profiles" section later in this chapter.

TABLE 9-5.   *Parameters for the CREATE USER Command in Oracle7*

When granting resource quotas in an Oracle7 database, the QUOTA parameter of the CREATE USER or ALTER USER command is used, as shown in the following listing. In this example, THUMPER is granted a quota of 100M in the USERS tablespace.

```
ALTER USER thumper
QUOTA 100M ON users;
```

This syntax is different from the Oracle Version 6 syntax for user resource quotas.

All of the parameters in the CREATE USER command may be altered via the ALTER USER command (except for the username).

Revoking Users

The process of revoking user access, like the user creation process, changed between Oracle Version 6 and Oracle7. Oracle7 uses a new command to completely remove the user from the database.

In Oracle7, the user can be completely dropped from the database via the DROP USER command. This command has one parameter, CASCADE, which drops all objects in the user's schema before dropping the user. If the user owns objects, then you must specify this parameter in order to drop the user. A sample DROP USER command is shown in the following listing.

```
DROP USER thumper CASCADE;
```

Any views, synonyms, procedures, functions, or packages that referenced objects in the schema of the dropped user will be marked as INVALID. If another user with the same name is created at a later date, there will be nothing for it to inherit from the previous user with that name.

System-Level Roles

System-level roles can be used in Oracle7 databases to distribute the availability of system-level commands used to manage the database.

Whereas Oracle Version 6 DBAs are limited to granting only CONNECT, RESOURCE, and DBA privileges, Oracle7 DBAs can either create customized system-level roles or use the ones that come with the database. The available privileges that can be granted via system-level roles are listed in Table 9-6. The "ANY" keyword in privilege signifies that the user has the privilege for all schemas in the database. If the keyword "ANY" is enclosed in brackets ("[ANY]"), then it is optional when granting that privilege.

Note that "ANY" and "PUBLIC" are not synonymous.

PRIVILEGE	CAPABILITIES GRANTED
Object Management:	
CREATE [ANY] CLUSTER	Create clusters.
CREATE ANY INDEX	Create any index.
CREATE [ANY] PROCEDURE	Create procedures, functions, or packages.
CREATE [ANY] SEQUENCE	Create sequences.
CREATE [ANY] SNAPSHOT	Create snapshots; must also have CREATE TABLE.
CREATE [PUBLIC] SYNONYM	Create [public] synonyms.
CREATE [ANY] TABLE	Create tables. The user must have a quota for a tablespace or have been granted UNLIMITED TABLESPACE.
CREATE [ANY] TRIGGER	Create triggers.
CREATE [ANY] VIEW	Create views.
ALTER ANY CLUSTER	Alter any cluster.
ALTER ANY INDEX	Alter any index.
ALTER ANY PROCEDURE	Alter any procedure, function, or package.
ALTER ANY SEQUENCE	Alter any sequence.
ALTER ANY SNAPSHOT	Alter any snapshot.
ALTER ANY TABLE	Alter any table. Also gives the user the ability to compile any view in any schema.
ALTER ANY TRIGGER	Enable, disable, or compile any trigger.
DROP ANY CLUSTER	Drop any cluster.
DROP ANY INDEX	Drop any index.
DROP ANY PROCEDURE	Drop any procedure, function, or package.
DROP ANY SEQUENCE	Drop any sequence.
DROP ANY SNAPSHOT	Drop any snapshot.
DROP ANY SYNONYM	Drop any private synonym.
DROP PUBLIC SYNONYM	Drop public synonyms.

TABLE 9-6.   *System-Level Privileges in Oracle7*

PRIVILEGE	CAPABILITIES GRANTED
DROP ANY TRIGGER	Drop any trigger.
DROP ANY VIEW	Drop any view.
BACKUP ANY TABLE	Perform an incremental export. See Chapter 10, "Optimal Backup and Recovery Procedures," for more details.
COMMENT ANY TABLE	Create comments for any table, view, or column.
DROP ANY TABLE	Drop any table.
LOCK ANY TABLE	Lock any table.
SELECT ANY TABLE	Select records from any table, view, or snapshot.
INSERT ANY TABLE	Insert records into any table or view.
UPDATE ANY TABLE	Update records in any table or view.
DELETE ANY TABLE	Delete rows from any table or view, and TRUNCATE any table or cluster.
ALTER SESSION	Alter session parameters.
CREATE SESSION	Connect to the database.
EXECUTE ANY PROCEDURE	Execute any procedure or function, and reference any public package variable.
SELECT ANY SEQUENCE	Select a value from any sequence.
Database Management:	
CREATE [PUBLIC] DATABASE LINK	Create links to other databases.
CREATE PROFILE	Create profiles for database users.
CREATE ROLE	Create roles.
CREATE ROLLBACK SEGMENT	Create rollback segments.
CREATE TABLESPACE	Create tablespaces.
CREATE USER	Create new users (see Table 9-5 for options).
ALTER PROFILE	Modify existing profiles.
ALTER RESOURCE COST	Change the costs of resources specified in the profiles.
ALTER ANY ROLE	Alter any role.

TABLE 9-6. *System-Level Privileges in Oracle7 (continued)*

PRIVILEGE	CAPABILITIES GRANTED
ALTER ROLLBACK SEGMENT	Alter rollback segments.
ALTER TABLESPACE	Alter tablespaces.
ALTER USER	Alter user.
DROP PROFILE	Drop an existing profile.
DROP PUBLIC DATABASE LINK	Drop a public database link.
DROP ANY ROLE	Drop any role.
DROP ROLLBACK SEGMENT	Drop an existing rollback segment.
DROP TABLESPACE	Drop a tablespace.
DROP USER	Drop a user. Append the "CASCADE" keyword if the user owns objects.
ALTER DATABASE	Issue ALTER DATABASE statements.
ALTER SYSTEM	Issue ALTER SYSTEM statements.
ANALYZE ANY	Analyze any table, cluster, or index
AUDIT ANY	Audit any schema object.
AUDIT SYSTEM	Audit system-level operations.
BECOME USER	Become another user; used by Import.
FORCE [ANY] TRANSACTION	Force the commit or rollback of [any] in-doubt distributed transactions in the local database.
GRANT ANY PRIVILEGE	Grant any of these system-level privileges.
GRANT ANY ROLE	Grant any role to a user.
MANAGE TABLESPACE	Manage the status of tablespaces (online/offline and begin backup/end backup states).
RESTRICTED SESSION	Can connect when the database has been started using STARTUP RESTRICT.
UNLIMITED TABLESPACE	Can use an unlimited amount of storage space in any tablespace. This overrides any resource quotas, and cannot be granted to roles.

TABLE 9-6. *System-Level Privileges in Oracle7 (continued)*

The WITH ADMIN OPTION clause is used to pass along to the grantee the ability to grant the privilege to other users.

SQL reference information for these options may be found in Appendix C, "SQL Reference for DBA Commands."

As described in Chapter 5, "Managing the Development Process," system-level privileges can be grouped into roles for different types of users. In the examples in that chapter, roles such as APPLICATION_DEVELOPER and APPLICATION_CREATOR were created. The roles described in that chapter cover almost all of the required user roles.

Several new system-level roles are needed to support DBA activities. The first of them, named OSOPER, is created via the Oracle7 Installer. Table 9-7 lists the system-level privileges granted to this role.

This role is created for use by the Systems Management personnel for the server on which the database resides (the "operators," hence the role's name). It has all of the privileges necessary to perform offline and online backups on the database (see Chapter 10, "Optimal Backup and Recovery Procedures," for information on these backup methods). If Systems Management personnel will also be performing exports of the database, then the EXP_FULL_DATABASE role (which is created with the database) should also be granted to their account.

Using this Oracle7 role avoids a security problem that exists in Oracle Version 6. In Oracle Version 6, performing backup and recovery operations requires the DBA privilege. Since there is no ability to separate system-level privileges (such as SELECT ANY TABLE) from the DBA privilege in Oracle Version 6, anyone who has the ability to back up the database also has the ability to query every table in it. Use of the OSOPER role avoids this problem.

PRIVILEGE

STARTUP

SHUTDOWN

ALTER DATABASE OPEN/MOUNT

ALTER DATABASE BACKUP

ARCHIVE LOG

RECOVER

RESTRICTED SESSION

TABLE 9-7. *System-Level Privileges for the OSOPER Role.*

If you choose not to install the OSOPER role via the Installer, you still may create a system-level role with these privileges, with whatever role name you choose, at a later date.

The account creation process may also be reexamined. Like the database backups process, DBA-level privileges are required to perform these functions. However, as seen from the privileges listed in Table 9-6, it is possible to select out a subset of privileges that are needed to create new users.

In Oracle7, a new system-level role called ACCOUNT_CREATOR can be created. It will only be able to create users; it will not be able to perform any other DBA-level commands. The commands that create this role are shown in the following listing.

```
CREATE ROLE application_creator;
GRANT CREATE SESSION, CREATE USER TO application_creator;
```

The first command in this listing creates a role called APPLICATION_CREATOR. The second command grants that role the ability to log in (CREATE SESSION) and create new accounts (CREATE USER). This role can then be granted to a centralized help desk, which will then be able to coordinate the creation of all new accounts.

Centralizing account creation helps to ensure that proper authorization procedures are followed when accounts are requested. The flexibility of system-level privileges and roles in Oracle7 allows this capability to be given to a user—in this case, a help desk—without also giving that user the ability to query data from the database.

Oracle7 includes three other system-level roles: CONNECT, RESOURCE, and DBA. These are intended for upward compatibility with Oracle Version 6 commands—specifically, they allow Oracle Version 6 users to be imported into Oracle7 databases.

The privileges associated with those roles are listed in Table 9-8.

ROLE	PRIVILEGES
CONNECT	ALTER SESSION, CREATE SESSION, CREATE CLUSTER, CREATE TABLE, CREATE VIEW, CREATE SYNONYM, CREATE SEQUENCE, CREATE DATABASE LINK
RESOURCE	CREATE CLUSTER, CREATE TABLE, CREATE PROCEDURE, CREATE SEQUENCE, CREATE TRIGGER
DBA	All system-level privileges WITH ADMIN OPTION

TABLE 9-8. *Privileges of the CONNECT, RESOURCE, and DBA Roles in Oracle7*

User Profiles

In Oracle7 databases, profiles can be used to place limits on the amount of system and database resources available to a user. If no profiles are created in a database, then the default profile, which specifies unlimited resources for all users, will be used.

The resources that can be limited via profiles are listed in Table 9-9.

As shown in Table 9-9, a number of resources may be limited for Oracle7 users. However, all of these restrictions are *reactive*; no action takes place until the user has exceeded the resource limit. Thus, profiles will not be of much assistance in preventing runaway queries from using large amounts of system resources before they reach their defined limit. Once the limit is reached, the query will be stopped.

RESOURCE	DESCRIPTION
SESSIONS_PER_USER	The number of concurrent sessions a user can have in an instance.
CPU_PER_SESSION	The CPU time, in hundredths of seconds, that a session can use.
CPU_PER_CALL	The CPU time, in hundredths of seconds, that a parse, execute, or fetch can use.
CONNECT_TIME	The number of minutes a session can be connected to the database.
IDLE_TIME	The number of minutes a session can be connected to the database without being actively used.
LOGICAL_READS_PER_SESSION	The number of data blocks that can be read in a session.
LOGICAL_READS_PER_CALL	The number of data blocks that can be read during a parse, execute, or fetch.
PRIVATE_SGA	The amount of private space a session can allocate in the SGA's Shared SQL Pool.
COMPOSITE LIMIT	The total resource cost for the session, in service unit. Costs for CPU_PER_SESSION, CONNECT_TIME, LOGICAL_READS_PER_SESSION, and PRIVATE_SGA factor into this calculation; they are set via the ALTER RESOURCE COST command.

TABLE 9-9. *Resources Limited by Profiles in Oracle7*

Profiles are created via the CREATE PROFILE command. The ALTER PROFILE command, shown in the following example, is used to modify existing profiles. In this example, the DEFAULT profile for the database is altered to allow a maximum idle time of one hour.

```
ALTER PROFILE DEFAULT
IDLE_TIME 60;
```

In general, the default profile should be used for all standard users; users who have exceptional requirements should have specialized profiles.

Tying Database Accounts to Host Accounts

Users are allowed to access a database once they have entered a valid username and password for that database. However, it is possible to take advantage of the operating system to provide an additional level of user authentication.

As in Oracle Version 6, a database account may be paired with an operating system account on the same server. The two account names will differ only in the prefix of the database account name. In Oracle7, the prefix defaults to "OPS$" but can be set to another value via the OS_AUTHENT_PREFIX parameter of the database's INIT.ORA file. This prefix can even be set to a null string, "", so that no prefix will be used.

For example, consider an operating system account named FARMER. The matching database account name for this user is OPS$FARMER. When the FARMER user is logged into his operating system account, he can access his OPS$FARMER account without specifying a password, as shown in the following listing.

```
> sqlplus /
```

The "/" takes the place of the username/password combination that would normally be required for access.

Accounts may be created with passwords. Considering the OPS$FARMER account again, its creation command would be in the following format.

```
CREATE USER ops$farmer
IDENTIFIED BY some_password
DEFAULT TABLESPACE users
TEMPORARY TABLESPACE temp;
```

Even though the password will not be used, it still may be specified. Because of this, it is possible to access the OPS$FARMER database account from a different operating system account if you know the password for the database account. The following listing shows a sample connection to the OPS$FARMER account from a different operating system account.

```
> sqlplus ops$farmer/some_password
```

There are two ways around this problem in Oracle7. First, you can create the account without a specific password, using the IDENTIFIED EXTERNALLY clause, as shown in the following listing. This clause bypasses the need for an explicit password for the account, while keeping the connection between the host account name and the database account name.

```
CREATE USER OPS$FARMER
IDENTIFIED EXTERNALLY
DEFAULT TABLESPACE users
TEMPORARY TABLESPACE temp;
```

When this clause is used, it forces the database to validate the operating system account being used to access the database. The operating system account name and the database account name must be identical (except for the database account name prefix).

The second option is to create the account with an impossible password. This method, described in the "Setting Impossible Passwords" section of this chapter, prevents the user from logging into the database account other than through the operating system account associated with it.

Password Protection

Both accounts and roles can be protected via passwords. Passwords for both are set when they are created, and may be modified via ALTER commands.

In Oracle7, the password for an account is set via the CREATE USER command, as shown in the following listing. In this example, the THUMPER account is created with an initial password of RABBIT.

```
CREATE USER thumper
IDENTIFIED BY rabbit;
```

Passwords for accounts should be changed via the ALTER USER command. A sample ALTER USER command is shown in the following listing.

```
ALTER USER thumper IDENTIFIED BY newpassword;
```

Passwords for Oracle7 roles are set at the time the role is created, via the CREATE ROLE command. It is not necessary to set a password for a role; if one is specified, then the password must be entered when the role is enabled by the user.

```
CREATE ROLE account_creator IDENTIFIED BY helpdesk_only;
```

The ALTER ROLE command is used to change the password associated with roles. Like user passwords, roles can also be IDENTIFIED EXTERNALLY, thereby enforcing a link between the host account name and the role name. Unlike user accounts, it is possible to have roles with no passwords (the default). It is also possible to remove a password from a role via the NOT IDENTIFIED clause, as shown in the following example.

```
ALTER ROLE account_creator NOT IDENTIFIED;
```

After this command has been executed, the "account_creator" role will not be password-protected.

Managing Privileges

Privileges give users access to data that they do not own. In Oracle7, *roles*—groups of privileges—are available to ease the administration of privileges. Explicit privileges are still available in Oracle7, and are in fact necessary in some circumstances.

Privileges are created via the GRANT command, and are recorded in the data dictionary. Access to tables, views, sequences—as well as synonyms for these—plus the ability to execute procedures, functions, packages, and snapshots can be granted to Oracle7 users. The privileges that may be granted on objects are listed in Table 9-10.

The WITH GRANT OPTION clause is used to pass along to the grantee the ability to make further grants on the base table. The following listing from SQL*Plus shows an example of this. In this example, the user named THUMPER grants the user named MCGREGOR both SELECT and partial UPDATE access on a table called EMPLOYEE, WITH GRANT OPTION. This user then grants one of these privileges to another user (named JFISHER).

```
GRANT SELECT, UPDATE (employee_name, address)
ON employee TO mcgregor
WITH GRANT OPTION;

CONNECT mcgregor/farmer
GRANT SELECT ON thumper.employee TO jfisher;
```

PRIVILEGE	CAPABILITIES GRANTED
SELECT	Can query the object.
INSERT	Can insert records into the table or view. In Oracle7, this privilege may be granted for specific columns in the table or view.
UPDATE	Can update records in the table or view. This privilege may be granted for specific columns in the table or view.
DELETE	Can delete records from the table or view.
ALTER	Can alter the table or sequence.
INDEX	Can create indexes on the table.
REFERENCES	Can create foreign keys that reference the table.
EXECUTE	Oracle7 only. Can execute the procedure, package, or function.

TABLE 9-10.   *Available Privileges in Oracle7*

Granting the privileges to PUBLIC makes them available to all users in the database.

The management of privileges can quickly become a time-consuming task. Each user must be granted the appropriate privileges for each object in a database application. Consider an application that has 20 tables and 30 users; 600 privileges (20 tables times 30 users) must be managed.

With the advent of roles in Oracle7, the management of such privileges became much easier. Roles are groups of privileges; the roles are then granted to users, greatly simplifying the privilege management process.

The following listing shows an example of the usage of roles. In this example, two roles are created. The first, APPLICATION_USER, is given the system-level privilege CREATE SESSION; a user who has been granted this role will be able to log into the database. The second role, DATA_ENTRY_CLERK, is granted privileges on tables.

```
CREATE ROLE application_user;
GRANT create session TO application_user;

CREATE ROLE data_entry_clerk;
GRANT SELECT, INSERT ON thumper.employee TO data_entry_clerk;
GRANT SELECT, INSERT ON thumper.time_cards TO data_entry_clerk;
GRANT SELECT, INSERT ON thumper.department TO data_entry_clerk;
```

Roles can be granted to other roles. For example, the APPLICATION_USER role can be granted to the DATA_ENTRY_CLERK role, as shown in this example.

```
GRANT application_user TO data_entry_clerk;
```

The role can then be granted to a user. This role can be dynamically enabled and disabled during the user's session.

```
GRANT data_entry_clerk TO mcgregor;
```

Roles and system privileges (such as CREATE TABLE) may be granted to users with the privilege to pass them on to other users. For these types of grants, the WITH ADMIN OPTION clause is used. In the following listing, the DATA_ENTRY_CLERK role created earlier is granted to a user (BPOTTER), along with the privilege to administer the role.

```
GRANT data_entry_clerk TO bpotter WITH ADMIN OPTION;
```

Given this privilege, the user BPOTTER can now grant and revoke the role to and from other users, and can drop the role as well.

In Oracle7, users who have table privileges via roles cannot create views based on those tables. This is because the grants made via a role are only valid while the user is logged in and the role is enabled. Thus, creation of views by non-owners requires explicit privileges on the tables.

The dynamic nature of roles is very useful for restricting users' privileges. If a role is enabled when a user starts an application (via the SET ROLE command), and then disabled upon leaving the application, then the user cannot take advantage of the role's privileges except when using the application.

For example, when MCGREGOR logs into an application, the command

```
SET ROLE data_entry_clerk;
```

may be executed. When this user leaves the application, the command

```
SET ROLE NONE;
```

will disable any privileges that had been granted via roles.

Revoking privileges and roles is done via the REVOKE command. You may either revoke some of a user's privileges (by explicitly listing them) or all of the user's privileges (via the ALL keyword). In the following example, a specific privilege is revoked for the EMPLOYEE table from one user, while another user's privileges are completely revoked.

```
REVOKE DELETE ON employee FROM peter;
REVOKE ALL ON employee FROM mcgregor;
```

In the following example, the role ACCOUNT_CREATOR is revoked from the user account named HELPDESK.

```
REVOKE account_creator FROM helpdesk;
```

Because user accounts in Oracle7 can be completely deleted via the

```
DROP USER username CASCADE;
```

command, privilege cleanup of deleted accounts has been virtually eliminated. REVOKE commands in Oracle7 are thus used mostly when users change status, or when applications move from one environment (such as Acceptance Test) to another (such as Production).

Listing Grants

Information about privileges that have been granted is stored in the data dictionary. This data is accessible via the data dictionary views.

In Oracle7, the data dictionary views listed in Table 9-11 can be used to list the privileges that have been granted within the database. User-level views are also available.

DATA DICTIONARY VIEW	CONTENTS
DBA_ROLES	Names of roles and their password status
DBA_ROLE_PRIVS	Users who have been granted roles
DBA_SYS_PRIVS	Users who have been granted system privileges
DBA_TAB_PRIVS	Users who have been granted privileges on objects
DBA_COL_PRIVS	Users who have been granted privileges on columns of tables
ROLE_ROLE_PRIVS	Roles that have been granted to other roles
ROLE_SYS_PRIVS	System privileges that have been granted to roles
ROLE_TAB_PRIVS	Table privileges that have been granted to roles

TABLE 9-11.   *DBA Views of Privileges in Oracle7*

For example, you may wish to display which system privileges have been granted to which roles. In that case, the following query would display that information.

```
SELECT
    role,              /*Name of the role*/
    privilege,         /*System privilege*/
    admin_option       /*Was ADMIN OPTION granted?*/
FROM role_sys_privs;
```

To retrieve table grants for users, you now have to look for two types of grants: explicit grants of privileges to users, and those that are granted via roles. To view the grants made via explicit grants, query the DBA_TAB_PRIVS view, as shown in the following listing.

```
SELECT
    grantee,           /*Recipient of the grant*/
    owner,             /*Owner of the object*/
    table_name,        /*Name of the object*/
    grantor,           /*User who made the grant*/
    privilege,         /*Privilege granted*/
    grantable          /*Was ADMIN OPTION granted?*/
FROM dba_tab_privs;
```

To view the table privileges granted via a role, find the user's records in DBA_ROLE_PRIVS and compare those to the role's table privileges (which are listed in ROLE_TAB_PRIVS).

```
SELECT
    dba_role_privs.grantee,          /*Recipient of the grant*/
    role_tab_privs.owner,            /*Owner of the object*/
    role_tab_privs.table_name,       /*Name of the object*/
    role_tab_privs.privilege,        /*Privilege granted*/
    role_tab_privs.grantable         /*Was ADMIN OPTION granted?*/
FROM dba_role_privs, role_tab_privs
WHERE dba_role_privs.granted_role = role_tab_privs.role
and dba_role_privs.grantee = 'some username';
```

This query will retrieve the role-granted table privileges for a particular user.

Limiting Available Commands: Product User Profiles

Within SQL*Plus, an additional level of security is provided—individual commands may be disabled for specific users. That way, users with the UPDATE privilege on a table can be prevented from using the SQL*Plus command-line interface to update the table in an uncontrolled fashion.

This capability allows DBAs to prevent users from accessing the operating system from within SQL*Plus (via the HOST command). This is useful when an application includes an option to access SQL*Plus, but you do not want the users to have access to the operating system.

In addition to revoking users' ability to use the HOST command from within SQL*Plus, you may also revoke their use of the CONNECT command. That will force them to stay within their own accounts. The following listing shows the results of these commands when this level of security is in place.

```
SQL> host
invalid command: host
SQL> connect system/manager
invalid command: connect
```

In each case, the "invalid command" message is returned. The user must remain in his or her own account.

To create this level of security, the *Product User Profile* tables must be created. The script for creating them is called pupbld.sql, and it is found in the $ORACLE_HOME/sqlplus/admin directory. This script creates several tables and views and should be run from within the SYSTEM account.

For SQL*Plus, the most important table is called PRODUCT_USER_PROFILE. The key columns for security purposes are listed in Table 9-12. Insert records into this table to create the desired level of security.

Roles can also be disabled via this table. To disable a role, set the ATTRIBUTE column to "ROLES", and place the role name in the CHAR_VALUE column. This is usually done in coordination with the disabling of the SET command (see Table 9-12).

Password Encryption and Trickery

Knowing how the database encrypts and sets passwords enables DBAs to perform a number of otherwise impossible tasks. These include the setting of impossible passwords and the ability to become other users, as described in the following sections.

COLUMN NAME	DESCRIPTION
PRODUCT	Set to "SQL*Plus". The name must be in mixed case, as shown here.
USERID	Username, in uppercase, for users whose commands are being disabled. The "%" wildcard can be used to specify multiple users. An entry for "%" used by itself will apply to all users.
ATTRIBUTE	The name, in uppercase, of the command being disabled. Disabling the "SET" command in SQL*Plus also disables SET ROLE and SET TRANSACTION.
CHAR_VALUE	Set to "DISABLED" (all capitals).

TABLE 9-12.   *Columns in PRODUCT_USER_PROFILE*

How Passwords Are Stored

When a password is specified for a user account or a role, the database stores the *encrypted* version of that password in the data dictionary. Setting the same password for two different accounts will result in different encryptions. For all passwords, the encrypted value is 16 characters long, and is comprised of numbers and capital letters.

How are passwords validated? When a password is entered during a user validation, that password is encrypted, and the encryption that is generated is compared to the one in the data dictionary for that account. If they match, then the password is correct and the authorization succeeds.

Setting Impossible Passwords

Knowing how the database stores passwords is important, because it adds new options to account security. What would happen if you could specify the encryption of a password, rather than the password itself? And what if the encryption you generated did not follow the format rules for encrypted passwords? The result would be an account that could never be logged into, since no password could generate the invalid encryption.

Consider the accounts and encrypted passwords selected by the following query. The query selects the USERNAME and PASSWORD fields from the DBA_USERS view. Output from the query is shown in Figure 9-1.

```
Username          Password
----------------  ---------------------------
MCGREGOR          1A2DD3CCEE354DFA
THUMPER           F3DE41CBB3AB4452
OPS$FARMER        4FF2FF1CBDE11332
```

FIGURE 9-1. *Sample Output from Encrypted Password Query*

```
SELECT
      username,           /*Username*/
      password            /*Encrypted password*/
FROM dba_users
WHERE username in ('MCGREGOR','THUMPER','OPS$FARMER');
```

Note that each of the encrypted passwords in Figure 9-1 is 16 characters in length.

Since the password is not stored in the data dictionary—but its encryption is—how does Import know what the passwords are? After all, when a Full Import is done from an export dump file, the passwords are imported as well.

There are two ways that Import could do this. It could insert the encrypted values directly into the data dictionary tables. However, that would be inconsistent with the way Import works. Instead, it executes an undocumented version of the GRANT CONNECT and CREATE USER commands. For an Oracle7 database, importing the MCGREGOR user from the database shown in the last listing would generate the following CREATE USER command:

```
CREATE USER mcgregor IDENTIFIED BY VALUES '1A2DD3CCEE354DFA';
```

In other words, Import uses the VALUES clause within the IDENTIFIED BY clause to specify the encrypted password for the user it is creating.

Import shouldn't get to have all the fun. You can use this same command to set an encryption for any account. As long as the encryption you set violates the encryption rules (16 characters, all capitals), it will be impossible to match during user authentication. The result will be an account that is only accessible from the correct operating system account on the server. In the following listing, the encryption is set to the phrase "no way". The DBA_USERS view is then requeried. The output from that query is shown in Figure 9-2.

```
ALTER USER ops$farmer IDENTIFIED BY VALUES 'no way';

SELECT
      username,             /*Username*/
      password              /*Encrypted password*/
FROM dba_users
WHERE username in ('MCGREGOR','THUMPER','OPS$FARMER');
```

It is now impossible to access the OPS$FARMER account except via the FARMER account on the server, and even then it is only accessible via the "/" clause. This capability is also useful for locking non-OPS$ accounts that should never be logged into directly, such as SYS.

Becoming Another User

Since the encrypted passwords can be set, it is possible to temporarily take over any account and then set it back to its original password. This allows you to become another user; this is most useful when testing applications or troubleshooting problems in Production.

Temporarily becoming another user requires going through the following steps:

1. Query DBA_USERS to determine the current encrypted password for the account.

2. Generate the ALTER USER command that will be needed to reset the encrypted password to its current value after you are done.

3. Spool the ALTER USER command to a file.

4. Change the user's password.

5. Access the user's account and perform your testing.

6. When the testing is complete, run the file containing the ALTER USER command to reset the user's encrypted password to its original value.

```
  Username        Password
  ----------      ----------------
  MCGREGOR        1A2DD3CCEE354DFA
  THUMPER         F3DE41CBB3AB4452
  OPS$FARMER      no way
```

FIGURE 9-2. *Sample Output showing modified Encryption.*

This process is automated via the following SQL*Plus script. This script automatically generates the command necessary to reset the user's account once your testing is complete.

```
REM*  become_another_user.sql
REM*
REM*  This script is valid for both Oracle7 and Oracle Version 6.
REM*  It generates the commands necessary to allow you to
REM*  temporarily become another user.
REM*
REM*  It MUST be run from a DBA account.
REM*
REM*  Input variables: The username of the account to be taken
REM*  over.
REM*
REM*  Steps 1, 2, and 3: Query DBA_USERS. Generate the ALTER USER
REM*  command that will be necessary to reset the password to its
REM*  present value.
REM*
set pagesize 0 feedback off verify off echo off termout off
REM*
REM*  Create a file called reset.sql to hold the commands
REM*  generated
REM*
spool reset.sql
REM*
REM*  Select the encrypted password from DBA_USERS.
REM*
SELECT 'alter user &&1 identified by values '||''''||
password||''''||';'
FROM dba_users WHERE username = upper('&&1');

prompt 'host rm -f reset.sql'
prompt 'exit'
spool off
exit
```

NOTE
In the SELECT statement, there are two sets of four single quotes.

This script generates as its output a script called reset.sql. This file will have three lines in it. The first line will contain the ALTER USER command, with the VALUES clause followed by the encrypted password. The second line will contain a host command that deletes the reset.sql file (since it will not be needed after it is used in Step 6). The third line contains an EXIT command to leave SQL*Plus. A sample reset.sql file is shown here:

```
alter user MCGREGOR identified by values '1A2DD3CCEE354DFA';
host rm -f reset.sql
exit
```

The "rm -f" command in the second line should be replaced by the appropriate file deletion command for your operating system.

You may now proceed with Steps 4 and 5, which involve changing the user's password (via the ALTER USER command), and accessing the account. These actions are shown in the following listing.

```
ALTER USER mcgregor IDENTIFIED BY my_turn;
CONNECT mcgregor/my_turn
```

You will now be logged into the MCGREGOR account. When you have completed your testing, log into SQL*Plus and run the reset.sql script shown above.

```
sqlplus system/manager @reset
```

If you are testing multiple accounts simultaneously, you may wish to embed the username in the "reset.sql" file name; otherwise, the first "reset.sql" file may be overwritten by later versions. If you are doing this for OPS$ accounts, be careful, since "$" is a special character in some operating systems (such as UNIX).

The account will now be reset to its original encrypted password—and thus its original password. The testing of the account took place without you needing to know what its password was, and without its password being destroyed.

Auditing

The database has the ability to audit all actions that take place within it. In Oracle Version 6, audit records are written to a table named SYS.AUD$ in the data dictionary; in Oracle7, these records may be written to either the SYS.AUD$ or the operating system's audit trail. The ability to use the operating system's audit trail is operating system-dependent.

Three different types of actions may be audited: login attempts, object accesses, and database actions. Each of these action types will be described in the following sections. When performing audits, the database's default functionality is to record both successful and unsuccessful commands; this may be modified when each audit type is set up.

To enable auditing in a database, the INIT.ORA file for the database must contain an entry for the AUDIT_TRAIL parameter. There are different values of this parameter for Oracle7 and Oracle Version 6. The applicable values for Oracle Version 6 are listed in Table 9-13.

The AUDIT_TRAIL values for Oracle7 are listed in Table 9-14. The values TRUE and FALSE are supported for backward compatibility with Oracle Version 6. TRUE is equivalent to DB, and FALSE is equivalent to NONE.

The AUDIT commands described in the following sections can be issued regardless of the setting of the AUDIT_TRAIL parameter. They will not be activated unless the database is started using an INIT.ORA AUDIT_TRAIL value that enables auditing.

If you elect to store the audit records in the SYS.AUD$ table, then that table's records should be periodically archived, and the table should then be TRUNCATE'd. Since it is in the data dictionary, this table is in the SYSTEM tablespace, and may cause space problems if its records are not periodically cleaned out.

AUDIT_TRAIL VALUE	DESCRIPTION
true	Enables auditing
false	Disables auditing

TABLE 9-13. *AUDIT_TRAIL Values for Oracle Version 6*

AUDIT_TRAIL VALUE	DESCRIPTION
NONE	Disables auditing
DB	Enables auditing, writing to the SYS.AUD$ table
OS	Enables auditing, writing to the operating system's audit trail (operating system-dependent)

TABLE 9-14. *AUDIT_TRAIL Values for Oracle7*

Login Audits

Every attempt to connect to the database can be audited. The command to begin auditing of login attempts is

```
AUDIT SESSION;
```

To audit only those connection attempts that result in successes or failures, use the commands shown in the following listing.

```
AUDIT SESSION WHENEVER SUCCESSFUL;
AUDIT SESSION WHENEVER NOT SUCCESSFUL;
```

If the audit records are stored in the SYS.AUD$ table, then they may be viewed via the DBA_AUDIT_SESSION (Oracle7) or DBA_AUDIT_CONNECT (Oracle Version 6) views.

The query shown in the following listing retrieves login audit records from the Oracle7 DBA_AUDIT_SESSION view. It lists the operating system account that was used ("OS_USERNAME"), the Oracle account name ("USERNAME"), and the terminal ID that was used ("TERMINAL"). The RETURNCODE column is evaluated: if it is 0, then the connection attempt succeeded; otherwise, two common error numbers are checked to determine the cause of the failure. The login and logoff times are also displayed.

```
SELECT
   os_username,            /*Operating system username used.*/
   username,               /*Oracle username of the account used.*/
   terminal,               /*Terminal ID used.*/
   decode(returncode,'0','Connected',
              '1005','FailedNull',
              '1017','Failed',returncode),     /*Failure check*/
   to_char(timestamp,'DD-MON-YY HH24:MI:SS'),  /*Login time*/
   to_char(logoff_time,'DD-MON-YY HH24:MI:SS') /*Logoff time*/
FROM dba_audit_session;
```

The error numbers that are checked are ORA-1005 and ORA-1017. These two error codes cover most of the login errors that occur. ORA-1005 is returned when a user enters a username but no password. ORA-1017 is returned when a user enters an invalid password. These error code numbers are the same for both Oracle Version 6 and Oracle7; the *Error Codes and Messages Manual* for new versions of the database should be checked before running this query, to make sure the meanings of these codes have not changed.

To disable session auditing, use the NOAUDIT command, as shown in this example.

```
NOAUDIT SESSION;
```

Action Audits

Any action affecting a database object—such as a table, database link, tablespace, synonym, rollback segment, user, or index—can be audited. The possible actions—such as CREATE, ALTER, and DROP—that can affect those objects can be grouped together during auditing. This reduces the amount of administrative effort necessary to establish and maintain the audit settings.

In Oracle7, all of the system-level commands can be audited. In Oracle Version 6, the only options are AUDIT CONNECT (which the AUDIT SESSION command in the last section accomplished), AUDIT RESOURCE, and AUDIT DBA. AUDIT RESOURCE groups together all those commands that require the RESOURCE privilege, such as CREATE TABLE. Oracle7 allows the Oracle Version 6 commands to be used, but it is preferable to specify the exact commands you are interested in, in order to avoid flooding the audit trail with noncritical entries.

For example, to audit all commands that affect roles, enter the command

```
AUDIT ROLE;
```

To disable this setting, enter the command

```
NOAUDIT ROLE;
```

The SQL command groupings for Oracle7 auditing are listed in Table 9-15. Each group can be used to audit all of the SQL commands that affect it (see Table 9-6 for a detailed listing of these commands). For example, the AUDIT ROLE command shown earlier will audit CREATE ROLE, ALTER ROLE, DROP ROLE, and SET ROLE commands.

Each action that can be audited is assigned a numeric code within the database. These codes are accessible via the AUDIT_ACTIONS view. The following query will display the available action codes for your database.

```
SELECT
      action,          /*Action code.*/
      name             /*Name of the action, such as ALTER USER.*/
FROM audit_actions;
```

Once the action code is known, the DBA_AUDIT_OBJECT view can be used to determine how an object was affected by the action. The query shown in the following listing retrieves login audit records from the Oracle7 DBA_AUDIT_OBJECT view. It lists the operating system account that was used ("OS_USERNAME"), the Oracle account name ("USERNAME"), and the terminal ID that was used ("TERMINAL"). The object owner ("OWNER") and name ("OBJ_NAME") are selected, along with the action code ("ACTION_NAME") for the action performed. The RETURNCODE column is evaluated: if it is 0, then the connection attempt succeeded; otherwise, the error number is reported. The login and logoff times are also displayed.

```
SELECT
   os_username,             /*Operating system username used.*/
   username,                /*Oracle username of the account used.*/
   terminal,                /*Terminal ID used.*/
   owner,                   /*Owner of the affected object.*/
   obj_name,                /*Name of the affected object.*/
   action_name,             /*Numeric code for the action.*/
   decode(returncode,'0','Success',returncode),   /*Failure check*/
   to_char(timestamp,'DD-MON-YY HH24:MI:SS')      /*Time stamp*/
   FROM dba_audit_object;
```

In Oracle7, you can also specify particular users to audit, using the BY [USERNAME] clause of the AUDIT command, as shown in the following listing. In this example, all UPDATE actions by the user MCGREGOR will be audited.

```
AUDIT UPDATE TABLE BY mcgregor;
```

SQL STATEMENT GROUP	AUDITED COMMANDS
CLUSTER	All statements affecting clusters.
DATABASE LINK	All statements affecting database links.
EXISTS	All statements that fail because an object already exists in the database; this is only available with Trusted Oracle.
INDEX	All statements affecting indexes.
NOT EXISTS	All statements that fail because a specified object does not exist.
PROCEDURE	All statements affecting procedures.
PROFILE	All statements affecting profiles.
PUBLIC DATABASE LINK	All statements affecting public database links.
PUBLIC SYNONYM	All statements affecting public synonyms.
ROLE	All statements affecting roles.
ROLLBACK SEGMENT	All statements affecting rollback segments.
SEQUENCE	All statements affecting sequences.
SESSION	All database logins.
SYNONYM	All statements affecting synonyms.
SYSTEM AUDIT	All AUDIT and NOAUDIT statements.
SYSTEM GRANT	All GRANT and REVOKE commands affecting system privileges and roles.
TABLE	All statements affecting tables.
TABLESPACE	All statements affecting tablespaces.
TRIGGER	All statments affecting triggers, including ALTER TABLE commands that enable or disable triggers.
USER	All statements affecting user accounts.
VIEW	All statements affecting views.

TABLE 9-15. *SQL AUDIT Options for Oracle7*

Object Audits

In addition to system-level actions on objects, data manipulation actions to objects can be audited. These may include auditing SELECT, INSERT, UPDATE, and DELETE operations against tables. Actions of this type are audited in a manner that is very similar to the Action Audits described in the previous section. The only difference is the addition of a new clause in the AUDIT command.

The additional clause for Object Audits is the BY SESSION or BY ACCESS clause. This specifies whether an audit record should be written once for each session (BY SESSION) or once for each time an object is accessed (BY ACCESS). For example, if a user executed four different UPDATE statements against the same table, then auditing BY ACCESS would result in four audit records being written—one for each table access. On the other hand, auditing the same situation BY SESSION would result in only one audit record being written.

Auditing BY ACCESS can therefore dramatically increase the rate at which audit records are written. It is generally used on a limited basis, to gauge the number of separate actions taking place during a specific time interval; when that testing is done, the auditing should be reverted to BY SESSION status.

Examples of these options are shown in the following listing. In the first command, all INSERT commands against the EMPLOYEE table are audited. In the second command, every command that affects the TIME_CARDS table is audited. In the third command, all DELETE operations against the DEPARTMENT table are audited, on a per session basis.

```
AUDIT INSERT ON thumper.employee;
AUDIT ALL ON thumper.time_cards;
AUDIT DELETE ON thumper.department BY SESSION;
```

The resulting audit records can be viewed via the query against the DBA_AUDIT_OBJECT view shown in the previous section.

Protecting the Audit Trail

Since the database audit trail table, SYS.AUD$, is stored within the database, any audit records that are written there must be protected. Otherwise, a user may attempt to delete his or her audit trail records after attempting unauthorized actions within the database.

The Oracle7 capability to write audit records to the operating system audit trail helps to get around this problem by storing the records external to the database. However, this option is not available in Oracle Version 6, and is not available for all operating systems for Oracle7.

If you must store the audit trail information in SYS.AUD$, then you *must* protect that table. First, audit actions against the table via the following command.

```
AUDIT ALL ON SYS.AUD$ BY ACCESS;
```

If any actions are made against the SYS.AUD$ table (inserts generated via audits of other tables don't count), then those actions will be recorded in the audit trail. Not only that, but actions against SYS.AUD$ can only be deleted by users who have the ability to CONNECT INTERNAL (i.e., are in the DBA group). Any actions made while connected as INTERNAL are automatically written to the audit trail.

Wherever possible, coordinate your database auditing and your operating system auditing. This will make it easier to track problems and coordinate security policies across the two environments. Since the system managers will most likely not want to see reams of audit trail entries, it also forces the DBA to analyze exactly which actions are the most critical to audit. Your aim should be to have an audit trail in which every record is significant. If it is not, then use the commands given in this chapter to modify the auditing options to reflect the true actions of interest.

Security in a Distributed Environment

Opening up a database to access from other servers also opens it up to potential security threats from those servers. Since such access comes via SQL*Net, modifications to SQL*Net parameters can provide most of the protection against unauthorized remote access.

Remote Account Access

Tying database accounts to server accounts helps the users on the local server to access the database with less effort. However, it also opens up the database to potential access from users on other servers.

The "OPS$" accounts, common to both Oracle Version 6 and Oracle7, provide a link between a host account name on the local server and a database account name. When this server is connected to a network, the question of what constitutes a "host account name" becomes clouded.

If a user on a remote server has the same account name as a user on the local server, then that remote user will be able to access the OPS$ account owned by the local user. Consider the OPS$FARMER user from earlier in this chapter. It is directly related to an account on the local server named FARMER. This allows a user *from the local server* to enter the command

```
> sqlplus /
```

and gain immediate access to the database.

But what it there was another user named FARMER, on a remote server? That user could access that same account on the local server, simply by specifying the proper SQL*Net connect string. In this case, assume that that local server is named "LOCAL", and that the instance ID is "LOC". If the TCP/IP protocol is used, then the SQL*Net V1 connect string to this database is 't:local:loc'.

This connect string is valid from *any* server. That means that the *remote* FARMER user can access the *local* OPS$FARMER account by entering the command

```
> sqlplus /@t:local:loc
```

This command specifies a connection to the OPS$ account associated with the account name being used, in the LOC database on the LOCAL server.

There are two problems that contribute to this security hole. First, SQL*Net is allowing an OPS$ connection across the network—that problem will be resolved in the next section. Second, different users have the same account name on different servers. The only way to resolve that is to have account names be unique across the entire network domain, not just for each server.

A second, related problem deals with DBA access across networked servers. If a user is a DBA on one server, then he or she has the ability to use the CONNECT INTERNAL command from within SQLDBA. A DBA on a *remote* server can also CONNECT INTERNAL to the *local* server if the TWO_TASK variable is used to point to the local database. This, in turn, gives that DBA full control over the local database.

Consider again the database identified by the SQL*NET V1 connect string 't:local:loc'. The remote DBA can set the TWO_TASK variable to be equal to this string. Full access to the local database will then be available. This is shown in the following listing.

```
> TWO_TASK=t:local:loc; export TWO_TASK
> sqldba lmode=y
SQLDBA> connect internal
```

In this example, the DBA on the remote first set the TWO_TASK variable equal to the chosen connect string, then used the *export* command (a UNIX Korn shell command that saves variable settings) to save the value of the TWO_TASK variable. The DBA then went into SQLDBA and was able to connect to the local database.

There are two sources of this problem as well. First, SQL*Net can allow DBA logins across servers—that problem will also be resolved in the next section. Second, when a server becomes networked, its administration becomes networked as well. Failing to address this and coordinate DBA activities across all servers may result in the rogue activity shown in these examples.

SQL*Net Settings

It is possible to close both of the security problems described in the last section via SQL*Net's startup parameters. The *opsoff* parameter disables access to OPS$ accounts for *remote* users; this access is still available to users on local server.

The *dbaoff* parameter, when used with the opsoff parameter, disables remote DBA access to local databases. Both of these parameters can be set when SQL*Net is started via the following command.

```
> orasrv dbaoff opsoff
```

See Chapter 15, "SQL*Net V1 and V2," and Chapter 16, "Networking in UNIX," for further information and options for SQL*Net.

CHAPTER 10

Optimal Backup and Recovery Procedures

The sight of a performer walking on a tightrope—untethered, unguarded, unprotected from a great fall—can be a fascinating sight. Every step must be perfect, each movement in unison with others to maintain a delicate balance.

Having a safety net in place beneath the performer makes the sight less spectacular somehow. And when the performer is held in place by ropes and a harness, the attraction is reduced even further until the audience turns away completely, looking for impending doom elsewhere.

An unprotected database is also a sight that will draw attention from thrill-seeking spectators. Fortunately, there are procedures that can be put in place to protect an Oracle database. These include both logical and physical backups, both of which have a number of options available. This chapter will not detail every possible option and recovery scenario; Oracle's documentation has already accomplished that. Rather, the focus will be on using the options in the most effective manner possible. You will see how to best integrate the available backup procedures with each other and with the operating system backups. Differences between the backup options in Oracle7 and Oracle Version 6 will also be highlighted.

When the system is in place, the recoverability of the database will be dependable—and while this may be rather boring to your spectators, a strong safety net is needed for every database.

Capabilities

There are three standard methods of backing up an Oracle database: *exports, cold backups*, and *hot (ARCHIVELOG) backups*. An export is a *logical* backup of the database; the other two backup methods are *physical* file backups. All three of these work with both Oracle Version 6 and Oracle7. There are differences between the two versions for the detailed implementation of these procedures, but the major capabilities are identical.

In the following sections, you will see each of these options fully described, with both Oracle Version 6 and Oracle7 options provided.

Logical Backups

A *logical backup* of the database involves reading a set of database records and writing them to a file. These records are read independent of their physical location. In Oracle, the *Export* utility is used to perform this type of database backup. To recover using the file generated from an export, Oracle's *Import* utility is used.

Export

Oracle's *Export* utility reads the database, including the data dictionary, and writes the output to a binary file called an *export dump file*. It may be performed for the full database, for specific users, or for specific tables. During exports, you may choose whether or not to export the data dictionary information associated with tables, such as the grants, indexes, and constraints associated with them. The file written by the export will contain the commands necessary to completely re-create all of the chosen objects.

Full database exports may be performed for all tables (called *Complete* exports), or for only those tables that have changed since the last export. There are two different types of incremental exports: *Incremental* and *Cumulative*. Incremental exports will export all tables that have changed since the last export, while cumulative exports will export all tables that have changed since the last full export.

The Export utility is also used to compress the extents of fragmented data segments. This functionality is described in Chapter 8, "Database Tuning."

Import

Once data has been exported, it may be imported via Oracle's *Import* utility. This utility reads the binary export dump file created by Export and executes the commands found there. For example, these commands may include a CREATE TABLE command, followed by an INSERT command to load data into the table.

The data that has been exported does not have to be imported into the same database, or the same schema, as was used to generate the export dump file. The export dump file may be used to create a duplicate set of the exported objects under a different schema, or in a separate database.

You can import either all or part of the exported data. If you import the entire export dump file from a Full export, then all of the database objects—including tablespaces, datafiles, and users—will be created during the import. However, it is often useful to precreate tablespaces and users, in order to specify the physical distribution of objects in the database.

If you are only going to import part of the data from the export dump file, then the tablespaces, datafiles, and users that will own and store that data must be set up prior to the import.

The data may also be imported into an Oracle database created under a higher version of the Oracle kernel. This is used between consecutive major releases of Oracle (such as from Oracle Version 6 to Oracle7). The reverse capability—importing from an export file created by a more recent major release—is not supported. When going between nonconsecutive major releases (for example, from Oracle Version 5 to Oracle7), it is recommended that you first import the data into the intermediate release (in this example, Oracle Version 6), then from that database into the later major release (Oracle7).

Physical Backups

Physical backups involve copying the files that comprise the database without regard to their logical content. These backups are also referred to as *file system backups*, since they involve using operating system file backup commands.

Oracle7 and Oracle Version 6 support two different types of physical file backups: the *cold* backup and the *hot* backup (also known as the "online" or "ARCHIVELOG" backup).

Cold Backups

Cold backups occur when the database has been shut down normally (that is, not due to instance failure). While it is "cold," the following files are backed up:

- All datafiles
- All control files
- All online redo logs
- The INIT.ORA file (optional)

It is easiest to back up the datafiles if the database file architecture uses a consistent directory structure. A sample of such an architecture is shown in the "Database File Layout" section of Chapter 4, "Physical Database Layouts."

Having all of these files backed up *while the database is closed* provides a complete image of the database as it existed at the time it was closed. The full set of these files could be retrieved from the backups at a later date and the database would be able to function. It is *not* valid to perform a file system backup of the database while it is open, unless a hot backup is being performed.

Hot (ARCHIVELOG) Backups

Hot backups first became available with Oracle Version 6. They can be used against any Oracle Version 6 or Oracle7 database that is running in ARCHIVELOG mode. In this mode, the online redo logs are archived, creating a full log of all transactions within the database.

Oracle writes to the online redo log files in a cyclical fashion; after filling the first log file, it begins writing to the second, until that one fills, and then begins writing to the third. Once the last online redo log file is filled, the LGWR (Log Writer) background process begins to overwrite the contents of the first redo log file.

When Oracle is run in ARCHIVELOG mode, the ARCH (Archiver) background process makes a copy of each redo log file before overwriting it. These archived redo log files are usually written to a disk device. They may also be written directly to a tape device, but this tends to be very operator-intensive.

You can perform file system backups of a database while that database is open, provided it is running in ARCHIVELOG mode. This involves setting each tablespace into a backup state, then backing up its datafiles, then restoring the tablespace to its normal state. The database can be fully recovered from such a backup, and can, via the archived redo logs, be rolled forward to any point in time. When the database is then opened, any committed transactions that were in the database at that time will have been restored.

While the database is open, the following files are backed up:

- All datafiles
- All archived redo log files
- One control file, via a special command

This is a very powerful backup procedure for two reasons. First, it provides full point-in-time recovery. Second, it allows the database to remain open during the file system backup. Thus, even databases that cannot be shut down due to user requirements can still have file system backups. Keeping the database open also keeps the SGA (memory) area of the database instance from being reset, as occurs during database startups. This will improve the database's performance by making better use of the available memory.

Implementations

In this section you will find the commands necessary to use each of the backup methods available in Oracle, as well as sample command files for performing them.

Export

The Export utility has three levels of functionality: *Full* mode, *User* mode, and *Table* mode.

In Full mode, the full database is exported. The entire data dictionary is read, and the DDL needed to re-create the full database is written to the export dump file. This includes all tablespaces, all users, and all of the objects, data, and privileges in their schemas.

In User mode, a user's objects are exported, as well as the data within them. All grants and indexes created by the user on the user's objects are also exported. Grants and indexes created by users other than the owner are not exported via this option.

In Table mode, a specified table is exported. Its structure, index, and grants are exported along with its data. Table mode can also export the full set of tables owned by a user (by specifying the schema owner, but no table names).

Export can be run either interactively or via command files. The run-time options that can be specified for Export are listed in Table 10-1.

KEYWORD	DESCRIPTION
USERID	Username/Password of the account running the export. If this is the first parameter after the "exp" command, then the "USERID" keyword does not have to be specified.
BUFFER	Size of the buffer used to fetch data rows. The default is system dependent; this value is usually set to a high value (>64000).
FILE	Name of the export dump file.
COMPRESS	A flag to indicate whether export should compress fragmented segments into single extents. This affects the STORAGE clauses that will be stored in the export file for those objects.
GRANTS	A flag to indicate whether grants on database objects will be exported.
INDEXES	A flag to indicate whether indexes on tables will be exported.
ROWS	A flag to indicate whether rows should be exported. If this is set to "N", then only the DDL for the database objects will be created in the export file.
CONSTRAINTS	A flag to indicate whether constraints on tables are exported.
FULL	If set to "Y", then a Full database export is performed.
OWNER	A list of database accounts to be exported; User exports of those accounts may then be performed.
TABLES	A list of tables to be exported; Table exports of those tables may then be performed.
RECORDLENGTH	The length, in bytes, of the dump export file record. Usually left at the default value unless you are going to transfer the export file between different operating systems.
INCTYPE	The type of export being performed (valid values are "COMPLETE" (default), "CUMULATIVE", and "INCREMENTAL"). The export types are described in the following sections.

TABLE 10-1. *Export Options*

KEYWORD	DESCRIPTION
RECORD	For Incremental exports, this flag indicates whether a record will be stored in data dictionary tables recording the export.
PARFILE	The name of a parameter file to be passed to Export. This file may contain entries for all of the parameters listed here.
ANALYZE	For Oracle7 only. A flag to indicate whether statistical information about the exported objects should be written to the export dump file.
CONSISTENT	For Oracle7 only. A flag to indicate whether a read-consistent version of all exported objects should be maintained. This is needed when tables that are related to each other are being modified by users during the Export process.
LOG	For Oracle7 only. The name of a file to which the log of the export will be written.
MLS	For Trusted Oracle only. A flag to indicate whether MLS labels should be exported.
MLS_LABEL_FORMAT	For Trusted Oracle only. This specifies the format for the MLS labels.

TABLE 10-1. *Export Options (continued)*

Note that a number of the parameters conflict with each other or may result in inconsistent instructions for Export. For example, setting FULL=Y and OWNER=HR would fail, since the FULL parameter calls for a Full export, while the OWNER parameter specifies a User export.

The default values for these options for Oracle7 and Oracle Version 6 are shown in Table 10-2. The parameters that are only available for Trusted Oracle ("MLS" and "MLS_LABEL_FORMAT") are not listed here.

These parameters may be displayed online via the following command.

```
exp help=Y
```

Note that in Oracle7, the GRANTS and CONSTRAINTS parameters now default to "Y".

KEYWORD	ORACLE7 DEFAULT VALUE	ORACLE VERSION 6 DEFAULT VALUE
USERID	undefined	undefined
BUFFER	system-dependent	system-dependent
FILE	EXPDAT.DMP	EXPDAT.DMP
COMPRESS	Y	Y
GRANTS	Y	N
INDEXES	Y	Y
ROWS	Y	Y
CONSTRAINTS	Y	N
FULL	N	N
OWNER	current user	current user
TABLES	undefined	undefined
RECORDLENGTH	system-dependent	system-dependent
INCTYPE	COMPLETE	COMPLETE
RECORD	Y	Y
PARFILE	undefined	undefined
ANALYZE	ESTIMATE	not available
CONSISTENT	N	not available
LOG	undefined	not available

TABLE 10-2. *Default Values for Export Parameters in Oracle7 and Oracle Version 6*

The COMPRESS=Y option alters the INITIAL parameter of the STORAGE clause for segments that have multiple extents. The total allocated space for that segment is thus compressed into a single extent. There are two important points to note concerning this functionality:

- First, it is the *allocated,* not the *used* space that is compressed. An empty table with 300M allocated to it in three 100M extents will be compressed into a single empty 300M extent. No space will be reclaimed.

- Second, if the tablespace is comprised of multiple datafiles, a segment may allocate space that is greater than the size of the largest datafile. In that case, using COMPRESS=Y would change the STORAGE clause to have an

INITIAL extent size that is greater than any datafile size. Since extents cannot span datafiles, this will fail during Import.

In the following example, the COMPRESS=Y option is used, as the HR and THUMPER owners are exported.

```
exp system/manager file=expdat.dmp compress=Y owner=(HR,THUMPER)
```

The LOG capability of Oracle7 is not available in Oracle Version 6. To log the output of an export command in Oracle Version 6, the operating system must be used to record the session output. In VMS, this can be done by running the Export in batch mode, and recording the batch output in a log file. In UNIX, the batch option is also available. An alternative in UNIX involves redirecting the command output to a log file, as shown in the following example. In this example, the Export is run with a parameter file called EXP.PAR, and its output is directed to a file called EXPDAT.LOG. The standard error is redirected to that log as well via the "2>&1" clause.

```
exp parfile=EXP.PAR >EXPDATA.LOG 2>&1
```

Complete Versus Incremental/Cumulative Exports

The INCTYPE Export parameter, when used with the FULL parameter, allows the DBA to export only those tables that have changed since the last Export. It is important to note that if any row in a table has changed, then every row of that table will be exported via an Incremental or Cumulative export. The available INCTYPE options are described in Table 10-3.

Complete exports form the basis for an export backup strategy. Incremental and Cumulative exports may be useful if very few of the database's tables change, and if those tables are very small. For example, in a decision support database that

OPTION	DESCRIPTION
COMPLETE	The default value. All tables specified will be exported.
INCREMENTAL	If FULL=Y, then this can be specified. Only those tables that contain rows that have changed since the last full export of any type will be exported.
CUMULATIVE	If FULL=Y, then this can be specified. This option exports all tables whose rows have changed since the last Cumulative or Complete export.

TABLE 10-3.   *INCTYPE Options for Export*

featured large, static tables, Incremental exports would be helpful. For databases using Incremental exports, Cumulative exports should be run periodically. The Incremental exports run prior to the last Cumulative export can then be discarded. During a recovery in such a database, you will need

- The last Complete export.
- The last Cumulative export.
- Every Incremental export since the last Cumulative or Complete export, whichever was run later.

Consistent Exports

During the process of writing the database's data to the export dump file, Export reads one table at a time. Thus, although the Export started at a specific point in time, each table is read at a different time. The data as it exists in each table at the moment Export starts to read *that table* is what will be exported. Since most tables are related to other tables (via primary and foreign key relationships), this may result in inconsistent data being exported if users are modifying data during the Export.

Consider the following scenario:

1. The Export begins.
2. Sometime during the Export, Table A is exported.
3. After Table A is exported, Table B, which has a foreign key to Table A, is exported.

What if transactions are occurring at the same time? Consider a transaction that involves both Table A and Table B, but does not commit until after Table A has been exported:

1. The Export begins.
2. A transaction against Table A and Table B begins.
3. Later, Table A is exported.
4. The transaction is committed.
5. Later, Table B is exported.

The transaction's data will be exported with Table B, but not with Table A (since the COMMIT had not yet occurred). The export dump file thus contains inconsistent data—in this case, foreign key records from Table B without matching primary key records from Table A.

To avoid this problem, there are two options. First, you should schedule Exports to occur when no one is making modifications to tables. Second, you can use a new option, CONSISTENT, with Oracle7. This option is only available for Complete exports; Incremental and Cumulative exports cannot use it.

When CONSISTENT=Y, the database will maintain a rollback segment to track any modifications made since the Export began. The rollback segment entries can then be used to re-create the data as it existed when the Export began. The result is a consistent set of exported data, with two major costs: the need for a very large rollback segment, and the reduced performance of the Export as it searches the rollback segment for changes.

Whenever possible, guarantee the consistency of exported data by running Exports while the database is mounted in DBA (Oracle Version 6) or RESTRICTED SESSION (Oracle7) mode. If you are unable to do this, then perform a CONSISTENT=Y export of the tables being modified, and a CONSISTENT=N export of the full database. This will minimize the performance penalties you incur while ensuring the consistency of the most frequently used tables.

Tablespace Exports

In order to defragment a tablespace, or to create a copy of its objects elsewhere, you will need to do a tablespace-level export. As you may have noted, there is not a "TABLESPACE=" parameter for Export. However, if your users are properly distributed among tablespaces, it is possible to use a series of User exports that, taken together, produce the desired result.

User exports record those database objects that are created by a user. However, there are certain types of user objects that are not recorded by User exports. Specifically, indexes and grants on tables owned by other accounts are not recorded via User exports.

Consider the case of two accounts, THUMPER and FLOWER. If THUMPER creates an index on one of FLOWER's tables, then a User export of THUMPER will not record the index (since THUMPER does not own the underlying table). A User export of FLOWER will also not record the index (since the index is owned by THUMPER). The same thing happens with grants: when a second account is capable of creating indexes and grants on objects, the usefulness of User exports rapidly diminishes.

Assuming that such *third-party objects* do not exist, or can be easily recreated via scripts, the next issue involves determining which users own objects in which tablespaces. This information is available via the data dictionary views. The following query maps users to tablespaces to determine their distribution of their objects. It does this by looking at the DBA_TABLES and DBA_INDEXES data dictionary views, and spools the output to a file called USER_LOCS.LST.

```
rem
rem    user_tablespace_maps.sql
```

```
rem
rem  This script maps user objects to tablespaces.
rem
set pagesize 60
break on owner on tablespace
column objects format A20
select
      owner,
      tablespace_name,
      count(*)||' tables' objects
from dba_tables
group by
      owner,
      tablespace_name
union
select
      owner,
      tablespace_name,
      count(*)||' indexes' objects
from dba_indexes
group by
      owner,
      tablespace_name

spool user_locs.lst
/
spool off
```

Sample output from this query is shown in Figure 10-1.

OWNER	TABLESPACE_NAME	OBJECTS
FLOWER	USERS	3 tables
		2 indexes
HR	HR_TABLES	27 tables
	HR_INDEXES	35 indexes
THUMPER	USERS	5 tables

FIGURE 10-1. *Sample Mapping of Users to Tablespaces*

The sample output shown in Figure 10-1 shows that the user account FLOWER owns tables and indexes in the USERS tablespace, and that THUMPER owns several tables in that tablespace as well. The user HR owns objects in both the HR_TABLES and the HR_INDEXES tablespaces.

Before determining the proper combinations of users to export for a tablespace, the inverse mapping—of tablespaces to users—should be done. The following query accomplishes this task. It queries the DBA_TABLES and DBA_INDEXES data dictionary views, and stores the output in a file called TS_LOCS.LST.

```
rem
rem    user_tablespace_maps.sql
rem
rem  This script maps user objects to tablespaces.
rem
set pagesize 60
break on tablespace on owner
column objects format A20
select
      tablespace_name,
      owner,
      count(*)||' tables' objects
from dba_tables
group by
      tablespace_name,
      owner
union
select
      tablespace_name,
      owner,
      count(*)||' indexes' objects
from dba_indexes
group by
      tablespace_name,
      owner

spool ts_locs.lst
/
spool off
```

The sample output shown in Figure 10-2 shows that the HR_TABLES tablespace contains objects from just one user (the HR account). The HR_INDEXES tablespace

TABLESPACE_NAME	OWNER	OBJECTS
HR_INDEXES	HR	35 indexes
HR_TABLES	HR	27 tables
USERS	FLOWER	3 tables
		2 indexes
	THUMPER	5 tables

FIGURE 10-2. *Sample Mapping of Users to Tablespaces*

is similarly isolated. The USERS tablespace, on the other hand, contains both tables and indexes, from several accounts.

The importance of properly distributing users' objects among tablespaces can be seen in Figures 10-1 and 10-2. Since the HR_TABLES tablespace only contains tables owned by the HR account (Figure 10-2), exporting the HR tables will export all of the objects in the HR_TABLES tablespace. As seen from Figure 10-1, HR does not own any tables anywhere else in the database. Because HR's tables are isolated to the HR_TABLES tablespace, and because that tablespace is only used by the HR account, a User export of HR will export all of the tables in HR_TABLES. Since the indexes on those tables are stored in HR_INDEXES, that tablespace can be defragmented at the same time, from the same export dump file.

```
exp system/manager file=hr.dmp owner=HR indexes=Y compress=Y
```

The tablespace can then be dropped and re-created, and the full export file can be imported. It will contain all of HR's tables and indexes. The following listing shows this process, using SQLDBA to manipulate the tablespaces. The full CREATE TABLESPACE commands are not shown since those details are not relevant to this example. In Oracle Version 6, the "lmode=Y" clause is not used.

```
sqldba lmode=Y
SQLDBA> connect internal
SQLDBA> drop tablespace hr_indexes including contents;
SQLDBA> drop tablespace hr_tables including contents;
SQLDBA> create tablespace hr_tables...
SQLDBA> create tablespace hr_indexes...
SQLDBA> exit

imp system/manager file=hr.dmp full=Y buffer=64000 commit=Y
```

Note that before reaching this point, you had to first analyze the distribution of users' objects in the database. If users are isolated to tablespaces, and if tablespaces are dedicated to users, then this process becomes simple.

What if HR had also owned objects in the USERS tablespace in this example? In that case, there would have been two alternatives. First, you could have queried the data dictionary views to determine the table names involved, and then specified all of HR's tables in the Export command via the TABLES parameter. Second, you could have exported HR's objects via a User export, dropped the HR_TABLES and HR_INDEXES tablespaces, dropped any HR objects located elsewhere in the database, re-created the HR_TABLES and HR_INDEXES tablespaces, and then performed the Import.

For the sample data given in Figures 10-1 and 10-2, re-creating the USERS tablespace requires performing User exports of both the THUMPER and the FLOWER accounts. Neither of these accounts owns objects in tablespaces other than USERS.

Note that this procedure *cannot* be used for tablespaces that contain temporary segments or rollback segments. The DROP TABLESPACE command will result in errors in those cases.

As noted previously, User exports do not export third-party grants and indexes. To determine if third-party grants or indexes exist, query the data dictionary views, as shown in the following queries.

The first set of queries searches for third-party grants. The queries are different for Oracle7 and Oracle Version 6 because of changes in privilege management between the two versions. The data dictionary view that shows this information also changed in name and structure between the two versions.

```
rem   Oracle7 version
rem
rem   third_party_grants.sql
rem
rem   This query searches for grants made by users
rem   other than the table owners.  These grants cannot
rem   be exported via User exports.
rem
break on grantor skip 1 on owner on table_name
select
      grantor,            /*Account that made the grant*/
      owner,              /*Account that owns the table*/
      table_name,         /*Name of the table*/
      grantee,            /*Account granted access*/
      privilege,          /*Privilege granted*/
      grantable           /*Was the privilege granted WITH ADMIN OPTION?*/
```

```
from dba_tab_privs
order by 1,2,3,4,5

spool third_parts_privs.lst
/
spool off


rem   Oracle Version 6  version
rem
rem   third_party_grants.sql
rem
rem   This query searches for grants made by users
rem   other than the table owners.  These grants cannot
rem   be exported via User exports.
rem
break on grantor skip 1 on owner on table_name
select
      grantor,               /*Account that made the grant*/
      owner,                 /*Account that owns the table*/
      table_name,            /*Name of the table*/
      grantee,               /*Account granted access*/
      select_priv,           /*Was SELECT privilege granted?*/
      insert_priv,           /*Was INSERT privilege granted?*/
      delete_priv,           /*Was DELETE privilege granted?*/
      update_priv,           /*Was UPDATE privilege granted?*/
      references_priv,       /*Was REFERENCES privilege granted?*/
      alter_priv,            /*Was ALTER privilege granted?*/
      index_priv             /*Was INDEX privilege granted?*/
from dba_tab_grants
order by 1,2,3,4

spool third_party_grants.lst
/
spool off
```

The query to search for third-party indexes did not change between Oracle Version 6 and Oracle7. As shown in the following listing, it queries the DBA_INDEXES data dictionary view to retrieve those records in which the index owner and the table owner columns do not have the same value.

```
rem
rem  third_party_indexes.sql
```

```
rem
rem  This query searches for indexes created by
rem  anyone other than the table owner.
rem
select
     owner,                    /*Owner of the index*/
     index_name,               /*Name of the index*/
     table_owner,              /*Owner of the table*/
     table_name                /*Name of the indexed table*/
from dba_indexes
where owner != table_owner

spool third_party_indexes.lst
/
spool off
```

If these queries show that third-party indexes or grants exist, and you plan to rely on User exports, then you must supplement those exports with scripts that generate the third-party grants and indexes. That is because those grants and indexes will not be recorded during User exports, only during Full exports.

Import

The *Import* utility reads the export dump file and runs the commands stored there. It may be used to selectively bring back objects or users from the export dump file.

When importing data from an Incremental or Cumulative export, you must first import from the most recent Incremental export, followed by the most recent Complete export. After that import is complete, the most recent Cumulative export must be imported, followed by all Incremental exports since that export.

Import can be run either interactively or via command files. The run-time options that can be specified for Import are listed in Table 10-4.

Note that a number of the parameters conflict with each other or may result in inconsistent instructions for Import. For example, setting FULL=Y and OWNER=HR would fail, since the FULL parameter calls for a Full import, while the OWNER parameter specifies a User import.

The default values for these options in Oracle7 and Oracle Version 6 are shown in Table 10-5. The "MLS" parameter, which is only available for Trusted Oracle, is not listed here.

Note the change in the IGNORE parameter between Oracle Version 6 and Oracle7. If IGNORE=Y (the default setting for Oracle Version 6), then CREATE TABLE errors will be ignored when encountered, and the data for those tables will be imported. When IGNORE=N, the CREATE TABLE errors will not be ignored,

KEYWORD	DESCRIPTION
USERID	Username/Password of the account running the import. If this is the first parameter after the "imp" command, then the "USERID" keyword does not have to be specified.
BUFFER	Size of the buffer used to fetch data rows. The default is system-dependent; this value is usually set to a high value (>64000).
FILE	Name of the export dump file to be imported.
SHOW	A flag to specify whether the file contents should be displayed, rather than executed.
IGNORE	A flag to indicate whether the Import should ignore errors encountered when issuing "CREATE" commands. This is used if the objects being imported already exist.
GRANTS	A flag to indicate whether grants on database objects will be imported.
INDEXES	A flag to indicate whether indexes on tables will be imported.
ROWS	A flag to indicate whether rows should be imported. If this is set to "N", then only the DDL for the database objects will be executed.
FULL	If set to "Y", then the full export dump file is imported.
FROMUSER	A list of database accounts whose objects should be read from the export dump file (when FULL="N").
TOUSER	A list of database accounts into which objects in the export dump file will be imported.
TABLES	A list of tables to be imported.
RECORDLENGTH	The length, in bytes, of the export dump file record. Usually left at the default value unless you are going to transfer the export file between different operating systems.
INCTYPE	The type of import being performed (valid values are "COMPLETE" (default), "CUMULATIVE", and "INCREMENTAL"). The export types are described in the following sections.

TABLE 10-4.   *Import Options*

KEYWORD	DESCRIPTION
COMMIT	A flag to indicate whether Import should COMMIT after each array (whose size is set by BUFFER). If this is set to "N", then Import will COMMIT after every table is imported. For large tables, COMMIT=N requires equally large rollback segments.
PARFILE	The name of a parameter file to be passed to Export. This file may contain entries for all of the parameters listed here.
INDEXFILE	Available for both Oracle Version 6 and Oracle7, but only documented in the latter. This very powerful option writes all of the CREATE TABLE, CREATE CLUSTER, and CREATE INDEX commands to a file, rather than running them. All but the CREATE INDEX commands will be commented out. This file can then be run (with slight modifications) after importing with INDEXES=N. It is very useful for separating tables and indexes into separate tablespaces.
DESTROY	For Oracle7 only. A flag to indicate whether the "CREATE TABLESPACE" commands found in dump files from Full exports will be executed (thereby destroying the datafiles in the database being imported into).
LOG	For Oracle7 only. The name of a file to which the log of the import will be written.
MLS	For Trusted Oracle only. A flag to indicate whether MLS labels should be imported.

TABLE 10-4. *Import Options* (continued)

and the Import will skip that table's data and move on to the next table. This is a very significant distinction if you plan to precreate the tables prior to the Import.

The DESTROY parameter is an Oracle7-only feature that is very useful for DBAs who run multiple databases on a single server. Since Full database Exports record the entire data dictionary, the tablespace and datafile definitions are written to the export dump file. The datafile definitions will include the full path name for the files. If this export dump file is used to migrate to a separate database on the same server, a problem may arise.

The problem is that when importing into the second database from the Full export of the first database, Import will execute the CREATE TABLESPACE commands found in the export dump file. These will instruct the database to create files in exactly the same directory, with the same name, as the files from the first

KEYWORD	ORACLE7 DEFAULT VALUE	ORACLE VERSION 6 DEFAULT VALUE
USERID	undefined	undefined
BUFFER	system-dependent	system-dependent
FILE	EXPDAT.DMP	EXPDAT.DMP
SHOW	N	N
IGNORE	N	Y
GRANTS	Y	Y
INDEXES	Y	Y
ROWS	Y	Y
FULL	N	N
FROMUSER	undefined	undefined
TOUSER	undefined	undefined
TABLES	undefined	undefined
RECORDLENGTH	system-dependent	system-dependent
INCTYPE	undefined	undefined
COMMIT	N	N
PARFILE	undefined	undefined
INDEXFILE	undefined	undefined
DESTROY	N	not available
LOG	undefined	not available

TABLE 10-5. *Default Values for Import Parameters in Oracle7 and Oracle Version 6*

database. Without using DESTROY=N (the default option), the first database's datafiles may be overwritten. The only other alternative when doing such an Import is to precreate all of the tablespaces, forcing the CREATE TABLESPACE commands to return errors (and thus not attempt to create any datafiles during the Import).

Rollback Segment Requirements

By default, the database will issue a COMMIT after every table is completely imported. Thus, if you have a table with 300M of data in it, then your rollback segments must accommodate a rollback segment entry that is at least that large. This is an unnecessary burden for the rollback segments. To shorten the sizes of the rollback segment entries, specify COMMIT=Y, along with a value for BUFFER. A COMMIT will then be executed after every BUFFER worth of data, as shown in the following example. In the first Import command shown, a commit is executed after every table is loaded. In the second command shown, a commit is executed after every 64,000 bytes of data are inserted.

```
imp system/manager file=expdat.dmp
imp system/manager file=expdat.dmp buffer=64000 commit=Y
```

How large should BUFFER be? BUFFER should be large enough to handle the largest single row to be imported. In tables with LONG datatypes, this may be greater than 64K. If you do not know the longest row length that was exported, start with a reasonable value (e.g., 50,000) and run the Import. If an IMP-00020 error is returned, then the BUFFER size is not large enough. Increase it and try the Import again.

When using COMMIT=Y, remember that a COMMIT is being performed for each BUFFER array. This implies that if the Import of a table fails, it is possible that some of the rows in that table may have already been Imported and committed. The partial load may then be either used or deleted prior to running the Import again.

Importing into Different Accounts

To move objects from one user to another user via Export/Import, export the owner of the objects. During the Import, specify the owner as the FROMUSER, and the account that is to own the objects as the TOUSER. For example, to export THUMPER's objects into the FLOWER account, execute the following commands. The first command exports the THUMPER owner, and the second command imports the THUMPER objects into the FLOWER account.

```
exp system/manager file=thumper.dat owner=thumper grants=N indexes=Y
      compress=Y rows=Y

imp system/manager file=thumper.dat FROMUSER=thumper TOUSER=flower
      rows=Y indexes=Y
```

Importing Structures That Failed to Import

The ROWS parameter is very useful for two reasons. First, it can be used to re-create just the database structure, without the tables' data, even if that data was exported. Second, it is often needed during successive Imports to recover objects that were not created during the first Import attempt. This is necessary because of the order in which objects are exported and imported.

When the Export program is run, it exports users in the order in which they were created in the database. A user's tables are then exported alphabetically. While this does not cause a problem during Exports, it may cause problems when those same objects are imported. The problems arise from the dependencies that may exist between objects in the database. If Import attempts to create an object (such as a view) before it creates the objects on which it depends, then an error will result. In such cases, the Import can be rerun, with ROWS=N and IGNORE=N, which will only import the structures that did not get imported during the first Import.

The following example shows this usage. The first Import attempts to bring in the entire export dump file. If there are failures during this Import, then a second pass is made to attempt to bring in those structures that failed the first time.

```
imp system/manager file=expdat.dmp full=Y commit=Y buffer=64000
```

During the import, several views fail with an ORA-00942 (table or view does not exist) error. Now run the Import a second time, with IGNORE=N and ROWS=N.

```
imp system/manager file=expdat.dmp ignore=N rows=N commit=Y buffer=64000
```

The IGNORE=N parameter in the second command tells Import to ignore any objects that were created during the first pass. It will only import those objects that failed. These are usually views that reference tables owned by multiple users.

Note that if a table referenced by a view is dropped, the view definition stays in the data dictionary. This definition can be exported, and the view creation will fail during an Import. In that case, since the view was invalid to begin with, a second Import will fail as well.

Using Import to Separate Tables and Indexes

Two Import options—INDEXFILE and INDEXES—can be used to reorganize the tablespace assignments of tables and indexes.

The INDEXFILE option is available but undocumented in Oracle Version 6. In Oracle7, it is documented. Using this option during an Import will result in the export dump file being read and, instead of being imported, its table and index creation scripts will be written to an output file. This file can be edited to alter the TABLESPACE and STORAGE parameters of the tables and indexes listed there. It may then be run via SQL*Plus to either precreate all objects prior to importing their data, or to create only specified objects (such as indexes).

When the indexfile is created, the CREATE INDEX scripts are the only ones that are not commented out via the REM command. This default functionality allows DBAs to separate a user's tables and indexes into separate tablespaces during Import. To do so, create the indexfile and alter the TABLESPACE clauses for the indexes. Then import the user, with INDEXES=N, so that the user's indexes will not be imported. Then run the altered indexfile to create the indexes in their new tablespace.

Note that the indexfile may contain entries for multiple users (if multiple users were exported). In practice, it is useful to separate the indexfile into multiple files, one for each user. This will make it easier to keep the tablespace assignments consistent. The following listing shows the steps involved in this process. In this example, THUMPER's objects are being copied into the FLOWER account, and the indexes are being separated from the tables in the process.

NOTE:
In Oracle7, the INDEXFILE parameter requires that either FULL=Y or a FROMUSER value is specified.

1. Export the user.

```
exp system/manager file=expdat.dmp owner=thumper
```

2. Create the indexfile from this export dump file.

```
imp system/manager file=expdat.dmp indexfile=indexes.sql
```

3. Edit the indexfile to change the TABLESPACE settings of the indexes.

4. Import the user, without its indexes.

```
imp system/manager file=expdat.dmp fromuser=thumper touser=flower
indexes=N commit=Y buffer=64000
```

5. Log into SQL*Plus as the user and run the altered indexfile to create the indexes.

```
sqlplus flower/password
SQL> @indexes
```

Importing Oracle Version 6 Exports into Oracle7
Oracle7 can read Oracle Version 6 export dump files. In the process of performing the Import, all CHAR datatypes from the Oracle Version 6 database will be changed to VARCHAR2 datatypes in Oracle7. All constraints specified for the Oracle Version 6 database will be imported into Oracle7, but only the NOT NULL constraints will be enabled; all others will be created in a DISABLED state.

Any users created in the Oracle Version 6 database can be imported into Oracle7. Users who have been granted CONNECT, RESOURCE, or DBA Privilege in Oracle Version 6 will be granted the roles with those names in Oracle7.

Cold Backups

A cold backup is a physical backup of the database files, made after the database has been shut down normally. While it is shut down, each of the files that is actively used by the database is backed up. These files thus capture a complete image of the database as it existed at the moment it was shut down.

The following files should be backed up during cold backups:

- All datafiles
- All control files
- All online redo logs
- The INIT.ORA file (optional)

It is easiest to back up the datafiles if the database file architecture uses a consistent directory structure. A sample of such an architecture is shown in the "Database File Layout" section of Chapter 4, "Physical Database Layouts."

In that architecture, all of the datafiles are located in directories at the same level on each device. Figure 10-3 shows a sample directory tree for a data disk named /db01.

Directories such as these should contain all of the datafiles, redo log files, and control files for a database. The only file needed for the cold backup that will not be in this location is the production INIT.ORA file, which should be in $ORACLE_HOME/dbs.

```
/db01
        /oracle
                /CASE
                        control1.dbf
                        sys01.dbf
                        tools.dbf
                /CC1
                        control1.dbf
                        sys01.dbf
                        tools.dbf
                /DEMO
                        control1.dbf
                        sys01.dbf
```

FIGURE 10-3. *Sample Directory Structure for a Data Disk*

If this directory structure is used, the backup commands are greatly simplified. The following listing shows a sample UNIX "tar" command, which is used here to back up files to a tape drive called "/dev/rmt/0hc". Because the directory structure is consistent, and the drives are named "/db01" through "/db09", the following command will back up all of the CC1 database's datafiles, redo log files, and control files.

```
> tar -cvf /dev/rmt/0hc /db0[1-9]/oracle/CC1
```

The "-cvf" flag is used to create a new "tar" saveset. To append the INIT.ORA file to this saveset, use the "-rvf" flag. This option, which appends files to the tape, is not available on all UNIX systems. If your installation does not support this, then the best alternative is to copy the files directly to a staging area on another disk (see "Database and Operating System Backups Integration" later in this chapter).

```
> tar -rvf /dev/rmt/0hc $ORACLE_HOME/dbs/initcc1.ora
```

These two commands, taken together, will back up all of the database's files to one tape device.

Since cold backups involve changes to the database's availability, they are usually scheduled to occur at night. A command file to automate these backups would resemble the following listing. In this example, the ORACLE_SID and ORACLE_HOME environment variables are set to point to the CC1 database. This database is then shut down, and the backup commands are executed. The database is then restarted.

```
ORACLE_SID=cc1; export ORACLE_SID
ORACLE_HOME=/orasw/v716; export ORACLE_HOME
sqldba command=shutdown immediate
insert backup commands like the "tar" commands here
sqldba command=startup
```

These examples are generic so that non-UNIX operating systems can use them with little modification. In VMS, for example, environment variables are set via instance-specific command files. For example, if the Oracle software home directory was DB01:[ORASW], then to set the environment variables, you would first go to the instance directory (via the SET DEF command). Once there, you would run the instance-specific ORAUSER file there. This is shown in the following example.

```
set def DB01:[ORASW.DB_instance_name]
@ORAUSER_DB_instance_name
```

The SQLDBA commands are the same across operating systems. The backup commands are operating system-specific. For VMS systems, the backup commands are of the form shown in the following example.

In this example, the VMS "Backup" command is used. The command is told to back up the files even if they have been marked as "NOBACKUP", and if they are interlocked (the "interl" parameter in this example). The "/log" clause logs the results of the backup command.

```
$Backup/ignore=(nobackup,interl)/log file tape1:oracle_backup.bck/sav
```

The file in this example is backed up to a tape device called "tape1". It is written to a saveset (as indicated by the "/sav" clause) called oracle_backup.bck. As with the UNIX "tar" command, you can back up multiple files at once via this command. The same backup command can be used to back up different files to savesets on the same tape. Those savesets will be appended to the tape.

Hot (ARCHIVELOG) Backups

Cold backups can only be done while the database is shut down. However, it is possible to perform physical file backups of a database while the database is open—provided the database is running in ARCHIVELOG mode and the backup is performed correctly. These backups are variously referred to as "hot" backups, "online" backups, or "ARCHIVELOG" backups.

Oracle writes to the online redo log files in a cyclical fashion; after filling the first log file, it begins writing the second until that one fills, and it then begins writing to the third. Once the last online redo log file is filled, the LGWR (Log Writer) background process begins to overwrite the contents of the first redo log file.

When Oracle is run in ARCHIVELOG mode, the ARCH background process makes a copy of each redo log file before overwriting it. These archived redo log files are usually written to a disk device. They may also be written directly to a tape device, but this tends to be very operator-intensive.

Getting Started

To make use of the ARCHIVELOG capability, the database must first be placed in ARCHIVELOG mode. The following commands show the Oracle7 and Oracle Version 6 commands needed to accomplish this. The order of the commands differs between the two versions. The Oracle7 version also features the clause "lmode=Y", which uses the line mode interface of SQLDBA (this interface is the only option in Oracle Version 6, and thus is not specified).

For Oracle7:

```
sqldba lmode=Y
SQLDBA> connect internal
SQLDBA> startup mount cc1;
SQLDBA> alter database archivelog;
SQLDBA> archive log start;
SQLDBA> alter database open;
```

For Oracle Version 6:

```
sqldba
SQLDBA> startup mount cc1;
SQLDBA> connect internal
SQLDBA> alter database archivelog;
SQLDBA> archive log start;
SQLDBA> alter database open;
```

Within both versions, the following command will display the current ARCHIVELOG status of the database from within SQLDBA:

```
archive log list
```

To change a database back to NOARCHIVELOG mode, use the following sets of commands.
For Oracle7:

```
sqldba lmode=Y
SQLDBA> connect internal
SQLDBA> startup mount cc1;
SQLDBA> alter database noarchivelog;
SQLDBA> alter database open;
```

For Oracle Version 6:

```
sqldba
SQLDBA> startup mount cc1;
SQLDBA> connect internal
SQLDBA> alter database noarchivelog;
SQLDBA> alter database open;
```

A database that has been placed in ARCHIVELOG mode will remain in that mode until it is placed in NOARCHIVELOG mode.

The location of the archived redo log files is determined by the settings in the database's INIT.ORA file. In Oracle7, it is usually set via the CONFIG.ORA file that is referenced as a parameter file in the INIT.ORA. The database files in Appendix A, "Database Creation Procedures," use this method for specifying the archived redo log file destination. The two parameters of note in those files are (with sample values):

```
log_archive_dest            = /db01/oracle/arch/CC1/arch
log_archive_start           = TRUE
```

In this example, the archived redo log files are being written to the directory "/db01/oracle/arch/CC1". The archived redo log files will all begin with the letters "arch", followed by a sequence number. For example, the archived redo log file directory may contain the files:

```
arch_170.dbf
arch_171.dbf
arch_172.dbf
```

Each of these files contains the data from a single online redo log. They are numbered sequentially, in the order in which they were created. In Oracle Version 6, they will all be the same size as the online redo log files; in Oracle7, the size varies but does not exceed their size of the online redo log files.

If the destination directory of the archived redo log files runs out of space, then ARCH will stop processing the online redo log data, and the database will stop itself. This situation can be resolved by adding more space to the archived redo log file destination disk, or by backing up the archived redo log files and then removing them from this directory.

Performing Online Database Backups

Once a database is running in ARCHIVELOG mode, it may be backed up while it is open and available to users. This capability allows round-the-clock database availability to be achieved while still guaranteeing the recoverability of the database.

Although hot backups can be performed during normal working hours, they should be scheduled for the times of the least user activity, for several reasons. First, the hot backups will use operating system commands to back up the physical files, and these commands will use most of the available I/O resources in the system (thus slowing down the interactive users). Second, while the tablespaces are being backed up, the manner in which transactions are written to the archived redo log files changes. If the physical block size of the operating system is less than the Oracle block size, then changing one record in a block will cause the record's entire block, not just the transaction data, to be written to the archived redo log file. This will use a great deal more space in the archived redo log file destination directory.

The command file for a hot backup is comprised of three parts:

1. A tablespace-by-tablespace backup of the datafiles, which in turn consists of

a) Setting the tablespace into backup state.

b) Backing up the tablespace's datafiles.

c) Restoring the tablespace to its normal state.

2. Backing up the archived redo log files, which consists of

a) Temporarily stopping the archiving process.

b) Recording which files are in the archived redo log destination directory.

c) Restarting the archiving process.

d) Backing up the archived redo log files, then deleting them.

3. Backing up the control file via the ALTER DATABASE BACKUP CONTROLFILE command.

A command file to perform a hot backup of a database will resemble the following listing. It is structured the same as the description just given. This example is for a UNIX database. In the first section, the environment variables ORACLE_SID and ORACLE_HOME are set for the database. SQLDBA is then used to put each tablespace in BEGIN BACKUP state. The datafiles associated with each tablespace are then backed up.

When the datafiles are being backed up, there are two choices available: they may be backed up directly to tape, or they may be backed up to disk. If you have enough disk space available, choose the latter option, since it will greatly reduce the time necessary for the backup procedures to complete. For this example, the datafiles will be written directly to tape.

```
#
# Sample Hot Backup Script for a UNIX File System database
#
# This script is for an Oracle7 database.  For Oracle Version 6,
# remove the "lmode=Y" clauses.  Everything else stays the same.
#
# Set up environment variables:
ORACLE_SID=cc1; export ORACLE_SID
ORACLE_HOME=/orasw/v716; export ORACLE_HOME
#
#     Step 1.  Perform a tablespace-by-tablespace backup
#     of the datafiles.  Set each tablespace, one at a time,
#     into BEGIN BACKUP state.  Then back up its datafiles
#     and return the tablespace to its normal state.
```

```
#
# Note for UNIX:  Set up an indicator for SQLDBA (called
# EOFarch1 here)so that the command file will stay within SQLDBA.
#
sqldba lmode=y <<EOFarch1
connect internal
REM
REM    Back up the SYSTEM tablespace
REM
alter tablespace SYSTEM begin backup;
!tar -cvf /dev/rmt/0hc /db01/oracle/CC1/sys01.dbf
alter tablespace SYSTEM end backup;
REM
REM  The SYSTEM tablespace has now been written to a
REM   tar saveset on the tape device /dev/rmt/0hc.  The
REM   rest of the tars must use the "-rvf" clause to append
REM   to that saveset.
REM
REM    Back up the RBS tablespace
REM
alter tablespace RBS begin backup;
!tar -rvf /dev/rmt/0hc /db02/oracle/CC1/rbs01.dbf
alter tablespace RBS end backup;
REM
REM    Back up the DATA tablespace
REM    For the purposes of this example, this tablespace
REM    will be comprised of two files, data01.dbf and data02.dbf.
REM    The * wildcard will be used in the file name.
REM
alter tablespace DATA begin backup;
!tar -rvf /dev/rmt/0hc /db03/oracle/CC1/data0*.dbf
alter tablespace DATA end backup;
REM
REM    Back up the INDEXES tablespace
REM
alter tablespace INDEXES begin backup;
!tar -rvf /dev/rmt/0hc /db04/oracle/CC1/indexes01.dbf
alter tablespace INDEXES end backup;
REM
REM    Back up the TEMP tablespace
REM
alter tablespace TEMP begin backup;
```

```
!tar -rvf /dev/rmt/0hc /db05/oracle/CC1/temp01.dbf
alter tablespace TEMP end backup;
REM
REM    Follow the same pattern to back up the rest
REM    of the tablespaces.
REM
REM
REM          Step 2.   Back up the archived redo log files.
REM
REM    First, stop the archiving process.  This will keep
REM    additional archived redo log files from being written
REM    to the destination directory during this process.
REM
archive log stop
REM
REM    Exit SQLDBA, using the indicator set earlier.
exit
EOFarch1
#
#   Record which files are in the destination directory.
#     Do this by setting an environment variable that is
#   equal to the directory listing for the destination directory.
#   For this example, the log_archive_dest is
#   /db01/oracle/arch/CC1.
#
FILES='ls /db01/oracle/arch/CC1/arch*.dbf'; export FILES
#
#   Now go back into SQLDBA and restart the
#   archiving process.  Set an indicator (called EOFarch2
#   in this example).
#
sqldba lmode=y <<EOFarch2
connect internal
archive log start;
exit
EOFarch2
#
#   Now back up the archived redo logs to the tape
#   device via the "tar" command, then delete them
#   from the destination device via the "rm" command.
#
tar -rvf /dev/rmt/0hc $FILES
```

```
rm -f $FILES
#
#     Step 3.  Back up the control file to a disk file.
#
sqldba lmode=y <<EOFarch3
alter database backup controlfile to
   'db01/oracle/CC1/CC1controlfile.backup';
exit
EOFarch3
#
#  Back up the control file to the tape.
#
tar -rvf /dev/rmt/0hc /db01/oracle/CC1/CC1controlfile.backup
#
#  End of hot backup script.
```

This backup script explicitly lists each datafile within each tablespace. Therefore, this backup procedure must be altered each time a datafile is added to the database.

Note that only one tablespace is in BEGIN BACKUP state at a time. This is done to minimize vulnerability to potential damage caused by database crashes. If the database is closed abnormally while a tablespace is in BEGIN BACKUP state, then it must be recovered from a prior backup. Using the one-at-a-time method shown here greatly reduces the possible impact of such a crash.

In the "Database and Operating System Backups Integration" section later in this chapter, this script will be modified to take advantage of file system backups performed by Systems Management personnel.

To back up an Oracle database in a VMS operating system, make several small changes to the backup script above:

1. Instead of the "#" signs in the UNIX script, use "$!" to signal a remark in the command file.

2. Remove the references to EOFarch1, EOFarch2, and EOFarch3. These aren't needed in VMS.

3. Replace the UNIX "tar" commands with VMS "Backup" commands, as shown earlier in this chapter.

4. Replace the UNIX "rm" command with a VMS "Delete" command.

5. Set up the environment variables that point to the instance via the instance-specific command file referred to earlier in this chapter.

6. When backing up the archived redo logs, set the "FILES" variable equal to the directory listing of the archived redo log destination directory.

Archived Redo Log File Backups

Since the archived redo log file destination directory may become full before the hot backup procedure is run, it is useful to have a backup procedure that only backs up that directory. The files in that directory can then be deleted, leaving space for new archived redo log files.

This procedure is simply a portion of the full hot backup process. It is a five-step process:

1. Temporarily stop the archiving process.

2. Record which files are in the archived redo log destination directory.

3. Restart the archiving process.

4. Back up the archived redo log files.

5. Delete those files from the destination directory.

The following command procedure performs this function. It is for UNIX databases using file systems. The "tar" command is used to back up the files to tape. For Oracle Version 6 databases, remove the "lmode=Y" clauses.

```
#      Step 1: Stop the archiving process. This will keep
#      additional archived redo log files from being written
#      to the destination directory during this process.
#
sqldba lmode=y <<EOFarch1
archive log stop;
REM
REM   Exit SQLDBA, using the indicator set earlier.
exit
EOFarch1
#
#      Step 2: Record which files are in the destination directory.
#      Do this by setting an environment variable that is
#   equal to the directory listing for the destination directory.
#   For this example, the log_archive_dest is
#   /db01/oracle/arch/CC1.
#
FILES='ls /db01/oracle/arch/CC1/arch*.dbf'; export FILES
#
#      Step 3: Go back into SQLDBA and restart the
```

```
#    archiving process. Set an indicator (called EOFarch2
#    in this example).
#
sqldba lmode=y <<EOFarch2
connect internal
archive log start;
exit
EOFarch2
#
#       Step 4. Back up the archived redo logs to the tape
#    device via the "tar" command, then delete them
#    from the destination device via the "rm" command.
#
tar -rvf /dev/rmt/0hc $FILES
#
#       Step 5. Delete those files from the destination directory.
#
rm -f $FILES
#
#       End of archived redo log file backup script.
```

The archived redo logs that are backed up via this procedure should be stored with the last previous hot backup.

Integration of Backup Procedures

Since there are three different methods for backing up the Oracle database, there is no need to have a single point of failure. Depending on your database's characteristics, one of the three methods should be chosen, and at least one of the two remaining methods should be used to back it up.

In the following sections you will see how to choose the primary backup method for your database, how to integrate logical and physical backups, and how to integrate database backups with file system backups.

Logical and Physical Backups Integration

Which backup method is appropriate for your database? Or rather, which backup method is appropriate to use as the *primary* backup method for your database?

The backup method selection process should take into account the characteristics of each method, as listed in Table 10-6.

As shown in Table 10-6, cold backups are the least flexible method of backing up the database. They are a point-in-time snapshot of the database; and since they are a physical backup, DBAs cannot selectively recover logical objects (such as tables) from them. Although there are times when they are appropriate, cold backups should normally be used as a fallback position in the event that the primary backup method fails.

Of the two remaining methods, which one is most appropriate? The answer depends on the nature of your database.

First, consider the recovery requirements. If your database is transaction-oriented, you will most likely want to use hot backups. Doing so will minimize the amount of transaction data lost in the event of a database failure. Using an Export-based strategy would limit you to only being able to go back to the data as it existed the last time the data was exported.

Next, consider the size of the database, and what objects you will likely be recovering. Given a standard recovery scenario—such as the loss of a disk—how long will it take for the data to be recovered? If a file is lost, the quickest way to recover it is usually via a physical backup, which again favors hot backups over exports.

There are, however, scenarios in which other methods are preferable. If the database is small, and transaction volume is very low, then either cold backups or Export will serve your needs. If you are only concerned about one or two tables, then use Export to selectively back them up. However, if the database is large, then the recovery time needed for Export/Import may be prohibitive. For such large, low-transaction environments, cold backups are appropriate.

Regardless of your choice for primary backup method, the final implementation should include an Export and a physical backup. This is necessary because these methods validate different things about the database: Export validates that it is logically sound, and physical backups that it is physically sound. Two sample integrations of these methods are shown in Table 10-7.

METHOD	TYPE	RECOVERY CHARACTERISTICS
Export	Logical	Can recover any database object to its status as of the moment it was exported.
Cold Backups	Physical	Can recover the database to its status as of the moment it was shut down.
Hot Backups	Physical	Can recover the database to its status at any point in time.

TABLE 10-6. *Comparison of Characteristics of Backup Methods*

DATABASE TYPE	HOT BACKUPS	COLD BACKUPS	EXPORTS
All sizes, transaction-intensive	Nightly	Weekly	Weekly
Small, mostly read-only	Not done	Weekly	Nightly
Large, mostly read-only	Not done	Nightly	Weekly

TABLE 10-7. *Sample Integration of Database Backup Methods*

As shown in Table 10-7, a good database backup strategy integrates logical and physical backups, based on the database's usage characteristics.

Other database activities may call for ad hoc backups. These may include cold backups before performing database upgrades, and exports during application migration between databases.

Database and Operating System Backups Integration

As described in this chapter, the DBA's backup activities involve a number of tasks normally assigned to a Systems Management group: monitoring disk usage, maintaining tapes, and so on. Rather than duplicate these efforts, it is best to integrate them. The database backup strategy should be modified so that the System Management personnel's file system backups will take care of all tape handling.

How is this to be done? It is usually accomplished by dedicating disk drives as destination locations for physical file backups. Instead of backing up files to tape drives, they will instead be written to other disks on the same server. Those disks should be targeted for backups by the System Management personnel's regular file system backups.

Consider the datafile backups shown earlier in the ARCHIVELOG backups section. The datafiles were written directly to tape via a "tar" command, as shown in this example:

```
REM
REM    Back up the RBS tablespace - directly to tape
REM
alter tablespace RBS begin backup;
!tar -rvf /dev/rmt/0hc /db02/oracle/CC1/rbs01.dbf
alter tablespace RBS end backup;
REM
```

Instead of backing the files up to tape, copy them to the target device for database file backups. For this example, "/db10" will be used as the device name. As shown in this listing, the RBS tablespace is put into BEGIN BACKUP state. Its files are then copied (here, via the UNIX "cp" command) to a new device, and the tablespace is returned to its normal state.

The commands in the following listing are executed from within SQLDBA.

```
REM
REM    Back up the RBS tablespace - to another disk (UNIX)
REM
alter tablespace RBS begin backup;
!cp /db02/oracle/CC1/rbs01.dbf /db10/oracle/CC1/backups
alter tablespace RBS end backup;
REM
```

The VMS version is identical, except for the operating system command used. In this case, the "Backup" command is used.

The commands in the following listing are executed from within SQLDBA.

```
REM
REM    Back up the RBS tablespace - to another disk (VMS)
REM
alter tablespace RBS begin backup;
!backup/ignore=(no backup, interl)DB01:[ORACLE.CC1]RBS01.DBF
DB10:[ORACLE.CC1.BACKUPS]
alter tablespace RBS end backup;
REM
```

To minimize the amount of space required for this task, you may also wish to have the operating system compress the file on the destination device once it has been copied there, if that option is available in your operating system.

This also changes the way in which archived redo log files are backed up. The new process is shown in the following listing. The UNIX "mv" command is used to move the files to the backup destination device. This does away with the need for the FILES environment variable that was used in the backup-to-tape method. As shown in this listing, the archiving process is temporarily stopped; when the files have all been moved, it is restarted.

```
#
# Procedure for moving archived redo logs to another device
#
# In Oracle Version 6 databases, drop the "lmode=y" command.
#
sqldba lmode=y <<EOFarch2
archive log stop;
!mv /db01/oracle/arch/CC1 /db10/oracle/arch/CC1
archive log start;
exit
EOFarch2
#
# end of archived redo log directory move.
```

The control file can also be automatically backed up to the backup destination device. The final distribution of files will resemble that shown in Table 10-8. In this example, the destination device is named "/db10".

The "/db10" device can then be backed up by the Systems Management file system backups. The DBA does not have to run a separate tape backup job.

DISK /DB01-/DB09	DISK /DB10
Datafiles	Copies of datafiles
Online redo logs	
Archived redo log file directory	Old archived redo log files
Control files	Backed up control file

TABLE 10-8. *File Distribution after Backups to a Destination Device*

Recovery Scenarios When Using These Procedures

Unless you test and validate your backup procedures, you cannot be certain that you will be able to recover from *any* type of database failure. Recovery thus begins with testing. Create a sample database and use your chosen procedures. Then test your ability to recover from different types of database failures.

On most of the servers that I have worked with, the mean time between failure (MTBF) for disks is between three and four years. Failures due to disk errors are the most common types encountered. The *Oracle7 Server Administrator's Guide* includes an exhaustive description of the recovery procedures needed for each type of possible failure. For Oracle Version 6, you should reference both the *Oracle Version 6 DBA Guide* and the online file named RECOVERY.DOC, which is found in the $ORACLE_HOME/rdbms/admin directory.

In the following sections you will see how to apply the integrated database backups to the three most common scenarios: instance failure, disk failure, and user failure. "User failure" occurs when users execute DDL commands (such as DROP TABLE) that they need to undo.

Instance Failure

Recovery from instance failure should be automatic. The database will need access to all of its control files, online redo log files, and datafiles, in their proper locations. Any uncommitted transactions that existed in the database will be rolled back. Following an instance failure, such as one brought on by a server failure, be sure to check the alert log for the database for any error messages when the database attempts to restart itself.

Media (Disk) Failure

Disk failure, also called *media failure*, occurs when a disk on which an active database file resides becomes unreadable by the database. This may occur due to a disk crash or to a compilation of read errors on the disk. Either way, the files on the disk must be replaced.

The disks on which *online redo log files* reside should always be mirrored. In Oracle7, this can be done by using redo log groups; in Oracle Version 6, the mirroring has to occur at the operating system level. Since these files are mirrored, they should never be lost due to a media failure.

This leaves three types of files to consider: control files, archived redo log files, and datafiles.

If the lost file is a *control file*, it is easy to recover regardless of the backup method chosen. Every database should have multiple copies of its control file (which the database will keep in sync), all stored on different devices. The sample database creation scripts in Appendix A, "Database Creation Procedures," create three control files for each database and locate them on three different drives. To recover from the loss of a control file, shut the database down and copy one of the remaining control files to the proper location.

If all control files are lost, you can use a command that became available in later releases of Oracle Version 6 called CREATE CONTROLFILE. This command has been expanded in functionality in Oracle7. It allows you to create a new control file for the database, specifying all of the datafiles, online redo logs, and database parameters that are in the database. If you are unsure of the parameters to use here, and you are running ARCHIVELOG backups, there is a helpful feature available in Oracle7. It is

```
alter database backup controlfile to trace;
```

The proper CREATE CONTROLFILE command will be written to a trace file. Do not use this command unless *all* of the control files have been lost.

If the lost file is an *archived redo log file*, you cannot recover it. For this reason, it is important that the archived redo log file destination device be mirrored as well. Archived redo log files should be regarded as being as important as the online redo log files.

If the lost file is a *datafile*, it can be recovered from the previous night's hot backup. Follow these steps:

1. Restore the lost file from the backup to its original location.

```
cp /db10/oracle/CC1/data01.dbf /db03/oracle/CC1/data01.dbf
```

2. Mount the database.

```
ORACLE_SID=cc1; export ORACLE_SID
ORACLE_HOME=/orasw/v716; export ORACLE_HOME
sqldba lmode=y
SQLDBA> connect internal
SQLDBA> startup mount cc1;
```

NOTE
For Oracle Version 6, the two SQLDBA commands shown for this step are reversed in order, and the "lmode=Y" clause is not applicable.

3. Recover the database. You will be prompted for the name of each archived redo log file that is needed for recovery.

```
SQLDBA> recover database;
```

When prompted, enter the file names for the requested archived redo log files.

4. Open the database.

```
SQLDBA> alter database open;
```

When the datafile is restored from the backup, the database will recognize that it is from an earlier point in time than the rest of the database. To bring it forward in time, it will apply the transactions it finds in the archived redo log files.

The datafiles may be recovered from either the hot or the cold backup (if the database was in ARCHIVELOG mode at the time). If there are complications with the recovery, such as corruption in the files, see the recovery documentation referred to earlier in this chapter for a full list of your options.

Recovering Accidentally Dropped or Altered Objects

Occasionally, users will make errors that they will not be able to roll back or undo. Such errors may consist of DDL commands, such as ALTER TABLE and DROP TABLE, or DML commands, such as UPDATE and DELETE.

In all such cases, the users' desire is to return to a point in time prior to the database event that they wish to retract. This calls for a point-in-time recovery.

The simplest type of point-in-time recovery uses the most recent export dump file. If the user can go back that far in time, then this may be an acceptable alternative. Use the Import commands shown earlier in this chapter to selectively import the objects and users desired.

This may not suffice. The users may need a more up-to-date version of the table—for example, as it existed an hour before the offending command was executed.

To perform a point-in-time recovery, you must be running in ARCHIVELOG mode.

1. There are two options for the first step for this method of recovery:

a) Back up the current database (via a cold backup, usually) and replace it with a prior version of itself, then roll that version forward in time to the desired time.

Or

b) Create a database with the same instance name on a different server, leaving the current database intact, while using the prior version of the primary database as the basis for the second database.

Regardless of the option chosen, the second step is:

2. Roll the temporary database forward in time, using the following command from within SQLDBA, in place of the RECOVER DATABASE command used for normal recoveries: The date is in the format "YYYY-MM-DD:HH24:MI:SS". The sample date below is for November 28 (11-28), 1993, at 2:40 p.m. (14:40).

```
SQLDBA> connect internal
SQLDBA> startup mount instance_name;
```

NOTE
For Oracle Version 6, those two commands are executed in reverse order.

```
SQLDBA> recover database until '1993-11-28:14:40:00';
```

3. While still in SQLDBA, execute the normal command to open the database, using the RESETLOGS option. This forces the database to reset the redo log sequence number information in the control files and the online redo log files. This in turn makes sure that any redo log entry data that followed the "RECOVER DATABASE UNTIL" time specification will not be applied to the database.

```
SQLDBA> alter database open resetlogs;
```

The database will now be opened and available, and will look as it did at the time specified during the "RECOVER DATABASE UNTIL" command. The dropped or altered objects can now be backed up via Export.

4. Export the logical objects that were affected.

```
> exp system/manager file=saved.dmp tables=(owner.tablename)
```

The altered or dropped objects are now recorded in the export dump file. The temporary database created in Step 1 can now be dropped.

Restore the production database to its old state. Then use the export dump file created in Step 4 to Import the altered/dropped objects back into the production database in their former state.

5. After restoring the production database, prepare it for the Import of the old version of the data. These preparations may involve dropping the objects that were altered by the users. Once this is complete, Import the earlier versions of those objects from the export dump file. The production database is thus returned to its state before Step 1, and the damaged objects have been replaced by their earlier incarnations.

```
> imp system/manager file=saved.dmp full=Y commit=Y buffer=64000
```

The emphasis in the integration of the available backup methods is placed on being able to recover from the most common types of failures. Since each method has different characteristics, the proper combination of methods will vary from database to database. Regardless of the methods chosen, they should be integrated with the regular file system backups and *tested*. Properly used, they will be able to support the recovery from any type of database crash.

PART 3

Supporting Packages

CHAPTER 11

Supporting Oracle*CASE

Throughout the discussions of DBA activities in this book, the same cycle of activity types keeps recurring: Plan-Do-Check-Act. This same cycle of activities can be utilized in application development as well. Oracle's version of this methodology, known as CASE*Method, is supported by its CASE (Computer Aided Software Engineering) tool, called Oracle*CASE.

Oracle*CASE—Overview

Oracle*CASE has several components, which are listed in Table 11-1.

COMPONENT	USAGE
CASE*Dictionary	Stores the application's data dictionary
CASE*Designer	Graphically depicts the relationships between entities in the application
CASE*Generator	Generates application code (in SQL*Forms, SQL*ReportWriter, etc.) based on the application's definitions

TABLE 11-1. *Oracle*CASE Components*

Of the components listed in Table 11-1, the CASE*Dictionary component has the least "flash." However, it is the component that has the greatest impact on the underlying database, and can occasionally place severe loads on the database. Supporting this component will be the focus of this chapter.

CASE*Dictionary 5.0.22, which supports both Oracle Version 6 and Oracle7, will be used as the basis for the technical details described here.

Database Structure

In order to best support Oracle*CASE, treat it as an application package. Give it its own database, separate from development work. Doing so will greatly enhance your flexibility when supporting CASE*Dictionary.

CASE*Dictionary uses SQL*Forms and SQL*Menu as its front-end tools. Therefore, these tools will need to be installed in the CASE database. Since little development work will be done in these tools in a CASE database, use their default installation configuration; this calls for a single set of the product tables, owned by the SYSTEM user. Before installing these tools in the database, make sure the SYSTEM user has the TOOLS tablespace as its default. The default tablespace setting for the SYSTEM user can be seen via the following query.

This query searches the DBA_USERS view for information about the default settings of the SYSTEM user.

```
select
    username,
    default_tablespace
from DBA_USERS
where username = 'SYSTEM';
```

Aside from SYSTEM, there are two other accounts that own objects needed by CASE*Dictionary: SYSCASE and CASEMGR.

SYSCASE owns 20 tables that form the basis of the CASE*Dictionary application. These tables should be stored in their own tablespace, and do not require much space.

The CASEMGR account, on the other hand, owns the tables that the users hit directly. It owns 21 tables and over 200 views. Depending on the size and number of applications that are modeled in the CASE*Dictionary application, the CASEMGR table sizes can grow rapidly. These tables should be stored in their own tablespace.

Database Access

Each user who needs access to CASE*Dictionary must have an account in the CASE database. Users only require CONNECT Privilege for the database, although some users may require RESOURCE Privilege to test the object creation SQL generated by the CASE tool.

Each user must be enrolled in SQL*Menu in order to access the CASE*Dictionary front-end menus. The two SQL*Menu groups used in CASE*Dictionary are listed in Table 11-2.

CASEMGR and SYSCASE should both be in the CMAN group. All other users should be enrolled in the CDICT group.

Therefore, a user who needs access to Oracle*CASE must first be set up as an SQL*Menu user, then be enrolled in the CDICT group. This process is performed by the SQL*Menu Administrator for the CASE database. It may be automated via the following steps.

Grant EXECUTE access to SQL*Menu to the user via the GENMENU command. The "-GE" flag specifies that the user should be granted ("G") EXECUTE ("E") access to the tool.

```
>GENMENU system/manager -GE username
```

SQL*MENU GROUP	USAGE
CMAN	Dictionary Manager; able to access all menus and run all options
CDICT	Dictionary User; may only access those options available via the Main Menu

TABLE 11-2. *CASE*Dictionary 5.0 SQL*Menu Groups*

Enroll the user in the CDICT group. To do this, go into SQL*Menu and access the Role Definition screen from the Action-Admin-Security menu. Display the Username window on this screen, and add the new user's name to the list of users with the CDICT role.

Once the user's SQL*Menu access has been established, the CASE*Dictionary access to the available application systems can be set up by the CASE Administrator. The user setup screens available within CASE*Dictionary automatically create 113 private synonyms in each user's account. To avoid this, be sure that CASE is isolated to its own database. If it is, then you can create public synonyms that are accessible to all users in place of the private synonyms created by the tool.

If you are using the private-synonym method with CASE*Dictionary 5.0 against an Oracle7 database, the database must have the Oracle Version 6 data dictionary catalog views installed for the user installation scripts to work. The procedures for creating these views are shown in the following listing. As shown in this listing, the catalog6.sql script in the $ORACLE_HOME/rdbms/admin directory must be run from the SYS account. This account is accessed via the "connect internal" command from within sqldba.

```
sqldba lmode=Y
SQLDBA> connect internal
SQLDBA> @$ORACLE_HOME/rdbms/admin/catalog6
```

The DBA's Role

Typically, the administration tasks for an Oracle*CASE database are divided into two sections: those which are application-specific (such as enrolling users and creating new versions of application models) and those which are DBA-specific.

The CASE Administrator must keep the DBA updated on the overall CASE strategy and schedule. The CASE*Dictionary tools for creating extracts of applications place enormous temporary loads on the database (see "Supporting Extracts," later in this chapter). Also, the versioning strategy used within the CASE tool will affect the space requirements. Failure of the CASE Administrator and DBA to coordinate these strategies will result in repeated failures within the application.

The DBA must plan a flexible database that is capable of handling a normal workload of many small transactions by many users. However, this same database must be capable of supporting a single transaction that may be as large as all of the CASE tables put together. The application of the logical database layout methods described in Chapter 3, "Logical Database Layouts," is therefore crucial.

Database Planning

The DBA must plan the CASE database as if it were two separate databases: one for use during application design and development, and one for support of large data manipulation transactions (*extracts*) performed by the CASE Administrator.

Extracts do not, as their name might suggest, write data from the CASE tables into a flat file external to the database. Rather, they create tables that are copies of the CASE tables, via commands like those shown in the following listing.

```
CREATE TABLE extract_table
AS SELECT * FROM CASE_table;
```

Note that this command combines a CREATE TABLE command with a single implicit INSERT command. The INSERT command creates a single transaction that holds all of the data from the CASE table for insert into the extract table. Since a transaction cannot span rollback segments, there must be a single rollback segment available that is large enough to handle such a transaction.

Therefore, a single large-volume rollback segment is needed, for use during the CASE Administrator's extracts. However, this does not reflect the day-to-day requirements of the application. Typically, a CASE environment features very low transaction volume. To support this transaction volume, rollback segments of 10M in size are usually sufficient. Create one rollback segment for every four to six active transactions. See Chapter 7, "Managing Rollback Segments," for information on how to monitor the amount of rollback segment data being written and the number of active transactions per rollback segment.

File Location and Sizes

Based on the discussions earlier in this chapter, the elements of a CASE*Dictionary database can be summarized in the listing shown in Table 11-3.

To improve the performance of the CASE application, you may wish to separate the indexes owned by CASEMGR and SYSCASE into different tablespaces. This will allow them to be stored apart from the tables that they index. Their files may also be stored on separate devices, thus minimizing contention.

To further minimize contention, the SYSTEM, RBS, CASEMGR, and SYSCASE tablespaces should all be stored on separate devices. Use the scripts given in Chapter 4, "Physical Database Layouts," to verify the I/O weights of each of the datafiles.

Most of these tablespaces will be 20M or less in size. The only possible exceptions are TEMP, RBS, RBS_2, and CASEMGR. Proper sizing of these

TABLESPACE	USAGE
SYSTEM	Data Dictionary
SYSCASE	Objects owned by SYSCASE user
CASEMGR	Objects owned by CASEMGR user
TOOLS	Product tables for SQL*Forms and SQL*Menu
RBS	Production rollback segments
RBS_2	One large rollback segment for extracts
TEMP	Temporary segments
USERS	User objects

TABLE 11-3. *CASE*Dictionary Database Elements*

tablespaces is dependent on how large your application model is and on the versioning strategy used.

Versioning Considerations

Versioning allows developers to maintain different versions of the same application. Since the application design's data is stored in the database, this means that two versions of the same application will double that application's storage requirements in the CASE tables.

The DBA must work with the CASE Administrator to make sure a consistent versioning strategy is in place for all application teams. If creating multiple versions of a CASE application is to be the exception to the rule, then the frequency of such exceptions must still be estimated. Those estimates should then be used to calculate the amount of additional space that CASE*Dictionary is likely to need.

Supporting Extracts

CASE*Dictionary's extract feature creates a set of temporary tables to hold a copy of an application system's design. The data in those tables can then be either exported to a file or imported into another CASE database. If a parent application system is specified, then the data of all of its dependent application systems is extracted as well.

The problems in supporting extracts lie in two areas: the transaction size and the inability to specify a rollback segment to use. These problems are caused by the way in which the extract tables are generated.

Extracts are run from within the CASE*Dictionary application, from the Application Migration/Bridge Menu. The scripts that run the extract do not contain any rollback segment specifications. Furthermore, they run transactions of the type shown in the following listing.

```
CREATE TABLE extract_table
AS SELECT * FROM CASE_table;
```

This command combines a CREATE TABLE command with a single implicit INSERT command. The INSERT command creates a single transaction that holds all of the data from the CASE table for insertion into the extract table. Since a transaction cannot span rollback segments, there must be a single rollback segment available that is large enough to handle such a transaction.

The objective when supporting extracts is thus twofold: to provide enough space for the temporary extract tables being created, and to force the transactions to use a rollback segment created specifically for this purpose.

Space Requirements

The storage requirements for extract tables mirror the storage requirements for the application design data. Therefore, at least 50 percent of the space in the CASEMGR tablespace must be unused before the extract starts.

The space used by the extract tables is only temporary. It is assumed by the application that those tables will be either exported to flat files or read into another CASE database. When the latter process occurs (via the "Load Application System into Dictionary" option of the Application Migration/Bridge Menu), the extract tables are automatically deleted when the process is complete.

Thus, the additional space in the CASEMGR tablespace is not used by the Production users, and is used for very short periods of time by the CASE Administrator during extracts. However, its existence is critical to the success of the extraction procedure.

Using Specialized Rollback Segments

How do you force a transaction to use a specific rollback segment, if you cannot edit the command that is being executed? By giving the database only one rollback segment to choose from.

Since the extract commands being run are not visible to the user, it is not possible to add a

```
SET TRANSACTION USE ROLLBACK SEGMENT EXTRACT_1
```

command to the command file. This command would point the transactions that follow to a specialized rollback segment. Since this is not an option, the database will assign the transaction to a rollback segment, using a round-robin method to select which rollback segment to use.

To remove the randomness in this selection process, schedule the extracts to occur at times when no one else is using the CASE database. Then use the instructions given in Chapter 7, "Managing Rollback Segments," to deactivate all but the extract load rollback segment (which should be in the RBS_2 tablespace). Then run the extract process. Once it completes, reactivate the production rollback segments.

Monitoring

There are several key areas of the CASE database that must be monitored to make sure they do not exceed acceptable ranges. These include the areas tracked by the Command Center monitoring application provided in Chapter 6, "Monitoring Multiple Databases." These include

- Free space trends for all tablespaces
- Extension of all rollback segments
- Extension of large data and index segments

Most Active Tables and Indexes

CASE*Dictionary is a heavily indexed application. The tables listed in Table 11-4 are the ones most likely to grow rapidly; therefore, their indexes are also likely to grow rapidly. Be sure to monitor them via the Command Center monitoring application. All of the tables listed are owned by the CASEMGR user.

OWNER	TABLE NAME
CASEMGR	CDI_TEXT
CASEMGR	SDD_ELEMENTS
CASEMGR	SDD_STRUCTURE_ELEMENTS
CASEMGR	SDW_VIRTUAL_OBJECTS
CASEMGR	SDW_VIRTUAL_RELATIONSHIPS

TABLE 11-4. *Most Active Tables in CASE*Dictionary 5.0*

Space Trend Monitoring

When monitoring the available free space, the most active tablespaces (those used for the CASEMGR and SYSCASE data) should be watched the most closely. The RBS and RBS_2 tablespaces should also be monitored for any changes in free space availability. It is particularly critical that these statistics be monitored immediately prior to creating the extract tables or loading a new application from extract tables.

CHAPTER 12

Supporting Oracle Financials

Since the earliest computer was essentially an electronic abacus, it is only fitting that computers be used for accounting. Oracle's accounting package, Oracle Financials, is an application developed and sold by Oracle to manage corporate accounting. It includes modules for the General Ledger (GL), Accounts Payable (AP), Purchase Orders (PO), Fixed Assets (FA), and other major financial categories. It is created using a wide variety of Oracle tools. Release 9 of Oracle Financials uses SQL*Forms 2.3 for its front-end forms. Release 10 is the first client-server version, using Oracle Forms 4.0. This chapter will focus on Release 9, although its implementation recommendations will be applicable to both versions.

Versions of Release 9 starting with 9.4.2 can be installed in Oracle Version 6 or Oracle7 databases. The database management information presented here applies to both.

Oracle Financials—Overview

From the DBA's perspective, Oracle Financials is a fairly complex application, even in those installations that do not use all of the modules. The following sections describe the key features of the database that you should be aware of.

Database Structure

Each module of Oracle Financials corresponds to an Oracle account. That account, such as "GL" for the General Ledger module, owns all of the tables and indexes for that module. Another account, "FND," owns the tables that SQL*Forms 2.3 uses to generate the front-end forms. Since SQL*Forms 2.3 code is interpreted, rather than compiled, these FND tables are queried by the applications during production usage of the forms.

Since each module's objects are created under its own account, create two tablespaces for each account: one for its tables (such as "GL_TABLES") and one for its indexes (such as "GL_INDEXES"). Separating the tables and indexes into different tablespaces may be done by editing the application creation scripts.

Even if you are not using all of the modules of Financials, each module's tables must be installed. Many of the views in Oracle Financials will query tables from multiple modules—and thus from multiple owners. Failing to install the unused modules will therefore cause the views to be unusable.

These views may present problems during database rebuilds. This is particularly true if developers create their own views, since the order in which the structures are imported may cause the view to be imported before its underlying tables are. In order to resolve this problem, you can run the import twice: first with only the structures being imported, then a second run to bring in the data. The second import will create any views that experienced errors during the first import. The two import commands are

```
imp system/manager file=export.dmp rows=N
imp system/manager file=export.dmp full=y buffer=64000 commit=Y
```

The first command imports all of the database structures, but none of the rows ("rows=N"). The second import brings in the structures and the data, with a commit point set for every 64,000 bytes of data imported.

This subject is described in greater detail in Chapter 10, "Optimal Backup and Recovery Procedures."

Database Access

Access to the Financials application is controlled within the application. Users log into the application as themselves, are validated, and are then logged into the modules they are using as the module owners. This means that all users of GL get logged in as GL.

This has the effect of removing the administration of user accounts from the DBA's tasks. The only accounts in a production Financials database will be those that belong to the module owners. The Financials *System Administrator* (SysAdmin) will be responsible for all user authorizations.

From an account management perspective, the DBA will only be involved in setting up the module owner accounts (such as GL and PO) and any accounts created for access to the Financials database from outside databases. These are typically created to allow query-only access to restricted views of Financials data.

The DBA must also grant Select access on the dynamic performance tables (the V$ tables) to all Financials users. This is accomplished via the commands shown in the following listing. The first command changes directory to the $ORACLE_HOME/rdbms/admin directory via the UNIX "cd" command. The second command starts SQLDBA in line mode (lmode=y). The user must then connect as SYS ("connect internal") and run the grants scripts (called monitor.sql). In Oracle7, this file is named utlmontr.sql.

```
cd $ORACLE_HOME/rdbms/admin
sqldba lmode=y
SQLDBA> connect internal
SQLDBA> @monitor
```

This script grants SELECT access to the dynamic performance tables to PUBLIC. Several of the triggers in the Financials front-end forms reference these views, and will fail if these grants are not made. These grants have to be regranted after every database rebuild.

Concurrent Managers

Oracle Financials features an internal job queue manager called the *concurrent manager*. This is a very flexible mechanism for scheduling jobs that access the database. A single Financials database can run several concurrent managers (but usually less than five). These are set up by the Financials SysAdmin and run as

STATUS	DESCRIPTION
Q	Waiting in the queue
R	Running
C	Completed

TABLE 12-1. *Status Values for Concurrent Requests*

background processes, waking up at specified intervals to check for jobs waiting to be executed.

Jobs in the concurrent manager queue are stored in a table called FND_CONCURRENT_REQUESTS, owned by the FND account. They will have one of the status values listed in Table 12-1.

Once a request has been run and completed, its record remains in the FND_CONCURRENT_REQUESTS table. These old records provide an audit trail of request submissions, but they do so at the expense of database space. Records of completed jobs should be archived to flat files on a regular scheduled basis and then deleted from the table. The Financials SysAdmin should be responsible for doing this, since the concurrent manager should be shut down during this process. If the FND_CONCURRENT_REQUESTS table begins extending, the DBA should advise the Financials SysAdmin to decrease the time between these data archiving operations.

The Financials SysAdmin can customize the concurrent managers. They can be restricted to run jobs of a particular type, or those run by a specific user. They may also be restricted based on the program run. These restrictions allow long-running reports to be done at off-peak hours. Doing this will greatly reduce the amount of rollback segment space needed by minimizing the inactive, in-use rollback segment data (see Chapter 7, "Managing Rollback Segments").

Although it is possible to configure the concurrent managers so that their processes run at a low operating system priority, this is not an optimal choice. The better solution is to run all jobs at the same priority *at their appropriate times*. The result? Better performance for everyone. The DBA should work with the Financials SysAdmin to evaluate system usage cycles and determine how jobs can be more effectively scheduled.

The Demo Database

Oracle delivers a full copy of a Demo database along with Financials. This is actually an export dump file, which is intended to be imported into a single user account (such as "MODEL90"). This account should point to its own tablespace. It will own all 1,003 tables (in Release 9.3.7) that make up Financials, as well as their associated views and indexes.

Since the demo database may be modified during training or demos, DBAs should be prepared to reimport this data periodically.

The DBA's Role

The DBA of an Oracle Financials database needs to work with the Financials SysAdmin to coordinate their activities for aspects of the application that affect database storage, access, and structure. The Financials SysAdmin will have a greater involvement in issues internal to the application, such as setting up the Financials segment codes.

Sizing for the Financials application is also the responsibility of the Financials SysAdmin. The database size required is dependent on a number of factors specific to the implementation of the application. The calculations needed to determine the proper size are in the Oracle Financials Installation Guide.

Financials is a modifiable package, so there must be a Development area established. Since the data is critical to corporate finances, a Test area is normally used as well. For further information on the development process, see Chapter 5, "Managing the Development Process."

The DBA must perform the following functions:

- Plan and create the database, given the sizes specified by the SysAdmin.

- Create Development, Test, and Production instances of the database.

- Create data and index tablespaces for each of the modules.

- Install the Demo database in its own tablespaces in the Development and Test databases.

- Monitor rollback segment usage.

- Monitor temporary segment usage.

- Monitor SGA (database memory area) usage.

- Monitor fragmentation of tables, indexes, and free space.

- Monitor the FND.FND_CONCURRENT_REQUESTS table for excessive records.

These tasks will be described in the following sections of this chapter.

Database Planning

Each implementation of Oracle Financials will be different. However, there are several general guidelines to follow when creating databases to support this application. The sections that follow will describe the generic structure that should be extended to fit your site's specific needs.

Separation of Development and Production

Since Oracle Financials uses Oracle tools such as SQL*Forms for its data entry and reporting capabilities, developers may create new reports and add them to the application. Because of this capability, the development of add-ons to Financials must be managed via a methodology based on the guidelines in Chapter 5, "Managing the Development Process."

Since the tools used to access Financials (such as SQL*Forms 2.3) may actively use the database during execution, all development must take place outside of the Production instance. Since a separate Development database will be needed, the Demo database (MODEL90) is unnecessary in the Production instance. The Demo database should be loaded into the Test database for system testing or training purposes.

Choosing the Size and Number of Rollback Segments

Choosing exact values for the size and number of rollback segments involves analyzing the transaction volumes within the database (see Chapter 7, "Managing Rollback Segments"). The required size for the production transactions will be different than that of the transactions required for closing periods and performing large data loads. To design the rollback segments effectively, you must force such large transactions into their own extra-large rollback segments. Several general guidelines can be established for the data entry transactions in Financials databases, based on three factors.

First, estimate the number of concurrent transactions—how many processes will be concurrently *writing* rollback data?

Second, estimate the size of the an "average" transaction. This can be done empirically using the Development database and the monitoring scripts given in Chapter 7, "Managing Rollback Segments." The size of the transactions is dependent on the manner in which the application is used. Users who commit records infrequently will require much larger rollback segment entries—and thus much larger rollback segments—than users who commit frequently. If you encounter rollback segment space problems during data entry usage, work with the users to determine if the errors are being caused by infrequent commits—this can be resolved by training. If this is not the case, then the next design step, which concerns scheduling, should be evaluated.

The third step is to evaluate how often transactions are manipulating data that is needed by other transactions or queries. This causes the rollback segments to maintain a set of *inactive, in use* (IIU) data—and this data may be overwritten at any time after the manipulating transaction completes. There are two types of actions that control the amount of IIU data needed: the scheduling of long-running queries and the amount of overlap between concurrent data manipulation transactions.

By scheduling long-running jobs to be executed during times when very little data entry activity is occurring, the amount of IIU data needed will be greatly reduced. This data is needed to maintain a read-consistent image of the data as it existed when the query began. To reduce the amount of IIU space needed in the rollback segments, the DBA should work with the Financials SysAdmin to schedule long-running queries to run when the tables they are querying are not being modified.

Avoid the temptation to run such queries at lower operating system priority than other jobs. Doing so only increases the length of time during which the IIU data must remain in the rollback segment—and thereby increases the likelihood that the IIU data will be overwritten, causing the query to fail.

Appropriate values for the three factors can be determined by setting up a Test environment that closely mirrors the eventual Production instance. The following scripts, taken from Chapter 7, "Managing Rollback Segments," can be used to measure the actual transaction characteristics.

To analyze the number of concurrent transactions, run the following query. It determines the number of processes that are writing data to rollback segments at this instant. It makes use of the V$LOCK dynamic performance table to establish a relationship between rollback segments (from V$ROLLNAME) and the processes (from V$PROCESS) that hold locks on those rollback segments.

The following query is for Oracle Version 6:

```
REM*
REM*   Username to Rollback Segment mapping for Oracle Version 6.
REM*
SELECT
    R.NAME ROLLBACK_SEG,
    L.PID    ORACLE_PID,
    P.SPID   SYSTEM_PID,
    NVL(P.USERNAME,'NO TRANSACTION') TRANSACTION,
```

```
    P.TERMINAL
FROM V$LOCK L, V$PROCESS P, V$ROLLNAME R
    WHERE L.PID = P.PID (+)
    AND TRUNC(L.ID1(+)/65536)=R.USN
    AND L.TYPE(+) = 'TX'
    AND L.LMODE(+) = 6
    ORDER BY R.NAME;
```

Sample output is shown in the following listing.

```
ROLLBACK_SEG    ORACLE_PID SYSTEM_PI TRANSACTION     TERMINAL
-------------- ---------- --------- -------------- --------
R1                                  NO TRANSACTION
R2                                  NO TRANSACTION
R3                                  NO TRANSACTION
R4                 14 23C08791 GL               VTA3901:
R5                 15 23C00516 AP               VTA3980:
R6                 22 23C00413 PO               VTA3872:
SYSTEM                              NO TRANSACTION
```

This shows that only three users are actively writing to the rollback segments (GL, AP, and PO). Each is writing to a rollback segment that no one else is using. Rollback segments R1, R2, R3, and SYSTEM are presently inactive. If there were more than one user using a rollback segment, there would be multiple records for that rollback segment. You may wish to add a break on the ROLLBACK_SEG column to make this stand out.

For Oracle7, two minor changes must be made to account for a change in the Oracle7 V$LOCK table. That table no longer has a 'PID' (Process ID) column, so the ADDR (address) column is used in its place for the join to V$PROCESS. The PID selected is now retrieved from V$PROCESS.

```
REM*
REM*  Username to Rollback Segment mapping for Oracle7.
REM*
SELECT
    R.NAME ROLLBACK_SEG,
    P.PID    ORACLE_PID,
    P.SPID   SYSTEM_PID,
    NVL(P.USERNAME,'NO TRANSACTION') TRANSACTION,
    P.TERMINAL
FROM V$LOCK L, V$PROCESS P, V$ROLLNAME R
    WHERE L.ADDR = P.ADDR (+)
    AND TRUNC(L.ID1(+)/65536)=R.USN
```

```
AND L.TYPE(+) = 'TX'
AND L.LMODE(+) = 6
ORDER BY R.NAME;
```

DBAs using the UNIX operating system may not be able to see the actual usernames via these queries. That is because of the way in which database processes are managed under UNIX. In those systems, a second process will be started to access the database during database connections, and its username may be null. In that case, the NVL performed for the 'TRANSACTION' field will return the value 'NO TRANSACTION', even though the PID (Process ID) will be shown.

To determine the size of the transactions, query the V$ROLLSTAT dynamic performance table. For Financials, this should be done over a specific time interval (such as during a regular day of usage, when no extraordinary transactions will be run). Large transactions, such as budget loads, should be measured separately via the same means.

To determine the changes in the values of the V$ROLLSTAT columns during a specific time interval, the system statistics scripts can be used. These are called *BSTAT.SQL* and *ESTAT.SQL* in Oracle Version 6, and *UTLBSTAT.SQL* and *UTLESTAT.SQL* in Oracle7. Running these scripts is described in Chapter 6, "Monitoring Multiple Databases."

The BSTAT/UTLBSTAT script creates a table that stores the current values in the V$ROLLSTAT table. When ESTAT/UTLESTAT is run at a later date, V$ROLLSTAT's values at that time will be compared to those that were stored. The difference will be reported. It is important that the database not be shut down between the running of the BSTAT/UTLBSTAT script and the ESTAT/UTLESTAT script. This is because the database resets the statistics in the V$ROLLSTAT table during system startup; therefore, the baseline values generated by BSTAT/UTLBSTAT would be of no use following a database restart.

In the UTLBSTAT script, the following commands are used to create the tables at the beginning of the time interval. The first two CREATE TABLE commands create tables called STATS$BEGIN_ROLL and STATS$END_ROLL, both with no records in them. The INSERT command then stores the current values from the V$ROLLSTAT table into STATS$BEGIN_ROLL.

```
drop table stats$begin_roll;
create table stats$begin_roll
as select * from v$rollstat where 0 = 1;

drop table stats$end_roll;
create table stats$end_roll
as select * from stats$begin_roll;

insert into stats$begin_roll select * from v$rollstat;
```

When UTLESTAT is run, it populates the STATS$END_ROLL table by querying the V$ROLLSTAT table for the then-current values. A table called *STATS$ROLL* is then created. Its sole purpose is to hold the results of a query that determines the difference between the records in STATS$BEGIN_ROLL and STATS$END_ROLL. This is the table that is queried to generate the output report from UTLESTAT.

```
insert into stats$end_roll select * from v$rollstat;

create table stats$roll
as select  e.usn undo_segment,
        e.gets-b.gets trans_tbl_gets,
    e.waits-b.waits trans_tbl_waits,
    e.writes-b.writes undo_bytes_written,
    e.rssize segment_size_bytes,
        e.xacts-b.xacts xacts,
    e.shrinks-b.shrinks shrinks,
        e.wraps-b.wraps wraps
    from stats$begin_roll b, stats$end_roll e
        where e.usn = b.usn;
```

The data in the STATS$ROLL table lists each rollback segment, and the statistics that accumulated during the time between the running of UTLBSTAT and UTLESTAT.

Querying the STATS$ROLL table will return the columns listed in Table 12-2 for the interval.

The columns of greatest interest for the transaction sizing process are the TRANS_TBL_GETS, TRANS_TBL_WAITS, and UNDO_BYTES_WRITTEN columns. If the amount of waits is nonzero, then a transaction had to wait before acquiring a lock in the header of the rollback segment. This indicates that there are not enough rollback segments available.

The UNDO_BYTES_WRITTEN column displays the total number of bytes written to the rollback segment during the interval, while the TRANS_TBL_GETS column shows the number of transactions that wrote to the rollback segments. The number and average transaction size (UNDO_BYTES_WRITTEN/TRANS_TBL_GETS) is thus known.

The BSTAT/ESTAT reports of Oracle Version 6 function in a similar manner to the UTLBSTAT/UTLESTAT reports shown above. Its rollback segment output contains the columns listed in Table 12-3 for the interval.

The number and volume of average transactions in the Test database is now known. Create rollback segments that are designed to handle four to six average transactions each. Follow the instructions in Chapter 7, "Managing Rollback

COLUMN NAME	DESCRIPTION
TRANS_TBL_GETS	The number of rollback segment header requests.
TRANS_TBL_WAITS	The number of rollback segment header requests that resulted in waits.
UNDO_BYTES_WRITTEN	The number of bytes written to the rollback segment.
SEGMENT_SIZE_BYTES	The size of the rollback segment, in bytes. Note that this column only considers the ending value.
XACTS	The number of active transactions.
SHRINKS	The number of shrinks that the rollback segment had to perform in order to stay at the OPTIMAL size.
WRAPS	The number of times a rollback segment entry wrapped from one extent into another.

TABLE 12-2.   *Columns Available in STATS$ROLL for Oracle7*

Segments" to determine the final number and size. For Financials, use an IIU percentage of 15 to 20 percent.

The Second Temporary Tablespace: TEMP_GL

The GL user in Financials databases has processing space requirements that exceed those of all the rest of the database users combined. It needs to have a large temporary tablespace available for its processing. Since its requirements are so

COLUMN NAME	DESCRIPTION
TRANS_TBL_GETS	The number of rollback segment header requests.
TRANS_TBL_WAITS	The number of rollback segment header requests that resulted in waits.
UNDO_BYTES_WRITTEN	The number of bytes written to the rollback segment.
SEGMENT_SIZE_BYTES	The size of the rollback segment, in bytes. Note that this column only considers the ending value.

TABLE 12-3.   *Columns Available in STATS$ROLL for Oracle Version 6*

unique, isolate its temporary tablespace from the rest of the users by creating a tablespace that is used only for GL's temporary segments. Start with a tablespace that is between 50 and 100 megabytes in size. Create it so that it has 20 to 50 divisions (as shown below) so that you can measure the actual usage in the tablespace. Then assign the GL user to this tablespace using the commands shown in the following listing.

```
CREATE TABLESPACE TEMP_GL
DATAFILE '/db01/oracle/FIN/temp_gl.dbf' SIZE 100M
DEFAULT STORAGE
(INITIAL 5M NEXT 5M PCTINCREASE 0);

ALTER USER GL TEMPORARY TABLESPACE TEMP_GL;

GRANT RESOURCE (50M) ON TEMP_GL TO GL;
```

In an Oracle7 database, the granting of space quota on a tablespace is done via the ALTER USER command, as shown in the following listing

```
ALTER USER gl QUOTA 50M on TEMP_GL;
```

In this example, the tablespace is created with a size of 100M. Its default storage parameters will use that space in 5M extents. Therefore, after a large GL transaction has completed, the number of free extents in the tablespace that are 5M in size will tell you how large the temporary segment became (if you are using Oracle Version 6). In Oracle7, this capability is no longer available, since the free space that is released by the temporary segment when the transaction completes is recombined with the rest of the free space in the tablespace. The only way to see the amount of free space used is to query the DBA_SEGMENTS table while the transaction is under way.

```
REM *
REM * How large are the temporary segments that are
REM *    currently in use?
REM *
REM * For Oracle Version 6 and Oracle7
REM *
SELECT
    EXTENTS,          /*How many extents does the temp segment have?*/
    BYTES,            /*How large is it, in bytes? */
    BLOCKS            /*How large is it, in Oracle blocks? */
FROM DBA_SEGMENTS
WHERE SEGMENT_TYPE = 'TEMPORARY';
```

This query will provide information about each of the temporary segments currently in use in the database. It displays the number of extents and total size of each such segment.

The final command in the example above granted the GL user RESOURCE privilege on the TEMP_GL tablespace. This privilege is not necessary to create temporary segments. Rather, its purpose is to allow the GL user to create several small tables that are stored apart from the GL production tables.

File Locations

The optimal file locations for the files used by the Financials database depend on your specific implementation of the application. However, there are several generic guidelines that can be used to establish a baseline configuration. The guidelines in Chapter 4, "Physical Database Layouts," can then be used to further refine their placements. Those guidelines include estimating the relative I/O weight for each file in the database.

Oracle software and the application software for Financials should be stored on separate disks to avoid concurrent I/O contention.

Online redo logs should be fairly large in size—5 to 10M each. There should be at least four of them for each Financials instance. Since they will typically experience heavy usage, they should be stored on a disk with little other activity.

The "FND" account should have two tablespaces: one for its tables, and one for its indexes. These tables and indexes will store the data used by the SQL*Forms applications. These tablespaces will generally have a high I/O weight (see Chapter 4, "Physical Database Layouts"), and they should be stored on separate devices to minimize concurrent I/O contention.

Each module (such as General Ledger) will need a pair of tablespaces: one for its tables and one for its indexes. These tablespaces should be created on different devices, to help minimize concurrent I/O contention. The main modules installed at your site (such as GL, FA, AP) should be separate across disks as well. That is, you should not store the GL tables on the same disk as the AP tables since entries into one module's tables may impact another module's tables, triggering concurrent I/O contention.

There should be at least two rollback segment tablespaces. Create one for the production data entry usage, and another (RBS_2) to be used during large data loads and month-end closings. They may be stored on the same device, since they are rarely used at the same time.

A small TOOLS directory will be needed to support the Oracle tools that are installed with Financials. It typically experiences very little I/O relative to the rest of the database files.

As previously noted, two temporary tablespaces are needed: TEMP for all users but GL, and TEMP_GL for the GL account's exclusive use. They may be stored on the same device. Of the two, TEMP_GL will experience far greater I/O. Its relative weight within the database is dependent on the way in which the application is being used. If many periods are open at once, then the processing requirements for postings will increase greatly, which will in turn increase the size of the temporary tables created by GL.

In the Development and Test databases, a DEMO tablespace will be needed to hold the objects created for the Demo account. This tablespace should be relatively dormant outside of training times.

Concurrent Managers

To minimize the amount of rollback segment space needed, encourage the use of the concurrent managers to schedule jobs appropriately. They allow jobs to be held until a specific start time, and run when there will be little interference from data manipulation transactions. Use the scripts given previously in the "Choosing the Size and Number of Rollback Segments" section of this chapter to determine how many processes are actively writing data while a report is being run. Whenever possible, that number should be zero.

INIT.ORA Parameters

There are several database initialization parameters that can be set (via the INIT.ORA initialization parameter file) to improve the performance of Oracle Financials. The major parameters to set are listed in the following sections.

SGA Size
The System Global Area (SGA) is the memory area that is available to the instance. Data that is read from the database is held in the SGA for quick retrieval by other users. Structural information about the database and the data returned by transactions is stored in the SGA. In Oracle7 databases, an additional area called the Shared SQL Area stores the parsed version of statements run against the database.

For Financials, make the SGA as large as possible given the memory available on your server. The Oracle Financials Installation Guide gives calculations for the minimum SGA size that should be used. In general, expect the data buffer cache in the Financials Production SGA to take between 10 and 20 percent of the server's memory. This value is set via the DB_BLOCK_BUFFERS parameter in the database's INIT.ORA file. Its initial value is dependent on the amount of memory available on the server.

Open Cursors
The INIT.ORA "open_cursors" parameter limits the number of open cursors (context areas) that can be simultaneously held by each user process. In Oracle Version 6,

the maximum value is 255; in Oracle7, it is operating system-dependent. For both versions it should be set to its maximum value for Financials users.

Optimizer Changes

When Oracle Version 6.0.33.1 was released, the internal Oracle optimizer was modified. One of the changes involved the manner in which nested sub-queries were handled by the optimizer. A side effect of this change was to slow down the performance of Financials reports that had been created with the previous optimizer functionality in mind.

To offset this change, a special INIT.ORA parameter must be used. Its first character is an underscore (_), and its entry is shown in the following listing.

```
_optimizer_undo_changes    = TRUE
```

Dictionary Cache Parameters

The dictionary cache within the SGA holds structural information about the database. In Oracle Version 6, DBAs can specify values for each individual cache within the dictionary cache. In Oracle7, the dictionary cache is part of the Shared SQL Area, so the sizes of the individual caches are set indirectly via the size specified for that area.

Having a dictionary cache that is too small prevents the database from taking full advantage of the SGA's performance benefits. If the space available to a cache is insufficient, it must dynamically choose which of its entries has been least recently used. This entry is then written back to disk and replaced by a newly-read entry.

As previously noted, Financials has over 1,000 tables (in Release 9.3.7, 1,003 tables). To accommodate the application's needs, the INIT.ORA entries listed in Table 12-4 can be used as a starting point. Use the memory monitoring scripts in Chapter 6, "Monitoring Multiple Databases," to determine which of the parameters should be raised or lowered.

PARAMETER	VALUE
DC_TABLES	1500
DC_OBJECTS	2000
DC_INDEXES	1500
DC_COLUMNS	4000
DC_SYNONYMS	1500

TABLE 12-4. *Recommended Settings for Major INIT.ORA Parameters for Oracle Financials in Oracle Version 6*

These parameters are for Oracle Version 6. For Oracle7, start with a Shared SQL Area size of 8M. Be sure to monitor it to determine if its size needs to be increased or decreased for your installation.

Block Size

To maximize performance within Financials, increase the Oracle block size used. Rather than using a 2048 byte block size, increase it to 4096. This will reduce the percentage of each block that is devoted to overhead. As a result, more data will be read with each I/O. This should in turn result in fewer I/Os being necessary to resolve a query, thus improving performance. The INIT.ORA entry for this parameter is

```
block_size    = 4096
```

Note that for Oracle7, this entry is stored in the config*DB_NAME*.ora file that is referenced by the database's INIT.ORA file.

Monitoring

Financials databases must be monitored closely. The Command Center monitoring application described in Chapter 6, "Monitoring Multiple Databases," captures the information most relevant for judging the health of a Financials database. This includes the current length of the rollback segments, the number of extents in tables and indexes, and the percentage of free space in tablespaces.

The following sections describe important aspects of these measurements for Financials databases.

Most Active Tables and Indexes

The tables and indexes that are most likely to extend depend on the specific modules that have been installed, and the manner in which they are being used. In general, several tables and their indexes experience growth spurts that cause them to become fragmented quickly. Since Financials is heavily indexed, expect the indexes to encounter problems first. The tables to monitor are listed in Table 12-5. Their indexes will be the ones most likely to extend.

The actual tables that will experience extension problems in your Financials database will vary. Creating and running a Command Center monitoring database (see Chapter 6, "Monitoring Multiple Databases") will greatly simplify the process of identifying problem areas. Note that most of the FND tables, since they define

OWNER	TABLE NAME
AP	AP_INVOICES
AP	AP_PAYMENT_SCHEDULES
GL	GL_BALANCES
GL	GL_BUDGET_INTERIM
GL	GL_SUMMARY_INTERIM
GL	GL_JE_LINES
PO	PO_VENDORS
PO	PO_VENDOR_SITES
RA	RA_CUSTOMER_TRX
RA	RA_CUSTOMER_TRX_LINES

TABLE 12-5. *Financials Tables Most Likely to Extend*

the application's forms interface, are fairly static and large in size. Other tables, such as GL.GL_CODE_COMBINATIONS, may experience great expansion during initial database load and setup, then become very static.

Space Trend Monitoring

Changes in the free space available within tablespaces must be monitored. The trending reports given in Chapter 6, "Monitoring Multiple Databases," display this information for each tablespace. The tablespaces most likely to experience changes in free space are the modules' tablespaces. Since Financials is a heavily indexed application, the free space in the modules' index tablespaces may decrease at a faster rate than their associated tables.

Tuning

Once the database has been planned, installed, and monitored, it may then be tuned. The estimates that were made earlier for Test databases can now be verified against Production.

Monitoring SGA Usage

In order to ensure that the SGA has been properly sized, the database's system monitoring scripts should be run. These scripts, called BSTAT.SQL and ESTAT.SQL for Oracle Version 6, and UTLBSTAT.SQL and UTLESTAT.SQL for Oracle7, create beginning and ending copies of the system statistics tables for a specific time interval. Their usage for monitoring the SGA is described in Chapter 6, "Monitoring Multiple Databases." The proper interpretation of the output report is also described in that chapter.

Verifying I/O Weights

After the database has been in use, the I/O weights that were estimated for the database files can be verified. To do this, use the calculations given in the "Verification of I/O Weighting Estimates" section of Chapter 4, "Physical Database Layouts."

The GL Optimizer

Oracle Version 6 uses a rule-based optimizer to determine the best access path to use to retrieve data. However, these rules fail to take into account the nature of the data: how it is distributed, how many rows are in each table, and how unique an index is, for example.

In order to enhance the performance of Oracle Financials, a cost-based optimizer was developed to serve the application. This optimizer populates the GL.GL_SEGMENT_RATIOS table, which is then used to determine which index should be used for each of the Financial Statement Generator (FSG) reports. When an FSG report is run, it then suppresses all but the most selective index for that report.

Since the FSG reports rely on the GL_SEGMENT_RATIOS table, they will only choose the proper index if the GL_SEGMENT_RATIOS table is up to date. The optimizer should be run to repopulate this table when the account structure of the general ledger changes, when the summary template structure changes, and periodically during regular usage (for example, following month-end closings). To run the GL optimizer, the Financials SysAdmin chooses the Optimizer option from the Financials Navigate/Setup/System menu. Although the DBA is not directly involved in this task, it has a direct effect on performance and appropriate schedule and should thus be coordinated between the DBA and the Financials SysAdmin.

CHAPTER 13

Supporting Oracle Utilities

The Oracle database provides a strong foundation for application data storage and manipulation. Oracle utilities are the tools with which those applications are built. These utilities include data entry tools, such as SQL*Forms, and reporting tools, such as SQL*ReportWriter. The Oracle utilities described in this book are listed in Table 13-1.

Usage of Export and Import is described in Chapter 10, "Optimal Backup and Recovery Procedures," and in Chapter 8, "Database Tuning." This chapter will provide additional information for the administration of these tools.

This chapter contains support notes that are applicable to all Oracle utilities, followed by notes for each of the utilities listed in Table 13-1. The only exceptions to this are Oracle*CASE, whose administrative tasks are fully described in Chapter

UTILITY	USAGE
Export	Performs logical backups of the database.
Import	Reads the output of Export operations and inserts it into the database.
Oracle*CASE	Models database entities and their relationships.
Programmatic Interfaces	Access the database via programs (such as Pro*C).
SQL*Forms	Creates data entry screens.
SQL*Loader	Performs bulk loads of data from flat files into Oracle tables.
SQL*Menu	Creates menus for applications.
SQL*Net	Communicates between databases.
SQL*Plus	Command-line interface for SQL commands.
SQL*ReportWriter	Creates reports against database data.
SQL*TextRetrieval	Performs text-based searches on database data.

TABLE 13-1.   *Oracle Utilities*

11, "Supporting Oracle*CASE," and SQL*Net, whose administrative tasks are fully described in Chapter 15, "SQL*Net V1 and V2."

Support Notes for All Oracle Utilities

Most of the utilities listed in Table 13-1 depend on underlying structures in the database. Table 13-2 lists the object dependencies of the utilities that will be described in this chapter.

The database must support these dependencies. As a DBA, there are several key points to address, including the location of the tables needed by the utilities, and the possibility of having multiple copies of the product tables.

Location of Product Tables

Although tables for several of these utilities are created under the SYSTEM schema, that does *not* mean that those tables have to be created in the SYSTEM tablespace. The best way to keep product tables from being created in the SYSTEM tablespace

UTILITY	DEPENDENT ON
Export	SYS-owned export views, plus tables to record incremental exports.
SQL*Forms	SYSTEM-owned tables and views to record forms definitions.
SQL*Menu	SYSTEM-owned tables and views to record menu definitions and privileges.
SQL*Plus	SYSTEM-owned tables and views to record user profile and help information.
SQL*ReportWriter	SYSTEM-owned tables and views to record reports definitions.
SQL*TextRetrieval	DBA account-owned tables and views to record text retrieval configuration, plus user-owned hit list tables.

TABLE 13-2. *Object Dependencies of Oracle Utilities*

is to precreate the database, using the procedures given in Appendix A, "Database Creation Procedures." Using those directions results in the following conditions:

- A tablespace called TOOLS is created for product tables.
- The SYSTEM user does not have RESOURCE Privilege on the SYSTEM tablespace.
- The SYSTEM user has RESOURCE Privilege on the TOOLS tablespace.
- The SYSTEM user has TOOLS as its default tablespace.

Once these conditions are established, the Oracle utilities should then be installed in the database. Any object created in the SYSTEM schema will automatically be placed in the TOOLS tablespace. This will help to keep the SYSTEM data dictionary tablespace from containing non-data dictionary tables.

User Copies of Product Tables

The Oracle utilities that create tables under the SYSTEM account also create public synonyms that point to these tables. Thus, any user in the database can access them without specifying the table owner.

For example, SQL*Forms 3.0 creates a table called FORM_TRIGGER under the SYSTEM schema. It grants SELECT, INSERT, UPDATE, and DELETE Privilege on this table to PUBLIC—that is, to all users. It then creates a public synonym called FORM_TRIGGER that points to this table via the following command.

```
CREATE PUBLIC SYNONYM form_trigger FOR system.form_trigger;
```

After those grants and synonyms have been created (via the iadgrants.sql script, in the $ORACLE_HOME/forms30/admin directory), any user can access the SYSTEM.FORM_TRIGGER table via the FORM_TRIGGER synonym.

Since the tables are being accessed solely via synonyms, *they do not have to be created under the SYSTEM schema.* They can be created under *any* account. Not only that, but multiple copies of the tables can be created under separate accounts.

This option is shown in Figure 13-1.

As shown in Figure 13-1(a), the default configuration calls for utility tables to be created in a single schema (usually the SYSTEM schema). Public synonyms are then available to all users. However, the option shown in Figure 13-1(b) is often useful. In this configuration, the main set of tables is still created under the SYSTEM schema. However, a second set of the utility tables is created under a second user account. This user will not access the SYSTEM set of tables, since having its own

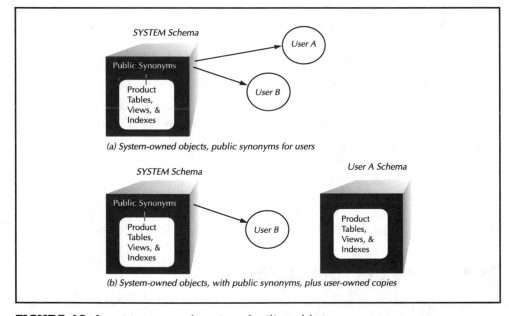

(a) System-owned objects, public synonyms for users

(b) System-owned objects, with public synonyms, plus user-owned copies

FIGURE 13-1. *User-owned copies of utility tables*

set of objects with the same names as the public synonyms will override the ability to use those synonyms.

Why do such a thing? There are several good reasons to consider the user-owned objects option. In environments in which multiple development teams are using the same tool, it is often useful to separate their efforts to minimize contention. Doing so will also reduce the rate at which a single set of tables would acquire additional storage space. Although creating the same applications under two sets of utility tables instead of one set will not decrease the tables' space requirements, it will make it easier to manage their space needs. It will also help to prevent the actions of one team from impacting the other.

You may also wish to use one set of the tables as a tool for maintaining a copy of an earlier version of the application. This is particularly useful for tools such as SQL*Menu 5.0, which dynamically looks at its tables while the application is executing.

There are two options for creating the second set of application objects: First, you can export the table structures needed from the SYSTEM user, and import them into a second user. This requires that you know the names of all of the tables you need. The following commands illustrate this process. See Chapter 10, "Optimal Backup and Recovery Procedures," for further information on the Export and Import options shown here.

```
exp system/manager file=forms_tables.dmp tables=(system.form_trigger,
    other tables)
imp system/manager file=forms_tables.dmp FROMUSER=SYSTEM TOUSER=APPLDEV1
    commit=Y buffer=64000
```

In this example, the SQL*Forms tables owned by the SYSTEM user are copied to the APPLDEV1 schema via the use of the FROMUSER and TOUSER clauses, following a Table export of the SQL*Forms tables.

The second option for creating sets of utility tables involves using the object creation scripts called by the Oracle installation program. Most of these scripts are found in the /admin directory of the appropriate tool. For example, for SQL*Forms 3.0, they are found in $ORACLE_HOME/forms30/admin. The table, view, and index creation scripts can be found there. The grants and synonym scripts should also be in that directory, but they are not necessary when creating a second set of the utility tables. Although you are creating a second set of the utility tables, leave the public synonyms pointing to the SYSTEM-owned tables in place.

Controlling Access to Utilities

If your users are able to access the server's operating system, then you may wish to add another level of security to your applications by controlling access to the Oracle utilities' executables. That is, you probably don't want users to be able to develop their own SQL*Forms 3.0 or SQL*Menu 5.0 applications. In order to prevent this, modify the operating system privileges so that they only have access to the modules they need. In the case of SQL*Forms 3.0, for example, they need access to RUNFORM30 but not to SQLFORMS30.

Product-Specific Support

In the following sections you will find product-specific information about supporting the utilities listed in Table 13-1, with the exceptions of SQL*Net and Oracle*CASE (which are covered in Chapter 15, "SQL*Net V1 and V2," and Chapter 11, "Supporting Oracle*CASE," respectively).

Export/Import

The Oracle Export utility reads data from the database and writes it to a binary file called an export dump file. This file can then be used by the Import utility to read data into a database.

How does Export know which objects to select, and in what order? To do this, Export makes use of a set of views created under the SYS user. The creation script for these views is called expvew.sql for Oracle Version 6; in Oracle7 it is named catexp.sql. It is located in the $ORACLE_HOME/rdbms/admin directory.

In certain circumstances, you may need to edit this view script. For example, if there is a single table in your database that is corrupt, and you wish to export the entire rest of the database, how can you do it? The easiest way is to modify the view that lists the tables that will be exported. This view is called EXUTAB.

To remove an object from the list of those that will be exported, edit the export view creation script. In the WHERE clause of the EXUTAB view, append the line

```
AND O$.NAME <> 'table name'
```

In the view's query, "O$" is the alias given to the SYS.OBJ$ table. This is a kernel table that holds information about all database objects. The "O$.NAME" column lists the names of the objects to be exported. By adding this additional clause to the view's WHERE clause, you eliminate any object with that name from the list of those to be exported.

Once the view has been modified, rerun the export view creation script to drop and re-create the EXUTAB view. All subsequent exports of that database will not export tables with the name you specified in your addition to the WHERE clause.

Export also makes use of several tables to record the status of Incremental exports (see Chapter 10, "Optimal Backup and Recovery Procedures," for details on this option). The tables are owned by SYS and should not be moved from the

ORACLE7	ORACLE VERSION 6
SYS.INCVID	SYS.INCVID
SYS.INCEXP	SYS.INCEXP
SYS.INCFIL	

TABLE 13-3. *Tables Used During Incremental Exports.*

SYSTEM tablespace. Their names for Oracle7 and Oracle Version 6 are listed in Table 13-3.

Programmatic Interfaces

The programmatic interfaces to Oracle allow application developers to write programs in 3GL programming languages that can access the database. Oracle supports a number of such programming languages, including C, FORTRAN, COBOL, and Ada.

As a DBA, the most important support note for the programmatic interfaces concerns upgrades to the database or operating system software. Since the users' programs use the Oracle kernel's software libraries, and since the operating system software libraries are also used, any modification to either library requires that the users' programs be relinked. This should take place any time the database software is upgraded (for example, from version 7.0.16 to 7.1) or the operating system software is upgraded.

SQL*Forms

The information given earlier in this chapter about moving application tables out of the SYSTEM tablespace and creating copies of them in non-SYSTEM schemas is completely applicable to SQL*Forms. In addition, SQL*Forms applications can have user exits linked to them. User exits are programs, written in one of the programmatic interfaces, that can be called directly from within a SQL*Forms application.

Linking a user exit to the SQL*Forms executables requires that the user exit's *link library* be added to the *link list* of the SQL*Forms executables. These libraries of programming routines are read each time the executables are relinked to the Oracle kernel. Adding the user exit libraries to the SQL*Forms link list ensures that the user exit will always be available within SQL*Forms.

User exits do not have to be linked to the production copy of the executables. Instead, a second copy of the executable can be created, leaving the original intact. Only the new copy of the executable will contain the user exit. This feature is useful for testing user exits before moving them to the production copy of the executable.

The methods for performing these links and the files involved are operating system-dependent; the instructions are in the Oracle *Installation and User's Guide* for the operating system.

SQL*Loader

SQL*Loader is a utility for loading data into Oracle tables from external files. As a DBA, you only have to be concerned with two aspects of its usage:

1. Are the tables and indexes properly sized for the data load that is expected?

2. Is the Direct Path option being used? (It is available only in Oracle7.)

The table and index size calculations (see Chapter 5, "Managing the Development Process") should take into account the data that is coming in via flat files. Typically, this data's length and volume are very well defined, so the sizing estimates should be accurate.

If it is a one-time load used for initial population of the data, then do not create the indexes until after the data has been loaded and the table's sizing has been verified.

The Direct Path option available in Oracle7 is a high-speed method for inserting data into tables. It bypasses the normal processing of INSERT statements and instead writes directly to the table's data blocks. When using Direct Path, the data in the flat file should be presorted. For large data loads, the performance gains are considerable.

Of course, someone must pay the cost for such gains. In this case, it is the tablespace used for temporary segments. When a Direct Path load is started, the table's indexes are placed in an invalid state for the duration of the load. As data is loaded into the table, the new index key values are written to a temporary segment. When the load completes, the old index values and the new values are merged, and the index once again becomes valid.

The implication of this for temporary segment storage space is considerable. SQL*Loader requires that enough space be available in the temporary tablespace to hold, at a minimum, the INITIAL extent sizes of all the indexes on the table being loaded. Since the Direct Path option is normally used on large data loads, the space requirements for the temporary tablespace are usually large. They are determined by the index sizing. For unsorted data loads, the temporary tablespace size requirements may be *twice* the index size requirements.

To determine the status of an index, query the DBA_INDEXES view, as shown in the following listing. Valid "STATUS" values are "DIRECT LOAD" and "VALID".

```
SELECT
      owner,          /*Owner of the index*/
      index_name,     /*Name of the index*/
      status          /*Either DIRECT PATH or VALID*/
FROM dba_indexes;
```

SQL*Menu

SQL*Menu is typically used as a companion tool to SQL*Forms. The information given earlier in this chapter about moving application tables out of the SYSTEM tablespace and creating copies of them in non-SYSTEM schemas is completely applicable to SQL*Menu. In addition, SQL*Menu applications can call SQL*Forms applications that have user exits linked to them. User exits are programs, written in one of the programmatic interfaces, that can be called directly from within a SQL*Forms application.

When a user exit is linked to a SQL*Forms executable, it should also be linked to the SQL*Menu executable that will be calling that form—for SQL*Menu 5.0, this is RUNMENU50.

Linking a user exit to the SQL*Menu executables requires that the user exit's *link library* be added to the *link list* of the SQL*Menu executables. These libraries of programming routines are read each time the executables are relinked to the Oracle kernel. Adding the user exit libraries to the SQL*Menu link list ensures that the user exit will always be available within SQL*Menu.

User exits do not have to be linked to the production copy of the executables. Instead, a second copy of the executable can be created, leaving the original intact. Only the new copy of the executable will contain the user exit. This feature is useful for testing user exits before moving them to the production copy of the executable.

The methods for performing these links and the files involved are operating system-dependent; the instructions are in the Oracle *Installation and User's Guide* for the operating system.

SQL*Plus

SQL*Plus is the command line interface to the Oracle database. There are two features of it that DBAs should be familiar with: the HELP table and the Product User Profile tables.

First, during installation of the SQL*Plus tool, the DBA will be asked if the SQL*Plus HELP table should be loaded. This table is very simple in structure. It contains the text from the *SQL*Plus Users Guide* for each of the available commands. However, most users of this tool should be experienced enough that they do not need this information available online. Even if they did want it online, the interface to the text in the HELP table is unwieldy. If you plan to load it, it will require around 20M of space in the database, and it will be created under the SYSTEM schema. Be sure that the SYSTEM user's default tablespace is set to the TOOLS tablespace before loading the HELP table.

To check the default tablespace assignment, query the DBA_USERS view, as shown in the following listing.

```
SELECT
      username,
      default_tablespace
FROM dba_users
WHERE username = 'SYSTEM';
```

The second SQL*Plus feature that concerns DBAs is the use of "*product user profile*" information. This set of tables and views allows DBAs to restrict which SQL*Plus commands are available to users. The use of these tables is described in Chapter 9, "Database Security and Auditing."

The product user profile tables should always be loaded. Before creating them, make sure that the SYSTEM user's default tablespace is set to TOOLS. Only two tables, PRODUCT_PROFILE and USER_PROFILE, will be created, along with several views.

The script that creates these tables and views is called pupbld.sql, and it is located in the $ORACLE_HOME/sqlplus/admin directory. It must be run from within SQL*Plus, when logged in as the SYSTEM user.

SQL*ReportWriter

SQL*ReportWriter is an Oracle report generation tool. Report definitions are stored in tables in the database.

The option of having user-based rather than centralized tables for SQL*ReportWriter is automated via the Oracle Installer. If you choose to have centralized tables, then you must first assign TOOLS as the default tablespace of the SYSTEM user. If you decide the users will have individual copies of the SQL*ReportWriter tables, the users' default tablespace settings should be set to the USERS tablespace.

As with the SQL*Forms tables, a centralized version should be used in Production environments and in isolated development databases. If multiple applications that use SQL*ReportWriter are being developed in the same database, then use multiple copies of the utility's tables.

SQL*TextRetrieval

SQL*TextRetrieval is a text-based searching tool. It allows users to search database fields (or external files) for keywords. The use of thesauri, synonym rings, proximity searching, and fuzzy matching is also supported.

SQL*TextRetrieval creates tables under a user who has DBA Privilege. This user does not have to be the SYSTEM user; this makes it very easy to point to the TOOLS tablespace instead of the SYSTEM tablespace. Separate user accounts can be created to use for the tutorial and demo tables.

This product requires that several other Oracle products be installed. Its administrative interface uses SQL*Forms and SQL*Menu for its front-end, and SQL*Plus and PL/SQL for its processing. When any of those products is upgraded, SQL*TextRetrieval should be relinked to make sure the product software libraries are in sync.

CHAPTER 14

Supporting Third-Party Tools

A large number of tools written by companies other than Oracle access the Oracle database. In addition to those tools written specifically for the Oracle database, tools written for other databases are often converted to support Oracle databases. These tools developed by companies other than Oracle are referred to as *third-party* tools.

Ad hoc query tools and application development tools are common types of third-party tools. When managing databases that are accessed by these tools, DBAs must take into consideration the same guidelines that apply to in-house applications. These guidelines, as discussed in Chapter 3, "Logical Database Layouts," and Chapter 5, "Managing the Development Process," call for consistent database configurations and planning.

TOOLS	DESCRIPTION
Forest & Trees	Decision support query tool
IQ for Windows	Ad hoc and batch query tool
PowerBuilder	Application development
PowerViewer	Ad hoc query tool portion of PowerBuilder tool set
Q+E	Ad hoc query tool
SQL*Assist	Ad hoc query tool
SQR	Report writer/4GL

TABLE 14-1.   *Third-Party Tools*

The third-party tools that will be discussed here are listed in Table 14-1.

In the following sections you will see descriptions of the database administration requirements for each of these tools.

Forest & Trees

Forest & Trees is a decision support query tool sold by Trinzic, Inc. It is used to develop canned queries that access the database, for use in business analysis. It is a Windows-based tool that requires SQL*Net for Windows in order to communicate with the host database across a network.

Version 3.01 of Forest & Trees supports both Oracle Version 6 and Oracle7. It does not require any modifications to the Oracle database structures, nor do its users require any special system privileges.

IQ for Windows

IQ for Windows is an ad hoc query tool sold by IQ Software for the Windows environment (using SQL*Net for Windows). There are also versions of this tool available for server operating systems (such as VMS and UNIX), so it can be used as a batch reporting tool as well. Version 3.02.14 of this tool is able to access both Oracle Version 6 and Oracle7.

No database modifications on the server are necessary to support this product. All modifications are made on the client installation.

Once installed, the product must be activated on the Windows client by means of an activation serial number. Once installation is complete, the following lines must be added to the c:\iqwin\IQCONFIG.DAT file for Oracle7 compliance:

```
##  These additions are for Oracle7 compliance
    G6 2000,2000
    G7 2000,2000
```

To access Oracle7, users specify a connect string to an Oracle7 database during Category setup.

PowerBuilder

PowerBuilder is an application development tool suite for the Windows environment (using SQL*Net for Windows), sold by PowerSoft. Version 2 of PowerBuilder supports Oracle Version 6; Version 3 of this product supports both Oracle Version 6 and Oracle7.

PowerBuilder requires several DBA actions in order for users to be able to use the tool. These involve table creations, table moves, grants, and catalog changes.

First, PowerBuilder creates a set of its own tables to manage database catalog information (the number and names of these tables changed from Version 2 to Version 3 of PowerBuilder). To create these tables, log into PowerBuilder as the SYSTEM user for the database. The first time that you use PowerBuilder to log into the SYSTEM account in a database, PowerBuilder will automatically create its tables under that account. Immediately check to make sure that these tables were not created in the SYSTEM tablespace. If they were, move them to the TOOLS tablespace via the methods described in Chapter 3, "Logical Database Layouts."

Once those tables have been created, grant SELECT, INSERT, UPDATE, and DELETE privilege on them to PUBLIC, and create public synonyms for them. Failing to do so will cause users to get "Insufficient privileges" errors when they attempt to access the database via PowerBuilder.

Although PowerBuilder 3.0 can access the Oracle7 database, it still requires that the Oracle Version 6 data dictionary catalog views be created. To create them, use the commands in the following listing. These commands use the UNIX "cd" command to go to the /rdbms/admin directory under $ORACLE_HOME. The CATALOG6.SQL file is then run to create the catalog views.

```
cd $ORACLE_HOME/rdbms/admin
sqldba
SQLDBA> connect internal
SQLDBA> catalog6
```

Whenever possible, prevent users from using the database painter or the database administrator of PowerBuilder to create database objects. PowerBuilder places quote marks (") around column and table names in CREATE TABLE commands—and doing so allows database objects to be created with invalid names. These names may include reserved words (such as DATE) and lowercase letters (which are then stored in the database's data dictionary tables as lowercase letters).

To access an Oracle7 database from the Windows client, create a new logon profile on the client (File-Connect-Setup-New). Enter a name for the new profile. Enter "OR7" for the DBMS to connect to Oracle7 (as opposed to "OR6" for Oracle Version 6 connections). The associated connect string for this profile must specify an Oracle7 instance. During PowerBuilder 3.0 installation on the Windows client, choose the "PowerSoft Oracle Interface" option of the "Database Development and Deployment Kit" installation screen.

PowerViewer

PowerViewer is an ad hoc query tool sold by PowerSoft as part of the PowerBuilder tool set. Version 3.0 of this tool accesses both Oracle Version 6 and Oracle7. It runs in the Windows environment, requiring SQL*Net for Windows to access remote databases. It does not require any modifications to the Oracle database structures, nor do its users require any special system privileges.

To access an Oracle7 database, create a new logon profile on the Windows client (File-Connect-Setup-New). Enter a name for the new profile. Enter "OR7" for the DBMS to connect to Oracle7 (as opposed to "OR6" for Oracle Version 6 connections). The associated connect string for this profile must specify an Oracle7 instance.

Q+E

Q+E is an ad hoc query tool that is part of the Microsoft Office tool set. Version 3.0 of this tool can be used against Oracle Version 6. Version 5.0 can be used against both Oracle Version 6 and Oracle7. It does not require any modifications to the Oracle database structures, nor do its users require any special system privileges.

Q+E can also be used to create tables in the database. Users of this functionality in Q+E should note that Version 5.0 does not allow creation of VARCHAR2 columns except via its SQL window. When the resulting table is viewed, the column may be listed as a CHAR column.

SQL * Assist

SQL*Assist is an ad hoc query tool that runs under many environments, including UNIX and VMS, and has the ability to store the query output in a number of formats, including SAS datasets. Version 3.21 of this tool supports both Oracle Version 6 and Oracle7. It does not require any modifications to the Oracle database structures, nor do its users require any special system privileges.

SQR

SQR defies description in a single sentence. It can be used as a report writer, a programming language, or a data load/unload utility. It has its own users' group and newsletter; product support is currently provided by MITI. It runs in a variety of operating systems (UNIX, VMS, Windows). It must be re-linked to the Oracle kernel each time that it or the kernel is upgraded. Relinking is accomplished by running the LINKSQR program in the program directory.

SQR also comes with a user exit called SQREXIT that can be linked with SQL*Forms. Applications created in SQL*Forms can then call SQR directly via user exit calls. However, if the called SQR program encounters an error, then the user will be disconnected from the database while still in the calling application. An ORA-3114 error will be returned, forcing the user to exit Oracle completely and then reconnect to the application.

Version 2.4.1 is the first version of SQR that is certified against both Oracle Version 6 and Oracle7. DBAs do not have to make any changes to the database to support this tool. As a matter of fact, you may wish to use its data unload/load utilities, provided via the EXPORT.SQR program. This program automatically generates two SQR programs: one for writing a table's data to a flat file, and another for inserting that data back into the database. Since these programs can be modified, this is equivalent to doing a selective export.

This program can be extended and modified by users. In its standard form, it trims timestamps off of date fields and does not handle stored carriage returns correctly. For further information on these modifications, see "Extending EXPORT.SQR" by Matthew Reagan, in the *Newsletter of the National SQR Users Group*, Volume 2, Issue 1. The National SQR Users Group can be reached via phone at 610/286-6204.

PART 4

Networked Oracle

CHAPTER 15

SQL*Net V1 and V2

I t's hard to find a computer these days that isn't tied into a network. Distributing computing power across servers and sharing information across networks greatly enhances the value of the computing resources available. Instead of being a stand-alone server, the server becomes an entry point for the information superhighway.

Databases can also be distributed; the Oracle tool *SQL*Net* functions as the on-ramp to the database information highway. It facilitates the sharing of data between databases, even if those databases are on different types of servers running different operating systems and communications protocols. It also allows for *client-server* applications to be created; the server can then function primarily for database I/O, while the CPU requirements of an application can be moved to the front-end client machines.

SQL*Net V1 works with Oracle Version 5, Oracle Version 6, and Oracle7. SQL*Net V2 is specific to Oracle7, and includes a number of new features that allow you to take advantage of some of Oracle7's new features. Both versions will be described here. The MultiProtocol Interchange, which is unique to SQL*Net V2, will also be covered.

The installation and configuration instructions for SQL*Net depend on the particular hardware, operating system, and communications software you are using. The material provided here will help you get the most out of your database networking, regardless of your configuration.

Overview of SQL*Net

Using SQL*Net distributes the work load associated with databases. Since many database queries are performed via applications, a server-based application forces the server to support both the CPU requirements of the application and the I/O requirements of the database (see Figure 15-1(a)). Using a *client-server* configuration allows this load to be distributed between two machines. The first, called the *client*, supports the application that initiates the request from the database. The backend machine on which the database resides is called the *server*. The client bears most of the CPU load, while the database server is dedicated to supporting queries, not applications. This distribution of resource requirements is shown in Figure 15-1(b).

When the client sends a database request to the server, the server receives and executes the SQL statement that is passed to it. The results of the SQL statement, plus any error conditions that are returned, are then sent back to the client.

In addition to client-server implementations, *server-server* configurations are often needed. In this type of environment, databases on separate servers share data with each other. Each server can then be physically isolated from every other server without being logically isolated from it. A typical implementation of this type involves corporate headquarters servers that communicate with departmental servers in various locations. Each server supports client applications, but it also has the ability to communicate with other servers in the network. This architecture is shown in Figure 15-2.

When one of the servers sends a database request to another server, the sending server acts like a client. The receiving server executes the SQL statement that is passed to it, and returns the results plus error conditions to the sender.

SQL*Net allows both of these architectures to become reality. When run on both the client and the server, it allows database requests made from one database (or application) to be passed to another database on a separate server. In most cases, machines can function both as clients and servers; the only exceptions are operating systems with single-user architectures, such as MS-DOS. In such cases, those machines can only function as clients.

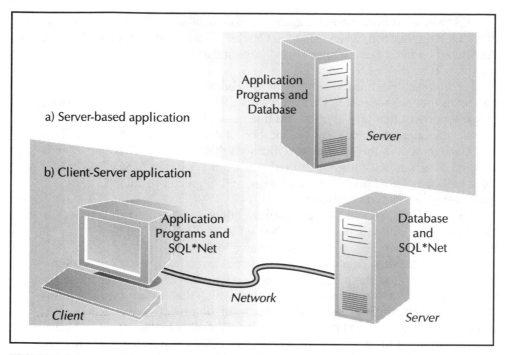

FIGURE 15-1. *Client-Server Architecture*

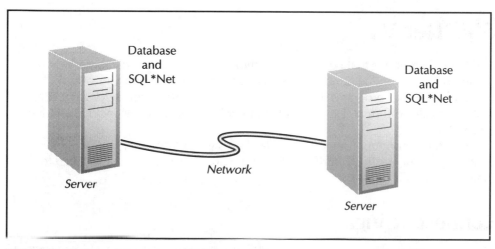

FIGURE 15-2. *Server-Server Architecture*

SQL*Net V1 supports queries against remote databases. SQL*Net V2 supports distributed queries too; when using the Oracle7 Distributed Option, it also supports distributed updates. See Chapter 17, "Managing Distributed Databases," for further information on distributed updates.

The end result of this functionality is the ability to communicate with all databases that are accessible via the network and SQL*Net. It is then possible to create synonyms that give applications true network transparency; the user who submits the query will not know the location of the data that is used to resolve it. The management of the network specifications that are needed in order to make location transparency a reality has been made much simpler in SQL*Net V2. This topic will be covered briefly in this chapter, and in greater detail in Chapter 17, "Managing Distributed Databases."

Each object in a database is uniquely identified by its owner and name. For example, there will only be one table named EMPLOYEE owned by the user HR; there cannot be two objects of the same name in the same schema.

Within distributed databases, two additional layers of object identification must be added. First, the name of the instance which accesses the database must be identified. Next, the name of the server on which that instance resides must be identified. Putting together these four parts of the object's name—its server, its instance, its owner, and its name—results in a *Fully Qualified Object Name* (*FQON*). In order to access a remote table, that table's FQON must be known. DBAs and application administrators can set up access paths to automate the selection of all four parts of the FQON. Although the basic methods for doing so are the same for both SQL*Net V1 and SQL*Net V2, the underlying technology is very different.

SQL*Net V1

SQL*Net V1 requires that both of the machines involved in the database communication run the same *communications protocol*. A communications protocol is a set of programs that configure data for transmission across a network in a standardized format. Examples of communications protocols include DECNet and TCP/IP.

In order to communicate between databases via SQL*Net V1, you will have to specify connect strings. In the next section you will see the details needed to create these.

Connect Strings

The server and instance portions of an object's FQON in SQL*Net V1 are identified by means of a *connect string*. This string specifies the communications protocol,

server name, and instance name to use when performing the query. The format for
a SQL*Net V1 connect string is

```
Protocol Prefix : Server Name : Instance Name
```

A fourth parameter, *buffer size*, can be added at the end, as shown in the
following listing.

```
Protocol Prefix : Server Name: Instance Name, Buffer Size
```

The buffer size is used to specify the size, in bytes, of the context area used
to pass data between SQL*Net and the communications protocol. The default is
protocol-specific, and can be decreased if memory consumption is a problem. For
TCP/IP, the default buffer size is 4096 bytes. Note that the buffer size parameter is
preceded by a comma, not by a colon like the other parameters.

The protocol prefix is a one-letter abbreviation for the communications
protocol that will be used to transfer the request across the network. For TCP/IP,
this is "T". For DECNet, it is "D". Thus, a SQL*Net connect string for a TCP/IP
connection will be in the following format.

```
T: Server Name :Instance Name, Buffer Size
```

If you are using the default buffer size with TCP/IP, and are accessing a
database whose instance ID is LOC on a server named HQ, then the connect string
would be

```
T:hq:loc
```

This connect string can be specified when executing queries on remote
databases, provided those remote servers are running SQL*Net V1 and the same
communications protocol as the HQ server. A user on a client machine could
connect to the HR account on the HQ server by entering the following command.

```
> sqlplus hr/puffinstuff@T:hq:loc;
```

The "@" sign tells the database to use the SQL*Net connect string that follows it to
determine the database to login to. If the username and password are correct for that
database, then a session is opened there and the user can begin using the database.

Aliases and Defaults

The configuration instructions for SQL*Net V1 are very operating system-specific.
In general, most implementations of SQL*Net allow a default connection to be

specified. If a host and instance name are not specified in the connect string, then the default will be used.

In some operating systems, aliases may be used to provide an additional level of location transparency. UNIX allows this via a file called /etc/sqlnet. The aliases defined in this file may then be used in place of full connect strings.

For example, the /etc/sqlnet file may contain the following line.

```
hq      t:hq:loc
```

The alias "hq" can now be used in place of the connect string "t:hq:loc". This has two direct benefits. First, it eliminates keystrokes from the connect string. Second, it makes it easier to manage changes to data locations. If the LOC instance is moved from the HQ server, this alias file can be quickly changed, and all users of the "hq" alias will then be redirected to the appropriate server.

To use an alias, specify it wherever a connect string would be used. For example, instead of entering

```
> sqlplus hr/puffinstuff@t:hq:loc
```

you could enter

```
> sqlplus hr/puffinstuff@hq
```

To override the public aliases set via the /etc/sqlnet file, a private alias file can be created. This file should be named .sqlnet and stored in your account's home directory.

Specific implementation details for UNIX are found in Chapter 16, "Networking in UNIX."

Further examples of the use of SQL*Net connect strings will be shown in the three "Usage Example" sections of this chapter.

Implementation

The implementation instructions for SQL*Net vary widely, depending on the server and the operating system it uses. This is because SQL*Net is very tightly coupled with the operating system's communication programs, and the protocols they use. Details of implementing SQL*Net V1 in the supported systems are provided in the *SQL*Net User's Guide* for the protocol you are using. Implementation details for UNIX are provided in this book in Chapter 16, "Networking in UNIX."

SQL*Net V2

SQL*Net V2 introduces a number of new features that both simplify its administration and increase its usefulness.

In SQL*Net V1, both servers that are communicating need to be running the same communications protocol. This may result in having servers and operating systems using protocols for which they are not well suited. For example, in order to have VAXes running DECNet communicate with UNIX servers running TCP/IP, either the UNIX server must run DECNet or the VAX must run TCP/IP. In both cases, you would be forcing the system to support a communications protocol that was not designed for it.

With SQL*Net V2, multiple protocols are supported during SQL*Net connections via a feature called the MultiProtocol Interchange (described in a later section of this chapter). SQL*Net V2 has as its foundation the Transparent Network Substrate (TNS), which resolves all server-level connectivity issues. The combination of the MultiProtocol Interchange and the TNS allows SQL*Net V2 connections to be made independent of the operating system and communications protocol run by each server.

SQL*Net V2 also has the capability to send and receive data requests in an asynchronous manner; this allows it to support the Oracle7 multithreaded server architecture. SQL*Net V1 does not have this capability.

Connect Descriptors

The server and instance portions of an object's FQON in SQL*Net V2 are identified by means of a *connect descriptor*. This descriptor specifies the communications protocol, server name, and instance name to user when performing the query. Because of the protocol-independence of SQL*Net V2, it also includes hardware connectivity information. The format for a SQL*Net V2 connect descriptor is shown in the following listing. The example shown here uses the TCP/IP protocol, and specifies a connection to an instance named LOC on a server named HQ. The keywords are protocol-specific.

```
(DESCRIPTION=
      (ADDRESS=
            (PROTOCOL=TCP)
            (HOST=HQ)
            (PORT=1521))
      (CONNECT DATA=
            (SID=loc)))
```

In this connect descriptor, the protocol is set to TCP/IP, the server ("HOST") is set to HQ, and the port on that host that should be used for the connection is port 1521 (which is the recommended port assignment for SQL*Net V2 in UNIX installations). The instance name is specified in a separate part of the descriptor, as the "SID" assignment.

The structure for this descriptor is consistent across all protocols. Also, the descriptors can be automatically generated via the SQL*Net V2 Configuration Tool provided by Oracle (and described later in this chapter). As previously noted, the keywords used by the connect descriptors are protocol-specific. The keywords to use and the values to give them are provided in the operating system-specific documentation for SQL*Net V2.

Service Names

Users are not expected to type in a SQL*Net V2 connect descriptor each time they want to access remote data. Indeed, they would probably mutiny at such a suggestion. Instead, the DBA can set up *service names* (aliases), which refer to these connect descriptors. Service names are stored in a file called TNSNAMES.ORA. This file should be copied to all servers on the database network. Every client should have a copy of this file. It should be generated via the SQL*Net V2 Configuration Tool, which is described later in this chapter.

A sample entry in the TNSNAMES.ORA file is shown in the following listing. This example assigns a service name of HQ to the connect descriptor given above.

```
HQ =(DESCRIPTION=
      (ADDRESS=
            (PROTOCOL=TCP)
            (HOST=HQ)
            (PORT=1521))
      (CONNECT DATA=
            (SID=loc)))
```

A user wishing to connect to the LOC instance on the HQ server can now use the "HQ" service name, as shown in this example.

```
> sqlplus hr/puffinstuff@HQ;
```

As in the SQL*Net V1 example, the "@" sign tells the database to use the SQL*Net connection that follows it to determine which database to login to. If the username and password are correct for that database, then a session is opened there and the user can begin using the database.

The creation of aliases for connect descriptors has already been accomplished via the use of service names. The use of synonyms to further enhance location transparency will be described in the "Usage Example: Database Links" section of this chapter.

Listeners

Each server on the network must contain a LISTENER.ORA file. This file lists the names and addresses of all of the TNS "*listener*" processes on the machine and the instances they support. These processes receive connections from SQL*Net V2 clients. Each server must have at least one listener process.
    A LISTENER.ORA file is comprised of four parts:

- A header section
- An Interprocess Calls (IPC) address definition section
- Instance definitions
- Operational Parameters

This file is automatically generated by the SQL*Net V2 Configuration Tool.

Supporting the SQL*Net V2 Configuration Tool

As previously noted, the TNSNAMES.ORA files and LISTENER.ORA files should be automatically generated via the SQL*Net V2 Configuration Tool. In order to use this tool, an account must first be created in the local database.
    The creation of this account is automated by a SQL*Plus script called NCSSCHEMA.SQL, located in the $ORACLE_HOME/network/config directory. This script, which must be run from an account with full DBA privileges, creates an account named NET_CONF, with a password of NET_CONF. It then creates the tables necessary to support the configuration tool.
    Before running the script, edit it to point the NET_CONF account's DEFAULT tablespace to one of your choosing. This can be specified in the CREATE USER command, as shown in the following listing.

```
CREATE USER net_conf IDENTIFIED BY net_conf
DEFAULT TABLESPACE tools;
```

After the NCSSCHEMA.SQL script has completed, alter the password of the NET_CONF account via the ALTER USER command, as shown in this example.

```
ALTER USER net_conf IDENTIFIED BY newpass;
```

The configuration tool is based on SQL*Forms 3.0, and should be run from the SQL*Forms directory. Access the tool via the net_conf command followed by the username (which is also "net_conf") and password to use, as shown in this example.

```
net_conf net_conf/newpass
```

The SQL*Net V2 Configuration Tool prompts the user for the information needed to set up the Listeners, Service Names, and MultiProtocol Interchanges.

The MultiProtocol Interchange

The MultiProtocol Interchange portion of SQL*Net V2 is used to establish database communication links between otherwise incompatible network protocols. The concept of a network *community* is used to determine whether a MultiProtocol Interchange is necessary.

A network community is a set of servers that communicate with each other via a single protocol. Examples of communities would include networks of UNIX servers using TCP/IP, or of VAX servers using DECNet. To transfer database requests from one community to another, a MultiProtocol Interchange must be used. This is shown graphically in Figure 15-3.

The advantage of a MultiProtocol Interchange is that all servers no longer have to be using the same communications protocol, as they did in SQL*Net V1. Because of this, each server can use the communications protocol that is best suited to its environment, and can still be able to transfer data back and forth with other databases. This communication takes place regardless of the communications protocols used on the remote servers; the MultiProtocol Interchange takes care of the differences between the protocols.

In environments with three or more network communities, multiple MultiProtocol Interchanges are used. They may be physically configured so that multiple access paths are available between servers. This is shown in Figure 15-4.

Multiple access paths can be used to transfer data from one community to another. The MultiProtocol Interchanges will select the most appropriate path based on path availability and network load. The relative cost of each path is specified via the SQL*Net V2 Configuration Tool when the MultiProtocol Interchanges are set up.

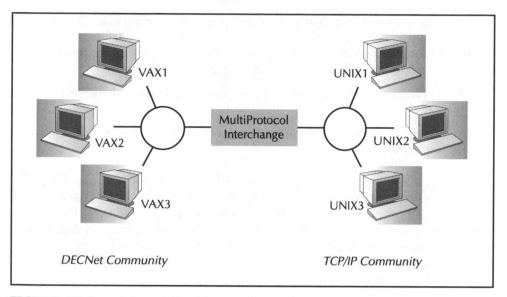

FIGURE 15-3.   *A Sample MultiProtocol Interchange*

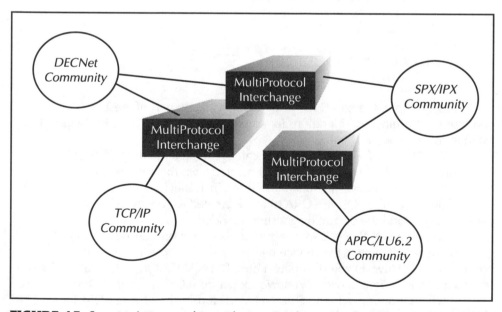

FIGURE 15-4.   *MultiProtocol Interchange Configuration for Three Communities*

Each MultiProtocol Interchange is comprised of three components:

- A Connection Manager, which manages a Listener process to detect connection requests, and uses data pumps to transfer data

- A Navigator, which chooses the best possible path through the TNS network

- The Interchange Control Utility, which is used to manage the Interchange's availability

The SQL*Net V2 Configuration Tool is used to establish the configuration of each of these components when a new MultiProtocol Interchange is created.

The network community in which a server exists should be added to the connect descriptors for its databases. A modified version of the connect descriptor shown earlier, with the "COMMUNITY" parameter added, is shown in the following listing. This is a modification to the TNSNAMES.ORA files that are distributed throughout the network.

```
HQ =(DESCRIPTION=
     (ADDRESS=
            (COMMUNITY=TCP.HQ.COMPANY)
            (PROTOCOL=TCP)
            (HOST=HQ)
            (PORT=1521))
     (CONNECT DATA=
            (SID=loc)))
```

In this example, the host "HQ" is identified as being part of the TCP/IP community. Naming considerations for communities are discussed in Chapter 17, "Managing Distributed Databases."

The TNSNAMES.ORA file is automatically generated via the SQL*Net V2 Configuration Tool. Other files that are generated from this tool for the MultiProtocol Interchanges include those listed in Table 15-1.

An additional file, SQLNET.ORA, may be created to specify additional diagnostics beyond the default diagnostics provided.

Although the SQL*Net V2 architecture makes location transparency available (particularly via the use of the service names in the TNSNAMES.ORA files), a new problem arises: How do you distribute a new TNSNAMES.ORA file to all of the servers and clients in a network? A new product from Oracle, called Oracle Names, will be coming out with SQL*Net V2.1. It uses the Oracle7 Distributed Option to manage the distribution of the network configuration files.

FILE NAME	DESCRIPTION
TNSNAV.ORA	Describes the communities of each MultiProtocol Interchange on the network.
TNSNET.ORA	Contains an overview of the layout of the network for all MultiProtocol Interchanges. Lists all the communities on the network and the relative cost of traversing them. Community costs are set during Interchange configuration, and reflect the throughput capability of the community. These costs are used to choose which of multiple available access paths should be used.
INTCHG.ORA	Contains parameters that control the behavior of each MultiProtocol Interchange.

TABLE 15-1. *MultiProtocol Interchange Files Created by the SQL*Net V2 Configuration Tool*

Usage Example: Client-Server Applications

There are several ad hoc query tools available that work in a client-server fashion. Consider the example of a query tool such as Q+E, operating in a Microsoft Windows environment on an MS-DOS PC. The PC is connected via a network card to a TCP/IP network, and is running a TCP/IP software package and SQL*Net V1 for Windows. The database that it will be accessing resides on a UNIX server on the same network. This configuration is depicted in Figure 15-5.

When the user runs Q+E within Windows, a username, password, and connection string to a database must be specified. The user enters a connection string in the format

```
T: Server Name : Instance Name
```

Since TCP/IP is being used, the protocol prefix is "T". When the user is connected to the database, he or she may then query from the tables available there. Every time a query is executed, the SQL statement for the query is sent to the server and executed. The data is then returned via SQL*Net and displayed on the client PC.

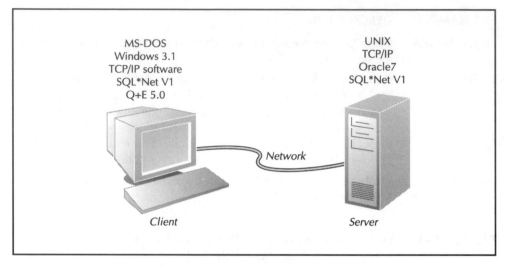

FIGURE 15-5. *Example Client-Server Configuration*

Usage Example: Database Links

For frequently used connections to remote databases, *database links* should be established. These specify the connection string (or connect descriptor) that is to be used, and may also specify the username to connect to in the remote database.

A database link is typically used to create local objects (such as views or synonyms) that access remote databases via server-server communications. This provides location transparency to the local users. When a database link is referenced by a SQL statement, it opens a session in the remote database and executes the SQL statement there. The data is then returned, and the remote session stays open in case it is needed again. Database links can be created as public links (by DBAs, making the link available to all users in the local database) or as private links.

The following SQL*Net V1 example creates a private database link called HR_LINK.

```
CREATE DATABASE LINK hr_link
CONNECT TO hr IDENTIFIED BY puffinstuff
USING 'T:hq:loc';
```

The CREATE DATABASE LINK command, as shown in this example, has three parameters:

1. The name of the link (HR_LINK, in this example).

2. The account to connect to (if none is specified, then the local username and password will be used in the remote database).

3. The connect string.

A public database link can be created by adding the keyword PUBLIC to the CREATE DATABASE LINK command, as shown in the following SQL*Net V2 example.

```
CREATE PUBLIC DATABASE LINK hr_link
CONNECT TO hr IDENTIFIED BY puffinstuff
USING 'HQ';
```

Note that in this example for SQL*Net V2, the connect string is not specified, but rather, the service name ("HQ") that was assigned to the connect descriptor. The mapping of service names to connect descriptors is done via the TNSNAMES.ORA file on the local machine. Therefore, if the "LOC" instance is moved to a different server, then the database links can be redirected to LOC's new location simply by distributing a TNSNAMES.ORA file that contains the modification.

To use these links, simply add them as suffixes to table names in commands. The following example creates a local view of a remote table, using the HR_LINK database link.

```
CREATE VIEW local_employee_view
AS
SELECT * FROM employee@hr_link
WHERE office='ANNAPOLIS';
```

The FROM clause in this example refers to "employee@hr_link". Since the HR_LINK database link specifies the server name, instance name, and owner name, the FQON for the table is known. If no account name had been specified, then the user's account name would have been used instead.

In this example, a view was created in order to limit the records that users could retrieve. If no such restriction is necessary, then a synonym can be used instead. This is shown in the following example.

```
CREATE PUBLIC SYNONYM employee FOR employee@hr_link;
```

Local users who query the local public synonym EMPLOYEE will automatically have their queries redirected to the EMPLOYEE table in the LOC instance on the HQ server. Location transparency has thus been achieved.

By default, a single SQL statement can use up to four database links. This limit can be increased via the OPEN_LINKS parameter in the database's INIT.ORA file.

Usage Example: The COPY Command

The SQL*Plus COPY command is an underutilitized, underappreciated command. It allows data to be copied between databases (or within the same database) via SQL*Plus. Although it allows the user to select which columns to copy, it works best when all of the columns of a table are being chosen. The greatest benefit of this command is its ability to COMMIT after each array of data has been processed; this in turn generates transactions that are of a manageable size.

Consider the case of a large table (again, using EMPLOYEE as the example). What if the EMPLOYEE table has 100,000 rows that use a total of 100M of space, and you need to make a copy of that table into a different database? The easiest option, using a database link, involves the following steps:

```
CREATE DATABASE LINK hr_link
CONNECT TO hr IDENTIFIED BY puffinstuff
USING 'T:hq:loc';

CREATE TABLE employee
AS
SELECT * FROM employee@hr_link;
```

The first command creates the database link, and the second command creates a new table based on all of the data in the remote table.

Unfortunately, this option taxes your rollback segments. In order for it to work, a transaction the size of the entire remote table (100M) must be supported. This in turn requires a rollback segment that is at least that large.

To break the transaction into smaller entries, use the SQL*Plus COPY command. The syntax for this command is

```
COPY FROM
remote username/remote password@connect string
TO
username/password@connect string
[APPEND|CREATE|INSERT|REPLACE]
table name
USING subquery;
```

If the current account is to be the destination of the copied data, then the local username, password, and connect string are not necessary.

To set the transaction entry size, use the SQL*Plus SET command to set a value for the ARRAYSIZE parameter. This determines the number of records that will be retrieved in each "batch." The COPYCOMMIT parameter tells SQL*Plus how many batches should be committed at one time. Thus, the following SQL*Plus script accomplishes the same data-copying goal that the CREATE TABLE AS command met; however, it breaks up the single transaction into multiple transactions. In this example, the data is committed after every 1,000 records. This reduces the transaction's rollback segment entry size needed from 100M to 1M.

```
set copycommit 1
set arraysize 1000
COPY FROM hr/puffinstuff@t:hq:loc -
CREATE employee -
USING -
SELECT * FROM employee
```

Except for the last line, each line in the COPY command must be terminated with a dash (-), since this is a SQL*Plus command.

The different data options within the COPY command are described in Table 15-2.

The feedback provided by this command is confusing at first. After the final commit is complete, the database reports to the user the number of records that were committed in the *last* batch. It does not report the total number of records committed (unless they are all committed in a single batch).

OPTION	DESCRIPTION
APPEND	Inserts the rows into the destination table. Automatically creates the table if it does not exist.
CREATE	Creates the table, then inserts the rows.
INSERT	Inserts the rows into the destination table if it exists; otherwise returns an error. When using INSERT, all columns must be specified in the USING subquery.
REPLACE	Drops the existing destination table and replaces it with a new table containing the copied data.

TABLE 15-2.   *Data Options for the COPY Command*

Tuning SQL*Net

Tuning SQL*Net applications is fairly straightforward: wherever possible, reduce the amount of data that is sent across the network, particularly for online transaction processing applications. The basic procedures that should be applied include

- The use of distributed objects, such as snapshots, to replicate static data to remote databases.

- The use of procedures to reduce the amount of data sent across the network. Rather than sending data back and forth, only the procedure's error status is returned.

- The use of the highest buffer size available for SQL*Net buffering.

- The use of SQL*Net V2 wherever applicable. SQL*Net V2 sends fewer network packets for overhead purposes than SQL*Net V1 does.

- Providing enough MultiProtocol Interchanges so that a single site on the network does not become a bottleneck for data transfer.

- Using homogenous servers wherever possible to eliminate the need for protocol interchange.

The first of these topics is discussed in detail in Chapter 8, "Database Tuning." The rest of the topics listed here are simply a matter of good planning. Using them effectively will help you turn your network into your own private information superhighway.

CHAPTER 16

Networking in UNIX

As a general rule, there is no general rule. And as for a standard version of UNIX, there isn't one of those either. This chapter will therefore concentrate on those networking elements that are common to most UNIX versions. Instructions for implementing SQL*Net V1 and V2 in UNIX will be provided. Since the TCP/IP communications protocol is commonly used for UNIX servers, that protocol will be featured.

Before a process can connect to a database on a server, there are several steps that the DBA must take in conjunction with the UNIX system administrator. The following sections describe each of these steps.

Identification of Hosts

A *host*, for the purposes of this chapter, will be defined as a server that is capable of communicating with another server via a network. Each host maintains a list of the hosts with which it can communicate. This list is maintained in a file called /etc/hosts. The "/etc" portion of the filename signifies that it is located in the /etc directory. This file contains the Internet address for the hosts, plus the host names. It may optionally include an alias for each host name. A sample portion of an /etc/hosts file is shown here:

```
127.0.0.1 nmhost
127.0.0.2 txhost
127.0.0.3 azhost arizona
```

In this example, there are three hosts listed. The first two entries assign host names ("nmhost" and "txhost") to Internet addresses. The third entry assigns both a host name ("azhost") and an alias ("arizona") to an Internet address.

Most networking software for PC clients emulates this. Within the network software directory structure, a file called HOSTS is maintained. This file lists the Internet address and host name for each host that the client can directly reach. The file is identical in structure to the UNIX /etc/hosts file.

The list of host names in the /etc/hosts file determines which host names can be specified in a SQL*Net connect string from this host. Therefore, you may wish to guarantee that no host's /etc/hosts file can be changed without distributing that change to all hosts on the network. Otherwise, you may create networks in which some hosts are dead ends.

Consider the /etc/hosts file given earlier. If that was the /etc/hosts file for the server known as txhost, then it would be able to reach two other servers (nmhost and azhost). However, what if no other server had txhost listed in *its* /etc/hosts file? The txhost server would be unreachable from the network.

That may be a desirable scenario from a security standpoint. It would serve to partially isolate the databases on txhost from the kinds of network security problems that were described in Chapter 9, "Database Security and Auditing." However, it is more often the case that hosts are added to the network in order to share information and resources. Inconsistent /etc/hosts files stand in the way of meeting that goal. The consistency of these files is usually maintained by a UNIX systems administrator.

Identification of Databases

All databases that are run on a host and are accessible to the network must be listed in a file named /etc/oratab. The "/etc" portion of the file name signifies that it is located in the /etc directory. This file is maintained by the DBA.

It is not necessary to make entries into this file for every database on the local server. However, UNIX servers are often used in client-server and server-server applications (see Chapter 15, "SQL*Net V1 and V2"). Each database used in such an application must be listed in the /etc/oratab file. It is therefore customary to list most of your databases in this file.

The components of an entry in this file are listed in Table 16-1.

The "Startup_Flag" component doesn't seem to fit; after all, why should a network connection care about the startup schedule for an instance? This flag is part of the entry because this file is also used (by default; it can be changed) during system startup to start the server's Oracle databases.

The three components are listed all on one line, separated only by colons (:). A sample /etc/oratab file is shown here.

```
LOC:/orasw/v716:Y
CC1:/orasw/v716:N
OLD:/orasw/v637:Y
```

This example shows entries for three instances, named LOC, CC1, and OLD. The first two instances have the same ORACLE_HOME; the third uses an older version of the Oracle kernel. Both LOC and OLD will be automatically started when the server starts; CC1 will have to be manually started.

COMPONENT	DESCRIPTION
ORACLE_SID	Instance name (Server ID).
ORACLE_HOME	Full path name of the root directory of the Oracle software used by the database.
Startup_Flag	Flag to indicate whether the instance should be started when the host is started. If set to "Y", then it will be started. If set to "N", then it will not be started.

TABLE 16-1. *Entry Components for /etc/oratab*

Once an instance is listed in the /etc/oratab file on an identified host on the network (via /etc/hosts), it can be accessed via SQL*Net connection strings. However, SQL*Net must be enabled in order for this to work. The next section describes the configuration of the SQL*Net server process in UNIX.

Identification of Services

A *server process* listens for connection requests from clients. It directs those requests to the proper UNIX socket, and the connection can then take place. The method of managing the SQL*Net server process changed between SQL*Net V1 and SQL*Net V2. The following sections describe these methods.

For SQL*Net V1

Services on a server are listed in a file called /etc/services. The "/etc" portion of the filename signifies that it is located in the /etc directory. Like the /etc/hosts file, this file is typically maintained by a UNIX systems administrator.

The SQL*Net service is called *orasrv* for SQL*Net V1. In SQL*Net V1, it should be assigned to port 1525 (SQL*Net V2 typically uses port 1521). The SQL*Net V1 entry in the /etc/services file is shown in the following illustration. As shown, there are three parts to the entry: the service name, the port number, and a protocol specification—in this example, TCP/IP is specified.

```
orasrv 1525/tcp
```

Although this modification to the /etc/services file assigns the SQL*Net server process to a port, it does not start that process. Starting the orasrv process is described in the "Starting the SQL*Net Server Process" section of this chapter.

For SQL*Net V2

In SQL*Net V2, the port specifications are made via the files that are distributed throughout the network. The TNSNAMES.ORA file on each host will include listings of *service names*, with their associated connect descriptors. These descriptors contain the connection information needed by SQL*Net V2. A sample entry for TNSNAMES.ORA is shown in the following listing.

```
HQ =(DESCRIPTION=
     (ADDRESS=
          (PROTOCOL=TCP)
          (HOST=HQ)
          (PORT=1521))
     (CONNECT DATA=
          (SID=loc)))
```

In this example, the service name HQ is given to a specific connect descriptor. That descriptor specifies the host ("HQ"), the protocol ("TCP"), the port ("1521"), and the instance ID ("loc").

In order for a client to connect to a database on a remote server via SQL*Net V2, the remote server must be running a SQL*Net V2 Listener process. This process, called TNSLSNR ("TNS Listener"), waits for connection attempts to the databases listed in the LISTENER.ORA file. This file lists all of the listeners on the server. The LISTENER.ORA file thus plays an important role in the server's ability to "listen" to outside connection requests. This file should be generated via the SQL*Net V2 Configuration Tool (see Chapter 15, "SQL*Net V1 and V2").

Starting the SQL*Net V2 Listener process is described in the next section.

Starting the SQL*Net Server Process

Because SQL*Net V1 and V2 differ in their server architecture, different procedures are needed to start the server processes. The following sections provide the necessary commands.

For SQL*Net V1

The orasrv process can be started manually. Simply type in the command shown in the following listing at the UNIX command prompt.

```
> orasrv
```

The parameters for the orasrv command are listed in Table 16-2. When used, they should be listed on the command line in the order listed in Table 16-2.

Unlike many other Oracle command parameters, the parameters listed in Table 16-2 are not specified in a KEYWORD=VALUE format (such as EXP FULL=Y for Full exports). Rather, the parameters, which are mostly flags, are entered without values.

PARAMETER DESCRIPTION

Mapfile	The name of the file used to map instance names (ORACLE_SID) to their Oracle software root directories (ORACLE_HOME). If not specified, this defaults to /etc/oratab. When specified, the keyword "Mapfile" is not used; only the new file name is specified (see the example).
I	A flag to indicate if in-band breaks are used. This is the default.
O	A flag to indicate if out-of-band breaks are used. The "I" and "O" parameters are mutually exclusive.
logon	A flag to indicate that SQL*Net activities should be written to a logfile.
logoff	A flag used to turn logging off. The "logon" and "logoff" parameters are mutually exclusive.
debugon	A flag to indicate that SQL*Net debugging activities should be started. These report a greater level of detail on connection attempts, and are written to the SQL*Net logfile.
debugoff	A flag used to turn debugging off. The "debugon" and "debugoff" parameters are mutually exclusive.
dbaon	A flag to indicate that users on remote servers will be able to CONNECT INTERNAL in the local databases. See Chapter 9, "Database Security and Auditing," for further details.
dbaoff	A flag used to prevent remote users from being able to CONNECT INTERNAL in the local databases. The "dbaon" and "dbaoff" parameters are mutually exclusive.
opson	A flag to indicate that users on remote servers will be able to take advantage of autologin accounts (which typically are prefixed with "OPS$") in the local databases. See Chapter 9, "Database Security and Auditing," for further details.
opsoff	A flag used to prevent remote users from using autologin accounts in local databases. The "opson" and "opsoff" parameters are mutually exclusive.
-O	Specifies the log file. This is followed immediately by the value for the "Logfile" parameter.
Logfile	The name of the log file that SQL*Net should use. Its default value is $ORACLE_HOME/tcp/log/orasrv.log. If that file already exists, then new log entries will be appended to it.

TABLE 16-2. *SQL*Net V1 ORASRV Parameters*

The two exceptions to this are the Mapfile and Logfile parameters. These parameter names are never typed on the command line. Instead, their values are specified, as shown in the following example.

```
> orasrv /etc/myoratab dbaoff opsoff
```

In this example, a file named /etc/myoratab will be used as the mapping file, in place of the default (/etc/oratab). Remote database and DBA connections are disabled as well.

The orasrv process should be owned by root, with a setuid root bit set; the necessary commands are shown in the following listing. They use the UNIX "chown" command to change the ownership, and the UNIX "chmod" command to modify its permissions.

```
> chown root orasrv
> chmod 4555 orasrv
```

To start SQL*Net automatically on system startups, modify the /etc/rc file. This file contains commands that are executed at system startup time. Modify it to include a specification for the location of $ORACLE_HOME, followed by an "su" command that starts the orasrv process. A sample set of commands is shown in the following listing.

```
ORACLE_HOME=/orasw/v637
su -oracle -c $ORACLE_HOME/bin/orasrv
```

In this example, the root directory for Oracle software is specified via the ORACLE_HOME environment variable. In the second line of the listing, the UNIX "su" command is used. This allows the user running the system startup (the "root" user) to run this command as the "oracle" user.

A third method of starting the orasrv process involves using the "start" option of the utililty that is used to control the process. This utility, called *tcpctl*, will be fully described in the next section, "Controlling the SQL*Net Server Process." The command that uses this utility to start the SQL*Net V1 server process is

```
> tcpctl start
```

The options available within tcpctl will be described in the "Controlling the SQL*Net Server Process" section of this chapter.

After starting SQL*Net V1, you can check that it is running by listing the active processes owned by the "oracle" account. You should see an entry for "orasrv" if the SQL*Net is running.

The following command can be used to perform this check. It uses the UNIX "ps -ef" command to list the system's active processes. The "grep orasrv" command then eliminates those rows that do not contain the term "orasrv."

```
> ps -ef | grep orasrv
```

Sample output for this command is shown here:

```
oracle    250     1 0 Feb 18 ? 0:00 orasrv
oracle 23757 23738 3 Feb 18 ? 0:01 grep orasrv
```

This output shows two processes: the "orasrv" process and the process that is checking for it.

For SQL*Net V2

The SQL*Net V2 Listener process is controlled by the Listener Control Utility, named LSNRCTL. The options available for this utility are described in the next section, "Controlling the SQL*Net Server Process." To start the listener, use the command

```
> LSNRCTL START
```

This will start the default listener (named LISTENER). If you wish to start a listener with a different name, include that listener's name as the second parameter following the LSNRCTL command. For example, if you created a listener called MY_LSNR, then you could start it via the following command.

```
> LSNRCTL START MY_LSNR
```

In the next section you will find descriptions of the other parameters available for the Listener Control Utility.

After starting a SQL*Net V2 Listener (such as "MY_LSNR"), you can check that it is running by using the "status" option of the Listener Control Utility.

The following command can be used to perform this check.

```
> LSNRCTL STATUS
```

Sample output for this command is shown in Figure 16-1.

```
LSNRCTL for SUNOS: Version 2.0.14.0.0
Copyright (c) Oracle Corporation 1992. All rights reserved.
Connecting to (ADDRESS=(PROTOCOL=IPC)(KEY=loc))
STATUS of the LISTENER
----------------------
Alias LISTENER
Version TNSLSNR for SUNOS: Version 2.0.14.0.0 Production
Start Date 30-DEC-93 10:32:00
Uptime 4 days 3 hr. 33 min. 2 sec
Trace Level OFF
Security OFF
Listener Parameter File
/orasw/v716/loc/network/admin/listener.ora
Listener Log File
/orasw/v716/loc/network/log/listener.log
Services Summary...
 loc
The command completed successfully.
```

FIGURE 16-1. *Sample Output of SQL*Net V2 Listener Status Check*

This output shows that the Listener has been started, and that it is currently supporting only one service ("loc"), as defined by its LISTENER.ORA file.

If you wish to see the operating system-level processes that are involved, use the following command. It uses the UNIX "ps -ef" command to list the system's active processes. The "grep tnslsnr" command then eliminates those rows that do not contain the term "tnslsnr".

```
> ps -ef | grep tnslsnr
```

Sample output for this command is shown here:

```
oracle  595    1 0 Feb 18 ? 0:00 /orasw/v716/bin/tnslsnr
                                  LISTENER -inherit
oracle 8791 8774 3 Feb 18 ? 0:01 grep tnslsnr
```

This output shows two processes: the "LISTENER" process and the process that is checking for it. The first line of output is wrapped to the second line here.

Controlling the SQL*Net Server Process

It may be necessary to modify the SQL*Net server processes periodically. Since you don't want to have to shut down and restart the server just to change the SQL*Net parameters, there are utilities available to manage them. The following sections describe these utilities: tcpctl for SQL*Net V1, and LSNRCTL for SQL*Net V2.

For SQL*Net V1

The tcpctl utility monitors the orasrv process. It also has the ability to stop, start, and modify that process. Its documented parameters are listed in Table 16-3.

The first four parameters—*start, stop, stat,* and *version*—are mutually exclusive. The last two parameters, *log* and *debug,* are used only in conjunction with the *start* parameter.

PARAMETER	DESCRIPTION
Start	Starts the orasrv process.
Stop	Stops the orasrv process.
Stat	Displays the status of orasrv. Status information includes if the process is running, when it started, the total number of connections, the Oracle SIDs being supported, and whether logging is enabled. This can be used to query the status of orasrv on a remote server.
Version	Displays the version number of orasrv. This can be used to query the status of orasrv on a remote server.
Log	A flag to indicate whether logging mode should be enabled. The default is no logging. Specifying "log" when starting orasrv via tcpctl is equivalent to using the orasrv "logon" parameter.
Debug	A flag to indicate whether debugging mode should be enabled. The default is to not perform debugging. Specifying "debug" when starting orasrv via tcpctl is equivalent to using the orasrv "debugon" parameter.

TABLE 16-3. *SQL*Net V1 TCPCTL Parameters*

Therefore, there are four possible tcpctl commands, with modifications available for three of them:

 To stop the orasrv process:

```
> tcpctl stop
```

■ To list status information for the orasrv process:

```
> tcpctl stat
```

This command may be modified. To list status information for an orasrv process on a remote host, add the host name, prefixed with "@," to the "tcpctl stat" command, as shown in the following listing.

```
> tcpctl stat @host_name
```

■ To list the version of orasrv being used:

```
> tcpctl version
```

This command may be modified. To list version information for an orasrv process on a remote host, add the host name, prefixed with "@", to the "tcpctl version" command, as shown in the following listing.

```
> tcpctl version @host_name
```

■ To start the orasrv process:

```
> tcpctl start
```

This command may be modified. To turn the logging and debugging modes on or off, use the log and debug parameters with a "tcpctl start" command, as shown in the following listing.

```
> tcpctl start log debug
```

In this example, the orasrv process will be started, with logging mode enabled and debugging mode enabled.

There are also a number of tcpctl parameters that are undocumented. They are listed in Table 16-4.

PARAMETER	DESCRIPTION
Debug=<level>	When used in conjunction with the "debug" parameter, this determines the level of trace information written to the log file. Generally used only when requested by Oracle support.
Opsrooton	Flag to indicate that the database should allow remote access to a local account named OPS$ROOT.
Opsrootoff	Flag to indicate that no remote access should be allowed to a local account named OPS$ROOT. This parameter may be used in conjunction with the "opson" parameter to allow only non-root remote autologins.
Port=<port>	Specifies the port to be used, if other than the default.
Listen=<queue size>	Specifies the length of the listen queue.
Timeout=<seconds>	Specifies how long a handshake with orasrv should be attempted before the attempt times out.
Forkon, Forkoff & Detachon, Detachoff	Tell SQL*Net how to run the orasrv process. The default is Detachon, which runs orasrv as a detached process.

TABLE 16-4. *Undocumented SQL*Net V1 TCPCTL Parameters*

For SQL*Net V2

The Listener Control Utility for SQL*Net V2 is named LSNRCTL. It is used to start, stop, and modify the Listener process on the server. Its parameters are listed in Table 16-5. Each of these parameters may be accompanied by a value; for all except the "SET PASSWORD" command, that value will be a Listener name. If no Listener name is specified, then the default ("LISTENER") will be used.

These commands do not all have to be entered on the same line. The DBA can enter the LSNRCTL command by itself and enter the LSNRCTL utility shell, from which all other commands can then be executed.

This small set of commands gives the DBA a great deal of control over the Listener process, as shown in the following examples. In most of these examples, the LSNRCTL command is first entered by itself. This places the user in the LSNRCTL utility (as indicated by the LSNRCTL prompt). The rest of the commands are entered from within this utility.

■ To stop the Listener:

PARAMETER	DESCRIPTION
SET PASSWORD	This command, when followed by the Listener's password, allows the user access to administrative options within LSNRCTL. The Listener's password is set via the PASSWORDS_*listener_name* parameters in the LISTENER.ORA file.
START	Starts the Listener.
STOP	Stops the Listener.
STATUS	Provides status information about the Listener, including the time it was started, its parameter file name, its log file, and the services it supports. This can be used to query the status of a Listener on a remote server.
VERSION	Displays version information for the Listener, TNS, and the protocol adapters.
SERVICES	Displays services available, along with its connection history. It also lists whether each service is enabled for remote DBA or autologin access.
RELOAD	Allows you to modify the Listener services after the Listener has been started. It forces SQL*Net to read and use the most current LISTENER.ORA file.
TRACE	Sets the trace level of the Listener to one of three choices: OFF, USER (limited tracing), and ADMIN (high level of tracing).

TABLE 16-5. *SQL*Net V2 LSNRCTL Parameters*

```
> lsnrctl
LSNRCTL> SET PASSWORD lsnr_password
LSNRCTL> STOP
```

■ To list status information for the Listener:

```
> lsnrctl status
```

To list the status of a Listener on another host, add a service name from that host as a parameter to the status command. The following example uses the "HQ" service name shown earlier in this chapter.

```
> lsnrctl status hq
```

■ To list version information about the Listener:

```
> lsnrctl version
```

■ To list information about the services supported by the Listener:

```
> lsnrctl
LSNRCTL> SET PASSWORD lsnr_password
LSNRCTL> SERVICES
```

■ To reload the services from the LISTENER.ORA file:

```
> lsnrctl
LSNRCTL> SET PASSWORD lsnr_password
LSNRCTL> RELOAD
```

■ To change the level of tracing performed:

```
>Isnrctl
LSNRCTL> SET PASSWORD lsnr_password
LSNRCTL> TRACE USER
```

■ To start the Listener process:

```
> lsnrctl
LSNRCTL> SET PASSWORD lsnr_password
LSNRCTL> START
```

Most of these commands require passwords. Therefore, it is not advisable to run them via batch commands, since that would involve either storing the password in a file or passing it as a parameter to a batch program.

Debugging Connection Problems

As described in this chapter, SQL*Net connections in UNIX require that a number of communication mechanisms be properly configured. The connections involve host-to-host communication, proper identification of services and databases, and proper configuration of the SQL*Net server processes. In the event of connection problems when using SQL*Net, it is important to eliminate as many of these components as possible.

Start by making sure that the host the connection is trying to reach is accessible via the network. This can be checked via the following command.

```
> telnet host_name
```

If this command is successful, then you will be prompted for a username and password on the remote host. If the "ping" command is available to you, then you may use it instead. This command, shown in the following listing, will check to see if the remote host is available and will return a status message.

```
> ping host_name
```

If the host is available on the network, then the next step is to check if SQL*Net is running. At the same time, you can check to see what parameters it is currently using; this is important if you are attempting a remote autologin access. The following commands will provide this information.

■ For SQL*Net V1:

```
> tcpctl stat @host_name
```

If the "@host_name" clause is left off, then the command will return the status of SQL*Net on the local server.

■ For SQL*Net V2:

```
> lsnrctl status service_name
```

The "service_name" clause should refer to the name of a service on the remote server. If it is not used, then the command will return the status of SQL*Net on the local server.

These two checks—of host availability and SQL*Net availability—will resolve over 90 percent of SQL*Net connection problems in server-server communications. The rest of the problems will result from difficulties with the database specification that is being used. These problems include invalid username/password combinations, down databases, and databases in need of recovery.

In client-server communications, the same principles for debugging connection problems apply. First verify that the remote host is accessible; most communications software for clients includes a *telnet* or *ping* function. If it is not accessible, then the problem may be on the client side. Verify that *other* clients are able to access the host on which the database resides. If they can, then the problem is isolated to the client. If they cannot, then the problem lies on the server side, and the server, its SQL*Net processes, and its databases should be checked.

CHAPTER 17

Managing Distributed Databases

Everyone knows somebody whose desk is a mess. Surely it wouldn't take too long to organize the papers by subject matter, file them in a comprehensible fashion, and clean up the mess. Of course, the desk's owner always replies that after everything was organized, it would never be found again.

Unless you want your databases to look like that desk, you need to plan their organization. As computers join ever-expanding local and wide area networks, local and remote databases will join in ever-expanding networks of databases. To take advantage of these distributed databases, you need to understand their capabilities, their management, and the monitoring and tuning considerations that are unique to them. The available data will then be organized *and* quickly retrievable—in stark contrast to the cluttered desk approach.

Overview of Distributed Databases

The *distributed database* architecture is based on the *server-server* configurations described in Chapter 15, "SQL*Net V1 and V2." In this type of environment, databases on separate servers (hosts) share data with each other. Each server can then be physically isolated from every other server without being logically isolated from it.

A typical implementation of this type involves corporate headquarters servers that communicate with departmental servers in various locations. Each server supports client applications, but it also has the ability to communicate with other servers in the network. This architecture is shown in Figure 17-1.

When one of the servers sends a database request to another server, the sending server acts like a *client*. The receiving server executes the SQL statement that is passed to it and returns the results plus error conditions to the sender.

SQL*Net allows this architecture to become reality. When run on all of the servers, SQL*Net allows database requests made from one database (or application) to be passed to another database on a separate server. It supports distributed queries and distributed updates when using the Oracle7 Distributed Option.

With this functionality, you can communicate with all of the databases that are accessible via your network and SQL*Net. You can then create synonyms that give applications true network transparency; the user who submits a query will not

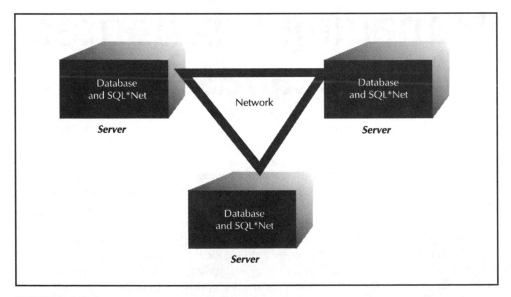

FIGURE 17-1. *Server-Server Architecture*

know the location of the data that is used to resolve it. The management of the network specifications that are needed to make location transparency a reality has been made much simpler in SQL*Net V2.

Remote Queries

It is possible for Oracle databases that are not using the Oracle7 Distributed Option to communicate, and even to perform, limited remote data manipulation tasks. The ability to perform remote queries is only one capability of a distributed database, and its usefulness is limited. It will only serve your needs if your data is isolated both logically and physically; that is, the "ownership" of the data can be ascribed to a single database, and there are no data dependencies between databases.

To query a remote database, a *database link* must be established. This specifies the SQL*Net connection string (or service name) that is to be used, and may also specify the username to connect to in the remote database. When a database link is referenced by an SQL statement, it opens a session in the remote database and executes the SQL statement there. The data is then returned, and the remote session stays open in case it is needed again. Database links can be created as public links (by DBAs, making the link available to all users in the local database) or as private links.

The following SQL*Net V2 example creates a public database link called HR_LINK.

```
CREATE PUBLIC DATABASE LINK hr_link
CONNECT TO hr IDENTIFIED BY puffinstuff
USING 'HQ';
```

The CREATE DATABASE LINK command, as shown in this example, has several parameters:

- The optional keyword PUBLIC, which allows DBAs to create links for all users in a database.

- The name of the link (hr_link, in this example).

- The account to connect to (if none is specified, then the local username and password will be used in the remote database).

- The service name ("HQ"). For SQL*Net V1, the connect string is used instead. See Chapter 15, "SQL*Net V1 and V2," for information on this.

To use this link, simply add it as a suffix to table names in commands. The following example queries a remote table by using the HR_LINK database link.

```
SELECT * FROM employee@hr_link
WHERE office='ANNAPOLIS';
```

Database links cannot be used to return values from fields with LONG datatypes. A sample remote query example is shown in Figure 17-2.

The FROM clause in this example refers to "employee@hr_link." Since the HR_LINK database link specifies the server name, instance name, and owner name, the full name of the table is known. If no account name had been specified in the database link, then the user's account name would have been used instead.

The detailed management of database links is described in the "Managing Distributed Data" section later in this chapter.

Remote Data Manipulation: Two-Phase Commit

In databases that are not using the Oracle7 Distributed Option, there is a limitation to the use of database links: they can only be used for data manipulation if the data is on the same server as the process that submits the command. That is, if a user on SERVER1 submits an UPDATE command via a database link to a

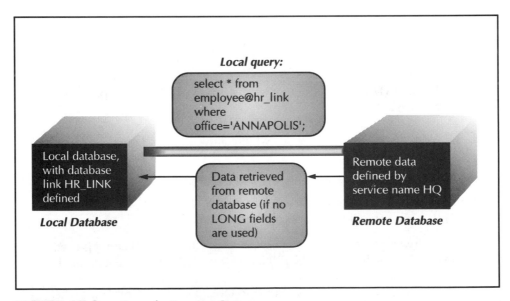

FIGURE 17-2. *Sample Remote Query*

database on SERVER2, then that transaction will fail unless the Oracle7 Distributed Option is used.

To achieve remote data manipulation, you'll need to support *Two-Phase Commit (2PC)*—and that's where the Oracle7 Distributed Option comes into play. 2PC allows groups of transactions across several nodes to be treated as a unit; either all of the transactions commit, or they all get rolled back. This is shown in Figure 17-3. In that figure, two UPDATE transactions are performed. The first UPDATE goes against a local table (EMPLOYEE); the second, against a remote table (EMPLOYEE@HR_LINK). After the two transactions are performed, a single COMMIT is then executed. If either transaction cannot commit, then both transactions will be rolled back.

Thus, the Distributed Option yields two important benefits: databases on other servers can be updated, and those transactions can be grouped together with others in a logical unit. This second benefit occurs because of the database's use of 2PC. Its two phases are

1. The *Prepare* phase. An initiating node called the *global coordinator* notifies all sites involved in the transaction to be ready to either commit or roll back the transaction.

2. The *Commit* phase. If there is no problem with the Prepare phase, then all sites commit their transactions. If a network or node failure occurs, then all sites roll back their transactions.

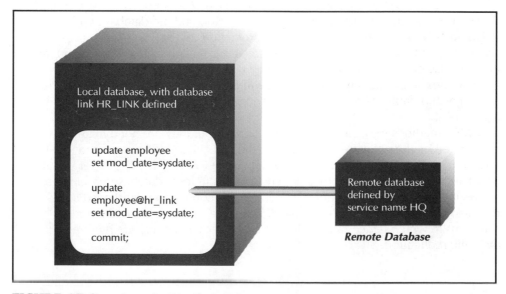

FIGURE 17-3. *Sample Distributed Transaction*

The use of 2PC is transparent to the users. The detailed management of distributed transactions is discussed in the "Managing Distributed Transactions" section later in this chapter.

Dynamic Data Replication

To improve the performance of queries that use data from remote databases, you may wish to replicate that data on the local server. There are several options for accomplishing this, depending on which Oracle7 option you are using.

If you are using the Oracle7 Procedural Option with the Distributed Option, you can use *database triggers* to replicate data from one table into another. For example, after every INSERT into a table, a trigger may fire to insert that same record into another table—and that table may be in a remote database. Thus, triggers can be used to enforce data replication in simple configurations. If the types of transactions against the base table cannot be controlled, then the trigger code needed to perform the replication will be unacceptably complicated.

When using the Oracle7 Distributed Option, you can use *snapshots* to replicate data between databases. You do not have to replicate an entire table, or limit yourself to data from just one table. When replicating a single table, you may use a WHERE clause to restrict which records are replicated, and may perform GROUP BY operations on the data. You can also join the table with other tables and replicate the result of the queries.

The data in the local snapshot of the remote table(s) will need to be refreshed. You can specify the refresh interval for the snapshot, and the database will automatically take care of the replication procedures. If the snapshot is a one-to-one replication of records in a remote table (called a *simple snapshot*), then the database can use a *snapshot log* to send over only transaction data; otherwise it is a *complex snapshot,* and the database will perform complete refreshes on the local snapshot table. The dynamic replication of data via snapshots is shown in Figure 17-4.

Other methods may be used to replicate data, but they are not dynamically maintained by the database. For example, the SQL*Plus COPY command (see the "Usage Example: The COPY Command" section of Chapter 15, "SQL*Net V1 and V2") can be used to create copies of remote tables in local databases, and it also allows the use of complex queries. However, this command would need to be repeated every time the data is changed. Therefore, its use is limited to those situations in which large, static tables are replicated; dynamic data requires dynamic replication.

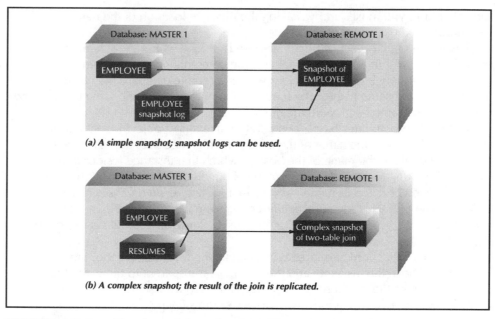

FIGURE 17-4. *Simple and Complex Snapshots*

Managing Distributed Data

Before you can worry about managing transactions against remote databases, you have to get the data there—and make it globally accessible to other databases. The following sections describe the requisite management tasks: enforcing location transparency, and managing the database links, triggers, and snapshots that are used to access the data.

The Infrastructure: Enforcing Location Transparency

Using hard-coded node names and database names in connect strings is like hard-coding account passwords in application programs. Neither will result in a system that is easily maintainable. To properly design your distributed databases for long-term use, you must start by making the physical location of the data transparent to the application.

The name of an object within a database is unique within the schema that owns it. Thus, within any single database, the combination of owner and object name will uniquely identify a table. However, a remote database may have an account with the same name, which may own an object with the same name. How can the object name be properly qualified?

Within distributed databases, two additional layers of object identification must be added. First, the name of the instance which accesses the database must be identified. Next, the name of the host on which that instance resides must be identified. Putting together these four parts of the object's name—its host, its instance, its owner, and its name—results in a *Fully Qualified Object Name* (*FQON*). The FQON is sometimes referred to as the *global object name*. To access a remote table, that table's FQON must be known. A sample is shown in Figure 17-5.

The goal of location transparency is to make the first three parts of the FQON—the host, the instance, and the schema—transparent to the user. It is even possible to make the object name itself transparent to the user (it may, for example, point instead to a view that joins two tables), but this chapter will keep that portion of the FQON intact as a point of reference.

The first three parts of the FQON are all specified via database links, so any effort at achieving location transparency should start there. First, consider a typical SQL*Net V2 database link:

```
CREATE PUBLIC DATABASE LINK hr_link
CONNECT TO hr IDENTIFIED BY puffinstuff
USING 'HQ';
```

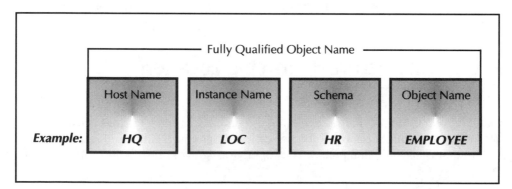

Fully Qualified Object Name			
Host Name	Instance Name	Schema	Object Name
HQ	LOC	HR	EMPLOYEE

Example:

FIGURE 17-5. *Fully Qualified Object Name*

By using a service name ("HQ"), the host and instance name are kept transparent. They are translated into their actual values via the local host's TNSNAMES.ORA file. A sample entry in this file, for this service name, is shown in the following listing.

```
HQ =(DESCRIPTION=
        (ADDRESS=
                (PROTOCOL=TCP)
                (HOST=HQ)
                (PORT=1521))
        (CONNECT DATA=
                (SID=loc)))
```

The two lines in bold in this listing fill in the two missing pieces of the FQON: when the "HQ" service name is used, the host name is "HQ", and the instance name is "LOC". This TNSNAMES.ORA file shows the parameters for the TCP/IP protocol; other protocols may use different keywords, but their usage is the same. They provide transparency for the server and instance name.

The HR_LINK database link, if created via the code given earlier in this section, will thus provide transparency for the first two parts of the FQON. But what if the data moves from the HR schema, or the HR account's password changes? The database link would have to be dropped and re-created. The same would be true if account-level security was required; it may be necessary to create and maintain multiple database links.

To resolve the transparency of the "schema" portion of the FQON, you can modify the way in which the database link is written. Consider the database link in the following listing (again, a public database link using an SQL*Net V2 syntax).

```
CREATE PUBLIC DATABASE LINK hr_link
USING 'HQ';
```

This database link leaves out the "connect to" line entirely. It will use what is known as a *default connection*. An example of this link being used is shown in the following listing.

```
SELECT * FROM employee@HR_LINK;
```

When this link is used, the database will resolve the FQON in the following manner:

1. It will search the local TNSNAMES.ORA file to determine the proper host name.

2. It will search the local TNSNAMES.ORA file to determine the proper instance name.

3. It will search the database link for a "connect to" specification. If none is found, then it will attempt to connect to the specified database using the *current user's* username and password.

4. It will search the FROM clause of the query for the object name.

Default connections are often used to access tables whose rows can be restricted based on the username that is accessing the table. For example, if the remote database had a table named HR.EMPLOYEE, and every employee was allowed to see his or her own record, then a database link with a specific connection, such as

```
CREATE PUBLIC DATABASE LINK hr_link
CONNECT TO hr IDENTIFIED BY puffinstuff
USING 'HQ';
```

would log in as the owner of the table (the "HR" account). If this specific connection is used, it is not possible to restrict the user's view of the records on the remote host. However, if a default connection is used, and a view is created on the remote host using the USER pseudocolumn, then only that user's data would be returned from the remote host. A sample database link and view of this type is shown in the following listing.

```
CREATE PUBLIC DATABASE LINK hr_link
USING 'HQ';

CREATE VIEW remote_emp
AS SELECT * FROM employee@HR_LINK
WHERE ename=user;
```

Either way, the data can be restricted. The difference is that when a default connection is used, the data can be restricted based on the username in the remote database; if a specific connection is used, then the data can be restricted after it has been returned to the local database. The default connection method thus reduces the amount of network traffic needed to resolve the query, as well as adding an additional level of location transparency to the data.

Using this method raises a different set of maintenance issues. The TNSNAMES.ORA files must be synchronized across the servers, and the username/password combinations in multiple databases must be synchronized. These issues are addressed in the next section, "Managing Database Links."

These options are not restricted to SQL*Net V2. Default connections can be used in database links against Oracle Version 6 and Oracle7 databases. These examples focus on the server-server connections typical of distributed databases; for further information on the use of defaults and aliases for location transparency in client-server and SQL*Net V1 environments, see Chapter 15, "SQL*Net V1 and V2," and Appendix D, "Configuration Guidelines for Client-Server Environments."

Managing Database Links

Information about public database links can be retrieved via the DBA_DB_LINKS data dictionary view. Private database links can be viewed via the USER_DB_LINKS data dictionary view. Whenever possible, separate your users among databases so that they may all share the same public database links. As a side benefit, these users will usually also be able to share public grants and synonyms.

The columns of the DBA_DB_LINKS data dictionary view are listed in Table 17-1. They are the same for both Oracle7 and Oracle Version 6.

Note that the number of database links that can be used by a single query is limited by the OPEN_LINKS parameter in the database's INIT.ORA file. Its default value is 4.

The managerial tasks involved for database links depend on the level to which you have implemented location transparency in your databases. They also depend on the version of SQL*Net you are using—users of SQL*Net V2.1 should see the following section, on the Oracle*Names product.

COLUMN NAME	DESCRIPTION
OWNER	Owner of the database link.
DB_LINK	Name of the database link (such as "HR_LINK" in this chapter's examples).
USERNAME	The name of the account that should be used to open a session in the remote database, if a specific connection is used.
PASSWORD	The password of the account that should be used to open a session in the remote database, if a specific connection is used.
HOST	The SQL*Net connect string that will be used to connect to the remote database.
CREATED	A timestamp that marks the creation date for the database link.

TABLE 17-1.   *Columns of DBA_DB_LINKS*

In the best-case scenario, default connections are used along with service names or aliases. In this case, the only requirements for successful maintenance are that the TNSNAMES.ORA file be consistent across hosts and that user account/password combinations be maintained globally. The file synchronization can be accomplished via the operating system—for example, by use of the UNIX "rcp" (remote copy) command to copy files to remote hosts.

Synchronizing account/password combinations is more difficult, but there are several alternatives. First, you may force all changes to user account passwords to go through a central authority. This central authority would have the responsibility for updating the password for the account in all databases in the network—a time-consuming task, but a valuable one.

Second, you may audit all user password changes; simply audit all ALTER USER commands. For Oracle Version 6, you'll also need to audit all GRANT CONNECT commands. These are the only commands that can be used to change a user's password. If they are detected, then the user should be contacted, and the password should then be changed on all databases available in the network.

Both of these require that the DBA access multiple databases, and that the DBA know exactly which databases to modify. The Oracle*Names product described in the next section both manages and implements the required tasks.

If any part of the FQON—such as a username—is embedded in the database link, then a change affecting that part of the FQON requires that the database link be dropped and re-created. For example, if the HR user's password was changed, then the HR_LINK database link with a specific connection defined earlier would be dropped:

```
DROP DATABASE LINK hr_link;
```

and the link would then be re-created, using the new account specification:

```
CREATE PUBLIC DATABASE LINK hr_link
CONNECT TO hr IDENTIFIED BY newpassword
USING 'HQ';
```

Location Transparency Made Easy: Using Oracle*Names

With Oracle*Names, all of the tasks of managing distributed databases are handled via a global naming service, available to all servers in a network. The service is used to store information about

- Connect strings
- Connect descriptors
- Database links
- Object aliases

This changes the way in which database links are resolved. Before, when a database link was specified, the database first looked at the user's private database links. If none with the matching name was found, then the available public database links were checked.

Oracle*Names adds an additional level to this. Now, if the first two checks do not return a match for the database link name, then the Oracle*Names server's list of global database link names is searched for the database link. If the link name is found there, Oracle*Names will return the link's specifications and resolve the query.

This greatly simplifies the administration of location transparency in a distributed environment. The information related to remote data access is now stored in a central location. The impact of this is felt every time a part of an FQON is modified. For example, if there were multiple links using specific connections to a single remote database, then a pre-Oracle*Names modification to the user's password would require dropping and re-creating multiple database links. With Oracle*Names, this change is made once.

Oracle*Names also supports the Domain Name Service (DNS) structure that Oracle introduced with SQL*Net V2. Oracle's DNS allows network hierarchies to be specified; thus, a server may be identified as HR.HQ.ACME.COM, which would be interpreted as the HR server in the HQ network of the ACME company. See the "Database Domains and Communities" section later in this chapter for information on this naming structure.

If connect descriptors are also stored in Oracle*Names, then the need for manually maintaining multiple copies of the TNSNAMES.ORA file rapidly diminishes. The centralized Oracle*Names server defines the relationships among the network objects. The database network may be divided into administrative regions, and the management tasks may be likewise divided. A change to one region will be transparently propagated to the other regions.

Oracle*Names will be available on a platform as soon as SQL*Net V2.1 is available for the platform.

Managing Database Triggers

If you are using the Oracle7 Procedural Option and the Distributed Option, and your data replication needs are fairly limited, then you can use database triggers to replicate data from one table into another. In general, this method is only used when the only type of data being sent to the remote database is either an INSERT or a DELETE. The code necessary to support UPDATE transactions is usually much more complex than a comparable snapshot; see the following sections for information on snapshots

Database triggers are executed when specific actions happen to specific tables. They can be executed for each row of a transaction, or for an entire transaction as a unit. When dealing with data replication, you will usually be concerned with each row of data.

Before creating the trigger, you must create a database link for the trigger to use. In this case, the link is created in the database that *owns* the data, accessible to the owner of the table being replicated.

```
CREATE PUBLIC DATABASE LINK trigger_link
USING 'REMOTE1';
```

This link, named "trigger_link", uses a service name ("REMOTE1") to specify the connection to a remote database. Since no specific connect string is specified, a default connection will be attempted instead. That will attempt to log into the "REMOTE1" database using the same username and password as the account that calls the link.

The trigger shown in the following listing uses this link. It is fired after every row is inserted into the EMPLOYEE table. Since it executes after the row has been inserted, the row's data has already been validated. It then inserts the same row into a remote table with the same structure, using the TRIGGER_LINK database link just defined. The remote table must already exist.

```
CREATE TRIGGER copy_data
AFTER INSERT ON employee
FOR EACH ROW
BEGIN
    INSERT INTO employee@TRIGGER_LINK
    VALUES
    (:new.empno, :new.ename, :new.deptno,
    :new.salary, :new.birth_date, :new.soc_sec_num);
END;
/
```

This trigger uses the "new" keyword to reference the values from the row that was just inserted into the local EMPLOYEE table.

To list information about triggers, use the DBA_TRIGGERS data dictionary view. The following query will list the "header" information about the trigger—its type, the statement that calls it, and the table on which it calls. This example shows the header information for the COPY_DATA trigger just created.

```
SELECT
    trigger_type,
    triggering_event,
    table_name
```

```
FROM dba_triggers
WHERE trigger_name = 'COPY_DATA';
```

Sample output from this query is shown here:

```
TYPE              TRIGGERING_EVENT        TABLE_NAME
----------------  ----------------------  ------------
AFTER EACH ROW    INSERT                  EMPLOYEE
```

The text of the trigger can also be queried from this view, as shown in the following listing.

```
SELECT
  trigger_body
FROM dba_triggers
WHERE trigger_name = 'COPY_DATA';
```

Sample output from this query is shown in Figure 17-6.

It is theoretically possible to create a trigger to replicate all possible permutations of data manipulation actions on the local database, but this quickly becomes difficult to manage. For a complex environment, it is best to consider the use of snapshots or manual data copies. However, for the limited circumstances described earlier, triggers are a very easy solution to implement.

```
TRIGGER_BODY
-------------------------------------------------------------
BEGIN
     INSERT INTO employee@TRIGGER_LINK
     VALUES
     (:new.empno, :new.ename, :new.deptno,
     :new.salary, :new.birth_date, :new.soc_sec_num);
END;
```

FIGURE 17-6.   *Sample Trigger Body Query Output for DBA_TRIGGERS*

Managing Snapshots

Snapshots are used to dynamically replicate data between distributed databases. The master table will be updatable, but the snapshots will be read-only. To use them, you must be using the Oracle7 Distributed Option. There are two types of snapshots available: *complex snapshots* and *simple snapshots*.

In a simple snapshot, each row is based on a single row in a single remote table. A row in a complex snapshot may be based on more than one row in a remote table—such as via a GROUP BY operation—or on the result of a multi-table join. Simple snapshots are thus a specific subset of the snapshots that can be created.

Since the snapshot will create several objects in the local database, the user creating the snapshot must have CREATE TABLE, CREATE VIEW, and CREATE INDEX privileges.

Before creating a snapshot, a database link to the source database should first be created in the local database. The following SQL*Net V2 example creates a private database link called HR_LINK (which has been used as an example throughout this chapter).

```
CREATE DATABASE LINK hr_link
CONNECT TO hr IDENTIFIED BY puffinstuff
USING 'HQ';
```

The syntax used to create the snapshot on the local server is shown in the following listing. In this example, the snapshot is given a name ("emp_dept_count"), and its storage parameters are specified. Its base query is given, as well as its refresh interval. In this case, the snapshot is told to immediately retrieve the master data, then to perform the snapshot operation again in seven days ("sysdate+7").

```
CREATE SNAPSHOT emp_dept_count
PCTFREE 5
TABLESPACE snap
STORAGE (INITIAL 100K NEXT 100K PCTINCREASE 0)
REFRESH COMPLETE
     START WITH sysdate
     NEXT sysdate+7
AS SELECT deptno, count(*) dept_count
FROM employee@hr_link
GROUP BY deptno;
```

NOTE
Because Oracle uses the name of the snapshot in the names of the database objects that support it, the snapshot's name should be kept to less than 23 characters.

NOTE
A snapshot query cannot reference tables or views owned by the user SYS.

Because the records in this snapshot will not correspond one-to-one with the records in the master table, this is a complex snapshot. That means that every time the snapshot is refreshed, the snapshot will need to be completely re-created.

When this snapshot is created, a table is created in the local database. Oracle will create a table called SNAP$_*snapshotname* to store the records from the snapshot's query. This table should not be altered in any way, although it may be indexed. A read-only view of this table, named after the snapshot, will be created as well. A second view, named MVIEW$_*snapshotname*, will be created as a view of the remote master table(s). This view will be used during refreshes.

To drop a snapshot, use the DROP SNAPSHOT command. An example of this is shown in the following listing.

```
DROP SNAPSHOT emp_dept_count;
```

The snapshot's storage parameters can be altered via the ALTER SNAPSHOT command, as shown in the following listing.

```
ALTER SNAPSHOT emp_dept_count PCTFREE 5;
```

To improve the snapshot's performance, you may wish to add an index to it. To do this, create the appropriate index on the underlying SNAP$_*snapshotname* table via the CREATE INDEX command.

To view data about snapshots, query the DBA_SNAPSHOTS data dictionary view. A sample query against this view is shown in the following listing.

```
SELECT
  name,           /*Name of the viewed used for the snapshot*/
  last_refresh,   /*Timestamp for the last refresh*/
  type,           /*Type of refresh used for automatic refreshes*/
  query           /*Query used to create the snapshot*/
FROM DBA_SNAPSHOTS;
```

This query will return the most-used information for the snapshot. Other information, such as the master table name and the name of the database link used, can also be retrieved via this view.

Enforcing Referential Integrity in Snapshots

The referential integrity between two related tables, both of which have simple snapshots to a remote database, may not be enforced in their snapshots. If the tables are refreshed at different times, or if transactions are occurring on the master tables during the refresh, then it is possible for the snapshots of those tables to not reflect the referential integrity of the master tables.

If, for example, EMPLOYEE and DEPT are related to each other via a primary key-foreign key relationship, then simple snapshots of these tables may contain violations of this relationship. These violations may include foreign keys without matching primary keys. In this example, that could mean employees in the EMPLOYEE snapshot with DEPTNO values that do not exist in the DEPT snapshot.

There are a number of potential solutions to this problem. First, time the refreshes to occur when the master tables are not in use. Second, perform the refreshes manually (see the following section for information on this) immediately after locking the master tables. Third, you may join the tables in the snapshot, creating a complex snapshot that will be based on the master tables (which will be properly related to each other).

Another option will become available with Oracle7.1. It will feature a modification to snapshot functionality that will allow the DBA to relate snapshots to each other. As a result of this, consistent simple snapshots can be generated.

Sizing and Storing Snapshots

The appropriate storage parameters for snapshots are derived from the data being selected. Since the data is being replicated, the source data is known and can be sized. Use the space calculations in Chapter 5, "Managing the Development Process," to size the snapshot.

If a complex snapshot is used, then the storage needs will vary. For example, the "EMP_DEPT_COUNT" snapshot shown in the previous section should use less space than its master table, since it performs a GROUP BY on the table and only returns two columns. For other complex snapshots—such as those involving joins and returning columns from multiple tables—the space needs for the snapshot may exceed those of any of the master tables involved. Therefore, always calculate the space for the local snapshot rather than relying on the storage parameters for the master tables.

Because of the nature of the snapshot data and objects, you may wish to create a tablespace that is dedicated to supporting them. The emphasis should be on providing enough contiguous space so that no snapshot refresh attempt will ever fail due to space availability problems.

Manual Snapshot Refreshes

The EMP_DEPT_COUNT snapshot defined earlier contained the following specifications about its refresh interval:

```
REFRESH COMPLETE
     START WITH sysdate
     NEXT sysdate+7
```

The "REFRESH COMPLETE" clause indicates that each time the snapshot is refreshed, it should be completely re-created. The available REFRESH options are listed in Table 17-2.

The "START WITH" clause tells the database when the snapshot should be refreshed. In this example, that is specified as "sysdate", so the database will replicate the data when the snapshot is created.

The "NEXT" clause is used to set the interval for the refreshes. This period will be measured from the time of the last refresh, whether it was done automatically by the database or manually by the DBA. In this example, a refresh will occur seven days after the most recent snapshot.

You may manually refresh the snapshot via the DBMS_SNAPSHOT package provided by Oracle. There is a procedure named REFRESH within this package that can be used to refresh a single snapshot. An example of the command's usage is shown in the following listing. In this example, the user first logs in to SQLDBA, then uses the EXECUTE command to execute the procedure. The parameters passed to the procedure are described following the example.

```
sqldba lmode=y
SQLDBA> connect internal
SQLDBA> EXECUTE dbms_snapshot.refresh('emp_dept_count','?');
```

REFRESH OPTION	DESCRIPTION
COMPLETE	The snapshot tables are completely regenerated using the snapshot's query and the master tables every time the snapshot is refreshed.
FAST	If a simple snapshot is used, then a snapshot log can be used to send only the changes to the snapshot table.
FORCE	The default value. If possible, it performs a FAST refresh; otherwise, it will perform a COMPLETE refresh.

TABLE 17-2. *Snapshot Refresh Options*

The REFRESH procedure of the DBMS_SNAPSHOT package, as shown in this listing, takes two parameters. The first is the name of the snapshot, which should be prefixed by the name of the snapshot's owner (if other than the user executing this command). The second parameter is the manual refresh option. The available values for the manual refresh option parameter are listed in Table 17-3.

Another procedure in the DBMS_SNAPSHOT package can be used to refresh all of the snapshots that are scheduled to be automatically refreshed. This procedure, named REFRESH_ALL, will refresh each snapshot separately. It does not accept any parameters. The following listing shows an example of its execution. In this example, the user first logs into SQLDBA, then uses the EXECUTE command to execute the procedure.

```
sqldba lmode=y
SQLDBA> connect internal
SQLDBA> EXECUTE dbms_snapshot.refresh_all;
```

Since the snapshots will be refreshed consecutively, they are not all refreshed at the same time. Therefore, a database or server failure during the execution of this procedure may cause the local snapshots to be out of sync with each other. If that happens, simply rerun this procedure after the database has been recovered.

Managing Snapshot Logs

A snapshot log is a table that maintains a record of modifications to the master table in a snapshot. It is stored in the same database as the master table and is only available for simple snapshots. The data in the snapshot log is used during Fast refreshes of the table's snapshots. If you are going to use this method, create the snapshot log before creating the snapshot.

MANUAL REFRESH OPTION	DESCRIPTION
F	Fast refresh
f	Fast refresh
C	Complete refresh
c	Complete refresh
?	Indicates that the default refresh option for the snapshot should be used

TABLE 17-3.   *Manual Refresh Option Values for the DBMS_SNAPSHOT.REFRESH Procedure*

To create a snapshot log, you must be able to create an AFTER ROW trigger on the table. This implies that you have CREATE TRIGGER and CREATE TABLE privileges, and that there is not already an AFTER ROW trigger on the table. You cannot specify a name for the snapshot log.

NOTE
Because Oracle uses the name of the master table in the names of the database objects that support its snapshot log, the master table's name should be kept to less than 23 characters.

Since the snapshot log is a table, it has the full set of table storage clauses available to it. The example in the following listing shows the creation of a snapshot log on a table named EMPLOYEE. The log will be placed in the DATA_2 tablespace, with the specified storage parameters.

```
CREATE SNAPSHOT LOG ON employee
TABLESPACE data_2
STORAGE(INITIAL 100k NEXT 50K PCTINCREASE 0)
PCTFREE 5;
```

The PCTFREE value for this table can be set very low, as shown in this example. The size of the snapshot log depends on the number of changes that will be processed during each refresh. The more frequently the snapshot is refreshed, the less space is needed for the snapshot log.

Just as snapshots create underlying tables, snapshot logs create a set of database structures. In the master table's database, the snapshot log creates a table named MLOG$_*tablename* to store the ROWID and a timestamp for the rows in the master table. This table will be used to identify the rows that have changed since the last refresh. An AFTER ROW trigger named TLOG$_*tablename*, which will populate the MLOG$_*tablename* table, is created on the master table. Do not alter either of these objects.

The storage parameters for the snapshot log can be modified via the ALTER SNAPSHOT LOG command. When using this command, specify the name of the master table, not its snapshot log table name. An example of altering the EMPLOYEE table's snapshot log is shown in the following listing.

```
ALTER SNAPSHOT LOG employee
PCTFREE 10;
```

Information about snapshot logs can be retrieved via the DBA_SNAPSHOT_LOGS data dictionary view. This view lists the owner of the snapshot log, its master table, its snapshot log table, and the trigger used. Since the snapshot log table is a segment in the database, and its name is known (MLOG$_*tablename*), its space usage can be tracked via the extent monitoring scripts provided in Chapter 6, "Monitoring Multiple Databases."

To drop a snapshot log, use the DROP SNAPSHOT LOG command, as shown in the following example.

```
DROP SNAPSHOT LOG ON employee;
```

This will drop the snapshot log and its associated objects from the database.

Managing Distributed Transactions

In databases using the Oracle7 Distributed Option, a single logical unit of work may include transactions against multiple databases. The example shown earlier in Figure 17-3 illustrates this: a COMMIT is submitted after two tables in separate databases have been updated. Oracle7 will transparently maintain the integrity between the two databases by ensuring that all of the transactions involved either commit or roll back as a group. This is accomplished automatically via Oracle7's Two-Phase Commit (2PC) mechanism.

The first phase of the 2PC is the Prepare phase. In this phase, each node involved in a transaction prepares the data that it will need to either commit or roll back the data. Once prepared, a node is said to be *in-doubt*. The nodes notify the initiating node for the transaction (known as the *global coordinator*) of their status.

Once all nodes are prepared, the transaction enters the Commit phase, and all nodes are instructed to commit their portion of the logical transaction. The databases all commit the data at the same logical time, preserving the integrity of the distributed data.

Resolving In-Doubt Transactions

Transactions against stand-alone databases may fail due to problems with the database server; for example, there may be a media failure. Working with distributed databases increases the number of potential failure causes. For example, a transaction against a remote database requires that the network used to access that database, and the remote host itself, be available.

When a distributed transaction is pending, an entry for that transaction can be viewed via the DBA_2PC_PENDING data dictionary view. When the transaction completes, its record is removed from that table. If the transaction is pending, but is not able to complete, then its record stays in DBA_2PC_PENDING.

The RECO (Recoverer) background process periodically checks the DBA_2PC_PENDING view for distributed transactions that failed to complete. Using the information there, the RECO process on a node will automatically attempt to recover the local portion of an in-doubt transaction. It then attempts to establish connections to any other databases involved in the transaction and resolves the distributed portions of the transaction. The related rows in the DBA_2PC_PENDING views in each database are then removed.

Thus, the recovery of distributed transactions is performed automatically by the RECO process. It is possible to manually recover the local portions of a distributed transaction, but this will usually result in inconsistent data between the distributed databases. This is counter to the purpose of distributed transactions, since they serve to enforce relationships between local and remote data. If a local recovery is performed, then the remote data will be out of sync.

To minimize the number of distributed recoveries necessary, you can influence the way that the distributed transaction is processed. This is accomplished via the use of *commit point strengths* to tell the database how to structure the transaction. These are described in the next section.

Commit Point Strength

Each set of distributed transactions, by its nature, references multiple hosts and databases. Of those, one host and database can normally be singled out as being the most reliable, or as owning the most critical data. This database is known as the *commit point site;* if data is committed there, then it is committed for all databases. If the transaction against the commit point site fails, then the transactions against the other nodes are rolled back. This site also stores information about the status of the distributed transaction.

The commit point site will be selected by Oracle based on each database's *commit point strength*. This is set via the INIT.ORA file, as shown in the following listing.

```
COMMIT_POINT_STRENGTH=100
```

The values set for the COMMIT_POINT_STRENGTH parameter are set on a relative scale, not on an absolute scale. In the preceding example, it was set to "100." If another database has a commit point strength of "200," then that database would be the commit point site for a distributed transaction involving those two databases. The value cannot exceed 255.

Since the scale is relative, set up a site-specific scale. Set the commit point on your most reliable database to 250. Then grade the other servers and databases relative to that one. If, for example, another database is only 80 percent as reliable as the most reliable database, then assign it a commit point strength of 200 (80 percent of 250). Fixing a single database at a definite point (in this case, 250) allows the rest of the databases to be graded on an even scale. This should result in the proper commit point site being used for each transaction.

Database Domains and Communities

All of the examples in this chapter have used the standard method for evaluating an object's FQON—using the object name in the query, and resolving the rest of the object name via a database link. This method will work across all platforms and networking options. However, networks that use a Domain Name Service (DNS) to name their hosts can take advantage of new networking features within Oracle7.

A *Domain Name Service* allows hosts within a network to be hierarchically organized. Each node within the organization is called a *domain*, and each domain is labelled by its function. These functions may include "COM" for companies and "EDU" for schools. Each domain may have many sub-domains. Therefore, each host will be given a unique name within the network; its name contains information about how it fits into the network hierarchy. Host names within a network are typically comprised of up to four parts; the left-most portion of the name is the host's name, and the rest of the name shows the domain to which the host belongs.

For example, a host may be named "HQ.MYCORP.COM". In this example, the host is named "HQ". It is identified as being part of the "MYCORP" sub-domain of the "COM" domain.

This is significant for two reasons. First, the host name is part of the FQON. Second, Oracle7 allows you to specify the DNS version of the host name in database link names, thus simplifying the management of distributed database connections.

To implement this, you first need to add two parameters to your INIT.ORA file for the database. The first of these, *DB_NAME*, may already be there. It should be set to the instance name. The second parameter is *DB_DOMAIN*, which is set to the DNS name of the database's host. It specifies the network domain in which the host resides. If a database named "LOC" was created on the "HQ.MYCORP.COM" server, then its INIT.ORA entries would be the same as the ones shown in the following listing.

```
DB_NAME = loc
DB_DOMAIN = hq.mycorp.com
```

To enable the usage of the database domain name, the GLOBAL_NAMES parameter must be set to TRUE in your INIT.ORA file, as shown in the following listing. If it is not set, then it will default to FALSE, and the database link names will not correspond to global database names (as shown earlier in this chapter).

```
GLOBAL_NAMES = true
```

Once these parameters have been set, the database must be shut down and restarted using this INIT.ORA file for the settings to take effect.

When using this method of creating global database names, the names of the database links that are created are the same as the databases to which they point. Thus, a database link that pointed to the "LOC" database listed earlier would be named LOC.HQ.MYCORP.COM. This is shown in the following listing.

```
CREATE PUBLIC DATABASE LINK loc.hq.mycorp.com
USING 'connect string';
```

In this configuration, it is still possible to create database links that do not contain the global database name of the database to which they point. In those cases, Oracle appends the local database's DB_DOMAIN value to the name of the database link. For example, if the database was within the "HQ.MYCORP.COM" domain, and the database link was named "LOC", then the database link name, when used, would be automatically expanded to "LOC.HQ.MYCORP.COM".

Using global database names thus establishes a link between the database name, database domain, and database link names. This, in turn, makes it easier to identify and manage database links. For example, you can create a public database link (with no connect string) in each database that points to every other database. Users within a database no longer need to guess at the proper database link to use; if they know the global database name, then they know the database link name. If a table is moved from one database to another, or if a database is moved from one host to another, it is easy to determine which of the old database links must be dropped and re-created. Using global database names is part of migrating from stand-alone databases to true networks of databases.

Database domains are often confused with communities. *Communities* are used by SQL*Net to identify a group of servers that communicate via the same communications protocol. For example, a community may be named "TCP.HQ.MYCORP.COM". That would identify it as being the community of servers using the TCP/IP protocol to communicate within the "HQ.MYCORP.COM" network domain. Thus, the network domain serves to help enforce the uniqueness of the SQL*Net community's name. The "TCP" portion of the community's name refers not to a host or database name, but to the communication protocol that the hosts share.

Since it is common for hosts in the same domain to share the same communications protocol, it is useful to make the network domain part of the SQL*Net community name. The ".COM" portion of the network domain name is usually left off the community name, since communities usually do not span that level of the network hierarchy. Thus, the TCP/IP community in this example would be named "TCP.HQ.MYCORP". Using a three-part community name also helps to reduce potential confusion between community names and network domain names.

Monitoring Distributed Databases

Most database-level monitoring systems, such as the Command Center database described in Chapter 6, "Monitoring Multiple Databases," analyze the performance of databases without taking their environments into account. However, there are several other key performance measures that must be taken into account for databases:

- The performance of the host
- The distribution of I/O across disks and controllers
- The usage of available memory

For distributed databases, several additional performance measures must be considered:

- The capacity of the network and its hardware
- The load on the network segments
- The usage of different physical access paths between hosts

None of these can be measured from within the database. This forces the focus of monitoring efforts to shift from database-centric to network-centric. The database becomes one part of the monitored environment, rather than the only part that is checked.

It is still necessary to monitor those aspects of the database that are critical to its success—such as the extensions of its segments and the free space in tablespaces. However, the *performance* of distributed databases cannot be measured except as part of the performance of the network that supports them. Therefore, all performance-related tests, such as stress tests, must be coordinated with the network management staff. That staff can also verify the effectiveness of your attempts to reduce the database load on the network.

The performance of the individual hosts can usually be monitored via a network monitoring package. This monitoring is thus performed in a top-down fashion—network to host to database. Use the monitoring system described in Chapter 6, "Monitoring Multiple Databases," as an extension to the network and host monitors.

Tuning Distributed Databases

When tuning a stand-alone database, the goal is to reduce the amount of time it takes to find data. The DBA can use a number of database structures and options to increase the likelihood that the data will be found in memory or in the first place that the database looks. These are described in Chapter 8, "Database Tuning."

When working with distributed databases, there is an additional consideration. Since data is now not only being found, but also being shipped across the network, the performance of a query is now made up of the performance of these two steps. You must therefore consider the ways in which data is being transferred across the network, with a goal of reducing the network traffic.

A simple way to reduce network traffic is to replicate data from one node to another. This can be done manually (via the SQL*Plus COPY command), or automatically by the database (via snapshots). This solution improves the performance of queries against remote databases by bringing the data across the network once—usually during a slow period on the local host. Local queries can then use the local copy of the data, eliminating the network traffic that would otherwise be required.

There are two problems with this solution: first, the local data may become out of sync with the remote data. This is an historic problem with derived data; it limits the usefulness of this option to tables whose data is fairly static. Even if a simple snapshot is used with a snapshot log, the data will not be refreshed continuously, only when scheduled.

The second problem with the replicated data solution is that the copy of the table cannot pass updates back to the master table. That is, if a snapshot is used to make a local copy of a remote table, then the snapshot cannot be updated. The same must hold true for tables created with the SQL*Plus COPY command; they are not the master tables and should be treated as read-only tables.

Thus, any updates against those tables must be performed against the master tables. If the table is frequently updated, then replicating the data will not improve your performance with the currently available technology. With later versions of Oracle7.1, this situation will be resolved. When Oracle7.1 goes into production, the ability to update local snapshots will be in Alpha-test. It is expected that this ability—called Update Anywhere—will be in production six months after Oracle7.1 goes into production. The application developers and DBAs will be able to customize how the database resolves errors that may result if multiple users update the same rows from different snapshots.

The type of snapshot to use depends on the nature of the application. Simple snapshots do not involve any data manipulation with the query—they are simply copies of rows from remote tables. Complex snapshots perform operations such as GROUP BY, CONNECT BY, or joins on the remote tables. Knowing which to use requires that you know the way in which the data is to be used by the local database.

Simple snapshots allow you to use snapshot logs. These are logs of the transactions made against the remote table. When it is time to refresh that table's snapshots, only the transactions from the snapshot log are sent across the network. Therefore, if the remote table is frequently modified, and you need frequent refreshes, then using a simple snapshot will improve the performance of the snapshot refresh process.

When a complex snapshot is refreshed, it has to completely rebuild the snapshot tables. This seems at first like a tremendous burden to put on the system—why not find a way to use simple snapshots instead? However, there are a number of advantages to complex snapshots:

- Tables chosen for replication are typically modified infrequently. Therefore, the refreshes can normally be scheduled for low-usage times in the local database, lessening the impact of full refreshes.

- Complex snapshots may replicate less data than simple snapshots.

The second point seems a little cryptic. After all, a complex snapshot involves more processing than a simple snapshot, so shouldn't it require more work for the network? Actually, it may require *less* work for the network, because more work is being done by the database.

Consider the case of two tables being replicated via snapshots. The users on the local database will always query the two tables together, via a join. As shown in Figure 17-7, there are two options. You can either use two simple snapshots (Figure 17-7(a)), or you can perform the join via a complex snapshot (Figure 17-7(b)). What is the difference in performance between the two?

If the tables are joined properly, then the complex snapshot, even if it returns all columns from both tables, should not send any more data across the network than the two simple snapshots will when they are first created. In fact, it will most likely send less data during its creation. When choosing between these two alternatives on the basis of performance, you need to consider two factors:

1. The performance of the refreshes.

2. The performance of queries against the snapshots.

The second of these criteria is usually the more important of the two. After all, the data is being replicated to improve query performance. If the users only access

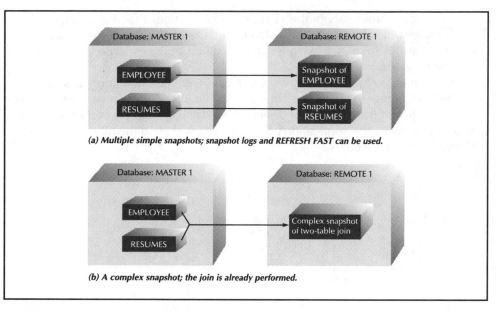

FIGURE 17-7. *Data Replication Options for Joins*

the tables via a specific join, then the complex snapshot has already performed the join for them. Performing the join against two simple snapshots will take longer. You cannot determine which of these options is preferable until the access paths that the users will use have been fully defined. If the tables are sometimes queried separately, or via a different join path, then you will need to use simple snapshots or multiple complex snapshots.

The performance of the refreshes won't concern your users. What may concern them is the validity of the data. If the remote tables are frequently modified, and are of considerable size, then you are almost forced to use simple snapshots with snapshot logs. Performing complete refreshes in the middle of a workday is generally unacceptable. Thus, it is the *frequency* of the refreshes, rather than the size of them, that determines which type of snapshot will have the better performance for the users. After all, they are most concerned about the performance of the system while they are using it; refreshes performed late at night do not affect them. If the tables need to be frequently synchronized, use simple snapshots with snapshot logs. Otherwise, custom complex snapshots should be used.

As was noted previously in this chapter, you may index the underlying SNAP$_tablename tables that are created by the snapshot in the local database. This should also help to improve query performance, at the expense of slowing down the refreshes.

Another means of reducing network traffic, via remote procedure calls, is described in Chapter 8, "Database Tuning." That chapter also includes information on tuning SQL and the application design. If the database was properly structured, then tuning the way the application processes data will yield the most significant performance improvements.

PART 5

Appendixes

APPENDIX A

Database Creation Procedures

The procedures provided here can be used to create a database that is in compliance with the logical and physical layout standards described in Chapter 3, "Logical Database Layouts" and Chapter 4, "Physical Database Layouts." The scripts created here provide the "7-Disk Compromise" discussed in Chapter 4. The code provided here creates the CC1 Command Center database described in Chapter 6, "Monitoring Multiple Databases." The SQL for both Oracle Version 6 and Oracle7 is provided.

The Oracle7 code is based on the SQL created by the Oracle installation program, with several modifications and customizations, particularly in the area of the rollback segment sizing. The Oracle Version 6 code mimics the Oracle7 code's logical and physical database layout conventions. Disk file and directory names are specific to UNIX.

The files provided here for Oracle7 are

FILENAME	DESCRIPTION
cr_CC1.sql	The SQL file to be called from within SQLDBA that actually creates the database.
initcc10.ora	The initial INIT.ORA file for the database creation.
initcc1.ora	The production INIT.ORA file for the database.
configcc1.ora	The CONFIG.ORA file for both production and initial database creation (assuming no archiving; to enable archiving, create a separate version for production).

For Oracle Version 6:

FILENAME	DESCRIPTION
cr_CC1.sql	The SQL file to be called from within SQLDBA that actually creates the database.
initcc10.ora	The initial INIT.ORA file for the database creation.
initcc11.ora	The second INIT.ORA file for the database creation.
initcc1.ora	The production INIT.ORA file for the database.

The Oracle7 suite will be listed first, followed by the Oracle Version 6 suite, in the order listed. The comments in the Oracle Version 6 scripts mimic those created by the Oracle7 database installation scripts, which in turn mimic the comments in the original OFA paper (see Chapter 3, "Logical Database Layouts").

Before running the cr_CC1.sql scripts, set your logical pointers to the name of the new database instance. In UNIX, this means setting the ORACLE_SID to the new instance name and ORACLE_HOME to the home directory of the version of the Oracle software you wish to use.

Oracle7 Scripts

The main database creation script is called cr_CC1.sql. It creates a database whose instance name is "CC1." This can be easily changed to whatever instance name you choose.

To specify a different instance name, change the name of the database creation file to use the new name (to cr_*new_db_name*.sql). Then change all references to "CC1" in the following scripts to use your new instance name. The "db_name" parameter in the INIT.ORA (Oracle Version 6) and configuration files (Oracle7) should also be renamed to reflect the new instance name.

Database Creation—The cr_CC1.sql Script

Before running this script, the user should have specified the database logicals (environment variables) to point to the CC1 database. In UNIX, this requires setting the ORACLE_SID environment variable to "CC1" and the ORACLE_HOME environment variable to the root directory of the Oracle software. This script should be run from the $ORACLE_HOME/dbs directory.

In this script, you will see the steps involved in creating a database that is compliant with the database design rules given in Chapter 3, "Logical Database Layout" and Chapter 4, "Physical Database Layout." This script consists of the following steps.

Initial Database Creation

1. Create the CC1 database, specifying the SYSTEM tablespace datafile and the online redo logs.

2. Create the Oracle7 catalog.

3. Create a second rollback segment (r0) in the SYSTEM tablespace.

4. Alter the new rollback segment to make it available. Other tablespaces can then be created.

Create New Tablespaces

5. Create a tablespace (RBS) for further rollback segments.

6. Create a tablespace (TEMP) for temporary segments.

7. Create a tablespace (TOOLS) for database products' tables.

8. Create a tablespace (TESTS) for tests of the CC1 monitoring application.

9. Create a DATA tablespace. For the CC1 monitoring application, name it CC.

10. Create an INDEXES tablespace. For the CC1 monitoring application, name it CCINDX.

Create Additional Rollback Segments

11. Create two rollback segments (r1,r2) in the RBS tablespace. For other applications, you will need to create more rollback segments (see Chapter 7, "Managing Rollback Segments").

12. Deactivate the second rollback segment (r0) in the SYSTEM tablespace.

Modify the SYS and SYSTEM Users

13. Alter the SYS and SYSTEM users' temporary tablespace designation to use TEMP.

14. Alter the SYSTEM user's default tablespace to use TOOLS.

15. Create the DBA synonyms for the SYSTEM user.

```
REM  Oracle7 database creation script for CC1
REM *
REM file: cr_CC1.sql
REM location:  $ORACLE_HOME/dbs
REM
REM  **Customize the file placements to your needs.**
REM
REM For this example, $ORACLE_HOME = /orasw/v7
REM *
REM * Set terminal output and command echoing on; log output
REM *
set termout on
set echo on
spool cr_CC1.log
REM Initial database creation
REM Step 1.  Create the database.  The control files will be
REM             created automatically when specified in the
REM             initcc10.ora file.
REM
REM * Start the <sid> instance (ORACLE_SID here must be set to
REM * <sid>).
REM *

connect internal
startup pfile=/orasw/v7/dbs/initcc10.ora nomount
```

```
REM * Create the <dbname> database.
REM * SYSTEM tablespace configuration guidelines:
REM *    General-Purpose ORACLE RDBMS              5Mb
REM *    Additional dictionary for applications   10-50Mb
REM * Redo Log File configuration guidelines:
REM *    Use 3+ redo log files to relieve log waits.
REM *    Use 2M per redo log file per connection to reduce
REM *    checkpoints.
REM *
create database "CC1"
    maxinstances 1
    maxlogfiles  16
    character set "US7ASCII"
    datafile
    '/db01/oracle/CC1/sys01.dbf' size    20M reuse
    logfile
    '/db05/oracle/CC1/redo01CC1.dbf'  size 2M reuse,
    '/db05/oracle/CC1/redo02CC1.dbf'  size 2M reuse,
    '/db05/oracle/CC1/redo03CC1.dbf'  size 2M reuse;

disconnect

REM * The database should already be started up at this point
REM * with: pfile=/orasw/v7/dbs/initcc10.ora

connect internal
REM
REM Step 2.   Create the Oracle7 catalog (data dictionary).
REM
REM # install data dictionary views:
@/orasw/v7/rdbms/admin/catalog.sql

REM Step 3.   Create a second rollback segment (r0) in SYSTEM.
REM
REM * Create additional rollback segment in SYSTEM.
REM *

connect internal
create rollback segment r0 tablespace system
storage (initial 16k next 16k minextents 2 maxextents 20);

REM Step 4.   Alter the new rollback segment to make it available.
```

```
REM              Further tablespaces can then be created.
REM
REM * Use ALTER ROLLBACK SEGMENT ONLINE to put r0 online without
REM * shutting down and restarting the database.
REM *
alter rollback segment r0 online;

REM Create new tablespaces
REM Step 5.   Create a tablespace (RBS) for rollback segments
REM
REM * Create a tablespace for rollback segments.
REM * Rollback segment configuration guidelines:
REM *   1 rollback segments for every 4 concurrent xactions.
REM *    All rollback segments the same size.
REM *

create tablespace rbs datafile
   '/db02/oracle/CC1/rbs01.dbf' size   10M reuse,
   '/db02/oracle/CC1/rbs02.dbf' size   10M reuse,
   '/db02/oracle/CC1/rbs03.dbf' size   10M reuse
default storage (
   initial    1M
   next       1M
   pctincrease 0
   minextents  9
   maxextents  50);

REM Step 6.   Create a tablespace (TEMP) for temporary segments.
REM
REM * Create a tablespace for temporary segments.
REM * Temporary tablespace configuration guidelines:
REM *
create tablespace temp datafile
   '/db05/oracle/CC1/temp01.dbf'      size   15M reuse
default storage (
   initial    500k
   next       500k
   pctincrease 0);

REM Step 7.   Create a tablespace (TOOLS) for products tools.
REM
REM * Create a tablespace for database tools.
```

```
REM *
create tablespace tools datafile
    '/db05/oracle/CC1/tools01.dbf'    size   20M reuse;


REM Step 8.  For the monitoring application, create a TESTS
REM              tablespace to be used when testing modifications.
REM
REM * Create a tablespace for database monitoring tests.
REM *
create tablespace tests datafile
    '/db05/oracle/CC1/tests01.dbf'    size   30M reuse;


REM Step 9.  Create a DATA tablespace.  For the CC1
REM              monitoring application, name it CC.
REM
REM * Create a tablespace for database monitoring tables.
REM *
create tablespace cc datafile
    '/db03/oracle/CC1/cc.dbf'         size   30M reuse;


REM Step 10.  Create an INDEXES tablespace.  For the CC1
REM               monitoring application, name it CCINDX.
REM
REM * Create a tablespace for database monitoring indexes.
REM *
create tablespace ccindx datafile
    '/db04/oracle/CC1/ccindx.dbf'     size   20M reuse;


REM Create additional rollback segments
REM Step 11.  Create two rollback segments in the RBS tablespace.
REM               For other applications, you will need to create
REM               more rollback segments (see Chapter 7, "Managing
REM               Rollback Segments").
REM
REM * Create rollback segments.  Use default storage.
REM *
create rollback segment r1 tablespace rbs
storage (optimal 9M);
create rollback segment r2 tablespace rbs
storage (optimal 9M);
```

```
REM Step 12.  Deactivate the second rollback segment (r0) in
REM               the SYSTEM tablespace.
REM
REM * Use ALTER ROLLBACK SEGMENT ONLINE to put rollback segments
REM * online without shutting down and restarting the database.
REM *
alter rollback segment r1 online;
alter rollback segment r2 online;

REM * Since we've created and brought online 2 more rollback
REM * segments, we no longer need the second rollback segment in
REM * the SYSTEM ts. Take it offline, but leave it in the SYSTEM
REM * tablespace. That way, it can be brought back online in case
REM * RBS has to be taken offline (if RBS_2 is not used).
alter rollback segment r0 offline;

REM drop rollback segment r0;
REM /*Keep this rollback segment available.*/

REM Modify the SYS and SYSTEM users.
REM Step 13.  Alter the SYS and SYSTEM users TEMPORARY TABLESPACE
REM               designation to user TEMP.
REM Step 14.  Alter the SYSTEM users DEFAULT TABLESPACE to use
REM               TOOLS.
REM *
alter user sys temporary tablespace temp;
alter user system quota 30M on tools
default tablespace tools temporary tablespace temp;

REM Step 15.  Create the DBA synonyms for the SYSTEM user.
REM
REM * For each DBA user, run DBA synonyms SQL script.  Each
REM * DBA USER created in the future needs to run this from its
REM * account.
REM *
connect system/manager
@/orasw/v7/rdbms/admin/catdbsyn.sql

spool off
```

Temporary Parameters–The initcc10.ora File

This file is called by Step 1 of the cr_CC1.sql script. It is used to mount the database. It is never used other than during database creation. It should be stored in the $ORACLE_HOME/dbs directory.

```
# Oracle7 initcc10.ora file, used during database creation.
#
# file:  initcc10.ora
# location:  $ORACLE_HOME/dbs
#
# include database configuration parameters
ifile                    = /orasw/v7/dbs/configcc1.ora
#
rollback_segments        = ()
db_files = 60
db_file_multiblock_read_count = 8
db_block_buffers = 500
shared_pool_size = 3500000
log_checkpoint_interval = 10000
processes = 50
dml_locks = 100
log_buffer = 8192
sequence_cache_entries = 10
sequence_cache_hash_buckets = 10
# audit_trail = true             # if you want auditing
# timed_statistics = true        # if you want timed statistics
max_dump_file_size = 10240       # limit trace file size to 5Mb
# log_archive_start = true       # if you want automatic archiving
mts_dispatchers="ipc,1"
mts_max_dispatchers=10
mts_servers=1
mts_max_servers=10
mts_service=dev7
mts_listener_address="(ADDRESS=(PROTOCOL=ipc)(KEY=dev7))"
```

Production Parameters–The initcc1.ora File

This file is not called directly by the database creation process. It is the INIT.ORA file that will be used during startup of the production database monitoring application. Its name contains the name of the instance it is used for (CC1).

In order to be used for a different instance, it must be renamed to use that instance's name in its filename.

This file should be stored in the $ORACLE_HOME/dbs directory. Note that it contains entries for the two rollback segments (r1 and r2) created during the database creation process. If you are using a different set of rollback segments, modify the "rollback segments" line to reflect their names.

```
# Oracle7 initcc1.ora file, production INIT.ORA file for CC1
#
# file:  initcc10.ora
# location:  $ORACLE_HOME/dbs
#
# include database configuration parameters
ifile                   = /orasw/v7/dbs/configcc1.ora
#
#rollback_segments       = (r0)
rollback_segments       = (r1,r2)
# tuning parameters
db_files = 60
db_file_multiblock_read_count = 8
db_block_buffers = 500
shared_pool_size = 3500000
log_checkpoint_interval = 10000
processes = 50
dml_locks = 100
log_buffer = 8192
sequence_cache_entries = 10
sequence_cache_hash_buckets = 10
# audit_trail = true              # if you want auditing
# timed_statistics = true         # if you want timed statistics
max_dump_file_size = 10240        # limit trace file size to 5Mb
#log_archive_start = true         # if you want automatic archiving
mts_dispatchers="ipc,1"
mts_max_dispatchers=10
mts_servers=1
mts_max_servers=10
mts_service=dev7
mts_listener_address="(ADDRESS=(PROTOCOL=ipc)(KEY=dev7))"
```

Database Configuration–The configcc1.ora File

This file specifies values for the database parameters that are usually not changed. It is called by the initcc10.ora file during Step 1 of the database creation. It is also called by the initcc1.ora file that is used during production.

This file should be located in the $ORACLE_HOME/dbs directory. Note that its name contains the instance name. To support a different instance, the file would have to be renamed. Its "db_name" parameter would also have to be changed to the new database name.

```
# Oracle7 Configuration file configcc1.ora
#
# file:   configcc1.ora
# location:   $ORACLE_HOME/dbs
#

control_files           = (/db01/oracle/CC1/ctrl1CC1.ctl,
                            /db02/oracle/CC1/ctrl2CC1.ctl,
                            /db03/oracle/CC1/ctrl3CC1.ctl)
background_dump_dest     = /orasw/v7/rdbms/log
core_dump_dest          = /orasw/v7/dbs
user_dump_dest          = /orasw/v7/rdbms/log
log_archive_dest        = /orasw/v7/arch/arch
db_block_size           = 2048

db_name                 = cc1
```

Oracle Version 6 Scripts

The main database creation script for Oracle Version 6 is called cr_CC1.sql. It creates a database whose instance name is "CC1." This can be easily changed to whatever instance name you choose.

These scripts are similar to the Oracle7 scripts, with four notable exceptions:

1. In Oracle Version 6, activating and deactivating rollback segments requires shutting down and restarting the database. The INIT.ORA files used during database startup will determine which rollback segments will be activated. This causes the order of the steps to be altered from that used for Oracle7.

2. In these scripts, the catalog views for Oracle Version 6 are automatically created via the "init_sql_files" parameter of the initcc10.ora file used during database creation.

3. In Oracle Version 6, there is no "config*db_name*.ora" file in the standard database creation script.

4. The method of granting RESOURCE quotas on tablespaces is slightly different between Oracle7 and Oracle Version 6.

Database Creation—The cr_CC1.sql Script

Before running this script, the user should have specified the database logicals to point to the CC1 database. In UNIX, this requires setting the ORACLE_SID environment variable to "CC1" and the ORACLE_HOME environment variable to the root directory of the Oracle software. This script should be run from the $ORACLE_HOME/dbs directory.

In this script, you will see the steps involved in creating a database that is compliant with the database design rules given in Chapter 3, "Logical Database Layout" and Chapter 4, "Physical Database Layout." This script consists of the following steps.

Initial Database Creation

1. Create the CC1 database, specifying the SYSTEM tablespace datafile and the online redo logs. The Oracle Version 6 catalog will be automatically created during database creation.

2. Create the DBA synonyms for the SYSTEM user.

3. Create a second rollback segment (r0) in the SYSTEM tablespace.

4. Shut the database down.

5. Restart the database using the initcc11.ora file to make the new rollback segment available. Other tablespaces can then be created.

Create Additional Rollback Segments

6. Create a tablespace (RBS) for further rollback segments.

7. Create two rollback segments (r1,r2) in the RBS tablespace. For other applications, you will need to create more rollback segments (see Chapter 7, "Managing Rollback Segments").

8. Shut the database down.

9. Restart the database using the production INIT.ORA file (initcc1.ora) to deactivate the second rollback segment (r0) in the SYSTEM tablespace.

Create New Tablespaces

10. Create a tablespace (TEMP) for temporary segments.

11. Create a tablespace (TOOLS) for database products' tables.

12. Create a tablespace (TESTS) for tests of the CC1 monitoring application.

13. Create a DATA tablespace. For the CC1 monitoring application, name it CC.

14. Create an INDEXES tablespace. For the CC1 monitoring application, name it CCINDX.

Modify the SYS and SYSTEM Users

15. Alter the SYS and SYSTEM users' temporary tablespace designation to use TEMP.

16. Alter the SYSTEM user's default tablespace to use TOOLS.

```
REM  Oracle Version 6 CC1 creation script
REM
REM file: cr_CC1.sql
REM location:  $ORACLE_HOME/dbs
REM
REM  **Customize the file placements to your needs.**
REM
REM For this example, $ORACLE_HOME = /orasw/v6
REM * Create CC1 database, instance name CC1
REM * Set terminal output and command echoing on, logging output.
set termout on
set echo on
spool cr_CC1
REM * Start the CC1 instance (ORACLE_SID must be set to CC1).
REM *
startup nomount pfile=$ORACLE_HOME/dbs/initcc10.ora
connect internal

REM Initial database creation
REM Step 1. Create the database, specifying the SYSTEM tablespace
REM        datafile and the online redo logs.  The Oracle Version 6
REM        catalog views will be automatically created during
REM        database creation via INITCC10.ora.  The control files
REM        will be created as specified in the initcc10.ora file.
REM
```

```
REM * Create the CC1 database.
REM *
create database CC1
logfile
   '/db05/oracle/CC1/redo01.dbf'    size    2m REUSE,
   '/db05/oracle/CC1/redo02.dbf'    size    2m REUSE,
   '/db05/oracle/CC1/redo03.dbf'    size    2m REUSE
maxlogfiles 60
datafile
   '/db01/oracle/CC1/sys01.dbf'    size    20m reuse
maxdatafiles 60;

REM Step 2.   Create the DBA synonyms for the SYSTEM user.
REM
REM * run DBA synonyms SQL script.
REM *
connect system/manager
@$ORACLE_HOME/rdbms/admin/dba_syn.sql

REM Step 3.   Create a second rollback segment (r0) in the SYSTEM
REM                tablespace.
REM
create rollback segment r0 tablespace system
storage (initial 16k next 16k minextents 2 maxextents 20);

REM Step 4.   Shut the database down.
REM Step 5.   Restart the database using the initcc11.ora file to
REM                make the new rollback segment (r0) available.
REM                Other tablespaces can then be created.
REM
disconnect
shutdown immediate
startup open CC1 pfile=$ORACLE_HOME/dbs/initcc11.ora
connect internal

REM Create new tablespaces
REM Step 6.   Create a tablespace (RBS) for further rollback
REM                segments.
REM
REM * Create a tablespace for rollback segments.  Default storage is for
REM * homogeneously-sized extents, with each rollback segment forced
```

```
REM * into a separate file with one additional file for extensions.
REM
create tablespace rbs
    datafile          '/db02/oracle/CC1/rbs01.dbf'  size    10m,
              '/db02/oracle/CC1/rbs02.dbf'  size    10m,
              '/db02/oracle/CC1/rbs03.dbf'  size    10m
    default storage  (initial   1M
              next       1M
              pctincrease 0
              minextents  9
              maxextents  50);

REM Step 7.   Create two rollback segments (r1,r2) in the RBS
REM               tablespace.  For other applications, you will need
REM               to create more rollback segments (see Chapter 7,
REM               "Managing Rollback Segments").
REM
REM * Create rollback segments.  Two rollback segments with
REM * 9 extents for users to lock on.
REM *
create rollback segment r1 tablespace rbs;
create rollback segment r2 tablespace rbs;

REM Step 8.   Shut the database down.
REM Step 9.   Restart the database using the production INIT.ORA
REM               file (initcc1.ora) to deactivate the second rollback
REM               segment (r0) in the SYSTEM tablespace.
REM
REM * Restart the instance to activate the additional rollback
REM * segments. This will disable the r0 rollback segment in the
REM * SYSTEM ts. Since we've created and brought online 2 more
REM * rollback segments,we no longer need the second rollback
REM * segment in the SYSTEM ts. Take it offline, but leave it in
REM * the SYSTEM tablespace. That way, it can be brought back
REM * online in case RBS has to be taken offline
REM * (if RBS_2 is not used).
REM *
disconnect
shutdown immediate
startup open CC1
```

```
connect internal

REM Create new tablespaces
REM Step 10.  Create a tablespace (TEMP) for temporary segments.
REM *
create tablespace temp
   datafile  '/db05/oracle/CC1/temp01.dbf'   size 15M
default storage (
   initial      500k
   next         500k
   pctincrease  0);
REM
REM     Step 11.  Create a tablespace (TOOLS) for database tools.
REM
create tablespace tools datafile
   '/db05/oracle/CC1/tools01.dbf'    size   20M reuse;
REM
REM Step 12.  Create a tablespace (TESTS) for tests of the CC1
REM               monitoring application.
REM
create tablespace tests
   datafile '/db05/oracle/CC1/tests.dbf'  size   30m;
REM
REM Step 13.  Create a DATA tablespace.  For the CC1 monitoring
REM               application, name it CC.
REM
create tablespace cc
       datafile  '/db03/oracle/CC1/cc.dbf'  size   30m;
REM
REM  Step 14.  Create an INDEXES tablespace.  For the CC1
REM               monitoring application, name it CCINDX.
REM
create tablespace ccindx
       datafile  '/db04/oracle/CC1/ccindx.dbf'  size   20m;
REM
REM Modify the SYS and SYSTEM users
REM Step 15.  Alter the SYS and SYSTEM users temporary tablespace
REM               designation to use TEMP.
REM Step 16.  Alter the SYSTEM users default tablespace to use
REM               TOOLs.
REM *
alter user sys temporary tablespace temp;
```

```
revoke resource from system;
revoke resource on system from system;
grant resource on tools to system;
alter user system default tablespace tools
temporary tablespace temp;

spool off
disconnect
```

Temporary Parameters(1)–The initcc10.ora File

```
# Oracle Version 6 initcc10.ORA file, for use during database creation.
#
# file:  initcc10.ora
# location:  $ORACLE_HOME/dbs
#
# instance initialization parameters, no rollback segments
#
context_area              = 2048
context_incr              = 2048
Control_files             = (/db01/oracle/CC1/control1.dbf,
                              /db02/oracle/CC1/control1.dbf,
                              /db03/oracle/CC1/control1.dbf)
db_block_buffers          = 1024
db_file_multiblock_read_count   = 8
db_name                   = CC1
dc_column_grants          = 150
dc_columns                = 2000
dc_constraint_defs        = 600
dc_constraints            = 450
dc_files                  = 75
dc_free_extents           = 150
dc_indexes                = 1000
dc_object_ids             = 150
dc_objects                = 700
dc_rollback_segments      = 75
dc_segments               = 150
dc_sequence_grants        = 60
dc_sequences              = 60
dc_synonyms               = 150
dc_table_grants           = 150
```

```
dc_tables                    = 700
dc_tablespace_quotas         = 75
dc_tablespaces               = 75
dc_used_extents              = 150
dc_usernames                 = 150
dc_users                     = 150
ddl_locks                    = 1000
dml_locks                    = 1000
enqueue_resources            = 2020
init_sql_files               = ($ORACLE_HOME/dbs/sql.bsq,
                               $ORACLE_HOME/rdbms/admin/catalog.sql,
                               $ORACLE_HOME/rdbms/admin/expvew.sql)
log_allocation               = 4096   # appropriate for 2Mb redo logs
log_buffer                   = 32768
log_checkpoint_interval      = 1024   #1024 blocks = 2Mb; once per file
open_cursors                 = 255
processes                    = 10
# rollback_segments          = (r0)
# rollback_segments          = ( )
row_cache_enqueues           = 2500
sequence_cache_entries       = 30
sequence_cache_hash_buckets     = 23
```

Temporary Parameters(2)–The initcc11.ora File

This file is called by Step 5 of the cr_CC1.sql script. It is used to restart the database in order to activate the r0 rollback segment created in Step 3. It is never used other than during database creation. It should be stored in the $ORACLE_HOME/dbs directory. It is identical to the initcc10.ora file except for the "rollback_segments" line.

```
# Oracle Version 6 initcc11.ORA file, for use during database
# creation.
# file:  initcc11.ora
# locations $ORACLE_HOME/dbs
#
# This init.ora file is used by the script to start instance
# CC1 with an additional rollback segment in the SYSTEM
# tablespace to add tablespaces to the database.  This file is
# functionally identical to the prior one except for the
# ROLLBACK_SEGMENTS parameter value.
#
```

```
context_area             = 2048
context_incr             = 2048
Control_files            =  (/db01/oracle/CC1/control1.dbf,
                             /db02/oracle/CC1/control1.dbf,
                             /db03/oracle/CC1/control1.dbf)
db_block_buffers         = 1024
db_file_multiblock_read_count   = 8
db_name                  = CC1
dc_column_grants         = 150
dc_columns               = 2000
dc_constraint_defs       = 600
dc_constraints           = 450
dc_files                 = 75
dc_free_extents          = 150
dc_indexes               = 1000
dc_object_ids            = 150
dc_objects               = 700
dc_rollback_segments     = 75
dc_segments              = 150
dc_sequence_grants       = 60
dc_sequences             = 60
dc_synonyms              = 150
dc_table_grants          = 150
dc_tables                = 700
dc_tablespace_quotas     = 75
dc_tablespaces           = 75
dc_used_extents          = 150
dc_usernames             = 150
dc_users                 = 150
ddl_locks                = 1000
dml_locks                = 1000
enqueue_resources        = 2020
init_sql_files           = ($ORACLE_HOME/dbs/sql.bsq,
                         $ORACLE_HOME/rdbms/admin/catalog.sql,
                         $ORACLE_HOME/rdbms/admin/expvew.sql)
log_allocation           = 4096  # appropriate for 2Mb redo logs
log_buffer               = 32768
log_checkpoint_interval  = 1024  #1024 blocks = 2Mb; once per file
open_cursors             = 255
processes                = 10
rollback_segments        = (r0)
# rollback_segments      = ( )
```

```
row_cache_enqueues        = 2500
sequence_cache_entries    = 30
sequence_cache_hash_buckets    = 23
```

Production Parameters–The initcc1.ora File

This file is the INIT.ORA file that will be used during production usage of the database monitoring application. It is called by Step 9 of the cr_CC1.sql script. Note that Step 9 does not indicate a file name to be used for the initialization parameters. Since none is named, the database will look for a file whose name is of the form init*db_name*.ora. In order to be used for a different instance, it must be renamed to use that instance's name in its file name.

This file should be stored in the $ORACLE_HOME/dbs directory. Note that it contains entries for the two rollback segments (r1 and r2) created during the database creation process. If you are using a different set of rollback segments, modify the "rollback segments" line to reflect their names.

```
# Oracle Version 6 production INIT.ORA file for CC1
#
# file: initcc1.ora
# location:  $ORACLE_HOME/dbs
#
# This init.ora file is the default startup file for instance
# CC1. It is functionally identical to both the previous init.ora
# files but for its ROLLBACK_SEGMENTS parameter value.
# default instance init parameters, production rollback segments
#
context_area            = 4096
context_incr            = 4096
control_files           = `(/db01/oracle/CC1/control1.dbf,
                /db02/oracle/CC1/control1.dbf,
                /db03/oracle/CC1/control1.dbf)
db_block_buffers        = 300
db_file_multiblock_read_count    = 8
db_name                 = CC1
dc_column_grants        = 150
dc_columns              = 500
dc_constraint_defs      = 100
dc_constraints          = 100
dc_files                = 75
dc_free_extents         = 150
dc_indexes              = 100
```

```
dc_object_ids            = 150
dc_objects               = 200
dc_rollback_segments     = 75
dc_segments              = 150
dc_sequence_grants       = 60
dc_sequences             = 60
dc_synonyms              = 150
dc_table_grants          = 150
dc_tables                = 100
dc_tablespace_quotas     = 75
dc_tablespaces           = 75
dc_used_extents          = 150
dc_usernames             = 150
dc_users                 = 50
ddl_locks                = 200
dml_locks                = 200
enqueue_resources        = 2020
init_sql_files           =   ($ORACLE_HOME/dbs/sql.bsq,
            $ORACLE_HOME/rdbms/admin/catalog.sql,
            $ORACLE_HOME/rdbms/admin/expvew.sql)
log_allocation           = 4096  # appropriate for 2Mb redo logs
log_buffer               = 32768
log_checkpoint_interval = 1024  #1024 blocks = 2Mb; once per file
log_archive_dest      = /db03/oracle/arch/arch.dbf
log_archive_start     = true
open_cursors             = 255
processes                = 10
# rollback_segments      = (r0)
rollback_segments        = (r1, r2)
row_cache_enqueues       = 2500
sequence_cache_entries  = 30
sequence_cache_hash_buckets    = 23
```

APPENDIX B

Database Installation Guidelines

Since Oracle is available on so many platforms, there is no single set of installation instructions that will suffice for all environments. This is particularly true since Oracle Version 6 is still supported; Oracle7's installation procedures are significantly different from earlier versions. Nonetheless, there are some standard guidelines that can be applied to any environment.

The Oracle installation program (the *Installer*) must accomplish several tasks:

1. Loading source files from tape

2. Creating and populating Oracle software directories

3. Compiling Oracle software

4. Creating Oracle databases

5. Creating the data dictionary catalog views

6. Creating database objects to support Oracle products and options

7. Creating miscellaneous database objects

8. Loading demonstration/help data for Oracle products

Before Step 1 ("Pre-install"), the server should be configured to support the type of database connectivity you will need. For example, if you are planning to query remote databases, then the servers involved in those queries should be attached to the network and properly configured for server-server communications. You must also make sure that there is adequate free space on the disks to hold the software you will be loading; the space requirements are dependent on which products you plan to install.

The Oracle pre-installation checklists in the operating system-specific installation guides provide disk space sizing information for the Oracle software directories. They also provide information for estimating the memory area required for the database users.

Use the Oracle Installer for the areas it is best at: loading the files from tape, creating the software directories, and compiling the software into executables. The tasks that involve direct manipulation of your databases should be done by you.

This is not a difficult set of tasks to assume, and it gives you tremendous control over the planning and implementation of your database. After creating the database to your specifications, you may wish to go back into the Installer and use it to create the database objects required for the products you will be using.

Therefore, the emphasis should be on taking over tasks number 4, 5, 6, and 7 of the previous list: creating the databases, creating the data dictionary catalogs, creating the database objects that will support your database products and options, and creating miscellaneous database objects.

Task number 8, which involves installing the product demonstration and help data, is not part of the standard database creation script. That is because it is not loaded for all environments; the demonstration demo, for example, is usually only used in Development and Test environments. Since it is not part of the standard installed software, treat it as an exception and use the Installer to load it.

Creating the Database

The first of these steps, creating the database, is described throughout this book. Appendix A, "Database Creation Procedures," provides a sample set of files that will accomplish the database creation. Manually creating the database yields numerous benefits:

■ You can set all of the database creation parameters. In Oracle Version 6, this is not the case when using the Installer. Notably, the Oracle Version 6 Installer does not allow you to specify a value for the MAXDATAFILES parameter. This value can only be changed by re-creating the entire database manually.

■ You have greater control over the rollback segment architecture. It is very unusual to find two databases that have the exact same transaction characteristics; those characteristics must be evaluated to determine the proper design for each database. See Chapter 7, "Managing Rollback Segments," for guidelines for choosing the proper number and size of rollback segments.

■ You can plan your logical database layouts. Oracle7's Installer is better in this regard, since it is designed with OFA in mind. That is, it does not assume that Oracle products tables should be stored in the SYSTEM tablespace. However, it assumes that no TOOLS_I or RBS_2 tablespace will be used. See Chapter 3, "Logical Database Layouts," for more information.

■ You can plan the physical database layouts. This is a classic case of planning before doing: it is difficult to plan the proper file locations while the Installer is prompting you for them. It is much better to plan the file locations before even starting the Installer. See Chapter 4, "Physical Database Layouts," for further information.

You may find it easiest to let Oracle create a database via the Installer first. Then exit the Installer, shut down the database, and delete its datafiles, while keeping the database creation scripts. These scripts can then be used as the basis for your own suite of database creation scripts.

A version of the database creation scripts suite is given in Appendix A, "Database Creation Procedures." When you change the drive designations, be sure that your file distribution complies with the guidelines given in Chapter 4, "Physical Database Layouts." Following those guidelines will reduce the likelihood of contention between the Oracle background processes.

When loading multiple versions of the Oracle software, use a directory structure similar to that shown in Figure B-1. This will keep the DBA scripts apart from the software directories, while maintaining a consistent directory structure for new versions. This example uses a device named "/orasw". A separate subdirectory is created for each installed database version.

Storing the datafiles at the same level in a directory hierarchy will simplify the management procedures. It also allows you to avoid putting the instance identifier in the file name; the instance identifier can be used as part of the directory path instead, as in the following sample directory structure listing. A sample disk

```
/orasw
        /v636
                /rdbms
                /dbs, etc.
        /v715
                /rdbms
                /dbs, etc.
        /dba
```

FIGURE B-1. *Disk Layout for Oracle Software*

hierarchy for data disks is shown in Figure B-2. In this example, a "/oracle"
directory is created on each disk. A subdirectory is then created for each instance
(in this example, CASE, CC1, and DEMO).

```
/db01
      /oracle
              /CASE
                      control1.dbf
                      sys01.dbf
                      tools.dbf
              /CC1
                      control1.dbf
                      sys01.dbf
                      tools.dbf
              /DEMO
                      control1.dbf
                      sys01.dbf
```

FIGURE B-2. *Disk Hierarchy for a Sample Data Disk*

Creating the Data Dictionary Catalog Views

The data dictionary catalogs are normally created as part of the database creation process; they are created in the scripts provided in Appendix A, "Database Creation Procedures." However, some third-party tools may require access to data dictionary views from earlier versions of the database. Specifically, some tools that work against both Oracle Version 6 and Oracle7 do so by relying on the Oracle Version 6 catalog view names. To support those tools, you must create the Oracle Version 6 catalog views in the Oracle7 database. (See Chapter 14, "Supporting Third-Party Tools," for examples.)

The view creation script for the Oracle7 data dictionary catalog is run during the database creation procedure provided in Appendix A, "Database Creation Procedures." The view creation script for the Oracle Version 6 data dictionary catalog, called CATALOG6.SQL, is located in $ORACLE_HOME/rdbms/admin. This script should be run from within SQLDBA, as shown in the following listing.

In this example, the UNIX "cd" command is used to change the current directory to the /rdbms/admin subdirectory under $ORACLE_HOME. Next, SQLDBA is run, and the DBA uses the CONNECT INTERNAL command to connect to the database's SYS account. The CATALOG6.SQL script is then run to create the Oracle Version 6 data dictionary views.

```
> cd $ORACLE_HOME/rdbms/admin
> sqldba lmode=y
SQLDBA> connect internal
SQLDBA> @catalog6
```

When the tools no longer require the Oracle Version 6 data dictionary catalog views, they can be dropped. Oracle has provided a script for this purpose, named DROPCAT6.SQL. Like CATALOG6.SQL, it is located in the $ORACLE_HOME/rdbms/admin directory. Its usage is shown in the following listing.

In this example, the UNIX "cd" command is used to change the current directory to the /rdbms/admin subdirectory under $ORACLE_HOME. Next, SQLDBA is run, and the DBA uses the CONNECT INTERNAL command to connect to the database's SYS account. The DROPCAT6.SQL script is then run to drop the Oracle Version 6 data dictionary views.

```
> cd $ORACLE_HOME/rdbms/admin
> sqldba lmode=y
SQLDBA> connect internal
SQLDBA> @dropcat6
```

Creating Database Objects to Support Oracle Products and Options

The scripts that the Installer uses to create database objects for Oracle products (such as Export) and options (such as the Procedural Option for Oracle7) are stored in the Oracle software directories as SQL scripts. In the Oracle7 versions, several of them have had significant amounts of documentation added to them to make it simpler to modify them.

Despite this additional documentation, it is still best to use the Installer to load these products and options. By the time you have reached this product installation step (task number 6), the database should be completely installed according to your plans, and there should be no chance that the Installer will override your plans. The one thing that the online scripts do not tell you is the one thing you need to know (and that the Installer *does* know): the interdependencies between the scripts.

For example, the objects needed for the Oracle7 Procedural Option are created via scripts. In the Oracle documentation, there are references to a file called CATPROC.SQL, located in the $ORACLE_HOME/rdbms/admin directory. As you might expect from its name, this script creates the data dictionary catalog views that are necessary for procedural objects and snapshots. But attempting to run this script by itself will result in errors. The problem is that the script is dependent on two other scripts: STANDARD.SQL, which creates PL/SQL packages for the Procedural Option, and DBMSSTDX.SQL, which includes extensions to the STANDARD package. The CATPROC.SQL script must be run after STANDARD.SQL and DBMSSTDX.SQL to avoid errors.

Unless you are constantly creating databases, relying on the Installer to coordinate these scripts is not burdensome. If, however, you need to fully automate the database creation process, then you will need to test the script combinations every time the database is upgraded.

Creating Miscellaneous Database Objects

There are several scripts that are run for almost every database. They are listed in Table B-1. All of the scripts have the suffix ".SQL" and are located in the $ORACLE_HOME/rdbms/admin directory. To run them, go into SQLDBA and CONNECT INTERNAL (as in the data dictionary catalog views examples).

ORACLE VERSION 6 SCRIPT	ORACLE7 SCRIPT	DESCRIPTION
XPLAINPL	UTLXPLAN	Creates the PLAN_TABLE table used by the EXPLAIN PLAN command to store the description of the statement execution path.
MONITOR	UTLMONTR	Grants access to the dynamic performance tables to PUBLIC.
BSTAT	UTLBSTAT	Creates a set of statistics tables at the start of a performance test.
ESTAT	UTLESTAT	Creates a set of statistics tables at the end of a performance test, and generates a report. See Chapter 6, "Monitoring Multiple Databases," for details on interpreting the report.

TABLE B-1. *Descriptions of Common Utility Scripts*

Oracle7 comes with a number of powerful application development tools that are described in Appendix A of the *Oracle7 Server Application Developer's Guide.* The scripts for creating these objects are not called by the Installer; it is left to the DBA to manually run them after creating the database.

The application development tools are listed in Table B-2, along with the scripts needed to create the supporting Oracle database objects. All of the scripts have the suffix ".SQL" and are located in $ORACLE_HOME/rdbms/admin. To run them, go into SQLDBA and CONNECT INTERNAL (as in the data dictionary catalog views examples). Print out the scripts if you choose to use these features, since these scripts are very well documented and contain relevant examples.

As DBA, you need to be aware of which applications are using these tools. Otherwise, the application may fail when you move it from one database to another (for example, from Acceptance Test to Production). These objects thus become part of the application—and they should be subject to the same code migration considerations that are applied to the application code itself.

You must be particularly careful with these scripts as well as the catalog scripts, since they are not all capable of being moved between databases via Export/Import. They must be run for each database in your environment. Any that you use regularly should be added to your standard database creation scripts.

TOOL	SCRIPT	DESCRIPTION
Mail Link	DBMSMAIL & UTLMAIL	Creates the package needed to send mail via Oracle*Mail. Upgrades the mail database so that it can be accessed via remote procedure calls.
Lock Management	DBMSLOCK	Allows developers to create user-defined locks.
Database Alerts	DBMSALRT	Creates database alert procedures, which allow applications to be notified whenever values of interest in the database change.
Database Pipes	DBMSPIPE	Allows sessions within the same instance to communicate with each other.
Procedural Output	DBMSOTPT	Allows users to output messages from procedures and triggers.
Procedure Descriptions	DBMSDESC	Allows developers to describe the arguments of a stored procedure.

TABLE B-2.   *Scripts Needed to Support Additional Oracle7 Tools*

APPENDIX C

SQL Reference for DBA Commands

This appendix offers brief summaries of each of the SQL DBA commands. The commands are arranged alphabetically.

This material is extracted from the *Oracle7 Server SQL Language Reference Manual* which documents all of the Oracle Server SQL commands. This appendix is copyrighted by Oracle Corporation, December 1992, Part Number 778-70-1292 and is included with the permission of Oracle Corporation. The *Oracle7 Server SQL Language Reference Manual* is a reference well worth having and can be obtained by contacting Oracle Corporation.

ALTER DATABASE

Purpose   To alter an existing database in one of these ways:

- mount the database
- convert an ORACLE Version 6 data dictionary when migrating to ORACLE7
- open the database
- choose archivelog or noarchivelog mode for redo log file groups
- perform media recovery
- add or drop a redo log file group or a member of a redo log file group
- rename a redo log file member or a data file
- backup the current control file
- create a new data file in place of an old one for recovery purposes
- take a data file online or offline
- enable or disable a thread of redo log file groups
- change the database's global name
- change the MAC mode
- equate the predefined label DBHIGH or DBLOW with an operating system label

Prerequisites   You must have ALTER DATABASE system privilege.

Syntax   ALTER DATABASE command ::=

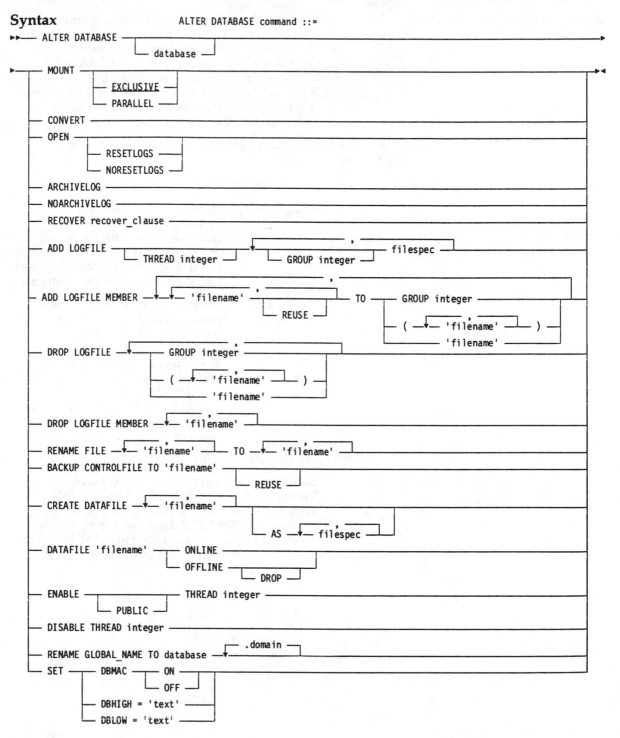

ALTER DATABASE

Keywords and Parameters

database

identifies the database to be altered. If you omit *database*, ORACLE alters the database identified by the value of the initialization parameter DB_NAME. You can only alter the database whose control files are specified by the initialization parameter CONTROL_FILES. Note that the *database* identifier is not related to the SQL*Net database specification.

You can only use the following options when the database is not mounted by your instance:

MOUNT

mounts the database.

EXCLUSIVE

mounts the database in exclusive mode. This mode allows the database to be mounted by only one instance at a time. You cannot use this option if another instance has already mounted the database.

PARALLEL

mounts the database in parallel mode. This mode allows the database to be mounted by multiple instances concurrently. You can only use this option if you are using ORACLE with the Parallel Server option. You cannot use this option if another option has mounted the database in exclusive mode.

The default is EXCLUSIVE.

CONVERT

completes the conversion of the ORACLE Version 6 data dictionary. After you use this option, the Version 6 data dictionary no longer exists in the ORACLE7 database. Only use this option when you are migrating to ORACLE7. For more information on using this option, see the *ORACLE7 Server Migration Guide*.

You can only use the following option when your instance has the database mounted, but not open:

OPEN   opens the database, making it available for normal use. You must mount the database before you can open it.

RESETLOGS   resets the current log sequence number to 1 and invalidates all redo entries in the online and archived redo log files. You must use this option to open the database after performing media recovery with a backup controlfile. After opening the database with this option, you should perform a complete database backup.

NORESETLOGS leaves the log sequence number and redo log files in their current state.

You can only specify these options after performing incomplete media recovery. In any other case, ORACLE uses the NORESETLOGS automatically.

You can only use the following options when your instance has the database mounted in exclusive mode, but not open:

ARCHIVELOG   establishes archivelog mode for redo log file groups. In this mode, the contents of a redo log file group must be archived before the group can be reused. This option prepares for the possibility of media recovery. You can only use this option after shutting down your instance normally or immediately with no errors and then restarting it, mounting the database in exclusive mode.

NOARCHIVELOG establishes noarchivelog mode for redo log files. In this mode, the contents of a redo log file group need not be archived so that the group can be reused. This mode does not prepare for recovery after media failure.

You can only use the following option when your instance has the database mounted in exclusive mode:

RECOVER performs media recovery. See the RECOVER clause. You only recover the entire database when the database is closed. You can recover tablespaces or data files when the database is open or closed, provided the tablespaces or data files to be recovered are not being used. You cannot perform media recovery if you are connected to ORACLE through the multi-threaded server architecture. You can also perform media recovery with the RECOVER SQL*DBA command.

You can use any of the following options when your instance has the database mounted, open or closed, and the files involved are not in use:

ADD LOGFILE adds one or more redo log file groups to the specified thread, making them available to the instance assigned the thread. If you omit the THREAD parameter, the redo log file group is added to the thread assigned to your instance. You need only use the THREAD parameter if you are using ORACLE with the Parallel Server option in parallel mode.

Each *filespec* specifies a redo log file group containing one or more members, or copies. See the syntax description of *filespec*.

You can choose the value of the GROUP parameter for each redo log file group. Each value uniquely identifies the redo log file group among all groups in all threads and can range from 1 to the MAXLOGFILES value. You cannot add multiple redo log file groups having the same GROUP value. If you omit this parameter, ORACLE generates its value automatically. You can examine the GROUP value for a redo log file group through the dynamic performance table V$LOG.

ADD LOGFILE MEMBER adds new members to existing redo log file groups. Each new member is specified by *'filename'*. If the file already exists, it must be the same size as the other group members and you must specify the REUSE option. If the file does not exist, ORACLE creates a file of the correct size. You cannot add a member to a group if all of the group's members have been lost through media failure.

You can specify an existing redo log file group in one of these ways:

GROUP parameter	You can specify the value of the GROUP parameter that identifies the redo log file group.
list of filenames	You can list all members of the redo log file group. You must fully specify each filename according to the conventions for your operating system.

DROP LOGFILE
drops all members of a redo log file group. You can specify a redo log file group in the same manners as the ADD LOGFILE MEMBER clause. You cannot drop a redo log file group if all of its members have been lost through media failure.

DROP LOGFILE MEMBER
drops one or more redo log file members. Each *'filename'* must fully specify a member using the conventions for filenames on your operating system.

You cannot use this clause to drop all members of a redo log file group that contain valid data. To perform this operation, use the DROP LOGFILE clause.

RENAME FILE
renames data files or redo log file members. This clause only renames files in the control file, it does not actually rename them on your operating system. You must specify each filename using the conventions for filenames on your operating system.

BACKUP CONTROLFILE
backs up the current control file to the specified *'filename'*. If the backup file already exists, you must specify the REUSE option.

CREATE DATAFILE
creates a new data file in place of an old one. You can use this option to recreate a data file that was lost with no backup. The *'filename'* must identify a file that is or was once part of the database. The *filespec* specifies the name and size of the new data file. If you omit the AS clause, ORACLE creates the new file with the same name and size as the file specified by *'filename'*.

ORACLE creates the new file in the same state as the old file when it was created. You must perform media recovery on the new file to return it to the state of the old file at the time it was lost.

You cannot create a new file based on the first data file of the SYSTEM tablespace unless the database was created in archivelog mode.

DATAFILE takes a data file online or offline. If any other instance has the database open, your instance must also have the database open:

ONLINE brings the data file online.

OFFLINE takes the data file offline.

DROP takes a data file offline when the database is in noarchivelog mode.

You can only use the following options when your instance has the database open:

ENABLE enables the specified thread of redo log file groups. The thread must have at least two redo log file groups before you can enable it.

PUBLIC makes the enabled thread available to any instance that does not explicitly request a specific thread with the initialization parameter THREAD.

If you omit the PUBLIC option, the thread is only available to the instance that explicitly requests it with the initialization parameter THREAD.

DISABLE disables the specified thread, making it unavailable to all instances. You cannot disable a thread if an instance using it has the database mounted.

RENAME GLOBAL_NAME changes the global name of the database. The *database* is the new database name and can be as long as eight bytes. The optional *domain*s specifies where the database is effectively located in the network hierarchy. Renaming your database automatically clears all data from the shared pool in the SGA. However, renaming your database does not change global references to your database from existing database links, synonyms, and stored procedures and functions on remote databases. Changing such references is the responsibility of the administrator of the remote databases.

For more information on global names, see Chapter 20 "Distributed Databases" of the *ORACLE7 Server Concepts Manual*.

SET   changes one of the following for your database:

DBMAC   changes the mode in which Trusted ORACLE is configured:

ON   configures Trusted ORACLE in DBMS MAC mode.

OFF   configures Trusted ORACLE in OS MAC mode.

DBHIGH   equates the predefined label DBHIGH to the operating system label specified by *'text'*.

DBLOW   equates the predefined label DBLOW to the operating system label specified by *'text'*.

You must specify labels in the default label format for your session. Changes made by this option take effect when you next start your instance. You can only use this clause if you are using Trusted ORACLE. For more information on this clause, see the *Trusted ORACLE7 Server Administrator's Guide*.

Usage Notes   For more information on using the ALTER DATABASE command for database maintenance, see Chapter 3 "Starting Up and Shutting Down" of the *ORACLE7 Server Administrator's Guide*.

ALTER PROFILE

Purpose

To add, modify, or remove a resource limit in a profile.

Prerequisites

You must have ALTER PROFILE system privilege.

If you are using Trusted ORACLE in DBMS MAC mode, your DBMS label must match the profile's creation label or you must satisfy one of these criteria:

- If the profile's creation label is higher than your DBMS label, you must have READUP and WRITEUP system privileges
- If the profile's creation label is lower than your DBMS label, you must have WRITEDOWN system privilege.
- If the profile's creation label and your DBMS label are noncomparable, you must have READUP, WRITEUP, and WRITEDOWN system privileges.

Syntax

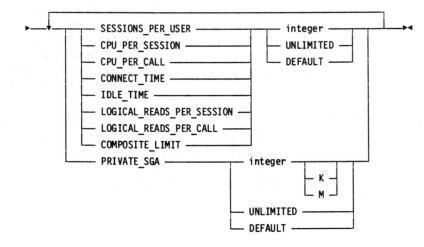

```
ALTER PROFILE command ::=

►►──── ALTER PROFILE profile LIMIT ────────────────────────────────►
```

Keywords and Parameters

profile   is the name of the profile to be altered.

integer   defines a new limit for a resource in this profile. For information on resource limits, see the CREATE PROFILE command.

UNLIMITED   specifies that this profile allows unlimited use of the resource.

DEFAULT   removes a resource limit from the profile. Any
                     user assigned the profile is subject to the limit on
                     the resource defined in the DEFAULT profile in
                     their subsequent sessions.

Usage Notes   Changes made to a profile with an ALTER PROFILE statement only
                     affect users in their subsequent sessions, not in their current sessions.

                     You cannot remove a limit from the DEFAULT profile.

ALTER RESOURCE COST

Purpose

To specify a formula to calculate the total resource cost used in a session. For any session, this cost is limited by the value of the COMPOSITE_LIMIT parameter in the user's profile.

Prerequisites

You must have ALTER RESOURCE COST system privilege.

If you are using Trusted ORACLE in DBMS MAC mode, your DBMS label must match DBLOW or you must have WRITEDOWN system privileges.

Syntax

ALTER RESOURCE COST command ::=

```
►►── ALTER RESOURCE COST ─┬── CPU_PER_SESSION integer ──────────┬──►◄
                          ├── CONNECT_TIME integer ──────────────┤
                          ├── LOGICAL_READS_PER_SESSION integer ─┤
                          └── PRIVATE_SGA integer ───────────────┘
```

Keywords and Parameters

integer   is the weight of each resource.

Usage Notes

The ALTER RESOURCE COST command specifies the formula by which ORACLE calculates the total resource cost used in a session. With this command, you can assign a weight to each of these resources:

CPU_PER_SESSION	The amount of CPU time used by a session measured in hundredths of seconds.
CONNECT_TIME	The elapsed time of a session measured in minutes.
LOGICAL_READS_PER_SESSION	The number of data blocks read during a session, including blocks read from both memory and disk.
PRIVATE_SGA	The number of bytes of private space in the System Global Area (SGA) used by a session. This limit only applies if you are using the multi-threaded server architecture and allocating private space in the SGA for your session.

ORACLE calculates the total resource cost by multiplying the amount of each resource used in the session by the resource's weight and summing the products for all four resources. Both the products and the total cost are expressed in units called *service units*.

Although ORACLE monitors the use of other resources, only these four can contribute to the total resource cost for a session. For information on all resources, see the CREATE PROFILE command later in this chapter.

The weight that you assign to each resource determines how much the use of that resource contributes to the total resource cost. Using a resource with a lower weight contributes less to the cost than using a resource with a higher weight. If you do not assign a weight to a resource, the weight defaults to 0 and use of the resource subsequently does not contribute to the cost. The weights you assign apply to all subsequent sessions in the database.

Once you have specified a formula for the total resource cost, you can limit this cost for a session with the COMPOSITE_LIMIT parameter of the CREATE PROFILE command. If a session's cost exceeds the limit, ORACLE aborts the session and returns an error. For information on establishing resource limits, see the CREATE PROFILE command. If you use the ALTER RESOURCE COST command to change the weight assigned to each resource, ORACLE uses these new weights to calculate the total resource cost for all current and subsequent sessions.

ALTER ROLE

Purpose

To change the authorization needed to enable a role.

Prerequisites

You must either have been granted the role with the ADMIN OPTION or have ALTER ANY ROLE system privilege.

If you are using Trusted ORACLE in DBMS MAC mode, your DBMS label must match the role's creation label or you must satisfy one of these criteria:

- If the role's creation label is higher than your DBMS label, you must have READUP and WRITEUP system privileges
- If the role's creation label is lower than your DBMS label, you must have WRITEDOWN system privilege.
- If the role's creation label and your DBMS label are noncomparable, you must have READUP, WRITEUP, and WRITEDOWN system privileges.

Syntax

```
ALTER ROLE command ::=

▶▶── ALTER ROLE role ──┬── NOT IDENTIFIED ──────────────────────────◀
                       └── IDENTIFIED ──┬── BY password ──┬──
                                        └── EXTERNALLY ───┘
```

Keywords and Parameters

The keywords and parameters in the ALTER ROLE command all have the same meaning as in the CREATE ROLE command. For information on these keywords and parameters, see the CREATE ROLE command.

ALTER ROLLBACK SEGMENT

Purpose

To alter a rollback segment in one of these ways:

- by bringing it online
- by taking it offline
- by changing its storage characteristics

Prerequisites

You must have ALTER ROLLBACK SEGMENT system privilege.

If you are using Trusted ORACLE in DBMS MAC mode, your DBMS label must match the rollback segment's creation label or you must satisfy one of these criteria:

- If the rollback segment's creation label is higher than your DBMS label, you must have READUP and WRITEUP system privileges
- If the rollback segment's creation label is lower than your DBMS label, you must have WRITEDOWN system privilege.
- If the rollback segment's creation label and your DBMS label are noncomparable, you must have READUP, WRITEUP, and WRITEDOWN system privileges.

Syntax

```
ALTER ROLLBACK SEGMENT command ::=

►►── ALTER ROLLBACK SEGMENT rollback_segment ──┬── ONLINE ──────────────────►◄
                                               ├── OFFLINE ─────────────
                                               └── STORAGE storage_clause ──┘
```

Keywords and Parameters

rollback_segment	specifies the name of an existing rollback segment.
ONLINE	brings the rollback segment online.
OFFLINE	takes the rollback segment offline.
STORAGE	changes the rollback segment's storage characteristics. See STORAGE clause.

Usage Notes

When you create a rollback segment, it is initially offline. An offline rollback segment is not available for transactions.

The ONLINE option brings the rollback segment online making it available for transactions by your instance. You can also bring a rollback segment online when you start your instance with the initialization parameter ROLLBACK_SEGMENTS.

The OFFLINE option takes the rollback segment offline. If the rollback segment does not contain information necessary to rollback any active transactions, ORACLE takes it offline immediately. If the rollback segment does contain information for active transactions, ORACLE makes the rollback segment unavailable for future transactions and takes it offline after all the active transactions are committed or rolled back. Once the rollback segment is offline, it can be brought online by any instance.

You cannot take the SYSTEM rollback segment offline.

You can tell whether a rollback segment is online or offline by querying the data dictionary view DBA_ROLLBACK_SEGS. Online rollback segments are indicated by a STATUS value of 'IN_USE'. Offline rollback segments are indicated by a STATUS value of 'AVAILABLE'.

For more information on making rollback segments available and unavailable, see Chapter 9 "Managing Rollback Segments" of the *ORACLE7 Server Administrator's Guide*.

The STORAGE clause of the ALTER ROLLBACK SEGMENT command affects future space allocation in the rollback segment. You cannot change the values of the INITIAL and MINEXTENTS for an existing rollback segment.

ALTER SYSTEM

Purpose

To dynamically alter your ORACLE instance in one of these ways:

- to enable or disable resource limits
- to manage shared server processes or dispatcher processes for the multi-threaded server architecture
- to explicitly switch redo log file groups
- to explicitly perform a checkpoint
- to verify access to data files
- to restrict logons to ORACLE to only those users with RESTRICTED SESSION system privilege
- to enable distributed recovery in a single-process environment
- to disable distributed recovery
- to manually archive redo log file groups or to enable or disable automatic archiving
- to clear all data from the shared pool in the System Global Area (SGA)
- to terminate a session

Prerequisites

You must have ALTER SYSTEM system privilege.

If you are using Trusted ORACLE in DBMS MAC mode, your DBMS label must be the equivalent of DBHIGH.

ALTER SYSTEM

Syntax

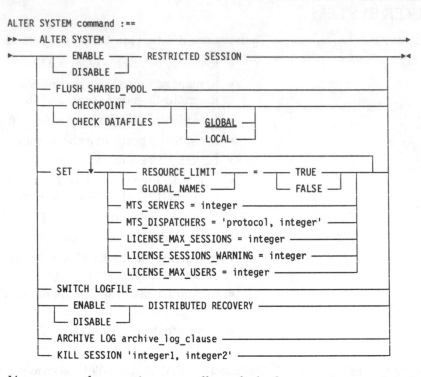

```
ALTER SYSTEM command :==
►►— ALTER SYSTEM —————————————————————————————————►
►— ┬─ ENABLE ──┬─ RESTRICTED SESSION ──────────────►◄
   │ └─ DISABLE ─┘
   ├─ FLUSH SHARED_POOL ─────────────────────────
   ├─ CHECKPOINT ───────────────────────
   │ └─ CHECK DATAFILES ─┘ ┬─ GLOBAL ─┬
   │                       └─ LOCAL ──┘
   ├─ SET ─┬─ RESOURCE_LIMIT ─┬─ = ─┬─ TRUE ──┬
   │       ├─ GLOBAL_NAMES ───┘     └─ FALSE ─┘
   │       ├─ MTS_SERVERS = integer ─────────
   │       ├─ MTS_DISPATCHERS = 'protocol, integer' ─
   │       ├─ LICENSE_MAX_SESSIONS = integer ─
   │       ├─ LICENSE_SESSIONS_WARNING = integer ─
   │       └─ LICENSE_MAX_USERS = integer ─
   ├─ SWITCH LOGFILE ───────────────────────────
   ├─ ┬─ ENABLE ──┬─ DISTRIBUTED RECOVERY ─────────
   │  └─ DISABLE ─┘
   ├─ ARCHIVE LOG archive_log_clause ─────────────
   └─ KILL SESSION 'integer1, integer2' ──────────
```

Keywords and Parameters

You can use these options regardless of whether your instance has the database dismounted or mounted, open or closed:

ENABLE RESTRICTED SESSION	allows only users with RESTRICTED SESSION system privilege to logon to ORACLE.
DISABLE RESTRICTED SESSION	reverses the effect of the ENABLE RESTRICTED SESSION option, allowing all users with CREATE SESSION system privilege to logon to ORACLE.
FLUSH SHARED_POOL	clears all data from the shared pool in the System Global Area (SGA).

You can use these options when your instance has the database mounted, open or closed:

CHECKPOINT   performs a checkpoint.

> GLOBAL   performs a checkpoint for all instances that have opened the database.
>
> LOCAL   performs a checkpoint only for the thread of redo log file groups for your instance. You can only use this option when your instance has the database open.
>
> If you omit both the GLOBAL and LOCAL options, ORACLE performs a global checkpoint.

CHECK DATAFILES   verifies access to online data files.

> GLOBAL   verifies that all instances that have opened the database can access all online data files.
>
> LOCAL   verifies that your instance can access all online data files.
>
> If you omit both the GLOBAL and LOCAL options, ORACLE uses GLOBAL by default.

You can only use these parameters and options when your instance has the database open:

RESOURCE_LIMIT   controls resource limits.

> TRUE   enables resource limits.
>
> FALSE   disables resource limits.

GLOBAL_NAMES   controls the enforcement of global naming:

> TRUE   enables the enforcement of global names.
>
> FALSE   disables the enforcement of global names.

MTS_SERVERS   specifies a new minimum number of shared server processes.

MTS_DISPATCHERS specifies a new number of dispatcher processes:

protocol	is the network protocol of the dispatcher processes.
integer	is the new number of dispatcher processes of the specified protocol.

You can specify multiple MTS_DISPATCHERS parameters in a single command for multiple network protocols.

LICENSE_MAX_SESSIONS
limits the number of sessions on your instance. A value of 0 disables the limit.

LICENSE_SESSIONS_WARNING
establishes a threshold of sessions over which ORACLE writes warning messages to the ALERT file for subsequent sessions. A value of 0 disables the warning threshold.

LICENSE_MAX_USERS
limits the number of users on your database. A value of 0 disables the limit.

SWITCH LOGFILE switches redo log file groups.

ENABLE DISTRIBUTED RECOVERY
enables distributed recovery. In a single-process environment, you must use this option to initiate distributed recovery.

DISABLE DISTRIBUTED RECOVERY
disables distributed recovery.

ARCHIVE LOG
manually archives redo log files or enables or disables automatic archiving. See the ARCHIVE LOG clause.

KILL SESSION
terminates a session. You must identify the session with both of these values from the V$SESSION:

integer1	is the value of the SID column.
integer2	is the value of the SERIAL# column.

Restricting Logons

By default, any user granted CREATE SESSION system privilege can log on to ORACLE. The ENABLE RESTRICTED SESSION option of the ALTER SYSTEM command prevents logons by all users except those having RESTRICTED SESSION system privilege. Existing sessions are not terminated.

You may want to restrict logons if you are performing application maintenance and you want only application developers with RESTRICTED SESSION system privilege to log on. To restrict logons, issue this statement:

```
ALTER SYSTEM
    ENABLE RESTRICTED SESSION
```

You can then terminate any existing sessions using the KILL SESSION clause of the ALTER SYSTEM command.

After performing maintenance on your application, issue this statement to allow any user with CREATE SESSION system privilege to log on:

```
ALTER SYSTEM
    DISABLE RESTRICTED SESSION
```

Clearing the Shared Pool

The FLUSH SHARED_POOL option of the ALTER SYSTEM command clears all information from the shared pool in the System Global Area (SGA). The shared pool stores this information:

- cached data dictionary information
- shared SQL and PL/SQL areas for SQL statements, stored procedures, functions, packages, and triggers

You might want to clear the shared pool before beginning performance analysis. To clear the shared pool, issue this statement:

```
ALTER SYSTEM
    FLUSH SHARED_POOL
```

This statement does not clear shared SQL and PL/SQL areas for SQL statements, stored procedures, functions, packages, or triggers that are currently being executed or for SQL SELECT statements for which all rows have not yet been fetched.

ALTER SYSTEM

Performing a Checkpoint

The CHECKPOINT clause of the ALTER SYSTEM command explicitly forces ORACLE to perform a checkpoint. You can force a checkpoint if you want to ensure that all changes made by committed transactions are written to the data files on disk. For more information on checkpoints, see Chapter 22 "Recovery Structure" of the *ORACLE7 Server Concepts Manual*. If you are using ORACLE with the Parallel Server option in parallel mode, you can specify either the GLOBAL option to perform a checkpoint on all instances that have opened the database or the LOCAL option to perform a checkpoint on only your instance.

This statement forces a checkpoint:

```
ALTER SYSTEM
    CHECKPOINT
```

ORACLE does not return control to you until the checkpoint is complete.

Checking Data Files

The CHECK DATAFILES clause of the ALTER SYSTEM command verifies access to all online data files. If any data file is not accessible, ORACLE writes a message to an ALERT file. You may want to perform this operation after fixing a hardware problem that prevented an instance from accessing a data file. For more information on using this clause, see the *ORACLE7 Parallel Server Administrator's Guide*.

This statement verifies that all instances that have opened the database can access all online data files:

```
ALTER SYSTEM
    CHECK DATAFILES GLOBAL
```

Using Resource Limits

When you start an instance, ORACLE enables or disables resource limits based on the value of the initialization parameter RESOURCE_LIMIT. You can issue an ALTER SYSTEM statement with the RESOURCE_LIMIT option to enable or disable resource limits for subsequent sessions.

Enabling resource limits only causes ORACLE to enforce the resource limits assigned to users. To choose resource limit values for a user, you must create a *profile*, or a set of limits, and assign that profile to the user. For more information on this process, see the CREATE PROFILE and CREATE USER commands.

This ALTER SYSTEM statement dynamically enables resource limits:

```
ALTER SYSTEM
    SET RESOURCE_LIMIT = TRUE
```

Enabling and Disabling Global Name Resolution

When you start an instance, ORACLE determines whether or not to enforce global name resolution for remote objects accessed in SQL statements based on the value of the initialization parameter GLOBAL_NAMES. You can subsequently enable or disable global names resolution while your instance is running with the GLOBAL_NAMES parameter of the ALTER SYSTEM command. You can also enable or disable global name resolution for your instance with the GLOBAL_NAMES parameter of the ALTER SESSION command.

Oracle Corporation recommends that you enable global name resolution. For more information on global name resolution and how ORACLE enforces it, see the section "Referring to Objects in Remote Databases" on page 2-13 of the *Oracle7 Server SQL Language Reference Manual* and Chapter 15 "Managing Distributed Databases" of the *ORACLE7 Server Administrator's Guide*.

Managing Processes for the Multi-Threaded Server

When you start your instance, ORACLE creates shared server processes and dispatcher processes for the multi-threaded server architecture based on the values of these initialization parameters:

MTS_SERVERS

This parameter specifies the initial and minimum number of shared server processes. ORACLE may automatically change the number of shared server processes if the load on the existing processes changes. While your instance is running, the number of shared server processes can vary between the values of the initialization parameters MTS_SERVERS and MTS_MAX_SERVERS.

MTS_DISPATCHERS

This parameter specifies one or more network protocols and the number of dispatcher processes for each protocol.

For more information on the multi-threaded server architecture, see Chapter 9 "Memory Structures and Processes" of the *ORACLE7 Server Concepts Manual*.

You can subsequently use the MTS_SERVERS and MTS_DISPATCHERS parameters of the ALTER SYSTEM command to perform one of these operations while the instance is running:

To create additional shared server processes: You can cause ORACLE to create additional shared server processes by increasing the minimum number of shared server processes.

To terminate existing shared server processes: ORACLE terminates these shared server processes only after they finish processing their current calls and only if the load on the server processes is not so high that it cannot be managed by the remaining processes.

To create more dispatcher processes for a specific protocol: You can create additional dispatcher processes up to a maximum across all protocols specified by the initialization parameter MTS_MAX_DISPATCHERS.

You cannot use this command to create dispatcher processes for network protocols that are not specified by the initialization parameter MTS_DISPATCHERS. To create dispatcher processes for a new protocol, you must change the value of the initialization parameter.

To terminate existing dispatcher processes for a specific protocol: ORACLE terminates these dispatcher processes only after their current user processes disconnect from the instance.

ALTER TABLESPACE

Purpose

To alter an existing tablespace in one of these ways:

- to add or rename data file(s)
- to change default storage parameters
- to take the tablespace online or offline
- to begin or end a backup

Prerequisites

If you have ALTER TABLESPACE system privilege, you can perform any of this command's operations. If you have MANAGE TABLESPACE system privilege, you can only perform these operations:

- to take the tablespace online or offline
- to begin or end a backup

If you are using Trusted ORACLE in DBMS MAC mode, your DBMS label must match the tablespace's creation label or you must satisfy one of these criteria:

- If the tablespace's creation label is higher than your DBMS label, you must have READUP and WRITEUP system privileges.
- If the tablespace's creation label is lower than your DBMS label, you must have WRITEDOWN system privilege.
- If the tablespace's creation label and your DBMS label are noncomparable, you must have READUP, WRITEUP, and WRITEDOWN system privileges.

If you are using Trusted ORACLE in DBMS MAC mode, to add a data file, your operating system process label must be the equivalent of DBHIGH.

Syntax

ALTER TABLESPACE command ::=

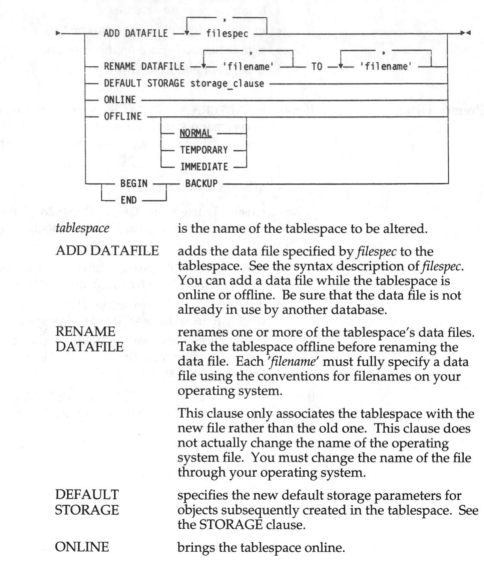

Keywords and Parameters

tablespace	is the name of the tablespace to be altered.
ADD DATAFILE	adds the data file specified by *filespec* to the tablespace. See the syntax description of *filespec*. You can add a data file while the tablespace is online or offline. Be sure that the data file is not already in use by another database.
RENAME DATAFILE	renames one or more of the tablespace's data files. Take the tablespace offline before renaming the data file. Each *'filename'* must fully specify a data file using the conventions for filenames on your operating system.
	This clause only associates the tablespace with the new file rather than the old one. This clause does not actually change the name of the operating system file. You must change the name of the file through your operating system.
DEFAULT STORAGE	specifies the new default storage parameters for objects subsequently created in the tablespace. See the STORAGE clause.
ONLINE	brings the tablespace online.

OFFLINE   takes the tablespace offline and prevents further access to its segments.

NORMAL   performs a checkpoint for all data files in the tablespace. All of these data files must be online. You need not perform media recovery on this tablespace before bringing it back online. You must use this option if the database is in noarchivelog mode.

TEMPORARY   performs a checkpoint for all online data files in the tablespace but does not ensure that all files can be written. Any offline files may require media recovery before you bring the tablespace back online.

IMMEDIATE   does not ensure that tablespace files are available and does not perform a checkpoint. You must perform media recovery on the tablespace before bringing it back online.

The default is NORMAL.

Before taking a tablespace offline for a long period of time, you may want to alter any users who have been assigned the tablespace as either a default or temporary tablespace. When the tablespace is offline, these users cannot allocate space for objects or sort areas in the tablespace. You can reassign users new default and temporary tablespaces with the ALTER USER command.

BEGIN BACKUP   signifies that an online backup is to be performed on the data files that comprise this tablespace. This option does not prevent users from accessing the tablespace. This option is used for control file and redo log record keeping. You must use this option before beginning an online backup.

While the backup is in progress, you cannot perform any of these operations:

- take the tablespace offline normally
- shutdown the instance
- begin another backup of the tablespace

END BACKUP signifies that an online backup of the tablespace is complete. Use this option as soon as possible after completing an online backup.

Usage Notes

If you are using Trusted ORACLE, data files that you add to a tablespace are labelled with the operating system equivalent of DBHIGH.

ALTER USER

Purpose

To change any of these characteristics of a database user:

- password
- default tablespace for object creation
- tablespace for temporary segments created for the user
- tablespace access and tablespace quotas
- limits on database resources
- default roles

Prerequisites

You must have ALTER USER privilege. However, you can change your own password without this privilege.

If you are using Trusted ORACLE in DBMS MAC mode, your DBMS label must match the user's creation label or you must satisfy one of these criteria:

- If the user's creation label is higher than your DBMS label, you must have READUP and WRITEUP system privileges.
- If the user's creation label is lower than your DBMS label, you must have WRITEDOWN system privilege.
- If the user's creation label and your DBMS label are noncomparable, you must have READUP, WRITEUP, and WRITEDOWN system privileges.

You can only change a user's default roles if your DBMS label matches the creation label of the user. Your DBMS label must also dominate the role's creation label or you must have READUP system privilege.

You can only establish a default or temporary tablespace if both your DBMS label and the user's creation label dominates the tablespace's creation label or if both you and the user have READUP system privilege.

You can only change a user's profile if both your DBMS label and the user's creation label dominate the profile's creation label or if both you and the user have READUP system privilege.

Syntax

ALTER USER command ::=

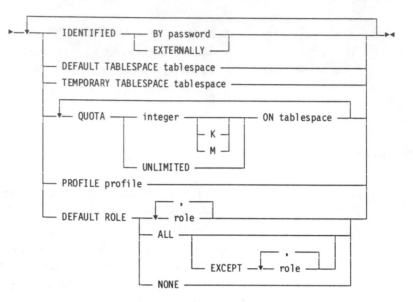

Keywords and Parameters

user		is the user to be altered.
IDENTIFIED		indicates how ORACLE permits user access.
	BY	specifies a new password for the user. The *password* does not appear in quotes and is not case-sensitive. The password can only contain single-byte characters from your database character set regardless of whether this character set also contains multi-byte characters.
	EXTERNALLY	indicates that ORACLE verifies user access with the operating system, rather than with a password. See the CREATE USER command.

Although you do not need privileges to change your own password, you must have ALTER USER system privilege to change from BY *password* to EXTERNALLY or vice-versa.

DEFAULT TABLESPACE   specifies the default tablespace for object creation.

TEMPORARY TABLESPACE   specifies the tablespace for the creation of temporary segments for operations such as sorting that require more space than is available in memory.

QUOTA   establishes a space quota of *integer* bytes on the tablespace for the user. This quota is the maximum space in *tablespace* that can be allocated for objects in the user's schema. You can use K or M to specify the quota in kilobytes or megabytes. You need not have quota on the tablespace to establish a quota on the tablespace for another user. See the CREATE USER command.

If you reduce an existing quota to a value below the space allocated for existing objects in the user's schema in the tablespace, no more space in the tablespace can be allocated to objects in the schema.

Note that an ALTER USER statement can contain multiple QUOTA clauses for multiple tablespaces.

UNLIMITED   places no limit on the space in the tablespace allocated to objects in the user's schema.

PROFILE   changes the user's profile to *profile*. In subsequent sessions, the user is subject to the limits defined in the new profile.

To assign the default limits to the user, assign the user the DEFAULT profile.

DEFAULT ROLE   establishes default roles for the user. ORACLE enables the user's default roles at logon. By default, all roles granted to the user are default roles.

ALL   makes all the roles granted to the user default roles, except those listed in the EXCEPT clause.

NONE   makes none of the roles granted to the user default roles.

Establishing Default Roles

The DEFAULT ROLE clause can only contain roles that have been granted directly to the user with a GRANT statement. You cannot use the DEFAULT ROLE clause to enable:

- roles not granted to the user
- roles granted through other roles
- roles managed by the operating system

Note that ORACLE enables default roles at logon without requiring the user to specify their passwords.

ANALYZE

Purpose

To perform one of these functions on an index, table, or cluster:

- to collect statistics about the object used by the optimizer and store them in the data dictionary
- to delete statistics about the object from the data dictionary
- to validate the structure of the object
- to identify migrated and chained rows of the table or cluster

Prerequisites

The object to be analyzed must be in your own schema or you must have the ANALYZE ANY system privilege.

If you are using Trusted ORACLE in DBMS MAC mode, your DBMS label must match the creation label of the object to be analyzed or you must satisfy one of these criteria:

- If the object's creation label is higher than your DBMS label, you must have READUP and WRITEUP system privileges
- If the object's creation label is lower than your DBMS label, you must have WRITEDOWN system privilege.
- If the object's creation label and your DBMS label are noncomparable, you must have READUP, WRITEUP, and WRITEDOWN system privileges.

If you want to list chained rows of a table or cluster into a list table, the list table must be in your own schema or you must have INSERT privilege on the list table or you must have INSERT ANY TABLE system privilege. If you are using Trusted ORACLE in DBMS MAC mode, the list table must also meet the criteria for the analyzed object described above.

ANALYZE

Syntax

ANALYZE command ::=

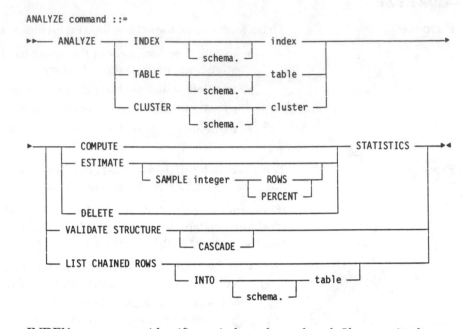

Keywords and Parameters

INDEX   identifies an index to be analyzed. If you omit *schema*, ORACLE assumes the index is in your own schema.

TABLE   identifies a table to be analyzed. If you omit *schema*, ORACLE assumes the table is in your own schema. When you collect statistics for a table, ORACLE also automatically collects the statistics for each of the table's indexes.

CLUSTER   identifies a cluster to be analyzed. If you omit *schema*, ORACLE assumes the cluster is in your own schema. When you collect statistics for a cluster, ORACLE also automatically collects the statistics for all the cluster's tables and all their indexes, including the cluster index.

COMPUTE STATISTICS   computes exact statistics about the analyzed object and stores them in the data dictionary.

ESTIMATE STATISTICS	estimates statistics about the analyzed object and stores them in the data dictionary.	
	SAMPLE	specifies the amount of data from the analyzed object ORACLE samples to estimate statistics. If you omit this parameter, ORACLE samples 1064 rows. If you specify more than half of the data, ORACLE reads all the data and computes the statistics.
	ROWS	causes ORACLE to sample *integer* rows of the table or cluster or *integer* entries from the index. The *integer* must be at least 1.
	PERCENT	causes ORACLE to sample *integer* percent of the rows from the table or cluster or *integer* percent of the index entries. The *integer* can range from 1 to 99.
DELETE STATISTICS	deletes any statistics about the analyzed object that are currently stored in the data dictionary.	
VALIDATE STRUCTURE	validates the structure of the analyzed object. If you use this option when analyzing a cluster, ORACLE automatically validates the structure of the cluster's tables.	
CASCADE	validates the structure of the indexes associated with the table or cluster. If you use this option when validating a table, ORACLE also validates the table's indexes. If you use this option when validating a cluster, ORACLE also validates all the clustered tables' indexes, including the cluster index.	
LIST CHAINED ROWS	identifies migrated and chained rows of the analyzed table or cluster. You cannot use this option when analyzing an index.	
	INTO	specifies a table into which ORACLE lists the migrated and chained rows. If you omit *schema*, ORACLE assumes the list table is in your own schema. If you omit this clause altogether, ORACLE assumes that the table is named CHAINED_ROWS. The list table must be on your local database.

ANALYZE

Collecting Statistics

You can collect statistics about the physical storage characteristics and data distribution of an index, table, or cluster and store them in the data dictionary. You can use the COMPUTE STATISTICS or ESTIMATE STATISTICS option to cause ORACLE to compute or estimate these statistics:

- Computation always provides exact values, but can take longer than estimation.
- Estimation is often much faster than computation and the results are usually nearly exact.

Use estimation, rather than computation, unless you feel you need exact values. Estimation is especially useful for tables that are concurrently being accessed by SELECT, INSERT, UPDATE, and DELETE statements. Since collecting statistics prevents these statements from accessing the table, using estimation instead of computation minimizes the time the table is unavailable. For the same reason, do not collect statistics on the tables, clusters, and indexes of your production applications during periods of high activity on your database.

Some statistics are always computed exactly, regardless of whether you specify computation or estimation. If you choose estimation and the time saved by estimating a statistic is negligible, ORACLE computes the statistic exactly.

If the data dictionary already contains statistics for the analyzed object, ORACLE updates the existing statistics with the new ones.

The statistics are used by the ORACLE optimizer to choose the execution plan for SQL statements that access analyzed objects. These statistics may also be useful to application developers who write such statements. For information on how these statistics are used, see Chapter 13 "The Optimizer" of the *ORACLE7 Server Concepts Manual.*

The following sections list the statistics for indexes, tables, and clusters.

Indexes

For an index, ORACLE collects these statistics:

- depth of the index from its root block to its leaf blocks*
- number of leaf blocks
- number of distinct index values
- average number of leaf blocks per index value
- average number of data blocks per index value
  (for an index on a table)
- clustering factor
  (how well ordered are the rows about the indexed values)

The statistics marked with asterisks (*) are always computed exactly.

These statistics appear in the data dictionary views USER_INDEXES, ALL_INDEXES, and DBA_INDEXES.

Tables

For a table, ORACLE collects these statistics:

- number of rows
- number of data blocks currently containing data *
- number of data blocks allocated to the table that have never been used *
- average available free space in each data block in bytes
- number of chained rows
- average row length, including the row's overhead, in bytes
- number of distinct values for each column
- maximum* and minimum* values for each column
  (Note that these are the second greatest and second least values)

The statistics marked with asterisks (*) are always computed.

These statistics all appear in the data dictionary views USER_TABLES, ALL_TABLES, and DBA_TABLES, except for the number of distinct values and the maximum and minimum values for each column which appear in USER_TAB_COLUMNS, ALL_TAB_COLUMNS, and DBA_TAB_COLUMNS.

Clusters

For an indexed cluster, ORACLE collects the average number of data blocks taken up by a single cluster key value and all of its rows. For a hash clusters, ORACLE collects the average number of data blocks taken up by a single hash key value and all of its rows. These statistics appear in the data dictionary views USER_CLUSTERS and DBA_CLUSTERS.

Deleting Statistics   With the DELETE STATISTICS option of the ANALYZE command, you can remove existing statistics about an object from the data dictionary. You may want to remove statistics if you no longer want the ORACLE optimizer to use them.

When you use the DELETE STATISTICS option on a table, ORACLE also automatically removes statistics for all the table's indexes. When you use the DELETE STATISTICS option on a cluster, ORACLE also automatically removes statistics for all the cluster's tables and all their indexes, including the cluster index.

Validating Structures   With the VALIDATE STRUCTURE option of the ANALYZE command, you can verify the integrity of the structure of an index, table, or cluster. If ORACLE successfully validates the structure, a message confirming its validation is returned to you. If ORACLE encounters corruption in the structure of the object, an error message is returned to you. In this case, drop and recreate the object.

Indexes   For an index, the VALIDATE STRUCTURE option verifies the integrity of each data block in the index and checks for block corruption. Note that this option does not confirm that each row in the table has an index entry or that each index entry points to a row in the table. You can perform these operations by validating the structure of the table.

When you use the VALIDATE STRUCTURE option on an index, ORACLE also collects statistics about the index for the data dictionary view INDEX_STATS. These statistics are not used by the ORACLE optimizer. Do not confuse these statistics with the statistics collected by the COMPUTE STATISTICS and ESTIMATE STATISTICS options.

Tables   For a table, the VALIDATE STRUCTURE option verifies the integrity of each of the table's data blocks and rows. You can use the CASCADE option to also validate the structure of all indexes on the table and to perform cross-referencing between the table and each of its indexes. For each index, the cross-referencing involves these validations:

- Each value of the tables's indexed column must match the indexed column value of an index entry. The matching index entry must also identify the row in the table by the correct ROWID.

- Each entry in the index identifies a row in the table. The indexed column value in the index entry must match that of the identified row.

Clusters

For a cluster, the VALIDATE STRUCTURE option verifies the integrity of each row in the cluster and automatically validates the structure of each of the cluster's tables. You can use the CASCADE option to also validate the structure of all indexes on the cluster's tables, including the cluster index.

ARCHIVE LOG clause

Purpose

To manually archive redo log file groups or to enable or disable automatic archiving.

Prerequisites

The ARCHIVE LOG clause must appear in an ALTER SYSTEM command. You must have the privileges necessary to issue this statement. For information on these privileges, see the ALTER SYSTEM command.

You must also have the OSDBA or OSOPER role enabled.

You can use most of the options of this clause when your instance has the database mounted, open or closed. Options that require your instance to have the database open are noted.

If you are using Trusted ORACLE in DBMS MAC mode, your DBMS label must be the equivalent of DBHIGH.

Syntax

```
ARCHIVE LOG archive_log_clause ::=
►►── ARCHIVE LOG ──┬──────────────────┬──────────────────────►
                   └── THREAD integer ─┘

►─┬──── SEQ integer ──────┬───────────────────────────────►◄
  │──── CHANGE integer ───│──┬── TO 'location' ──┬
  │──── CURRENT ──────────│  └──────────────────┘
  │──── GROUP integer ────│
  │──── LOGFILE 'filename' ┤
  │──── NEXT ─────────────│
  │──── ALL ──────────────│
  │──── START ────────────┘
  └──── STOP ──────────────
```

Keywords and Parameters

THREAD   specifies thread containing the redo log file group to be archived. You only need to specify this parameter if you are using ORACLE with the Parallel Server option in parallel mode.

SEQ   manually archives the online redo log file group identified by the log sequence number *integer* in the specified thread. If you omit the THREAD parameter, ORACLE archives the specified group from the thread assigned to your instance.

CHANGE

manually archives the online redo log file group containing the redo log entry with the system change number (SCN) specified by *integer* in the specified thread. If the SCN is in the current redo log file group, ORACLE performs a log switch. If you omit the THREAD parameter, ORACLE archives the groups containing this SCN from all enabled threads. You can only use this option when your instance has the database open.

CURRENT

manually archives the current redo log file group of the specified thread, forcing a log switch. If you omit the THREAD parameter, ORACLE archives the current redo log file groups from all enabled threads. You can only use this option when your instance has the database open.

GROUP

manually archives the online redo log file group with the specified GROUP value. You can determine the GROUP value for a redo log file group by examining the data dictionary view DBA_LOG_FILES. If you specify both the THREAD and GROUP parameters, the specified redo log file group must be in the specified thread.

LOGFILE

manually archives the online redo log file group containing the redo log file member identified by *'filename'*. If you specify both the THREAD and LOGFILE parameters, the specified redo log file group must be in the specified thread.

NEXT

manually archives the next online redo log file group from the specified thread that is full but has not yet been archived. If you omit the THREAD parameter, ORACLE archives the earliest unarchived redo log file group from any enabled thread.

ALL

manually archives all online redo log file groups from the specified thread that are full but have not been archived. If you omit the THREAD parameter, ORACLE archives all full unarchived redo log file groups from all enabled threads.

START

enables automatic archiving of redo log file groups. You can only enable automatic archiving for the thread assigned to your instance.

TO	specifies the location to which the redo log file group is archived. The value of this parameter must be a fully-specified file location following the conventions of your operating system. If you omit this parameter, ORACLE archives the redo log file group to the location specified by the initialization parameter LOG_ARCHIVE_DEST.
STOP	disables automatic archiving of redo log file groups. You can only disable automatic archiving for the thread assigned to your instance.

Usage Notes

You must archive redo log file groups in the order in which they are filled. If you specify a redo log file group for archiving with the SEQ or LOGFILE parameter and earlier redo log file groups are not yet archived, ORACLE returns an error. If you specify a redo log file group for archiving with the CHANGE parameter or CURRENT option and earlier redo log file groups are not yet archived, ORACLE archives all unarchived groups up to and including the specified group.

You can also manually archive redo log file groups with the ARCHIVE LOG SQL*DBA command. For information on this command, see the *ORACLE7 Server Utilities User's Guide*.

You can also choose to have ORACLE archive redo log files groups automatically. For information on automatic archiving, see Chapter 17 "Archiving Redo Information" of the *ORACLE7 Server Administrator's Guide*. Note that you can always manually archive redo log file groups regardless of whether automatic archiving is enabled.

AUDIT (SQL Statements)

Purpose
To choose specific SQL statements for auditing in subsequent user sessions. To choose particular schema objects for auditing, use the AUDIT command (Schema Objects).

Prerequisites
You must have AUDIT SYSTEM system privilege.

If you are using Trusted ORACLE in DBMS MAC mode, your DBMS label must dominate the creation label of the users whose SQL statements you are auditing.

Syntax
AUDIT command (SQL Statements) ::=

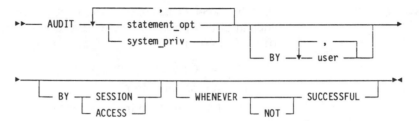

Keywords and Parameters

statement_opt
chooses specific SQL statements for auditing. For a list of these statement options and the SQL statements they audit, see Table C-1 and Table C-2.

system_priv
chooses SQL statements that are authorized by the specified system privilege for auditing. For a list of all system privileges and the SQL statements that they authorize, see Table C-4 under the GRANT (System Privileges and Roles) section.

BY *user*
chooses only SQL statements issued by specified users for auditing. If you omit this clause, ORACLE audits all users' statements.

BY SESSION
causes ORACLE to write a single record for all SQL statements of the same type issued in the same session.

BY ACCESS
causes ORACLE to write one record for each audited statement.

If you specify statement options or system privileges that audit Data Definition Language statements, ORACLE automatically audits by access regardless of whether you specify the BY SESSION or BY ACCESS option.

AUDIT (SQL Statements)

	For statement options and system privileges that audit other types of SQL statements, you can specify either the BY SESSION or BY ACCESS option. BY SESSION is the default.
WHENEVER SUCCESSFUL	chooses auditing only for SQL statements that complete successfully.
	NOT chooses auditing only for statements that fail, or result in errors.
	If you omit the WHENEVER clause, ORACLE audits SQL statements regardless of success or failure.

Auditing

Auditing keeps track of operations performed by database users. For each audited operation, ORACLE produces an audit record containing this information:

- user performing the operation
- type of operation
- object involved in the operation
- date and time of the operation

ORACLE writes audit records to the audit trail. The audit trail is a database table that contains audit records. You can review database activity by examining the audit trail through data dictionary views. For information on these views, see Appendix B "Data Dictionary Reference" of the *ORACLE7 Server Administrator's Guide*.

How to Audit

To generate audit records, you must perform these steps:

Enable auditing: You must enable auditing with the initialization parameter AUDIT_TRAIL.

Specify auditing options: To specify auditing options, you must use the AUDIT command. Auditing options choose which SQL commands, operations, database objects, and users ORACLE audits. After you specify auditing options, they appear in the data dictionary. For information on data dictionary views containing auditing options see Appendix B "Data Dictionary Reference" of the *ORACLE7 Server Administrator's Guide*.

You can specify auditing options regardless of whether auditing is enabled. However, ORACLE does not generate audit records until you enable auditing.

Auditing options specified by the AUDIT command (SQL Statements) apply only to subsequent sessions, rather than to current sessions.

Statement Options

Table C-1 lists the statement options and the statements that they audit.

TABLE C-1
Statement Auditing Options

Statement Option	SQL Statements and Operations
CLUSTER	CREATE CLUSTER ALTER CLUSTER DROP CLUSTER TRUNCATE CLUSTER
DATABASE LINK	CREATE DATABASE LINK DROP DATABASE LINK
EXISTS	All SQL statements that fail because an object, part of an object, or value already exists in the database. This option is only available with Trusted ORACLE.
INDEX	CREATE INDEX ALTER INDEX DROP INDEX
NOT EXISTS	All SQL statements that fail because a specified object does not exist.
PROCEDURE	CREATE FUNCTION CREATE PACKAGE CREATE PACKAGE BODY CREATE PROCEDURE DROP FUNCTION DROP PACKAGE DROP PROCEDURE
PROFILE	CREATE PROFILE ALTER PROFILE DROP PROFILE
PUBLIC DATABASE LINK	CREATE PUBLIC DATABASE LINK DROP PUBLIC DATABASE LINK
PUBLIC SYNONYM	CREATE PUBLIC SYNONYM DROP PUBLIC SYNONYM
ROLE	CREATE ROLE ALTER ROLE DROP ROLE SET ROLE

continued on the next page

AUDIT (SQL Statements)

Statement Option	SQL Statements and Operations
ROLLBACK SEGMENT	CREATE ROLLBACK SEGMENT ALTER ROLLBACK SEGMENT DROP ROLLBACK SEGMENT
SEQUENCE	CREATE SEQUENCE DROP SEQUENCE
SESSION	Logons
SYNONYM	CREATE SYNONYM DROP SYNONYM
SYSTEM AUDIT	AUDIT (SQL Statements) NOAUDIT (SQL Statements)
SYSTEM GRANT	GRANT (System Privileges and Roles) REVOKE (System Privileges and Roles)
TABLE	CREATE TABLE DROP TABLE TRUNCATE TABLE
TABLESPACE	CREATE TABLESPACE ALTER TABLESPACE DROP TABLESPACE

TRIGGER	CREATE TRIGGER
	ALTER TRIGGER
	    with ENABLE and DISABLE options
	DROP TRIGGER
	ALTER TABLE
	    with ENABLE ALL TRIGGERS
	    and DISABLE ALL TRIGGERS clauses

USER	CREATE USER ALTER USER DROP USER
VIEW	CREATE VIEW DROP VIEW

**Short Cuts for
System Privileges and
Statement Options**

ORACLE provides short cuts for specifying system privileges and statement options. With these shortcuts, you can specify auditing for multiple system privileges and statement options at once:

CONNECT   This short cut is equivalent to specifying the CREATE SESSION system privilege.

RESOURCE   This short cut is equivalent to specifying these system privileges:

- ALTER SYSTEM
- CREATE CLUSTER
- CREATE DATABASE LINK
- CREATE PROCEDURE
- CREATE ROLLBACK SEGMENT
- CREATE SEQUENCE
- CREATE SYNONYM
- CREATE TABLE
- CREATE TABLESPACE
- CREATE VIEW

DBA   This short cut is equivalent to the SYSTEM GRANT statement option and these system privileges:

- AUDIT SYSTEM
- CREATE PUBLIC DATABASE LINK
- CREATE PUBLIC SYNONYM
- CREATE ROLE
- CREATE USER

ALL   This short cut is equivalent to specifying all statement options shown in Table C-1, but not the additional statement options shown in Table C-2.

ALL PRIVILEGES   This short cut is equivalent to specifying all system privileges.

Oracle Corporation encourages you to choose individual system privileges and statement options for auditing, rather than these short cuts. These short cuts may not be supported in future versions of ORACLE.

AUDIT (SQL Statements)

Additional Statement Options

Table C-2 lists additional statement options and the SQL statements and operations that they audit. Note that these statement options are not included in the ALL short cut.

TABLE C-2
Additional Statement Auditing Options

Statement Option	SQL Statements and Operations
ALTER SEQUENCE	ALTER SEQUENCE
ALTER TABLE	ALTER TABLE
COMMENT TABLE	COMMENT ON TABLE table, view, snapshot COMMENT ON COLUMN table.column, view.column, snapshot.column
DELETE TABLE	DELETE FROM table, view
EXECUTE PROCEDURE	Execution of any procedure or function or access to any variable or cursor inside a package.

GRANT PROCEDURE	GRANT privilege ON procedure, function,
	    package
	REVOKE privilege ON procedure,
	    function, package

GRANT SEQUENCE	GRANT privilege ON sequence REVOKE privilege ON sequence
GRANT TABLE	GRANT privilege ON table, view, snapshot REVOKE privilege ON table, view, snapshot
INSERT TABLE	INSERT INTO table, view
LOCK TABLE	LOCK TABLE table, view
SELECT SEQUENCE	Any statement containing sequence.CURRVAL or sequence.NEXTVAL
SELECT TABLE	SELECT FROM table, view, snapshot
UPDATE TABLE	UPDATE table, view

AUDIT (Schema Objects)

Purpose
To choose a specific schema object for auditing. To choose particular SQL commands for auditing, use the AUDIT command (SQL Statements).

Prerequisites
The object you choose for auditing must be in your own schema or you must have AUDIT ANY system privilege.

If you are using Trusted ORACLE in DBMS MAC mode, your DBMS label must match the object's creation label or you must satisfy one of these criteria:

- If the object's creation label is higher than your DBMS label, you must have READUP and WRITEUP system privileges
- If the object's creation label is lower than your DBMS label, you must have WRITEDOWN system privilege.

If the object's creation label and your DBMS label are noncomparable, you must have READUP, WRITEUP, and WRITEDOWN system privileges.

Syntax

```
AUDIT command (Schema Objects) ::=
```

AUDIT (Schema Objects)

Keywords and Parameters

object_opt specifies a particular operation for auditing. Table C-3 shows each object option and the types of objects for which it applies.

schema is the schema containing the object chosen for auditing. If you omit *schema*, ORACLE assumes the object is in your own schema.

object identifies the object chosen for auditing. The object must be one of these types:

- table
- view
- sequence
- stored procedure, function, or package
- snapshot

You can also specify a synonym for a table, view, sequence, procedure, stored function, package, or snapshot.

DEFAULT establishes the specified object options as default object options for subsequently created objects.

BY SESSION means that ORACLE writes a single record for all operations of the same type on the same object issued in the same session.

BY ACCESS means that ORACLE writes one record for each audited operation.

If you omit both of these options, ORACLE audits by session.

WHENEVER SUCCESSFUL chooses auditing only for SQL statements that complete successfully.

NOT chooses auditing only for statements that fail, or result in errors.

If you omit the WHENEVER clause entirely, ORACLE audits all SQL statements, regardless of success or failure.

Auditing

Auditing keeps track of operations performed by database users. For a brief conceptual overview of auditing including how to enable auditing, see the AUDIT command (SQL Statements). Note that auditing options established by the AUDIT command (Schema Objects) apply to current sessions as well as to subsequent sessions.

Object Options

TABLE C-3
Object Auditing Options

Table C-3 shows the object options you can choose for each type of object.

Object Option	Tables	Views	Sequences	Procedures Functions Packages	Snapshots
ALTER	✓		✓		
AUDIT	✓	✓	✓	✓	
COMMENT	✓	✓			
DELETE	✓	✓			
EXECUTE				✓	
GRANT	✓	✓	✓	✓	
INDEX	✓				
INSERT	✓	✓			
LOCK	✓	✓			
RENAME	✓	✓		✓	
SELECT	✓	✓	✓		✓
UPDATE	✓	✓			

The name of each object option specifies a command to be audited. For example, if you choose to audit a table with the ALTER option, ORACLE audits all ALTER TABLE statements issued against the table. If you choose to audit a sequence with the SELECT option, ORACLE audits all statements that use any of the sequence's values.

Short Cuts for
Object Options

ORACLE provides a short cut for specifying object auditing options:

ALL   This short cut is equivalent to specifying all object options applicable for the type of object. You can use this short cut rather than explicitly specifying all options for an object.

Default Auditing

You can use the DEFAULT option of the AUDIT command to specify auditing options for objects that have not yet been created. Once you have established these default auditing options, any subsequently created object is automatically audited with those options. Note that the default auditing options for a view are always the union of the auditing options for the view's base tables.

If you change the default auditing options, the auditing options for previously-created objects remain the same. You can only change the auditing options for an existing object by specifying the object in the ON clause of the AUDIT command.

CREATE CONTROLFILE

Purpose

To recreate a control file in one of these cases:

- All copies of your existing control files have been lost through media failure.
- You want to change the name of the database.
- You want to change the maximum number of redo log file groups, redo log file members, archived redo log files, data files, or instances that can concurrently have the database mounted and open.

Warning: Oracle Corporation recommends that you perform a full backup of all files in the database before using this command.

Prerequisites

You must have the OSDBA role enabled. The database must not be mounted by any instance.

If you are using Trusted ORACLE in DBMS MAC mode, your operating system label must be the equivalent of DBHIGH.

Syntax

```
CREATE CONTROLFILE command ::=
```

Keywords and Parameters

REUSE

specifies that existing control files identified by the initialization parameter CONTROL_FILES can be reused, thus ignoring and overwriting any and all information they may currently contain. If you omit this option and any of these control files already exist, ORACLE returns an error.

SET DATABASE	changes the name of the database. The name of a database can be as long as eight bytes.
DATABASE	specifies the name of the database. The value of this parameter must be the existing database name established by the previous CREATE DATABASE statement or CREATE CONTROLFILE statement.
LOGFILE	specifies the redo log file groups for your database. You must list all members of all redo log file groups. These files must all exist. See the syntax description of *filespec*.
RESETLOGS	ignores the contents of the files listed in the LOGFILE clause. Each *filespec* in the LOGFILE clause must specify the SIZE parameter. ORACLE assigns all redo log file groups to thread 1 and enables this thread for public use by any instance. After using this option, you must open the database using the RESETLOGS option of the ALTER DATABASE command.
NORESETLOGS	specifies that all files in the LOGFILE clause should be used as they were when the database was last open. These files must be the current redo log files rather than restored backups. ORACLE reassigns the redo log file groups to the threads to which they were previously assigned and re-enables the threads as they were previously enabled. If you specify GROUP values, ORACLE verifies these values with the GROUP values when the database was last open.
DATAFILE	specifies the data files of the database. You must list all data files. These files must all exist, although they may be restored backups that require media recovery. See the syntax description of *filespec*.
MAXLOGFILES	specifies the maximum number of redo log file groups that can ever be created for the database. ORACLE uses this value to determine how much space in the control file to allocate for the names of redo log files. The default and maximum values depend on your operating system. The value that you specify should not be less than the greatest GROUP value for any redo log file group.
	Note that the number of redo log file groups accessible to your instance is also limited by the initialization parameter LOG_FILES.

MAXLOGMEMBERS specifies the maximum number of members, or copies, for a redo log file group. ORACLE uses this value to determine how much space in the control file to allocate for the names of redo log files. The minimum value is 1. The maximum and default values depend on your operating system.

MAXLOGHISTORY specifies the maximum number of archived redo log file groups for automatic media recovery of the ORACLE Parallel Server. ORACLE uses this value to determine how much space in the control file to allocate for the names of archived redo log files. The minimum value is 0. The default value is a multiple of the MAXINSTANCES value and varies depending on your operating system. The maximum value is limited only by the maximum size of the control file. Note that this parameter is only useful if you are using ORACLE with the Parallel Server option in both parallel mode and archivelog mode.

MAXDATAFILES specifies the maximum number of data files that can ever be created for the database. The minimum value is 1. The maximum and default values depend on your operating system. The value you specify should not be less than the total number of data files ever in the database, including those for tablespaces that have been dropped.

Note that the number of data files accessible to your instance is also limited by the initialization parameter DB_FILES.

MAXINSTANCES specifies the maximum number of instances that can simultaneously have the database mounted and open. This value takes precedence over the value of the initialization parameter INSTANCES. The minimum value is 1. The maximum and default values depend on your operating system.

ARCHIVELOG establishes the mode of archiving the contents of redo log files before reusing them. This option prepares for the possibility of media recovery as well as instance recovery.

NOARCHIVELOG establishes the initial mode of reusing redo log files without archiving their contents. This option prepares for the possibility of instance recovery but not media recovery.

If you omit both the ARCHIVELOG and NOARCHIVELOG options, ORACLE chooses noarchivelog mode by default. After creating the control file, you can change between archivelog mode and noarchivelog mode with the ALTER DATABASE command.

Usage Notes

Oracle Corporation recommends that you take a full backup of all files in the database before issuing a CREATE CONTROLFILE statement.

When you issue a CREATE CONTROLFILE statement, ORACLE creates a new control file based on the information you specify in the statement. If you omit any of the options from the statement, ORACLE uses the default options, rather than the options for the previous control file. After successfully creating the control file, ORACLE mounts the database in exclusive mode. You then must perform media recovery before opening the database. Oracle Corporation recommends that you then shutdown the instance and take a full backup of all files in the database.

For more information on using this command, see Chapter 19 "Recovering a Database" of the *ORACLE7 Server Administrator's Guide*.

When you create a control file in Trusted ORACLE, it is labeled with your DBMS label. The control file cannot be used unless it is labeled at the operating system equivalent of DBHIGH. If you issue a CREATE CONTROLFILE statement in DBMS MAC mode, Trusted ORACLE automatically switches to OS MAC mode. You can then return to DBMS MAC mode by issuing an ALTER DATABASE statement with the SET DBMAC ON clause.

CREATE DATABASE

Purpose

To create a database, making it available for general use, with these options:

- to establish a maximum number of instances, data files, redo log files groups, or redo log file members
- to specify names and sizes of data files and redo log files
- to choose a mode of use for the redo log

Warning: This command prepares a database for initial use and erases any data currently in the specified files. Only use this command when you understand its ramifications.

Prerequisites

You must have the OSDBA role enabled.

If you are using Trusted ORACLE and you plan to use the database in DBMS MAC mode, your operating system label should be the equivalent of DBLOW.

Syntax

```
CREATE DATABASE command ::=
```

```
►►── CREATE DATABASE ──────────────────────────────────►
                    └─ database ─┘
```

```
►──┬────────────────────────────────────┬──►◄
   ├── CONTROLFILE REUSE ────────────────┤
   │                        ,            │
   ├── LOGFILE ─┬──────────────┬─ filespec ─┤
   │            └─ GROUP integer ─┘          │
   ├── MAXLOGFILES integer ──────────────┤
   ├── MAXLOGMEMBERS integer ────────────┤
   ├── MAXLOGHISTORY integer ────────────┤
   │                        ,            │
   ├── DATAFILE ─┬─ filespec ─┬──────────┤
   ├── MAXDATAFILES integer ─────────────┤
   ├── MAXINSTANCES integer ─────────────┤
   ├──┬── ARCHIVELOG ──┬─────────────────┤
   │  └── NOARCHIVELOG ─┘                │
   ├── EXCLUSIVE ────────────────────────┤
   └── CHARACTER SET charset ────────────┘
```

Keyword and Parameters

database

is the name of the database to be created and can be up to eight bytes long. ORACLE writes this name into the control file. If you subsequently issue an ALTER DATABASE statement and that explicitly specifies a database name, ORACLE verifies that name with the name in the control file.

The *database* cannot be a SQL*DBA reserved word. These reserved words appear in the *ORACLE7 Server Utilities User's Guide*. If you omit *database* from a CREATE DATABASE statement, ORACLE uses the name specified by the initialization parameter DB_NAME.

CONTROLFILE REUSE

reuses existing control files identified by the initialization parameter CONTROL_FILES, thus ignoring and overwriting any information they currently contain. This option is usually used only when you are recreating a database, rather than creating one for the first time. You cannot use this option if you also specify a parameter value that requires that the control file be larger than the existing files. These parameters are MAXLOGFILES, MAXLOGMEMBERS, MAXLOGHISTORY, MAXDATAFILES, and MAXINSTANCES.

If you omit this option and any of the files specified by CONTROL_FILES already exist, ORACLE returns an error message.

LOGFILE

specifies one or more files to be used as redo log files. Each *filespec* specifies a redo log file group containing one or more redo log file members, or copies. See the syntax description of *filespec*. All redo log files specified in a CREATE DATABASE statement are added to redo log thread number 1.

You can also choose the value of the GROUP parameter for the redo log file group. Each value uniquely identifies a redo log file group and can range from 1 to the value of the MAXLOGFILES parameter. You cannot specify multiple redo log file groups having the same GROUP value. If you omit this parameter, ORACLE generates its value automatically. You can examine the GROUP value for a redo log file group through the dynamic performance table V$LOG.

If you omit the LOGFILE clause, ORACLE creates two redo log file groups by default. The names and sizes of the default files vary depending on your operating system.

MAXLOGFILES   specifies the maximum number of redo log file groups that can ever be created for the database. ORACLE uses this value to determine how much space in the control file to allocate for the names of redo log files. The default, minimum, and maximum values vary depending on your operating system.

The number of redo log file groups accessible to your instance is also limited by the initialization parameter LOG_FILES.

MAXLOGMEMBERS   specifies the maximum number of members, or copies, for a redo log file group. ORACLE uses this value to determine how much space in the control file to allocate for the names of redo log files. The minimum value is 1. The maximum and default values vary depending on your operating system.

MAXLOGHISTORY   specifies the maximum number of archived redo log files for automatic media recovery of ORACLE with the Parallel Server option. ORACLE uses this value to determine how much space in the control file to allocate for the names of archived redo log files. The minimum value is 0. The default value is a multiple of the MAXINSTANCES value and varies depending on your operating system. The maximum value is limited only by the maximum size of the control file. Note that this parameter is only useful if you are using the ORACLE with the Parallel Server option in parallel mode and archivelog mode.

DATAFILE   specifies one or more files to be used as data files. See the syntax description of *filespec*. These files all become part of the SYSTEM tablespace. If you omit this clause, ORACLE creates one data file by default. The name and size of this default file depends on your operating system.

MAXDATAFILES specifies the maximum number of data files that can ever be created for the database. The minimum value is 1. The maximum and default values depend on your operating system.

The number of data files accessible to your instance is also limited by the initialization parameter DB_FILES.

MAXINSTANCES specifies the maximum number of instances that can simultaneously have this database mounted and open. This value takes precedence over the value of the initialization parameter INSTANCES. The minimum value is 1. The maximum and default values depend on your operating system.

ARCHIVELOG establishes archivelog mode for redo log file groups. In this mode, the contents of a redo log file group must be archived before the group can be reused. This option prepares for the possibility of media recovery.

NOARCHIVELOG establishes noarchivelog mode for redo log files groups. In this mode, the contents of a redo log file group need not be archived before the group can be reused. This option does not prepares for the possibility of media recovery.

The default is noarchivelog mode. After creating the database, you can change between archivelog mode and noarchivelog mode with the ALTER DATABASE command.

EXCLUSIVE mounts the database in exclusive mode after it is created. This mode allows only your instance to access the database. ORACLE automatically mounts the database in exclusive mode after creating it, so this keyword is entirely optional.

For multiple instances to access the database, you must first create the database, close and dismount the database, and then mount it in parallel mode. For information on closing, dismounting, and mounting the database, see the ALTER DATABASE command.

CHARACTER SET specifies the character set the database uses to store data. You cannot change the database character set after creating the database. The supported character sets and default value of this parameter depends on your operating system.

CREATE DATABASE

Usage Notes

This command erases all data in any specified data files that already exist to prepare them for initial database use. If you use the command on an existing database, all data in the data files is lost.

After creating the database, this command mounts it in exclusive mode and opens it, making it available for normal use.

If you create a database using Trusted ORACLE, it is labeled with your operating system label and is created in OS MAC mode. If you plan to use the database in DBMS MAC mode, be sure you set values for DBHIGH and DBLOW. For more information on creating Trusted ORACLE databases, see the *Trusted ORACLE7 Server Administrator's Guide*.

CREATE DATABASE LINK

Purpose

To create a database link. A *database link* is an object in the local database that allows you to access objects on a remote database or to mount a secondary database in read-only mode. The remote database can be either an ORACLE or a non-ORACLE database.

Prerequisites

To create a private database link, you must have CREATE DATABASE LINK system privilege. To create a public database link, you must have CREATE PUBLIC DATABASE LINK system privilege. Also, you must have CREATE SESSION privilege on a remote database. SQL*Net must be installed on both the local and remote databases.

Syntax

CREATE DATABASE LINK command ::=

```
►►─── CREATE ─────────────────── DATABASE LINK dblink ──────────────────►
              └─ PUBLIC ─┘

►──────────────────────────────────────────────────────────────────────►◄
    └─ CONNECT TO user IDENTIFIED BY password ─┘  └─ USING 'connect_string' ─┘
```

Keyword and Parameters

PUBLIC

creates a public database link available to all users. If you omit this option, the database link is private and is available only to you.

dblink

is the complete or partial name of the database link.

CONNECT TO *user* IDENTIFIED BY *password*

is the username and password used to connect to the remote database. If you omit this clause, the database link uses the username and password of each user who uses the database link.

USING

specifies either:

- the database specification of a remote database
- the specification of a secondary database for a read-only mount.

For information on specifying remote databases, see the *SQL*Net User's Guide* for your specific SQL*Net protocol.

Read-only mounts are only available in Trusted ORACLE and can only be specified for public database links. For information on specifying read-only mounts, see the *Trusted ORACLE7 Server Administrator's Guide*.

CREATE DATABASE LINK

Usage Notes

You cannot create a database link in another user's schema and you cannot qualify *dblink* with the name of a schema. Since periods are permitted in names of database links, ORACLE interprets the entire name, such as RALPH.LINKTOSALES, as the name of a database link in your schema rather than as a database link named LINKTOSALES in the schema RALPH.

Once you have created a database link, you can use it to refer to tables and views on the remote database. You can refer to a remote table or view in a SQL statement by appending *@dblink* to the table or view name. You can query a remote table or view with the SELECT command. If you are using ORACLE with the distributed option, you can also access remote tables and views in any of these commands:

- DELETE
- INSERT
- LOCK TABLE
- UPDATE

The number of different database links that can appear in a single statement is limited to the value of the initialization parameter OPEN_LINKS.

When you create a database link in Trusted ORACLE, it is labeled with your DBMS label.

For SQL*Net V2, the *connect string* clause is replaced by a *service name*. See Chapter 15, "SQL*Net V1 and V2," for details.

CREATE PROFILE

Purpose

To create a profile. A *profile* is a set of limits on database resources. If you assign the profile to a user, that user cannot exceed these limits.

Prerequisites

You must have CREATE PROFILE system privilege.

Syntax

CREATE PROFILE command ::=

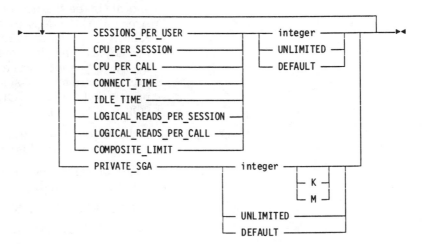

Keywords and Parameters

profile   is the name of the profile to be created.

SESSIONS_PER_USER
     limits a user to *integer* concurrent sessions.

CPU_PER_SESSION limits the CPU time for a session. This value is expressed in hundredths of seconds.

CPU_PER_CALL limits the CPU time for a call (a parse, execute, or fetch). This value is expressed in hundredths of seconds.

CONNECT_TIME limits the total elapsed time of a session. This value is expressed in minutes.

IDLE_TIME   limits periods of continuous inactive time during a session. This value is expressed in minutes. Long-running queries and other operations are not subject to this limit.

LOGICAL_READS_PER_SESSION

    limits the number of data blocks read in a session, including blocks read from memory and disk, to *integer* blocks.

LOGICAL_READS_PER_CALL

    limits the number of data blocks read for a call to process a SQL statement (a parse, execute, or fetch) to *integer* blocks.

PRIVATE_SGA   limits the amount of private space a session can allocate in the shared pool of the System Global Area (SGA) to *integer* bytes. You can also use the K or M to specify this limit in kilobytes or megabytes. This limit only applies if you are using the multi-threaded server architecture. The private space for a session in the SGA includes private SQL and PL/SQL areas, but not shared SQL and PL/SQL areas.

COMPOSITE_LIMIT limits the total resource cost for a session. You must express the value of this parameter in service units.

    ORACLE calculates the total resource cost as a weighted sum of these resources:

- CPU_PER_SESSION
- CONNECT_TIME
- LOGICAL_READS_PER_SESSION
- PRIVATE_SGA

    For information on how to specify the weight for each session resource see the ALTER RESOURCE COST command.

UNLIMITED   indicates that a user assigned this profile can use an unlimited amount of this resource.

DEFAULT   omits a limit for this resource in this profile. A user assigned this profile is subject to the limit for this resource specified in the DEFAULT profile.

Usage Notes

In Trusted ORACLE, the new profile is automatically labeled with your DBMS label.

Using Profiles

A *profile* is a set of limits on database resources. You can use profiles to limit the database resources available to a user for a single call or a single session. ORACLE enforces resource limits in these ways:

- If a user exceeds the CONNECT_TIME or IDLE_TIME session resource limit, ORACLE rolls back the current transaction and ends the session. When the user process next issues a call to ORACLE, an error message is returned.
- If a user attempts to perform an operation that exceeds the limit for other session resources, ORACLE aborts the operation, rolls back the current statement, and immediately returns an error. The user can then commit or roll back the current transaction. The user must then end the session.
- If a user attempts to perform an operation that exceeds the limit for a single call, ORACLE aborts the operation, rolls back the current statement, and returns an error message, leaving the current transaction intact.

How to Limit Resources

To specify resource limits for a user, you must perform both of these operations:

Enable resource limits: You can enable resource limits through one of these ways:

- You can enable resources limits with the initialization parameter RESOURCE_LIMIT.
- You can enable resource limits dynamically with the ALTER SYSTEM command. See the ALTER SYSTEM command.

Specify resource limits: To specify a resource limit for a user, you must perform these steps:

1. Create a profile that defines the limits using the CREATE PROFILE command.
2. Assign the profile to the user using the CREATE USER or ALTER USER command.

Note that you can specify resource limits for users regardless of whether resource limits are enabled. However, ORACLE does not enforce these limits until you enable them.

CREATE PROFILE

The DEFAULT Profile

ORACLE automatically creates a default profile named DEFAULT. This profile initially defines unlimited resources. You can change the limits defined in this profile with the ALTER PROFILE command.

Any user who is not explicitly assigned a profile is subject to the limits defined in the DEFAULT profile. Also, if the profile that is explicitly assigned to a user omits limits for some resources or specifies DEFAULT for some limits, the user is subject to the limits on those resources defined by the DEFAULT profile.

CREATE ROLE

Purpose

To create a role. A *role* is a set of privileges that can be granted to users or to other roles.

Prerequisites

You must have CREATE ROLE system privilege.

Syntax

```
CREATE ROLE command ::=

►►── CREATE ROLE role ─────────────────────────────────────────────►◄
                      ├─ NOT IDENTIFIED ──────────────────────┤
                      └─ IDENTIFIED ──┬─ BY password ──┬───────┘
                                      └─ EXTERNALLY ───┘
```

Keywords and Parameters

role

is the name of the role to be created. Oracle Corporation recommends that the *role* contain at least one single-byte character regardless of whether the database character set also contains multi-byte characters.

NOT IDENTIFIED

indicates that a user granted the role need not be verified when enabling it.

IDENTIFIED

indicates that a user granted the role must be verified when enabling it with the SET ROLE command:

BY *password*

The user must specify the *password* to ORACLE when enabling the role. The password can only contain single-byte characters from your database character set regardless of whether this character set also contains multi-byte characters.

EXTERNALLY

The operating system verifies the user enabling to the role. Depending on the operating system, the user may have to specify a password to the operating system when enabling the role.

If you omit both the NOT IDENTIFIED option and the IDENTIFIED clause, the role defaults to NOT IDENTIFIED.

CREATE ROLE

Usage Notes

In Trusted ORACLE, the new role is automatically labeled with your DBMS label.

Using Roles

A *role* is a set of privileges that can be granted to users or to other roles. You can use roles to administer database privileges. You can add privileges to a role's privilege domain and then grant the role to a user. The user can then enable the role and exercise the privileges in the role's privilege domain. For information on enabling roles, see the ALTER USER command.

A role's privilege domain contains all privileges granted to the role and all privileges in the privilege domains of the other roles granted to it. A new role's privilege domain is initially empty. You can add privileges to a role's privilege domain with the GRANT command.

When you create a role, ORACLE grants you the role with ADMIN OPTION. The ADMIN OPTION allows you to perform these operations:

- grant the role to another user or role
- revoke the role from another user or role
- alter the role to change the authorization needed to access it
- drop the role

Roles Defined by ORACLE

Some roles are defined by SQL scripts provided on your distribution media. These roles are predefined:

- CONNECT
- RESOURCE
- DBA
- EXP_FULL_DATABASE
- IMP_FULL_DATABASE

The CONNECT, RESOURCE, and DBA roles are provided for compatibility with previous versions of ORACLE. Oracle encourages you to design your own roles for database security, rather rely on these roles. These roles may not be created automatically by future versions of ORACLE.

The EXP_FULL_DATABASE and IMP_FULL_DATABASE roles are provided for convenience in using the Import and Export utilities. For more information on these roles, see Table C-5 under GRANT (System Privileges and Roles).

ORACLE also creates other roles that authorize you to administer the database. On many operating systems, these roles are called OSOPER and OSDBA. Their names may be different on your operating system.

CREATE ROLLBACK SEGMENT

Purpose

To create a rollback segment. A *rollback segment* is an object that is used by ORACLE to store data necessary to reverse, or undo, changes made by transactions.

Prerequisites

You must have CREATE ROLLBACK SEGMENT system privilege. Also, you must have either space quota on the tablespace to contain the rollback segment or UNLIMITED TABLESPACE system privilege.

If you are using Trusted ORACLE in DBMS MAC mode, your DBMS label must dominate the tablespace's label.

Syntax

```
CREATE ROLLBACK SEGMENT command ::=
```

```
►►── CREATE ──┬──────────────┬── ROLLBACK SEGMENT rollback_segment ──────►
              └── PUBLIC ──┘
```

```
►──┬─────────────────────────────────────────────────────────────────►◄
   │   ┌──────────────────────────┐
   └───┤── TABLESPACE tablespace ──┤
       └── STORAGE storage_clause ─┘
```

Keyword and Parameters

PUBLIC
   specifies that the rollback segment is *public* and is available to any instance. If you omit this option, the rollback segment is private and is only available to the instance naming it in its initialization parameter ROLLBACK_SEGMENTS.

rollback_segment
   is the name of the rollback segment to be created.

TABLESPACE
   identifies the tablespace in which the rollback segment is created. If you omit this option, ORACLE creates the rollback segment in the SYSTEM tablespace.

STORAGE
   specifies the characteristics for the rollback segment. See the STORAGE clause.

CREATE ROLLBACK SEGMENT

Usage Notes

The tablespace must be online for you to add a rollback segment to it.

When you create a rollback segment, it is initially offline. To make it available for transactions by your ORACLE instance, you must bring it online through one of these means:

- ALTER ROLLBACK SEGMENT command
- ROLLBACK_SEGMENTS initialization parameter

For more information on creating rollback segments and making them available, see Chapter 9 "Managing Rollback Segments" of the *ORACLE7 Server Administrator's Guide*.

A tablespace can have multiple rollback segments. Generally, multiple rollback segments improve performance. For a discussion of the optimum number and size of the rollback segments, see Chapter 23 "Tuning Contention" of the *ORACLE7 Server Administrator's Guide*.

When you create a rollback segment in Trusted ORACLE, it is labeled with your DBMS label.

CREATE SYNONYM

Purpose
To create a synonym. A *synonym* is an alternative name for a table, view, sequence, procedure, stored function, package, snapshot, or another synonym.

Prerequisites
To create a private synonym in your own schema, you must have CREATE SYNONYM system privilege.

To create a private synonym in another user's schema, you must have CREATE ANY SYNONYM system privilege. If you are using Trusted ORACLE in DBMS MAC mode, your DBMS label must dominate the creation label of the owner of schema to contain the synonym.

To create a PUBLIC synonym, you must have CREATE PUBLIC SYNONYM system privilege.

Syntax

CREATE SYNONYM command ::=

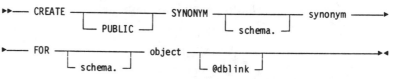

Keywords and Parameters

PUBLIC
creates a public synonym. Public synonyms are accessible to all users. If you omit this option, the synonym is private and is accessible only within its schema.

schema
is the schema to contain the synonym. If you omit *schema*, ORACLE creates the synonym in your own schema.

synonym
is the name of the synonym to be created.

FOR
identifies the object for which the synonym is created. If you do not qualify *object* with *schema*, ORACLE assumes that the object is in your own schema. The *object* can be of these types:

- table
- view
- sequence
- stored procedure, function, or package
- snapshot
- synonym

The object cannot be contained in a package. Note that the object need not currently exist and you need not have privileges to access the object.

You can use a complete or partial *dblink* to create a synonym for an object on a remote database where the object is located. If you specify *dblink* and omit *schema*, the synonym refers to an object in the schema specified by the database link. Oracle Corporation recommends that you specify the schema containing the object in the remote database.

If you omit *dblink*, ORACLE assumes the object is located on the local database.

Usage Notes

In Trusted ORACLE, the new synonym is automatically labeled with your DBMS label.

A synonym can be used to stand for its base object in any Data Manipulation Language statement:

- SELECT
- INSERT
- UPDATE
- DELETE
- EXPLAIN PLAN
- LOCK TABLE

Synonyms can also be used in these Data Definition Language statements:

- AUDIT
- NOAUDIT
- GRANT
- REVOKE
- COMMENT

Synonyms are used for security and convenience. Creating a synonym for an object allows you to:

- reference the object without specifying its owner
- reference the object without specifying the database on which it is located
- provide another name for the object

Synonyms provide both data independence and location transparency; synonyms permit applications to function without modification regardless of which user owns the table or view and regardless of which database holds the table or view.

Scope of Synonyms

A private synonym name must be distinct from all other objects in its schema. ORACLE attempts to resolve references to objects at the schema level before resolving them at the PUBLIC synonym level. ORACLE only uses a public synonym when resolving references to an object if both of these cases are true:

- the object is not prefaced by a schema
- the object is not followed by a database link

For example, assume the schemas SCOTT and BLAKE each contain tables named DEPT and the user SYSTEM creates a PUBLIC synonym named DEPT for BLAKE.DEPT. If the user SCOTT then issues the following statement, ORACLE returns rows from SCOTT.DEPT:

```
SELECT *
    FROM dept
```

To retrieve rows from BLAKE.DEPT, the user SCOTT must preface DEPT with the schema name:

```
SELECT *
    FROM blake.dept
```

If the user ADAM's schema does not contain an object named DEPT, then ADAM can access the DEPT table in BLAKE's schema by using the public synonym DEPT:

```
SELECT *
    FROM dept
```

CREATE TABLESPACE

Purpose

To create a tablespace. A *tablespace* is an allocation of space in the database that can contain objects.

Prerequisites

You must have CREATE TABLESPACE system privilege. Also, the SYSTEM tablespace must contain at least two rollback segments including the SYSTEM rollback segment.

Syntax

```
CREATE TABLESPACE command ::=
```

```
►►── CREATE TABLESPACE tablespace ─ DATAFILE ──┬─ filespec ─┬──────►
                                               └─────◄──────┘
                                                      ,

►──┬──────────────────────────────────────────┬────────────────►◄
   └──┬─ DEFAULT STORAGE storage_clause ─┬─────┘
      ├─────────── ONLINE ───────────────┤
      └─────────── OFFLINE ──────────────┘
```

Keywords and Parameters

tablespace	is the name of the tablespace to be created.
DATAFILE	specifies the data file or files to comprise the tablespace. See the syntax description of *filespec*.
DEFAULT STORAGE	specifies the default storage parameters for all objects created in the tablespace. For information on storage parameters, see the STORAGE clause.
ONLINE	makes the tablespace available immediately after creation to users who have been granted access to the tablespace.
OFFLINE	makes the tablespace unavailable after immediately after creation.

If you omit both the ONLINE and OFFLINE options, ORACLE creates the tablespace online by default. The data dictionary view DBA_TABLESPACES indicates whether each tablespace is online or offline.

Usage Notes

A *tablespace* is an allocation of space in the database that can contain any of these segments:

- data segments
- index segments
- rollback segments
- temporary segments

All databases have at least one tablespace, SYSTEM, which ORACLE creates automatically when you create the database.

After creating a tablespace, you can subsequently use the ALTER TABLESPACE command to take it online or offline or add data files to it.

Many schema objects have associated segments that occupy space in the database. These objects are located in tablespaces. The user creating such an object can optionally specify the tablespace to contain the object. The owner of the schema containing the object must have space quota on the object's tablespace. You can assign space quota on a tablespace to a user with the QUOTA clause of the CREATE USER or ALTER USER commands.

CREATE USER

Purpose

To create a database *user*, or an account through which you can log in to the database, and establish the means by which ORACLE permits access by the user. You can optionally assign these properties to the user:

- default tablespace
- temporary tablespace
- quotas for allocating space in tablespaces
- profile containing resource limits

Prerequisites

You must have CREATE USER system privilege.

If you are using Trusted ORACLE in DBMS MAC mode, you must meet additional prerequisites to perform the optional assignments of this statement:

- To assign a default or temporary tablespace, your DBMS label must dominate the tablespace's creation label.
- To assign a profile, your DBMS label must dominate the profile's creation label.

Syntax

```
CREATE USER command ::=
```

Keywords and Parameters

user

is the name of the user to be created. This name can only contain characters from your database character set and must follow the rules described in the section "Object Naming Rules" on page 2-3 of the *Oracle7 Server SQL Language Reference Manual*. Oracle Corporation recommends that the *user* contain at least one single-byte character regardless of whether the database character set also contains multi-byte characters.

IDENTIFIED	indicates how ORACLE permits user access:

    BY *password*   The user must specify this password to logon. The password can only contain single-byte characters from your database character set regardless of whether this character set also contains multi-byte characters.

    EXTERNALLY   ORACLE verifies user access through the operating system.

DEFAULT TABLESPACE	identifies the default tablespace for objects that the user creates. If you omit this clause, objects default to the SYSTEM tablespace.
TEMPORARY TABLESPACE	identifies the tablespace for the user's temporary segments. If you omit this clause, temporary segments default to the SYSTEM tablespace.
QUOTA	allows the user to allocate space in the tablespace and optionally establishes a quota of *integer* bytes. This quota is the maximum space in the tablespace the user can allocate. You can also use the K or M to specify the quota in kilobytes or megabytes.

    UNLIMITED   allows the user to allocate space in the tablespace without bound.

PROFILE	assigns the profile named profile to the user. The profile limits the amount of database resources the user can use. If you omit this clause, ORACLE assigns the DEFAULT profile to the user.

Usage Notes

If you create a new user in Trusted ORACLE, the user's creation label is your DBMS label.

Verifying Users Through Your Operating System

The EXTERNALLY option causes ORACLE to verify access to the user through the operating system, rather than with a password. Such a user can only be accessed from a single operating system account. At logon, ORACLE compares the username and the current operating system account name. The username must match the account name prefixed by the value of the initialization parameter OS_AUTHENT_PREFIX.

CREATE USER

Establishing Tablespace Quotas for Users

To create an object or a temporary segment, the user must allocate space in some tablespace. To allow the user to allocate space, use the QUOTA clause. A CREATE USER statement can have multiple QUOTA clauses, each for a different tablespace. Other clauses can appear only once.

Note that you must use QUOTA clauses to allow the user to allocate space in the default and temporary tablespaces. Note also that you need not have a quota on a tablespace in order to establish a quota for another user on that tablespace.

Granting Privileges to a User

For a user to perform any database operation, the user's privilege domain must contain a privilege that authorizes that operation. A user's privilege domain contains all privileges granted to the user and all privileges in the privilege domains of the user's enabled roles. When you create a user with the CREATE USER command, the user's privilege domain is empty.

Note: To logon to ORACLE, a user must have CREATE SESSION system privilege. After creating a user, you should grant the user this privilege.

DROP DATABASE LINK

Purpose   To remove a database link from the database.

Prerequisites   To drop a private database link, the database link must be in your own schema. To drop a PUBLIC database link, you must have DROP PUBLIC DATABASE LINK system privilege.

If you are using Trusted ORACLE in DBMS MAC mode, your DBMS label must match the database link's creation label or you must satisfy one of these criteria:

- If the database link's creation label is higher than your DBMS label, you must have READUP and WRITEUP system privileges
- If the database link's creation label is lower than your DBMS label, you must have WRITEDOWN system privilege.
- If the database link's creation label and your DBMS label are noncomparable, you must have READUP, WRITEUP, and WRITEDOWN system privileges.

Syntax

```
DROP DATABASE LINK command ::=
```

```
►►── DROP ──┬──────────┬── DATABASE LINK dblink ──────────────►◄
            └─ PUBLIC ─┘
```

Keywords and Parameters

PUBLIC   must be specified to drop a PUBLIC database link.

dblink   specifies the database link to be dropped.

Usage Notes   You cannot drop a database link in another user's schema and you cannot qualify *dblink* with the name of a schema. Since periods are permitted in names of database links, ORACLE interprets the entire name, such as RALPH.LINKTOSALES, as the name of a database link in your schema rather than as a database link named LINKTOSALES in the schema RALPH.

DROP PROFILE

Purpose

To remove a profile from the database.

Prerequisites

You must have DROP PROFILE system privilege.

If you are using Trusted ORACLE in DBMS MAC mode, your DBMS label must match the profile's creation label or you must satisfy one of these criteria:

- If the profile's creation label is higher than your DBMS label, you must have READUP and WRITEUP system privileges
- If the profile's creation label is lower than your DBMS label, you must have WRITEDOWN system privilege.
- If the profile's creation label and your DBMS label are noncomparable, you must have READUP, WRITEUP, and WRITEDOWN system privileges.

Syntax

```
DROP PROFILE command ::=

►►── DROP PROFILE profile ─────────────────────────────►◄
                          └─ CASCADE ─┘
```

Keywords and Parameters

profile   is the name of the profile to be dropped.

CASCADE   deassigns the profile from any users to whom it is assigned. ORACLE automatically assigns the DEFAULT profile to such users. You must specify this option to drop a profile that is currently assigned to users.

Usage Notes

You cannot drop the DEFAULT profile.

DROP ROLE

Purpose
To remove a role from the database.

Prerequisites
You must have been granted the role with the ADMIN OPTION or have DROP ANY ROLE system privilege.

If you are using Trusted ORACLE in DBMS MAC mode, your DBMS label must match the role's creation label or you must satisfy one of these criteria:

- If the role's creation label is higher than your DBMS label, you must have READUP and WRITEUP system privileges
- If the role's creation label is lower than your DBMS label, you must have WRITEDOWN system privilege.

If the role's creation label and your DBMS label are noncomparable, you must have READUP, WRITEUP, and WRITEDOWN system privileges.

Syntax
```
DROP ROLE command ::=

►►──── DROP ROLE role ─────────────────────────────────────────►◄
```

Keywords and Parameters

role   is the role to be dropped.

Usage Notes
When you drop a role, ORACLE revokes it from all users and roles to whom it has been granted and removes it from the database.

DROP ROLLBACK SEGMENT

Purpose   To remove a rollback segment from the database.

Prerequisites   You must have DROP ROLLBACK SEGMENT system privilege.

If you are using Trusted ORACLE in DBMS MAC mode, your DBMS label must match the rollback segment's creation label or you must satisfy one of these criteria:

- If the rollback segment's creation label is higher than your DBMS label, you must have READUP and WRITEUP system privileges
- If the rollback segment's creation label is lower than your DBMS label, you must have WRITEDOWN system privilege.
- If the rollback segment's creation label and your DBMS label are noncomparable, you must have READUP, WRITEUP, and WRITEDOWN system privileges.

Syntax

```
DROP ROLLBACK SEGMENT command ::=

►►── DROP ROLLBACK SEGMENT rollback_segment ──────────────────►◄
```

Keywords and Parameters   *rollback_segment*   is the name the rollback segment to be dropped.

Usage Notes   When you drop a rollback segment, all space allocated to the rollback segment returns to the tablespace.

You can only drop a rollback segment that is offline. To determine whether a rollback segment is offline, query the data dictionary view DBA_ROLLBACK_SEGS. Offline rollback segments have the value 'AVAILABLE' in the STATUS column. You can take a rollback segment offline with the OFFLINE option of the ALTER ROLLBACK SEGMENT command.

You cannot drop the SYSTEM rollback segment.

DROP SYNONYM

Purpose
To remove a synonym from the database.

Prerequisites
If you want to drop a private synonym, either the synonym must be in your own schema or you must have DROP ANY SYNONYM system privilege. If you want to drop a PUBLIC synonym, either the synonym must be in your own schema or you must have DROP ANY PUBLIC SYNONYM system privilege.

If you are using Trusted ORACLE in DBMS MAC mode, your DBMS label must match the synonym's creation label or you must satisfy one of these criteria:

- If the synonym's creation label is higher than your DBMS label, you must have READUP and WRITEUP system privileges
- If the synonym's creation label is lower than your DBMS label, you must have WRITEDOWN system privilege.
- If the synonym's creation label and your DBMS label are noncomparable, you must have READUP, WRITEUP, and WRITEDOWN system privileges.

Syntax
```
DROP SYNONYM command ::=
```

```
►►── DROP ──┬─────────────┬── SYNONYM ──┬───────────┬── synonym ──────►◄
            └─ PUBLIC ─┘                └─ schema. ─┘
```

Keywords and Parameters

PUBLIC   must be specified to drop a public synonym.

schema   is the schema containing the synonym. If you omit *schema*, ORACLE assumes the synonym is in your own schema.

synonym   is the name of the synonym to be dropped.

Usage Notes
You can change the definition of a synonym by dropping and recreating it.

DROP TABLESPACE

Purpose

To remove a tablespace from the database.

Prerequisites

You must have DROP TABLESPACE system privilege. No rollback segments in the tablespace can be assigned active transactions.

If you are using Trusted ORACLE in DBMS MAC mode, your DBMS label must match the tablespace's creation label or you must satisfy one of these criteria:

- If the tablespace's creation label is higher than your DBMS label, you must have READUP and WRITEUP system privileges
- If the tablespace's creation label is lower than your DBMS label, you must have WRITEDOWN system privilege.
- If the tablespace's creation label and your DBMS label are noncomparable, you must have READUP, WRITEUP, and WRITEDOWN system privileges.

Syntax

```
DROP TABLESPACE command ::=

►►─── DROP TABLESPACE tablespace ──────────────────────────────►

►─┬──────────────────────────────────────────────────┬─►◄
  └─ INCLUDING CONTENTS ─┬────────────────────────┬─┘
                         └─ CASCADE CONSTRAINTS ─┘
```

Keywords and Parameters

tablespace

is the name of the tablespace to be dropped.

INCLUDING CONTENTS

drops all the contents of the tablespace. You must specify this clause to drop a tablespace that contains any database objects. If you omit this clause, and the tablespace is not empty, ORACLE returns an error message and does not drop the tablespace.

CASCADE CONSTRAINTS

drops all referential integrity constraints from tables outside the tablespace that refer to primary and unique keys in the tables of the tablespace. If you omit this option and such referential integrity constraints exist, ORACLE returns an error message and does not drop the tablespace.

Usage Notes

You can drop a tablespace regardless of whether it is online or offline. Oracle Corporation recommends that you take the tablespace offline before dropping it to ensure that no SQL statements in currently running transactions access any of the objects in the tablespace.

You may want to alter any users who have been assigned the tablespace as either a default or temporary tablespace. After the tablespace has been dropped, these users cannot allocate space for objects or sort areas in the tablespace. You can reassign users new default and temporary tablespaces with the ALTER USER command.

You cannot drop the SYSTEM tablespace.

DROP USER

Purpose   To remove a database user and optionally remove the user's objects.

Prerequisites   You must have DROP USER system privilege.

If you are using Trusted ORACLE in DBMS MAC mode, your DBMS label must match the user's creation label or you must satisfy one of these criteria:

- If the user's creation label is higher than your DBMS label, you must have READUP and WRITEUP system privileges
- If the user's creation label is lower than your DBMS label, you must have WRITEDOWN system privilege.
- If the user's creation label and your DBMS label are noncomparable, you must have READUP, WRITEUP, and WRITEDOWN system privileges.

Syntax

```
DROP USER command ::=

►►── DROP USER user ─────────────────────────────►◄
                   └─ CASCADE ─┘
```

Keywords and Parameters

user	is the user to be dropped.
CASCADE	drops all objects in the user's schema before dropping the user. You must specify this option to drop a user whose schema contains any objects.

Usage Notes   ORACLE does not drop users whose schemas contain objects. To drop such a user, you must perform one of these actions:

- explicitly drop the user's objects before dropping the user
- drop the user and objects together using the CASCADE option

If you specify the CASCADE option and drop tables in the user's schema, ORACLE also automatically drops any referential integrity constraints on tables in other schemas that refer to primary and unique keys on these tables. The CASCADE option causes ORACLE to invalidate, but not drop, these objects in other schemas:

- views or synonyms for objects in the dropped user's schema
- stored procedures, functions, or packages that query objects in the dropped user's schema

ORACLE does not drop snapshots on tables or views in the user's schema or roles created by the user.

EXPLAIN PLAN

Purpose

To determine the execution plan ORACLE follows to execute a specified SQL statement. This command inserts a row describing each step of the execution plan into a specified table. If you are using cost-based optimization, this command also determines the cost of executing the statement.

Prerequisites

To issue an EXPLAIN PLAN statement, you must have the privileges necessary to insert rows into an existing output table that you specify to hold the execution plan.

You must also have the privileges necessary to execute the SQL statement for which you are determining the execution plan. If the SQL statement accesses a view, you must have privileges to access any tables and views on which the view is based. If the view is based on another view that is based on a table, you must have privileges to access both the other view and its underlying table.

To examine the execution plan produced by an EXPLAIN PLAN statement, you must have the privileges necessary to query the output table.

If you are using Trusted ORACLE in DBMS MAC mode, your DBMS label must dominate the output table's creation label or you must satisfy one of these criteria:

- If the output table's creation label is higher than your DBMS label, you must have READUP and WRITEUP system privileges.
- If the output table's creation label and your DBMS label are noncomparable, you must have READUP, WRITEUP, and WRITEDOWN system privileges.

EXPLAIN PLAN

Syntax

EXPLAIN PLAN command ::=

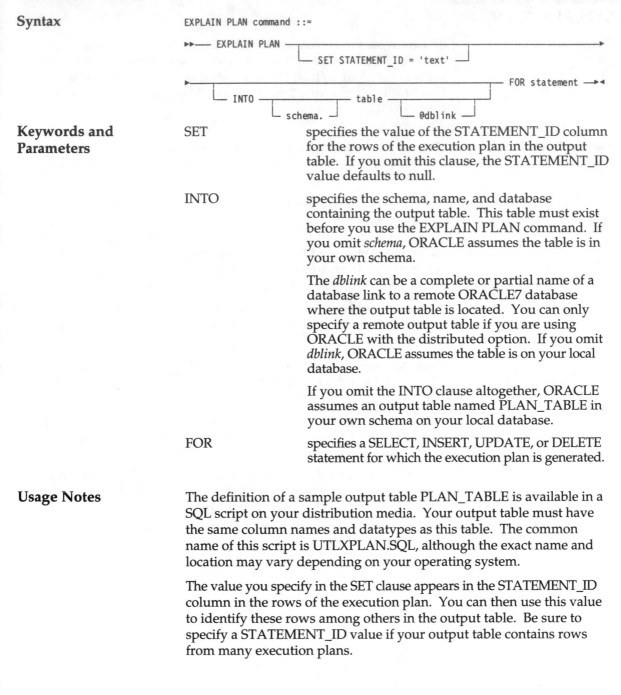

Keywords and Parameters

SET
    specifies the value of the STATEMENT_ID column for the rows of the execution plan in the output table. If you omit this clause, the STATEMENT_ID value defaults to null.

INTO
    specifies the schema, name, and database containing the output table. This table must exist before you use the EXPLAIN PLAN command. If you omit *schema*, ORACLE assumes the table is in your own schema.

    The *dblink* can be a complete or partial name of a database link to a remote ORACLE7 database where the output table is located. You can only specify a remote output table if you are using ORACLE with the distributed option. If you omit *dblink*, ORACLE assumes the table is on your local database.

    If you omit the INTO clause altogether, ORACLE assumes an output table named PLAN_TABLE in your own schema on your local database.

FOR
    specifies a SELECT, INSERT, UPDATE, or DELETE statement for which the execution plan is generated.

Usage Notes

The definition of a sample output table PLAN_TABLE is available in a SQL script on your distribution media. Your output table must have the same column names and datatypes as this table. The common name of this script is UTLXPLAN.SQL, although the exact name and location may vary depending on your operating system.

The value you specify in the SET clause appears in the STATEMENT_ID column in the rows of the execution plan. You can then use this value to identify these rows among others in the output table. Be sure to specify a STATEMENT_ID value if your output table contains rows from many execution plans.

Since the EXPLAIN PLAN command is a Data Manipulation Language command, rather than a Data Definition Language command, ORACLE does not implicitly commit the changes made by an EXPLAIN PLAN statement. If you want to keep the rows generated by an EXPLAIN PLAN statement in the output table, you must commit the transaction containing the statement.

You can also issue the EXPLAIN PLAN command as part of the SQL trace facility. For information on how to use the SQL trace facility and how to interpret execution plans, see Appendix B "Performance Diagnostic Tools" of the *ORACLE7 Server Application Developer's Guide*.

Filespec

Purpose

To either specify a file as a data file or specify a group of one or more files as a redo log file group.

Prerequisites

A *filespec* can appear in either CREATE DATABASE, ALTER DATABASE, CREATE TABLESPACE, or ALTER TABLESPACE commands. You must have the privileges necessary to issue one of these commands. For information on these privileges, see the CREATE DATABASE, ALTER DATABASE, CREATE TABLESPACE, and ALTER TABLESPACE.

Syntax

filespec (Data Files) ::=

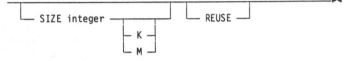

filespec (Redo Log File Groups) ::=

Keywords and Parameters

'filename'   is the name of either a data file or a redo log file member. A redo log file group can have one or more members, or copies. Each *'filename'* must be fully specified according to the conventions for your operating system.

SIZE   specifies the size of the file. If you omit this parameter, the file must already exist.

K   specifies the size in kilobytes.

M   specifies the size in megabytes.

If you omit K and M, the size is specified in bytes.

REUSE   allows ORACLE to reuse an existing file. If the file already exists, ORACLE verifies that its size matches the value of the SIZE parameter. If the file does not exist, ORACLE creates it. If you omit this option, the file must not already exist and ORACLE creates the file.

The REUSE option is only significant when used with the SIZE option. If you omit the SIZE option, ORACLE expects the file to exist already. Note that whenever ORACLE uses an existing file, the file's previous contents are lost.

GRANT (System Privileges and Roles)

Purpose

To grant system privileges and roles to users and roles. To grant object privileges, use the GRANT command (Object Privileges).

Prerequisites

To grant a system privilege, you must either have been granted the system privilege with the ADMIN OPTION or have been granted GRANT ANY PRIVILEGE system privilege.

To grant a role, you must either have been granted the role with the ADMIN OPTION or have been granted GRANT ANY ROLE system privilege or have created the role.

If you are using Trusted ORACLE in DBMS MAC mode, your DBMS label must dominate both the label at which the system privilege or role was granted to you and the creation label of the grantee user or role.

Syntax

```
GRANT command (System Privileges and Roles) ::=
```

Keywords and Parameters

system_priv	is a system privilege to be granted.
role	is a role to be granted.
TO	identifies users or roles to which system privileges and roles are granted.
	PUBLIC — grants system privileges or roles to all users.
WITH ADMIN OPTION	allows the grantee to grant the system privilege or role to other users or roles. If you grant a role with ADMIN OPTION, the grantee can also alter or drop the role.

Usage Notes

You can use this form of the GRANT command to grant both system privileges and roles to users, roles, and PUBLIC:

If you grant a privilege to a user: ORACLE adds the privilege to the user's privilege domain. The user can immediately exercise the privilege.

If you grant a privilege to a role: ORACLE adds the privilege to the role's privilege domain. Users who have been granted and have enabled the role can immediately exercise the privilege. Other users who have been granted the role can enable the role and exercise the privilege.

If you grant a privilege to PUBLIC: ORACLE adds the privilege to the privilege domains of each user. All users can immediately perform operations authorized by the privilege.

If you grant a role to a user: ORACLE makes the role available to the user. The user can immediately enable the role and exercise the privileges in the role's privilege domain.

If you grant a role to another role: ORACLE adds the granted role's privilege domain to the grantee role's privilege domain. Users who have been granted the grantee role can enable it and exercise the privileges in the granted role's privilege domain.

If you grant a role to PUBLIC: ORACLE makes the role available to all users. All users can immediately enable the role and exercise the privileges in the roles privilege domain.

A privilege or role cannot appear more than once in the list of privileges and roles to be granted. A user, role, or PUBLIC cannot appear more than once in the TO clause.

You cannot grant roles circularly. For example, if you grant the role BANKER to the role TELLER, you cannot subsequently grant TELLER to BANKER. Also, you cannot grant a role to itself.

GRANT (System Privileges and Roles)

System Privileges

Table C-4 lists system privileges and the operations that they authorize. You can grant any of these system privileges with the GRANT command.

TABLE C-4
System Privileges

System Privilege	Operations Authorized
ALTER ANY CLUSTER	Allows grantee to alter any cluster in any schema.
ALTER ANY INDEX	Allows grantee to alter any index in any schema.
ALTER ANY PROCEDURE	Allows grantee to alter any stored procedure, function, or package in any schema.
ALTER ANY ROLE	Allows grantee to alter any role in the database.
ALTER ANY SEQUENCE	Allows grantee to alter any sequence in any schema.
ALTER ANY SNAPSHOT	Allows grantee to alter any snapshot in any schema.
ALTER ANY TABLE	Allows grantee to alter any table or view in any schema.
ALTER ANY TRIGGER	Allows grantee to enable, disable, or compile any database trigger in any schema.
ALTER DATABASE	Allows grantee to alter the database.
ALTER PROFILE	Allows grantee to alter profiles.
ALTER RESOURCE COST	Allows grantee to set costs for session resources.
ALTER ROLLBACK SEGMENT	Allows grantee to alter rollback segments.
ALTER SESSION	Allows grantee to issue ALTER SESSION statements.
ALTER SYSTEM	Allows grantee to issue ALTER SYSTEM statements.
ALTER TABLESPACE	Allows grantee to alter tablespaces.

continued on the next page

System Privilege	Operations Authorized
ALTER USER	Allows grantee to alter any user. This privilege authorizes the grantee to change another user's password or authentication method, assign quotas on **any** tablespace, set default and temporary tablespaces, and assign a profile and default roles.
ANALYZE ANY	Allows grantee to analyze any table, cluster, or index in any schema.
AUDIT ANY	Allows grantee to audit any object in any schema using AUDIT (Schema Objects) statements.
AUDIT SYSTEM	Allows grantee to issue AUDIT (SQL Statements) statements.
BECOME USER	Allows the grantee to use the Import utility to import objects in the schemas of other users.
BACKUP ANY TABLE	Allows grantee to use the Export utility to export objects in the schemas of other users.
COMMENT ANY TABLE	Allows grantee to comment on any table, view, or column in any schema.
CREATE ANY CLUSTER	Allows grantee to create a cluster in any schema. Behaves similarly to CREATE ANY TABLE .
CREATE ANY INDEX	Allows grantee to create an index in any schema on any table in any schema.
CREATE ANY PROCEDURE	Allows grantee to create stored procedures, functions, and packages in any schema.
CREATE ANY SEQUENCE	Allows grantee to create a sequence in any schema.
CREATE ANY SNAPSHOT	Allows grantee to create snapshots in any schema.
CREATE ANY SYNONYM	Allows grantee to create private synonyms in any schema.
CREATE ANY TABLE	Allows grantee to create tables in any schema. The owner of the schema containing the table must have space quota on the tablespace to contain the table.

continued on the next page

GRANT (System Privileges and Roles)

System Privileges (continued)

System Privilege	Operations Authorized
CREATE ANY TRIGGER	Allows grantee to create a database trigger in any schema associated with a table in any schema.
CREATE ANY VIEW	Allows grantee to create views in any schema.
CREATE CLUSTER	Allows grantee to create clusters in own schema.
CREATE DATABASE LINK	Allows grantee to create private database links in own schema.
CREATE PROCEDURE	Allows grantee to create stored procedures, functions, and packages in own schema.
CREATE PROFILE	Allows grantee to create profiles.
CREATE PUBLIC DATABASE LINK	Allows grantee to create public database links.
CREATE PUBLIC SYNONYM	Allows grantee to create public synonyms.
CREATE ROLE	Allows grantee to create roles.
CREATE ROLLBACK SEGMENT	Allows grantee to create rollback segments.
CREATE SESSION	Allows grantee to connect to the database.
CREATE SEQUENCE	Allows grantee to create sequences in own schema.
CREATE SNAPSHOT	Allows grantee to create snapshots in own schema.
CREATE SYNONYM	Allows grantee to create synonyms in own schema.
CREATE TABLE	Allows a grantee to create tables in own schema. To create a table, the grantee must also have space quota on the tablespace to contain the table.
CREATE TABLESPACE	Allows grantee to create tablespaces.
CREATE TRIGGER	Allows grantee to create a database trigger in own schema.

continued on the next page

System Privileges (continued)

System Privilege	Operations Authorized
CREATE USER	Allows grantee to create users. This privilege also allows the creator to assign quotas on **any** tablespace, set default and temporary tablespaces, and assign a profile as part of a CREATE USER statement.
CREATE VIEW	Allows grantee to create views in own schema.
DELETE ANY TABLE	Allows grantee to delete rows from tables or views in any schema or truncate tables in any schema.
DROP ANY CLUSTER	Allows grantee to drop clusters in any schema.
DROP ANY INDEX	Allows grantee to drop indexes in any schema.
DROP ANY PROCEDURE	Allows grantee to drop stored procedures, functions, or packages in any schema.
DROP ANY ROLE	Allows grantee to drop roles.
DROP ANY SEQUENCE	Allows grantee to drop sequences in any schema.
DROP ANY SNAPSHOT	Allows grantee to drop snapshots in any schema.
DROP ANY SYNONYM	Allows user to drop private synonyms in any schema.
DROP ANY TABLE	Allows grantee to drop tables in any schema.
DROP ANY TRIGGER	Allows grantee to drop database triggers in any schema.
DROP ANY VIEW	Allows grantee to drop views in any schema.
DROP PROFILE	Allows grantee to drop profiles.
DROP PUBLIC DATABASE LINK	Allows grantee to drop public database links.
DROP PUBLIC SYNONYM	Allows grantee to drop public synonyms.
DROP ROLLBACK SEGMENT	Allows grantee to drop rollback segments.
DROP TABLESPACE	Allows grantee to drop tablespaces.

continued on the next page

GRANT (System Privileges and Roles)

System Privilege	Operations Authorized
DROP USER	Allows a grantee to drop users.
EXECUTE ANY PROCEDURE	Allows grantee to execute procedures or functions (stand-alone or packaged) or reference public package variables in any schema.
FORCE ANY TRANSACTION	Allows grantee to force the commit or rollback of any in-doubt distributed transaction in the local database. Also allows the grantee to induce the failure of a distributed transaction.
FORCE TRANSACTION	Allows grantee to force the commit or rollback of own in-doubt distributed transactions in the local database.
GRANT ANY PRIVILEGE	Allows grantee to grant any system privilege.
GRANT ANY ROLE	Allows grantee to grant any role in the database.
INSERT ANY TABLE	Allows grantee to insert rows into tables and views in any schema.
LOCK ANY TABLE	Allows grantee to lock tables and views in any schema.
MANAGE TABLESPACE	Allows grantee to take tablespaces offline and online and begin and end tablespace backups.
READUP	Allows grantee to query data having an access class higher than the grantee's session label. This privilege is only available in Trusted ORACLE.
RESTRICTED SESSION	Allows grantee to logon after the instance is started using the SQL*DBA STARTUP RESTRICT command.
SELECT ANY SEQUENCE	Allows grantee to reference sequences in any schema.
SELECT ANY TABLE	Allows grantee to query tables, views, or snapshots in any schema.

continued on the next page

System Privileges (continued)

System Privilege	Operations Authorized
UNLIMITED TABLESPACE	Allows grantee to use an unlimited amount of **any** tablespace. This privilege overrides any specific quotas assigned. If you revoke this privilege from a user, the grantee's schema objects remain but further tablespace allocation is denied unless authorized by specific tablespace quotas. You cannot grant this system privilege to roles.
UPDATE ANY TABLE	Allows grantee to update rows in tables and views in any schema.
WRITEDOWN	Allows grantee to create, alter, and drop schema objects and to insert, update, and delete rows having access classes lower than the grantee's session label. This privilege is only available in Trusted ORACLE.
WRITEUP	Allows grantee to create, alter, and drop schema objects and to insert, update, and delete rows having access classes higher than the grantee's session label. This privilege is only available in Trusted ORACLE.

TABLE C-5
Roles Defined by ORACLE

Role	System Privileges and Roles Granted
CONNECT	ALTER SESSION CREATE CLUSTER CREATE DATABASE LINK CREATE SEQUENCE CREATE SESSION CREATE SYNONYM CREATE TABLE CREATE VIEW
RESOURCE	CREATE CLUSTER CREATE PROCEDURE CREATE SEQUENCE CREATE TABLE CREATE TRIGGER
DBA	All system privileges WITH ADMIN OPTION EXP_FULL_DATABASE role IMP_FULL_DATABASE role
EXP_FULL_DATABASE	SELECT ANY TABLE BACKUP ANY TABLE INSERT, UPDATE, DELETE ON sys.incexp, sys.incvid, sys.incfil
IMP_FULL_DATABASE	BECOME USER WRITEDOWN (in Trusted ORACLE)

Roles Defined by ORACLE

Some roles are created automatically by ORACLE. When you create a database, ORACLE creates these roles and grants them certain system privileges. Table C-5 lists each predefined role and its system privileges.

Note: If you grant the RESOURCE or DBA role to a user, ORACLE implicitly grants the UNLIMITED TABLESPACE system privilege to the user.

The CONNECT, RESOURCE, and DBA are provided for compatibility with previous versions of ORACLE. The SQL script SQL.BSQ creates these roles, grants privileges to them, and grants the DBA role with ADMIN OPTION to the users SYS and SYSTEM. This script is available on your distribution media, although its exact name and location may vary depending on your operating system. Oracle Corporation encourages you to design your own roles for database security, rather than rely on these roles. These roles may not be automatically created by future versions of ORACLE.

The EXP_FULL_DATABASE and IMP_FULL_DATABASE roles are provided for convenience in using the Import and Export utilities. The SQL script CATEXP.SQL creates these roles, grants privileges to them, and grants them to the DBA role. This script is available on your distribution media, although its exact name and location may vary depending on your operating system.

ADMIN OPTION

A grant with the ADMIN OPTION supersedes a previous identical grant without the ADMIN OPTION. If you grant a system privilege or role to user without the ADMIN OPTION, and then subsequently grant the privilege or role to the user with the ADMIN OPTION, the user has the ADMIN OPTION on the privilege or role.

A grant without the ADMIN OPTION does not supersede a previous grant with the ADMIN OPTION. To revoke the ADMIN OPTION on a system privilege or role from a user, you must revoke the privilege or role from the user altogether and then grant the privilege or role to the user without the ADMIN OPTION.

Granting Roles Through Your Operating System

Some operating systems have facilities that grant operating system privileges to operating system users. You can use such facilities to grant roles to ORACLE users with the initialization parameter OS_ROLES. If you choose to grant roles to users through operating system facilities, you cannot also grant roles to users with the GRANT command, although you can use the GRANT command to grant system privileges to users and system privileges and roles to other roles.

GRANT (Object Privileges)

Purpose

To grant privileges for a particular object to users and roles. To grant system privileges and roles, use the GRANT command (System Privileges and Roles).

Prerequisites

The object must be in your own schema or you must have been granted the object privileges with the GRANT OPTION.

If you are using Trusted ORACLE in DBMS MAC mode, your DBMS label must dominate the label at which the object privilege was granted to you and the creation label of the grantee user or role.

Syntax

GRANT command (Object Privileges) ::=

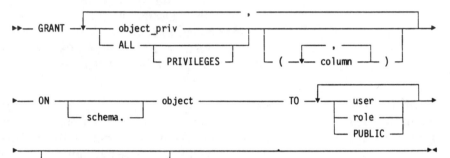

Keywords and Parameters

object_priv

is an object privilege to be granted. You can substitute any of these values:

- ALTER
- DELETE
- EXECUTE
- INDEX
- INSERT
- REFERENCES
- SELECT
- UPDATE

ALL
PRIVILEGES

grants all the privileges for the object that you have been granted with the GRANT OPTION. The user who owns the schema containing an object automatically has all privileges on the object with the GRANT OPTION.

column	specifies a table or view column on which privileges are granted. You can only specify columns when granting the INSERT, REFERENCES, or UPDATE privilege. If you do not list columns, the grantee has the specified privilege on all columns in the table or view.
ON	identifies the object on which the privileges are granted. If you do not qualify *object* with *schema*, ORACLE assumes the object is in your own schema. The object can be one of these types:

- table
- view
- sequence
- procedure, function, or package
- snapshots
- synonym for a table, view, sequence, snapshot, procedure, function, or package

TO	identifies users or roles to which the object privilege is granted.
	PUBLIC grants object privileges to all users.
WITH GRANT OPTION	allows the grantee to grant the object privileges to other users and roles. The grantee must be a user or PUBLIC, rather than a role.

Usage Notes

You can use this form of the GRANT statement to grant object privileges to users, roles, and PUBLIC:

If you grant a privilege to a user: ORACLE adds the privilege to the user's privilege domain. The user can immediately exercise the privilege.

If you grant a privilege to a role: ORACLE adds the privilege to the role's privilege domain. Users who have been granted and have enabled the role can immediately exercise the privilege. Other users who have been granted the role can enable the role and exercise the privilege.

If you grant a privilege to PUBLIC: ORACLE adds the privilege to the privilege domain of each user. All users can immediately exercise the privilege.

A privilege cannot appear more than once in the list of privileges to be granted. A user or role cannot appear more than once in the TO clause.

GRANT (Object Privileges)

Object Privileges

Each object privilege that you grant authorizes the grantee to perform some operation on the object. Table C-6 summarizes the object privileges that you can grant on each type of object.

TABLE C-6
Object Privileges

Object Privilege	Tables	Views	Sequences	Procedure Functions Packages	Snapshots
ALTER	✓		✓		
DELETE	✓	✓			
EXECUTE				✓	
INDEX	✓				
INSERT	✓	✓			
REFERENCES	✓				
SELECT	✓	✓	✓		✓
UPDATE	✓	✓			

Table Privileges

These object privileges authorize operations on a table:

ALTER   allows the grantee to change the table definition with the ALTER TABLE command.

DELETE   allows the grantee to remove rows from the table with the DELETE command.

INDEX   allows the grantee to create an index on the table with the CREATE INDEX command.

INSERT   allows the grantee to add new rows to the table with the INSERT command.

REFERENCES   allows the grantee to create a constraint that refers to the table. You cannot grant this privilege to a role.

SELECT   allows the grantee to query the table with the SELECT command.

UPDATE   allows the grantee to change data in the table with the UPDATE command.

Any one of these object privileges allows the grantee to lock the table in any lockmode with the LOCK TABLE command.

View Privileges	These object privileges authorize operations on a view:

DELETE   allows the grantee to remove rows from the view with the DELETE command.

INSERT   allows the grantee to add new rows to the view with the INSERT command.

SELECT   allows the grantee to query the view with the SELECT command.

UPDATE   allows the grantee to change data in the view with the UPDATE command.

Any one of these object privileges allows the grantee to lock the view in any lockmode with the LOCK TABLE command.

To grant a privilege on a view, you must have that privilege with the GRANT OPTION on all of the view's base tables.

Sequence Privileges

These object privileges authorize operations on a sequence:

ALTER   allows the grantee to change the sequence definition with the ALTER SEQUENCE command.

SELECT   allows the grantee to examine and increment values of the sequence with the CURRVAL and NEXTVAL pseudocolumns.

Procedure, Function, and Package Privileges

This object privilege authorizes operations on a procedure, function, or package:

EXECUTE   allows the grantee to execute the procedure or function or to access any program object declared in the specification of a package.

Snapshot Privileges

This object privilege authorizes operations on a snapshot:

SELECT   allows the grantee to query the snapshot with the SELECT command.

Synonym Privileges

The object privileges available for a synonym are the same as the privileges for the synonym's base object. Granting a privilege on a synonym is equivalent to granting the privilege on the base object. If you grant a user a privilege on a synonym, the user can use either the synonym name or the base object name in the SQL statement that exercises the privilege.

NOAUDIT (SQL Statements)

Purpose To stop auditing chosen by the AUDIT command (SQL Statements). To stop auditing chosen by the AUDIT command (Schema Objects), use the NOAUDIT command (Schema Objects).

Prerequisites You must have AUDIT SYSTEM system privilege.

If you are using Trusted ORACLE in DBMS MAC mode, your DBMS label must match the label at which the auditing option was set or you must satisfy one of these criteria:

- If the auditing option was set at a label higher than your DBMS label, you must have READUP and WRITEUP system privileges.
- If the auditing option was set at a label lower than your DBMS label, you must have WRITEDOWN system privilege.
- If the auditing option was set at a label noncomparable to your DBMS label, you must have READUP, WRITEUP, and WRITEDOWN system privileges.

Syntax

```
NOAUDIT command (SQL Statements) ::=
```

Keywords and Parameters

statement_opt is a statement option for which auditing is stopped. For a list of the statement options and the SQL statements they audit, see Table C-1 and Table C-2.

system_priv is a system privilege for which auditing is stopped. For a list of the system privileges and the statements they authorize, see Table C-1.

BY stops auditing only for SQL statements issued by specified users in their subsequent sessions. If you omit this clause, ORACLE stops auditing for all users' statements.

WHENEVER SUCCESSFUL	stops auditing only for SQL statements that complete successfully.
NOT	stops auditing only for statements that result in ORACLE errors.
	If you omit the WHENEVER clause entirely, ORACLE stops auditing for all statements, regardless of success or failure.

Usage Notes

A NOAUDIT statement (SQL Statements) reverses the effect of a previous AUDIT statement (SQL Statements). Note that the NOAUDIT statement must have the same syntax as the previous AUDIT statement. For information on auditing specific SQL commands, see the AUDIT command (SQL Statements).

NOAUDIT (Schema Objects)

Purpose

To stop auditing chosen by the AUDIT command (Schema Objects). To stop auditing chosen by the AUDIT command (SQL Statements), use the NOAUDIT command (SQL Statements).

Prerequisites

The object on which you stop auditing must be in your own schema or you must have AUDIT ANY system privilege.

If you are using Trusted ORACLE in DBMS MAC mode, your DBMS label must match the label at which the auditing option was set or you must satisfy one of these criteria:

- If the auditing option was set at a label higher than your DBMS label, you must have READUP and WRITEUP system privileges.
- If the auditing option was set at a label lower than your DBMS label, you must have WRITEDOWN system privilege.
- If the auditing option was set at a label noncomparable to your DBMS label, you must have READUP, WRITEUP, and WRITEDOWN system privileges.

Syntax

```
NOAUDIT command (Schema Objects) ::=
```

Keywords and Parameters

object_opt

stops auditing for particular operations on the object. For a list of these options, see Table C-3.

ON

identifies the object on which auditing is stopped. If you do not qualify *object* with *schema*, ORACLE assumes the object is in your own schema.

WHENEVER SUCCESSFUL

stops auditing only for SQL statements that complete successfully.

NOT

option stops auditing only for statements that result in ORACLE errors.

If you omit the WHENEVER clause entirely, ORACLE stops auditing for all statements, regardless of success or failure.

Usage Notes   For information on auditing specific schema objects, see the AUDIT command (Schema Objects).

RECOVER clause

Purpose
To perform media recovery.

Prerequisites
The RECOVER clause must appear in an ALTER DATABASE statement. You must have the privileges necessary to issue this statement. For information on these privileges, see the ALTER DATABASE command.

You must also have the OSDBA role enabled. You cannot be connected to ORACLE through the multi-threaded server architecture. Your instance must have the database mounted in exclusive mode.

Syntax

RECOVER recover_clause ::=

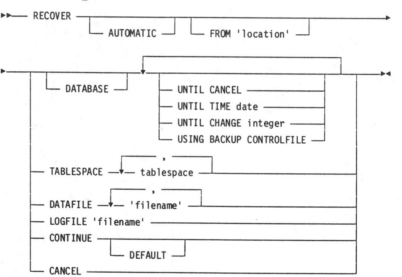

Keywords and Parameters

AUTOMATIC automatically generates the names of the redo log files to apply during media recovery. If you omit this option, ORACLE prompts you for names of redo log files and you must specify them by issuing ALTER DATABASE statements with the LOGFILE parameter.

FROM specifies the location from which the archived redo log file group is read. The value of this parameter must be a fully-specified file location following the conventions of your operating system. If you omit this parameter, ORACLE assumes the archived redo log file group is in the location specified by the initialization parameter LOG_ARCHIVE_DEST.

DATABASE | recovers the entire database. This is the default option. You can only use this option when the database is closed.

UNTIL CANCEL | performs cancel-based recovery. This option recovers the database until you cancel recovery by issuing an ALTER DATABASE statement with a RECOVER clause containing the CANCEL option.

UNTIL TIME | performs time-based recovery. This parameter recovers the database to the time specified by the *date*. The *date* must be a character literal in the format 'YYYY-MM-DD:HH24:MI:SS'.

UNTIL CHANGE | performs change-based recovery. This parameter recovers the database to a transaction consistent state immediately prior to the system change number (SCN) specified by *integer*.

USING BACKUP CONTROLFILE | specifies that a backup control file is being used instead of the current control file.

TABLESPACE | recovers only the specified tablespaces. You can use this option if the database is open or closed, provided the tablespaces to be recovered are not being used.

DATAFILE | recovers the specified data files. You can use this option when the database is open or closed, provided the data files to be recovered are not being used.

LOGFILE | continues media recovery by applying the specified redo log file.

CONTINUE | continues multi-instance recovery after it has been interrupted to disable a thread.

CONTINUE DEFAULT | continues recovery by applying the redo log file that ORACLE has automatically generated.

CANCEL | terminates cancel-based recovery.

Usage Notes

Oracle Corporation recommends that you use the SQL*DBA RECOVER command rather than the ALTER DATABASE command with the RECOVER clause to perform media recovery. For most purposes, the RECOVER command is easier to use than the ALTER DATABASE command. For information on this command, see the *ORACLE7 Server Utilities User's Guide*. For more information on media recovery, see Chapter 19 "Recovering a Database" of the *ORACLE7 Server Administrator's Guide*.

RECOVER clause

You can use the ALTER DATABASE command with the RECOVER clause if you want to write your own specialized media recovery application using SQL.

REVOKE (System Privileges and Roles)

Purpose

To revoke system privileges and roles from users and roles. To revoke object privileges from users and roles, use the REVOKE command (Object Privileges).

Prerequisites

You must have been granted the system privilege or role with the ADMIN OPTION. Also, you can revoke any role if you have the GRANT ANY ROLE system privilege.

If you are using Trusted ORACLE in DBMS MAC mode, your DBMS label must match the label at which the system privilege or role was granted or you must satisfy one of these criteria:

- If the label at which the system privilege or role was granted is higher than your DBMS label, you must have READUP and WRITEUP system privileges
- If the label at which the system privilege or role was granted is lower than your DBMS label, you must have WRITEDOWN system privilege.
- If the label at which the system privilege or role is noncomparable to your DBMS label, you must have READUP, WRITEUP, and WRITEDOWN system privileges.

Syntax

```
REVOKE command (System Privileges and Roles) ::=
```

Keywords and Parameters

system_priv is a system privilege to be revoked. For a list of the system privileges, see Table C-4.

role is a role to be revoked. For a list of the roles predefined by ORACLE, see Table C-5.

FROM identifies users and roles from which the system privileges or roles are revoked.

PUBLIC revokes the system privilege or role from all users.

REVOKE (System Privileges and Roles)

Usage Notes

You can use this form of the REVOKE command to revoke both system privileges and roles from users, roles, and PUBLIC:

If you revoke a privilege from a user: ORACLE removes the privilege from the user's privilege domain. Effective immediately, the user cannot exercise the privilege.

If you revoke a privilege from a role: ORACLE removes the privilege from the role's privilege domain. Effective immediately, users with the role enabled cannot exercise the privilege. Also, other users who have been granted the role and subsequently enable the role cannot exercise the privilege.

If you revoke a privilege from PUBLIC: ORACLE removes the privilege from the privilege domain of each user who has been granted the privilege through PUBLIC. Effective immediately, such users can no longer exercise the privilege. Note that the privilege is not revoked from users who have been granted the privilege directly or through roles.

If you revoke a role from a user: ORACLE makes the role unavailable to the user. If the role is currently enabled for the user, the user can continue to exercise the privileges in the role's privilege domain as long as it remains enabled. However, the user cannot subsequently enable the role.

If you revoke a role from another role: ORACLE removes the revoked role's privilege domain from the revokee role's privilege domain. Users who have been granted and have enabled the revokee role can continue to exercise the privileges in the revoked role's privilege domain as long as the revokee role remains enabled. However, other users who have been granted the revokee role and subsequently enable it cannot exercise the privileges in the privilege domain of the revoked role.

If you revoke a role from PUBLIC: ORACLE makes the role unavailable to all users who have been granted the role through PUBLIC. Any user who has enabled the role can continue to exercise the privileges in its privilege domain as long as it remains enabled. However, users cannot subsequently enable the role. Note that the role is not revoked from users who have been granted the privilege directly or through other roles.

REVOKE (System Privileges and Roles)

The REVOKE command can only revoke privileges and roles that have been granted directly with a GRANT statement. The REVOKE command cannot perform these operations:

- revoke privileges or roles not granted to the revokee
- revoke roles granted through the operating system
- revoke privileges or roles granted to the revokee through roles

A system privilege or role cannot appear more than once in the list of privileges and roles to be revoked. A user, a role, or PUBLIC cannot appear more than once in the FROM clause.

REVOKE (Object Privileges)

Purpose

To revoke object privileges for a particular object from users and roles. To revoke system privileges or roles, use the REVOKE command (System Privileges and Roles).

Prerequisites

You must have previously granted the object privileges to each user and role.

If you are using Trusted ORACLE in DBMS MAC mode, your DBMS label must match the label at which you granted the object privilege or you must satisfy one of these criteria:

- If the label at which you granted the object privilege is higher than your DBMS label, you must have READUP and WRITEUP system privileges.
- If the label at which you granted the object privilege is lower than your DBMS label, you must have WRITEDOWN system privilege.
- If the label at which you granted the object privilege is noncomparable to your DBMS label, you must have READUP, WRITEUP, and WRITEDOWN system privileges.

Syntax

REVOKE command (Object Privileges) ::=

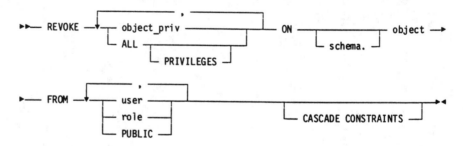

Keywords and Parameters

object_priv   is an object privilege to be revoked. You can substitute any of these values:

- ALTER
- DELETE
- EXECUTE
- INDEX
- INSERT
- REFERENCES
- SELECT
- UPDATE

ALL PRIVILEGES   revokes all object privileges that you have granted to the revokee.

ON   identifies the object on which the object privileges are revoked. This object can be one of these types:

- table
- view
- sequence
- procedure, stored function, or package
- snapshot
- synonym for a table, view, sequence, procedure, stored function, package, or snapshot

If you do not qualify *object* with *schema*, ORACLE assumes the object is in your own schema.

FROM   identifies users and roles from which the object privileges are revoked.

PUBLIC   revokes object privileges from all users.

CASCADE CONSTRAINTS   drops any referential integrity constraints that the revokee has defined using REFERENCES privilege that you are now revoking. You must specify this option along with the REFERENCES privilege or the ALL PRIVILEGES option if the revokee has exercised the REFERENCES privilege to define a referential integrity constraint.

REVOKE (Object Privileges)

Usage Notes

You can use this form of the REVOKE command to revoke object privileges from both users and roles:

If you revoke a privilege from a user: ORACLE removes the privilege from the user's privilege domain. Effective immediately, the user cannot exercise the privilege.

If you revoke a privilege from a role: ORACLE removes the privilege from the role's privilege domain. Effective immediately, users with the role enabled cannot exercise the privilege. Other users who have been granted the role cannot exercise the privilege after enabling the role.

If you revoke a privilege from PUBLIC: ORACLE removes the privilege from the privilege domain of each user who has been granted the privilege through PUBLIC. Effective immediately, all such users are restricted from exercising the privilege. Note that the privilege is not revoked from users who have been granted the privilege directly or through roles.

You can only use the REVOKE command to revoke object privileges that you previously granted directly to the revokee. You cannot use the REVOKE command to perform these operations:

- revoke object privileges that you did not grant to the revokee
- revoke privileges granted through the operating system
- revoke privileges granted to roles granted to the revokee

A privilege cannot appear more than once in the list of privileges to be revoked. A user, a role, or PUBLIC cannot appear more than once in the FROM clause.

Object Privileges

Each object privilege authorizes some operation on an object. By revoking an object privilege, you prevent the revokee from performing that operation. For a summary of the object privileges for each type of object, see Table C-6.

Revoking Multiple Identical Grants

Multiple users may grant the same object privilege to the same user, role, or PUBLIC. To remove the privilege from the grantee's privilege domain, all grantors must revoke the privilege. If even one grantor does not revoke the privilege, the grantee can still exercise the privilege by virtue of that grant.

Cascading Revokes   Revoking an object privilege that a user has either granted or exercised to define an object or a referential integrity constraint has cascading effects:

- If you revoke an object privilege from a user who has granted the privilege to other users or roles, ORACLE also revokes the privilege from the grantees.

- If you revoke an object privilege from a user whose schema contains a procedure, function, or package that contains SQL statements that exercise the privilege, the procedure, function, or package can no longer be executed.

- If you revoke an object privilege on an object from a user whose schema contains a view on that object, ORACLE invalidates the view.

- If you revoke REFERENCES privilege from a user who has exercised the privilege to define referential integrity constraints, you must specify the CASCADE CONSTRAINTS option. ORACLE then revokes the privilege and drops the constraints.

SET ROLE

Purpose

To enable and disable roles for your current session.

Prerequisites

You also must already have been granted the roles that you name in this statement.

If you are using Trusted ORACLE in DBMS MAC mode, your DBMS label must dominate the label at which these roles were granted to you.

Syntax

SET ROLE command ::=

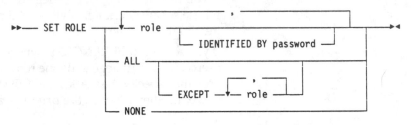

Keywords and Parameters

role

    is a role to be enabled for the current session. Any roles not listed are disabled for the current session.

    password   is the password for a role. If the role has a password, you must specify the password to enable the role.

ALL
EXCEPT

    enables all roles granted to you for the current session, except those listed in the EXCEPT clause. Roles listed in the EXCEPT clause must be roles granted directly to you; they cannot be roles granted to you through other roles. You cannot use this option to enable roles with passwords that have been granted directly to you.

    If you list a role in the EXCEPT clause that has been granted to you both directly and through another role, the role is still enabled by virtue of your enabling the role to which it has been granted.

NONE

    disables all roles for the current session.

Default Privilege Domain

At logon ORACLE establishes your default privilege domain by enabling your default roles. Your default privilege domain contains all privileges granted explicitly to you and all privileges in the privilege domains of your default roles. You can then perform any operations authorized by the privileges in your default privilege domain.

Changing Your Privilege Domain

During your session, you can change your privilege domain with the SET ROLE command. The SET ROLE command changes the roles currently enabled for your session. You can change your enabled roles any number of times during a session. The number of roles that can be concurrently enabled is limited by the initialization parameter MAX_ENABLED_ROLES.

You can use the SET ROLE command to enable or disable any of these roles:

- roles that have been granted directly to you
- roles granted to you through other roles

You cannot use the SET ROLE command to enable roles that you have not been granted either directly or through other roles.

Your current privilege domain is also changed in these cases:

- if you are granted a privilege
- if one of your privileges is revoked
- if one of your enabled roles is revoked
- if the privilege domain of one of your enabled roles is changed

If none of these conditions occur and you do not issue the SET ROLE command, your default privilege domain remains in effect for the duration of your session. In the last two cases, the change in your privilege domain does not take effect until you logon to ORACLE again or issue a SET ROLE statement.

You can determine which roles are in your current privilege domain at any time by examining the SESSION_ROLES data dictionary view.

To change your default roles, use the ALTER USER command.

SET TRANSACTION

Purpose	To perform one of these operations on your current transaction:

- establish your current transaction as either a read-only or a read-write transaction
- assign your current transaction to a specified rollback segment

Prerequisites

A SET TRANSACTION statement must be the first statement in your transaction. However, every transaction need not begin with a SET TRANSACTION statement.

Syntax

```
SET TRANSACTION command ::=

►►── SET TRANSACTION ──┬── READ ONLY ──────────────────────┬──►◄
                       ├── READ WRITE ──────────────────────┤
                       └── USE ROLLBACK SEGMENT rollback_segment ──┘
```

Keywords and Parameters

READ ONLY	establishes the current transaction as a read-only transaction.
READ WRITE	establishes the current transaction as a read-write transaction.
USE ROLLBACK SEGMENT	assigns the current transaction to the specified rollback segment. This option also establishes the transaction as a read-write transaction.

You cannot use the READ ONLY option and the USE ROLLBACK SEGMENT clause in a single SET TRANSACTION statement or in different statements in the same transaction. Read-only transactions do not generate rollback information and therefore are not assigned rollback segments.

Usage Notes

The operations performed by a SET TRANSACTION statement affect only your current transaction, not other users or other transactions. Your transaction ends whenever you issue a COMMIT or ROLLBACK statement. Note also that ORACLE implicitly commits the current transaction before and after executing a Data Definition Language statement.

Establishing Read-only Transactions

The default state for all transactions is statement level read consistency. You can explicitly specify this state by issuing a SET TRANSACTION statement with the READ WRITE option.

You can establish transaction level read consistency by issuing a SET TRANSACTION statement with the READ ONLY option. After a transaction has been established as read-only, all subsequent queries in that transaction only see changes committed before the transaction began. Read-only transactions are very useful for reports that run multiple queries against one or more tables while other users update these same tables.

Only these statements are permitted in a read-only transaction:

- SELECT (except statements with the FOR UPDATE clause)
- LOCK TABLE
- SET ROLE
- ALTER SESSION
- ALTER SYSTEM

INSERT, UPDATE, and DELETE statements and SELECT statements with the FOR UPDATE clause are not permitted. Any Data Definition Language statement implicitly ends the read-only transaction.

The read consistency that read-only transactions provide is implemented in the same way as statement-level read consistency. Every statement by default uses a consistent view of the data as of the time the statement is issued. Read-only transactions present a consistent view of the data as of the time that the SET TRANSACTION READ ONLY statement is issued. Read-only transactions provide read consistency is for all nodes accessed by distributed queries as well as local queries.

You cannot toggle between transaction level read consistency and statement level read consistency in the same transaction. A SET TRANSACTION statement can only be issued as the first statement of a transaction.

Assigning Transactions to Rollback Segments

If you issue a Data Manipulation Language statement in a transaction, ORACLE assigns the transaction to a rollback segment. The rollback segment holds the information necessary to undo the changes made by the transaction. You can issue a SET TRANSACTION statement with the USE ROLLBACK SEGMENT clause to choose a specific rollback segment for your transaction. If you do not choose a rollback segment, ORACLE chooses one randomly and assigns your transaction to it.

SET TRANSACTION

This statement allows you to assign transactions of different types to rollback segments of different sizes:

- Assign OLTP transactions, or small transactions containing only a few Data Manipulation Language statements that modify only a few rows, to small rollback segments if there are no long-running queries concurrently reading the same tables. Small rollback segments are more likely to remain in memory.

- Assign transactions that modify tables that are concurrently being read by long-running queries to large rollback segments so that the rollback information needed for the read consistent queries is not overwritten.

- Assign transactions with bulk Data Manipulation Language statements, or statements that insert, update, or delete large amounts of data, to rollback segments large enough to hold the rollback information for the transaction.

STORAGE clause

Purpose
To specify storage characteristics for tables, indexes, clusters, and rollback segments, and the default storage characteristics for tablespaces.

Prerequisites
The STORAGE clause can appear in commands that create or alter any of these objects:

- clusters
- indexes
- rollback segments
- snapshots
- snapshot logs
- tables
- tablespaces

To change the value of a STORAGE parameter, you must have the privileges necessary to issue one of these commands.

Syntax

STORAGE storage_clause ::=

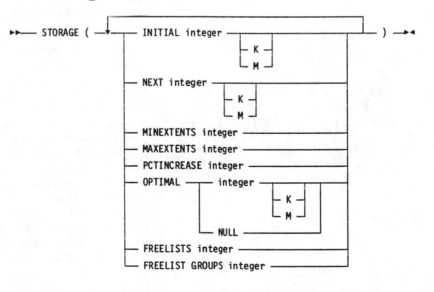

STORAGE clause

Keywords and Parameters

INITIAL

specifies the size in bytes of the object's first extent. ORACLE allocates space for this extent when you create the object. You can also use K or M to specify this size in kilobytes or megabytes. The default value is the size of 5 data blocks. The minimum value is the size of 2 data blocks. The maximum value varies depending on your operating system. ORACLE rounds values up to the next multiple of the data block size.

NEXT

specifies the size in bytes of the next extent to be allocated to the object. You can also use K or M to specify the size in kilobytes or megabytes. The default value is the size of 5 data blocks. The minimum value is the size of 1 data block. The maximum value varies depending on your operating system. ORACLE rounds values up to the next multiple of the data block size.

PCTINCREASE

specifies the percent by which each extent after the second grows over the previous extent. The default value is 50, meaning that each subsequent extent is 50% larger than the preceding extent. The minimum value is 0, meaning all extents after the first are the same size. The maximum value varies depending on your operating system.

You cannot specify PCTINCREASE for rollback segments. Rollback segments always have a PCTINCREASE value of 0.

ORACLE rounds the calculated size of each new extent up to the next multiple of the data block size.

MINEXTENTS

specifies the total number of extents allocated when the segment is created. This parameter allows you to allocate a large amount of space when you create an object, even if the space available is not contiguous. The default and minimum value is 1, meaning that ORACLE only allocates the initial extent, except for rollback segments for which the default and minimum value is 2. The maximum value varies depending on your operating system.

If the MINEXTENTS value is greater than 1, then ORACLE calculates the size of subsequent extents based on the values of the INITIAL, NEXT, and PCTINCREASE parameters.

MAXEXTENTS   specifies the total number of extents, including the first, that ORACLE can allocate for the object. The minimum value is 1. The default and maximum values vary depending your data block size.

OPTIMAL   specifies an optimal size in bytes for a rollback segment. You can also use K or M to specify this size in kilobytes or megabytes. ORACLE tries to maintain this size for the rollback segment by dynamically deallocating extents when their data is no longer needed for active-transactions. ORACLE deallocates as many extents as possible without reducing the total size of the rollback segment below the OPTIMAL value. This parameter is only for rollback segments and not for other objects.

    NULL   specifies no optimal size for the rollback segment, meaning that ORACLE never deallocates the rollback segment's extents. This is the default behavior.

    The value of this parameter cannot be less than the space initially allocated for the rollback segment specified by the MINEXTENTS, INITIAL, NEXT, and PCTINCREASE parameters. The maximum value varies depending on your operating system. ORACLE rounds values to the next multiple of the data block size.

FREELIST GROUPS   specifies the number of groups of free lists for a table, cluster, or index. The default and minimum value for this parameter is 1. Only use this parameter if you are using ORACLE with the Parallel Server option in parallel mode.

FREELISTS   specifies the number of free lists for each of the free list groups for the table, cluster, or index. The default and minimum value for this parameter is 1, meaning that each free list group contains one free list. The maximum value of this parameter depends on the data block size. If you specify a FREELISTS value that is too large, ORACLE returns an error message indicating the maximum value.

You can only specify the FREELISTS parameter in CREATE TABLE, CREATE CLUSTER, and CREATE INDEX statements. You can only specify the FREELIST GROUPS parameter in CREATE TABLE and CREATE CLUSTER statements.

Usage Notes

The STORAGE parameters affect both how long it takes to access data stored in the database as well as how efficiently space in the database is used. For a discussion of the effects of these parameters, see Chapter 22 "Tuning I/O" of the *ORACLE7 Server Administrator's Guide*.

When you create a tablespace, you can specify values for the STORAGE parameters. These values serve as default STORAGE parameter values for segments allocated in the tablespace.

When you create a cluster, index, rollback segments, snapshot, snapshot log, or table, you can specify values for the STORAGE parameters for the segments allocated to these objects. If you omit any STORAGE parameter, ORACLE uses the value of that parameter specified for the tablespace, except in the case of an index. If you create an index and omit a STORAGE parameter, ORACLE, allocates extents in one of these ways:

- If the table on which the index is created has no rows, ORACLE allocates extents using the default STORAGE parameter values for the tablespace.
- If the table contains rows and the size of the resulting index is less than or equal to 25 data blocks, ORACLE disregards the default STORAGE parameters for the tablespace and allocates a single extent large enough for the entire index.
- If the size of the resulting index is more than 25 data blocks, ORACLE disregards the default STORAGE parameters for the tablespace and allocates five extents of equal size to hold the index.

When you alter a cluster, index, rollback segment, snapshot, snapshot log, or table, you can change the values of STORAGE parameters. These new values only affect future extent allocations. For this reason, you cannot change the values of the INITIAL and MINEXTENTS parameter. If you change the value of the NEXT parameter, the next allocated extent will have the specified size, regardless of the size of the most-recently allocated extent and the value of the PCTINCREASE parameter. If you change the value of the PCTINCREASE parameter, ORACLE calculates the size of the next extent using this new value and the size of the most recently allocated extent.

When you alter a tablespace, you can change the values of STORAGE parameters. These new values serve as default values only to subsequently allocated segments (or subsequently created objects).

TRUNCATE

Purpose

To remove all rows from a table or cluster.

Prerequisites

The table or cluster must be in your schema or you must have DELETE ANY TABLE system privilege.

If you are using Trusted ORACLE, your DBMS label must match the creation label of the table or cluster or you must satisfy one of these criteria:

- If the creation label of the table or cluster is higher than your DBMS label, you must have READUP and WRITEUP system privileges
- If the creation label of the table or cluster is lower than your DBMS label, you must have WRITEDOWN system privilege.
- If the creation label of the table or cluster is noncomparable to your DBMS label, you must have READUP, WRITEUP, and WRITEDOWN system privileges.

Syntax

```
TRUNCATE command ::=

►►─ TRUNCATE ─┬─ TABLE ──────────────── table ────────────────────►◄
             │          └─ schema. ─┘           ┌─ DROP ──── STORAGE ─┐
             └─ CLUSTER ─────────────── cluster ─┘  └─ REUSE ─┘
                        └─ schema. ─┘
```

Keywords and Parameters

TABLE

specifies the schema and name of the table to be truncated. If you omit *schema*, ORACLE assumes the table is in your own schema. This table cannot be part of a cluster.

When you truncate a table, ORACLE also automatically deletes all data in the table's indexes.

CLUSTER

specifies the schema and name of the cluster to be truncated. If you omit *schema*, ORACLE assumes the cluster is in your own schema. You can only truncate an indexed cluster, not a hash cluster.

When you truncate a cluster, ORACLE also automatically deletes all data in the cluster's tables' indexes.

DROP STORAGE

deallocates the space from the deleted rows from the table or cluster. This space can subsequently be used by other objects in the tablespace.

REUSE STORAGE leaves the space from the deleted rows allocated to the table or cluster. This space can be subsequently used only by new data in the table or cluster resulting from inserts or updates.

The DROP STORAGE or REUSE STORAGE option that you choose also applies to the space freed by the data deleted from associated indexes.

If you omit both the REUSE STORAGE and DROP STORAGE options, ORACLE uses the DROP STORAGE option by default.

Usage Notes

You can use the TRUNCATE command to quickly remove all rows from a table or cluster. Removing rows with the TRUNCATE command is faster than removing them with the DELETE command for these reasons:

- The TRUNCATE command is a Data Definition Language command and generates no rollback information.
- Truncating a table does not fire the table's DELETE triggers.
- Truncating the master table of a snapshot does not record any changes in the table's snapshot log.

The TRUNCATE command allows you to optionally deallocate the space freed by the deleted rows. The DROP STORAGE option deallocates all but the space specified by the table's MINEXTENTS parameter.

Deleting rows with the TRUNCATE command is also more convenient than dropping and recreating a table for these reasons:

- Dropping and recreating invalidates the table's dependent objects, while truncating does not.
- Dropping and recreating requires you to regrant object privileges on the table, while truncating does not.
- Dropping and recreating requires you to recreate the table's indexes, integrity constraints, and triggers and respecify its STORAGE parameters, while truncating does not.

You cannot individually truncate a table that is part of a cluster. You must either truncate the cluster, delete all rows from the table, or drop and recreate the table.

You cannot truncate the parent table of an enabled referential integrity constraint. You must disable the constraint before truncating the table.

TRUNCATE

If you truncate the master table of a snapshot, ORACLE does not record the removed rows in the snapshot log. For this reason, a fast refresh does not remove the rows from the snapshot. Snapshots based on a truncated table must be refreshed completely for ORACLE to remove their rows.

You cannot roll back a TRUNCATE statement.

APPENDIX D

Configuration Guidelines for Client-Server Environments

Since Oracle supports so many different configurations and platforms, there is no single set of specifications that will be valid for every client-server environment. However, there are a number of general procedures that apply to the configuration of client-server environments. These guidelines are based on the communications details from Chapter 15, "SQL*Net V1 and V2," and Chapter 16, "Networking in UNIX."

Overview of Client-Server Processing

Using a *client-server* configuration allows the CPU and processing load of an application to be distributed between two machines. The first, called the *client,* supports the application that initiates the request from the database. The back-end machine on which the database resides is called the *server.* The client may bear most of the CPU load, while the database server is dedicated to supporting queries, not applications. This distribution of resource requirements is shown in Figure D-1.

When the client sends a database request to the server (via SQL*Net), the server receives and executes the SQL statement that is passed to it. The results of the SQL statement, plus any error conditions that are returned, are then sent back to the client.

To use a client-server architecture, the client and server machines must be capable of communicating with each other. This implies that there is a hardware connection between the two machines. Each machine must support a communications protocol that allows them to interchange data. With SQL*Net V1, both machines must use the same protocol. When using SQL*Net V2, the MultiProtocol Interchange may be used to resolve compatibility problems between various protocol communities (see Chapter 15, "SQL*Net V1 and V2").

Two examples will be used in this appendix. First, consider a client that is running Microsoft Windows 3.1 and SQL*Net V1. It is connected via an *NIC* (*Network Interface Card*) to an Ethernet network. The server with which it hopes to communicate is also located on that network. To make this example generic,

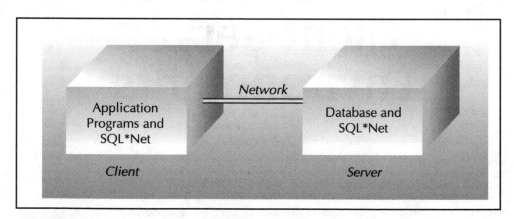

FIGURE D-1.   *Client-Server Architecture*

assume that the server is running UNIX and both machines are running the TCP/IP protocol. This generic configuration will be used as an illustration throughout this appendix.

This configuration is shown graphically in Figure D-2.

A second architecture, which involves adding a file server to the configuration, will be described as a modification to this configuration.

For the client and server to communicate, several steps must be taken:

- The server must be configured to accept communications via the network.

- The server must identify which databases are available for network logins.

- The server must be running SQL*Net.

- The client must be configured to communicate via the network.

- The client must have adequate memory and disk resources available.

- The client must have SQL*Net installed and specify a connect string.

If any of these steps is skipped, then the client application will be unable to communicate with the database on the server.

Configuring the Server

Server configurations are described in Chapter 16, "Networking in UNIX." The server must identify which hosts it can communicate with, specify which databases are available, and run the SQL*Net server process.

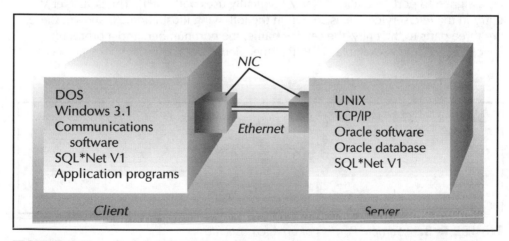

FIGURE D-2. *Sample Client-Server Configuration*

Identifying Available Hosts

A *host,* for the purposes of this example, will be defined as a server that is capable of communicating with another server via a network. Each host maintains a list of the hosts with which it can communicate. This list is maintained in a file called /etc/hosts. The "/etc" portion of the file name signifies that it is located in the /etc directory. This file contains the Internet address for the hosts, plus the host names. It may optionally include an alias for each host name. A sample portion of an /etc/hosts file is shown in Figure D-3.

In this example, there are five hosts listed. The first two entries assign host names ("nmhost" and "txhost") to Internet addresses. The third entry assigns both a host name ("azhost") and an alias ("arizona") to an Internet address. The fourth entry maps the "hq" server to its Internet address. The fifth entry, "mypc", maps the client PC's Internet address to its host name.

Identifying Available Services

A *server process* listens for connection requests from clients. It directs those requests to the proper UNIX socket, and the connection can then take place. The services for both SQL*Net V1 and V2 are described in Chapter 16, "Networking in UNIX," and in Chapter 15, "SQL*Net V1 and V2." The examples in this chapter will focus on the SQL*Net V1 installation.

Services on a UNIX server are listed in a file called /etc/services. The "/etc" portion of the file name signifies that it is located in the /etc directory. Like the /etc/hosts file, this file is typically maintained by a UNIX systems administrator.

The SQL*Net service is called *orasrv* for SQL*Net V1. In SQL*Net V1, it should be assigned to port 1525 (SQL*Net V2 typically uses port 1521). The SQL*Net V1 entry in the /etc/services file is shown in the following illustration. As shown, there are three parts to the entry: the service name, the port number, and a protocol specification (in this example, TCP/IP is specified).

```
127.0.0.1    nmhost
127.0.0.2    txhost
127.0.0.3    azhost arizona
127.0.0.4    hq
127.4.2.11   mypc
```

FIGURE D-3. *Sample Portion of an /etc/hosts file*

```
orasrv 1525/tcp
```

Identifying Available Databases

All databases that are run on a UNIX host and are accessible to the network must be listed in a file named /etc/oratab. The "/etc" portion of the file name signifies that it is located in the /etc directory. This file is maintained by the DBA. Each database used in a client-server application must be listed in the /etc/oratab file.

A sample /etc/oratab file is shown here:

```
LOC:/orasw/v716:Y
CC1:/orasw/v716:N
OLD:/orasw/v637:Y
```

There are three components to each entry in the /etc/oratab file, separated only by colons (:). The entries' components, which are fully described in Chapter 16, "Networking in UNIX," are the instance name (ORACLE_SID), Oracle software root directory (ORACLE_HOME), and a flag to indicate if the instance should be started on host startup (which is a necessary flag, but irrelevant to SQL*Net communications).

This example shows entries for three instances: LOC, CC1, and OLD (the first components in each entry). The first two instances have the same ORACLE_HOME; the third uses an older version of the Oracle kernel (as shown in the second component of the entries). Both LOC and OLD will be automatically started when the server starts; CC1 will have to be manually started (by virtue of the "Y" and "N" flags in the third component of each entry).

Once an instance is listed in the /etc/oratab file on an identified host on the network (via /etc/hosts), it can be accessed via SQL*Net connection strings. However, SQL*Net must be enabled for this to work. The next section describes the configuration of the SQL*Net server process in UNIX.

Starting SQL*Net

In the Windows-to-UNIX example, if the database application will be using SQL*Net V1, then the orasrv process must be started on the server. All of the available parameters for this process are listed in Chapter 16, "Networking in UNIX."

The following command starts the orasrv process.

```
> orasrv
```

For details on security problems in distributed computing environments, see the "Security in Distributed Environments" section of Chapter 9, "Database Security and Auditing."

The *tcpctl* utility may also be used to start the orasrv process. This utility can also be used to verify the status of SQL*Net. The first command in the following listing uses the "start" option to start SQL*Net. The second command in this listing uses the "stat" option to verify that SQL*Net is available.

```
> tcpctl start
> tcpctl stat
```

For a full description of the options for the tcpctl utility, and for information on the analogous SQL*Net V2 commands, see Chapter 16, "Networking in UNIX."

Configuring the Client

Before any communications can begin, the client machine must be physically connected to a network, and must have network communications software installed on it. The Network Interface Card (NIC) in your client machine must be supported by the communications software. See the *Setting up SQL*Net* guide for your client operating system for a list of the supported communications packages. Be sure to check this listing every time you upgrade either the communications package or the client's SQL*Net version.

To configure the example Microsoft Windows 3.1 client for SQL*Net TCP/IP, you must run Windows in enhanced mode. SQL*Net TCP/IP for Windows does not support standard mode or real mode.

Identifying Available Hosts

Just as the server machine must identify its available hosts, the client machine must also specify the hosts to which it can connect. This is typically done via the use of a HOSTS file, which is identical in structure to the server's /etc/hosts file.

The HOSTS file contains the Internet address for the hosts, plus the host names. It may optionally include an alias for each host name. A sample portion of a HOSTS file is shown here:

```
127.0.0.1 nmhost
127.0.0.2 txhost
127.0.0.3 azhost arizona
127.0.0.4 hq
```

In this example, there are four hosts listed. The first two entries assign host names ("nmhost" and "txhost") to Internet addresses. The third entry assigns both a host name ("azhost") and an alias ("arizona") to an Internet address. The fourth entry assigns an Internet address to the "hq" server.

The location of this file in the client's directory structure is dependent on the communications package in use.

Identifying Available Services

Just as the server machine must have a file to define the services it uses, the client machine must also have a way of specifying the services that it will connect to. On the server machine, this file is called /etc/services. On the client machine, it is called SERVICES. The SQL*Net portion of the services file should be identical on both machines. The SERVICES file for the sample configuration is shown here:

```
orasrv 1525/tcp
```

This file will be used by the communications software to attach to the proper communications socket on the UNIX server when an SQL*Net connection is attempted.

Identifying the Client Configuration

SQL*Net for Windows provides a local configuration file, called ORACLE.INI, that can be used to customize the client environment. You can also specify these parameters at the DOS command line, via the SET command, but it is simpler to create and distribute a standard configuration file.

The ORACLE.INI file is a series of entries, similar in form to an INIT.ORA file, in which parameters are set equal to values. The only difference in syntax between the two types of files is that the ORACLE.INI file does not accept spaces around the equal signs. These parameters are only read when you start the Oracle RDBMS or an Oracle tool on the client.

The available parameters are listed in Table D-1. The most significant parameters are shaded.

PARAMETER	DESCRIPTION
DYNAMIC_MEMORY	For DOS only. Specifies the number of bytes, in kilobytes, that SQLPME will reserve in extended memory for DOS products.
LOCAL	Defines a default SQL*Net connect string when no driver is specified. This allows users to log in to a remote database without specifying a full connect string.
ORACLE_HOME	The root directory for Oracle software; this entry is automatically created when the database is installed on the client. For Windows, defaults to \ORAWIN.
ORACLE_SPOOLER	The command Oracle will use when spooling listings to a printer. For Windows, DOS, and OS/2, defaults to PRINT.
REMOTE	Defines the default SQL*Net connect string to use when connecting via a local database. This enables users of a local database on the client to connect to remote databases without specifying all of the connection parameters.
SQLNET	Sets aliases for database connect strings; similar in function to the /etc/sqlnet file (see Chapter 16, "Networking in UNIX").
SQLPATH	Defines the path used to find the local LOGIN.SQL file.
SQLNET_USERNAME	Allows SQL*Net users to access OPS$ autologin accounts. This parameter is set to the server operating system account name. The user can then log in to the remote database without specifying a username and password.
TCP_HOSTS_FILE	The name of the client file used to specify available hosts.
TCP_SERVICES_FILE	The name of the client file used to specify available services.
TCP_VENDOR	Specifies which virtual socket library transport to use. This is communications software-specific.

TABLE D-1. *ORACLE.INI Parameters for the Client*

The SQLNET parameter allows you to approximate the SQL*Net V2 service name functionality in SQL*Net V1. By relying on the database alias names, you add a layer of location transparency to any applications that use the database across the network.

Client Machine Specifications

Can your Windows client support these requirements? To do so, it will have to meet the following minimum specifications:

Hardware:

- IBM, Compaq, or 100 percent compatible PC with an 80286 processor (or higher)
- Enough hard-disk space to store the files for your operating system, SQL*Net, your communications software, and your applications software
- A disk drive to use during installations
- An NIC for network communications

Memory:

- Enough memory to run your network software, SQL*Net, and your application software; a minimum of 5M is recommended

Software:

- Microsoft Windows 3.1
- SQL*Net TCP/IP for Windows, Version 1.1 or higher
- Network communications software

The SQL*Net TCP/IP for Windows software takes 100K of disk space, and approximately 120K of memory. When sizing your client machine, keep in mind that the application front-end programs, operating system, and communications software will require far greater resources than SQL*Net will.

If your processor is slow, then programs will usually run (just slower than you'd like). If not enough memory is available, then applications may not run at all. For that reason, be sure that you have at least 5M of memory on the PC—the more, the better.

Running SQL*Net

Now that the machines are set up and ready to talk, all you have to do is make sure that the tool you will be using to communicate with the remote database is properly configured. As noted in Chapter 14, "Supporting Third-Party Tools," there are often changes required to tools when you change from Oracle Version 6 to Oracle7 databases. There may also be differences between tools in the syntax of the database connect string. For example, some tools require that the entire connect string be entered in lowercase and enclosed in double quotes (though this is an isolated case). Be sure to test the connections thoroughly each time the network hardware, communications software, operating system, or SQL*Net version is changed.

Adding a File Server to the Configuration

To better distribute the resources required for a database application, you may choose to add a *file server* to the architecture. In this design, the Oracle software and application software may be stored on the file server. The result of this design is that no direct logins are made to the database server; rather, it exists solely to service database requests. This allows the database server to be tuned for this purpose.

In this architecture, it is usually preferable to use UNIX workstations for clients instead of PC clients. As shown in Figures D-4 and D-5, this allows two different architectures to be considered. In Figure D-4, the workstations send SQL*Net requests to the database server. The file server, which is *NFS mounted* to the database server, handles all requests for application and Oracle software. This "mounting" process enables the files on the file server to be accessed as if they were on the database server.

The second option is to have the client workstations NFS mounted on the file servers. The file servers would still contain the Oracle software and application software. The clients would thus be mounted as part of the file server that contains the Oracle code. The file server would communicate with the database server via the network, as shown in Figure D-5.

Using either of these configurations does two things: it adds a layer of complexity to the system administration, and it adds a great many capabilities to your architecture. First, consider the new capabilities:

- No users log directly into the database server. Therefore, memory and system resources can be tuned exclusively to handle database requests.

- Users can be separated by class. That is, developers can be physically separated from users.

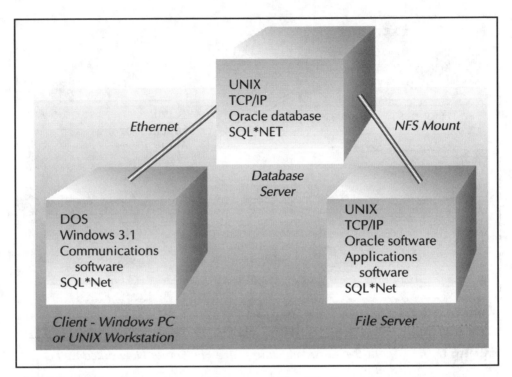

FIGURE D-4. *Client-Server Architecture with a File Server Networked to the Server*

■ Different user classes can access different executables. This can be used to test new versions of code, or to prevent user access to development tools (see Chapter 9, "Database Security and Auditing").

These capabilities add a layer of complexity to the administration of the system. When designing the administrative tools for this type of system, consider

■ The mechanisms you will use to keep the files on the file servers in sync.

■ The mechanisms you will use to keep the operating system parameters of the file servers in sync.

■ The network capacity. Now that the servers can be tuned for specific uses, do not skimp on the network that allows them to communicate.

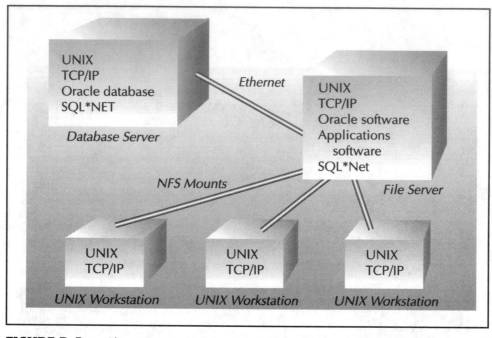

FIGURE D-5. *Client-Server Architecture with a File Server Networked to the Clients*

■ The security issues inherent in distributed environments. See Chapter 9, "Database Security and Auditing," regarding potential problems with remote autologins and remote DBA activities.

■ The memory and disk capacity of the file servers. Having introduced them as a benefit to the architecture, do not turn them into a system bottleneck.

When implementing applications in this type of environment, avoid hard-coding server names into the application's connect strings. With SQL*Net V2, this is done via the use of service names. In SQL*Net V1, you can use aliases (see "Identifying the Client Configuration," earlier in this chapter) or synonyms for database links (see Chapter 15, "SQL*Net V1 and V2"). The addition of file servers to the database application configuration adds a good deal of flexibility to the architecture; to take full advantage of it, you'll need to design for full location transparency.

Index

B

C

L

M

S

T

U

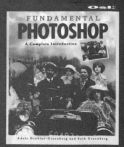

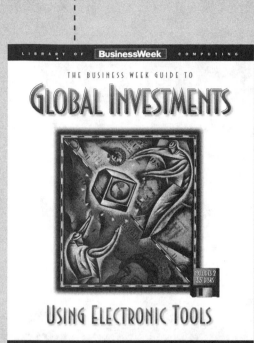
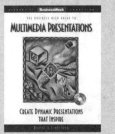

Think Fast
PASSING
LANE AHEAD

ORDER BOOKS DIRECTLY FROM OSBORNE/MC GRAW-HILL.

For a complete catalog of Osborne's books, call 510-549-6600 or write to us at 2600 Tenth Street, Berkeley, CA 94710

Call Toll-Free: *1-800-822-8158*
*24 hours a day, 7 days a week
in U.S. and Canada*

Mail this order form to:
*McGraw-Hill, Inc.
Blue Ridge Summit, PA 17294-0840*

Fax this order form to:
717-794-5291

EMAIL
*7007.1531@COMPUSERVE.COM
COMPUSERVE GO MH*

Ship to:

Name _____

Company _____

Address _____

City / State / Zip _____

Daytime Telephone: _____
(We'll contact you if there's a question about your order.)

ISBN #	BOOK TITLE	Quantity	Price	Total
0-07-88				
0-07-88				
0-07-88				
0-07-88				
0-07-88				
0-07088				
0-07-88				
0-07-88				
0-07-88				
0-07-88				
0-07-88				
0-07-88				
0-07-88				

Shipping & Handling Charge from Chart Below	
Subtotal	
Please Add Applicable State & Local Sales Tax	
TOTAL	

Shipping & Handling Charges

Order Amount	U.S.	Outside U.S.
Less than $15	$3.45	$5.25
$15.00 - $24.99	$3.95	$5.95
$25.00 - $49.99	$4.95	$6.95
$50.00 - and up	$5.95	$7.95

*Occasionally we allow other selected
companies to use our mailing list. If you
would prefer that we not include you in
these extra mailings, please check here:* ☐

METHOD OF PAYMENT

☐ Check or money order enclosed (payable to Osborne/McGraw-Hill)

☐ AMERICAN EXPRESS   ☐ DISCOVER   ☐ MasterCard   ☐ VISA

Account No. ☐☐☐☐☐☐☐☐☐☐☐☐☐☐☐☐

Expiration Date _____

Signature _____

In a hurry? Call 1-800-822-8158 anytime, day or night, or visit your local bookstore.

Thank you for your order

Code BC640SL